D0218760

American Experiences

American Experiences

READINGS IN AMERICAN HISTORY

★ ★ ★

Volume II   From 1877

Seventh Edition

★

Randy Roberts

Purdue University

★

James S. Olson

Sam Houston State University

PEARSON

Longman

New York   San Francisco   Boston
London   Toronto   Sydney   Tokyo   Singapore   Madrid
Mexico City   Munich   Paris   Cape Town   Hong Kong   Montreal

Executive Editor: Michael Boezi
Executive Marketing Manager: Sue Westmoreland
Supplements Editor: Brian Belardi
Media Supplements Editor: Melissa Edwards
Production Manager: Stacey Kulig
Project Coordination, Text Design, and Electronic Page Makeup: Carlisle Publishing
Services
Cover Design Manager: Wendy Ann Fredericks
Cover Designer: Susan Koski Zucker
Cover Photo: Fine Art Photographic Library/CORBIS
Photo Researcher: Vivette Porges
Senior Manufacturing Buyer: Alfred C. Dorsey
Printer and Binder: R.R. Donnelley and Sons
Cover Printer: R.R. Donnelley and Sons

For permission to use copyrighted material, grateful acknowledgment is made to the
copyright holders on p. 351, which are hereby made part of this copyright page.

Library of Congress Cataloging-in-Publication Data

Copyright © 2008 by Pearson Education, Inc.

All rights reserved. No part of this publication may be reproduced, stored in a
retrieval system, or transmitted, in any form or by any means, electronic, mechanical,
photocopying, recording, or otherwise, without the prior written permission of the
publisher. Printed in the United States.

Please visit us at www.ablongman.com

ISBN 13: 978-0-321-48701-8
ISBN 10: 0-321-48701-X

5 6 7 8 9 10—DOH—15 14 13

To Our Families

Contents

★ ★ ★

*Indicates new article

Preface

American History instructors enjoy talking about the grand sweep of the American past. Many note the development of unique traditions such as the American political tradition and the American diplomatic tradition. They employ the article *the* so often that they depict history as a seamless garment and Americans as all cut from the same fabric. Nothing could be further from the truth. America is a diverse country, and its population is the most ethnically varied in the world—white and black, Indian and Hispanic, rich and poor, male and female. No single tradition can encompass this variety. *American Experiences* shows the complexity and richness of the nation's past by focusing on the people—how they coped with, adjusted to, or rebelled against America. The readings examine Americans as they worked and played, fought and made love, lived and died.

We designed *American Experiences* as a supplement to the standard textbooks used in college survey classes in American history. Unlike other readers, it covers ground not usually found in textbooks. For example, instead of a discussion of the political impact of the Populist movement, we explore *The Wizard of Oz* as a Populist parable. In short, *American Experiences* presents different slants on standard and not-so-standard topics.

We have tested each essay in classrooms so that *American Experiences* reflects not only our interest in social history but also student interests in American history in general. We have selected essays that are readable, interesting, and help illuminate important aspects of America's past. For example, to show the nature of the class system in the South and to introduce the topic of Southern values, we selected one essay on gouging matches in the Southern backcountry. As an introduction to the conventional and medical view of women in the late nineteenth century, we selected an essay about Lizzie Borden. Each essay, then, serves at least two purposes: to tell a particular story well and to help illustrate the social or political landscape of America.

This reader presents a balanced picture of the experiences of Americans. The characters in these volumes are not exclusively white males from the Northeast, whose eyes are continually focused on Boston, New York, and Washington. Although their stories are certainly important, so too are the stories of blacks adjusting with dignity to a barbarous labor system, Hispanics coming to terms with Anglo culture, and women striving for increased opportunities in a gender-restricted society. We have looked at all of these stories and, in doing so, we have assumed that Americans express themselves in a variety of ways: through work, sex, and games, as well as politics and diplomacy.

Changes to the Seventh Edition

During the past four years, we have solicited a variety of opinions from colleagues and students about the selections for Volume 2 of *American Experiences*. Based on that feedback, we have made a number of changes in the seventh edition, always with the intent of selecting articles that undergraduate students will find interesting and informative. The new articles for the second volume of this edition are:

- Marty Jones, "Hollywood Scapegoat: The Roscoe Arbuckle Case"
- Bernard Asbell, "F.D.R.'s Extra Burden"
- Mark Bernstein, "Inventing Broadcast Journalism" and Edward R. Murrow, "For Most of It I Have No Words"
- H. H. Wubben, "American Prisoners of War in Korea: A Second Look at the 'Something New in History' Theme"
- Joshua Zeitz, "Boomer Century"
- Douglas Little, "Arabs, Israelis, and American Orientalism"

American Experiences is divided into standard chronological and topical parts. Each part is introduced by a brief discussion of the major themes of the period or topic. In turn, each selection is preceded by a short discussion of how it fits into the part's general theme. We employed this method to give students some guidance through the complexity of the American experience. At the conclusion of each selection is a series of study questions and a brief bibliographic essay. These are intended to further the usefulness of *American Experiences* for students as well as teachers.

We would like to acknowledge the help of our reviewers and thank them for their efforts: Anna Bates, Aquinas College; Paul E. Doutrich, York College of Pennsylvania; Steve Goodson, State University of West Georgia; Cheryl T. Kalny, St. Norbert College; Dennis Lythgoe, University of Utah; Timothy R. Mahoney, University of Nebraska; Marc Maltby, Owensboro Community and Technical College; Constance M. McGovern, Frostburg State University; Johnny S. Moore, Radford University; Susan E. Myers-Shirk, Middle Tennessee State University; and Richard Pate, Danville Area Community College.

Randy Roberts
James S. Olson

American Experiences

I

★ ★ ★

Reconstruction and the West

Although the Civil War did not begin as a crusade against slavery, it ended that way. The Emancipation Proclamation and Thirteenth Amendment to the Constitution made human bondage in the United States illegal, and during Reconstruction Republicans worked diligently to extend full civil rights to southern blacks. Despite the concerted opposition of President Andrew Johnson, the Radical Republicans in Congress pushed through a strong legislative program. The Civil Rights Act of 1866 and the Fourteenth and Fifteenth Amendments to the Constitution were all basically designed to bring the emancipated slaves into the political arena and build a respectable Republican party in the South. Both of these goals were stillborn, however, when Congress removed the troops from the last southern states. In 1877, the old planter elite resumed its control of southern politics. They disfranchised and relegated blacks to second-class citizenship, and the South became solidly Democratic. The South had indeed been brought back into the Union, but the grandiose hopes for a true reconstruction of southern life would not be realized for more than a century.

Genuine change in the southern social structure required more than most northerners could accept. Confiscation and redistribution of the plantations among poor whites and former slaves was too brazen an assault on property rights; northern businessmen feared that someday their own workers might demand similar treatment. Nor were northerners prepared for real social change. Advocating political rights for blacks was one thing; true social equality was quite another. Prejudice ran deep in the American psyche, too deep in the 1870s to allow for massive social change. Finally, most Americans were growing tired of the debate over civil rights and becoming preoccupied with business, money, and economic growth. Heavy industry in the East and vacant land in the West were absorbing their energies.

Just as Reconstruction was coming to an end, out West, ambitious farmers were rapidly settling the frontier, anxious to convert the land into an agricultural empire. Civilization was forever replacing a wilderness mentality with familiar political, economic, and social institutions. Already the "Old West" was becoming the stuff of which nostalgia is made. Normal, if somewhat eccentric, people were being transformed into larger-than-life heroes as American society tried to maintain its rural, individualistic roots. Back East, cities and factories were announcing a future of bureaucracies, interest groups, crowds, and enormous industrial production. America would never be the same again. The cult of western heroes helped people forget the misery of the Civil War and vicariously preserve a disappearing way of life.

READING 1

★ ★ ★

Knights of the Rising Sun

Allen W. Trelease

Periodically, even today, Ku Klux Klansmen rally in America, burning crosses on the lawns of new black neighbors, painting swastikas on the walls of a Jewish synagogue, or marching on Martin Luther King Jr.'s birthday somewhere in small-town, southern America. They remain a dark legacy of the Civil War, which killed more than 600,000 Americans, and the institution of slavery. When the war ended, the South lay in ruins. For the next 12 years, northern Republicans tried to "reconstruct" the South in a chaotic crusade that mixed retribution, corruption, and genuine idealism. Intent on punishing white southerners for their disloyalty while enfranchising millions of former slaves, the northern Republicans, especially the "Radicals," tried to extend full civil rights via the Fourteenth and Fifteenth Amendments, but for a variety of reasons the attempt failed. By 1877, political power in the South had reverted to the white elite.

A major factor in the failure of Radical Republicans to "reconstruct" the South was the rise of the Ku Klux Klan. Enraged at the very thought of black political power, Klansmen resorted to intimidation and violence, punishing southern blacks even suspected of sympathizing with Radical goals for the South. In "Knights of the Rising Sun," historian Allen Trelease describes Klan activities in Texas during the late 1860s. Isolated from the main theaters of the Civil War, much of Texas remained unreconstructed, and the old white elite, along with their Klan allies, succeeded in destroying every vestige of black political activity and in eliminating the Republican party from the state's political life.

Large parts of Texas remained close to anarchy through 1868. Much of this was politically inspired despite the fact that the state was not yet reconstructed and took no part in the national election. In theory the Army was freer to take a direct hand in maintaining order than was true in the states which had been readmitted, but the shortage of troops available for this duty considerably lessened that advantage. At least twenty counties were involved in the Ku Klux terror, from Houston north to the Red River. In Houston itself Klan activity was limited to the holding of monthly meetings in a gymnasium and posting notices on lampposts, but in other places there was considerable violence.

By mid-September disguised bands had committed several murders in Trinity County, where two lawyers and both justices of the peace in the town of Sumter were well known as Klansmen. Not only did the crimes go unpunished, but Conservatives used them to force a majority of the Negroes to swear allegiance to the Democratic party; in return they received the familiar protection papers supposedly guaranteeing them against further outrage. "Any one in this community opposed to the Grand Cyclops and his imps is in danger of his life," wrote a local Republican in November. In Washington County the Klan sent warning notices to Republicans and committed at least one murder. As late as January 1869 masked parties were active around Palestine, shaving heads, whipping, and shooting among the black population, as well as burning down their houses. The military arrested five or six men for these offenses, but the Klan continued to make the rounds of Negroes' and Union men's houses, confiscating both guns and money. Early in November General J. J. Reynolds, military commander

in the state, declared in a widely quoted report that "civil law east of the Trinity river is almost a dead letter" by virtue of the activities of Ku Klux Klans and similar organizations. Republicans had been publicly slated for assassination and forced to flee their homes, while the murder of Negroes was too common to keep track of. These lawless bands, he said, were "evidently countenanced, or at least not discouraged, by a majority of the white people in the counties where [they] are most numerous. They could not otherwise exist." These statements did not endear the general to Conservative Texans, but they were substantially true.

The worst region of all, as to both Klan activity and general banditry, remained northeast Texas. A correspondent of the Cincinnati *Commercial* wrote from Sulphur Springs early in January 1869:

Armed bands of banditti, thieves, cut-throats and assassins infest the country; they prowl around houses, they call men out and shoot or hang them, they attack travellers upon the road, they seem almost everywhere present, and are ever intent upon mischief. You cannot pick up a paper without reading of murders, assassinations and robbery. . . . And yet not the fourth part of the truth has been told; not one act in ten is reported. Go where you will, and you will hear of fresh murders and violence. . . . The civil authority is powerless—the military insufficient in number, while hell has transferred its capital from pandemonium to Jefferson, and the devil is holding high carnival in Gilmer, Tyler, Canton, Quitman, Boston, Marshall and other places in Texas.

Judge Hardin Hart wrote Governor Pease in September to say that on account of "a regularly organized band which has overrun the country" he could not hold court in Grayson, Fannin, and Hunt counties without a military escort.

Much of this difficulty was attributable to outlaw gangs like those of Ben Bickerstaff and

"Texas: The Knights of the Rising Sun" from *White Terror: The Ku Klux Klan Conspiracy and Southern Reconstruction* by Allen W. Trelease. Copyright © 1971 by Allen W. Trelease. Reprinted by permission of the author.

Cullen Baker, but even their activities were often racially and politically inspired, with Negroes and Union men the chief sufferers. Army officers and soldiers reported that most of the population at Sulphur Springs was organized into Ku Klux clubs affiliated with the Democratic party and some of the outlaws called themselves Ku Klux Rangers. At Clarksville a band of young men calling themselves Ku Klux broke up a Negro school and forced the teacher to flee the state.

White Conservatives around Paris at first took advantage of Klan depredations among Negroes by issuing protection papers to those who agreed to join the Democratic party. But the marauding reached such proportions that many freedmen fled their homes and jobs, leaving the crops untended. When a body of Klansmen came into town early in September, apparently to disarm more blacks, some of the leading citizens warned them to stop. The freedmen were not misbehaving, they said, and if they needed disarming at a later time the local people would take care of it themselves. Still the raiding continued, and after a sheriff's posse failed to catch the culprits the farmers in one neighborhood banded together to oppose them by force. (Since the Klan had become sacred among Democrats, these men claimed that the raiding was done by an unauthorized group using its name. They carefully denied any idea of opposing the Klan itself.) Even this tactic was ineffective so far as the county as a whole was concerned, and the terror continued at least into November. The Freedmen's Bureau agent, Colonel DeWitt C. Brown, was driven away from his own farm thirty miles from Paris and took refuge in town. There he was subjected to constant threats of assassination by Klansmen or their sympathizers. From where he stood the Klan seemed to be in almost total command.

The Bureau agent at Marshall (like his predecessor in the summer) suspected that the planters themselves were implicated in much of the terrorism. By driving Negroes from their homes just before harvest time the Klan enabled many landowners to collect the crop without having to pay the laborers' share.

Jefferson and Marion County remained the center of Ku Klux terrorism, as the Cincinnati reporter pointed out. A garrison of twenty-six men under Major James Curtis did little to deter violence. Bands of hooded men continued to make nocturnal depredations on Negroes in the surrounding countryside during September and October as they had for weeks past. "Whipping the freedmen, robbing them of their arms, driving them off plantations, and murdering whole families are of daily, and nightly occurrence," wrote the local Bureau agent at the end of October, "all done by disguised parties whom no one can testify to. The civil authorities never budge an inch to try and discover these midnight marauders and apparently a perfect apathy exists throughout the whole community regarding the general state of society. Nothing but martial law can save this section as it is at present. . . ." Inside town, Republicans hardly dared go outdoors at night, and for several weeks the county judge, who was afraid to go home even in the daytime, slept at the Army post. The local Democratic newspapers, including the *Ultra Ku Klux*, encouraged the terror by vying with one another in the ferocity of their denunciations of Republicans.

Major Curtis confirmed this state of affairs in a report to General Reynolds:

Since my arrival at the Post. . . . [in mid-September] I have carefully observed the temper of the people and studied their intentions. I am constrained to say that neither are pacific. The amount of unblushing fraud and outrage perpetrated upon the negroes is hardly to be believed unless witnessed. Citizens who are esteemed respectable do not hesitate to take every unfair advantage. My office is daily visited by large numbers of unfortunates who have had money owing them, which they have been unable to obtain. The moral sense of the community appears blunted and gray headed apologists for such men as Baker and Bicker-staff can be met on all the street corners. . . . The right of franchise in this section is a farce. Numbers of negroes have been killed for daring to be Radicals, and their houses have so often been broken into by their Ku Klux neighbors in search of arms that they are now pretty well defenceless. The civil officers cannot and will not punish these outrages. Calvary armed with double barrelled shotguns would soon scour the country and these desperadoes be met on their own ground. They do not fear the arms that the troops now have, for they shoot from behind hedges and fences or at night and then run. No more notice is taken here of the death of a Radical negro than of a mad dog. A democratic negro however, who was shot the other day by another of his stripe, was followed to his grave through the streets of this city by a long procession in carriages, on horseback, and on foot. I saw some of the most aristocratic and respectable white men in this city in the procession.

On the same night that Curtis wrote, the new Grand Officers of the Knights of the Rising Sun were installed in the presence of a crowd of 1,200 or 1,500 persons. "The town was beautifully illuminated," a newspaper reported, "and the Seymour Knights and the Lone Star Club turned out in full uniform, with transparencies and burners, in honor of the occasion." Sworn in as Grand Commander for the ensuing twelve months was Colonel William P. Saufley, who doubled as chairman of the Marion County Democratic executive committee. Following the installation "able and patriotic speeches" were delivered by several notables, including a Democratic Negro.

As usual, the most hated Republican was the one who had the greatest Negro following. This was Captain George W. Smith, a young Union army veteran from New York who had settled in Jefferson as a merchant at the end of the war. His business failed, but the advent of Radical Reconstruction opened the prospect of a successful political career; at the age of twenty-four Smith was elected to the state constitutional convention by the suffrage of the Negro majority around Jefferson. At the convention, according to a perhaps overflattering posthumous account, he was recognized as one of the abler members. "In his daily life he was correct, almost austere. He never drank, smoked, chewed, nor used profane language." However, "he was odious as a negro leader, as a radical, as a man who could not be cowed, nor scared away." Smith may also have alienated his fellow townspeople by the strenuous efforts he made to collect debts they owed him. Even a few native Republicans like Judge Charles Caldwell, who was scarcely more popular with Conservatives, refused to speak from the same platform with him. As his admirer pointed out, Smith "was ostracized and his life often threatened. But he refused to be scared. He sued some of his debtors and went to live with colored people." One day, as he returned from a session of the convention, his carpetbag—perhaps symbolically—was stolen, its contents rifled, and a list of them published in a local newspaper.

The beginning of the end for Smith came on the night of October 3, after he and Anderson Wright, a Negro, had spoken at a Republican meeting. As he opened the door of a Negro cabin to enter, Smith was fired upon by four men outside including Colonel Richard P. Crump, one of Jefferson's leading gentry. Smith drew his revolver and returned the fire, wounding two of the assailants and driving them away. He then went to Major Curtis at the Army post. Here Crump, with the chief of police and others, soon arrived bearing a warrant for his arrest on a charge of assault. The attackers' original intention to kill Smith now assumed greater urgency because he and several Negroes present had recognized their assailants. Smith objected strenuously to their efforts to get custody of him, protesting that it was equivalent to signing his death warrant. Nevertheless Curtis turned him over to the civil authorities on their assurance of his safety. Smith was taken off to jail and a small civilian guard was posted around it. The major was uneasy, however, and requested reinforcements from his superior, but they were refused.

The next day there were signs in Jefferson of an assembling of the Knights of the Rising Sun. Hoping to head off a lynching, Curtis dispatched sixteen soldiers (the greater part of his command) to help guard the jail. At 9 p.m., finally, a signal was sounded—a series—of strokes on a bell at the place where the Knights held their meetings. About seventy members now mobilized under the command of Colonel Saufley and proceeded to march in formation toward the jail; they were in disguise and many carried torches. The jail building lay in an enclosed yard where at that time four black men were confined for a variety of petty offenses. One of the prisoners was Anderson Wright, and apparently the real reason for their being there was that they had witnessed the previous night's attempt to murder Smith; they may even have been fellow targets at that time. When the Knights reached this enclosure they burst through it with a shout and overpowered the guard, commanded by a young Army lieutenant. The invaders then turned to the Negro prisoners and dragged them into some adjoining woods. Wright and a second man, Cornelius Turner, managed to escape from them, although Wright was wounded; the other two prisoners were shot nearly to pieces. As soon as Major Curtis heard the shooting and firing he came running with his remaining soldiers; but they too were quickly overpowered. Repeatedly the major himself tried to prevent the mob from entering the jail building in which Smith was confined, only to be dragged away from the door each time. They had no trouble unlocking the door, for city marshall Silas Nance, who possessed the key, was one of the conspirators.

At first Smith tried to hold the door shut against their entry. Eventually failing at this, he caught the foremost man, pulled him into the room, and somehow killed him. "It is common talk in Jefferson now," wrote a former Bureau agent some months later, "that Capt. Smith killed the first man who entered—that the Knights of the Rising Sun afterward buried him secretly with their funeral rites, and it was hushed up, he being a man from a distance. It is an established fact that one Gray, a strong man, who ventured into the open door, was so beaten by Capt. Smith that he cried, 'Pull me out! He's killing me!' and he was dragged out backward by the leg." All this took place in such darkness that the Knights could not see their victim. Some of them now went outside and held torches up to the small barred window of Smith's cell. By this light they were able to shoot him four times. "The door was burst open and the crowd surged in upon him as he fell, and then, man after man, as they filed around fired into the dying body. This refinement of barbarity was continued while he writhed and after his limbs had ceased to quiver, that each one might participate in the triumph."

Once the mob had finished its work at the jail it broke up into squads which began patrolling the town and searching for other Republican leaders. County Judge Campbell had anticipated trouble earlier in the evening and taken refuge as usual at Major Curtis' headquarters. Judge Caldwell was hated second only to Smith after his well-publicized report as chairman of the constitutional convention's committee on lawlessness. Hearing the shooting around the jail, he fled from his home into the woods. In a few moments twenty-five or thirty Knights appeared at the house, looking for him. Some of the party were for killing him, and they spent two hours vainly trying to learn his whereabouts from his fifteen-year-old son, who refused to tell. Another band went to the house of G. H. Slaughter, also a member of the convention, but he too escaped.

The next day the few remaining white Republicans in town were warned by friends of a widely expressed desire to make a "clean

By 1868 the Ku Klux Klan had become a full-fledged terrorist organization involving community members of all classes and ranks, many of whom were veterans of the Confederate army.

them to stay and offered their protection. But the Republicans recalled the pledge to Smith and departed as quickly as they could, some openly and others furtively to avoid ambush.

White Conservatives saw these events—or at least their background and causes—in another light. They regarded Smith as "a dangerous, unprincipled carpet-bagger" who "lived almost entirely with negroes, on terms of perfect equality." Whether there was evidence for it or not, they found it easy to believe further that this "cohabitation" was accompanied by "the most unbridled and groveling licentiousness"; according to one account he walked the streets with Negroes in a state of near-nudity. For at least eighteen months he had thus "outraged the moral sentiment of the city of Jefferson," defying the whites to do anything about it and threatening a race war if they tried. This might have been overlooked if he had not tried repeatedly to precipitate such a collision. As head of the Union League he delivered inflammatory speeches and organized the blacks into armed mobs who committed assaults and robberies and threatened to burn the town. When part of the city did go up in flames earlier in the year Smith was held responsible. Overlooking the well-attested white terrorism which had prevailed in the city and county for months, a Democratic newspaper claimed that all had been peace and quiet during Smith's absence at the constitutional convention. But on his return he resumed his incendiary course and made it necessary for the whites to arm in self-defense.

According to Conservatives the initial shooting affray on the night of October 3 was precipitated by a group of armed Negroes with Smith at their head. They opened fire on Crump and his friends while the latter were on their way to protect a white man whom Smith had threatened to attack. Democrats did not dwell over-long on the ensuing lynching, nor did they bother to explain the killing of the Negro prisoners. In fact the affair was made deliberately mysterious and a bit romantic in their telling. According to the Jef-

sweep" of them. Most of them stayed at the Haywood House hotel the following night under a military guard. Meanwhile the KRS scoured the city looking for dangerous Negroes, including those who knew too much about the preceding events for anyone's safety. When Major Curtis confessed that the only protection he could give the white Republicans was a military escort out of town, most of them decided to leave. At this point some civic leaders, alarmed at the probable effects to the town and themselves of such an exodus under these circumstances, urged ferson *Times*, both the soldiers and the civilians on guard at the jail characterized the lynch party as "entirely sober and apparently well disciplined." (One of the party later testified in court that at least some of them had put on their disguises while drinking at a local saloon.) "After the accomplishment of their object," the *Times* continued, "they all retired as quietly and mysteriously as they came—none knowing who they were or from whence they came." (This assertion, it turned out, was more hopeful than factual.)

The *Times* deplored such proceedings in general, it assured its readers, but in this case lynching "had become . . . an unavoidable necessity. The sanctity of home, the peace and safety of society, the prosperity of the country, and the security of life itself demanded the removal of so base a villain." A month later it declared: "Every community in the South will do well to relieve themselves [*sic*] of their surplus Geo. Smiths, and others of like ilk, as Jefferson rid herself of hers. This is not a healthy locality for such incendiaries, and no town in the South should be." Democratic papers made much of Judge Caldwell's refusal to appear publicly with Smith—which was probably inspired by his Negro associations. They claimed that Smith's fellow Republicans were also glad to have him out of the way, and noted that the local citizens had assured them of protection. But there was no mention of the riotous search and the threats upon their lives which produced that offer, nor of their flight from the city anyway.

The Smith affair raises problems of fact and interpretation which appeared in almost every Ku Klux raid across the South. Most were not so fully examined or reported as this, but even here it is impossible to know certainly where the truth lay. Republican and Democratic accounts differed diametrically on almost every particular, and both were colored by considerations of political and personal interest. But enough detailed and impartial evidence survives to sustain the Republican case on most counts. Negro and Re-

publican testimony concerning the actual events in October is confirmed by members of the KRS who turned state's evidence when they were later brought to trial. Smith's prior activities and his personal character are less clear. Republicans all agreed later that he was almost puritanical in his moral code and that he was hated because of his unquestioned social associations and political influence with the blacks. He never counseled violence or issued threats to burn the town, they insisted; on the contrary, the only time he ever headed a Negro crowd was when he brought a number of them to help extinguish the fire which he was falsely accused of starting.

As elsewhere in the South, the logic of some of the charges against Smith is not convincing. Whites had a majority in the city and blacks in the county. Theoretically each could gain by racial violence, offsetting its minority status. But Conservatives always had the advantage in such confrontations. They were repeatedly guilty of intimidating the freedmen, and in case of an open collision everyone (including Republicans) knew they could win hands down. Democrats were certainly sincere in their personal and political detestation of Smith; almost as certainly they were sincere in their fears of his political activity and what it might lead to. From their viewpoint an open consorter with and leader of Negroes was capable of anything. It was easy therefore to believe the worst and attribute the basest motives without clear evidence. If some Negroes did threaten to burn the town—often this was a threat to retaliate for preceding white terrorism—it was easy to overlook the real cause and attribute the idea to Smith. The next step, involving hypocrisy and deliberate falsehood in some cases, was to charge him with specific expressions and activities which no other source substantiates and which the logic of the situation makes improbable. Men who practiced or condoned terrorism and murder in what they conceived to be a just cause would not shrink from character assassination in the same cause.

Interestingly enough, most of the character assassination—in Smith's case and generally—followed rather than preceded Ku Klux attacks. This did not arise primarily from a feeling of greater freedom or safety once the victim was no longer around to defend himself; some victims, unlike Smith, lived to speak out in their own behalf. Accusations after the fact were intended rather to rationalize and win public approval of the attack once it had occurred; since these raids were the product of at least semisecret conspiracy there was less need to win public approval beforehand. Sometimes such accusations were partially true, no doubt, and it was never easy for persons at a distance to judge them; often it is no easier now. Democrats tended to believe and Republicans to reject them as a matter of course. The *Daily Austin Republican* was typical of Radical papers in its reaction to Democratic newspaper slurs against Smith after his death: "We have read your lying sheets for the last *eighteen* months, and this is the first time you have made any such charges. . . ." It was surely justified in charging the Democratic editors of Texas with being accessories after the fact in Smith's murder.

The military authorities had done almost nothing to stop KRS terrorism among the Negroes before Smith's murder, and this violence continued for at least two months afterward. Similar conditions prevailed widely, and there were too few troops—especially cavalry—to patrol every law-less county. But the murder of a white man, particularly one of Smith's prominence and in such a fashion, aroused officials to unwonted activity. The Army recalled Major Curtis and sent Colonel H. G. Malloy to Jefferson as provisional mayor with orders to discover and bring to justice the murderers of Smith and the two freedmen killed with him. More troops were also sent, amounting ultimately to nine companies of infantry and four of cavalry. With their help Malloy arrested four of Jefferson's leading men on December 5.

Colonel W. P. Saufley, whom witnesses identified as the organizer of the lynching, would have been a fifth, but he left town the day before on business, a Democratic newspaper explained, apparently unaware that he was wanted. (This business was to take him into the Cherokee Indian Nation and perhaps as far as New York, detaining him so long that the authorities never succeeded in apprehending him.) That night the KRS held an emergency meeting and about twenty men left town for parts unknown while others prepared to follow.

General George P. Buell arrived soon afterward as commandant, and under his direction the arrests continued for months, reaching thirty-seven by early April. They included by common repute some of the best as well as the worst citizens of Jefferson. Detectives were sent as far as New York to round up suspects who had scattered in all directions. One of the last to leave was General H. P. Mabry, a former judge and a KRS leader who was serving as one of the counsel for the defense. When a soldier revealed that one of the prisoners had turned state's evidence and identified Mabry as a leader in the lynching, he abruptly fled to Canada.

The authorities took great pains to recover Anderson Wright and Cornelius Turner, the Negro survivors of the lynching, whose testimony would be vital in the forthcoming trials. After locating Wright, General Buell sent him with an Army officer to find Turner, who had escaped to New Orleans. They traveled part of the way by steamboat and at one point, when the officer was momentarily occupied elsewhere, Wright was set upon by four men. He saved himself by jumping overboard and made his way to a nearby Army post, whence he was brought back to Jefferson. Buell then sent a detective after Turner, who eventually was located, and both men later testified at the trial.

The intention of the authorities was to try the suspects before a military commission, as they were virtually sure of acquittal in the civil courts. Defense counsel (who consisted ultimately of eleven lawyers—nearly the whole Jefferson bar) made every effort to have the case transferred; two of them even went to Washington to appeal personally to Secretary of War Schofield, but he refused to interfere. R. W. Loughery, the editor of both the Jefferson *Times* and the *Texas Republican* in Marshall, appealed to the court of public opinion. His editorials screamed indignation at the "terrible and revolting ordeal through which a refined, hospitable, and intelligent people are passing, under radical rule," continually subject to the indignity and danger of midnight arrest. He also sent requests to Washington and to Northern newspapers for intercession against Jefferson's military despotism. The prisoners, he said, were subject to brutal and inhuman treatment. Loughery's *ex parte* statement of the facts created a momentary ripple but no reversal of policy. In reality the prisoners were treated quite adequately and were confined in two buildings enclosed by a stockade. Buell released a few of them on bond, but refused to do so in most cases for the obvious reason that they would have followed their brothers in flight. Although they seem to have been denied visitors at first, this rule was lifted and friends regularly brought them extra food and delicacies. The number of visitors had to be limited, however, because most of the white community regarded them as martyrs and crowded to the prison to show their support.

After many delays the members of the military commission arrived in May and the trial got under way; it continued into September. Although it proved somewhat more effective than the civil courts in punishing Ku Klux criminals, this tribunal was a far cry from the military despotism depicted by its hysterical opponents. The defense counsel presented their case fully and freely. Before long it was obvious that they would produce witnesses to swear alibis for most or all of the defendants. Given a general public conspiracy of this mag-

nitude, and the oaths of KRS members to protect each other, this was easy to do; and given the dependence of the prosecution by contrast on Negro witnesses whose credibility white men (including Army officers) were accustomed to discounting, the tactic was all too effective. The results were mixed. At least fourteen persons arrested at one time or another never went to trial, either for lack of evidence or because they turned state's evidence. Seventeen others were tried and acquitted, apparently in most cases because of sworn statements by friends that they were not present at the time of the lynching. Only six were convicted. Three of these were sentenced to life terms, and three to a term of four years each in the Huntsville penitentiary. General Reynolds refused to accept the acquittal of Colonel Crump and three others, but they were released from custody anyway, and the matter was not raised again. Witnesses who had risked their lives by testifying against the terrorists were given help in leaving the state, while most of the defendants returned to their homes and occupations. The arrests and trials did bring peace to Jefferson, however. The Knights of the Rising Sun rode no more, and the new freedom for Radicals was symbolized in August by the appearance of a Republican newspaper.

Relative tranquillity came to northeast Texas generally during the early part of 1869. Some Republicans attributed this to the election of General Grant, but that event brought no such result to other parts of the South. Both Ben Bickerstaff and Cullen Baker were killed and their gangs dispersed, which certainly helped. The example of military action in Jefferson likely played a part; it was accompanied by an increase of military activity throughout the region as troops were shifted here from the frontier and other portions of the state. Immediately after the Smith lynching in October, General Reynolds ordered all civil and military officials to "arrest, on the spot any person wearing a mask or otherwise disguised." Arrests did increase, but it was probably owing less to this order than to the more efficient concentration of troops. In December the Bureau agent in Jefferson had cavalry (for a change) to send out after men accused of Ku Klux outrages in Upshur County. Between October 1868 and September 1869 fifty-nine cases were tried before military commissions in Texas, chiefly involving murder or aggravated assault; they resulted in twenty-nine convictions. This record was almost breathtaking by comparison with that of the civil courts.

The Texas crime rate remained high after 1868. Organized Ku Klux activity declined markedly, but it continued in sporadic fashion around the state for several years. A new state government was elected in November 1869 and organized early the next year under Republican Governor E. J. Davis. In his first annual message, in April 1870, Davis called attention to the depredations of disguised bands. To cope with them he asked the legislature to create both a state police and a militia, and to invest him with the power of martial law. In June and July the legislature responded affirmatively on each count. The state police consisted of a mounted force of fewer than 200 men under the state adjutant general; in addition, all county sheriffs and their deputies and all local marshals and constables were considered to be part of the state police and subject to its orders. In November 1871 a law against armed and disguised persons followed. Between July 1870 and December 1871 the state police arrested 4,580 persons, 829 of them for murder or attempted murder. Hundreds of other criminals probably fled the state to evade arrest. This activity, coupled with occasional use of the governor's martial law powers in troubled localities, seems to have diminished lawlessness by early 1872. There still remained the usual problems of prosecuting or convicting Ku Klux offenders, however, and very few seem to have been punished legally.

Study Questions

1. Why was Klan terrorism so rampant in Texas? Did the federal government possess the means of preventing it?

2. What was the relationship between the Ku Klux Klan in Texas and the Democratic party?

3. How did well-to-do white planters respond to the Ku Klux Klan?

4. What were the objectives of the Ku Klux Klan in Texas?

5. Who were the white conservatives? How did they interpret Klan activities?

6. Why did the state government try to curtail Klan activities in the early 1870s? Did state officials succeed?

Bibliography

The book that created two generations of stereotypes by vindicating the South and indicting the North is William A. Dunning's *Reconstruction, Political and Economic* (1907). The first major dissent came from W. E. B. DuBois's classic

Black Reconstruction in America, 1860–1880 (1935). It was not until the civil rights movement of the 1960s that historians engaged in a fresh look at Reconstruction. John Hope Franklin's *Reconstruction After the Civil War* (1961) took Dunning to task, as did Kenneth Stampp in *The Era of Reconstruction* (1965). For a look at political corruption during the era of Reconstruction, see Mark W. Summers, *The Era of Good Stealings* (1993). Since its inception in the 1870s, the Ku Klux Klan rose and fell, then rose and fell again, and then resurrected again, waxing and waning in rhythm with American debates over race, immigration, and ethnicity. Allan Trelease's *White Terrorism: The Ku Klux Klan Conspiracy and Southern Reconstruction* (1971) is a good place to begin a study of the early Klan. Also see Stanley F. Horn, *Invisible Empire: The Story of the Ku Klux Klan, 1866–1871* (1969). For general histories of the Klan, see Wyn Craig Wade, *Fiery Cross: The KKK in America* (1986) and Mark David Chalmers, *Hooded Americanism: The History of the Ku Klux Klan* (1981). For the recent history of the Klan, see Mark David Chalmers, *Backfire: How the KKK Helped the Civil Rights Movement* (2003).

READING 2

★ ★ ★

A Road They Did Not Know

Larry McMurtry

The battle remains, even today, over 125 years later, shrouded in mystery and a pop-culture fog. The great Sioux warrior chiefs—Crazy Horse and Sitting Bull—took on one of the U.S. Army's most flamboyant officers, and when the dust settled, all of the white soldiers, including Lieutenant Colonel George Armstrong Custer, were dead, killed in a tactical blunder of epic proportions. The death of Custer and the troops in his 7th Cavalry captured the American imagination in the 1870s; and since then, it has continued to inspire curiosity, awe, and inquiry. It has spawned a scholarly literature and a mythology un-equaled in U.S. history. In the following article, one of America's most gifted novelists—Larry McMurtry—deciphers exactly what happened on June 25–26, 1876, at the Battle of the Little Big Horn, why it happened, and what it has meant to Americans.

By the summer of 1875 a crisis over the Black Hills of South Dakota could no longer be postponed. Lt. Col. George Armstrong Custer had made a grand announcement that there was gold in the hills, and it caught the nation's attention. After that miners could not be held back. The government was obviously going to find a way to take back the Black Hills, but just as obviously, it was not going to be able to do so without difficulty and without criticism. The whites in the peace party were vocal; they and others of various parties thought the government ought to at least *try* to honor its agreements, particularly those made as solemnly and as publicly as the one from 1868 giving the Sioux the Black Hills and other lands. So there ensued a period of wiggling and squirming, on the part of the government and the part of the Sioux, many of whom had become agency Indians by this time. The free life of the hunting Sioux was still just possible, but only in certain areas: the Powder River, parts of Montana, and present-day South Dakota west of the Missouri River, where the buffalo still existed in some numbers.

By this time most of the major Indian leaders had made a realistic assessment of the situation and drawn the obvious conclusion, which was that their old way of life was rapidly coming to an end. One way or another they were going to have to walk the white man's road—or else fight until they were all killed. The greatest Sioux warriors, Crazy Horse and Sitting Bull, were among the most determined of the hostiles; two others, Red Cloud and Spotted Tail, rivals at this point, both had settled constituencies. They were administrators essentially, struggling to get more food and better goods out of their respective agents. As more and more Indians came in and enrollment lists swelled, this became a full-time job, and a vexing and frustrating one at that.

There were of course many Indians who tried to walk a middle road, unwilling to give up the old ways completely but recognizing that the presence of whites in what had once been their country was now a fact of life. Young Man Afraid of His Horses, son of the revered Old Man Afraid of His Horses, was one of the middle-of-the-roaders.

The whites at first tried pomp and circumstance, bringing the usual suspects yet again to Washington, hoping to tempt them—Red Cloud, Spotted Tail, anyone—to sell the Black Hills. They would have liked to have had Sitting Bull and Crazy Horse at this grand parley, or even a moderate, such as Young Man Afraid of His Horses, but none of these men or any of the principal hostiles wanted anything to do with this mini-summit. Red Cloud and Spotted Tail had no authority to sell the Black Hills, or to do anything about them at all, a fact the white authorities should have realized by this time. There were still thousands of Sioux on the northern plains who had not given their consent to anything. The mini-summit fizzled.

Many Indians by this time had taken to wintering in the agencies and then drifting off again once the weather improved. Thousands came in, but when spring came, many of them went out again.

Crazy Horse, who was about thirty-five years old, enjoyed in 1875–76 what was to be his last more or less unharassed winter as a free Indian. How well or how clearly he realized that his time was ending, we don't know. Perhaps he still thought that if the people fought fiercely and didn't relent, they could beat back the whites, not all the way to the Platte perhaps, but at least out of the Powder River country. We don't really know what he was thinking and should be cautious about making him more geopolitically attuned than he may have been. At this juncture nobody had really agreed to anything, but as the spring of 1876 approached, the Army directed a number of its major players toward the

Larry McMurtry, "A Road They Did Not Know," *American Heritage*, 50 (February–March 1999), 52–65.

northern plains. To the south, on the plains of Texas, the so-called Red River War was over. The holdouts among the Comanches and the Kiowas had been defeated and their horse herd destroyed. Ranald S. Mackenzie and Nelson A. Miles both distinguished themselves in the Red River War and were soon sent north to help subdue the Cheyennes and the northern Sioux. Gen. George Crook was already in the field, and Col. John Gibbon, Gen. Alfred Terry, and, of course, George Armstrong Custer were soon on their way.

By March of 1876 a great many Indians were moving north, toward Sitting Bull and the Hunkpapa band of Sioux, ready for a big hunt and possibly for a big fight with the whites, if the whites insisted on it, as in fact they did. The Little Bighorn in eastern Montana was the place chosen for this great gathering of native peoples, which swelled with more and more Indians as warmer weather came.

General Crook—also known as Three Stars, or the Grey Fox—struck first. He located what the scout Frank Grouard assured him was Crazy Horse's village, made a dawn attack, captured the village, destroyed the ample provender it contained (some of which his own hungry men could happily have eaten), but killed few Indians. Where Crazy Horse actually was at this time is a matter much debated, but the camp Crook destroyed seems not to have been his. For Crook the encounter was more vexation than triumph. The Sioux regrouped that night and got back most of their horses, and the fight drove these peace-seeking Indians back north toward Sitting Bull. Crook continued to suppose that he had destroyed Crazy Horse's village; no doubt some of the Indian's friends were there, but the man himself was elsewhere.

A vast amount had been written about the great gathering of Indians who assembled in Montana in the early summer of 1876. It was to be the last mighty grouping of native peoples on the Great Plains of America. For the older people it evoked memories of earlier summer gatherings—reunions of a sort—such as had once been held at Bear Butte, near Crazy Horse's birthplace. Many of these Indians probably knew that what was occurring was in the nature of a last fling; there might be no opportunity for such a grand occasion again. Most of the Indians who gathered knew that the soldiers were coming, but

Sitting Bull

Lt. Col. George Armstrong Custer

they didn't care; their numbers were so great that they considered themselves invincible. Many Indians, from many tribes, remembered it as a last great meeting and mingling, a last good time. Historically, from this point on, there is a swelling body of reminiscence about the events of the spring and summer of 1876. Indeed, from the time the armies went into the field in 1876 to the end of the conflict, there is a voluminous memoir literature to be sifted through—most of it military memoirs written by whites. Much of this found its way into the small-town newspapers that by then dotted the plains. These memoirs are still emerging. In 1996 four letters written by the wife of a captain who was at Fort Robinson when Crazy Horse was killed were discovered and published. The woman's name was Angie Johnson. It had taken more than a century for this literature to trickle out of the attics and scrapbooks of America, and it is still trickling. Of course it didn't take that long for the stately memoirs of Generals Sheridan and Sherman and Miles and the rest to be published.

Though the bulk of this memoir literature is by white soldiers, quite a few of the Sioux and the Cheyennes who fought at the Little Bighorn managed to get themselves interviewed here and there. It is part of the wonder of the book *Son of the Morning Star* that Evan S. Connell has patiently located many of these obscurely published reminiscences from both sides of the fight and placed them in his narrative in such a way as to create a kind of mosaic of firsthand comment. These memoirs don't answer all the questions, or even very many of them, but it is still nice to know what the participants *thought* happened, even if what we're left with is a kind of mesquite thicket of opinion, dense with guessing, theory, and speculation. Any great military conflict—Waterloo, Gettysburg, et cetera—leaves behind a similar confusion, a museum of memories but an extremely untidy one. Did the general say that or do this? Was Chief Gall behind Custer or in front of him or nowhere near him? The mind that is

troubled by unanswered and possibly unanswerable questions should perhaps avoid military history entirely. Battles are messy things. Military historians often have to resort to such statements as "it would at this juncture probably be safe to assume. . . ." Stephen E. Ambrose is precisely right (and uncommonly frank) when he says plainly that much of the fun of studying the Battle of the Little Bighorn is the free rein it offers to the imagination. Once pointed toward this battle, the historical imagination tends to bolt; certainly the field of battle that the Indians called the Greasy Grass has caused many imaginations to bolt.

What we know for sure is that when June rolled around in 1876, there were a great many Indians, of several tribes, camped in southern Montana, with a fair number of soldiers moving west and north to fight them. Early June of that year may have been a last moment of confidence for the Plains Indians: They were many, they had meat, and they were in *their* place. Let the soldiers come.

This buildup of confidence was capped by what was probably the best-reported dream vision in Native American history—namely, Sitting Bull's vision of soldiers falling upside down into camp. This important vision did not come to the great Hunkpapa spontaneously; instead it was elaborately prepared for. Sitting Bull allowed a friend to cut one hundred small pieces of flesh from his arms, after which he danced, staring at the sun until he fainted. When he came out of his swoon, he heard a voice and had a vision of soldiers as numerous as grasshoppers falling upside down into camp. There were some who were skeptical of Sitting Bull—he could be a difficult sort—but this vision, coming as it did at the end of a great Sun Dance, convinced most of his people that if the soldiers did come, they would fall. (It is worth mentioning that Sitting Bull had mixed luck with visions. Not long before his death a meadowlark, speaking in Sioux, told him that his own people would kill him—which is what occurred.)

Shortly after this great vision of soldiers falling had been reported and considered, some Cheyenne scouts arrived with the news that General Crook was coming from the south with a lot of soldiers and a considerable body of Crow and Shoshone scouts. This was a sign that Sitting Bull had not danced in vain, although Crook never got very close to the great encampment, because Crazy Horse, Sitting Bull, and a large force immediately went south to challenge him on the Rosebud Creek, where the first of the two famous battles fought that summer was joined.

When the Indians attacked, Crook's thousand-man force was very strung out, with soldiers on both sides of the river, in terrain that was broken and difficult. Crow scouts were the first to spot the great party from the north; by common agreement the Crows and Shoshones fought their hearts out that day, probably saving Crook from the embarrassment of an absolute rout. But Crazy Horse, Black Twin, Bad Heart Bull, and many others were just as determined. Once or twice Crook almost succeeded in forming an effective battle line, but Crazy Horse and the others kept dashing right into it, fragmenting Crook's force and preventing a serious counterattack. There was much close-quarter, hand-to-hand fighting. In a rare anticipation of women in combat, a Cheyenne woman rushed in at some point and saved her brother, who was surrounded. (The Cheyennes afterward referred to the Battle of the Rosebud as the Battle Where the Girl Saved Her Brother.) Crook struggled all day, trying to mount a strong offensive, but the attackers were so persistent that they thwarted him. Finally the day waned, and shadows began to fall across the Rosebud. The Indians, having enjoyed a glorious day of battle, went home. They had turned Three Stars back, allowing him nowhere near the great gathering on the Little Bighorn.

Because the Indians left the field when the day was over, Crook claimed a victory, but nobody believed him, including, probably, himself. The Battle of the Rosebud was one of his most frustrating memories. It was indeed a remarkable battle between forces almost equally matched; in some ways it was more interesting than the fight at the Little Bighorn eight days later. Neither side could mount a fully decisive offensive, and both sides suffered unusually high casualties but kept fighting. The whites had no choice, of course; their adversaries in this case fought with extreme determination. The body count for the two sides varies with the commentator. Among historians who have written about the battle, George Hyde puts Crook's loss as high as fifty-seven men, a number that presumably includes many Crows and Shoshones who fell that day. Stephen Ambrose says it was twenty-eight men; Stanley Vestal says it was ten; and Robert Utley and Evan Connell claim it was nine. The attacking Sioux and Cheyennes may themselves have lost more than thirty men, an enormous casualty rate for a native force. Accustomed as we are to the wholesale slaughter of the two world wars, or even of the Civil War, it is hard to keep in mind that when Indian fought Indian, a death count of more than three or four was unusual.

At the end of the day, General Crook at last accepted the advice his scouts had offered him earlier, which was that there were too many Indians up ahead for him to fight.

Had the full extent of Crook's difficulties on the Rosebud been known to the forces moving west into Montana, the sensible officers—that is, Gibbon and Terry—would have then proceeded with extreme caution, but it is unlikely that any trouble of Crook's would have slowed Custer one whit. Even if he had known that the Indians had sent Crook packing, it is hard to imagine that he would have proceeded differently. He had plenty of explicit—and, at the last, desperate—warnings from his own scouts, but he brushed these aside as he hurried the 7th Cavalry on to its doom. He plainly did not want to give his pessimistic scouts the time of day. He refused the offer of extra troops and also refused a Gatling gun, for fear that it might slow him down and allow the Indians to get away. It was only in the last minutes of his life that Custer finally realized that the Indians were fighting, not running. Custer was convinced that he could whip whatever body of Indians he could persuade to face him. He meant to win, he meant to win alone, and he meant to win rapidly, before any other officers arrived to dilute his glory.

Custer, that erratic egotist, has been studied more than enough; he has even been the subject of one of the best books written about the West, Evan Connell's *Son of the Morning Star.* Historians have speculated endlessly about why he did what he did at the Little Bighorn on the twenty-fifth of June, 1876; and yet what he did was perfectly in keeping with his nature. He did what he had always done: push ahead, disregard orders, start a fight, win it unassisted if possible, then start another fight. He had seldom done otherwise, and there was no reason at all to expect him to do otherwise in Montana that summer.

It may be true, as several writers have suggested, that he was covertly running for president that summer. The Democratic National Convention was just convening; a flashy victory and a timely telegram might have put him in contention for the nomination. Maybe, as Connell suggests, he thought he could mop up on the Sioux, race down to the Yellowstone River, hop on the steamer *Far West,* and make it to the big opening of the Philadelphia Centennial Exposition on July 4. So he marched his men most of the night and flung them into battle when—as a number of Indians noted—they were so tired their legs shook as they dismounted. As usual, he did only minimal reconnaissance, and convinced himself on no evidence whatever that the Indians must be running away from him, not toward him. The highly experienced scouts who were with him—the half-breed Mitch Bouyer and the Arikara Bloody Knife and the Crow Half Yellow Face—all told Custer that they would die if they descended into the valley where the Indians were. None of them, in all their many years on the plains, had ever seen anything to

match this great encampment. All the scouts knew that the valley ahead was for them the valley of death. Half Yellow Face, poetically, told Custer that they would all go home that day by a road they did not know. The fatalism of these scouts is a story in itself. Bouyer, who knew exactly what was coming, sent the young scout Curly away but then himself rode on with Custer, to his death.

Whatever they said, what wisdom they offered, Custer ignored. It may be that he *was* running for president, but it is hard to believe that he would have done anything differently even if it had been an off year politically. Maj. Marcus Reno and Capt. Frederick Benteen, whom he had forced to split off, both testified much later that they didn't believe Custer had any plan when he pressed his attack. He was—and long had been—the most aggressive general in the American army. It didn't matter to him how many Indians there were. When he saw an enemy, he attacked, and would likely have done so even if he had had no political prospects.

In the week between the fight on the Rosebud and the one at the Little Bighorn, Crazy Horse went back to the big party. The great General Crook had been whipped; the Indians felt invincible again. Everyone knew that more soldiers were coming, but no one was particularly concerned. These soldiers could be whipped in turn.

Some commentators have suggested that a sense of doom and foreboding hung over the northern plains during this fatal week; Indian and soldier alike were said to feel it. Something dark and terrible was about to happen— and yet it was high summer in one of the most beautiful places in Montana, the one time when that vast plain is usually free of rain clouds or snow clouds. But this summer, Death was coming to a feast, and many felt his approach. On the morning of the battle, when most of the Sioux and Cheyennes were happily and securely going about their domestic business, never supposing that any soldiers would be foolish enough to attack them,

Crazy Horse, it is said, marked a bloody hand in red pigment on both of his horse's hips and drew an arrow and a bloody scalp on both sides of his horse's neck. Oglala scouts had been keeping watch on Custer, following his movements closely. Crazy Horse either knew or sensed that the fatal day had come.

The Battle of the Little Bighorn, June 25 and 26, 1876, is one of the most famous battles in world history. I doubt that any other American battle—not the Alamo, not Gettysburg—has spawned a more extensive or more diverse literature. There are books, journals, newsletters, one or another of which has by now printed every scrap of reminiscence that has been dredged up. Historians, both professional and amateur, have poured forth voluminous speculations, wondering what would have happened if somebody—usually the unfortunate Major Reno—had done something differently, or if Custer hadn't foolishly split his command, or if and if and if. Though the battle took place more than 120 years ago, debate has not much slackened. In fact the sudden rise in Native American studies has resulted in increased reprinting of Indian as opposed to white reminiscences; now the Sioux and the Cheyennes are pressing the debate.

A number of white historians have argued that one or another Indian leader made the decisive moves that doomed Custer and the 7th; for these historians the battle was decided by strategy and generalship, not numbers. Both Stephen Ambrose and Mari Sandoz have written many pages about the brilliance of Crazy Horse in flanking Custer and seizing the high ground—today called Custer Hill—thus ending Custer's last hope of establishing a defensive position that might have held until reinforcements arrived. Others argue for their favorite chief, whether Gall, Two Moon, or another. Evan Connell, in his lengthy account of the battle, scarcely mentions Crazy Horse's part in it. All these arguments, of course, depend on Indian memory, plus study of the battleground itself. To me they seem to be permanently ambiguous, potent rather than conclusive. It is indeed an area of study where historians can give free rein to their imaginations; what Stephen Ambrose doesn't mention is that the Sioux and the Cheyennes, in remembering this battle, might be giving *their* imaginations a little running room as well. A world in which all whites are poets and all Indians sober reporters is not the world as most of us know it.

We are likely never to know for sure who killed Custer. He had his famous hair short for this campaign; had it still been long, many Indians might have recognized him. It is as well to keep in mind that as many as two thousand horses may have been in motion during this battle; between the dust they raised and the gun smoke, the scene would have become phantasmagorical; it would have been difficult for anyone to see well, or far. It is thus little wonder that no one recognized Custer. At some sharp moment Custer must have realized that his reasoning had been flawed. The Indians he had assumed were running away were actually coming to kill him, and there were a lot of them. Whether he much regretted his error is doubtful. Fighting was what Custer did, battle thrilled him, and now he was right in the dead thick of the biggest Indian fight of all. He may have enjoyed himself right up to the moment he fell.

For his men, of course, it was a different story. They had been marching since the middle of the night; a lot of them were so tired they could barely lift their guns. For them it was dust, weariness, terror, and death.

No one knows for certain how many Indians fought in this battle, but two thousand is a fair estimate, give or take a few hundred. Besides their overpowering numbers they were also highly psyched by the great Sun Dance and their recent victory over Crook. When Major Reno and his men appeared at the south end of the great four-mile village, the Indians were primed. Reno might have charged them and produced, at least, disarray, but he didn't; the Indians soon chased him back across the Little Bighorn and up a bluff, where he survived, just barely. A lucky shot hit Bloody Knife, the Arikara scout, square in the head; Major Reno, standing near, was splattered with his brain matter. Some think this gory accident undid Major Reno, but we will never know the state of his undoneness, if any. Gall, the Hunkpap a warrior, who, by common agreement, was a major factor in this battle, soon had fifteen hundred warriors mounted and ready to fight. If Reno *had* charged the south end of the village, he might have been massacred as thoroughly as Custer.

Exactly when Crazy Horse entered the battle is a matter of debate. Some say he rode out and skirmished a little with Reno's men; others believe he was still in his lodge when Reno arrived and that he was interested only in the larger fight with Custer. Most students of the battle think that when it dawned on Custer that he was in a fight for survival, not glory, he turned north, toward the high ground, hoping to establish a defensive redoubt on the hill, or rise, that is now named for him. But Crazy Horse, perhaps at the head of as many as a thousand warriors himself, flanked him and seized that high ground, sealing Custer's doom while, incidentally, making an excellent movie role for Errol Flynn and a number of other leading men.

So Crazy Horse may have done it, but it was Gall and *his* thousand or so warriors who turned back Reno and then harried Custer so hard that the 7th Cavalry—the soldiers who fell into camp, as in Sitting Bull's vision—could never really establish *any* position. If Crazy Horse did flank Custer, it was of course good quarter-backing, but it hardly seems possible now to insist that any one move was decisive. Gall and his men might have finished Custer without much help from anyone; Gall had lost two of his wives and three of his children early in the battle and was fighting out his anger and his grief.

From this distance of years the historians can argue until their teeth rot that one man or another was decisive in this battle, but all these arguments are unprovable now. What's certain is that George Armstrong Custer was very foolish, a glory hound who ignored orders, skipped or disregarded his reconnaissance, and charged, all but blindly, into a situation in which, whatever the quality of Indian generalship, he was quickly overwhelmed by numbers.

What I think of when I walk that battleground is dust. Once or twice in my life I rode out with as many as thirty cowboys; I remember the dust that small, unhurried group made. The dust of two thousand milling, charging horses would have been something else altogether; the battleground would soon have been a hell of dust, smoke, shooting, hacking; once the two groups of fighting men closed with each other, visibility could not have been good. Custer received a wound in the breast and one in the temple, either of which would have been fatal. His corpse was neither scalped nor mutilated. Bad Soup, a Hunkpapa, is said to have pointed out Custer's corpse to White Bull. "There he lies," he said. "He thought he was going to be the greatest man in the world. But there he is."

Most of the poetic remarks that come to us from this battle are the work of writers who interviewed Indians, or those who knew Indians, who thought they remembered Bad Soup saying something, or Half Yellow Face making (probably in sign) the remark about the road we do not know, or Bloody Knife staring long at the sun that morning, knowing that he would not be alive to see it go down behind the hills that evening. All we can conclude now is that Bloody Knife and Bad Soup and Half Yellow Face were right, even if they didn't say the words that have been attributed to them.

Hundreds of commentators, from survivors who fought in the battle to historians who would not be born until long years after the dust had settled in the valley of the Little

Bighorn, have developed opinions about scores of issues that remain, in the end, completely opaque. Possibly Crazy Horse fought as brilliantly as some think—we will never really know—but he and Sitting Bull and Two Moon survived the battle and Custer didn't. General Grant, no sentimentalist, put the blame for the defeat squarely on Custer, and said so bluntly. The Indians made no serious attempt to root out and destroy Reno, though they could have. Victory over Long Hair was enough; Custer's famous 1868 dawn attack on the Cheyenne chief Black Kettle was well avenged.

The next day, to Major Reno's vast relief, the great gathering broke up, the Indians melting away into the sheltering vastness of the plains.

What did the Sioux and Cheyenne leaders think at this point? What did they feel? Several commentators have suggested that once the jubilation of victory subsided, a mood of foreboding returned. Perhaps the tribes recognized that they were likely never to be so unified again, and they were not. Perhaps the leaders knew that they were likely never to have such a one-sided military victory again either—a victory that was thrown them because of the vainglory of one white officer.

Or perhaps they didn't think in these terms at all—not yet. With the great rally over, the great battle won, they broke up and got on with their hunting. Perhaps a few did reckon that something was over now, but it is doubtful that many experienced the sense of climax and decline as poetically as Old Lodge Skins in Thomas Berger's novel *Little Big Man:* "Yes, my son," he says, "it is finished now, because what more can you do to an enemy than beat him? Were we fighting red men against red men—the way we used to, because that is a man's profession, and besides it is enjoyable—it would now be the turn of the other side to whip us. We would fight as hard as ever and perhaps win again, but they would definitely start with an advantage, because that is the *right* way. There is no permanent winning or losing when things move, as they should, in a circle. . . .

"But white men, who live in straight lines and squares, do not believe as I do. With them it is everything or nothing: Washita or Greasy Grass. . . . Winning is all they care about, and if they can do that by scratching a pen across a paper or saying something into the wind, they are much happier. . . ."

Old Lodge Skins was right about the Army's wanting to win. Crook's defeat at the Rosebud had embarrassed the Army, and the debacle at the Little Bighorn shamed it. The nation, of course, was outraged. By August of 1876 Crook and Terry were lumbering around with a reassuring force of some four thousand soldiers. Naturally they found few Indians. Crazy Horse was somewhere near Bear Butte, harrying the miners in the Black Hills pretty much as the mood struck him. There was a minor engagement or two, of little note. The Indians were not suicidal; they left the massive force alone. Crook and Terry were such respecters now that they were bogged down by their own might.

In the fall of that year, the whites, having failed to buy the Black Hills, simply took them, with a travesty of a treaty council at which the Indians lost not only the Black Hills but the Powder River, the Yellowstone, and the Bighorns. By the end of what was in some ways a year of glory, 1876, Crazy Horse had to face the fact that his people had come to a desperate pass. It was a terrible winter, with sub-zero temperatures day after day. The Indians were ragged and hungry; the soldiers who opposed them were warmly clothed and well equipped. The victories of the previous summer were, to the Sioux and the Cheyennes, now just memories. They had little ammunition and were hard pressed to find game enough to feed themselves.

During this hard period, with the soldiers just waiting for spring to begin another series of attacks, Sitting Bull decided to take himself and his people to Canada. Crazy Horse perhaps considered this option and then rejected it because in Canada the weather was even colder, or maybe he just didn't want to leave home. But in early May of 1877, he had eleven hundred people with him, and more than two thousand horses, when he came into Red Cloud agency at Fort Robinson in northwestern Nebraska. Probably neither the generals nor Crazy Horse himself ever quite believed that a true surrender had taken place, but this august event, the surrender of "Chief" Crazy Horse, was reported in *The New York Times* on May 8, 1877.

Study Questions

1. What happened to Native Americans on the Great Plains in the nineteenth century, and why did so many Indian leaders feel that they had no choice but to "either walk the white man's road" or die fighting?

2. Describe Crazy Horse and Sitting Bull.

3. What role did General George Crook play in the events leading up to Little Big Horn?

4. Why, in early June 1876, did the Indians consider themselves invincible in the face of the invading white army?

5. Describe the personality of Lieutenant Colonel George Armstrong Custer.

6. When Custer's troops went into battle, what disadvantages did they face? How did Custer's personality contribute to their problems? What miscalculations did Custer make just prior to the battle?

7. What happened to the Sioux and to the Black Hills after the battle?

Bibliography

For general surveys of the "conquest" of the American West, see Patricia Nelson Limerick, *The Legacy of Conquest: The Unbroken Past of the American West* (1987), *"It's Your Misfortune and None of My Own": A History of the American West* (1991); and Robert Hine and John Mack Faragher, *The American West: A New Interpretive History* (2000). Excellent studies of the Plains Indians include Morris W. Foster, *Being Comanche: A Social History of an American Indian Community* (1991) and Catherine Price, *The Oglala People, 1841–1879* (1996). For biographies of the major figures involved in the Battle of the Little Big Horn, see John G. Neihardt, *Black Elk Speaks: Being the Life Story of a Holy Man of the Oglala Sioux* (1961); Mari Sandoz, *Crazy Horse: The Strange Man of the Oglalas* (1961); Stephen Ambrose, *Crazy Horse and Custer: The Parallel Lives of Two American Warriors* (1996); Robert M. Utley, *Cavalier in Buckskin: George Armstrong Custer and the Western Military Frontier* (1988); and *The Lance and the Shield: The Life and Times of Sitting Bull* (1993).

2

★ ★ ★

The Gilded Age

Change dominated the American scene during the last quarter of the nineteenth century. Noted throughout most of the century for its agricultural output, America suddenly became an industrial giant, and by 1900 it led the world in industrial production. Unfettered by governmental codes and regulations, industrialists created sprawling empires. In 1872, Scottish immigrant Andrew Carnegie built his first steel mill, and his holdings steadily expanded until, almost 30 years later, he sold his steel empire to J. Pierpont Morgan for close to a half billion dollars. In oil, meatpacking, and other industries the pattern was the same—a handful of ruthless, efficient, and farsighted men dominated and directed America's industrial growth.

Just as important as the ambitious industrialists were the millions of men and women who provided the muscle that built the industries and ran the machines. Some came from the country's farmlands, victims of dropping agricultural prices or of the loneliness and boredom of farm life. Others were immigrants who came to the United States to escape poverty and political oppression. Crowded into booming cities, the workers—native and immigrant alike—labored long and hard for meager rewards.

The changes wrought by industrial growth and urban expansion created an atmosphere characterized by excitement and confusion. Some people, such as Andrew Carnegie and John D. Rockefeller, moved from relatively humble origins to fabulous wealth and impressive social standing. Each symbolized the possibility of rising from rags to riches. New opportunities created new wealth, and the important older American families were forced to make room for the new. As a result, wealthy Americans went to extraordinary lengths to display their status. J. P. Morgan bought yachts and works of art, whereas other industrialists built mansions along the rocky shore of Newport, Rhode Island. Both the boats and houses marked the owners as men who had "arrived." The clubs, restaurants, and resorts of the late nineteenth century were part of an attempt to define the new American aristocracy.

Other people suffered during this time of change. For example, the social and economic positions of farmers declined during the late nineteenth century. Once considered the "salt of the earth" and "the backbone of America," they were instead viewed as ignorant rubes and country bumpkins. Outmatched by unpredictable weather, expanding railroads, and declining prices produced by overexpansion, they consistently tried to overcome their problems by working harder, organizing cooperatives, and forming political parties. They labored heroically, but most of their efforts and organizations ended in failure.

Minority and ethnic Americans similarly faced difficult battles. Most of them were locked out of the opportunities available to educated white male Americans. It was also difficult for women to improve their social and economic positions. They experienced the excitement of the period from a distance, but they knew the pain and frustration firsthand.

READING 3

★ ★ ★

American Assassin: Charles J. Guiteau

James W. Clarke

Abraham Lincoln, James Garfield, William McKinley, Huey Long, John Kennedy, Robert Kennedy, Martin Luther King Jr.—our history has been too often altered by an assassin's bullet. Some of America's political assassins were clearly insane; others were motivated by political beliefs or dark personal desires. It is sometimes difficult to determine where political partisanship ends and insanity begins. In "American Assassin," James W. Clarke recounts the case of Charles J. Guiteau, a tireless self-promoter who shot President James A. Garfield on July 2, 1881. Guiteau was certainly unusual; part con-man, part religious fanatic, he believed he was destined for some sort of greatness. But was he insane? And if so, was his insanity a legal defense for his actions? These and other questions had to be answered by the jurors who sat in judgment of Guiteau. In an age before Sigmund Freud's work, when individuals were held responsible for their own actions, these questions were difficult, if not impossible, to fully answer.

With the single exception of Richard Lawrence, there has been no American assassin more obviously deranged than Charles Guiteau. Unlike Lawrence [who attempted to assassinate Andrew Jackson], however, who could be described as a paranoid schizophrenic, Guiteau was not paranoid. Indeed, he possessed a rather benign view of the world until shortly before he was hanged. On the gallows, he did lash out at the injustice of his persecutors, but even then his anger was tempered by a sense of martyrdom, glories anticipated in the next world, and a dying man's belief that in the future a contrite nation would erect monuments in his honor.

That Lawrence was confined in mental hospitals for the remainder of his life and Guiteau hanged can be attributed primarily to two facts: Jackson survived; Garfield did not. For certainly the symptoms of severe mental disturbance in Guiteau's case, although of a different sort, were as striking as in Lawrence's. As we will see, the convenient label and implied motive—"disappointed office-seeker"—that has been attached to Guiteau by writers and historians confuses symptoms with causes.

Religion, Law, and Politics

Charles Julius Guiteau was born on September 8, 1841, in Freeport, Illinois. His mother, a quiet, frail woman, died seven years later of complications stemming from a mind-altering "brain fever" she had initially contracted during her pregnancy with Charles. In addition to Charles, she was survived by her husband, Luther, an intensely religious man and Charles' older brother and sister, John and Frances.

From the beginning, people noticed that little Julius, as he was called (until he dropped the name in his late teens because "there was too much of the Negro about it"), was different. Luther Guiteau soon became exasperated with his inability to discipline his unruly and annoying youngest son and, as a result, Julius was largely raised by his older sister and her husband, George Scoville. Years later, in 1881, Scoville would be called to represent the accused assassin at his trial.

Although plagued by a speech impediment, for which he was whipped by his stern father, Guiteau was, in his fashion, a rather precocious youngster who learned to read quickly and write well. An annoying aversion to physical labor was observed early and remained with him the rest of his life. At the age of eighteen, Charles became interested in furthering his education and, against his father's will, used a small inheritance he had received from his grandfather to enter the University of Michigan.

His father, who was scornful of secular education, had urged his son to seek a scripture-based education at the utopian Oneida Community in New York. The curriculum there focused on study of the Bible. The elder Guiteau had hopes that his errant son might also acquire some self-discipline in a more authoritarian God-fearing environment.

After a couple of semesters at Ann Arbor, Charles, as he was now called, decided to heed his father's advice and transfer to Oneida where, in addition to religious instruction, he had recently learned that they practiced free love. With sex and the Lord on his mind, he enthusiastically entered the New York commune in June 1860. Like his father, Charles now believed that Oneida was the first stage in establishing the Kingdom of God on Earth.

Not long after his arrival, Charles came to believe that he had been divinely ordained to lead the community because, as he announced with a typical lack of humility, he alone possessed the ability. Since no one else had received this revelation, Charles soon found himself at odds with the community leadership. Moreover, the Oneida leaders believed that Charles' vigorously protested need

Clarke, James W., *American Assassins: The Darker Side of Politics.* Copyright © 1982 by Princeton University Press. Excerpt. pp. 198–214, reprinted by permission of Princeton University Press.

of increasing periods for contemplative pursuits was merely evidence of the slothfulness his father had hoped they would correct.

Other tensions also began to build. Young Charles was becoming increasingly frustrated because the young women of the community were not responding to his amorous overtures. Convinced of his personal charm, this nervous, squirrel-like little man was annoyed because these objects of his intended affection were so unresponsive. Adding insult to injury they soon laughingly referred to him as Charles "Gitout."

As his position within the community continued to deteriorate, Charles became more isolated and alienated until, in April 1865, he left for New York City. He wrote to his father to explain his decision after arriving in Hoboken:

Dear Father:

I have left the community. The cause of my leaving was because I could not conscientiously and heartily accept their views on the labor question. They wanted to make a hard-working businessman of me, but I could not consent to that, and therefore deemed it expedient to quietly withdraw, which I did last Monday. . . .

I came to New York in obedience to what I believed to be the call of God for the purpose of pursuing an independent course of theological and historical investigation. With the Bible for my textbook and the Holy Ghost for my schoolmaster, I can pursue my studies without interference from human dictation. In the country [Oneida] my time was appropriated, but now it is at my own disposal, a very favorable change. I have procured a small room, well furnished, in Hoboken, opposite the city, and intend to fruitfully pursue my studies during the next three years.

Then he announced a new scheme:

*And here it is proper to state that the energies of my life are now, and have been for months, pledged to God, to do all that within me lies to extend the sovereignty of Jesus Christ by plac-*ing at his disposal a powerful daily paper. I am persuaded that theocratic presses are destined, in due time, to supersede to a great extent pulpit oratory. There are hundreds of thousands of ministers in the world but not a single daily theocratic press. It appears to me that there is a splendid chance for some one to do a big thing for God, for humanity and for himself.*

With a new suit of clothes, a few books, and a hundred dollars in his pocket, he planned to publish his own religious newspaper that would, he was convinced, spearhead a national spiritual awakening.

In another lengthy letter to his father, Charles continued to detail his plans for the "Theocratic Daily" that would "entirely discard all muddy theology, brain philosophy and religious cant, and seek to turn the heart of men toward the living God." Buoyed with an ill-founded sense of well-being and enthusiasm, Charles went on euphorically: "I claim that I am in the employ of Jesus Christ and Co., the very ablest and strongest firm in the universe, and that what I can do is limited only by their power and purpose." And knowing full well that *he* would edit the paper, he announced confidently:

Whoever edits such a paper as I intend to establish will doubtless occupy the position of Target General to the Press, Pulpit, and Bench of the civilized world; and if God intends me for that place, I fear not, for I know that He will be "a wall of fire round me," and keep me from all harm.

Confidently expecting to promote the Kingdom of God without the restrictions of the Oneida Community and, not incidentally, also enjoy wealth and fame in the process, Guiteau sought financial backing for the paper in New York City. In a flurry of optimistic salesmanship, he scurried about presenting his proposal to prospective subscribers and advertisers; they, as it turned out, were not impressed with this odd little entrepreneur and his religious views. Soon finding himself short of money, somewhat discouraged, and tiring of a diet of dried beef, crackers, and lemonade that he ate in his dingy Hoboken room, Charles returned to Oneida after only three months in the big city.

But his return only confirmed his original reservations about the place, and he soon left again—this time more embittered by his experiences there than ever before. Again without money, Charles wrote to the Community requesting a $9,000 reimbursement—$1,500 a year for the six years he had spent there. When the community refused to pay, Charles sued, threatening to make public the alleged sexual, as well as financial, exploitation employed by the Oneida leadership—especially its founder, John Humphrey Noyes.

Undoubtedly bitter about the rejection he had endured in this sexually permissive environment, Charles lashed out in an unintentionally amusing attack on both Noyes and the Oneida women. Charging that Noyes lusted after little girls, Guiteau angrily told a reporter: "All the girls that were born in the Community were forced to cohabit with Noyes at such an early period it dwarfed them. The result was that most of the Oneida women were small and thin and homely."

Obviously stung by such criticism, Noyes threatened to bring extortion charges against Guiteau. In a letter to Charles' father, who was mortified by his son's behavior, he advised that Charles had admitted to, among other sins, stealing money, frequenting brothels, and being treated for a venereal ailment. Noyes added that Charles also had apparently thrown in the towel, so to speak, in an uninspired battle with masturbation. Such appraisals confirmed his father's sad suspicion that Charles' real purpose in going to Oneida was "the free exercise of his unbridled lust." Charles' "most shameful and wicked attack" and subsequent episodes convinced Luther Guiteau that his prodigal son was "absolutely insane." In despair, he wrote to his oldest son John that, unless something stopped him,

Charles would become "a fit subject for the lunatic asylum."

Having thus incurred his father's anger and facing the prospects of a countersuit for extortion, Charles abandoned his legal claim and left New York for Chicago. There, given the standards of the day, he began to practice law, after a fashion. In 1869, he married a young woman he had met at the Y.M.C.A., a Miss Annie Bunn. After only one memorably incoherent attempt to argue a case, his practice of law was reduced to collecting delinquent bills for clients. By 1874, the law practice and marriage had both failed, the latter as a result of his adultery with a "high toned" prostitute and the occasional beatings he used to discipline his beleaguered wife.

When his marriage ended, Charles wandered back to New York. Continually borrowing small sums of money that he never repaid voluntarily, Guiteau soon found himself, as usual, in trouble with creditors. Resentful of such unseemly harassment, he wrote an indignant letter to his brother John addressing him as "Dear Sir." This and other letters reveal the unfounded arrogance and unintentional humor of a man with only the most tenuous grasp of the reality of his position:

Your letter from Eaton . . . dated Nov. 8, '72, received. I got the $75 on my supposed responsibility as a Chicago lawyer. I was introduced to Eaton by a gentleman I met at the Young Men's Christian Association, and it was only incidentally that your name was mentioned.

I wrote to Eaton several times while at Chicago, and he ought to have been satisfied, but he had the impertinence to write you and charge me with fraud, when he knew he let me have the money entirely upon my own name and position. Had he acted like a "white" man, I should have tried to pay it long ago. I hope you will drop him.

Yours truly,
CHARLES J. GUITEAU

A few days after this letter was written, Charles' exasperated brother himself became the target of an angry response when he requested a repayment of a small loan:

J. W. GUITEAU: NEW YORK, March 13th, 1873 Find $7 enclosed. Stick it up your bung-hole and wipe your nose on it, and that will remind you of the estimation in which you are held by.

CHARLES J. GUITEAU

Sign and return the enclosed receipt and I will send you $7, but not before, and that, I hope, will end our acquaintance.

Disdainful of the pettiness of such small lenders, Charles confidently launched another major venture in the publishing business: he wanted to purchase the Chicago *Inter-Ocean* newspaper. But businessmen and bankers, from whom he sought financial backing, were unimpressed and not a little skeptical about this seedy little man with a confidential manner. Frustrated but ever the undaunted optimist, Charles turned again to religion.

Impressed with the bountiful collection plates at the Chicago revival meetings of Dwight Moody where he served as an usher in the evening services, Charles decided to prepare himself for the ministry. After a short period of voracious reading in Chicago libraries, he soon had himself convinced that he alone had ascertained the "truth" on a number of pressing theological questions. With familiar enthusiasm, he launched his new career with pamphlets and newspaper advertisements. Adorned with sandwich board posters, Charles walked the streets inviting all who would listen to attend his sermons on the physical existence of hell, the Second-Coming, and so forth. The self-promotion campaign was repeated in one town after another as he roamed between Milwaukee, Chicago, New York, and Boston.

In handbills, Charles proclaimed himself "the Eloquent Chicago Lawyer." His performances, in fact, followed a quite different pattern: a bombastic introduction that soon deteriorated into a series of incoherent nonsequiturs, whereupon he would end inconclusively and abruptly dash from the building amid the jeers and laughter of his audiences—the whole episode lasting perhaps ten to fifteen minutes. With his dubious reputation as an evangelist growing, Charles darted from one town to another leaving in his path a growing accumulation of indignant audiences and unpaid bills. Often arrested, he was periodically jailed for short periods between 1877 and 1880 when he again turned his attention to politics.

The Garfield Connection

Describing himself as a "lawyer, theologian, and politician," Guiteau threw himself into the Stalwart faction's fight for the 1880 Republican presidential nomination in New York. When a third term was denied the Stalwart's choice, Ulysses S. Grant, the nomination went to a darkhorse, James A. Garfield. Guiteau quickly jumped on the Garfield bandwagon. In New York, he began to hang around the party headquarters and, as he was to remind people later, he did work on the "canvass" for the candidate. In his view, his most noteworthy contribution to the campaign and Garfield's subsequent election, however, was an obscure speech he wrote (and may have delivered once in Troy, New York) entitled, "Garfield vs. Hancock." A few weeks before, the same speech had been entitled "Grant vs. Hancock." Undeterred by the change in candidates, the speech, Guiteau later claimed, originated and developed the issue that won the election for Garfield. That issue, in brief, was the claim that if the Democrats gained the presidency it would mean a resumption of the Civil War because the Democrats had only sectional, rather than national, loyalties. In a personal note, dated March 11, 1881, to the newly appointed secretary of state, James G. Blaine, Guiteau explained his claim:

I think I have a right to claim your help on the strength of this speech. It was sent to our leading editors and orators in August. It was the first shot in the rebel war claim idea, and it was their idea that elected Garfield . . . . I will talk with you about this as soon as I can get a chance. There is nothing against me. I claim to be a gentleman and a Christian.

Indeed, from the moment the election results were in, Guiteau had begun to press his claims in letters to Garfield and Blaine. He also became a familiar figure at the Republican party headquarters in New York, confident that he would be rewarded for his efforts with a consulship appointment; the only question remaining, he believed, was the location. Would it be Paris, Vienna, or some other post of prominence? With this in mind, he moved from New York to Washington on March 5, 1881, where he began to badger not only the President's staff but Blaine and the president himself in the corridors of the White House. Striking a posture of gallingly unwarranted familiarity with those he encountered, he also let loose a barrage of "personal" notes written in the same annoying style. Typical is the following:

[Private]
GEN'L GARFIELD
    From your looks yesterday I judge you did not quite understand what I meant by saying "I have not called for two or three weeks." I intended to express my sympathy for you on account of the pressure that has been on you since you came into office.
    I think Mr. Blaine intends giving me the Paris consulship with your and Gen. Logan's approbation, and I am waiting for the break in the Senate.
    I have practiced law in New York and Chicago, and presume I am well qualified for it.

I have been here since March 5, and expect to remain some little time, or until I get my commission.

Very respectfully,
CHARLES GUITEAU
AP'L 8

Shortly before he had written to the secretary of state to inquire whether President Hayes' appointments to foreign missions would expire in March 1881, as he expected. Learning that they would, Guiteau became more persistent in pressing his claims for an appointment to the missions of either Vienna, Paris, or possibly Liverpool. Earlier he had written again to Garfield, whom he had never met, to advise him of his plans to wed a wealthy and cultured woman (whose acquaintance, also, he had not at that time, or ever, made). Such unknowingly ludicrous acts were intended, in the bizarre judgment of Charles J. Guiteau, to enhance his already eminent qualifications for a foreign ministry.

In the meantime, the newspapers were filled with the controversy that had developed between the new President and the boss-dominated Stalwart faction of the Republican party over patronage appointments in New York. Finally, on May 13, 1881, the two most powerful of the Stalwart bosses, Roscoe Conkling and Tom "Me Too" Platt of New York, resigned their Senate seats in protest over the President's failure to follow their preferences in his patronage appointments. In so doing, they discounted the fact that Garfield had accepted their man, "Chet" Arthur, as his running mate and vice president. Angrily condemning the beleaguered Garfield's disloyalty and traitorous tactics, the resignations triggered numerous editorial attacks and denunciations of the President and his mentor Blaine, which were to continue until July 2, 1881.

On the same day the resignations were announced, Guiteau once again approached Blaine with his by now familiar blandishments, only to have the exasperated secretary roar, "Never bother me again about the Paris consulship as long as you live!" But Guiteau persisted. A week later, he wrote again to the President:

[Private]
General GARFIELD:

I have been trying to be your friend; I don't know whether you appreciate it or not, but I am moved to call your attention to the remarkable letter from Mr. Blaine which I have just noticed.

According to Mr. Farwell, of Chicago, Blaine is "a vindictive politician" and "an evil genius," and you will "have no peace till you get rid of him."

This letter shows Mr. Blaine is a wicked man, and you ought to demand his immediate resignation; otherwise you and the Republican party will come to grief. I will see you in the morning, if I can, and talk with you.

Very respectfully
CHARLES GUITEAU
May 23

If past behavior is any clue to the future, at this point Guiteau would have begun to consider yet another occupational change, returning again perhaps with his typical enthusiastic optimism to theology or law. Previously, Guiteau had accepted failure with remarkable equanimity, sustained always by the exalted opinion he had of himself. As one scheme after another collapsed—his leadership aspirations at Oneida, his journalistic ventures, the law practice, and the evangelistic crusade— his bitterness and disappointment were short-lived as he moved on to other careers. His confidence in his own ability and the Horatio Alger-like opportunities that abounded in nineteenth-century America remained unshaken. Even his angry exchanges with the Oneida establishment possessed the tone of someone who enjoyed the battle as well as the spoils; certainly these exchanges reflected none of the desperation of the all-time loser that he, in fact, was. In Guiteau's delusional world, these frustrations were merely temporary setbacks in a career that was, he remained convinced, destined for wealth and fame.

Now, for the first time in his oddly chaotic life, Guiteau found himself sharing his outsider status with men he admired: Conkling and Platt and the other Stalwarts. And it was in this realization—not the denial of the various appointments he had sought—that his assassination scheme germinated. Indeed, a month later, on June 16, he wrote in his "Address to the American People":

I conceived of the idea of removing the President four weeks ago. Not a soul knew of my purpose. I conceived the idea myself. I read the newspapers carefully, for and against the administration, and gradually the conviction settled on me that the President's removal was a political necessity, because he proved a traitor to the men who made him, and thereby imperiled the life of the Republic. At the late Presidential election, the Republican party carried every Northern State. Today, owing to the misconduct of the President and his Secretary of State, they could hardly carry ten Northern States. They certainly could not carry New York, and that is the pivotal State.

Ingratitude is the basest of crimes. That the President, under the manipulation of his Secretary of State, has been guilty of the basest ingratitude to the Stalwarts admits of no denial. . . . In the President's madness he has wrecked the once grand old Republican party; and for this he dies. . . .

I had no ill-will to the President.

This is not murder. It is a political necessity. It will make my friend Arthur President, and save the Republic. I have sacrificed only one. I shot the President as I would a rebel, if I saw him pulling down the American flag. I leave my justification to God and the American people.

I expect President Arthur and Senator Conkling will give the nation the finest administration it has ever had. They are honest and have plenty of brains and experience.

[signed] CHARLES GUITEAU

Later, on June 20, he added this even more bizarre postscript:

The President's nomination was an act of God. The President's election was an act of God. The President's removal is an act of God. I am clear in my purpose to remove the President. Two objects will be accomplished: It will unite the Republican party and save the Republic, and it will create a great demand for my book, "The Truth." This book was written to save souls and not for money, and the Lord wants to save souls by circulating the book.

CHARLES GUITEAU

It is unlikely that Guiteau would have chosen the course of action he did without the sense that he was in good company—"a Stalwart of the Stalwarts," as he liked to describe himself. In his distorted mind, to "remove" the President, as he euphemistically described it, would provide the same status and recognition he had sought in a consul-ship appointment, and, more importantly, in every hare-brained scheme he had botched since the time he first entered the Oneida Community to establish the Kingdom of God on Earth. In this last grandly deluded plan, his aspirations in theology, law, and politics were to culminate in a divinely inspired and just act "to unite the Republican party and save the Republic" and, not incidentally, launch a new career for Charles Guiteau not only as a lawyer, theologian, and politician, but as a national hero with presidential aspirations.

Charles J. Guiteau, assassin of President James Garfield (1881). Much of the public viewed his insanity plea as a dodge, arguing that Guiteau's methodical planning and self-seeking motives could not be the product of a disturbed mind.

With this in mind, on June 8, Guiteau borrowed fifteen dollars and purchased a silver-mounted English revolver. He planned to have it, along with his papers, displayed after the assassination at the Library of the State Department or the Army Medical Museum. To prepare for the big event, he began target practice on the banks of the Potomac. After stalking the President for several weeks and bypassing at least two opportunities to shoot him, Guiteau rose early on Saturday, July 2, 1881. He had rented a room a few days before at the Riggs House and, on this morning, began preparations to meet the President at the Baltimore and Potomac Railroad Station. The President was scheduled to leave that morning for a vacation trip. Downing a hearty breakfast, which he charged to his room, he pocketed the last of a series of bizarre explanations:

July 2, 1881

To the White House:

The President's tragic death was a sad necessity, but it will unite the Republican party and save the Republic. Life is a fleeting dream, and it matters little when one goes. A human life is of small value. During the war thousands of brave boys went down without a tear. I presume the President was a Christian, and that he will be happier in Paradise than here.

It will be no worse for Mrs. Garfield, dear soul, to part with her husband this way than by natural death. He is liable to go at any time anyway.

I had no ill-will towards the President. His death was a political necessity. I am a lawyer, a theologian, a politician. I am a Stalwart of the Stalwarts. I was with General Grant and the rest of our men in New York during the canvass. I have some papers for the press, which I shall leave with Byron Andrews and his co-journalists at 1440 N.Y. Ave., where all the reporters can see them.

I am going to jail.

[signed] CHARLES GUITEAU

Guiteau then walked to the banks of the Potomac where after taking a few final practice shots he proceeded to the railroad station to await the President's arrival. Once at the station, he used the men's room, had his shoes shined, and, after estimating that his assignment would be completed shortly before the President's train was scheduled to leave, he reserved a hackman for an anticipated 9:30 arrest and departure to the District Prison. He had already checked the prison's security, lest in the emotion of the moment he might be attacked by crowds who had not had time to realize what a great patriotic service he had just

rendered. He was convinced that after his explanation was published the wisdom and justice of his act would be appreciated. Until such time, however, he had taken a further precaution of drafting a letter requesting that General Sherman see to his safekeeping in jail. The letter, which fell from his pocket during the scuffle that followed the shooting, read as follows:

To GENERAL SHERMAN:

I have just shot the President. I shot him several times, as I wished him to go as easily as possible. His death was a political necessity. I am a lawyer, theologian and politician. I am a Stalwart of the Stalwarts. I was with General Grant and the rest of our men in New York during the canvass. I am going to jail. Please order out your troops and take possession of the jail at once.

Very respectfully,
[signed] CHARLES GUITEAU

So it was with this completely distorted view of reality that Charles Guiteau fired two shots into the President's back as he walked arm-in-arm with Secretary Blaine toward the waiting train. The President, failing to respond to treatment, lingered two and a half months before dying on September 19, 1881.

The Trial

Throughout his lengthy seventy-two-day trial, Guiteau's delusional state was apparent to anyone inclined to acknowledge it. His brother-in-law, George Scoville, represented him at the trial and entered a plea of insanity. In Scoville's opening statement for the defense, he described in some detail the history of mental illness in the Guiteau family: at least two uncles, one aunt, and two cousins, not to mention his mother who died of "brain fever" but was probably insane. He went on to mention the highly eccentric behavior of his father that, at least one physician thought, properly qualified him for this category. It should also be noted that Guiteau's sister, Frances, the wife of George Scoville, behaved so strangely during her brother's trial that her probable insanity was noted by one participating physician who had occasion to observe her closely. And indeed, her husband later had her declared insane and institutionalized in October 1882, after her brother's execution.

This seemingly overwhelming evidence of a hereditary affliction was ignored or discounted by expert witnesses and finally the jury. Also discounted were the defendant's own delusional symptoms evident in the past schemes, bizarre letters to prominent persons he had never met, and his distorted conception of reality, which was apparent in his remarks throughout the trial and to the day he was executed. Scoville's line of defense was rejected by the defendant himself and greatly resented by John W. Guiteau, Charles' older bother. In a letter to Scoville, dated October 20, 1881, shortly after the trial began, John denied the history of family insanity described by the defense. Rather than heredity, he argued indignantly, most of the cases Scoville cited could be explained by self-induced factors such as insobriety and "mesmerism"; the others, specifically his parents' symptoms, he categorically denied. Falling into line with previous diagnoses of the causes of Charles' problems, most notably that of leaders of the Oneida Community, John Guiteau wrote: "I have no doubt that masturbation and self-abuse is at the bottom of his [Charles'] mental imbecility."

As for Charles himself, thoroughly contemptuous of his brother-in-law's legal abilities, he drafted his own plea, which read as follows:

I plead not guilty to the indictment and my defense is threefold:

1. Insanity, in that it was God's act and not mine. The Divine pressure on me to remove the President was so enormous that it destroyed my free agency, and therefore I am not legally responsible for my act.

Throughout his trial, Guiteau would acknowledge only this interpretation of insanity; that is, he was insane only in the sense that he did something that was not his will but God's. He did not accept the idea that he was in any way mentally deficient. Typical of his remarks on this issue made throughout the trial is the following:

. . . the Lord interjected the idea [of the President's removal] into my brain and then let me work it out my own way. That is the way the Lord does. He doesn't employ fools to do his work; I am sure of that; he gets the best brains he can find.

His plea continued describing two rather novel circumstances that, he claimed, were the Lord's will just as the assassination:

2. The President died from malpractice. About three weeks after he was shot his physicians, after careful examination, decided he would recover. Two months after this official announcement he died. Therefore, I say he was not fatally shot. If he had been well treated he would have recovered.

The third circumstance had to do with the court's jurisdiction:

3. The President died in New Jersey and, therefore, beyond the jurisdiction of this Court. This malpractice and the President's death in New Jersey are special providences, and I am bound to avail myself of them in my trial in justice to the Lord and myself.

He went on to elaborate:

I undertake to say that the Lord is managing my case with eminent ability, and that he had a special object in allowing the President to die in New Jersey. His management of this case is worthy of Him as the Deity, and I have entire confidence in His disposition to protect me, and to send me forth to the world a free and innocent man.

The jury's guilty verdict notwithstanding, it was clear that Guiteau had no grasp of the reality of his situation. Almost to the last, he believed he would be acquitted, at which point, he planned to begin a lecture tour in Europe and later return to the United States in time to re-enter politics as a presidential contender in 1884. He was confident that the jury, like the great majority of Americans, would recognize that Garfield's "removal" was divinely ordained and that the Almighty himself was responsible. He was convinced they would recognize that he was only an instrument in the Master's hands.

Contrary to some assessments, there was no evidence of paranoia in his behavior. Buoyed by a delusion-based optimism, he mistook the crowds of curious on-lookers at the jail as evidence of respect and admiration: bogus checks for incredible sums of money and ludicrous marriage proposals that were sent to him by cranks were sincerely and gratefully acknowledged; and promotional schemes evolved in his distorted mind to market his ridiculous books and pamphlets—all this while anticipating a run for the presidency in 1884! Meanwhile, in high spirits, the poor wretch ate heartily and slept well in a small cell located both literally and figuratively in the shadow of the gallows.

The Execution

When at the very last he realized that there was no hope for survival, his anger was, considering the circumstances, tempered much as it had been during his dispute with the Oneida Community. There were warnings of divine retribution for the ungrateful new president, Chester Arthur, the unfair prosecuting attorneys, and the jury, but again his anger lacked the intensity and desperation of someone facing death. As the execution date approached, Charles,

realizing failure once again, simply set his sights elsewhere as he had on many previous occasions. Eschewing politics, the presidency, the Stalwarts, and the law that had failed him, the lawyer and politician once again became the theologian. Anticipating an other-worldly position at the side of the Almighty, Charles walked serenely to the gallows. Earlier he had given the letter below to the chaplain who stood by him at the last:

Washington, D.C.
June 29, 1882

TO THE REV. WILLIAM W. HICKS:
I, Charles Guiteau, of the City of Washington, in the District of Columbia, now under sentence of death, which is to be carried into effect between the hours of twelve and two o'clock on the 30th day of June, a.d., 1882, in the United States jail in the said District, do hereby give and grant to you my body after such execution; provided, however, it shall not be used for any mercenary purposes.

And I hereby, for good and sufficient considerations, give, deliver and transfer to said Hicks my book entitled "The Truth and Removal" and copyright thereof to be used by him in writing a truthful history of my life and execution.

And I direct that such history be entitled "The Life and Work of Charles Guiteau"; and I hereby solemnly proclaim and announce to all the world that no person or persons shall ever in any manner use my body for any mercenary purpose whatsoever.

And if at any time hereafter any person or persons shall desire to honor my remains, they can do it by erecting a monument whereon shall be inscribed these words: "Here lies the body of Charles Guiteau, Patriot and Christian. His soul is in glory."

[signed] CHARLES GUITEAU
Witnesses: Charles H. Reed
James Woodward

Before the noose was placed around his neck, he was given permission to read his "last dying prayer" to the crowd of faces gazing up at him from the prison yard below. Comparing his situation to that of Christ at Calvary, Guiteau condemned President Arthur's ingratitude "to the man that made him and saved his party and land" and warned of divine retribution.

After completing his prayer, he again looked thoughtfully out over the crowd before announcing in a loud clear voice:

I am now going to read some verses which are intended to indicate my feelings at the moment of leaving this world. If set to music they may be rendered effective. The idea is that of a child babbling to his mamma and his papa. I wrote it this morning about 10 o'clock.

Then with childlike mournfulness, Guiteau read:

I am going to the Lordy. I am so glad.
  I am going to the Lordy. I am so glad.
  I am going to the Lordy. Glory, hallelujah; glory hallelujah.
  I am going to the Lordy;
  I love the Lordy with all my soul; glory, hallelujah.
  And that is the reason I am going to the Lord.
  Glory, hallelujah; glory, hallelujah. I am going to the Lord.

I saved my party and my land; glory, hallelujah.
  But they have murdered me for it, and that is the reason
  I am going to the Lordy.
  Glory, hallelujah; glory, hallelujah. I am going to the Lordy.
  I wonder what I will do when I get to the Lordy;
  I guess that I will weep no more when I get to the Lordy.
  Glory, hallelujah!
  I wonder what I will see when I get to the Lordy,
  I expect to see most splendid things, beyond all earthly conception.

As he neared completion, he raised his voice to a very high pitch and concluded with

When I am with the Lordy, glory, hallelujah!
  Glory, hallelujah! I am with the Lord.

Whereupon attendants strapped his legs, adjusted the noose, and placed a black hood over his head as Rev. Hicks prayed, "God the Father be with thee and give thee peace evermore." Guiteau, according to his own request, signaled the hangman by dropping a slip of paper from his fingers. As the trap sprung, Charles Guiteau slipped confidently into eternity with "Glory, Glory, Glory" on his lips.

Conclusion

Although the debate on the true state of Guiteau's mental condition was to continue among physicians for some years afterward, a brief article in the *Medical News* a day after the execution seems to have been representative of the prevailing view of the medical profession. While conceding that the neurologists who testified to the assassin's obvious insanity may have been correct, society would still be better, the editors reasoned, for having rid itself of such persons. As a further practical matter, it is unlikely that in 1881 any jury in the country would have acquitted the president's assassin whatever his mental condition.

Study Questions

1. Was Guiteau's life before the assassination consistent with his plea of insanity?

2. What were the political motivations for Guiteau's actions?

3. What were the problems with evaluating the evidence presented by the experts on insanity? Did Guiteau, according to the author, actually suffer from paranoia?

4. How would you describe Guiteau's religious beliefs? In your opinion, did those values inhibit his ability to interpret reality?

5. Was the verdict of the jury just? Could any other verdict have been reasonably justified?

Bibliography

The most thoughtful and thought-provoking exploration of the Guiteau episode is Charles E. Rosenberg, *The Trial of the Assassin Guiteau* (1968). Also see Kenneth D. Ackerman, *The Dark House: The Surprise Election and Political Murder of President James A. Garfield* (2003). However, some contemporary articles also make interesting reading. John P. Gray, a leading late-nineteenth-century American expert on insanity and an important witness in the Guiteau trial, presented his conclusions in "The United States vs. Charles J. Guiteau," *American Journal of Insanity* 38 (1882). Edward C. Spitzka, the other major expert in the case, offered his opinion in "A Contribution to the Question on the Mental Status of Guiteau and the History of His Trial," *Alienist and Neurologist* 4 (1883). The most recent work on American political assassinations is James W. Clarke, *American Assassins: The Darker Side of Politics* (1982). Clarke provides a good general bibliography on the subject. For the politics of the period, see H. Wayne Morgan, *From Hayes to McKinley: National Party Politics, 1877–1896* (1969) and John M. Taylor, *Garfield of Ohio: The Available Man* (1970).

READING 4

★ ★ ★

The Wizard of Oz: Parable on Populism

Henry M. Littlefield

The late nineteenth century was not a period known for its social justice. Angry and exploited workers found little sympathy in the halls of government. During strikes, federal authorities consistently intervened on the side of management rather than labor, even though strikes were usually responses to wage cuts. In the 1894 Pullman strike, for example, President Grover Cleveland sided with the rights of property over the rights of labor and crushed the strike. Thus, the newly formed unions won few concessions for their members. At the end of the century, the work week for the "average" industrial worker was almost 60 hours. The average skilled worker earned 20 cents an hour, twice as much as the average unskilled worker.

Life on the farms in the Midwest and South was probably even worse than life in the northern industries. Technological innovations and scientific farming techniques led to increased production, which in turn sent prices spiraling downward. Discriminatory railroad rates and the government's tight money policies further weakened the economic positions of farmers. As a result, farmers faced an economic depression that cost many their farms. Returning to his midwestern home in 1889, writer Hamlin Garland noted, "Nature was as bountiful as ever . . . but no splendor of cloud, no grace of sunset could conceal the poverty of these people; on the contrary, they brought out, with a more intolerable poignancy, the gracelessness of these homes, and the sordid quality of the mechanical routine of these lives." In the following essay, Henry M. Littlefield takes a fascinating look at Lyman Frank Baum's *The Wonderful Wizard of Oz* and the light it shed on the workers' and farmers' plight in the late nineteenth century.

On the deserts in North Africa in 1941 two tough Australian brigades went to battle singing,

Have you heard of the wonderful wizard,
  The wonderful Wizard of Oz,
And he is a wonderful wizard,
  If ever a wizard there was.

It was a song they had brought with them from Australia and would soon spread to England. Forever afterward it reminded Winston Churchill of those "buoyant days." Churchill's nostalgia is only one symptom of the world-wide delight found in an American fairy tale about a little girl and her odyssey in the strange land of Oz. The song he reflects upon came from a classic 1939 Hollywood production of the story, which introduced millions of people not only to the land of Oz, but to a talented young lady named Judy Garland as well.

Ever since its publication in 1900 Lyman Frank Baum's *The Wonderful Wizard of Oz* has been immensely popular, providing the basis for a profitable musical comedy, three movies and a number of plays. It is an indigenous creation, curiously warm and touching, although no one really knows why. For despite whole-hearted acceptance by generations of readers, Baum's tale has been accorded neither critical acclaim, nor extended critical examination. Interested scholars, such as Russell B. Nye and Martin Gardiner, look upon *The Wizard of Oz* as the first in a long and delightful series of Oz stories, and understandably base their appreciation of Baum's talent on the totality of his works.

The Wizard of Oz is an entity unto itself, however, and was not originally written with a sequel in mind. Baum informed his readers in 1904 that he had produced *The Marvelous Land of Oz* reluctantly and only in answer to well over a thousand letters demanding that he create another Oz tale. His original effort remains unique and to some degree separate from the books which follow. But its uniqueness does not rest alone on its peculiar and transcendent popularity.

Professor Nye finds a "strain of moralism" in the Oz books, as well as "a well-developed sense of satire," and Baum stories often include searching parodies on the contradictions in human nature. The second book in the series, *The Marvelous Land of Oz,* is a blatant satire on feminism and the suffragette movement. In it Baum attempted to duplicate the format used so successfully in *The Wizard,* yet no one has noted a similar play on contemporary movements in the latter work. Nevertheless, one does exist, and it reflects to an astonishing degree the world of political reality which surrounded Baum in 1900. In order to understand the relationship of *The Wizard* to turn-of-the-century America, it is necessary first to know something of Baum's background.

Born near Syracuse in 1856, Baum was brought up in a wealthy home and early became interested in the theater. He wrote some plays which enjoyed brief success and then, with his wife and two sons, journeyed to Aberdeen, South Dakota, in 1887. Aberdeen was a little prairie town and there Baum edited the local weekly until it failed in 1891.

For many years Western farmers had been in a state of loud, though unsuccessful, revolt. While Baum was living in South Dakota not only was the frontier a thing of the past, but the Romantic view of benign nature had disappeared as well. The stark reality of the dry, open plains and the acceptance of man's Darwinian subservience to his environment served to crush Romantic idealism.

Hamlin Garland's visit to Iowa and South Dakota coincided with Baum's arrival. Henry Nash Smith observes,

From Henry M. Littlefield, "The Wizard of Oz: Parable on Populism" in *American Quarterly,* Vol. 16 (Spring 1964). © The Johns Hopkins University Press. Reprinted by permission.

Garland's success as a portrayer of hardship and suffering on Northwestern farms was due in part to the fact that his personal experience happened to parallel the shock which the entire West received in the later 1880s from the combined effects of low prices, . . . grasshoppers, drought, the terrible blizzards of the winter of 1886–1887, and the juggling of freight rates . . . .

As we shall see, Baum's prairie experience was no less deeply etched, although he did not employ naturalism to express it.

Baum's stay in South Dakota also covered the period of the formation of the Populist party, which Professor Nye likens to a fanatic "crusade." Western farmers had for a long time sought governmental aid in the form of economic panaceas, but to no avail. The Populist movement symbolized a desperate attempt to use the power of the ballot. In 1891 Baum moved to Chicago where he was surrounded by those dynamic elements of reform which made the city so notable during the 1890s.

In Chicago Baum certainly saw the results of the frightful depression which had closed down upon the nation in 1893. Moreover, he took part in the pivotal election of 1896, marching in "torch-light parades for William Jennings Bryan." Martin Gardiner notes besides, that he "consistently voted as a Democrat . . . and his sympathies seem always to have been on the side of the laboring classes." No one who marched in even a few such parades could have been unaffected by Bryan's campaign. Putting all the farmers' hopes in a basket labeled "free coinage of silver," Bryan's platform rested mainly on the issue of adding silver to the nation's gold standard. Though he lost, he did at least bring the plight of the little man into national focus.

Between 1896 and 1900, while Baum worked and wrote in Chicago, the Great Depression faded away and the war with Spain thrust the United States into world prominence. Bryan maintained midwesterner's control over the Democratic party, and often spoke out against American policies toward Cuba and the Philippines. By 1900 it was evident that Bryan would run again, although now imperialism and not silver seemed the issue of primary concern. In order to promote greater enthusiasm, however, Bryan felt compelled once more to sound the silver leitmotif in his campaign. Bryan's second futile attempt at the presidency culminated in November 1900. The previous winter Baum had attempted unsuccessfully to sell a rather original volume of children's fantasy, but that April, George M. Hill, a small Chicago publisher, finally agreed to print *The Wonderful Wizard of Oz*.

Baum's allegiance to the cause of Democratic Populism must be balanced against the fact that he was not a political activist. Martin Gardiner finds through all of his writings "a theme of tolerance, with many episodes that poke fun at narrow nationalism and ethnocentrism." Nevertheless, Professor Nye quotes Baum as having a desire to write stories that would "bear the stamp of our times and depict the progressive fairies of today."

The Wizard of Oz has neither the mature religious appeal of a *Pilgrim's Progress*, nor the philosophic depth of a *Candide*. Baum's most thoughtful devotees see in it only a warm, cleverly written fairy tale. Yet the original Oz book conceals an unsuspected depth, and it is the purpose of this study to demonstrate that Baum's immortal American fantasy encompasses more than heretofore believed. For Baum created a children's story with a symbolic allegory implicit within its story line and characterizations. The allegory always remains in a minor key, subordinated to the major theme and readily abandoned whenever it threatens to distort the appeal of the fantasy. But through it, in the form of a subtle parable, Baum delineated a midwesterner's vibrant and ironic portrait of this country as it entered the twentieth century.

We are introduced to both Dorothy and Kansas at the same time:

Dorothy lived in the midst of the great Kansas prairies, with Uncle Henry, who was a farmer, and Aunt Em, who was the farmer's wife. Their house was small, for the lumber to build it had to be carried by wagon many miles. There were four walls, a floor and a roof, which made one room; and this room contained a rusty-looking cooking stove, a cupboard for the dishes, a table, three or four chairs, and the beds.

When Dorothy stood in the doorway and looked around, she could see nothing but the great gray prairie on every side. Not a tree nor a house broke the broad sweep of flat country that reached to the edge of the sky in all directions. The sun had baked the plowed land into a gray mass, with little cracks running through it. Even the grass was not green, for the sun had burned the tops of the long blades until they were the same gray color to be seen everywhere. Once the house had been painted, but the sun blistered the paint and the rains washed it away, and now the house was as dull and gray as everything else.

When Aunt Em came there to live she was a young, pretty wife. The sun and wind had changed her, too. They had taken the sparkle from her eyes and left them a sober gray; they had taken the red from her cheeks and lips, and they were gray also. She was thin and gaunt, and never smiled now. When Dorothy, who was an orphan, first came to her, Aunt Em had been so startled by the child's laughter that she would scream and press her hand upon her heart whenever Dorothy's merry voice reached her ears; and she still looked at the little girl with wonder that she could find anything to laugh at.

Uncle Henry never laughed. He worked hard from morning till night and did not know what joy was. He was gray also, from his long beard to his rough boots, and he looked stern and solemn, and rarely spoke.

It was Toto that made Dorothy laugh, and saved her from growing as gray as her other surroundings. Toto was not gray; he was a little black dog, with long silky hair and small black eyes that twinkle merrily on either side of his funny, wee nose. Toto played all day long, and Dorothy played with him, and loved him dearly.

Hector St. John de Crèvecoeur would not have recognized Uncle Henry's farm; it is straight out of Hamlin Garland. On it a deadly environment dominates everyone and everything except Dorothy and her pet. The setting is Old Testament and nature seems grayly impersonal and even angry. Yet it is a fearsome cyclone that lifts Dorothy and Toto in their house and deposits them "very gently—for a cyclone—in the midst of a country of marvelous beauty." We immediately sense the contrast between Oz and Kansas. Here there are "stately trees bearing rich and luscious fruits . . . gorgeous flowers . . . and birds with . . . brilliant plumage" sing in the trees. In Oz "a small brook rushing and sparkling along" murmurs "in a voice very grateful to a little girl who had lived so long on the dry, gray prairies."

Trouble intrudes. Dorothy's house has come down on the wicked Witch of the East, killing her. Nature, by sheer accident, can provide benefits, for indirectly the cyclone has disposed of one of the two truly bad influences in the Land of Oz. Notice that evil ruled in both the East and the West; after Dorothy's coming it rules only in the West.

The wicked Witch of the East had kept the little Munchkin people "in bondage for many years, making them slave for her night and day." Just what this slavery entailed is not immediately clear, but Baum later gives us a specific example. The Tin Woodman, whom Dorothy meets on her way to the Emerald City, had been put under a spell by the Witch of the East. Once an independent and hardworking human being, the Woodman found

Dorothy and her friends prepare to "follow the yellow brick road." The spectacularly successful 1939 film based on The Wizard of Oz *came out during another Great Depression and prefigured happiness in "Somewhere Over the Rainbow."*

Tin Woodman's situation has an obvious parallel in the condition of many Eastern workers after the depression of 1893. While Tin Woodman is standing still, rusted solid, he deludes himself into thinking he is no longer capable of that most human of sentiments, love. Hate does not fill the void, a constant lesson in the Oz books, and Tin Woodman feels that only a heart will make him sensitive again. So he accompanies Dorothy to see if the Wizard will give him one.

Oz itself is a magic oasis surrounded by impassable deserts, and the country is divided in a very orderly fashion. In the North and South the people are ruled by good witches, who are not quite as powerful as the wicked ones of the East and West. In the center of the land rises the magnificent Emerald City ruled by the Wizard of Oz, a successful humbug whom even the witches mistakenly feel "is more powerful than all the rest of us together." Despite these forces, the mark of goodness, placed on Dorothy's forehead by the Witch of the North, serves as protection for Dorothy throughout her travels. Goodness and innocence prevail even over the powers of evil and delusion in Oz. Perhaps it is this basic and beautiful optimism that makes Baum's tale so characteristically American—and midwestern.

Dorothy is Baum's Miss Everyman. She is one of us, levelheaded and human, and she has a real problem. Young readers can understand her quandary as readily as can adults. She is good, not precious, and she thinks quite naturally about others. For all of the attractions of Oz Dorothy desires only to return to the gray plains and Aunt Em and Uncle Henry. She is directed toward the Emerald City by the good Witch of the North, since the Wizard will surely be able to solve the problem of the impassable deserts. Dorothy sets out on the Yellow Brick Road wearing the Witch of the East's magic Silver Shoes. Silver shoes walking on a golden road; henceforth Dorothy becomes the innocent agent of Baum's ironic view of the silver issue. Remember, neither

that each time he swung his axe it chopped off a different part of his body. Knowing no other trade he "worked harder than ever," for luckily in Oz tinsmiths can repair such things. Soon the Woodman was all tin. In this way Eastern witchcraft dehumanized a simple laborer so that the faster and better he worked the more quickly he became a kind of machine. Here is a Populist view of evil Eastern influences on honest labor which could hardly be more pointed.

There is one thing seriously wrong with being made of tin; when it rains rust sets in. Tin Woodman had been standing in the same position for a year without moving before Dorothy came along and oiled his joints. The

Dorothy, nor the good Witch of the North, nor the Munchkins understand the power of these shoes. The allegory is abundantly clear. On the next to last page of the book Baum has Glinda, Witch of the South, tell Dorothy, "Your Silver Shoes will carry you over the desert . . . . If you had known their power you could have gone back to your Aunt Em the very first day you came to this country." Glinda explains, "All you have to do is to knock the heels together three times and command the shoes to carry you wherever you wish to go." William Jennings Bryan never outlined the advantages of the silver standard any more effectively.

Not understanding the magic of the Silver Shoes, Dorothy walks the mundane—and dangerous—Yellow Brick Road. The first person she meets is a Scarecrow. After escaping from his wooden perch, the Scarecrow displays a terrible sense of inferiority and self-doubt, for he has determined that he needs real brains to replace the common straw in his head. William Allen White wrote an article in 1896 entitled "What's the Matter with Kansas?" In it he accused Kansas farmers of ignorance, irrationality, and general muddle-headedness. What's wrong with Kansas are the people, said Mr. White. Baum's character seems to have read White's angry characterization. But Baum never takes White seriously and so the Scarecrow soon emerges as innately a very shrewd and very capable individual.

The Scarecrow and the Tin Woodman accompany Dorothy along the Yellow Brick Road, one seeking brains, the other a heart. They meet next the Cowardly Lion. As King of Beasts he explains, "I learned that if I roared very loudly every living thing was frightened and got out of my way." Born a coward, he sobs, "Whenever there is danger my heart begins to beat fast." "Perhaps you have heart disease," suggests Tin Woodman, who always worries about hearts. But the Lion desires only courage and so he joins the party to ask help from the Wizard.

The Lion represents Bryan himself. In the election of 1896 Bryan lost the vote of Eastern labor, though he tried hard to gain their support. In Baum's story the Lion, on meeting the little group, "struck at the Tin Woodman with his sharp claws." But, to his surprise, "he could make no impression on the tin, although the Woodman fell over in the road and lay still." Baum here refers to the fact that in 1896 workers were often pressured into voting for McKinley and gold by their employers. Amazed, the Lion says, "he nearly blunted my claws," and he adds even more appropriately, "When they scratched against the tin it made a cold shiver run down my back." The King of Beasts is not after all very cowardly, and Bryan, although a pacifist and an anti-imperialist in a time of national expansion, is not either. The magic Silver Shoes belong to Dorothy, however. Silver's potent charm, which had come to mean so much to so many in the Midwest, could not be entrusted to a political symbol. Baum delivers Dorothy from the world of adventure and fantasy to the real world of heartbreak and desolation through the power of Silver. It represents a real force in a land of illusion, and neither the Cowardly Lion nor Bryan truly needs or understands its use.

All together now the small party moves toward the Emerald City. Coxey's Army of tramps and indigents, marching to ask President Cleveland for work in 1894, appears no more naively innocent than this group of four characters going to see a humbug Wizard, to request favors that only the little girl among them deserves.

Those who enter the Emerald City must wear green glasses. Dorothy later discovers that the greenness of dresses and ribbons disappears on leaving, and everything becomes a bland white. Perhaps the magic of any city is thus self-imposed. But the Wizard dwells here and so the Emerald City represents the national Capitol. The Wizard, a little bumbling old man, hiding behind a facade of papier mâché and noise, might be any president from Grant to McKinley. He comes straight from the fairgrounds in Omaha, Nebraska, and he symbolizes the American criterion for leadership—he is able to be everything to everybody.

As each of our heroes enters the throne room to ask a favor the Wizard assumes different shapes, representing different views toward national leadership. To Dorothy, he appears as an enormous head, "bigger than the head of the biggest giant." An apt image for a naive and innocent little citizen. To the Scarecrow he appears to be a lovely, gossamer fairy, a most appropriate form for an idealistic Kansas farmer. The Woodman sees a horrible beast, as would any exploited Eastern laborer after the trouble of the 1890s. But the Cowardly Lion, like W. J. Bryan, sees a "Ball of Fire, so fierce and glowing he could scarcely bear to gaze upon it." Baum then provides an additional analogy, for when the Lion "tried to go nearer he singed his whiskers and he crept back tremblingly to a spot nearer the door."

The Wizard has asked them all to kill the Witch of the West. The golden road does not go in that direction and so they must follow the sun, as have many pioneers in the past. The land they now pass through is "rougher and hillier, for there were no farms nor houses in the country of the West and the ground was untilled." The Witch of the West uses natural forces to achieve her ends; she is Baum's version of sentient and malign nature.

Finding Dorothy and her friends in the West, the Witch sends forty wolves against them, then forty vicious crows and finally a great swarm of black bees. But it is through the power of a magic golden cap that she summons the flying monkeys. They capture the little girl and dispose of her companions. Baum makes these Winged Monkeys into an Oz substitute for the plains Indians. Their leader says, "Once . . . we were a free people, living happily in the great forest, flying from tree to tree, eating nuts and fruit, and doing just as we pleased without calling anybody

master." "This," he explains, "was many years ago, long before Oz came out of the clouds to rule over this land." But like many Indian tribes Baum's monkeys are not inherently bad; their actions depend wholly upon the bidding of others. Under the control of an evil influence, they do evil. Under the control of goodness and innocence, as personified by Dorothy, the monkeys are helpful and kind, although unable to take her to Kansas. Says the Monkey King, "We belong to this country alone, and cannot leave it." The same could be said with equal truth of the first Americans.

Dorothy presents a special problem to the Witch. Seeing the mark on Dorothy's forehead and the Silver Shoes on her feet, the Witch begins "to tremble with fear, for she knew what a powerful charm belonged to them." Then "she happened to look into the child's eyes and saw how simple the soul behind them was, and that the little girl did not know of the wonderful power the Silver Shoes gave her." Here Baum again uses the silver allegory to state the blunt homily that while goodness affords a people ultimate protection against evil, ignorance of their capabilities allows evil to impose itself upon them. The Witch assumes the proportions of a kind of western Mark Hanna or Banker Boss, who, through natural malevolence, manipulates the people and holds them prisoner by cynically taking advantage of their innate innocence.

Enslaved in the West, "Dorothy went to work meekly, with her mind made up to work as hard as she could; for she was glad the Wicked Witch had decided not to kill her." Many Western farmers have held these same grim thoughts in less mystical terms. If the Witch of the West is a diabolical force of Darwinian or Spencerian nature, then another contravening force may be counted upon to dispose of her. Dorothy destroys the evil Witch by angrily dousing her with a bucket of water. Water, that precious commodity which the drought-ridden farmers on the Great Plains needed so badly, and which if correctly used could create an agricultural paradise, or at least dissolve a wicked witch. Plain water brings an end to malign nature in the West.

When Dorothy and her companions return to the Emerald City they soon discover that the Wizard is really nothing more than "a little man, with a bald head and a wrinkled face." Can this be the ruler of the land?

Our friends looked at him in surprise and dismay.

"I thought Oz was a great Head," said Dorothy . . . . "And I thought Oz was a terrible Beast," said the Tin Woodman. "And I thought Oz was a Ball of Fire," exclaimed the Lion. "No; you are all wrong," said the little man meekly. "I have been making believe."

Dorothy asks if he is truly a great Wizard. He confides, "Not a bit of it, my dear; I'm just a common man." Scarecrow adds, "You're more than that . . . you're a humbug." The Wizard's deception is of long standing in Oz and even the witches were taken in. How was it accomplished? "It was a great mistake my ever letting you into the Throne Room," the Wizard complains. "Usually I will not see even my subjects, and so they believe I am something terrible." What a wonderful lesson for youngsters of the decade when Benjamin Harrison, Grover Cleveland and William McKinley were hiding in the White House. Formerly the Wizard was a mimic, a ventriloquist and a circus balloonist. The latter trade involved going "up in a balloon on circus day, so as to draw a crowd of people together and get them to pay to see the circus." Such skills are as admirably adapted to success in late-nineteenth-century politics as they are to the humbug wizardry of Baum's story. A pointed comment on midwestern political ideals is the fact that our little Wizard comes from Omaha, Nebraska, a center of Populist agitation. "Why that isn't very far from Kansas," cries Dorothy. Nor, indeed, are any of the characters in the wonderful land of Oz.

The Wizard, of course, can provide the objects of self-delusion desired by Tin Woodman, Scarecrow and Lion. But Dorothy's hope of going home fades when the Wizard's balloon leaves too soon. Understand this: Dorothy wishes to leave a green and fabulous land, from which all evil has disappeared, to go back to the gray desolation of the Kansas prairies. Dorothy is an orphan, Aunt Em and Uncle Henry are her only family. Reality is never far from Dorothy's consciousness and in the most heartrending terms she explains her reasoning to the Good Witch Glinda,

Aunt Em will surely think something dreadful has happened to me, and that will make her put on mourning; and unless the crops are better this year than they were last I am sure Uncle Henry cannot afford it.

The Silver Shoes furnish Dorothy with a magic means of travel. But when she arrives back in Kansas she finds, "The Silver Shoes had fallen off in her flight through the air, and were lost forever in the desert." Were the "her" to refer to America in 1900, Baum's statement could hardly be contradicted.

Current historiography tends to criticize the Populist movement for its "delusions, myths and foibles," Professor C. Vann Woodward observed recently. Yet *The Wonderful Wizard of Oz* has provided unknowing generations with a gentle and friendly midwestern critique of the Populist rationale on these very same grounds. Led by naive innocence and protected by goodwill, the farmer, the laborer and the politician approach the mystic holder of national power to ask for personal fulfillment. Their desires, as well as the Wizard's cleverness in answering them, are all self-delusion. Each of these characters carries within him the solution to his own problem, were he only to view himself objectively. The fearsome Wizard turns out to be nothing more than a common man, capable of shrewd but mundane answers to these self-induced needs. Like any good politician he gives the people what they want. Throughout the story Baum poses a central thought; the American desire for symbols of fulfillment is illusory. Real needs lie elsewhere.

Thus the Wizard cannot help Dorothy, for of all the characters only she has a wish that is selfless, and only she has a direct connection to honest, hopeless human beings. Dorothy supplies real fulfillment when she returns to her aunt and uncle, using the Silver Shoes, and cures some of their misery and heartache. In this way Baum tells us that the silver crusade at least brought back Dorothy's lovely spirit to the disconsolate plains farmer. Her laughter, love and goodwill are no small addition to that gray land, although the magic of silver has been lost forever as a result.

Noteworthy too is Baum's prophetic placement of leadership in Oz after Dorothy's departure. The Scarecrow reigns over the Emerald City, the Tin Woodman rules in the West and the Lion protects smaller beasts in "a grand old forest." Thereby farm interests achieve national importance, industrialism moves West and Bryan commands only a forest full of lesser politicians.

Baum's fantasy succeeds in bridging the gap between what children want and what they should have. It is an admirable example of the way in which an imaginative writer can teach goodness and morality without producing the almost inevitable side effect of nausea. Today's children's books are either saccharine and empty, or boring and pedantic. Baum's first Oz tale—and those which succeed it—are immortal not so much because the "heartaches and nightmares are left out" as that "the wonderment and joy" are retained.

Baum declares, "The story of 'The Wonderful Wizard of Oz' was written solely to pleasure children of today." In 1963 there are very few children who have never heard of the Scarecrow, the Tin Woodman or the Cowardly Lion, and whether they know W. W. Denslow's original illustrations of Dorothy, or Judy Garland's whimsical characterization, is immaterial. *The Wizard* has become a genuine piece of American folklore because, knowing his audience, Baum never allowed the consistency of the allegory to take precedence over the theme of youthful entertainment. Yet once discovered, the author's allegorical intent seems clear, and it gives depth and lasting interest even to children who only sense something else beneath the surface of the story. Consider the fun in picturing turn-of-the-century America, a difficult era at best, using these ready-made symbols provided by Baum. The relationships and analogies outlined above are admittedly theoretical, but they are far too consistent to be coincidental, and they furnish a teaching mechanism which is guaranteed to reach any level of student.

The Wizard of Oz says so much about so many things that it is hard not to imagine a satisfied and mischievous gleam in Lyman Frank Baum's eye as he had Dorothy say, "And oh, Aunt Em! I'm so glad to be at home again!"

Study Questions

1. Why was Lyman Frank Baum in a good position to understand the problems of workers in the late nineteenth century?

2. What sort of picture does *The Wonderful Wizard of Oz* paint of farm life? What was the effect of agrarian labor on the farmers themselves?

3. How does the story detail the complexities of the silver issue? Does Baum seem to feel that the gold standard was the major problem facing the farmers?

4. How does the Tin Woodman dramatize the plight of the northern industrial worker? How does the Scarecrow symbolize the plight of the farmers?

5. In what ways is the Cowardly Lion similar to William Jennings Bryan?

6. What roles do the good and bad witches play in the story?

7. Is *The Wonderful Wizard of Oz* an effective parable?

Bibliography

Martin Gardiner and Russell B. Nye, *The Wizard of Oz and Who He Was* (1957), examine Baum and his works. The best studies of the Populist movement are John D. Hicks, *The Populist Revolt* (1931); C. Vann Woodward, *Tom Watson: Agrarian Rebel* (1938); Lawrence Goodwyn, *Democratic Promise: The Populist Movement in America* (1976); Robert C. McMath Jr., *Populist Vanguard: A History of the Southern Farmers' Alliance* (1975); and Stanley B. Parsons, *The Populist Context: Rural Versus Urban Power on a Great Plains Frontier* (1973). Paul W. Glad, *McKinley, Bryan, and the People* (1964) and Robert F. Durden, *The Climax of Populism: The Election of 1896* (1965) examine the crucial election of 1896. For industrial working conditions in the late nineteenth century, see Herbert G. Gutman, *Work, Class, and Society in Industrializing America* (1976); David Brody, *Steelworkers in America: The Nonunion Era* (1960); Albert Rees, *Real Wages in Manufacturing, 1890–1914* (1961); and Paul Krause, *The Battle for Homestead: Politics, Culture, and Steel, 1880–1892* (1992). Also see Steven Hahn, *The Roots of Southern Populism* (1983).

READING 5

★ ★ ★

She Couldn't Have Done It, Even If She Did

Kathryn Allamong Jacob

There is something infinitely compelling and fascinating about an unsolved murder. England has Jack the Ripper, and although it has been more than 100 years since the last Ripper murder was committed, historians of the crimes still speculate on the identity of the murderer. The American equivalent to Jack the Ripper is Lizzie Borden, who very likely killed her father and stepmother on August 2, 1892. Although she was judged innocent of the murders, strong circumstantial evidence points toward her guilt. However, in a larger sense the jury was more concerned with the physical and psychological nature of upper-class womanhood than with the actual crimes. As Kathryn Allamong Jacob writes, during the summer of 1893 "the entire Victorian conception of womanhood was on trial for its life." The question most commonly asked that summer was to the point: How could a well-bred woman, who by her very nature was innocent, childlike, and moral, commit such a horrible crime? The answer of most well-bred men, and of all 12 of the prosperous Yankee jurors, was that she could not. An examination of the case thus illuminates an entire cultural landscape, casting light especially on American attitudes toward women. Were women, as a writer for *Scribner's* believed, "merely large babies . . . short-sighted, frivolous, and [occupying] an intermediate stage between children and men . . ."? Or was there something more to the issue?

During the summer of 1893, Americans riveted their attention on the town of New Bedford, Massachusetts, where Lizzie Andrew Borden was being tried for the gruesome ax murder of her father and stepmother. All other news paled in comparison, for here, in southeastern Massachusetts, not only a particular woman, but the entire Victorian conception of womanhood, was on trial for its life.

The drama began in August of 1892 at Number 92 Second Street in Fall River, Massachusetts, the home of Andrew Jackson Borden, whose family coat of arms prophetically bore a lion holding a battle-ax. The household consisted of Andrew, seventy; Abby Gray Borden, sixty-five, his wife; his two daughters, Lizzie Andrew and Emma Lenora, aged thirty-two and forty-two; and Bridget Sullivan, twenty-six, an Irish servant who had been with the family for nearly three years.

Andrew Borden began his business career as an undertaker. It was rumored that he had cut the feet off corpses to make them fit into undersized coffins, but however ill-gotten his initial profits, Borden invested them wisely. By 1892 he was worth nearly half a million dollars, served as a director of several banks and as a board member of three woolen mills, and had built the imposing A. J. Borden Building on Main Street as a testimony to his business acumen. To keep his fortunes increasing, Borden foreclosed, undercut, overcharged, and hoarded without flinching.

Borden's first wife, Sarah, had died in 1862 after bearing him three daughters, only two of whom survived past infancy. Two years later, he married Abby Gray, a thirty-eight-year-old spinster. Nothing suggests that Abby was anything but kind to the two little girls whose stepmother she became, but they never returned her affection. After her marriage, Abby

became a compulsive eater. Only a little over five feet tall, by 1892 she weighed more than two hundred pounds.

Emma, the older daughter, still lived at home at age forty-two. By all accounts, she was dowdy and narrow-minded. Lizzie Borden, ten years younger, also lived at home. Otherwise tightfisted, Andrew Borden doted on his younger daughter: over the years he lavished on Lizzie expensive gifts—a diamond ring, a sealskin cape, even a Grand Tour of Europe. Lizzie worshiped her father in return, and even gave him her high school ring to wear as a token of her affection.

Like her sister, Lizzie had evidently given up hope of marriage, but she led a more active life, centered around good works and the Central Congregational Church, where she taught a Sunday-school class of Chinese children, the sons and daughters of Fall River laundrymen. Though she loathed doing housework, she enthusiastically helped cook the church's annual Christmas dinner for local newsboys. In addition to being secretary-treasurer of the Christian Endeavor, Lizzie was active in the Ladies' Fruit and Flower Mission, the Women's Christian Temperance Union, and the Good Samaritan Charity Hospital.

Lizzie's Christian charity did not extend to her own home. The Borden family was not happy. While Emma tolerated her stepmother, Lizzie openly disliked her. Ill feelings increased in 1887, when Andrew gave Abby a house for the use of her sister. Seeking peace, Andrew gave his daughters a house of greater value to rent out, but they were not placated. A dressmaker later remembered making the mistake of referring to Abby as Lizzie's "mother," causing Lizzie to snap, "Don't call her that to me. She is a mean thing and we hate her."

Even the house Lizzie lived in vexed her. Its Grant-era furnishings contrasted sharply with her stylish clothes. There was no bath and no electricity, though such conveniences were common elsewhere in town. Beside the water closet in the basement stood a pile of old newspapers for sanitary purposes. No interior

"She Couldn't Have Done It, Even If She Did" by Kathryn Allamong Jacob, from *American Heritage* 29 (February/March, 1978) pp. 42–53. Reprinted by permission.

space was wasted on hallways. Rooms simply opened into one another, making it difficult for anyone to pass through unnoticed. Lizzie longed to live "on the hill," Fall River's most elegant neighborhood and the symbol of the social prominence she craved. While her father's wealth entitled her to live there, Andrew insisted on living on déclassé Second Street.

On Tuesday, August 2, 1892, strange things began to happen in the Borden house. Mr. and Mrs. Borden and Bridget suffered severe vomiting; Lizzie later claimed she felt queasy the next day. Emma, on vacation in Fairhaven, was spared. Over Andrew's objections, Abby waddled across the street to Dr. Bowen's to tell him she feared they had been poisoned. When he learned that the previous night's dinner had been warmed-over fish, the doctor laughingly sent her home.

The next day, Uncle John Morse, brother of the first Mrs. Borden, arrived unexpectedly on business. Like Andrew, Morse was single-minded in his pursuit of wealth, and the two men had remained friends. That evening, Lizzie visited Miss Alice Russell, a friend of Emma's. Miss Russell later testified that their conversation had been unsettling. Lizzie had spoken of burglary attempts on the Borden home, of threats against her father from unknown enemies. "I feel as if something was hanging over me that I cannot throw off . . .," she said. "Father has so much trouble. . . ." Though Miss Russell tried to reassure her, Lizzie left on an ominous, but prescient, note: "I am afraid somebody will do something."

On Thursday morning, August 4, Bridget rose about six and lit the breakfast fire. Around seven, the elder Bordens and their guest sat down to eat in the dining room. Lizzie did not appear downstairs till nine. By then, Mrs. Borden had begun dusting the downstairs and Morse had left the house to visit relatives across town. Lizzie told Bridget she did not feel well enough to eat breakfast, but sat in the kitchen sipping coffee. About twenty after nine, Andrew, too, left the house, setting off downtown to oversee his investments. Perhaps ten minutes later, Abby Borden went upstairs to tidy the guest room, and Bridget went outside to begin washing the downstairs windows. Only Lizzie and Abby remained in the house; Abby was never seen alive again.

Perhaps because of the oppressive heat, Andrew broke his long-established routine by coming home for lunch at a quarter of eleven, an hour and a half early. Bridget later testified that she had just begun scrubbing the inside of the windows when she heard him struggling with the frontdoor lock and let him in. Lizzie, by her own admission, was coming down the stairs from the second floor where Abby's body lay. (At the Borden trial the following year, the prosecution would produce witnesses who testified that Abby's body, lying on the guest-room floor, was clearly visible from the staircase, while the defense claimed it was almost completely obscured by a bed). Andrew asked Lizzie about Abby's whereabouts, according to Bridget, and Lizzie told him that Abby had received a note asking her to attend a sick friend.

Bridget finished her windows and climbed the back stairs to her attic room to rest at about eleven. Andrew lay down on the parlor sofa to nap. On the guest-room floor above him lay Abby's bleeding corpse. The house was hot and silent. Within minutes, Bridget recalled, she was awakened by Lizzie calling, "Come down quick; father's dead; somebody came in and killed him."

Little was left of Andrew's face. Half an eye hung from its socket. Doctors testified that a single ax blow had killed him; nine others had been gratuitous. Shortly after the police arrived, Bridget and a neighbor ventured upstairs for a sheet to cover the hideous sight, and there they found Abby. Her plump body lay face down in a pool of blood, her head and neck a bloody mass. Those first on the scene noted that Lizzie remained remarkably calm throughout the ordeal. While one woman claimed that there were tears in her eyes, several others testified that Lizzie's eyes were dry and her hands steady.

News traveled fast from neighbor to neighbor and even before the evening presses rolled, everyone in Fall River seemed to know of the horrifying incident. A local reporter recalled that "The cry of murder swept through the city like a typhoon . . . murder committed under the very glare of the midday sun within three minutes walk of the City Hall. . . ." By the next day, the story was front-page news throughout the country and when, after two days, no crazed ax-wielder was produced, newspapers which had praised the police began to question their competence. Trial transcripts suggest that the police did err on the side of caution. If the victims had not been so prominent, matters would have been simpler. The *New York Times* appreciated this fact, and on August 6 noted that "The police are acting slowly and carefully in the affair giving way, no doubt, to feelings of sentiment because of the high social standing of the parties involved." No systematic search of the Borden house was conducted until thirty-two hours after the murders. Out of deference to the bereaved daughters, neither Lizzie nor Emma, who had been summoned home from her vacation, was closely questioned for nearly three days.

Yet, by Saturday, the day of the funerals, the police felt that they had little choice but to arrest Lizzie. She alone, they felt, had had the opportunity to commit the murders. They found it hard to believe that anyone could have passed through the house unseen by Lizzie, who claimed to have been on the first floor while Abby was being murdered above. It also strained credibility to assert, as Lizzie did, that Abby's 210-pound body had crashed to the floor without a sound. Furthermore, despite a reward offered by the Borden sisters, no sender of the note that Lizzie claimed had called Abby to town could be found.

Lizzie's own contradictory answers to the first questions put to her by police were highly damaging. When asked her whereabouts when her father was killed, she gave different answers to different interrogators: "In the backyard"; ". . . in the loft getting a piece of iron for sinkers"; ". . . up in the loft eating pears." The closed barn loft would have been so insufferably hot that day that few would have visited it voluntarily, much less lingered to eat pears. Furthermore, an officer who claimed to have been the first to examine the loft after the crimes testified that the dust on the floor was undisturbed by footprints or trailing skirts.

In Lizzie's favor was the fact that she had been neat and clean when first seen after the murders. The police were certain that the murderer would have been covered with blood. (Medical experts would later examine the trajectories of the spurting blood and argue otherwise, but belief in a blood-drenched killer persisted.)

Though puzzled by Lizzie's cleanliness, police were certain that they had found the murder weapon. Lying in a box of dusty tools, stored high on a chimney jog in the basement, was a hatchet head. It was neither rusty nor old, though it had been freshly rubbed in ashes, perhaps to make it appear so. Moreover, its wooden handle, from which blood would have been difficult to remove, had been broken off near the head.

When the news broke that Lizzie was under suspicion, newspaper readers were horrified—not over the possibility that Lizzie might have murdered her parents, but that the police would harbor such horrid thoughts. The Boston *Globe* expressed its readers' indignation: "The only person that the government can catch is one whose innocence placed her in its power; the poor, defenseless child, who ought to have claimed by very helplessness their protection."

Angry letters denouncing the police flooded newspaper offices from New York to Chicago. Editorials appeared castigating the brutish officers who would suspect a grieving daughter of such a crime. Americans were certain that well-brought-up daughters could not commit murder with a hatchet on sunny summer mornings. And their reaction was not entirely without rationale.

Throughout the 1890s nearly every issue of *Forum, Arena, Scribner's, North American Review, Popular Science Monthly,* and *Harper's* (one of Lizzie's favorites) carried at least one article attesting to the gentleness, physical frailty, and docility of the well-bred American woman. Many of these articles were written in response to the growing number of women who were demanding equal rights, and were written with the intention of proving women hopelessly unable to handle the sacred privileges of men. After having read many such articles written by "learned gentlemen"—and antifeminist women—by the summer of 1892, men and women, regardless of how they stood on women's rights, felt certain that Lizzie Borden could not have hacked her parents to death. Physical and psychological frailties simply made it impossible.

Popular theories about women's physiological and psychological makeup took on new importance to followers of the Borden case. After detailed anatomical analysis, scientists confidently declared that the women of their era differed little from their prehistoric sisters. They spoke with assurance of women's arrested evolution. The fault, they agreed, lay in her reproductive capacity, which sapped vital powers that in men contributed to ever-improving physique and intellect.

The defects of the female anatomy included sloping shoulders, broad hips, underdeveloped muscles, short arms and legs, and poor coordination. To those who believed Lizzie innocent, evidence was abundant that no short-armed, uncoordinated, weakling of a woman could swing an ax with enough force to crash through hair and bone almost two dozen times.

But there was more to it than that. Having already noted women's smaller frame, anatomists should hardly have been surprised to find her skull proportionately smaller than man's, yet they held up this revelation, too, as further proof of her inferiority. Rather than follow intellectual

pursuits, for which they were woefully ill-equipped, women were advised to accept their intended roles as wives and mothers. After all, they were reminded, "Woman is only womanly when she sets herself to man 'like perfect music unto noble works.' "

Spinsters like Lizzie were, as one author charitably put it, "deplorable accidents," but they were not wholly useless. The nation's old maids were urged to devote themselves to Christian charities and to teaching—a "reproductive calling." Lizzie's devotion to good works and the church followed this prescription precisely. Compelling indeed was the image of this pious daughter serving steaming bowls of soup to indigent newsboys and diligently trying to bring the gospel to the heathen Chinese of Fall River.

While anatomists studied the size of woman's skull, psychologists examined its contents. Among the qualities found to be essentially female were spiritual sensitivity, a good memory for minutiae, and a great capacity for "ennobling love." These positive attributes, however, could not obscure the psychologists' basic premise; women were illogical, inconsistent, and incapable of independent thought.

It is no accident that these traits bore striking resemblance to those attributed to children. As one psychologist pointed out in *Scribner's:* "Women are merely large babies. They are shortsighted, frivolous and occupy an intermediate stage between children and men. . . ."

Several authors manfully chuckled over women's inability to plan and think things through. Clearly the murderer of the Bordens had planned things quite well. Not only had "he" managed to murder two people and elude the police, but "he" had shown remarkable tenacity by hiding for more than an hour after murdering Abby in order to do the same to Andrew.

Woman was considered man's superior in one area only: the moral sphere. She was thought to possess more "natural refinement," "diviner instincts," and stronger "spiritual sensibility" than man. She was inherently gentle, and abhorred cruelty—hardly the virtues of an ax murderer. Woman was also truthful, though some authors attributed her inability to lie to a lack of intelligence rather than to innate goodness. When reporters interviewed Lizzie's friends, the young women repeatedly mentioned her honesty.

Lizzie benefited greatly from the prevailing stereotypes of feminine delicacy and docility: her cause was also served by the widely accepted stereotype of the female criminal. Ironically, the same periodicals which carried articles about women's gentle nature also carried enough sordid stories of crimes committed by them to cast considerable doubt on their moral superiority. But writers did not find the situation paradoxical. To them, there were clearly two types of women: the genteel ladies of their own class and those women beneath them. Gentlemen authors believed that the womanly instincts of gentleness and love were the monopoly of upper-class women.

Scientists could hardly charge women of their own class with propensities toward violence without casting doubt on their own good breeding. For lower-class women with whom they had no intimate ties (at least none to which they would admit), the situation was quite different. These writers made it very clear that no woman servant, housekeeper, prostitute, nurse, washerwoman, barmaid, or factory girl could be above suspicion.

Several authors even believed that the female criminal had to look the part. In an article in *North American Review,* August, 1895, one criminologist thoughtfully provided the following description: "[She] has coarse black hair and a good deal of it. . . . She has often a long face, a receding forehead, overjutting brows, prominent cheekbones, an exaggerated frontal angle as seen in monkeys and savage races, and nearly always square jaws."

She could also be marked by deep wrinkles, a tendency toward baldness, and numerous moles. Other authors noted her long middle fingers, projecting ears, and overlapping teeth. While Lizzie had a massive jaw, her hair was red, her teeth were straight, and her ears flat. Perhaps fortunately for Bridget, a member of the suspect servant class, she was mole-free and brown-haired, and she did not have protruding middle fingers.

Criminal women supposedly exhibited neither the aversion to evil nor the love of mankind which ennobled their upper-class sisters. Among their vices were said to be great cruelty, passionate temper, a craving for revenge, cunning greed, rapacity, contempt for truth, and vulgarity. Such women were thought to be "erotic," but incapable of devoted love. Certainly the Bordens' murderer had been exceedingly cruel. But, while Lizzie was admittedly fond of money and volunteered her dislike of her stepmother, few would have called her rapacious or vengeful, and erotic was hardly an adjective one would have applied to the chaste treasurer of the Fruit and Flower Mission.

The ferocity of the criminal woman fascinated many authors. A favorite murderess was Catherine Hayes, who, in 1890, stabbed her husband to death, cut off his head with a penknife, and boiled it. But then, Mrs. Hayes was a mill worker. One writer did admit that murders might be committed by well-bred women; their weapon would be poison, however, rather than a penknife or an ax, because its passivity appealed to their nature.

Lizzie's attorneys skillfully exploited these two stereotypes—the genteel young woman and the wart-ridden murderess—to their client's advantage throughout the Borden trial. Even before the case reached court, the press had firmly implanted in the public mind a clear picture of Lizzie as bereaved daughter. The image-making began with the very first—and entirely false—story about Lizzie printed in the Boston *Globe* on the day after the murders; "The young woman, with her customary cheery disposition, evidenced her feelings in the tuneful melody from *Il Trovatore,* her favorite opera, which she was singing as she returned to the house. . . . One glance into the living room changed her from a buoyant-spirited young woman into a nervous wreck, every fiber of her being palpitating with the fearful effects of that look. . . ."

In the dozens of articles that followed, Lizzie became the embodiment of genteel young womanhood. A reporter who interviewed her friends found "not one unmaidenly nor a single deliberately unkind act." Voicing the belief of many, he concluded, "Miss Borden, without a word from herself in her own defense, is a strong argument in her own favor."

The attributes of womanliness which vindicated Lizzie did not apply to Bridget. A servant, semiliterate, nearly friendless, Catholic and Irish, Bridget was the perfect target for suspicion. To the dismay of many, no evidence or motive ever could be found to implicate her in the deaths of her employers. Nevertheless, the police received dozens of letters urging her arrest. One man wrote demanding that Bridget and "her Confessor"—that is, her priest—be thrown into prison until she admitted her guilt.

The inquest began in Fall River on August 9. Two pharmacists from Smith's Drug Store testified that Lizzie had been shopping for poison on the afternoon before the murders. She had not asked for arsenic, which was sold over the counter, they said, but for the more lethal prussic acid, claiming she needed it to clean her sealskin cape. On the stand, Lizzie steadfastly denied the pharmacists' story, even denied knowing where Smith's Drug Store was, though it had been there for fourteen years on a street not five minutes from the house in which she had lived since childhood.

Lizzie's own testimony was full of contradictions. Discrepancies in her story might have been explained by hysteria or grief, but she had displayed neither. On August 5, a reporter at the murder scene for the Providence *Journal* noted: "She wasn't the least bit scared or worried. Most women would faint at seeing their father dead, for I never saw a more horrible sight. . . . She is a woman of remarkable nerve and self-control."

Such self-control seemed unnatural in an age when women were expected to swoon, and many people were alarmed by it. The reverend Mr. Buck, Lizzie's minister, reassured her champions that "her calmness is the calmness of innocence." Her lawyer, Mr. Jennings, sought to explain away her inconsistent answers by noting that "she was having her monthly illness" on the day of the murders, thereby evoking embarrassed nods of understanding.

Public sentiment on Lizzie's behalf rose to extraordinary heights. In full agreement with their pastor, her church declared her innocent. Ecclesiastical supporters were joined by several noted feminists. Mary Livermore, Susan Fessenden (president of the Women's Christian Temperance Union), and Lucy Stone took up the cudgels on Lizzie's behalf. Livermore declared her arrest to be another outrage perpetrated by "the tyrant man." Lizzie became the sacrificial lamb, the simple, warmhearted girl offered up by corrupt police to the altar of a power-hungry district attorney.

Nonetheless, the judge ordered her arrest at the inquest's end.

Reporters found Lizzie disappointingly composed after the indictment. With no tears to report, they concentrated on her cherry trimmed hat and the two ministers on whose arms she leaned as she went off to jail in Taunton, the county seat. The horrible cell that awaited her was described in detail. In fact, Lizzie was not confined to a cell, but spent much of her time in the matron's room. Little mention was made of the flowers that graced the prison's window sill, or the lace-edged pillow slips brought by Emma, or of the meals which Lizzie had sent over from Taunton's best hotel.

When the preliminary hearing before Judge Blaisdell began in late November, reporters from more than forty out-of-town newspapers attended. Police held back huge crowds while ladies and gentlemen from Fall River's elite filed into the courtroom to claim the best seats.

A new piece of evidence, damaging to Lizzie's cause, was introduced. She had turned over to the police a spotlessly clean, fancy, blue bengaline dress that she swore she had worn on the day of the murders. Women in New England were surprised. No one wore party dresses of bengaline, a partly woolen fabric, around the house in the August heat. While witnesses swore that Lizzie was indeed wearing blue that day, none could swear that this dress was the one they had seen. To confound the problem, Alice Russell reluctantly admitted that she had seen Lizzie burn a blue cotton dress in the kitchen stove three days after the murders. The dress was soiled, she said Lizzie had told her, with brown paint—a color, noted the prosecutor, not unlike that of dried blood.

Except for rubbing her shoe buttons together, Lizzie sat quietly and displayed little interest. On the very last day, however, she broke into sobs as she heard her lawyer declare that no "person could have committed that crime unless his heart was black as hell." Delighted newspaper artists sketched a tearful Lizzie listening to Mr. Jennings as he asked: "Would it be the stranger, or would it be the one bound to the murdered man by ties of love? . . . what does it mean when we say the youngest daughter? The last one whose baby fingers have been lovingly entwined about her father's brow? Is there nothing in the ties of love and affection?"

Judge Blaisdell listened to all the evidence. It was no stranger who sat before him, but the daughter of a family he knew well. Jennings' image of the twining baby fingers was compelling, but so was the evidence prosecutor Hosea Knowlton produced. The judge finally began to speak: "Suppose for a single moment that *a man* was standing there. He was found close by that guestchamber which to Mrs. Borden was a chamber of death. Suppose that *a man* had been found in the vicinity of Mr. Borden and the only account he could give of himself was the unreasonable one that he was out in the barn looking for sinkers, that he was in the yard. . . . Would there be any question in the minds of men what should be done with such a man?" The judge's voice broke, but he continued: ". . . the judgment of the court is that you are probably guilty and you are ordered to wait the action of the Superior Court."

The trial began in New Bedford, Massachusetts, on June 5, 1893. Reporters from all over the East Coast converged on the town. Every hotel room within miles was reserved. Fences had to be erected around the courthouse to control the crowds.

Lizzie's newly inherited fortune of several hundred thousand dollars bought her excellent counsel. George Robinson, former governor of the state, was a masterful orator with a politician's shrewd sense of public opinion: at his suggestion, Lizzie went into mourning for the first time since the murders. Laboring against him were District Attorneys Hosea Knowlton and William Moody (a future U.S. Supreme Court justice), as able as Robinson, but with a distaste for flamboyance. Among the three judges who would hear Lizzie's case was Justice Justin Dewey, whom Robinson had elevated to the bench while governor.

One hundred and forty-eight men awaited jury selection. It was assumed that all had formed opinions; they were asked only if their minds were still open enough to judge the evidence fairly. The first man called claimed he could never convict a woman of a capital offense and was dismissed. Of the final twelve, the foreman was a real estate broker and sometime politician, two were manufacturers, three were mechanics, and six were farmers with considerable acreage. Not one foreign-

*Lizzie Borden, accused of the ax murders of her
father and stepmother in Fall River,
Massachusetts (August 1892), was acquitted by
an all-male jury that refused to believe that a
well-bred woman could be capable of such an act.*

Knowlton produced medical experts from
Harvard who testified that any average-sized
woman could have swung an ax with force
enough to commit the murders, and that the
trajectory of blood would have been away
from the assailant: Lizzie's tidy appearance
minutes after the crimes had no bearing on
her guilt or innocence. Robinson blithely discounted their testimony by asking the jurymen whether they put more store in Harvard
scientists than in their own New England
common sense.

Though Lizzie later professed to be shocked
at his bill of $25,000, Robinson was worth every
penny. As she sat before the jury, a Sunday-
school teacher and loving youngest daughter,
the jurymen, nearly all of whom were fathers
themselves, heard Robinson conclude: "If the
little sparrow does not fall unnoticed, then indeed in God's great providence, this woman
has not been alone in this courtroom."

The jury was sent off to deliberate with
what one reporter called Judge Dewey's "plea
for the innocent." The other two judges were
said to have been stunned by his lack of ob-
jectivity. Though Dewey was indeed grateful
to Robinson for his judgeship, a more compelling reason for his unswerving belief in
Lizzie's innocence may have been the three
daughters he had at home, the eldest of whom
was Lizzie's age.

The jurors who filed out with Dewey's plea
ringing in their ears were bewhiskered, respectable, family men. If they could believe
that a gentlewoman could pick up a hatchet
such as surely lay in their own basements, and
by murdering her parents become an heiress,
what could they think next time they looked
into their own girls' eyes?

They returned in one hour. The *New York
Times* reported that Lizzie's "face became
livid, her lips were compressed as she tottered
to her feet to hear the verdict!" Before the
clerk could finish asking for it, the foreman
cried, "Not guilty!" Lizzie dropped to her seat
as an enormous cheer went up from the

sounding name was among them. Nearly all
were over fifty: all were good Yankees.

The first blow to the prosecution came
when Judge Dewey ruled Lizzie's damaging
inquest testimony inadmissible and barred
evidence regarding the alleged attempt to buy
poison. While these rulings made Knowlton's
task more difficult, his biggest worry was that
jury men believed, as did the Boston *Globe*, in
the "moral improbability that a woman of refinement and gentle training . . . could have
conceived and executed so bloody a butch-
ery." As he repeatedly reminded the jury, "We
must face this case as men, not gallants."

spectators who climbed onto the benches, waving hats and handkerchiefs and weeping.

It would have been difficult for any jury to convict "beyond all reasonable doubt" on the circumstantial evidence presented. However, in the nearby bar to which the jurors dashed, a reporter learned that there had been no debate at all among the twelve. All exhibits were ignored. Their vote had been immediate and unanimous. It was only to avoid the impression that their minds had been made up in advance that they sat and chatted for an hour before returning with their verdict.

The following morning, Americans found reflected in the headlines their own joy that the jury had been so wise. Lizzie and Emma returned to Second Street.

Fall River society, which had defended her throughout her ordeal, fell away thereafter, and Lizzie was left pretty much alone. Undaunted, she determined to have all the things she had missed in her youth. With what some considered indiscreet haste, she bought a large house on the hill and named it Maplecroft. She also asked to be called Lisbeth and stopped going to the church whose parishioners had defended her so energetically. Matters were not improved when townspeople learned that she had bought and destroyed every available copy of local reporter Edwin Porter's *The Fall River Tragedy,* which had included portions of her inquest testimony.

Lizzie sealed her isolation in 1904 by striking up a friendship with Nance O'Neil, a Boston actress. The following year, to her neighbors' horror, Lizzie gave a party—complete with caterers and potted palms—for Miss O'Neil and her troupe. That night, Emma quietly moved out and never spoke to or saw Lizzie again.

Lizzie continued to live at Maplecroft in increasing isolation. Undoubtedly, she heard the nasty rhyme children began to sing to the tune of "Ta-Ra-Ra Boom-De-Ay!":

Lizzie Borden took an ax
And gave her mother forty whacks;
When she saw what she had done,
She gave her father forty-one!

Lizzie Borden died on June 1, 1927, at the age of sixty-six in Fall River. Emma died ten days later in New Hampshire. Few gravestones conceal a puzzle more intricate than that sealed away by the imposing Borden monument in Oak Grove Cemetery. The truth about the events on Second Street lies buried there along with Andrew, Abby, Emma, and Lizzie, but back then, in the summer of 1893, most Americans knew in their hearts that no young lady like Lizzie could have murdered her parents with an ax. Reputable authors in respectable magazines assured them their intuition was correct. They did not even want to think that it could be otherwise.

Study Questions

1. How did Lizzie Borden's class and social standing influence the way she was treated by legal authorities?

2. What were the physical, psychological, intellectual, and moral characteristics that popular magazines in the late nineteenth century attributed to well-bred women? How closely did Lizzie conform to these expectations?

3. What did late-nineteenth-century writers mean by such concepts as "arrested evolution" and "deplorable accidents"? How do these concepts indicate a sexually biased society?

4. In what area were women considered superior to men? Why was this so?

5. How did popular attitudes toward upper-class and lower-class women differ? Why were many people more inclined to suspect Bridget Sullivan than Lizzie Borden of the crime?

6. How was Lizzie's behavior during the entire episode interpreted?

7. Why was the trial politically and symbolically significant?

Bibliography

The Borden murder case has been examined and reexamined. Victoria Lincoln, *Lizzie Borden, a Private Disgrace* (1967) and Robert Sullivan, *Goodbye Lizzie Borden* (1974) argue that she was indeed guilty of the crimes. Edward D. Radin, *Lizzie Borden: The Untold Story* (1961) views the case from a different perspective. Recent historical scholarship has only begun to explore the complexities of American attitudes toward women. Lois W. Banner, *Women in Modern America: A Brief History* (1974, second edition 1984) presents a fine introduction to the topic and a good bibliography. Other useful studies on women in the late nineteenth century include John S. Haller Jr., and Robin M. Haller, *The Physician and Sexuality in Victorian America* (1974); G. J. Barker-Benfield, *The Horrors of the Half-Known Life: Male Attitudes Toward Women and Sexuality in Nineteenth-Century America* (1976); Linda Gordon, *Woman's Body, Woman's Right: A Social History of Birth Control in America* (1976); and Lois Banner, *American Beauty* (1983). Two other books present different views of the role of women in America. Kate Chopin, *The Awakening* (1980) is a wonderful novel written with depth and sensitivity. Questions of isolation and alienation in a small American town are touched upon in Michael Lesy, *Wisconsin Death Trip* (1973).

★ ★ ★

War and Peace in a New Century

The period between the assassination of William McKinley in 1901 and America's entry into the Great War in 1917 has been labeled as the Progressive Era. In character and tone the years mirrored the first Progressive president, Theodore Roosevelt. Animated and energetic, T. R. used the presidency as a "bully pulpit," readily giving his opinion on a variety of subjects, ranging from literature and politics to football and divorce. Roosevelt believed that America's greatness was the result of its Anglo-Saxon heritage. Although he hoped to bring a "Square Deal" to all Americans, his reforming impulse was conservative in nature; he maintained that only through moderate reform could America preserve its traditional social, economic, and political structure. He had no sympathy for such "radical fanatics" as socialists or anarchists, nor did he trust the masses of American people who lacked his breeding and education. His answer for any sort of mob action was "taking ten or a dozen of their leaders out, standing . . . them against a wall, and shooting them dead."

Despite their ethnocentricity and self-righteousness, Roosevelt and the next two Progressive presidents—William Howard Taft and Woodrow Wilson—did attempt to curb some of the worst abuses of the urban-industrial society. They saw legislation through Congress that limited the number of hours that women and children could work and enacted the Pure Food and Drug Act (1906) and the Meat Inspection Act (1906). However, other Progressives, often with the support of the president, supported Prohibition and antidivorce legislation, thereby seeking to regulate the private lives of millions of Americans.

A major shortcoming of the Progressive movement was the general reluctance to support minority and ethnic groups. Such Progressives as James K. Vardaman and Theodore G. Bilbo, both from Mississippi, supported forward-looking legislation for whites but were violent race-baiters. Progressives rarely attacked the Jim Crow system in the South or introduced antilynching legisla-

In 1901, Theodore Roosevelt said that he believed in the adage, "Speak softly and carry a big stick; you will go far." With this concept behind his foreign policy, he became a powerful arbitrator of many world disputes.

tion in Congress. Segregation within the federal government expanded under Woodrow Wilson.

Similarly, vocal and independent labor unions and women's rights organizations seldom found support among influential Progressives. Margaret Sanger's birth control movement met strong opposition from middle-class men and women who saw it as a threat to family and morality. Such radical working-class organizations as the Industrial Workers of the World (the IWW, or "Wobblies") were not embraced by the mainstream of the Progressive movement.

The Progressive movement, however, did not really survive World War I. As a result of the Spanish-American War of 1898, the United States had acquired new territories in the distant Pacific, requiring a two-ocean navy and leaving Americans with global responsibilities. Those responsibilities eventually complicated and compromised the reform spirit. The Great War of 1914–1918 damaged the reform impulses of Progressivism. It inspired skepticism, pessimism, and ultimately cynicism, and in the death-filled trenches of Western Europe, the Progressive movement met its demise.

The following essays deal with different characteristics of the Progressive movement. Confronted by the powerful forces of urbanization and industrialization, Americans attempted—sometimes successfully, often unsuccessfully—to come to terms with their changing society. Amidst that attempt, World War I complicated Progressivist dreams with the reality of horror, stupidity, and mass death.

READING 6

★ ★ ★

Teddy Roosevelt and the Rough Riders

Robert J. Maddox

Anchored off the coast of Cuba, aboard the *Yucatan*, Theodore Roosevelt received news on the evening of June 21, 1898, that he and his men, a volunteer cavalry regiment dubbed the Rough Riders, should disembark from the safety of the ship and join the fighting ashore. It was a welcomed invitation, celebrated with cheers, war dances, songs, boasts, and toasts. "To the officers—may they get killed, wounded, or promoted," urged one toast that captured the mood aboard ship.

Who were these Rough Riders who seemed so bent on winning glory? As one of them told Roosevelt, "Who would not risk his life for a star?" And who was Theodore Roosevelt, the energetic rich kid who lusted after fame and perhaps had his eyes—albeit nearsighted—focused on the presidency? Robert J. Maddox retells this story of Theodore Roosevelt, the Rough Riders, and America's "splendid little war" with Spain. In the process he tells a great deal about the future president and the nation that made him its hero.

The war against Spain in 1898 was one of the more popular conflicts in American history. Victory came easily, there were relatively few casualties, and the cause seemed just in the minds of most people. From it the United States acquired the Philippine Islands, Puerto Rico, Guam, and a virtual protectorate over Cuba. The nation acquired several heroes as well, Admiral Dewey to name one, but none more colorful than the flamboyant Teddy Roosevelt. His exploits in Cuba, at the head of his Rough Riders, made him a legend in his own lifetime and helped make him president of the United States.

Roosevelt was in the prime of his life when the war broke out. Not yet forty years old, he possessed an imposing if somewhat overweight physique which he kept fit by almost daily exercise. In this regard he was a self-made man. Spindly and a trifle owlish as a youngster, Roosevelt, through what one of his biographers termed the "Cult of Strenuosity," had built up his body by relentless physical activity. Only one of his faculties had failed to respond—his eyesight. Cursed from boyhood with extreme nearsightedness, which grew worse over the years, Roosevelt was very self-conscious about this weakness in an otherwise healthy organism. During the war he was so worried it would betray him in combat that he had at least a half-dozen pairs of spectacles sewn in various parts of his uniform as insurance.

Mentally, Roosevelt was a complex individual. Exceedingly bright, he read voraciously, and penned his own books and articles without the help of a ghostwriter. He was, or would become, friendly with some of the leading intellectuals of the era. One side of him, however, remained boyish until the day he died. "You must always remember," a British diplomat wrote a friend some years later, "that the

An 1889 photo shows Teddy Roosevelt as colonel of the Rough Riders. Teddy's uniforms, which had extra spectacles sewn into them, were tailored by Brooks Brothers to ensure a proper fit.

President [Roosevelt] is about six." Without in any way belittling his patriotism, it seems safe to say that Teddy's enthusiasm for fighting the Spaniards stemmed at least as much from his desire to have a "bully" time doing it.

No one ever accused Roosevelt of being a pacifist. During the 1880s and 1890s the United States had gotten into a number of scrapes with other nations over issues large and small. Almost invariably T. R. had called for the most militant actions in response to these situations, and had denounced those who urged caution. War to him was not a catastrophe to be avoided; it could be a tonic to the nation's bloodstream. A country too long at peace, he believed, tended to grow soft and

"Teddy Roosevelt and the Rough Riders" by Robert J. Maddox. This article is reprinted from the November 1977 issue of *American History Illustrated* 12, pp. 8–15, 18–19, with the permission of Cowles History Group, Inc. Copyright *American History Illustrated* magazine.

effeminate, while war encouraged "manliness," a characteristic he prized above all else.

Before 1897 Roosevelt had held no office which dealt directly with military or foreign affairs. He had served in the New York state legislature as federal Civil Service Commissioner, and as a commissioner of the New York City Police Department. Despite having held such prestigious jobs for a man of his years, Roosevelt's political future was clouded by his tendency to alienate some of those who could help him and by the strident views on foreign policy which he never hesitated to voice—often to the great embarrassment of his own party. When, as a reward for his services in the election of 1896, T. R.'s friends began pushing for his appointment as Assistant Secretary of the Navy in the new Republican administration, they encountered stiff opposition. The president-elect himself had reservations about Teddy, but named him anyway. "I hope he has no preconceived plans," McKinley said wistfully, "which he would wish to drive through the moment he got in."

McKinley hoped in vain. Within two months of his appointment, Roosevelt wrote the well-known naval expert, Captain Alfred Thayer Mahan, that:

If I had my way, we would annex those islands [Hawaii] tomorrow. If that is impossible, I would establish a protectorate. ... I believe we should build the Nicaraguan Canal at once, and should build a dozen new battleships, half of them on the Pacific Coast. I am fully alive to the danger from Japan.

These and similar sentiments clearly demonstrated that T. R. had no intention of vanishing into the bureaucracy. Nor did he. A short time later, when Secretary of the Navy John D. Long went on vacation, one newspaper reported that Roosevelt soon had "the whole Navy bordering on a war footing. It remains only to sand down the decks and pipe to quarters for action." Teddy did not try to conceal his delight in being left to mind the store. "The Secretary is away," he wrote in one letter, "and I am having immense fun running the Navy." One story had it that when asked about his Assistant Secretary, Long dourly responded "Why 'Assistant'?"

Sticking pins in maps and running around on inspection tours must have amused him, but Roosevelt wanted some real action. Spain provided the most likely source. Once the possessor of a world empire, Spain by this time was a minor power clinging grimly to its few remaining territories. One of these, Cuba, lay less than 100 miles from American shores, and for several years had smoldered with insurrection against Spanish domination. Though he refrained from speaking out publicly, Roosevelt, in private talks and correspondence, recommended war against Spain almost from the day he became assistant secretary. American honor demanded it, he said, and a brief war would help rekindle martial instincts which had flagged through years of peace. There would be an additional dividend, he wrote on one occasion, that being "the benefit done our military forces by trying both the Army and Navy in actual practice."

Roosevelt did not bring on the war with Spain, of course, however much he tried. Cuban propaganda, sensationalist American newspapers, and jingoes in and outside Congress, combined to keep talk of war before the public. Still, through 1897, President McKinley refused to be stampeded, and the Spanish government (which very much wished to avoid war) repeatedly gave in to American demands over the treatment of Cuba.

Then, early in 1898, two events occurred which made war virtually inevitable. First, a letter critical of McKinley, written by the Spanish minister in Washington, was stolen from the mails and reprinted in the American press. Trivial in itself, this blunder enraged many Americans. More important, the warship *Maine* blew up in a Cuban harbor with the loss of more than 200 sailors. Though not a shred of evidence has ever emerged to indicate that the Spanish were responsible, most Americans (abetted by much of the press) assumed that they were and demanded revenge. McKinley simply was not strong enough to stand against this pressure. On April 10 he asked Congress for what amounted to a declaration of war.

Well before the war began Roosevelt had told others that if it came he would not be content to remain in Washington. He was true to his word. By March he was beseeching New York state officials to permit him to raise a regiment of volunteers, which unit, he promised, would be "jim-dandy." That he had never served in the military, let alone seen combat, fazed Teddy not at all. He was greatly miffed when his generous offer was spurned.

Roosevelt, as usual, had other irons in the fire. Due to the minuscule size of the regular army, Congress had authorized the recruitment of three volunteer cavalry regiments from the Southwest. Because of his political connections, which he used to the utmost, Roosevelt was offered the command of one of these units. Modesty suddenly descended upon him. Estimating that it might take him a month or so to familiarize himself thoroughly with military procedures and tactics, T. R. asked that his friend, Captain Leonard Wood (at that time a military surgeon), be promoted to colonel and given command of the regiment. He would be satisfied with a mere lieutenant-colonelcy and would serve under Wood. Roosevelt's light could not be hidden, however, and from the start the First Volunteer Cavalry was known as "Roosevelt's Rough Riders."

Teddy was eager to get going. Quickly ordering the appropriate uniforms from Brooks Brothers (to ensure a proper fit), he began complaining that the war might be over before he could get into it—"it will be awful if we miss the fun." At last, in early May, he set out for San Antonio, Texas, where the First Volunteers were undergoing preliminary training. He arrived to the welcome of a brass band and "his boys."

And what a group it was. "Mingling among the cowboys and momentarily reformed bad men from the West," Henry Pringle has written, "were polo players and steeplechase riders from the Harvard, Yale, and Princeton clubs of New York City." Though from time to time Roosevelt protested against the carnival atmosphere which pervaded the camp, he enjoyed himself hugely. After one period of mounted drill, for instance, he told his men to "drink all the beer they want, which I will pay for" and had a few himself. Colonel Wood admonished Teddy for this kind of behavior, which the latter admitted was out of place. "Sir," Roosevelt replied, "I consider myself the damnedest ass within ten miles of this camp."

Two weeks after Teddy arrived in San Antonio, the Rough Riders were ordered to report to the Tampa, Florida, staging area for the expedition against Cuba. By this time they had been transformed from an undisciplined group in civilian clothes to an undisciplined group in uniform. Tampa was, if possible, even more chaotic than San Antonio had been. Units of Regulars, National Guard, and volunteers milled about with little overall direction and inadequate facilities. Some units were without arms, others had arms but no ammunition, still others lacked uniforms, bedding, or tents. It was a mess. "No head," Roosevelt wrote angrily in his diary, "a breakdown of both the railroad and military systems of the country."

With an aroused public clamoring for action, the War Department ordered the expedition to sail despite its obvious lack of preparation. At this point the Rough Riders had what amounted to their first engagement of the war—against other American soldiers. Port Tampa lay about nine miles from Tampa, where the troops were quartered, with only a single track railway connecting them. The orders sent to individual regiments included no scheduling, so it was up to each unit to get to the port as best it could. A mad scramble ensued to commandeer whatever rolling stock was available. The Rough Riders were lucky enough to come upon an engine with some coal cars which they promptly seized. But the excitement was not yet over. Arriving at the port, Roosevelt and Wood found that the ship allotted to them was also designated for two regiments and there was not enough space for all three. As Teddy later recounted the episode:

Accordingly, I ran at full speed to our train; and leaving a strong guard with the baggage I double-quicked the rest of the regiment up to the boat just in time to board her as she came into the quay and then to hold her against the 2d Regulars and the 71st, who had arrived a little too late. ... There was a good deal of expostulation, but we had possession.

It was a false alarm. On the eve of departure another message arrived from the War Department. "Wait until you get further orders before you sail," it read. "Answer quick." As things turned out the officers and men of the expeditionary force spent almost two weeks sweating and cursing in the tightly packed ships at anchor under the Florida sun. At last, on June 14, thirty-two steamers moved out of Port Tampa heading slowly toward Cuba. The Fifth Army Corps, as it was designated, consisted of two divisions and an independent brigade of infantry, a division of dismounted cavalry, four batteries of field artillery, and some auxiliary troops. The Rough Riders were aboard, of course, but like the other cavalry units they had nothing to ride. Because of the lack of space, the only animals brought along were horses for the officers and mules for carrying supplies.

Eventually the flotilla reached Cuba and landings were made virtually unopposed in several places. The debarkations resembled the disorder which had reigned at Tampa Bay. The men and equipment were brought ashore in helter-skelter fashion by an assortment of launches and other small boats. The animals were even less fortunate: They were driven off the sides of ships and left to fend for themselves. Some reached shore safely, others swam to watery graves. Once again, Teddy was unwilling to trust luck. Recognizing the

captain of a small vessel which drew alongside as a man he had known in the Navy Department, Roosevelt directed that the ship be used solely for getting the Rough Riders ashore as quickly as possible. After spending weeks aboard what they referred to as "prison hulks," the men must have appreciated the initiative of their second-in-command.

The course of the Cuban campaign cannot be recounted in detail here. The most charitable single word to describe it is "muddled." The commander of the Fifth Corps was General William R. Shafter, a rather lethargic man who weighed well over 300 pounds. Suffering from the heat since arriving in Florida, Shafter, during the latter part of the fighting, had to be transported reclining on a barn door. His immediate subordinates were three other general officers, who seemed at least as much concerned with outdoing one another as with fighting the Spaniards. One of them, "Fighting Joe" Wheeler, had last seen combat as a Confederate officer during the Civil War. During moments of stress, it was reported, he became confused as to who his opponents were and several times referred to them as "those Yankees." Fortunately for the Americans, the Spanish were in even worse shape. Although some individual Spanish troops and units fought well, they were badly led and defeatism permeated the defending forces.

Once a semblance of order was created on the beach, preparations were made for the expedition's advance against the main target, the harbor city of Santiago, less than twenty miles west along the coastline. The only available overland route, however, swung inland through jungles which provided excellent concealment for defenders. The movement took place in fits and starts and was not without incident—and losses. The Spanish fought a brief rearguard action at a place called Las Guásimas, for instance, during which sixteen Americans were killed and another fifty wounded. The Rough Riders took part in this engagement, as did some regular units, and there is evidence to indicate that Wood and

Roosevelt led their men into an ambush. In later years Roosevelt indignantly denied any such thing and claimed that "every one of the officers had full knowledge of where he would find the enemy." In any event, Teddy boasted, "...we wanted the first whack at the Spaniards and we got it."

Finally, by the end of June, American forces were within striking distance of Santiago. Their way was blocked by a series of fortifications and trenches located on a chain of hills surrounding the city—the most prominent of which was San Juan Hill. The difficulty in moving supplies and ammunition by pack animal along narrow jungle trails caused the troops to remain before Santiago for several days. The plan of attack was simple. One division would move several miles north to attack a stronghold at El Caney, the rest of the units would march head-on against the San Juan and nearby hills. Both assaults began on the morning of July 1.

From where they had grouped, American troops had to push through several miles of jungle and ford a stream before reaching clear ground in front of the hills. They began taking losses while still in the jungle. There were only two trails they could use and Spanish artillery had these zeroed in. One column had at its head an observation balloon pulled along by men holding guy ropes. It proved to be of little help to the Americans, but showed Spanish artillery-men exactly where the enemy was. Fortunately for the men underneath it, the bag was pierced several times and settled gently to the ground before it could cause even greater damage.

The jungle ended abruptly at a stream which ran along its edge roughly parallel to the Spanish lines on the ridges. Across the stream there were several hundred yards of meadowlands before reaching the slopes. As the troops emerged from the jungle, therefore, they were exposed to withering Spanish rifle fire from above. What little order there was broke down as the advancing columns began clogging up at the jungle's edge. Some

units refused to cross the stream, others became disorganized as they tried to move through and get into position. The situation presented a cruel dilemma to American commanders. To attack with insufficient numbers of men would be to risk defeat. To wait until all units were deployed would mean exposing those who crossed the stream first to an extended period under the crippling fire. Finally, a little past noon and before elements in the rear had left the jungle, the assault began.

San Juan Hill was the main objective. Somewhat to the right and much closer to American lines lay Kettle Hill, assigned to the dismounted cavalry. Since Colonel Wood earlier had taken command of a brigade, Roosevelt now led the Rough Riders. This was what he had been waiting for, and he would not be found wanting. Showing complete disdain for enemy bullets, Teddy galloped around on his horse, Little Texas, exhorting his men to form up for attack. They were joined by elements from several other regiments, including black troops from the 10th Cavalry. Roosevelt waved his hat and the men moved forward. "By this time we were all in the spirit of the thing and greatly excited by the charge," he wrote later, "the men cheering and running forward between shots. . . . I . . . galloped toward the hill. . . ."

According to his own account Roosevelt quickly moved ahead of the men, preceded only by his orderly, Henry Bardshar, "who had run ahead very fast in order to get better shots at the Spaniards. . . ." About forty yards from the crest Teddy encountered a wire fence and jumped off Little Texas, letting the horse run free. Almost immediately he saw Bardshar shoot down two Spaniards who emerged from the trenches. Soon Roosevelt and Bardshar were surrounded by the rest of the men as they swarmed over the hill, capturing or killing the few Spanish troops who had not retreated. The charge up Kettle Hill was over.

From their newly won position, Roosevelt and his men had an excellent view of the assault against San Juan Hill. Earlier artillery barrages had failed to cause much damage to the breastworks, and the black powder used in American guns produced smoke which drew Spanish counterfire. Now, however, three Gatling guns opened up with good effect. "They went b-r-r-r, like a lawn mower cutting grass over our trenches," a Spanish officer said later. "We could not stick a finger up when you fired without getting it cut off." Still the Spaniards held their positions as the ragged blue lines moved forward. Despite heavy losses, the Americans pushed doggedly up the hill. At last, just before they reached the top, the Spanish defenders fired a last volley and fled.

Beyond Kettle Hill and to the right of San Juan lay another ridge from which the enemy kept shooting. Rallying his men again, Roosevelt led them down the far side of Kettle, across the intervening valley, and up the slopes. "I was with Henry Bardshar, running up at the double," Teddy later recalled, "and two Spaniards leaped from the trenches and fired at us, not ten yards away. As they turned to run I closed in and fired twice, missing the first and killing the second. My revolver was from the sunken battleship *Maine*." Again the Americans drove the Spanish before them. When they took possession of these crests, "we found ourselves overlooking Santiago."

Although the Americans had won the day, the battle for Santiago was not yet over. The Spanish had about 16,000 men to defend the city, the Americans an equal number to take it. The latter were exhausted from their attacks and lacked reserves, food, and ammunition. By July 3, two days after the initial assaults, the Americans had lost 224 men killed and 1,370 wounded. The result was a stand-off. Spanish units did not attempt to break out of the ring; the Americans were in no shape to move against the city's defenses. "Tell the president for Heaven's sake to send us every regiment and above all every battery possible," Roosevelt wrote a friend. "We have

won so far at a heavy cost, but the Spaniards fight very hard and charging these intrenchments against modern rifles is terrible. . . . We *must* have help—thousands of men, batteries, and *food* and ammunition." Fortunately, the Spanish launched no major counterattacks.

While the men dug themselves into the hills, the battle for Santiago was decided by another engagement—at sea. A Spanish fleet had been bottled up in Santiago Harbor for some time: Shafter's expedition was supposed to take the city, thereby forcing the Spanish ships to leave the harbor or surrender. At 9:30 A.M. on July 3, Spanish ships began coming out singly under the guns of the blockaders. It was a courageous but futile effort. Despite some bungling on the part of the U.S. Navy, all the opposing ships were sunk or disabled. After two weeks of negotiation Shafter received the surrender of Santiago, and less than a month after that the Spanish government sued for peace.

Although the war had ended in complete victory for the United States, it came in for a great deal of criticism in the period following. Charges of incompetence were leveled against the top echelons, there were undignified exchanges between generals and admirals over who deserved credit for which victory, and the condition of the men returning from Cuba caused a public outcry. Many troops died from tropical illnesses, and still others from food poisoning caused by tainted meat.

It was probably for these reasons that Roosevelt's star came to shine so brightly. He had performed heroically, after all, and he was sufficiently subordinate in rank to escape any blame about the war's mismanagement.

Teddy himself was not loath to accept the limelight; indeed, he eagerly sought it. Almost immediately he began campaigning for the governorship of New York state and, lest anyone forget his exploits, kept the Rough Rider bugler at his side during his speeches. Roosevelt had other assets, of course, but being the "Hero of San Juan Hill" (he was not disposed to argue about which hill he had climbed) did him no harm. He had become fixed in the national mind as Colonel Teddy Roosevelt of the Rough Riders.

"I would honestly rather have my position of colonel," Roosevelt had told his men at their mustering-out ceremony, "than any other position on earth." No doubt he meant it at the time. As governor of New York, and later as president of the United States, he looked back fondly on his days in Cuba and the men who had served with him. In both positions he tried to accommodate as many as possible of the former Rough Riders who petitioned him for a job. His loyalty, if not his judgment, could scarcely be questioned. In one case he tried to have appointed as territorial marshal a man who, it was found, was serving time in prison for homicide. Undaunted, Teddy later tried to have the person installed as warden of the very prison in which he had been confined. "When I told this to John Hay," Roosevelt said, "he remarked (with a brutal absence of feeling) that he believed the proverb ran, 'Set a Rough Rider to catch a thief.'"

For once in his life, Teddy was at a loss for a reply.

Study Questions

1. What character traits inclined Roosevelt toward war? What events led the United States to war with Spain?

2. What sorts of men joined the Rough Riders?

3. What problems did the United States have mobilizing for war?

4. What role did the Battles of Kettle Hill and San Juan Hill play in the war in Cuba?

5. How did Roosevelt capitalize on his newly won fame?

Bibliography

The best overview of the Spanish-American War is David Trask, *The War with Spain in 1898* (1981). Shorter, but still useful is Frank Freidel, *The Splendid Little War* (1958). For a provocative study of the intersection between gender studies and military history, see Kristin Hoganson, *Fighting for American Manhood, How Gender Politics Provoked the Spanish-American and Philippine-American Wars* (2000). Theodore Roosevelt's own account of his moments of glory is *The Rough Riders* (1899). Among the more readable biographies of Roosevelt are Edmund Morris, *The Rise of Theodore Roosevelt* (1979) and his more recent *Theodore Rex* (2001), and David McCullough, *Mornings on Horseback* (1981). More scholarly biographies are G. Wallace Chessman, *Theodore Roosevelt and the Politics of Power* (1969) and Howard K. Beals, *Theodore Roosevelt and the Rise of America to World Power* (1956). On the war also see Gerald F. Linderman, *The Mirror of War: American Society and the Spanish-American War* (1974) and H. Wayne Morgan, *America's Road to Empire* (1965). Also see Stuart C. Miller, *"Benevolent Assimilation": The American Conquest of the Philippines, 1899–1903* (1982).

READING 7

★ ★ ★

Living and Dying in Packingtown, Chicago from *The Jungle*

Upton Sinclair

In the late fall of 1904, Upton Sinclair, a young and ambitious novelist imbued with a zealous sense of socialism, traveled to Chicago to gather information about the horrors and abuses of the meatpacking industry. For the next seven weeks, as a cold fall gave way to a brutal winter, Sinclair lived in the workers' ghetto of Packingtown, talked with workers, and studied the meatpacking industry.

On Christmas Day of 1904, he began writing *The Jungle*, the story of Jurgis Rudkus. A Lithuanian immigrant of great strength, Rudkus came to America full of hope—only to be used, abused, and discarded by the unfeeling powers of Packingtown. Sinclair wrote frantically for three months, stopping only occasionally to eat or sleep. He poured all his emotions into Rudkus's story, hoping to show Americans how evil the industry—and by extension, capitalism—had become. He recorded the stench and unhealthy conditions of Packingtown and the dangers of working in the packinghouses. Of the work, one historian wrote, "Each job had its own dangers: the dampness and cold of the packing rooms and hide cellar, the sharp blade of the beef boner's knife, the noxious dust of the wood department and fertilizer plant, the wild charge of a half-crazed steer on the killing floor." The following selection from *The Jungle* describes some of the working and living conditions in Packingtown.

During this time that Jurgis was looking for work occurred the death of little Kristoforas, one of the children of Teta Elzbieta. Both Kristoforas and his brother, Juozapas, were cripples, the latter having lost one leg by having it run over, and Kristoforas having congenital dislocation of the hip, which made it impossible for him ever to walk. He was the last of Teta Elzbieta's children, and perhaps he had been intended by nature to let her know that she had had enough. At any rate he was wretchedly sick and undersized; he had the rickets, and though he was over three years old, he was no bigger than an ordinary child of one. All day long he would crawl around the floor in a filthy little dress, whining and fretting; because the floor was full of draughts he was always catching cold, and snuffling because his nose ran. This made him a nuisance, and a source of endless trouble in the family. For his mother, with unnatural perversity, loved him best of all her children, and made a perpetual fuss over him—would let him do anything undisturbed, and would burst into tears when his fretting drove Jurgis wild.

And now he died. Perhaps it was the smoked sausage he had eaten that morning—which may have been made out of some tubercular pork that was condemned as unfit for export. At any rate, an hour after eating it, the child had begun to cry with pain, and in another hour he was rolling about on the floor in convulsions. Little Kotrina, who was all alone with him, ran out screaming for help, and after a while a doctor came, but not until Kristoforas had howled his last howl. No one was really sorry about this except poor Elzbieta, who was inconsolable. Jurgis announced that so far as he was concerned the child would have to be buried by the city, since they had no money for a funeral; and at this the poor woman almost went out of her senses, wringing her hands and screaming with grief and despair. Her child to be buried in a pauper's grave! And her stepdaughter to stand by and hear it said without protesting! It was enough to make Ona's father rise up out of his grave to rebuke her! If it had come to this, they might as well give up at once, and be buried all of them together! . . . In the end Marija said that she would help with ten dollars; and Jurgis being still obdurate, Elzbieta went in tears and begged the money from the neighbors, and so little Kristoforas had a mass and a hearse with white plumes on it, and a tiny plot in a graveyard with a wooden cross to mark the place. The poor mother was not the same for months after that; the mere sight of the floor where little Kristoforas had crawled about would make her weep. He had never had a fair chance, poor little fellow, she would say. He had been handicapped from birth. If only she had heard about it in time, so that she might have had the great doctor to cure him of his lameness! . . . Some time ago, Elzbieta was told, a Chicago billionaire had paid a fortune to bring a great European surgeon over to cure his little daughter of the same disease from which Kristoforas had suffered. And because this surgeon had to have bodies to demonstrate upon, he announced that he would treat the children of the poor, a piece of magnanimity over which the papers became quite eloquent. Elzbieta, alas, did not read the papers, and no one had told her; but perhaps it was as well, for just then they would not have had the carfare to spare to go every day to wait upon the surgeon, nor for that matter anybody with the time to take the child.

All this while he was seeking for work, there was a dark shadow hanging over Jurgis; as if a savage beast were lurking somewhere in the pathway of his life, and he knew it, and yet could not help approaching the place. There are all stages of being out of work in Packingtown, and he faced in dread the prospect of reaching the lowest. There is a place that waits for the lowest man—the fertilizer plant!

The men would talk about it in awe-stricken whispers. Not more than one in ten

Upton Sinclair, "Living and Dying in Packingtown, Chicago." From Upton Sinclair, *The Jungle*. Chicago, 1905.

had ever really tried it; the other nine had contented themselves with hearsay evidence and a peep through the door. There were some things worse than even starving to death. They would ask Jurgis if he had worked there yet, and if he meant to; and Jurgis would debate the matter with himself. As poor as they were and making all the sacrifices that they were, would he dare to refuse any sort of work that was offered to him, be it as horrible as ever it could? Would he dare to go home and eat bread that had been earned by Ona, weak and complaining as she was, knowing that he had been given a chance, and had not had the nerve to take it? And yet he might argue that way with himself all day, and one glimpse into the fertilizer-works would send him away again shuddering. He was a man, and he would do his duty; he went and made application—but surely he was not also required to hope for success.

The fertilizer-works of Durham's lay away from the rest of the plant. Few visitors ever saw them, and the few who did would come out looking like Dante, of whom the peasants declared that he had been into hell. To this part of the yards came all the "tankage" and waste products of all sorts; here they dried out the bones—and in suffocating cellars where the daylight never came you might see men and women and children bending over whirling machines and sawing bits of bones into all sorts of shapes, breathing their lungs full of the fine dust, and doomed to die, every one of them, within a certain definite time. Here they made the blood into albumen, and made other foul-smelling things into things still more foul-smelling. In the corridors and caverns where it was done you might lose yourself as in the great caves of Kentucky. In the dust and the steam the electric lights would shine like far-off twinkling stars—red and blue, green and purple stars, according to the color of the mist and the brew from which it came. For the odors in these ghastly charnel-houses there may be words in Lithuanian, but

there are none in English. The person entering would have to summon his courage as for a cold-water plunge. He would go on like a man swimming under water; he would put his handkerchief over his face, and begin to cough and choke; and then, if he were still obstinate, he would find his head beginning to ring, and the veins in his forehead to throb, until finally he would be assailed by an overpowering blast of ammonia fumes, and would turn and run for his life, and come out half-dazed.

On top of this were the rooms where they dried the "tankage," the mass of brown stringy stuff that was left after the waste portions of the carcasses had had the lard and tallow dried out of them. This dried material they would then grind to a fine powder, and after they had mixed it up well with a mysterious but inoffensive brown rock which they brought in and ground up by the hundreds of carloads for that purpose, the substance was ready to be put into bags and sent out to the world as any one of a hundred different brands of standard bone-phosphate. And then the farmer in Maine or California or Texas would buy this, at say twenty-five dollars a ton, and plant it with his corn; and for several days after the operation the fields would have a strong odor, and the farmer and his wagon and the very horses that had hauled it would all have it too. In Packingtown the fertilizer is pure, instead of being a flavoring, and instead of a ton or so spread on several acres under the open sky, there are hundreds and thousands of tons of it in one building, heaped here and there in haystack piles, covering the floor several inches deep, and filling the air with a choking dust that becomes a blinding sandstorm when the wind stirs.

It was to this building that Jurgis came daily, as if dragged by an unseen hand. The month of May was an exceptionally cool one, and his secret prayers were granted; but early in June there came a record-breaking hot spell, and after that there were men wanted in the fertilizer-mill.

The boss of the grinding room had come to know Jurgis by this time, and had marked him for a likely man; and so when he came to the door about two o'clock this breathless hot day, he felt a sudden spasm of pain shoot through him—the boss beckoned to him! In ten minutes more Jurgis had pulled off his coat and overshirt, and set his teeth together and gone to work. Here was one more difficulty for him to meet and conquer!

His labor took him about one minute to learn. Before him was one of the vents of the mill in which the fertilizer was being ground—rushing forth in a great brown river, with a spray of the finest dust flung forth in clouds. Jurgis was given a shovel, and along with half a dozen others it was his task to shovel this fertilizer into carts. That others were at work he knew by the sound, and by the fact that he sometimes collided with them; otherwise they might as well not have been there, for in the blinding dust-storm a man could not see six feet in front of his face. When he had filled one cart he had to grope around him until another came, and if there was none on hand he continued to grope till one arrived. In five minutes he was, of course, a mass of fertilizer from head to feet; they gave him a sponge to tie over his mouth, so that he could breathe, but the sponge did not prevent his lips and eyelids from caking up with it and his ears from filling solid. He looked like a brown ghost at twilight—from hair to shoes he became the color of the building and of everything in it, and for that matter a hundred yards outside it. The building had to be left open, and when the wind blew Durham and Company lost a great deal of fertilizer.

Working in his shirt-sleeves, and with the thermometer at over a hundred, the phosphates soaked in through every pore of Jurgis's skin, and in five minutes he had a headache, and in fifteen was almost dazed. The blood was pounding his brain like an engine's throbbing; there was a frightful pain in the top of his skull, and he could hardly control his hands.

Still, with the memory of his four months' siege behind him, he fought on, in a frenzy of determination; and half an hour later he began to vomit—he vomited until it seemed as if his innards must be torn to shreds. A man could get used to the fertilizer-mill, the boss had said, if he would only make up his mind to it; but Jurgis now began to see that it was a question of making up his stomach.

At the end of that day of horror, he could scarcely stand. He had to catch himself now and then, and lean against a building and get his bearings. Most of the men, when they came out, made straight for a saloon—they seem to place fertilizer and rattlesnake poison in one class. But Jurgis was too ill to think of drinking—he could only make his way to the street and stagger on to a car. He had a sense of humor, and later on, when he became an old hand, he used to think it fun to board a streetcar and see what happened. Now, however, he was too ill to notice it—how the people in the car began to gasp and sputter, to put their handkerchiefs to their noses, and transfix him with furious glances. Jurgis only knew that a man in front of him immediately got up and gave him a seat; and that half a minute later the two people on each side of him got up; and that in a full minute the crowded car was nearly empty—those passengers who could not get room on the platform having gotten out to walk.

Of course Jurgis had made his home a miniature fertilizer-mill a minute after entering. The stuff was half an inch deep in his skin—his whole system was full of it, and it would have taken a week not merely of scrubbing, but of vigorous exercise, to get it out of him. As it was, he could be compared with nothing known to men, save that newest discovery of the savants, a substance which emits energy for an unlimited time, without being itself in the least diminished in power. He smelt so that he made all food at the table taste, and set the whole family to vomiting; for himself it was three days before he could keep anything upon his stomach—he might wash his hands, and use a knife and fork, but were not his mouth and throat filled with the poison?

And still Jurgis stuck it out! In spite of splitting headaches he would stagger down to the plant and take up his stand once more, and begin to shovel in the blinding clouds of dust. And so at the end of the week he was a fertilizer man for life—he was able to eat again, and though his head never stopped aching, it ceased to be so bad that he could not work.

So there passed another summer. It was a summer of prosperity, all over the country, and the country ate generously of packing-house products, and there was plenty of work for all the family, in spite of the packers' efforts to keep a superfluity of labor. They were again able to pay their debts and to begin to save a little sum; but there were one or two sacrifices they considered too heavy to be made for long—it was too bad that the boys should have to sell papers at their age. It was utterly useless to caution them and plead with them; quite without knowing it, they were taking on the tone of their new environment. They were learning to swear in voluble English; they were learning to pick up cigar-stumps and smoke them, to pass hours of their time gambling with pennies and dice and cigarette-cards; they were learning the location of all the houses of prostitution on the "Levée," and the names of the "madames" who kept them, and the days when they gave their state banquets, which the police captains and the big politicians all attended. If a visiting "country-customer" were to ask them, they could show him which was "Hinky-dink's" famous saloon, and could even point out to him by name the different gamblers and thugs and "hold-up men" who made the place their headquarters. And worse yet, the boys were getting out of the habit of coming home at night. What was the use, they would ask, of wasting time and energy and a possible car-fare riding out to the stockyards every night when the weather was pleasant and they could crawl under a truck or into an empty doorway and sleep exactly as well? So long as they brought home a half dollar for each day, what mattered it when they brought it? But Jurgis declared that from this to ceasing to come at all would not be a very long step, and so it was decided that Vilimas and Nikalojus should return to school in the fall, and that instead Elzbieta should go out and get some work, her place at home being taken by her younger daughter.

Little Kotrina was like most children of the poor, prematurely made old; she had to take care of her little brother, who was a cripple, and also of the baby; she had to cook the meals and wash the dishes and clean house, and have supper ready when the workers came home in the evening. She was only thirteen, and small for her age, but she did all this without a murmur; and her mother went out, and after trudging a couple of days about the yards, settled down as a servant of a "sausage-machine."

Elzbieta was used to working, but she found this change a hard one, for the reason that she had to stand motionless upon her feet from seven o'clock in the morning till half-past twelve, and again from one till half-past five. For the first days it seemed to her that she could not stand it—she suffered almost as much as Jurgis had from the fertilizer—and would come out at sundown with her head fairly reeling. Besides this, she was working in one of the dark holes, by the electric light, and the dampness, too, was deadly—there were always puddles of water on the floor, and a sickening odor of moist flesh in the room. The people who worked here followed the ancient custom of nature, whereby the ptarmigan is the color of dead leaves in the fall and of snow in winter, and the chameleon, who is black when he lies upon a stump and turns green when he moves to a leaf. The men and women who worked in this department were precisely the color of the "fresh country sausage" they made.

The sausage-room was an interesting place to visit, for two or three minutes, and pro-

Chicago's meatpacking industry grew up with little or no government control. These sausage makers at Armour & Co. worked in extreme temperatures and without adequate ventilation, causing many to faint or to vomit from the stench.

vided that you did not look at the people; the machines were perhaps the most wonderful things in the entire plant. Presumably sausages were once chopped and stuffed by hand, and if so it would be interesting to know how many workers had been displaced by these inventions. On one side of the room were the hoppers, into which men shoveled loads of meat and wheelbarrows full of spices; in these great bowls were whirling knifes that made two thousand revolutions a minute, and when the meat was ground fine and adulterated with potato-flour, and well mixed with water, it was forced to the stuffing-machines on the other side of the room. The latter were tended by women; there was a sort of spout, like the nozzle of a hose, and one of the women would take a long string of "casing" and put the end over the nozzle and then work the whole thing on, as one works on the finger of a tight glove. This string would be twenty or thirty feet long, but the woman would have it all on in a jiffy; and when she had several on, she would press a lever, and a stream of sausage-meat would be shot out, taking the casing with it as it came. Thus one might stand and see appear, miraculously born from the machine, a wriggling snake of sausage of incredible length. In front was a big pan which caught these creatures, and two more women who seized them as fast as they appeared and twisted them into links. This was for the uninitiated the most perplexing work of all; for all that the woman had to give was a single turn of the wrist; and in some way she contrived to give it so that instead of an endless chain of sausages, one after another, there grew under her hands a bunch of strings, all dangling from a single centre. It was quite like the feat of a prestidigitator—for the woman worked so fast that the eye could literally not follow her, and there was only a mist of motion, and tangle after tangle of sausages appearing. In the midst of the mist, however, the visitor would suddenly notice the tense set face, with the two wrinkles graven in the forehead, and the ghastly pallor of the cheeks; and then he would suddenly recollect that it was time he was going on. The woman did not go on; she stayed right there—hour after hour, day after day, year after year, twisting sausage-links and racing with death. It was piece-work, and she was apt to have a family to keep alive; and stern and ruthless economic laws had arranged it that she could only do this by working just as she did, with all her soul upon her work, and with never an instant for a glance at the well-dressed ladies and gentlemen who came to stare at her, as at some wild beast in a menagerie.

With one member trimming beef in a cannery, and another working in a sausage factory, the family had a firsthand knowledge of the great majority of Packingtown swindles. For it was the custom, as they found, whenever meat was so spoiled that it could not be used for anything else, either to can it or else to chop it up into sausage. With what had been told them by Jonas, who had worked in the pickle-rooms, they could now study the whole of the spoiled-meat industry on the inside, and read a new and grim meaning into that old Packingtown jest—that they use everything of the pig except the squeal.

Jonas had told them how the meat that was taken out of pickle would often be found sour, and how they would rub it up with soda to take away the smell, and sell it to be eaten on free-lunch counters; also of all the miracles of chemistry which they performed, giving to any sort of meat, fresh or salted, whole or chopped, any color and any flavor and any odor they chose. In the pickling of hams they had an ingenious apparatus, by which they saved time and increased the capacity of the plant—a machine consisting of a hollow needle attached to a pump; by plunging this needle into the meat and working with his foot, a man could fill a ham with pickle in a few seconds. And yet, in spite of this, there would be hams found spoiled, some of them with an odor so bad that a man could hardly bear to be in the room with them. To pump into these the packers had a second and much stronger pickle which destroyed the odor—a process

known to the workers as "giving them thirty percent." Also, after the hams had been smoked, there would be found some that had gone to the bad. Formerly these had been sold as "Number Three Grade," but later on some ingenious person had hit upon a new device, and now they would extract the bone, about which the bad part generally lay, and insert in the hole a white-hot iron. After this invention there was no longer Number One, Two, and Three Grade—there was only Number One Grade. The packers were always originating such schemes—they had what they called "boneless hams," which were all the odds and ends of pork stuffed into casing; and "California hams," which were the shoulders, with big knuckle-joints, and nearly all the meat cut out; and fancy "skinned hams," which were made of the oldest hogs, whose skins were so heavy and coarse that no one would buy them—that is, until they had been cooked and chopped fine and labelled "head cheese"!

It was only when the whole ham was spoiled that it came into the department of Elzbieta. Cut up by the two-thousand-revolutions-a-minute flyers, and mixed with half a ton of other meat, no odor that ever was in a ham could make any difference. There was never the least attention paid to what was cut up for sausage; there would come all the way back from Europe old sausage that had been rejected, and that was mouldy and white—it would be dosed with borax and glycerine, and dumped into the hoppers, and made over again for home consumption. There would be meat that had tumbled out on the floor, in the dirt and sawdust, where the workers had tramped and spit uncounted billions of consumption germs. There would be meat stored in great piles in rooms; and the water from leaky roofs would drip over it, and thousands of rats would race about on it. It was too dark in these storage places to see well, but a man could run his hand over these piles of meat and sweep off handfuls of the dried dung of rats. These rats were nuisances, and the packers would put poisoned bread out for them; they would die, and then rats, bread, and meat would go into the hoppers together. This is no fairy story and no joke; the meat would be shovelled into carts, and the man who did the shovelling would not trouble to lift out a rat even when he saw one—there were things that went into the sausage in comparison with which a poisoned rat was a tidbit. There was no place for the men to wash their hands before they ate their dinner, and so they made a practice of washing them in the water that was to be ladled into the sausage. There were the butt-ends of smoked meat, and the scraps of corned beef, and all the odds and ends of the waste of the plants, that would be dumped into old barrels in the cellar and left there. Under the system of rigid economy which the packers enforced, there were some jobs that it only paid to do once in a long time, and among these was the cleaning out of the waste-barrels. Every spring they did it; and in the barrels would be dirt and rust and old nails and stale water—and cart load after cart load of it would be taken up and dumped into the hoppers with fresh meat, and sent out to the public's breakfast. Some of it they would make into "smoked" sausage—but as the smoking took time, and was therefore expensive, they would call upon their chemistry department, and preserve it with borax and color it with gelatine to make it brown. All of their sausage came out of the same bowl, but when they came to wrap it they would stamp some of it "special," and for this they would charge two cents more a pound.

Such were the new surroundings in which Elzbieta was placed, and such was the work she was compelled to do. It was stupefying, brutalizing work; it left her no time to think, no strength for anything. She was part of the machine she tended, and every faculty that was not needed for the machine was doomed to be crushed out of existence. There was only one mercy about the cruel grind—that it gave her the gift of insensibility. Little by little she sank into a torpor—she fell silent. She would meet Jurgis and Ona in the evening, and the three would walk home together, often without saying a word. Ona, too, was falling into the habit of silence—Ona, who had once gone about singing like a bird. She was sick and miserable, and often she would barely have strength enough to drag herself home. And there they would eat what they had to eat, and afterwards, because there was only their misery to talk of, they would crawl into bed and fall into a stupor and never stir until it was time to get up again, and dress by candlelight, and go back to the machines. They were so numbed that they did not even suffer much from hunger, now; only the children continued to fret when the food ran short.

Yet the soul of Ona was not dead—the souls of none of them were dead, but only sleeping; and now and then they would waken, and these were cruel times. The gates of memory would roll open—old joys would stretch out their arms to them, old hopes and dreams would call to them, and they would stir beneath the burden that lay upon them, and feel its forever immeasurable weight. They could not even cry out beneath it; but anguish would seize them, more dreadful than the agony of death. It was a thing scarcely to be spoken—a thing never spoken by all the world, that will not know its own defeat.

They were beaten; they had lost the game, they were swept aside. It was not less tragic because it was so sordid, because it had to do with wages and grocery bills and rents. They had dreamed of freedom; of a chance to look about them and learn something; to be decent and clean, to see their child grow up to be strong. And now it was all gone—it would never be! They had played the game and they had lost. Six years more of toil they had to face before they could expect the least respite, the cessation of the payments upon the house; and how cruelly certain it was that they could never stand six years of such a life as they were living! They were lost, they were going down—and there was no deliverance for them, no hope; for all the help it gave them the vast city in which they lived might have been an ocean waste, a wilderness, a desert, a tomb. So often this mood would come to Ona, in the nighttime, when something wakened her; she would lie, afraid of the beating of her own heart, fronting the blood-red eyes of the old primeval terror of life. Once she cried aloud, and woke Jurgis, who was tired and cross. After that she learned to weep silently—their moods so seldom came together now! It was as if their hopes were buried in separate graves.

Jurgis, being a man, had troubles of his own. There was another spectre following him. He had never spoken of it, nor would he allow any one else to speak of it—he had never acknowledged its existence to himself. Yet the battle with it took all the manhood that he had—and once or twice, alas, a little more. Jurgis had discovered drink.

He was working in the steaming pit of hell; day after day, week after week—until now there was not an organ of his body that did its work without pain, until the sound of ocean breakers echoed in his head day and night, and the buildings swayed and danced before him as he went down the street. And from all the unending horror of this there was a respite, a deliverance—he could drink! He could forget the pain, he could slip off the burden; he would see clearly again, he would be master of his brain, of his thoughts, of his will. His dead self would stir in him, and he would find himself laughing and cracking jokes with his companions—he would be a man again, and master of his life.

It was not an easy thing for Jurgis to take more than two or three drinks. With the first drink he could eat a meal, and he could persuade himself that that was economy; with the second he could eat another meal—but there would come a time when he could eat no more, and then to pay for a drink was an unthinkable extravagance, a defiance of the age-long instincts of his hunger-haunted class. One day, however, he took the plunge, and drank up all that he had in his pockets, and went home half "piped," as the men phrase it.

He was happier than he had been in a year; and yet, because he knew that the happiness would not last, he was savage, too—with those who would wreck it, and with the world, and with his life; and then again, beneath this, he was sick with the shame of himself. Afterward, when he saw the despair of his family, and reckoned up the money he had spent, the tears came into his eyes, and he began the long battle with the spectre.

It was a battle that had no end, that never could have one. But Jurgis did not realize that very clearly; he was not given much time for reflection. He simply knew that he was always fighting. Steeped in misery and despair as he was, merely to walk down the street was to be put upon the rack. There was surely a saloon on the corner—perhaps on all four corners, and some in the middle of the block as well; and each one stretched out a hand to him—each one had a personality of its own, allurements unlike any other. Going and coming—before sunrise and after dark—there was warmth and a glow of light, and the steam of hot food, and perhaps music, or a friendly face, and a word of good cheer. Jurgis developed a fondness for having Ona on his arm whenever he went out on the street, and he would hold her tightly, and walk fast. It was pitiful to have Ona know of this—it drove him wild to think of it; the thing was not fair, for Ona had never tasted drink, and so could not understand. Sometimes, in desperate hours, he would find himself wishing that she might learn what it was, so that he need not be ashamed in her presence. They might drink together, and escape from the horror—escape for a while, come what would.

So there came a time when nearly all the conscious life of Jurgis consisted of a struggle with the craving for liquor. He would have ugly moods, when he hated Ona and the whole family, because they stood in his way. He was a fool to have married; he had tied himself down, and made himself a slave. It was all because he was a married man that he was compelled to stay in the yards; if it had not been for that he might have gone off like Jonas, and to hell with the packers. There were single men in the fertilizer-mill—and those few were working only for a chance to escape. Meantime, too, they had something to think about while they worked—they had the memory of the last time they had been drunk, and the hope of the time when they would be drunk again. As for Jurgis, he expected to bring home every penny; he could not even go with the men at noontime—he was supposed to sit down and eat his dinner on a pile of fertilizer dust.

This was not always his mood, of course; he still loved his family. But just now was a time of trial. Poor little Antanas, for instance—who had never failed to win him with a smile—little Antanas was not smiling just now, being a mass of fiery red pimples. He had had all the diseases that babies are heir to, in quick succession—scarlet fever, mumps, and whooping-cough in the first year, and now he was down with the measles. There was no one to attend him but Kotrina; there was no doctor to help him because they were too poor, and children did not die of the measles—at least not often. Now and then Kotrina would find time to sob over his woes, but for the greater part of the time he had to be left alone, barricaded upon the bed. The floor was full of draughts, and if he caught cold he would die. At night he was tied down, lest he should kick the covers off him, while the family lay in their stupor of exhaustion. He would lie and scream for hours, almost in convulsions; and then when he was worn out, he would lie whimpering and wailing in his torment. He was burning up with fever, and his eyes were running sores; in the daytime he was a thing uncanny and impish to behold, a plaster of pimples and sweat, a great purple lump of misery.

Yet all this was not really cruel as it sounds, for sick as he was, little Antanas was the least unfortunate member of that family. He was quite able to bear his sufferings—it was as if

he had all these complaints to show what a prodigy of health he was. He was the child of his parents' youth and joy; he grew up like the conjurer's rose bush, and all the world was his oyster. In general, he toddled around the kitchen all day with a lean and hungry look—the portion of the family's allowance that fell to him was not enough, and he was unrestrainable in his demand for more. Antanas was but little over a year old, and already no one but his father could manage him.

It seemed as if he had taken all of his mother's strength—had left nothing for those that might come after him. Ona was with child again now, and it was a dreadful thing to contemplate; even Jurgis, dumb and despairing as he was, could not but understand that yet other agonies were on the way, and shudder at the thought of them.

For Ona was visibly going to pieces. In the first place she was developing a cough, like the one that had killed old Dede Antanas. She had had a trace of it ever since that fatal morning when the greedy street-car corporation had turned her out into the rain; but now it was beginning to grow serious, and to wake her up at night. Even worse than that was the fearful nervousness from which she suffered; she would have frightful headaches and fits of aimless weeping; and sometimes she would come home at night shuddering and moaning, and would fling herself down upon the bed and burst into tears. Several times she was quite beside herself and hysterical; and then Jurgis would go half mad with fright. Elzbieta would explain to him that it could not be helped, that woman was subject to such things when she was pregnant; but he was hardly to be persuaded, and would beg and plead to know what had happened. She had never been like this before, he would argue—it was monstrous and unthinkable. It was the life she had to live, the accursed work she had to do, that was killing her by inches. She was not fitted for it—no woman was fitted for it, no woman ought to be allowed to do such work; if the world could not keep them alive any other way it ought to kill them at once and be done with it. They ought not to marry, to have children; no workingman ought to marry—if he, Jurgis, had known what a woman was like, he would have had his eyes torn out first. So he would carry on, becoming half hysterical himself, which was an unbearable thing to see in a big man; Ona would pull herself together and fling herself into his arms, begging him to stop, to be still, that she would be better, it would be all right. So she would lie and sob out her grief upon his shoulder, while he gazed at her, as helpless as a wounded animal, the target of unseen enemies.

Study Questions

1. What was health care like for children in Packingtown?

2. What sort of men worked in the fertilizer plants? What were the hazards of the job?

3. How did the constant demand for money affect families?

4. What were the abuses of the "spoiled-meat" industry?

5. What response was Upton Sinclair hoping to achieve with *The Jungle?*

Bibliography

On the life of Upton Sinclair, see Floyd Dell, *Upton Sinclair: A Study in Social Protest* (1927); Jon Yoder, *Upton Sinclair* (1975); Leon Harris, *Upton Sinclair, American Rebel* (1975); and his own *The Autobiography of Upton Sinclair* (1962). Three good books on the literature of the period are Daniel Aaron, *Writers of the Left* (1969); James Burkhart Gilbert, *Writers and Partisans: A History of Literary Radicalism in America* (1968); and Larzer Ziff, *The American 1890s: Life and Times of a Lost Generation* (1966). On the meatpacking industry, Packingtown, and the lives of the workers, consult Louis Carroll Wade, *Chicago's Pride: The Stockyards, Packingtown, and Environs in the Nineteenth Century* (1987) and James R. Barrett, *Work and Community in the Jungle: Chicago's Packinghouse Workers* (1988).

READING 8

★ ★ ★

Rose Schneiderman and the Triangle Shirtwaist Fire

Bonnie Mitelman

The progress Americans made during the Progressive Era depended on one's perspective. For middle-class Americans, progress was visible everywhere. Real income rose and the government worked to ensure order and efficiency in the industrial world. For their part, most large industrialists cooperated with the government's effort to impose order, which often resulted in the elimination of bothersome competition. For example, leading meatpackers supported the Meat Inspection Act of 1906. The act raised inspection standards, thereby driving out small competitors and guaranteeing the quality of American meat on the competitive world market.

America's working class, however, had reason to question the nature of the "progress" that was being made. The men and women who labored in industrial America often performed uncreative, repetitive tasks at a pace set by machines. Possibly worse than the monotony of industrial life was the danger of it. Machines were blind and uncaring; they showed no sympathy for tired or bored workers who allowed their fingers to move too close to moving cogs. Injuries were common, and far too often industrialists were as unsympathetic as their machines. And for most unskilled workers, labor unions were weak and unrecognized by leading industrialists and manufacturers. In the following essay, Bonnie Mitelman discusses the 1911 Triangle Waist Company fire, a tragedy in which 146 workers died. The fire and its results raise serious questions about the extent and nature of progress during the early twentieth century.

On Saturday afternoon, March 25, 1911, in New York City's Greenwich Village, a small fire broke out in the Triangle Waist Company, just as the 500 shirtwaist employees were quitting for the day. People rushed about, trying to get out, but they found exits blocked and windows to the fire escape rusted shut. They panicked.

As the fire spread and more and more were trapped, some began to jump, their hair and clothing afire, from the eighth and ninth floor windows. Nets that firemen held for them tore apart at the impact of the falling bodies. By the time it was over, 146 workers had died, most of them young Jewish women.

A United Press reporter, William Shepherd, witnessed the tragedy and reported, "I looked upon the heap of dead bodies and I remembered these girls were the shirtwaist makers. I remembered their great strike of last year in which these same girls had demanded more sanitary conditions and more safety precautions in the shops. These dead bodies were the answer."

The horror of that fire touched the entire Lower East Side ghetto community, and there was a profuse outpouring of sympathy. But it was Rose Schneiderman, an immigrant worker with a spirit of social justice and a powerful way with words, who is largely credited with translating the ghetto's emotional reaction into meaningful, widespread action. Six weeks following the tragedy, and after years of solid groundwork, with one brilliant, well-timed speech, she was able to inspire the support of wealthy uptown New Yorkers and to swing public opinion to the side of the labor movement, enabling concerned civic, religious, and labor leaders to mobilize their efforts for desperately needed safety and industrial reforms.

The Triangle fire, and the deaths of so many helpless workers, seemed to trigger in Rose

"Rose Schneiderman and the Triangle Fire" by Bonnie Mitelman, from *American History Illustrated* 16 (July, 1981), pp. 38–47. Copyright © 1981 by Historical Times, Inc.

Schneiderman an intense realization that there was absolutely nothing or no one to help working women except a strong union movement. With fierce determination, and the dedication, influence, and funding of many other people as well, she battled to regulate hours, wages, and safety standards and to abolish the sweatshop system. In so doing, she brought dignity and human rights to all workers.

The dramatic "uprising of the 20,000" of 1909–1910, in which thousands of immigrant girls and women in the shirtwaist industry had endured three long winter months of a general strike to protest deplorable working conditions, had produced some immediate gains for working women. There had been agreements for shorter working hours, increased wages, and even safety reforms, but there had not been formal recognition of their union. At Triangle, for example, the girls had gained a 52-hour-week, a 12–15 percent wage increase, and promises to end the grueling subcontracting system. But they had not gained the only instrument on which they could depend for lasting change: a viable trade union. This was to have disastrous results, for in spite of the few gains that they seemed to have made, the workers won no rights or bargaining power at all. In fact, "The company dealt only with its contractors. It felt no responsibility for the girls."

There were groups as well as individuals who realized the workers' importance, but their attempts to change the situation accomplished little despite long years of hard work. The Women's Trade Union League and the International Ladies' Garment Workers' Union, through the efforts of Mary Dreier, Helen Marot, Leonora O'Reilly, Pauline Newman, and Rose Schneiderman had struggled unsuccessfully for improved conditions: the futility that the union organizers were feeling in late 1910 is reflected in the WTUL minutes of December 5 of that year.

A scant eight months after their historic waistmakers' strike, and three months before the deadly Triangle fire, a Mrs. Malkiel (no doubt Theresa Serber Malkiel, who wrote the legendary account of the strike, *The Diary of a Shirtwaist Striker: A Story of the Shirtwaist Makers' Strike in New York*) is reported to have come before the League to urge action after a devastating fire in Newark, New Jersey killed twenty-five working women. Mrs. Malkiel attributed their loss to the greed and negligence of the owners and the proper authorities. The WTUL subsequently demanded an investigation of all factory buildings and it elected an investigation committee from the League to cooperate with similar committees from other organizations.

The files of the WTUL contain complaint after complaint about unsafe factory conditions; many were filled out by workers afraid to sign their names for fear of being fired had their employers seen the forms. They describe factories with locked doors, no fire escapes, and barred windows. The *New York Times* carried an article which reported that fourteen factories were found to have no fire escapes, twenty-three had locked doors, and seventy-eight had obstructed fire escapes. In all, according to the article, 99 percent of the factories investigated in New York were found to have serious fire hazards.

Yet no action was taken.

It was the Triangle fire that emphasized, spectacularly and tragically, the deplorable safety and sanitary conditions of the garment workers. The tragedy focused attention upon the ghastly factories in which most immigrants worked; there was no longer any question about what the strikers had meant when they talked about safety and sanitary reform, and about social and economic justice.

The grief and frustration of the shirtwaist strikers were expressed by one of them, Rose Safran, after the fire: "If the union had won we would have been safe. Two of our demands were for adequate fire escapes and for open doors from the factories to the street. But the bosses defeated us and we didn't get the open doors or the better fire escapes. So our friends are dead."

The families of the fire victims were heartbroken and hysterical, the ghetto's *Jewish Daily Forward* was understandably melodramatic, and the immigrant community was completely enraged. Their Jewish heritage had taught them an emphasis on individual human life and worth; their shared background in the *shtetl* and common experiences in the ghetto had given them a sense of fellowship. They were, in a sense, a family—and some of the most helpless among them had died needlessly.

The senseless deaths of so many young Jewish women sparked within these Eastern Europeans a new determination and dedication. The fire had made reform absolutely essential. Workers' rights were no longer just socialist jargon: They were a matter of life and death.

The Triangle Waist Company was located on the three floors of the Asch Building, a 10-story, 135-foot-high structure at the corner of Greene Street and Washington Place in Greenwich Village. One of the largest shirtwaist manufacturers, Triangle employed up to 900 people at times, but on the day of the fire, only about 500 were working.

Leon Stein's brilliant and fascinating account of the fire, entitled simply *The Triangle Fire*, develops and documents the way in which the physical facilities, company procedures, and human behavior interacted to cause this great tragedy. Much of what occurred was ironic, some was cruel, some stupid, some pathetic. It is a dramatic portrayal of the eternal confrontation of the "haves" and the "have-nots," told in large part by those who survived.

Fire broke out at the Triangle Company at approximately 4:45 P.M. (because time clocks were reportedly set back to stretch the day, and because other records give differing times of the first fire alarm, it is uncertain exactly what time the fire started), just after pay envelopes had been distributed and employees were leaving their work posts. It was a small fire at first, and there was a calm, controlled effort to extinguish it. But the fire began to spread, jumping from one pile of debris to another, engulfing combustible shirtwaist fabric. It became obvious that the fire could not be snuffed out, and the workers tried to reach the elevators or stairway. Those who reached the one open stairway raced down eight flights of stairs to safety; those who managed to climb onto the available passenger elevators also got out. But not everyone could reach the available exits. Some tried to open the door to a stairway and found it locked. Others were trapped between long working tables or behind the hordes of people trying to get into the elevators or out through the one open door.

Under the work tables, rags were burning; the wooden floors, trim, and window frames were also afire. Frantically, workers fought their way to the elevators, to the fire escape, and to the windows—to any place that might lead to safety.

Fire whistles and bells sounded as the fire department raced to the building. But equipment proved inadequate, as the fire ladders reached only to the seventh floor. And by the time the firemen connected their hoses to douse the flames, the crowded eighth floor was completely ablaze.

For those who reached the windows, there seemed to be a chance for safety. The *New York World* describes people balancing on window sills, nine stories up, with flames scorching them from behind, until firemen arrived: "The nets were spread below with all promptness. Citizens were commandeered into service, as the firemen necessarily gave their attention to the one engine and hose of the force that first arrived. The catapult force that the bodies gathered in the long plunges made the nets utterly without avail. Screaming girls and men, as they fell, tore the nets from the grasp of the holders, and the bodies struck the sidewalks and lay just as they fell. Some of the bodies ripped big holes through the life nets."

One reporter who witnessed the fire remembered how:

A young man helped a girl to the window sill on the ninth floor. Then he held her out deliberately, away from the building, and let her drop. He held out a second girl the same way and let her drop. He held out a third girl who did not resist. They were all as unresisting as if he were helping them into a street car instead of into eternity. He saw that a terrible death awaited them in the flames and his was only a terrible chivalry. He brought around another girl to the window. I saw her put her arms around him and kiss him. Then he held her into space— and dropped her. Quick as a flash, he was on the window sill himself. His coat fluttered upwards—the air filled his trouser legs as he came down. I could see he wore tan shoes.

Those who had rushed to the fire escape found the window openings rusted shut. Several precious minutes were lost in releasing them. The fire escape itself ended at the second floor, in an airshaft between the Asch Building and the building next door. But too frantic to notice where it ended, workers climbed onto the fire escape one after another until, in one terrifying moment, it collapsed from the weight, pitching the workers to their death.

Those who had made their way to the elevators found crowds pushing to get into the cars. When it became obvious that the elevators could no longer run, workers jumped down the elevator shafts, landing on the tops of the cars, or grabbing for cables to ease their descent. Several died, but incredibly, some did manage to save themselves this way. One man was found, hours after the fire, beneath an elevator car in the basement of the building, nearly drowned by the rapidly rising water from the firemen's hoses.

Several people, among them Triangle's two owners, raced to the roof, and from there were led to safety. Others never had that chance. "When Fire Chief Croker could make his way into the [top] three floors," states one account of the fire, "he found sights that utterly staggered . . . he saw as the smoke drifted away bodies burned to the bare bones. There were skeletons bending over sewing machines."

The day after the fire, the *New York Times* announced that "the building was fireproof. It shows hardly any signs of the disaster that overtook it. The walls are as good as ever, as are the floors: nothing is worse for the fire except that furniture and 14 [*sic*] of the 600 men and girls that were employed in its upper three stories."

The building *was* fireproof. But there had never been a fire drill in the factory, even though the management had been warned about the possible hazard of fire on the top three floors. Owners Max Blanck and Isaac Harris had chosen to ignore these warnings in spite of the fact that many of their employees were immigrants who could barely speak English, which would surely mean panic in the event of a crisis.

The *New York Times* also noted that Leonora O'Reilly of the League had reported Max Blanck's visit to the WTUL during the shirtwaist strike, and his plea that the girls return to work. He claimed a business reputation to maintain and told the Union leaders he would make the necessary improvements right away. Because he was the largest manufacturer in the business, the League reported, they trusted him and let the girls return.

But the improvements were never made. And there was nothing that anybody could or would do about it. Factory doors continued to open in instead of out, in violation of fire regulations. The doors remained bolted during working hours, apparently to prevent workers from getting past the inspectors with stolen merchandise. Triangle had only two staircases where there should have been three, and those two were very narrow. Despite the fact that the building was deemed fireproof, it had

wooden window frames, floors, and trim. There was no sprinkler system. It was not legally required.

These were the same kinds of conditions which existed in factories throughout the garment industry; they had been cited repeatedly in the complaints filed with the WTUL. They were not unusual nor restricted to Triangle; in fact, Triangle was not as bad as many other factories.

But it was at Triangle that the fire took place.

The *Jewish Daily Forward* mourned the dead with sorrowful stories, and its headlines talked of "funerals instead of weddings" for the dead young girls. The entire Jewish immigrant community was affected, for it seemed there was scarcely a person who was not in some way touched by the fire. Nearly everyone had either been employed at Triangle themselves, or had a friend or relative who had worked there at some time or another. Most worked in factories with similar conditions, and so everyone identified with the victims and their families.

Many of the dead, burned beyond recognition remained unidentified for days, as searching family members returned again and again to wait in long lines to look for their loved ones. Many survivors were unable to identify their mothers, sisters, or wives; the confusion of handling so many victims and so many survivors who did not understand what was happening to them and to their dead led to even more anguish for the community. Some of the victims were identified by the names on the pay envelopes handed to them at quitting time and stuffed deeply into pockets or stockings just before the fire. But many bodies remained unclaimed for days, with bewildered and bereaved survivors wandering among them, trying to find some identifying mark.

Charges of first- and second-degree manslaughter were brought against the two men who owned Triangle, and Leon Stein's book artfully depicts the subtle psychological and

An unsafe work environment at the Triangle Waist Company caused the deaths of 146 workers when a fire broke out in the building in 1911. The tragedy brought labor issues to national attention.

sociological implications of the powerful against the oppressed, and of the Westernized, German-Jewish immigrants against those still living their old-world, Eastern European heritage. Ultimately, Triangle owners Blanck and Harris were acquitted of the charges against them, and in due time they collected their rather sizable insurance.

The shirtwaist, popularized by Gibson girls, had come to represent the newfound freedom of females in America. After the fire, it symbolized death. The reaction of the grief-stricken Lower East Side was articulated by socialist lawyer Morris Hillquit:

The girls who went on strike last year were trying to readjust the conditions under which they were obliged to work. I wonder if there is not some connection between the fire and that strike. I wonder if the magistrates who sent to jail the girls who did picket duty in front of the Triangle shop realized last Sunday that some responsibility may be theirs. Had the strike been successful, these girls might have been alive today and the citizenry of New York would have less of a burden upon its conscience.

For the first time in the history of New York's garment industry there were indications that the public was beginning to accept responsibility for the exploitation of the immigrants. For the first time, the establishment seemed to understand that these were human beings asking for their rights, not merely troublemaking anarchists.

The day after the Triangle fire a protest meeting was held at the Women's Trade Union League, with representatives from twenty leading labor and civic organizations. They formed "a relief committee to cooperate with the Red Cross in its work among the families of the victims, and another committee . . . to broaden the investigation and research on fire hazards in New York factories which was already being carried on by the League."

The minutes of the League recount the deep indignation that members felt at the indifference of a public which had ignored their pleas for safety after the Newark fire. In an attempt to translate their anger into constructive action, the League drew up a list of forceful resolutions that included a plan to gather delegates from all of the city's unions to make a concerted effort to force safety changes in factories. In addition, the League called upon all workers to inspect factories and then report any violations to the proper city authorities and to the WTUL. They called upon the city to immediately appoint organized workers as unofficial inspectors. They resolved to submit the following fire regulations suggestions: compulsory fire drills, fireproof exits, unlocked doors, fire alarms, automatic sprinklers, and regular inspections. The League called upon the legislature to create the Bureau of Fire Protection and finally, the League underscored the absolute need for all workers to organize themselves at once into trade unions so that they would never again be powerless.

The League also voted to participate in the funeral procession for the unidentified dead of the Triangle fire.

The city held a funeral for the dead who were unclaimed. "More than 120,000 of us were in the funeral procession that miserable rainy April day," remembered Rose Schneiderman. "From ten in the morning until four in the afternoon we of the Women's Trade Union League marched in the procession with other trade-union men and women, all of us filled with anguish and regret that we had never been able to organize the Triangle workers."

Schneiderman, along with many others, was absolutely determined that this kind of tragedy would never happen again. With single-minded dedication, they devoted themselves to unionizing the workers. The searing example of the Triangle fire provided them with the impetus they needed to gain public support for their efforts.

They dramatized and emphasized and capitalized on the scandalous working conditions of the immigrants. From all segments of the community came cries for labor reform. Stephen S. Wise, the prestigious reform rabbi, called for the formation of a citizens' committee. Jacob H. Schiff, Bishop David H. Greer, Governor John A. Dix, Anne Morgan (of *the* Morgans) and other leading civic and religious leaders collaborated in a mass meeting at the Metropolitan Opera House on May 2 to protest factory conditions and to show support for the workers.

Several people spoke at the meeting on May 2, and many in the audience began to grow restless and antagonistic. Finally, 29-year-old Rose Schneiderman stepped up to the podium.

In a whisper barely audible, she began to address the crowd.

I would be a traitor to these poor burned bodies, if I came here to talk good fellowship. We have tried you good people of the public and we have found you wanting. The old Inquisition had its rack and its thumbscrews and its instruments of torture with iron teeth. We know what these things are today: the iron teeth are our necessities, the thumbscrews the high-powered and swift machinery close to which we must work, and the rack is here in the fireproof structures that will destroy us the minute they catch on fire.

This is not the first time girls have burned alive in the city. Every week I must learn of the untimely death of one of my sister workers. Every year thousands of us are maimed. The life of men and women is so cheap and property is so sacred. There are so many of us for one job it matters little if 140-odd are burned to death.

We have tried you, citizens, we are trying you now, and you have a couple of dollars for the sorrowing mothers and daughters and sisters by way of a charity gift. But every time the workers come out in the only way they know to protest against conditions which are unbearable, the strong hand of the law is allowed to press down heavily upon us.

Public officials have only words of warning to us—warning that we must be intensely orderly and must be intensely peaceable, and they have the workhouse just back of all their warnings. The strong hand of the law beats us back when we rise into the conditions that make life bearable.

I can't talk fellowship to you who are gathered here. Too much blood had been spilled. I know from my experience it is up to the working people to save themselves. The only way they can save themselves is by a strong working-class movement.

Her speech has become a classic. It is more than just an emotional picture of persecution; it reflects the persuasive sadness and profound understanding that comes from knowing, finally, the cruel realities of life, the perspective of history, and the nature of human beings.

The devastation of that fire and the futility of the seemingly successful strike that had preceded it seemed to impart an undeniable truth to Rose Schneiderman: they could not fail again. The events of 1911 seemed to have made her, and many others, more keenly aware than they had ever been that the work-

ers' fight for reform was absolutely essential. If they did not do it, it would not be done.

In a sense, the fire touched off in Schneiderman an awareness of her own responsibility in the battle for industrial reform. This fiery socialist worker had been transformed into a highly effective labor leader.

The influential speech she gave did help swing public opinion to the side of the trade unions, and the fire itself had made the workers more aware of the crucial need to unionize. Widespread support for labor reform and unionization emerged. Pressure from individuals, such as Rose Schneiderman, as well as from groups like the Women's Trade Union League and the International Ladies' Garment Workers' Union, helped form the New York State Factory Investigating Commission, the New York Citizens' Committee on Safety, and other regulatory and investigatory bodies. The League and Local 25 (the Shirtwaist Makers' Union of the ILGWU) were especially instrumental in attaining a new Industrial Code for New York State, which became "the most outstanding instrument for safeguarding the lives, health, and welfare of the millions of wage earners in New York State and . . . in the nation at large."

It took years for these changes to occur, and labor reform did not rise majestically, Phoenix-like, from the ashes of the Triangle fire. But that fire, and Rose Schneiderman's whispered plea for a strong working-class movement, had indeed become the loud, clear call for action.

Study Questions

1. How successful had workers at the Triangle Waist Company been in gaining better working conditions before the fire? What were their major successes and failures?

2. What were the major labor concerns of the female immigrant workers?

3. Why did the fire lead to so many deaths? How did the design of the building contribute to the tragedy?

4. What was the Jewish community's reaction to the fire? How did the funeral help unify reform-minded people in New York City?

5. What role did Rose Schneiderman play in the aftermath of the tragedy? How did the fire influence the American labor movement?

Bibliography

As Mitelman indicates, the best treatment of the tragedy is Leon Stein, *The Triangle Fire* (1962). For a recent interpretation of the events, see David Von Drehle, *Triangle: The Fire That Changed America* (2003). Leslie Woodcock Tentler, *Wage-Earning Women: Industrial Work and Family Life in the United States, 1900–1930* (1979), treats the difficulties faced by working women. Useful treatments of the same theme are Susan Estabrook Kennedy, *If All We Did Was to Weep at Home: A History of White Working Class Women in America* (1979), and Barbara Mayer Wertheimer, *We Were There: The Story of Working Women in America* (1977). Meredith Tax, *The Rising of the Women: Feminist Solidarity and Class Conflict, 1880–1917* (1982), examines the successes and failures of middle-class and working-women to unite female laborers. Two excellent introductions to general issues that concerned workers are Herbert Gutman, *Work, Culture and Society in Industrializing America* (1977), and David Montgomery, *Workers' Control in America: Studies in the History of Work, Technology, and Labor Struggles* (1979). Moses Rischin, *The Promised City: New York's Jews, 1870–1940* (1970); Arthur S. Goren, *New York Jews and the Quest for Community: The Kehillah Experiment, 1908–1922* (1970); and Irving Howe, *World of Our Fathers: The Journey of the Eastern European Jews to America and the Life They Found and Made* (1976), treat the Jewish experience in America.

READING 9

★ ★ ★

Jack Johnson Wins the Heavyweight Championship

Randy Roberts

For the most part, the Progressive movement was a for-whites-only affair. During the first 20 years of the twentieth century, Asian and black Americans faced open and violent discrimination. On the West Coast, Japanese and Chinese immigrants confronted a humiliating series of discriminatory laws, while in the South and even North blacks were equally hard-pressed. In their presidencies, neither Theodore Roosevelt nor Woodrow Wilson made any attempt to alter the social structure of the Jim Crow South, where the lives of the blacks were unequal to the lives of the whites. Although blacks retained some political and civil rights in the North, they still suffered from social and economic discrimination.

Some blacks responded to the injustice. Booker T. Washington was willing to forego social and political equality for economic opportunities. W. E. B. Du Bois demanded more; he worked for full equality. Other blacks lodged less articulate protests through their actions. They refused to live within the narrow borders proscribed for them by white society. Often these blacks were labeled "bad niggers." White authorities hated and punished them, but in black communities they were regarded as heroes and legends. The most famous of these real-life renegades was Jack Johnson, the first black heavyweight champion. He defeated white boxers, married white women, enraged white authorities, and lived by his own laws. In the following selection, historian Randy Roberts uses Johnson's fight with Tommy Burns as an opportunity to examine the racial attitudes of the early twentieth century.

A fterwards concerned whites said it should never have taken place. John L. Sullivan, who by 1908 had quit drinking and become a moral crusader, said, "Shame on the money-mad Champion! Shame on the man who upsets good American precedents because there are Dollars, Dollars, Dollars in it." A dejected sports columnist wrote, "Never before in the history of the prize ring has such a crisis arisen as that which faces the followers of the game tonight." The sadness these men felt could only be expressed in superlatives—greatest tragedy, deepest gloom, saddest day, darkest night. The race war had been fought. Armageddon was over. The Caucasian race had lost. Twenty years after the event, and after a few more such Armageddons, Alva Johnston tried to explain the mood of the day: "The morale of the Caucasian race had been at a low ebb long before the great blow fell in 1908. The Kaiser had been growing hysterical over the Yellow Peril. Africa was still celebrating the victory of Emperor Menelik of Abyssinia over the Italians. Dixie was still in ferment because Booker T. Washington . . . had had a meal at the White House. Then . . . Jack Johnson won the World Heavyweight Championship from Tommy Burns. The Nordics had not been so scared since the days of Tamerlane."

Black ghetto dwellers and sharecroppers rejoiced. In cities from New York to Omaha, blacks smiled with delight. "Today is the zenith of Negro sports," observed a *Colored American Magazine* editor. Other black publications felt such qualifications were too conservative. The *Richmond Planet* reported that "no event in forty years has given more genuine satisfaction to the colored people of this country than has the single victory of Jack Johnson." Joy and pride spilled over into arrogance, or so some whites believed. The cotton-buying firm of Logan and Bryan predicted that Johnson's victory would encourage other blacks to enter boxing, thereby creating a shortage of field labor. Independent of Logan and Bryan's report, the black writer Jim Nasium counseled black youths to consider seriously a boxing career—where else could they face whites on an equal footing? In that last week of 1908 social change seemed close at hand. The implication of most reports was that Jack Johnson had started a revolution.

How had it all come about? When Burns arrived in Perth in August 1908, the world did not seem in any immediate danger. He was treated like a conquering hero. From Perth to Sydney he was cheered and fêted. Mayors and members of Parliament courted Burns as if he were visiting royalty. When the train made its normal 6 A.M. stop at Abury, men stood shivering in the cold to greet Burns. And at Sydney, at a more civilized hour, more than 8,000 people cheered the champion. Speeches were made and applause modestly received. An Australian politician, Colonel Ryrie, extolled the virtues of boxing, telling the gathering that the sport produced sturdy young men needed for battle, "not those milksops who cry out against it."

At these August occasions Burns was frequently asked about Johnson. Would he fight the black champion? If so, where? When? Burns patiently answered the questions like a saint repeating a litany. He would fight Johnson when the right purse was offered. The place was not important. In fact, Australia was as good as—if not better than—any other place. As Burns told a Melbourne reporter: "There are a lot of newspaper stories that I don't want to fight Johnson. I do want to fight him, but I want to give the white boys a chance first." And since the early English settlers had exterminated the Tasmanians, there were a lot of white boys in Australia.

Listening to Burns was an ambitious promoter. Hugh D. "Huge Deal" McIntosh was an American success story with an Australian setting. As a boy he worked in the Broken Hill mines and as a rural laborer, but early in life he

Reprinted with the permission of The Free Press, a division of Simon & Schuster from *Papa Jack: Jack Johnson and the Era of White Hopes* by Randy Roberts. Copyright © 1983 by The Free Press.

realized that a man could make more money using his brain than his back. His fortune was made as a pie salesman in Australian parks and sporting events, but his career included tours as a racing cyclist, a boxer, a waiter, a newspaper publisher, a member of parliament, a theatrical impresario, and other assorted jobs. All these stints equipped him with enough gab and gall to become a first-rate boxing promoter. It was McIntosh who had invited Burns to Australia to defend his title against Aussie boxers. A student of maps and calendars, he knew that when Teddy Roosevelt's Great White Fleet, then cruising about the Pacific, dropped anchor in Australia a heavyweight championship fight would prove a good draw. With this in mind, he rented a market garden at Rushcutter's Bay, on the outskirts of Sydney, and built an open-air stadium on it. By mid-summer he was ready for Burns.

In June he matched Burns against Bill Squires, whom the champion had already knocked out twice, once in the United States and once in France. In defense of Squires, however, it was noted by the press that in his second fight with Burns he had lasted eight rounds, seven longer than the first fight. On his home continent Squires did even better. He was not knocked out until the thirteenth round. Though the fight was not particularly good, the overflowing stadium pleased McIntosh mightily. More than 40,000 people showed up for the fight, including American sailors from the Great White Fleet, but only 15,000 could be seated in the stadium. The 25,000 others milled about outside, listening to the noise made by lucky spectators watching the fight.

Less than two weeks later Burns again defended his title, this time against Bill Lang in Melbourne before 19,000 spectators. Like the stadium at Rushcutter's Bay, South Melbourne Stadium had been hurriedly constructed on McIntosh's orders—it was built in twelve days—and the result had been worth the effort. In the two fights Burns made more than $20,000 and McIntosh grossed about

$100,000, half of which was clear profit. In addition, both fights had been filmed, and revenue from this pioneering effort was much greater than anticipated. Burns, McIntosh, and the Australian boxing public were all exceedingly pleased.

In late October Johnson arrived, and the pulse of Australia picked up a beat. The fight had already been arranged. McIntosh guaranteed Burns $30,000. Before such a sum the color line faded. Therefore, when Johnson landed at Perth he was in an accommodating mood. "How does Burns want it? Does he want it fast and willing? I'm his man in that case. Does he want it flat footed? Goodness, if he does, why I'm his man again. Anything to suit; but fast or slow, I'm going to win." After eight years of trying Johnson was about to get his chance to fight for the heavyweight title.

Short of money, Johnson and Fitzpatrick set up their training quarters in the inexpensive Sir Joseph Banks Hotel in Botany, far less plush than the Hydro Majestic Hotel at Medlow Bath, where Burns trained. Yet Johnson, like Burns, trained in earnest. Johnson looked relaxed—he joked, smiled, made speeches, and played the double bass—but the men and women who watched him train failed to notice that he was also working very hard. Each morning he ran; each afternoon he exercised and sparred with Bill Lang, who imitated Burns's style. Johnson knew that Burns—short, inclined toward fatness, addicted to cigars and strong drink—was nonetheless a very good boxer. In Bohum Lynch's opinion, Burns was a "decidedly good boxer" who, though unorthodox, had a loose and easy style. And in the weeks before the fight Johnson showed by his training that he did not take Burns lightly.

Nor did he disregard the power of Australian racism. He feared that in the emotionally charged atmosphere of an interracial championship fight he might not be given an even break. His concern was not unfounded. An editorial in Sydney's *Illustrated Sporting and Dramatic News* correctly indicated the racial temper of Australian boxing fans: "Citizens who have never prayed before are supplicating Providence to give the white man a strong right arm with which to belt the coon into oblivion." But of more concern to Johnson than white men's prayers were his suspicions of McIntosh as promoter and self-named referee. Several times the two quarreled in public, and they nearly came to blows when Johnson greeted the promoter with "How do, Mr. McIntosh? How do you drag yourself away from Tahmy?" McIntosh, a big, burly, muscular man, thereafter began carrying a lead pipe wrapped in sheet music. As he told his friend Norman Lindsay, it was in case "that black bastard" ever "tries any funny business."

As the bout drew closer, the racial overtones destroyed the holiday atmosphere. It seemed as if all Australia were edgy. In the name of civilization, Protestant reformers spoke words that fell on deaf ears. The fight, said the Sydney Anglican Synod, with "its inherent brutality and dangerous nature" would surely "corrupt the moral tone of the community." But the community was worried less about being corrupted than about the implication of a Johnson victory. Lindsay, whom McIntosh hired to draw posters to advertise the fight, visually portrayed the great fear. Across Sydney could be seen his poster showing a towering black and a much smaller white. As Richard Broome has suggested, "Thus must have evoked the deepest feelings Australians held about the symbols of blackness and whiteness and evoked the emotiveness of a big man versus a small man and the populous coloured races versus the numerically smaller white race." Clearly, the *Australian Star* editors had this in mind when they printed a cartoon showing the fight being watched by representatives of the white and black races. Underneath was a letter that predicted that "this battle may in the future be looked back upon as the first great battle of an inevitable race

war. . . . There is more in this fight to be considered than the mere title of pugilistic champion of the world."

Racial tension was nothing new to Australia. Race had mattered since the colony's founding. Partly it was an English heritage, passed down from the conquerors of Ireland, Scotland, and Wales—and absolute belief in the inferiority of everything and everyone non-English. In Australia, however, it had developed its own unique characteristics. There common English prejudices had been carried to extremes, and when confronted with dark-skinned natives, the Australians did not shrink from the notion of genocide. The most shocking example of racial relations was the case of the small island of Tasmania off the southeast coast of Australia. When the English first settled the island there were perhaps a few thousand Tasmanians. Short but long-legged, these red-brown people were described as uncommonly friendly natives. But the friendliness soon died, as British colonists hunted, raped, enslaved, abducted, or killed the Tasmanians. Slowly the race died off, until in 1876 Truganini, the very last survivor, died. Her passing struck many Australians as sad—but inevitable. As a correspondent for the *Hobart Mercury* wrote, "I regret the death of the last of the Tasmanian aborigines, but I know that it is the result of the *fiat* that the black shall everywhere give place to the white."

For Australia the problem was that other darker races had not given way fast enough in the generation after the death of Truganini. Though Social Darwinists preached the virtues of the lightskinned, by 1909 Australians felt threatened by the "lower" races. Increasingly after 1900 Australians demonstrated anxiety over their Oriental neighbors. Immigration restrictions aimed at keeping the country white were proposed and adopted. So bitter had the struggle become that in 1908, the year of the Johnson-Burns fight, the *Australia Bulletin* changed its banner from

"Australia for Australians" to "Australia for the white men."

Johnson and Burns became both an example of and a contribution to the fears of white Australians. Small, white Burns became the symbol of small, white Australia, nobly battling against the odds. Burn's defense was his brain and pluck, his desire to stave off defeat through intelligence and force of will. Johnson became the large, vulgar, corrupt, and sensual enemy. Reports said that he ignored training and instead wenched and drank. He had strength and size but lacked heart—in fact, he *should* win but probably would not. This last report gave rise to the rumor that the fight was fixed. Even the *New York Times* endorsed this view, as did the betting line that made Burns a 7 to 4 favorite.

Cool rains washed Sydney on Christmas night, the eve of the fight. To allow filming, the fight was not scheduled to begin until 11 A.M., but by 6 A.M. an orderly crowd of more than 5,000 was waiting at the gate. The stadium would be filled to capacity; yet interest was much more widespread. Throughout Australia men milled around newspaper offices hoping to hear a word about the progress of the fight. Inside the stadium at Rushcutter's Bay all Christmas cheer had vanished. The mood and tone of the day, from the gray, overcast sky to the uneasy quiet of the spectators, was eulogistic.

Johnson entered the ring first. Despite his dull gray robe his mood was almost carefree. There were a few cheers—though not many—as he slipped under the upper strand of the ropes, but calls of "coon" and "nigger" were more common. He smiled, bowed grandly, and threw kisses in every direction. He liked to strut the stage, and the vicious insults did not outwardly affect him. If anything, his smile became broader as he was more abused. In a country exhilarated by the discovery of gold, Johnson's gold-toothed smile ironically attracted only hate. Satisfied that he was not the crowd's favorite, he retired to his corner,

where Sam Fitzpatrick massaged his shoulders and whispered words of assurance into an unlistening ear.

By contrast, when Burns climbed into the ring, the stadium was filled with sound. Burns did not seem to notice. For a time it looked as if he had come into the ring expecting something other than a fight. He was dressed in a worn blue suit, more appropriate for a shoe salesman than the heavyweight champion. Methodically he removed the suit, folded it neatly, and put it in a battered wicker suitcase. Yet even in his short, tight boxing trunks he looked out of place. Jack London, covering the fight for the *New York Herald*, wrote that Burns looked "pale and sallow, as if he had not slept all night, or as if he had just pulled through a bout with fever." Pacing nervously in his corner, he avoided looking across the ring at Johnson.

Burns examined the bandages on Johnson's hands. He did this carefully, looking for hard tape or other unnatural objects. Satisfied, he returned to his corner. Johnson, however, was upset by the tape on Burns's elbows. He asked Burns to remove it. Burns refused. Johnson—suddenly serious—said he would not fight until the tape was removed. Still Burns refused. McIntosh tried to calm the two fighters. He was unsuccessful. The crowd, sensing an unexpected confrontation but not aware of the finer details, sided with Burns and used the moment as a pretext to shout more insults at Johnson, who smiled as if complimented on a new necktie but still refused to alter his protest. Finally, Burns removed the tape. Johnson nodded, satisfied.

McIntosh called the fighters to the center of the ring. He went over the do's and don'ts and the business of what punches would or would not be allowed. Then he announced that in the event that the police stopped the fight, he would render a decision based on who was winning at the time. The unpopular "no decision" verdict would not be given. Both Johnson and Burns had earlier agreed to this procedure. The fighters returned to their corners. A few moments later the bell rang. The color line in championship fights was erased.

Watching films of Johnson boxing is like listening to a 1900 recording of Enrico Caruso played on a 1910 gramophone. When Johnson fought Burns, film was still in its early days, not yet capable of capturing the subtleties of movement. Nuance is lost in the furious and stilted actions of the figures, which move about the screen in a Chaplinesque manner, as if some drunken cutter had arbitrarily removed three of every four frames. When we watch fighters of Johnson's day on film, we wonder how they could have been considered even good. That some of them were champions strains credulity. They look like large children, wrestling and cuffing each other, but not actually fighting like real boxers, not at all like Ali captured in zoom-lensed, slow-motion, technological grace. But the film misleads.

It was no Charlie Chaplin that shuffled out of his corner in round one to meet Tommy Burns. It was a great boxer who at age thirty was in his physical prime. No longer thin, Johnson was well-muscled, with a broad chest and thick arms and legs. His head was shaved in the style of the eighteenth-century bare-knuckle fighters, and his high cheekbones gave his face a rounded appearance. Although he had fought often, his superb defensive skills had kept his face largely unmarked. Like his mother he had a broad, flat nose and full lips, but his eyes were small and oddly Oriental when he smiled. He was famous for his clowning, but this stereotype of a black man obscured the more serious reality. He was often somber, and even when he smiled and acted like a black-faced minstrel, he could be serious. What he thought, he believed, was his own affair. His feelings could not be easily read on his face.

Both boxers began cautiously. Johnson flicked out a few probing jabs, designed more to test distance than to do any physical damage. Although Burns was much smaller than Johnson, he was considered a strong man with a powerful punch. Johnson clinched, tested Burns's strength, then shifted to long-range sparring. He allowed Burns to force the action, content to parry punches openhanded. Burns tried to hit Johnson with long left hooks, which fell short. Johnson feinted a long left of his own, but in the same motion he lowered his right shoulder, pivoted from the waist, stepped forward with his right foot, and delivered a perfect right uppercut. It was Johnson's finest weapon, and some ring authorities claim there never has been a fighter who could throw the punch as well as Johnson. Burns was caught flatfooted, leaning into the punch. His momentum was stopped and he fell backward. His head hit heavily on the floor. He lay still. The referee started to count.

"The fight," Jack London wrote only hours after it ended, "there was no fight. No Armenian massacre could compare with the hopeless slaughter that took place in the Sydney stadium today." From the opening seconds of the first round it was clear who would win. At least it was clear to London. It was a fight between a "colossus and a toy automation," between a "playful Ethiopian and a small and futile white man," between a "grown man and a naughty child." And through it all, London and the 20,000 white supporters of Burns watched in horror as their worst fears materialized.

"Hit the coon in his stomach." Burns needed no reminder. After surviving the first-round knockdown, he shifted to a different strategy, one he had thought about before. In the days before the fight, when reporters asked about his battle plan, he had smiled knowingly at his white chroniclers and said he would move in close and hit the black fighter where all black fighters were weak—in the stomach. This theory was hardly novel; it had long been considered axiomatic that black boxers had weak stomachs and hard heads. So thoroughly was the view accepted that black boxers took it for granted that white fighters would attack the body. Peter

Jackson once told Fred Dartnell, "They are all after my body. Hit a nigger in the stomach and you'll settle him, they say, but it never seems to occur to them that a white man might just as quickly be beaten by a wallop in the same region." Sam Langford agreed: blacks hated to be hit by a hard punch to the stomach, but so too did whites.

Boxing was not immune to the scientific explanations of the day. Polygenists believed—and Darwinists did not deny—that the black race was an "incipient species." Therefore, whites maintained, physically blacks and whites were very different. Burns, for example, assumed that Johnson not only had a weak stomach but lacked physical endurance. So he believed that the longer the fight lasted the better were his chances. Behind these stereotypes rested the science of the day. Writing only a year before in the *North American Review,* Charles F. Woodruff claimed that athletes raised in southern climates lacked endurance: "The excessive light prods the nervous system to do more than it should, and in time such constant stimulation is followed by irritability and finally by exhaustion." Only athletes from the colder northern latitudes had enough stamina to remain strong during the course of a long boxing match. Therefore, Burns, a Canadian, had reason to remain hopeful. By contrast, Johnson, raised about as far south as one could travel in the United States and only a generation or two removed from Africa, had to win quickly or not at all. At least, this was what Burns and his white supporters hoped.

Burns's strategy was thus founded on the racist belief that scientists, armed with physiological and climatological evidence, had proved that blacks were either inferior to whites, or—as in the case of harder heads— superior because of some greater physiological inferiority; that is to say, blacks had thicker skulls because they had smaller brains. Burns never questioned that his abdominal strength and his endurance were superior to Johnson's. Nor did he doubt that his

white skin meant that his desire to win and willingness to accept pain were greater than Johnson's. But above all, he was convinced that as a white he could outthink Johnson, that he could solve the problems of defense and offense more quickly than his black opponent. Burns's faith, in short, rested ultimately on the color of his skin.

Burns forgot, however, that he was facing a boxer liberated from the myths of his day. Johnson's stomach was not weak, and, more important, he knew it was not. As the fight progressed, he exposed the fallacy of Burns's theory. He started to taunt Burns. "Go on, Tommy, hit me here," Johnson said pointing to his stomach. When Burns responded with a blow to Johnson's midsection, Jack laughed and said to try again. "Is that all the better you can do, Tommy?" Another punch. "Come on, Tommy, you can hit harder than that, can't you?" And so it continued; Johnson physically and verbally was destroying the white man's myths.

Burns fought gamely, but without success. Johnson did not try for a knockout; he was content to allow the fight to last until the later rounds. Partly his decision was based on economics. The bout was being filmed, and few boxing fans in America would pay to watch pictures of pressmen, seconds, and other boxers for five minutes as a buildup for a fight that lasted only half a minute. But more important was Johnson's desire for revenge. He hated Burns and wanted to punish him. And he did. By the second round Burns's right eye was discolored and his mouth was bloody. By the middle rounds Burns was bleeding from a dozen minor facial cuts. Blood ran over his shoulders and stained the canvas ring. Before the white audience, Johnson badly punished Burns. And he enjoyed every second of it.

But punishment was not enough. Johnson wanted also to humiliate Burns. He did this verbally. From the very first round Johnson insulted Burns, speaking with an affected English accent, so that "Tommy" became "Tahmy." Mostly what Johnson said was ba-

The first African American man to gain the heavyweight boxing championship of the world was Jack Johnson, who held the title from 1908 to 1915.

nal: "Poor little Tahmy, who told you you were a fighter?" Or, "Say little Tahmy, you're not fighting. Can't you? I'll have to show you how." Occasionally, when Burns landed a punch, Johnson complimented him: "Good boy, Tommy; good boy, Tommy." In almost every taunt Johnson referred to Burns in the diminutive. It was always "Tommy Boy"; or "little Tommy." And always a derisive smile accompanied the words.

Sometimes Johnson sought to emasculate Burns verbally. Referring to Burns's wife, Johnson said, "Poor little boy, Jewel won't know you when she gets you back from this fight." Once when Burns landed what looked

to be an effective punch, Johnson laughed: "Poor, poor Tommy. Who taught you to hit? Your mother? You a woman?" Crude, often vulgar and mean, Johnson's verbal warfare was nevertheless effective.

Burns responded in kind. Bohum Lynch, who was a great fan of Burns, admitted that his champion's ring histrionics included baleful glaring, foot stomping, and mouth fighting. He often called Johnson a "cur" or a "big dog." At other times, when he was hurt or frustrated, he said, "Come on and fight, nigger. Fight like a white man." Burns's comments, however, were self-defeating. When Johnson insulted Burns, the champion lost control and fought recklessly. But Burns's taunts pleased Johnson, who responded by fighting in an even more controlled way than before. Johnson gained particular strength from Burns's racist statements. It was like playing the Dozens, where accepting abuse with an even smile and concealing one's true emotions were the sign of a sure winner.

When Johnson was not insulting Burns, he was talking to ringsiders. Usually he just joked about how easy the fight was and what he would do with the money he won from betting on the bout. That the ringsiders hated Johnson and screamed racial insults did not seem to bother him. Only rarely did Johnson show his disgust with the white audience. Once as he moved from his corner at the start of a round he spat a mouthful of water toward the press row, but such actions were unusual. More common was the smile—wide, detached, inscrutable. In describing the grin, Jack London came closest to the truth: it was "the fight epitomized." It was the smile of a man who has mastered the rules to a slightly absurd game.

After a few rounds the only question that remained unanswered was not who would win but how much punishment Burns could take. By the middle rounds that too was evident—he could survive great amounts of punishment. His eyes were bruised and discolored, his mouth hung open, his jaw was swollen and looked broken, and his body was splotched with his own blood. In the corner between rounds his seconds sponged his face with champagne, which was popularly believed to help revive hurt fighters. It did not help Burns. Yet at the bell he always arose to face more punishment and insults. For the white spectators, Burns's fortitude was itself inspiring. As Bohum Lynch wrote, "To take a beating any time, even from your best friend, is hard work. But to take a beating from a man you abhor, belonging to a race you despise, to know that he is hurting you and humiliating you with the closest attention to detail, and the coldest deliberation . . . this requires pluck."

By the thirteenth round everyone but Burns and Johnson was surfeited with the carnage. Spectators, left with nothing and nobody to cheer, now yelled for the fight to be stopped. After the thirteenth round police entered the ring. They talked with McIntosh, then with Burns. The white champion refused to concede. He insisted that he could win. But in the fourteenth Burns was again severely punished. A hard right cross knocked him to the canvas. He arose at the count of eight but was wobbly. Again policemen climbed into the ring, only this time there was no talking. The fight was stopped, although Burns—dazed, covered with blood, but still game—screamed at the police to give him another chance.

Everywhere was a stunned silence as the spectators accepted that the inevitable was now the actual. It had happened. A black man now wore the crown that had once belonged to Sullivan, Corbett, and Jeffries. As far as Australia was concerned, an "archetypal darkness" had replaced sweetness and light; the barbarian had defeated the civilized man. As the *Daily Telegraph* observed in doggerel:

And yet for all we know and feel,
  For Christ and Shakespeare,
    knowledge, love,
  We watch a white man bleeding reel,
  We cheer a black with bloodied glove.

The imagery in which the fight was reported clearly reflects the white Australian attitude toward Johnson. He was portrayed as a destructive beast. *Fairplay,* the liquor trades weekly, called Johnson "a huge primordial ape," and the *Bulletin's* cartoons likened him to a shaven-headed reptile. He was the discontented black and yellow masses that haunted the Australian mind. Journalist Randolph Bedford, perhaps the most unabashedly racist reporter at the fight, depicted it in ominous terms: "Yet the white beauty faced the black unloveliness, forcing the fight, bearing the punishment as if it were none . . . weight and reach were ebbing against intrepidity, intelligence and lightness . . . . His courage still shone in his eyes; his face was disfigured and swollen and bloodied. He was still beauty by contrast—beautiful but to be beaten; clean sunlight fighting darkness and losing."

In America the fight was not viewed in quite so maudlin a manner. Certainly the white American press was not pleased by the result, but it generally tried to dismiss it in a light-hearted mood. Perhaps, reporters reasoned, all was not lost. "Br'er Johnson is an American anyway," commented a reporter for the *Omaha Sunday Bee.* Then, too, boxing had declined so much in recent years that some experts wondered if the fight meant anything at all. Though John L. Sullivan criticized Burns for fighting Johnson, he added that "present day bouts cannot truly be styled prize fights, but only boxing matches." A fine distinction, but Sullivan believed it was enough to invalidate Johnson's claim as heavyweight champion. And certainly even if Johnson were the champion, reporters all agreed that he was far below the likes of Sullivan, Corbett, or Jeffries.

Though the mood had not yet reached a crisis stage, the fight's portent was still most unsettling to American whites. This was especially true about the manner in which blacks celebrated Johnson's victory. It was reported that the Manassas Club, a Chicago organization of wealthy blacks who had white wives, hired white waiters to serve the food at their banquet. And one of their members said that "Johnson's victory demonstrates the physical superiority of the black over the Caucasian. The basis of mental superiority in most men is physical superiority. If the negro can raise his mental standard to his physical eminence, some day he will be a leader among men." In other parts of the country blacks were reported as acting rude to whites and being swelled by false pride.

Johnson's actions in Australia did little to calm Caucasian fears. Turning against the sportsmanlike tradition of praising one's opponent, Johnson openly said that Burns was a worthless boxer: "He is the easiest man I ever met. I could have put him away quicker, but I wanted to punish him. I had my revenge." Nor was Johnson discreet about the company with whom he was seen in public. Hattie McClay, his companion who had remained in the background during the weeks before the fight, was now prominently on display. Dressed in silk and furs, she seemed as prized a possession of Johnson's as his gold-capped teeth.

Johnson now seemed more apt to emphasize racial issues that irritated whites. Interviewed during the days after the fight, he told reporters that he had the greatest admiration for the aboriginal Australians. Commenting on their weapons, he said, "Your central Australian natives must have been men of genius to have turned out such artistic and ideal weapons." Nor, he hinted, was he any less a genius. He understood human nature: because he defeated Burns he could expect to be hated by all whites. But, he added, he could find solace in his favorite books—*Paradise Lost, Pilgrim's Progress,* and *Titus Andronicus.* His comments achieved their purpose; everywhere white Australians snorted in disgust.

But his choice of books certainly did not reflect his own attitude. Unlike Milton's Adam, Johnson did not practice the standard Christian virtues.

Burns left Australia soon after the fight. A richer man by some $30,000, he nevertheless was bitter and filled with hatred. Johnson, however, decided to stay for a while in Australia. His side of the purse, a mere $5,000, was hardly enough to make the venture profitable. He hoped instead to capitalize on his fame by touring Australia as a vaudeville performer. It was common for any famous boxer to make such tours. In 1908 he had toured in America and Canada with the Reilly and Woods Big Show and had enjoyed the experience. He loved the limelight and, unlike other boxers, put on a good show. He demonstrated a few boxing moves, sang several songs, danced, and played the bass fiddle. During his Australian tour he actually made more money than he had in his fight with Burns. Not until mid-February was he ready to go home.

He had changed. The Johnson who left Australia in February was not the same man who had arrived in October. Inwardly, perhaps, he was much the same. But outwardly he was different. He was more open about his beliefs and his pleasures, less likely to follow the advice of white promoters and managers. Undoubtedly he believed the title of world champion set him apart from others of his race. And in this he was right. He would never be viewed as just another black boxer. But he was wrong in his assumption that the crown carried with it some sort of immunity against the dictates of whites and traditions of white society. Now more than ever Johnson was expected to conform. And now more than ever Johnson felt he did not have to. The collision course was set.

Study Questions

1. How did the promoters of the Johnson-Burns fight use racism to build up the gate? How did the racial attitudes of white Australians compare with those of white Americans?

2. How did Burns demonstrate racial stereotypes by the manner in which he fought Johnson?

3. What was the reaction of white Australians and Americans to Jack Johnson's victory?

4. What was Johnson's attitude toward white society?

5. How else might one use sports or popular culture to demonstrate racial attitudes?

Bibliography

The section is taken from Randy Roberts, *Papa Jack: Jack Johnson and the Era of White Hopes* (1983). Finis Farr, *Black Champion: The Life and Times of Jack Johnson* (1965), provides a readable popular history of the boxer, and Al-Tony Gilmore, *Bad Nigger! The National Impact of Jack Johnson* (1975), traces the newspaper reaction to Johnson. Johnson's image in black folklore is treated by William Wiggins, "Jack Johnson as Bad Nigger: The Folklore of His Life," *Black Scholar* (1969), and Lawrence W. Levine, *Black Culture and Black Consciousness: Afro-American Folk Thought from Slavery to Freedom* (1977). A number of books trace the evolution of white attitudes toward blacks. Among the best are George M. Fredrickson, *The Black Image in the White Mind: The Debate on Afro-American Character and Destiny, 1817–1914* (1971); Thomas F. Gossett, *Race: The History of an Idea in America* (1965); and John S. Haller Jr., *Outcasts from Evolution: Scientific Attitudes of Racial Inferiority, 1859–1900* (1971).

READING 10

★ ★ ★

The Trench Scene

Paul Fussell

For the generation that fought it, World War I was the Great War. It came after almost one hundred years of general European peace, and it shattered not only nations and people but also a system of thought, a worldview. Before the Great War, intellectuals talked seriously and earnestly about human progress and the perfectability of societies and individuals. Men and women, they agreed, were reasonable creatures, fully capable of ordering their lives and environment. The terrible slaughter of Verdun and the Somme, the mud and lice and rats of the trenches, the horrors of poison gases and bullet-torn bodies draped over barbed-wire barriers—these unspeakable barbarities silenced talk of progress. Ernest Hemingway spoke for his generation when he wrote about the impact of the Great War: "I was always embarrassed by the words *sacred, glorious,* and *sacrifice* and the expression *in vain.* . . . I had seen nothing sacred, and the things that were glorious had no glory and the sacrifices were like the stockyards at Chicago if nothing was done with the meat except to bury it. There were many words that you could not stand to hear and finally only the names of places had dignity . . . . Abstract words such as *glory, honor, courage,* or *hallow* were obscene beside the concrete names of villages, the number of roads, the names of rivers, the numbers of regiments and the dates."

In the following essay, literary historian Paul Fussell discusses the Great War as experienced by millions of soldiers who served time in the trenches of the Western Front. In these ditches some 7,000 British soldiers were killed or wounded daily between 1914 and 1918. Though not in such horrendous numbers, Americans too died in the trenches of France, and the experience of mass death transformed American society. The United States went into the war to "make the world safe for democracy" but emerged from the war pessimistic, cynical, and discouraged. As Fussell observes, "To be in the trenches was to experience an unreal, unforgettable enclosure and constraint, as well as a sense of being unoriented and lost." This was the aspect of the Great War that changed the temper of Western culture.

The idea of "the trenches" has been assimilated so successfully by metaphor and myth ("Georgian complacency died in the trenches") that it is not easy now to recover a feeling for the actualities. *Entrenched*, in an expression like *entrenched power*, has been a dead metaphor so long that we must bestir ourselves to recover its literal sense. It is time to take a tour.

From the winter of 1914 until the spring of 1918 the trench system was fixed, moving here and there a few hundred yards, moving on great occasions as much as a few miles. London stationers purveying maps felt secure in stocking "sheets of 'The Western Front' with a thick wavy black line drawn from North to South alongside which was printed 'British Line.'" If one could have gotten high enough to look down at the whole line at once, one would have seen a series of multiple parallel excavations running for 400 miles down through Belgium and France, roughly in the shape of an *S* flattened at the sides and tipped to the left. From the North Sea coast of Belgium the line wandered southward, bulging out to contain Ypres, then dropping down to protect Béthune, Arras, and Albert. It continued south in front of Montidier, Compiégne, Soissons, Reims, Verdun, St. Mihiel, and Nancy, and finally attached its southernmost end to the Swiss border at Beurnevisin, in Alsace. The top forty miles—the part north of Ypres—was held by the Belgians; the next ninety miles, down to the river Ancre, were British; the French held the rest, to the south.

Henri Barbusse estimates that the French front alone contained about 6,250 miles of trenches. Since the French occupied a little more than half the line, the total length of the numerous trenches occupied by the British must come to about 6,000 miles. We thus find over 12,000 miles of trenches on the Allied side alone. When we add the trenches of the Central Powers, we arrive at a figure of about 25,000 miles, equal to a trench sufficient to circle the earth. Theoretically it would have been possible to walk from Belgium to Switzerland entirely below ground, but although the lines were "continuous," they were not entirely seamless: occasionally mere shell holes or fortified strongpoints would serve as a connecting link. Not a few survivors have performed the heady imaginative exercise of envisioning the whole line at once. Stanley Casson is one who, imagining the whole line from his position on the ground, implicitly submits the whole preposterous conception to the criterion of the "normally" rational and intelligible. As he remembers, looking back from 1935:

Our trenches stood on a faint slope, just overlooking German ground, with a vista of vague plainland below. Away to right and left stretched the great lines of defense as far as eye and imagination could stretch them. I used to wonder how long it would take for me to walk from the beaches of the North Sea to that curious end of all fighting against the Swiss boundary; to try to guess what each end looked like; to imagine what would happen if I passed a verbal message, in the manner of the parlor game, along to the next man on my right to be delivered to the end man of all up against the Alps. Would anything intelligible at all emerge?

Another imagination has contemplated a similar absurd transmission of sound all the way from north to south. Alexander Aitken remembers the Germans opposite him celebrating some happy public event in early June, 1916, presumably either the (ambiguous) German success at the naval battle of Jutland (May 31–June 1) or the drowning of Lord Kitchener, lost on June 5 when the cruiser *Hampshire* struck a mine and sank off the Orkney Islands. Aitken writes, "There had been a morning in early June when a tremendous tincanning and beating of shell-gongs

From *The Great War and Modern Memory* by Paul Fussell. Copyright © 1975 by Oxford University Press, Inc, Reprinted by permission of the author.

had begun in the north and run south down their lines to end, without doubt, at Belfort and Mulhausen on the Swiss frontier." Impossible to believe, really, but in this mad setting, somehow plausible.

The British part of the line was normally populated by about 800 battalions of 1,000 men each. They were concentrated in the two main sectors of the British effort: the Ypres Salient in Flanders and the Somme area in Picardy. Memory has given these two sectors the appearance of two distinguishable worlds. The Salient, at its largest point about nine miles wide and projecting some four miles into the German line, was notable for its terrors of concentrated, accurate artillery fire. Every part of it could be covered from three sides, and at night one saw oneself almost surrounded by the circle of white and colored lights set up by the Germans to illuminate the ground in front of their trenches or to signal to the artillery behind them. The "rear area" at Ypres was the battered city itself, where the troops harbored in cellars or in the old fortifications built by Vauban in the seventeenth century. It was eminently available to the German guns, and by the end of the war Ypres was flattened to the ground, its name a byword for a city totally destroyed. Another war later, in 1940, Colin Perry—who was not born until four years after the Great War—could look at the ruins of London and speak of "the Ypres effect of Holborn." If the character of the Ypres sector was concentration and enclosure, inducing claustrophobia even above ground, the Somme was known—at least until July 1, 1916—for its greater amplitude and security. German fire came generally from only one direction; and troops at rest could move further back. But then there was the Somme mud; although the argument about whether the mud wasn't really worse at Ypres was never settled.

Each of these two sectors had its symbolic piece of ruined public architecture. At Ypres it was the famous Cloth Hall, once a masterpiece of medieval Flemish civic building. Its gradual destruction by artillery and its pathetic final dissolution were witnessed by hundreds of thousands, who never forgot this eloquent emblem of what happens when war collides with art. In the Somme the memorable ruined work of architecture, connoting this time the collision of the war with religion and the old pieties, was the battered Basilica in the town of Albert, or "Bert," as the troops called it. The grand if rather vulgar red and white brick edifice had been built a few years before the war, the result of a local ecclesiastic's enthusiasm. Together with his townsmen he hoped that Albert might become another Lourdes. Before the war 80,000 used to come on pilgrimages to Albert every year. The object of veneration inside the church was a statue of the Virgin, said to have been found in the Middle Ages by a local shepherd. But the statue of the Virgin never forgotten by the hordes of soldiers who passed through Albert was the colossal gilded one on top of the battered tall tower of the Basilica. This figure, called Notre Dame des Brebiéres, originally held the infant Christ in outstretched arms above her; but now the whole statue was bent down below the horizontal, giving the effect of a mother about to throw her child—in disgust? in sacrifice?—into the debris-littered street below. To Colonel Sir Maurice Hankey, Secretary of the War Committee, it was "a most pathetic sight." Some said that the statue had been bent down by French engineers to prevent the Germans from using it to aim at. But most—John Masefield among them—preferred to think it a victim of German artillery. Its obvious symbolic potential (which I will deal with later) impressed itself even on men who found they could refer to it only facetiously, as "The Lady of the Limp."

The two main British sectors duplicated each other also in their almost symbolic road systems. Each had a staging town behind: for Ypres it was Poperinghe (to the men, "Pop"); for the Somme, Amiens. From these towns troops proceeded with augmenting but usually well-concealed terror up a sinister road to the town of operations, either Ypres itself or Albert. And running into the enemy lines out of Ypres and Albert were the most sinister roads of all, one leading to Menin, the other to Bapaume, both in enemy territory. These roads defined the direction of ultimate attack and the hoped-for breakout. They were the goals of the bizarre inverse quest on which the soldiers were ironically embarked.

But most of the time they were not questing. They were sitting or lying or squatting in places below the level of the ground. "When all is said and done," Sassoon notes, "the war was mainly a matter of holes and ditches." And in these holes and ditches extending for ninety miles, continually, even in the quietest times, some 7,000 British men and officers were killed and wounded daily, just as a matter of course. "Wastage," the Staff called it.

There were normally three lines of trenches. The front-line trench was anywhere from fifty yards or so to a mile from its enemy counterpart. Several hundred yards behind it was the support trench line. And several hundred yards behind that was the reserve line. There were three kinds of trenches: firing trenches, like these; communication trenches, running roughly perpendicular to the line and connecting the three lines; and "saps," shallower ditches thrust out into No Man's Land, providing access to forward observation posts, listening posts, grenade-throwing posts, and machine gun positions. The end of a sap was usually not manned all the time: night was the favorite time for going out. Coming up from the rear, one reached the trenches by following a communication trench sometimes a mile or more long. It often began in a town and gradually deepened. By the time pedestrians reached the reserve line, they were well below ground level.

A firing trench was supposed to be six to eight feet deep and four or five feet wide. On the enemy side a parapet of earth or sandbags rose about two or three feet above the ground. A corresponding "parados" a foot or so high was often found on top of the friendly side. Into the sides of trenches were dug one- or two-man holes ("funk-holes"), and there were deeper dugouts, reached by dirt stairs, for use as command posts and officers' quarters. On the enemy side of a trench was a fire-step two feet high on which the defenders were supposed to stand, firing and throwing grenades, when repelling attack. A well-built trench did not run straight for any distance: that would have been to invite enfilade fire. Every few yards a good trench zigzagged. It had frequent traverses designed to contain damage within a limited space. Moving along a trench thus involved a great deal of weaving and turning. The floor of a proper trench was covered with wooden duckboards, beneath which were sumps a few feet deep designed to collect water. The walls, perpetually crumbling, were supported by sandbags, corrugated iron, or bundles of sticks or rushes. Except at night and in half-light, there was of course no looking over the top except through periscopes, which could be purchased in the "Trench Requisites" section of the main London department stores. The few snipers on duty during the day observed No Man's Land through loopholes cut in sheets of armor plate.

The entanglements of barbed wire had to be positioned far enough out in front of the trench to keep the enemy from sneaking up to grenade-throwing distance. Interestingly, the two novelties that contributed most to the personal menace of the war could be said to be American inventions. Barbed wire had first appeared on the American frontier in the late nineteenth century for use in restraining animals. And the machine gun was the brainchild of Hiram Stevens Maxim (1840–1916), an American who, disillusioned with native patent law, established his Maxim Gun Company in England and began manufacturing his guns in 1889. He was finally knighted for his efforts. At first the British regard for barbed wire was on a par with Sir Douglas Haig's understanding of the machine gun. In the autumn of 1914, the first wire Private Frank Richards saw emplaced before the British positions was a single strand of agricultural wire found in the vicinity. Only later did the manufactured article begin to arrive from England in sufficient quantity to create the thickets of mock-organic rusty brown that helped give a look of eternal autumn to the front.

The whole British line was numbered by sections, neatly, from right to left. A section, normally occupied by a company, was roughly 300 yards wide. One might be occupying front-line trench section 51; or support trench S 51, behind it; or reserve trench SS 51, behind both. But a less formal way of identifying sections of trench was by place or street names with a distinctly London flavor. *Piccadilly* was a favorite; popular also were *Regent Street* and *Strand;* junctions were *Hyde Park Corner* and *Marble Arch.* Greater wit—and deeper homesickness—sometimes surfaced in the naming of the German trenches opposite. Sassoon remembers "Durley's" account of the attack at Delville Wood in September, 1916: "Our objective was Pint Trench, taking Bitter and Beer and clearing Ale and Vat, and also Pilsen Lane." Directional and traffic control signs were everywhere in the trenches, giving the whole system the air of a parody modern city, although one literally "underground."

The trenches I have described are more or less ideal, although not so ideal as the famous exhibition trenches dug in Kensington Gardens for the edification of the home front. These were clean, dry, and well furnished, with straight sides and sandbags neatly aligned. R. E. Vernède writes his wife from the real trenches that a friend of his has just returned from viewing the set of ideal ones. He "found he had never seen anything at all like it before." And Wilfred Owen calls the Kensington Gardens trenches "the laughing stock of the army." Explaining military routines to civilian readers, Ian Hay labors to give the impression that the real trenches are iden-

tical to the exhibition ones and that they are properly described in the language of normal domesticity a bit archly deployed:

The firing-trench is our place of business—our office in the city, so to speak. The supporting trench is our suburban residence, whither the weary toiler may betake himself periodically (or, more correctly, in relays) for purposes of refreshment and repose.

The reality was different. The British trenches were wet, cold, smelly, and thoroughly squalid. Compared with the precise and thorough German works, they were decidedly amateur, reflecting a complacency about the British genius for improvisation. Since defense offered little opportunity for the display of pluck or swank, it was by implication derogated in the officers' *Field Service Pocket Book.* One reason the British trench system was so haphazard and ramshackle was that it had originally taken form in accord with the official injunction: "The choice of a [defensive] position and its preparation must be made with a view to economizing the power expended on defense in order that the power of offense may be increased." And it was considered really useless to build solid fortifications anyway: "An occasional shell may strike and penetrate the parapet, but in the case of shrapnel the damage to the parapet will be trifling, while in the case of a shell filled with high explosive, the effect will be no worse on a thin parapet than on a thick one. It is, therefore, useless to spend time and labor on making a thick parapet simply to keep out shells." The repeatedly revived hopes for a general breakout and pursuit were another reason why the British trenches were so shabby. A typical soldier's view is George Coppard's:

The whole conduct of our trench warfare seemed to be based on the concept that we, the British, were not stopping in the trenches for long, but were tarrying awhile on the way to

Berlin and that very soon we would be chasing Jerry across country. The result, in the long term, meant that we lived a mean and impoverished sort of existence in lousy scratch holes.

In contrast, the German trenches, as the British discovered during the attack on the Somme, were deep, clean, elaborate, and sometimes even comfortable. As Coppard found on the Somme, "Some of the [German] dugouts were thirty feet deep, with as many as sixteen bunk beds, as well as door bells, water tanks with taps, and cupboards and mirrors." They also had boarded walls, floors, and ceilings; finished wooden staircases; electric light; real kitchens; and wallpaper and overstuffed furniture, the whole protected by steel outer doors. Foreign to the British style was a German dugout of the sort recalled by Ernst Jünger:

At Monchy . . . I was master of an underground dwelling approached by forty steps hewn in the solid chalk, so that even the heaviest shells at this depth made no more than a pleasant rumble when we sat there over an interminable game of cards. In one wall I had a bed hewn out . . . . At its head hung an electric light so that I could read in comfort till I was sleepy. . . . The whole was shut off from the outer world by a dark-red curtain with rod and rings. . . .

As these examples suggest, there were "national styles" in trenches as in other things. The French trenches were nasty, cynical, efficient, and temporary. Kipling remembered the smell of delicious cooking emanating from some in Alsace. The English were amateur, vague, *ad hoc*, and temporary. The German were efficient, clean, pedantic, and permanent. Their occupants proposed to stay where they were.

Normally the British troops rotated trench duty. After a week of "rest" behind the lines, a unit would move up—at night—to relieve a unit in the front-line trench. After three days to a week or more in that position, the unit would move back for a similar length of time to the support trench, and finally back to the reserve. Then it was time for a week of rest again. In the three lines of trenches the main business of the soldier was to exercise self-

Trench warfare was a common practice during World War I. Here, U.S. troops set up trench artillery in France.

control while being shelled. As the poet Louis Simpson has accurately remembered:

Being shelled is the main work of an infantry soldier, which no one talks about. Everyone has his own way of going about it. In general, it means lying face down and contracting your body into as small a space as possible. In novels [The Naked and the Dead is an example] you read about soldiers, at such moments, fouling themselves. The opposite is true. As all your parts are contracting, you are more likely to be constipated.

Simpson is recalling the Second War, but he might be recalling the First. While being shelled, the soldier either harbored in a dugout and hoped for something other than a direct hit or made himself as small as possible in a funk-hole. An unlucky sentry or two was supposed to be out in the open trench in all but the worst bombardments, watching through a periscope or loophole for signs of an attack. When only light shelling was in progress, people moved about the trenches freely, and we can get an idea of what life there was like if we posit a typical twenty-four hours in a frontline trench.

The day began about an hour before first light, which often meant at about 4:30. This was the moment for the invariable ritual of morning stand-to (short for the archaic formal command for repelling attack, "Stand to Arms"). Since dawn was the favorite time for launching attacks, at the order to stand-to everyone, officers, men, forward artillery observers, and visitors, mounted the fire-step, weapon ready, and peered toward the German line. When it was almost full light and clear that the Germans were not going to attack that morning, everyone "stood down" and began preparing breakfast in small groups. The rations of tea, bread, and bacon, brought up in sandbags during the night, were broken out. The bacon was fried in mess-tin lids over small, and if possible smokeless, fires. If the men

were lucky enough to be in a division whose commanding general permitted the issue of the dark and strong government rum, it was doled out from a jar with the traditional iron spoon, each man receiving about two table-spoonsful. Some put it into their tea, but most swallowed it straight. It was a precious thing, and serving it out was almost like a religious ceremonial, as David Jones recalls in *In Parenthesis*, where a corporal is performing the rite:

O have a care—don't spill the precious
O don't jog his hand—ministering; do take
*   care.*
O please—give the poor bugger elbow room.

Larger quantities might be issued to stimulate troops for an assault, and one soldier remembers what the air smelled like during a British attack: "Pervading the air was the smell of rum and blood." In 1922 one medical officer deposed before a parliamentary committee investigating the phenomenon of "shell shock": "Had it not been for the rum ration I do not think we should have won the war."

During the day the men cleaned weapons and repaired those parts of the trench damaged during the night. Or they wrote letters, deloused themselves, or slept. The officers inspected, encouraged, and strolled about looking nonchalant to inspirit the men. They censored the men's letters and dealt with the quantities of official inquiries brought them daily by runner. How many pipe-fitters had they in their company? Reply immediately. How many hairdressers, chiropodists, bicycle repairmen? Daily "returns" of the amount of ammunition and the quantity of trench stores had to be made. Reports of the nightly casualties had to be sent back. And letters of condolence, which as the war went on became form letters of condolence, had to be written to the relatives of the killed and wounded. Men went to and fro on sentry duty or working parties, but no one showed himself above the trench. After evening stand-to, the real work began.

Most of it was aboveground. Wiring parties repaired the wire in front of the position. Digging parties extended saps toward the enemy. Carrying parties brought up not just rations and mail but the heavy engineering materials needed for the constant repair and improvement of the trenches: timbers, A-frames, duckboards, stakes and wire, corrugated iron, sandbags, tarpaulins, pumping equipment. Bombs and ammunition and flares were carried forward. All this ant-work was illuminated brightly from time to time by German flares and interrupted very frequently by machine gun or artillery fire. Meanwhile night patrols and raiding parties were busy in No Man's Land. As morning approached, there was a nervous bustle to get the jobs done in time, to finish fitting the timers, filling the sandbags, pounding in the stakes, and then returning mauls and picks and shovels to the Quartermaster Sergeant. By the time of stand-to, nothing human was visible above ground anywhere, but every day each side scrutinized the look of the other's line for significant changes wrought by night.

Flanders and Picardy have always been notorious for dampness. It is not the least of the ironies of the war for the British that their trenches should have been dug where the water-table was the highest and the annual rainfall the most copious. Their trenches were always wet and often flooded several feet deep. Thigh-boots or waders were issued as standard articles of uniform. Wilfred Owen writes his mother from the Somme at the beginning of 1917: "The waders are of course indispensable. In 2 1/2 miles of trench which I waded yesterday there was not one inch of dry ground. There is a mean depth of two feet of water." Pumps worked day and night but to little effect. Rumor held that the Germans not only could make it rain when they wanted it to—that is, all the time—but had contrived some shrewd technical method for conducting the water in their lines into the British positions—perhaps piping it underground. Ultimately there was no defense against the water but humor. "Water knee deep and up to the waist in places," one soldier notes in his diary. "Rumors of being relieved by the Grand Fleet." One doesn't want to dwell excessively on such discomforts, but here it will do no harm to try to imagine what, in these conditions, going to the latrine was like.

The men were not the only live things in the line. They were accompanied everywhere by their lice, which the professional delousers in rest positions behind the lines, with their steam vats for clothes and hot baths for troops, could do little to eliminate. The entry *lousy* in Eric Partridge's *Dictionary of Slang and Unconventional English* speaks volumes: "Contemptible; mean; filthy. . . . English till 20th C, when, especially after the Great War, colloquial and used as a mere pejorative." *Lousy with*, meaning *full of*, was "originally military" and entered the colloquial word-hoard around 1915: "That ridge is lousy with Fritz."

The famous rats also gave constant trouble. They were big and black, with wet, muddy hair. They fed largely on the flesh of cadavers and on dead horses. One shot them with revolvers or coshed them to death with pick handles. Their hunger, vigor, intelligence, and courage are recalled in numerous anecdotes. One officer notes from the Ypres Salient: "We are fairly plagued with rats. They have eaten nearly everything in the mess, including the tablecloth and the operations orders! We borrowed a large cat and shut it up at night to exterminate them, and found the place empty next morning. The rats must have eaten it up, bones, fur, and all, and dragged it to their holes."

One can understand rats eating heartily there. It is harder to understand men doing so. The stench of rotten flesh was over everything, hardly repressed by the chloride of lime sprinkled on particularly offensive sites. Dead horses and dead men—and parts of both—were sometimes not buried for months and often simply became an element of parapets and trench walls. You could smell the front line miles before you could see it. Lingering

pockets of gas added to the unappetizing atmosphere. Yet men ate three times a day, although what they ate reflected the usual gulf
between the ideal and the actual. The propa-
gandist George Adam announced with satisfaction that "the food of the army is based
upon the conclusions of a committee, upon
which sat several eminent scientists." The result, he asserted, is that the troops are "better
fed than they are at home." Officially, each
man got daily: 1 1/4 pounds fresh meat (or 1
pound preserved meat), 1 1/4 pounds bread, 4
ounces bacon, 3 ounces cheese, 1/2 pound
fresh vegetables (or 2 ounces dried), together
with small amounts of tea, sugar, and jam.
But in the trenches there was very seldom
fresh meat, not for eating, anyway; instead
there was "Bully" (tinned corned-beef) or
"Maconochie" (ma-cón-o-chie), a tinned
meat-and-vegetable stew named after its manufacturer. If they did tend to grow tedious in
the long run, both products were surprisingly
good. The troops seemed to like the Maconochie best, but the Germans favored the
British corned beef, seldom returning from a
raid on the British lines without taking back
as much as they could carry. On trench duty
the British had as little fresh bread as fresh
meat. "Pearl Biscuits" were the substitute.
They reminded the men of dog biscuits, although, together with the Bully beef, they
were popular with the French and Belgian
urchins, who ran (or more often strolled)
alongside the railway trains bringing troops
up to the front, soliciting gifts by shouting,
"Tommee! Bull-ee! Bee-skee!" When a company was out of the line, it fed better. It was
then serviced by its company cookers—stoves
on wheels—and often got something approaching the official ration, as it might also
in a particularly somnolent part of the line,
when hot food might come up at night in the
large covered containers known as Dixies.

Clothing and equipment improved as the
war went on, although at the outset there was
a terrible dearth and improvisation. During
the retreat from Mons, as Frank Richards tes-
tifies, "A lot of us had no caps: I was wearing
a handkerchief knotted at the four corners—
the only headgear I was to wear for some
time." Crucial supplies had been omitted: "We
had plenty of small-arm ammunition but no
rifle-oil or rifle-rag to clean our rifles with. We
used to cut pieces off our shirts . . . some of
us who had bought small tins of vaseline . . .
for use on sore heels or chafed legs, used to
grease our rifles with that." At the beginning
line officers dressed very differently from the
men. They wore riding-boots or leather put-
tees; melodramatically cut riding breeches;
and flare-skirted tunics with Sam Browne
belts. Discovering that this costume made
them special targets in attacks (German gunners were instructed to fire first at the people
with the thin knees), by the end they were
dressing like the troops, wearing wrap put-
tees; straight trousers bloused below the knee;
Other Ranks' tunics with inconspicuous insignia, no longer on the cuffs but on the shoulders; and Other Ranks' web belts and
haversacks. In 1914 both officers and men
wore peaked caps, and it was rakish for officers to remove the grommet for a "Gor-
blimey" effect. Steel helmets were introduced
at the end of 1915, giving the troops, as Sassoon observed, "a Chinese look." Herbert
Read found the helmets "the only poetic thing
in the British Army, for they are primeval in
design and effect, like iron mushrooms." A
perceptive observer could date corpses and
skeletons lying on disused battlefields by their
evolving dress. A month before the end of the
war, Major P. H. Pilditch recalls, he

*spent some time in the old No Man's Land of
four years' duration . . . . It was a morbid but
intensely interesting occupation tracing the
various battles amongst the hundreds of
skulls, bones and remains scattered thickly
about. The progress of our successive attacks
could be clearly seen from the types of equipment on the skeletons, soft cloth caps denoting
the 1914 and early 1915 fighting, then respira-
tors, then steel helmets marking attack in*

1916. Also Australian slouch hats, used in the costly and abortive attack in 1916.

To be in the trenches was to experience an unreal, unforgettable enclosure and constraint, as well as a sense of being unoriented and lost. One saw two things only: the walls of an unlocalized, undifferentiated earth and the sky above. Fourteen years after the war J. R. Ackerley was wandering through an unfrequented part of a town in India. "The streets became narrower and narrower as I turned and turned," he writes, "until I felt I was back in the trenches, the houses upon either side being so much of the same color and substance as the rough ground between." That lost feeling is what struck Major Frank Isherwood, who writes his wife in December, 1914. "The trenches are a labyrinth, I have already lost myself repeatedly . . . . You can't get out of them and walk about the country or see anything at all but two muddy walls on each side of you." What a survivor of the Salient remembers fifty years later are the walls of dirt and the ceiling of sky, and his eloquent optative cry rises as if he were still imprisoned there: "To be out of this present, ever-present, eternally present misery, this stinking world of sticky, trickling earth ceilinged by a strip of threatening sky." As the only visible theater of variety, the sky becomes all-important. It was the sight of the sky, almost alone, that had the power to persuade a man that he was not already lost in a common grave.

Study Questions

1. What was the effect of World War I on the landscape of Europe?

2. In theory, how were the trenches supposed to be constructed? What was life supposed to be like in the ideal trench? How did reality differ from theory?

3. What national differences were there in the construction and maintenance of trenches? What do the differences tell us about the different national characters and war aims?

4. Describe the sights, sounds, and smells of life in the trenches. How did trench life affect the soldiers?

5. What does Fussell mean when he describes the experience as "unreal"? How did trench life breed "a sense of being unoriented and lost"?

Bibliography

This selection is taken from Fussell's award-winning *The Great War and Modern Memory* (1975), the best discussion of the impact of the war on modern culture. Robert Wohl, *The Generation of 1914* (1979), re-creates the experiences of the men who fought and wrote about the war. Three good military overviews of the war are James L. Stokesbury, *A Short History of World War I* (1981); B. H. Liddell Hart, *The Real War, 1914–1918* (1930); and Cyril Falls, *The Great War* (1959). S. B. Fay, *The Origins of World War* (2 vols., 1928–1930); L. Albertini, *The Origins of the War of 1914* (3 vols., 1952–1957); and Fritz Fischer, *Germany's Aims in the First World War* (1967), discuss the complex origins of the war. The best studies of America's entry into the war are E. R. May, *The*

First World War and American Isolation (1957); P. Devlin, *Too Proud to Fight: Woodrow Wilson's Neutrality* (1975); and Barbara Tuchman, *The Zimmerman Telegram* (1958). Tuchman's *Guns of August* (1994) chronicles the first 30 days of the war. Military studies that give the reader a sense of the problems faced by the typical soldier include Martin Middlebrooks, *The First Day on the Somme* (1971); Alister Horne, *The Price of Glory: Verdun, 1916* (1962); Leon Wolff, *In Flanders Field* (1958); Barrie Pitt, *The Last Act* (1962); and John Keegan, *The Face of Battle: A Study of Agincourt, Waterloo, and the Somme* (1976). Two recent books are especially good: John Keegan, *The First World War* (2000) and Gary Mead, *The Doughboys: America and the First World War* (2000).

Heroes, Villains, and Society in the 1920s

The year 1920 ushered in a decade that historians steadfastly refuse to discuss in anything less than superlative terms. The decade brings to mind Charles Dickens's description of the revolutionary years of the eighteenth century in his novel *A Tale of Two Cities:* "It was the best of times, it was the worst of times . . . it was the season of Light, it was the season of Darkness, it was the spring of hope, it was the winter of despair, we had everything before us, we had nothing before us." If a decade may be said to have a personality, then the 1920s had the personality of a child—sometimes laughing and playful, at other times brooding, brutal, and ugly.

The first and perhaps most widely read book about the decade was Frederick Lewis Allen's *Only Yesterday: An Informal History of the 1920s.* Published in 1931 during the midst of the Great Depression, *Only Yesterday* describes a carefree decade that began with the end of the Great War and ended with the stock market crash. Allen paints a decade that roars with excitement, a decade brimming with bathtub gin, bootleg liquor, and bubbling champagne. Gangsters, movie sex goddesses, athletic heroes, and fabulous moneymakers seem to come alive on the pages of *Only Yesterday.* In sweeping terms Allen examines the "revolution in manners and morals," the "aching disillusionment" of intellectuals, and the crass materialism of millions of Americans.

Allen was not necessarily wrong. The sexual mores of the youth were changing, and there was evidence of intellectual disillusionment and crass materialism. The problem with the book is that its sweeping generalizations are simply too sweeping. In addition, too much of the activity of the decade is left out. The economic plight of rural Americans, the rise of the Ku Klux Klan, urban-rural tensions, racial injustice, nativism, and religious revivalism are just a few of the subjects that Allen does not treat. As a result, *Only Yesterday* is a flawed and unbalanced classic.

THE AMERICAN
FLAPPER - 1927

In recent years historians have explored the areas where Allen did not venture. And they have presented a different view of the 1920s, viewing the decade as a period of transition where older rural and newer urban attitudes uneasily coexisted. Although the country was becoming increasingly urban and bureaucratic, many Americans clung tightly to the more traditional values of their parents and grandparents. In an effort to preserve these values, they supported a variety of movements such as the Society for the Preservation of New England Antiquities, the Ku Klux Klan, and the National Origins Act of 1924.

If rural America resisted change, most of urban America accepted it. Spectators filled movie theaters and athletic stadiums to watch others perform, and entertainment became a product that was packaged and marketed by business executives. Millions of Americans worshipped at the altar of business efficiency and organization. Even crime became more organized and efficient. By 1929 the debate between rural and urban America was decided. The future belonged to the cities.

READING 11

★ ★ ★

The Black Sox Scandal

Dean Smith

Every few years or so, fat-bellied, middle-aged journalists start complaining that baseball "isn't what it used to be," that the American pastime is "in trouble," that the game is "in a crisis from which it may never recover." And yet, in spite of their nostalgic reflections about "the good old days," baseball is alive and well. Men's and women's softball leagues fill city recreation parks every night of the week, and Little Leaguers are playing more baseball than ever before. Fantasy baseball groups have sprouted in small towns and large cities all over the country, and junior high school boys have turned baseball cards into big business. America still loves baseball.

But there was a time when baseball was in real trouble. In 1921, headlines in newspapers across the country let Americans know that eight members of the Chicago White Sox were accused of conspiring to lose the 1919 World Series. The ensuing investigation and trial became symbolic of American life in the post–World War I years, when doubts about the country's future seemed endemic. It became known as the Black Sox Scandal, and in the following article Dean Smith describes the controversy and its significance in the 1920s.

When Jim Crusinberry, the *Chicago Tribune's* ace baseball writer, entered the lobby of the Sinton Hotel in Cincinnati that evening of September 30, 1919, he stumbled onto one of the most remarkable scenes of his career.

Perched atop a chair in the lobby was a wildly gesturing man whom he immediately recognized as Abe Attell, former world featherweight boxing champion and consort of New York gamblers. Attell had $1,000 bills in both hands and he was screaming his head off to anyone who would listen, offering to bet on the Cincinnati Reds to beat the Chicago White Sox—any amount, and at even money—in the World Series which was to open the following day at Redland Park.

Crusinberry's nose for news twitched like a bloodhound's. Even in those free-wheeling days of American sport, gamblers usually exercised more discretion than Attell was displaying. And why was he betting against the White Sox? The awesome Sox, one of the finest teams ever assembled up to that time, were top-heavy favorites to crush the so-so Reds in the Series. In most quarters, one had to offer at least 4-to-1 odds to bet on Chicago. Yet here was Attell betting big on Cincinnati, and at even money!

For most of the next two years, Crusinberry pursued his big story. Although thwarted repeatedly by baseball officialdom, underworld silence, and his cautious sports editor, he put the pieces together at last. With other tenacious reporters, he forced a Chicago grand jury to investigate the case that exploded over the sporting world as the Black Sox Scandal.

For nearly six decades American sports buffs have been discussing and analyzing the Black Sox legend, and still the complete story may never be told. What has been established is that eight members of the 1919 White Sox team conspired with two combinations of gamblers to throw the World Series to the Reds, and that the White Sox did indeed lose, five games to three. None of the sinning players, forever tarred in history as the Black Sox, ever received all the money promised for the fix, and several may have gotten no money at all.

What they did get was lifetime exile from organized baseball—an edict decreed and enforced by Commissioner Kenesaw Mountain Landis—despite the fact that the jury in a Cook County trial found them all innocent.

The Black Sox Scandal had an immense impact on a nation struggling to resume "normalcy" in the wake of World War I. To many Americans in that era of innocence, baseball was an almost religious rite, and the World Series was its most holy sacrament. The heroes of the Great American Game were assumed to be as pure as saints—despite considerable evidence to the contrary—and the heresy of desecrating the game for gambler's gold was unthinkable. When the stink of the Black Sox sellout fouled the air, an entire nation was sickened.

This early 20th-century scandal did incalculable damage to America's self-image as a moral nation, disillusioned millions of youthful fans, and helped set the tone for the licentious decade of the 1920's. Teapot Dome, the Prohibition era, corruption in high places, and the public acceptance of "everybody's doing it" raised questions about the value of personal integrity that remain to the present.

To reconstruct the story of the Black Sox tragedy, return to the Sinton Hotel and September 30, 1919. Jim Crusinberry was only one of many who had heard the rumor of an impending White Sox sellout. Hugh Fullerton, syndicated columnist of the *Chicago Herald and Examiner*, wired this cryptic warning to his newspaper clients: "Don't bet on Series. Ugly rumors afloat."

Jack Doyle, whose New York billiard academy was one of the nation's biggest gambling centers, estimated that $2,000,000 was wagered

"The Black Sox Scandal" by Dean Smith. This article is reprinted from the January 1977 issue of *American History Illustrated* 11, pp. 16–25, with the permission of Cowles History Group, Inc. Copyright *American History Illustrated* magazine.

in his establishment the night before the Series opener. "You couldn't miss it … the thing had an odor," he said later. "I saw smart guys take even money on the Sox who should have been asking for 5-to-1 odds."

The Series fix was one of the worst-kept secrets in the history of infamy. As the betting odds shifted dramatically, Cincinnati was buzzing with rumors. Chick Gandil, the Chicago first baseman and admitted ringleader of the sellout, recalled in a *Sports Illustrated* confession nearly four decades later that even a clerk in a downtown stationary store whispered to him on the eve of the opener, "I have it firsthand that the Series is in the bag."

Everybody knew, and yet nobody knew for sure. Who was bribing whom—and to do what? To complicate the situation, a story popped up that some Chicago gamblers were out to insure a White Sox victory by getting ace Cincinnati pitcher Dutch Ruether drunk the night before the opener.

The White Sox should have needed no help at all. Owner Charles Comiskey, revered as "The Old Roman," had built a magnificent ball club in Chicago. There was Eddie Collins, probably the best second baseman in baseball, and Buck Weaver, without a peer at third base. "Shoeless Joe" Jackson was a virtual illiterate, but there was no better hitter and left fielder in the game. Happy Felsch in center and Shano Collins in right rounded out a great Chicago outfield. Chick Gandil at first base was so tough he could play his position without a glove. And Swede Risberg was one of the great shortstops of the era. Behind the plate was the superb Ray Schalk.

The pitching staff was a little thin, especially with Red Faber on the injured list, but Eddie Cicotte, Claude Williams, and Dickie Kerr were a match for anything Cincinnati could throw against them. As for manager Kid Gleason, he was a canny veteran who knew the game inside out and did a passable job of welding his moody and contentious athletes into a team that had dominated the American League.

The first post–World War Series had been lengthened to best five games of nine to insure a bigger box office take (it was returned to best four-of-seven shortly thereafter), and a nation weary of war and sacrifice was eager for the spectacle to begin.

The tragic prelude to the opener at Cincinnati on October 1, 1919, is still difficult to piece together. Conflicting grand jury and court testimony, countless published revelations and "authentic" analyses—but a paucity of reliable source material—combine to create a knotty problem for the historian. Eliot Asinof's *Eight Men Out*, generally regarded as the most comprehensive book on the subject, says the Black Sox plot had its beginning when Gandil contacted Boston gambler Joseph (Sport) Sullivan some three weeks before the 1919 Series and offered to "put the Series in the bag" for $80,000. Gandil, in his 1956 revelation, declared it was Sullivan who first suggested to him that the Series might be fixed.

At any rate, Gandil first enlisted pitcher Eddie Cicotte in the plot and then shortstop Swede Risberg and pitcher Claude Williams. The team's top three hitters—Buck Weaver, Joe Jackson, and Happy Felsch—were reluctant enlistees. Gandil felt sure that those seven could guarantee a White Sox defeat. They could ground out in crucial spots, feed a fat pitch to a slugger with men on base, barely miss a fly ball—all without detection. The seven were soon joined by an eighth conspirator through sheer accident. Utility infielder Fred McMullin, a man hardly in a position to affect the Series outcome, was lying behind a locker one afternoon and overheard Gandil discussing the plan with Risberg. McMullin demanded a part of the action, and he was included to buy his silence.

Consorting with gamblers was not a new occupation for Gandil, who for years had sold information on starting pitchers and other useful baseball tips to the betting fraternity. "We all mixed with gamblers," Gandil explained later, "and most of them were honest."

Such shady associations were a fact of baseball life in 1919, and nobody seemed to care very much.

The eight Chicago players assembled in Gandil's room at the Ansonia Hotel in New York City on the evening of September 21st to discuss strategy. The eight were not particularly good friends and were united on only one subject: their common hatred for Comiskey, whom they regarded as a tightfisted tyrant who paid his players less than did any other owner in major league baseball.

Gandil and Felsch, for example, were earning only a little more than $4,000 a year; Cicotte's 1919 salary was about $5,000 (and he a 29-game winner with an earned run average of 1.82!); and the great Jackson, batting .375 for the season, earned only $6,000—compared with the $10,000 Cincinnati paid its leading hitter, Ed Roush.

The eight agreed to deal with the gamblers, although Weaver is said to have suggested that they take the fix money and win

the Series, anyhow. The evidence is conclusive that the superlative third baseman never threw a game or received a dime from the gamblers. He spent the rest of his life protesting his innocence and trying to restore his good name.

Even before arrangements could be made with Sullivan, word of the fix attempt leaked out. Cicotte was approached by gambler William T. (Sleepy Bill) Burns, a former pitcher who had made money in Texas oil, to let him bid on the action. Soon two gambling combinations—unknown to each other—were negotiating with the Chicago eight.

It was common knowledge in the far-flung American gambling community that only one man, Arnold Rothstein of New York City, could put up enough money to engineer a project as grandiose as the fixing of a World Series. Burns hurriedly consulted with a small-time gambler named Billy Maharg in Philadelphia, and together they rushed to Rothstein with the proposition.

"Shoeless" Joe Jackson and seven other players on the Chicago White Sox were charged with accepting money to throw the 1919 World Series.

Rothstein would not see them personally, but told his ambitious lieutenant, Abe Attell, to check it out. Attell was entranced with the sheer audacity of the idea, so Rothstein agreed to discuss the matter with Burns. But the gambling king, known far and wide as "The Big Bankroll," turned Burns down flat and advised him to forget this wild scheme.

Attell could not put the lucrative idea out of his mind, however, and he decided to step into the big time on his own. He called Burns and told him a lie that could have bought Abe a concrete casket: Rothstein had changed his mind, said Attell, and would put up $100,000 if Burns could get the eight White Sox to go along. It was sheer bluff on Attell's part. Certainly he could not lay his hands on the money the players were demanding, but he put up a confident front and prayed he could get the cash somewhere.

Meanwhile, Sullivan was busy, too. He also sought out Rothstein and somehow made a better impression on the shrewd New Yorker than had Burns. Rothstein assigned an aide named Nat Evans to work out the details of the Series fix with Sullivan and the players.

So Gandil and his co-conspirators began their comic opera dealings with two sets of gamblers, holding clandestine meetings in hotel rooms and hoping the rival fixers would never meet. The players demanded cash in advance, but the gamblers were untrusting souls who refused payment except after each game Chicago lost. Only Cicotte held out for his money beforehand, so Sullivan gave Gandil $10,000 to clinch the deal. The money mysteriously appeared under Cicotte's pillow at the Sinton Hotel the night before the Series opener.

According to the Black Sox legend, Rothstein demanded that Cicotte "give a sign" that the fix was on by hitting the first Cincinnati batter with a pitch. Whether or not Cicotte agreed, we will never know for sure, but for whatever reason—the heat of the 90-degree afternoon, the screaming throng of 30,500 in

Redland Park, nerves made jumpy by his Judas role, or a shouted threat from the stands that "there's a guy looking for you with a rifle"—Cicotte's second pitch to Cincinnati leadoff hitter Maurice Rath strayed inside and hit him in the small of the back.

It was not Cicotte's day. He was driven from the mound in the fourth inning as the Reds waltzed to a 9–1 victory. Even the Cincinnati pitcher, Dutch Ruether, connected for two triples to the humiliation of the proud Sox. The next day Claude Williams, a left-hander famous for his control, was shockingly wild and the Reds won again, 4–2.

Meanwhile, rumors of the fix had reached manager Gleason and owner Comiskey. Late at night after the first game, according to one version of the story, Comiskey woke John Heydler, president of the National League and a member of baseball's National Commission, and poured out his fears that the White Sox had sold out to the gamblers. Heydler then woke Ban Johnson, president of the American League and a bitter enemy of Comiskey's, and relayed the Chicago owner's apprehensions.

"That's the yelp of a beaten cur!" sneered Johnson, who terminated the conversation abruptly and went back to bed.

The gamblers were equally indisposed to conversation. Sullivan disappeared after the first game. Attell was in town, but he was very vague about specifics of the payoff to Gandil. "The money is all out on bets," he told the ringleader. "You'll have to give me another day."

According to Asinof's version, Attell did come up with $10,000 after the second game, the money going to Gandil. Gandil later denied receiving any of the money for himself, but he did manage somehow to buy a big new car immediately after the Series.

Chicago had lost the first two games and, aside from Gandil and Cicotte, none of the White Sox conspirators had received so much as a "thank you" from either gambling combination. Understandably, they were now ready to forget the entire arrangement and play to win. With rookie Dickie Kerr pitching a three-hit shutout before 29,126 rabid fans at Chicago's Comiskey Park, the White Sox cruised to a 3–0 triumph. Gandil himself drove in two of the Chicago runs.

Unfortunately for Attell, Burns, and their colleagues, the news of the White Sox rebirth of spirit had not reached them. As they ruefully reported later, they lost all their previous winnings betting on the Reds in the third game and had no further participation in the Series machinations. But Sullivan was still very much in the game. Fearful that the White Sox players had revolted, he came up with $20,000, part of the bankroll reportedly supplied by Rothstein.

Now it was time for the fourth game and Cicotte's chance to redeem himself. The spitball ace pitched a strong five-hitter, but his mates were powerless at the plate and Cincinnati walked away with a 2–0 win. Williams gave up only four hits in the fifth game, but again the White Sox bats were silent and the Reds had their fourth victory, 5–0.

At this point Sullivan made the last of the gamblers' payments, this one purportedly $15,000.

Only one game away from losing the Series, the White Sox miraculously returned to their regular season form in the sixth game. Kerr won it, 5–4, with Gandil's hit providing the winning margin in the 10th inning. Cicotte was brilliant in the seventh game, winning 4–1, and suddenly the White Sox looked like winners again.

The gamblers were more than a little nervous, even with the paid-off Williams slated to pitch the eighth game in Chicago. To be sure of his position, Sullivan (according to Williams' wife) employed a professional persuader to remind Williams of the unpleasant consequences in store for him and his family if he should win.

A well-known gambler telephoned reporter Fullerton before the game and told him to "watch out for the biggest first inning you ever saw." It arrived on schedule, with Williams surrendering four runs in the first frame. The fired-up Reds raced off to a 10–1 lead before Chicago scored four in the eighth to close the final Cincinnati victory margin to 10–5.

The lowly Reds had pulled off the baseball upset of the decade. But had they really outplayed the White Sox, or had the eight Chicago conspirators handed the Series to them in return for tainted money?

The debate continues to this day.

One of the leading advocates of the "no fix" theory, Victor Luhrs, in his book *The Great Baseball Mystery*, declares the indications are overwhelming that Cincinnati would have won the Series anyhow. In his summary Luhrs admits that Williams' poor pitching cost the White Sox the second and eighth games and that he quite probably was an intentional loser. Gandil and Risberg, he says, did not give their best efforts and McMullin (who appeared only twice as a pinch hitter) did not play enough to permit a judgment. But he stoutly defends Jackson, Weaver, Felsch, and Cicotte, crediting all four with playing their best.

Dr. Harold Seymour, in his book *Baseball—The Golden Age*, concluded that the box scores do not indicate that the Series was thrown. "In fact," says he, "the Black Sox on the whole actually made a better showing in the games than the Clean Sox (the other Chicago players)."

Joe Jackson, for example, led both teams at the plate with a .375 average, and Weaver ended with a .324 batting effort. Gandil's timely hitting won two games, and both Weaver and Jackson played errorless ball. Clean Eddie Collins, on the other hand, made two errors and batted an anemic .224; the other unblemished Chicago regulars did little better.

The rumors of a fix continued for many months, despite the best efforts of investigative reporters to dig out the truth. Comiskey offered a $20,000 reward (soon reduced to $10,000) for information on any skullduggery. But he ignored tips supplied by at least one gambler and never answered a letter from the remorseful Jackson, written by his wife, offering to tell what he knew. Apparently baseball officialdom had decided to sweep the dirt under the rug and hope it would be forgotten.

But the Chicago *Tribune's* Jim Crusinberry would not forget.

Crusinberry devoted every spare moment to tracking down leads, and at last—on a rainy New York afternoon in July 1920—the first crack in the wall of silence appeared. The telephone rang in the hotel room when Crusinberry was relaxing with columnist Ring Lardner. It was Kid Gleason, and he spoke in an excited whisper.

"I'm at Dinty Moore's," he told Crusinberry, "and Abe Attell is at the bar, drinking and starting to talk. Come on over and get close enough to listen." Within minutes, Crusinberry and Lardner were eavesdropping on a fascinating conversation.

"So it was Arnold Rothstein who put up the dough for the fix," they heard Gleason say. "That was it, Kid," answered Attell. "You know, Kid, I hated to do that to you, but I thought I was going to make a lot of money and I needed it, and then the big guy double-crossed me, and I never got but a small part of what he promised."

Attell rambled on for half an hour, naming the participants. At last Crusinberry had the information for his block-busting story. But his sports editor, wary of a libel suit, refused to print it. Frustrated and angry, Crusinberry decided to take matters into his own hands. He wrote an open letter to the *Tribune*, demanding a grand jury investigation of the Series fix, and persuaded Chicago businessman Fred M. Loomis to sign it. The strategy worked. The Cook County grand jury agreed to the probe, and on September 21, 1920 subpoenas were sent to baseball owners, managers, players, writers, and gamblers.

Six days later the first sensational revelation hit the newspapers. Enterprising Jimmy Isaminger, a writer for the Philadelphia *North American*, tracked down gambler Billy Maharg—a cohort of Burns and Attell—and got him to talk. Maharg knew only part of the story, of course, but his statement exploded like a bombshell. He implicated Cicotte as the chief fixer, said Attell had betrayed Burns and himself, and declared that the first, second, and eighth Series games had been thrown by the Chicago eight—who immediately became known as the Black Sox.

The ink was still damp on the Isaminger story when Gleason sought out the tormented Cicotte and persuaded him to confess. Weeping through much of his sensational testimony before the grand jury the following day, Cicotte admitted receiving $10,000, confessed that he had served up pitches that anyone could hit, and said he did it for his wife and children.

Jackson next took the stand, nervously admitting that he got $5,000 of the $20,000 promised him. As he was leaving the courthouse following his testimony, the most poignant incident of the whole sordid scandal took place. Several ragged youngsters crowded around him and one asked pleadingly, "Say it ain't so, Joe!"

All America fervently joined in that plea.

Historians may note with some amusement that the original Associated Press quote of the remark was a more grammatical "It isn't true, is it, Joe?" But several other reporters who were there quoted it in the street jargon in which it was probably uttered.

Williams testified next, admitting that he got $5,000 for his part in the fix. Then came Felsch, who also confessed $5,000, but insisted that he had done nothing to throw any of the games.

Although the White Sox were battling for the American League pennant in the final week of the season, Comiskey immediately suspended all seven active players. (Gandil had "retired" from baseball before the start of the 1920 season.) With the Chicago team decimated, Cleveland breezed to the league championship.

The grand jury indicted all eight Chicago players, along with gamblers Attell, Burns, Hal Chase, and "Rachael Brown," the name used by Rothstein aide Nat Evans. Rothstein himself escaped indictment. The New York gambling king made an appearance before the grand jury, storming in outraged innocence, and somehow convinced everyone that he had not participated in any way.

When the Black Sox trial finally began, on June 27, 1921, the prosecution made an electrifying announcement: All the players' signed confessions had mysteriously disappeared from the files! American League President Ban Johnson accused Rothstein of paying $10,000 to arrange the theft, upon which Rothstein threatened him with a $250,000 slander suit. He never carried out the threat.

Free of the damning confessions, the players all denied their earlier testimony and pleaded innocent. None testified during the trial.

All through a blazing hot July the sensational trial dragged on in the sweltering Chicago courtroom. The defense was conducted by several of the most expensive lawyers of the day (who paid them was never proved), and the crowded courtroom was noisily in support of the players. Burns turned state's evidence, and the other gamblers all avoided prosecution through legal maneuvers.

The outcome teetered in the balance as the mountain of testimony piled up. Then, on August 2, both legal teams rested their cases and Judge Hugo Friend made his charge to the jury:

The State must prove that it was the intent of the ballplayers and gamblers charged with conspiracy through the throwing of the World Series to defraud the public and others, and not merely to throw ball games.

The tricky bit of semantics was all the jury needed. The judge said taking bribes was not enough—throwing ball games was not enough. To be legally guilty, the players must have intended to defraud the public. How could anybody prove that?

In just two hours, forty-seven minutes the jury brought in "not guilty" verdicts on all concerned. The hushed courtroom erupted in wild cheering and, incredibly, members of the jury hoisted several of the Black Sox to their shoulders and paraded them triumphantly around the courtroom. Flushed with victory, Gandil spotted Ban Johnson, rushed to his side, and declared: "Goodbye, good luck, and to hell with you!"

The Black Sox celebrated their triumph at an Italian restaurant after the verdict was read—the same restaurant, incidentally, where the jurors dined and congratulated themselves—and toasted the immediate resumption of their baseball careers. But they did not reckon with the stern morality of white-haired Judge Kenesaw Mountain Landis, who had been installed as Commissioner of Baseball following the grim days of the grand jury investigation. Landis had said upon taking office that the Black Sox would never play again, but that was before the trial. Surely, the players reasoned, the judge would not dare to overrule a court of law.

But he did just that. Landis's statement after the trial was a verdict of doom:

Regardless of the verdict of juries, no player that throws a ball game ... [or] sits in a conference with a bunch of crooked players and gamblers where the ways and means of throwing games are planned and discussed, and does not promptly tell his club about it, will ever play professional baseball.

He added one more shocker: In addition to the eight Black Sox, he slapped a lifetime ban on Joe Gedeon of the St. Louis Browns, who had told the grand jury he made money betting on Cincinnati at the suggestion of Swede Risberg.

The players screamed, hired lawyers, and got petitions signed—but all to no avail. None of them ever played in organized baseball again. Landis was as unbending as iron, and many years later he went so far as to deny Jackson's petition to manage the Greenville, South Carolina, club in the low-low minors.

Part of the Black Sox legend is that Landis's stiff punishments saved baseball in its darkest hour. A glance at the soaring major league gate receipts in 1920 and 1921, however, seems to show that the sporting public would have supported the game whether or not the Black Sox had been punished. But the old judge's decision undoubtedly discouraged future cozy dealings between players and gamblers. Baseball never has suffered another scandal.

So the chastened Black Sox were cast out to make a living the best way they could. Weaver ran a Chicago drug store. Cicotte farmed near Detroit and then worked at an automobile plant. Williams ran a Chicago poolroom for a time and then started a nursery business in California. Felsch opened a tavern in Milwaukee. Risberg worked on a Minnesota dairy farm before opening a tavern in northern California. Gandil became a plumber in California. McMullin took one job and then another.

Jackson operated a restaurant, and later a liquor store, in South Carolina.

All eight are now dead.

Though most of them protested varying degrees of innocence throughout their lives, Gandil declared in his 1956 confession, "To this day, I feel that we got what we had coming."

Baseball survived and thrived, but it was never again the gloriously pure American rite it once had been. Too many little boys—of all ages—had suffered sobering disillusionment.

Perhaps Nelson Algren, who had idolized Swede Risberg, said it best many years later in his superb short story "The Silver-Colored Yesterday":

I traded off my Risberg bat ... and I flipped the program from that hot and magic Sunday when Cicotte was shutting out everybody forever, and a triumphant right-hander's wind had blown all the score cards across home plate, into the Troy Street gutter. I guess that was one way of learning what Hustletown, sooner or later, teaches all its sandlot sprouts. "Everybody's out for The Buck. Even big leaguers."

Even Swede Risberg.

Study Questions

1. Why did the little boy's comment "Say it ain't so, Joe" come to symbolize the public's reaction to the entire scandal?

2. What actually happened? Did the players really throw the World Series?

3. Who were the major characters in the scandal?

4. What decision did Judge Landis reach? Do you agree with the decision?

5. How would you compare the punishment given to the players in 1921 with contemporary professional athletes who gamble or find themselves with drug problems?

Bibliography

In recent years the history of sport in the United States has enjoyed increasing scholarly respectability. For a general survey, see Benjamin Rader, *American Sports: From the Age of Folk Games to the Age of Spectators* (1983). Stephen Reiss, *Touching Base: Professional Baseball and American Culture in the Progressive Era* (1980) is an especially useful examination of baseball in early-twentieth-century America. Also see David Q. Voigt, *American Baseball, Vol. 1: From Gentlemen's Sport to the Commissioner System* (1966). On the scandal itself, see Eliot Asinof, *Eight Men Out: The Black Sox and the 1919 World Series* (1963). For a discussion of the mood of the 1920s in the United States, see Roderick Nash, *The Nervous Generation: American Thought, 1917–1930* (1970). Organized crime in the 1920s has also generated scholarly literature. Herbert Asbury, *Sucker's Progress: An Informal History of Gambling in America* (1938) is a good, if dated, survey. Also see Jenna Joselit, *Our Gang: Jewish Crime and Politics in One American Community* (1983) and Humbert S. Nelli, *The Business of Crime: Italians and Syndicate Crime in the United States* (1981). For a discussion of the Black Sox Scandal, see Robert C. Cottrell, *Blackball, the Black Sox, and the Babe: Baseball's Crucial 1920 Season* (2001); and Daniel A. Nathan, *Saying It's So: A Cultural History of the Black Sox Scandal* (2003).

READING 12

★ ★ ★

Hollywood Scapegoat: The Roscoe Arbuckle Case

Marty Jones

Illusive and fragile, often quickly won and just as swiftly lost, stardom was the great contribution early Hollywood made to American culture. The motion picture industry manfactured and sold stars, men and women larger than life who had a certain "something" that millions of other people desired. Between 1917 and 1921, Roscoe "Fatty" Arbuckle was one of Hollywood's most unlikely stars. On screen in scores of films, Arbuckle was the innocent, overweight, bumbling comedic hero, the character who almost in spite of himself always saved the heroine. Americans loved "Fatty" Arbuckle, and studio heads paid him more than a million dollars to star in their productions.

The money, stardom, and love ended fast. In 1921, during a wild Labor Day party that Arbuckle hosted in his suite of the St. Francis Hotel in San Francisco, an obscure actress named Virginia Rappe became very ill from internal bleeding. Four days later she died. False statements led to the arrest of Arbuckle, who was charged with rape and murder. Although there was no credible evidence to link him to either crime, the case went to trial. Before Arbuckle was found not guilty, his career was destroyed and Hollywood was changed. In "Hollywood Scapegoat," Marty Jones shows how the Arbuckle case highlighted a clash of values in the United States. He also details how shrewd studio leaders used the case to strengthen the position of their industry.

On the afternoon of April 12, 1922, Roscoe Arbuckle stepped out of a San Francisco courthouse feeling as if the weight of the world had been lifted from his shoulders. For eight months after being charged with causing the death of a 27-year-old woman, he feared that the accusation would not only destroy his livelihood and fortune, but also cause him to spend the rest of his life behind bars. Now, posing for photographers with the jury that had acquitted him after a mere five minutes of deliberation, Roscoe beamed a familiar smile recognized the world over as that of movie comedian "Fatty" Arbuckle.

While the news brought cheers among Arbuckle's supporters, it was a blow to certain persons and organizations whose interests would have been better served by a verdict of guilty. From the moment the popular silent-screen clown had been accused of a rape that led to the death of a little-known actress, inaccurate and salacious stories in the press had fueled an anti-Arbuckle cottage industry. Editorials railed against the man. Sermons condemned him. It was reported that cowboys in a Wyoming theater opened fire with their pistols at Arbuckle's on-screen image. Given the controversy, all the comedian's movies were withdrawn from theaters. Roscoe's substantial salary was withheld as his hefty legal bills mounted.

The comedian believed acquittal would change all that. Questioned on the courthouse steps, a confident Arbuckle told reporters: "After the quick vindication that I have received today, I am sure the Americans will be fair and just. I am due for a comeback."

He was wrong. In the eight months since the Arbuckle scandal erupted, the Hollywood that Roscoe knew had changed forever. He now faced an industry in which there was no room for a movie star whose notoriety polarized the national debate on modern morality. A week to the day after being declared innocent, Roscoe "Fatty" Arbuckle was banned from motion pictures.

This was the first action taken by Will Hays in his role as head of the Motion Picture Producers and Distributors of America (MPPDA). Hays had been hired by a consortium of Hollywood's power elite to clean up the film industry. During his 28-year tenure, the "czar of the movies" became a figure synonymous with Hollywood censorship. What few people realized in 1922—but what has come to be understood since then—was that until Hays formally established the Motion Picture Production Code eight years later, his office served largely as a public relations front controlled by a handful of the industry's most powerful moguls. Incredibly, the men behind the destruction of Fatty Arbuckle's career

Roscoe "Fatty" Arbuckle.

"Hollywood Scapegoat: The Roscoe Arbuckle Case," by Marty Jones, American History 40 (June, 2005), pp. 40–47.

were none other than the comedian's own employers, Paramount studio heads Jesse Lasky and Adolph Zukor.

Both Lasky and Zukor had a fortune invested in Roscoe's contract and stacks of uncirculated Arbuckle comedies. Yet the two men chose to take a multimillion dollar bath. To understand their reasoning, it is necessary to consider the film industry as it existed at the beginning of the 1920s.

From the earliest days of the nickelodeon, the movies had been under the watchful eyes of American's moral guardians. They claimed that the "flickers," with their stark depictions of social ills and sexual liberation, should be confined to burlesque houses away from children and decent folk. Their protests only increased as one community after another opened movie houses that screened affordable daily entertainment to feed the fastest-growing pop culture movement of the new century.

In time, the moralists' ire was directed toward Hollywood, a city whose name had become synonymous not only with its most famous export but also with a phenomenon no one had anticipated: the movie star. Audiences embraced top film players with an unprecedented enthusiasm, adopting their fashions and mimicking their behavior. An insatiable hunger to learn more about those celebrities spawned yet another creation: the fan magazine. The lives of the stars offscreen became intertwined with the roles they portrayed on screen. The studios willingly played up this angle. Publicists were hired and biographies were created to reaffirm for the public that, for example, the Pennsylvania-bred Tom Mix was indeed a cowboy, or that Mary Pickford—in reality a shrewd businesswoman—was the epitome of innocence. The lives of the stars, like the movies themselves, became works of fiction.

This blurred line between fact and fantasy lay at the heart of the issue: If the movies were immoral, their opponents reasoned, it was because the people who made them were im-

moral. Hollywood was a haven for loose behavior, irresponsibility and disrespect for tradition. Its influence was corrupting the nation. It was a modern-day Babylon that needed cleansing.

The anti-Hollywood crowd, allied with reform politicians and sympathetic newspapers, was a powerful and vocal group. A reform movement in the 1910s and '20s could be an effective agent of change no matter what the target: This was an age when the temperance movement succeeded in enacting prohibition. And more and more, reformers were targeting the movies with a cry for censorship.

In the absence of a reaction from the film industry to these pleas, communities organized groups to determine standards for films to be shown within their own borders. As a result, expensive studio productions were going unseen on moral grounds due to the whims of the local committees. As these homegrown organizations found themselves reviewing an increasing amount of Hollywood product, movements for censorship began to take a much broader scope. Various states formed their own review boards. Since the specter of federal government control was what the film industry feared the most, the studio bosses began mulling ways to enact their own standards for censorship before the government did it for them.

Enter Roscoe "Fatty" Arbuckle. As a teenage saloon singer, the Southern California native was in the right place at the right time when the burgeoning film studios came to recruit local talent. On screen, Fatty was an impish overgrown boy, distinguishable from his fellow derby-wearing clowns by his round yet muscular girth. Off screen, Roscoe (never Fatty to his friends) was a generous and affable soul, a man who lived large with an appetite for fun. His career grew as Hollywood grew, and he watched the town evolve from dusty streets among fruit orchards into a community of palm-lined boulevards fronting the lush lawns of spacious estates. By the early 1920s, Arbuckle was at the top of his profession: famous worldwide, beloved in his community and among the best-paid stars in the business.

On Labor Day weekend of 1921, the 34-year-old Roscore ventured upstate to San Francisco for a fun-filled getaway. With two friends in tow, Roscoe arrived in the Golden Gate city late Saturday afternoon and checked into a suite with two bedrooms, each with its own bath, on the 12th floor of the luxurious St. Francis Hotel. The trio contacted a bootlegger and word was spread among a handful of Bay Area acquaintances that the party had started.

By Monday morning, Labor Day, Suite 1220 was the scene of roaring Jazz Age revelry. Bootleg liquor flowed freely. Music blared from a Victrola. Couples paired off. Dozens of people were in and out of the suite at various times. Midafternoon, Roscoe and an actress named Virginia Rappe (pronounced "rap-PAY") were missing from the suite's main room for about 10 minutes. They were next seen when Roscoe exited one of the bedrooms, saying there was something wrong with the girl on the bed. Most of the guests observed a drunken hysterical girl, tearing at her clothing as she writhed with an internal pain that she could not describe. Rappe was dismissed as a victim of too much bathtub gin. Hotel management was contacted, and the young woman was moved to another room to sleep it off. The party resumed and few gave a second thought to the absent guest. Back in his Hollywood home on Friday, September 9, Roscoe was stunned to learn that the actress had died and he was wanted in San Francisco for questioning. It was alleged that the large man had forced sex upon the small-framed girl, rupturing her bladder in the process. For three days she lay in agony before dying. Hours after Roscoe returned to the Bay Area, charges were filed. The next morning's headlines heralded Hollywood's first high-profile murder scandal: ARBUCKLE HELD FOR MURDER!

For some time there had been antagonism in San Francisco toward Hollywood. As the most developed and luxurious of all West Coast towns, the bay city had become a vacation playground for the young and wealthy of filmland, who routinely left the residuals of their bootleg booze and sex parties to be dealt with by local officials. California women, who had gained suffrage 10 years before the national passage of the 19th Amendment, were a powerful influence on San Francisco politics by 1921. At the time of Arbuckle's arrest, their efforts had been focused on cleaning up prostitution and sexual licentiousness. A Hollywood star could not have found a less sympathetic town in which to be charged with a crime.

Two Bay Area notables in particular had ulterior motives for promoting the scandal. One was San Francisco District Attorney Matthew Brady, a reform-minded ex-judge who was preparing a run for governor. Brady intended to try Arbuckle based on information supplied by a party guest named Maude Delmont. She told Brady that a leering, drunken Arbuckle had dragged Rappe into the bedroom and kept her behind the locked door while she cried for help. During the three days Rappe lay dying, she told Delmont, "Roscoe did this to me." This information seemed like a godsend to the ambitious Brady. What better credential to campaign with than that of the man who tamed the moral corruption of Hollywood?

The other man in the mix was William Randolph Hearst. The legendary publishing magnate knew no scruples when it came to selling newspapers. Despite the credo that the accused are innocent until proved guilty, Hearst knew that a guilty Arbuckle played better on the newsstand. The affair became a case study in yellow journalism, with outright fabrications contributing to legends that persist today (e.g., Roscoe raped Virginia with a Coke bottle, Roscoe pranced the room wearing Virginia's panties on his head, etc.). When Hearst cameramen were denied access to Roscoe in his cell, a composite mock-up was created and passed off as the real thing. The public ate it all up. Years later, Hearst would boast that the Arbuckle affair had sold more papers than America's entry into World War I. At the very least, Hearst's efforts ensured that Roscoe would be found guilty in the court of public opinion.

Abetting the controversy were the voices of the ever-present anti-Hollywood crowd. In the scandal they found every justification for their denunciation of the film industry. Ministers and editorialists had a field day. Additionally, news of bootleg liquor's role in the case prompted anti-alcohol leagues to leap into the fray. (Arbuckle would be charged separately for violating the Volsted Act, and he would pay a fine.) Determined that someone should be held accountable for the corruption of America, groups such as the Women's Vigilant Committee of San Francisco demanded that Arbuckle be convicted to set an example.

All this happened without regard to due process. Before a grand jury could convene, District Attorney Brady learned that Delmont's story had holes in it. Further investigation suggested that her tale was entirely of her own creation since she had not even been present in the suite when Arbuckle and Rappe were alone together. The deeper Brady probed into his star witness' background, the more distressing the discoveries: Delmont had a history of making dubious claims and an outstanding arrest warrant for bigamy, and there was the possibility that she had been plotting to set Roscoe up for extortion. Brady knew she would be destroyed under cross-examination.

With his political aspirations on the line, Brady opted to press forward without the testimony of the very person who had brought the charges. He would attempt to try the case with secondary witnesses and circumstantial evidence, which resulted in the judge reducing the charge from murder to involuntary manslaughter. When Brady failed to bring

forth the sole accuser, Roscoe's attorney entered a motion that the case be dropped. The judge denied it with this declaration: "We are not trying Roscoe Arbuckle alone…we are trying our present day morals, our present day social conditions, our present day looseness of thought and lack of social balance. The issue here is really truly larger than the guilt or innocence of this poor, unfortunate man; the issue is universal and grows out of conditions, which are a matter of comment and notoriety and apprehension to every true lover and protector of our American institutions."

His point was clear: Roscoe Arbuckle wasn't on trial, Hollywood was.

Lasky, Zukor and the other studio moguls should have seen it coming. For years they had been using their collective power and influence to protect their industry from such scrutiny. Covering up news of stars' indiscretions was standard operating procedure. In fact, five years earlier Paramount had dealt with a lesser-known Arbuckle controversy. At a stag party during a publicity tour in Boston, some of the hired female "escorts" turned out to be minors. Although it has never been established that Roscoe was directly involved, the studio nonetheless shelled out $100,000 in hush money to the district attorney in order to protect their star comedian's reputation.

But in the hostile San Francisco climate, the moguls—all of them relocated East Coast businessmen—found that they could not buy influence. Aware that their livelihoods were in the cross hairs, they ordered all studio employees—directors, actors, essentially anyone who could vouch for Roscoe's good character—to sit mum lest their own careers suffer collateral damage.

To deflect attention from the scandal, the industry heads agreed that it was necessary to appease Hollywood's loudest critics. It was noted that Major League Baseball had recently faced a similar public relations problem after the 1919 "Black Sox" World Series scandal. In order to restore respectability to their sport, the owners had appointed a public figure with an honest reputation as baseball's first commissioner. Using this template, the studio moguls sought a de facto commissioner for the movies.

That's when they found Will Hays. In 1920, as chairman of the Republican National Committee, Hays was a key figure in securing Ohio Senator Warren G. Harding's nomination for, and election to, the presidency. In turn, Harding made Hays his postmaster general. As a high-profile cabinet member who espoused solid Presbyterian virtues, Hays was seen as a pillar of respectability. One mogul declared that if Hays could convince a majority of Americans to vote for Harding, he would be the perfect man to change the public's perception of Hollywood.

It was a consortium of the top moguls, among them Zukor, Lasky, Marcus Lowes of Lowes Pictures, Samuel Goldwyn of Metro and William Fox of 20th Century Fox, that conceived the MPPDA. Although not created as a censor, the office promised to act as a watchdog over the kind of corrupting influence of which Hollywood was most often accused. Hays was offered $100,000 per year to head the organization. It was a shrewd move. With a cabinet member at its helm, the MPPDA acquired the aura of government intervention without being a government agency.

Meanwhile, 500 miles north of Hollywood, the circus was underway in San Francisco. The case had all the hallmarks one has since come to expect of showbiz scandals: a celebrity defendant, surrounded by the best counsel money could buy—"the million-dollar defense," as the press dubbed it—and a victim, posthumously elevated to sainthood by one side and subjected to the worst of character assassinations by the other. One witness was so pressured from both sides that she escaped through a window while under guard and fled the country. Seemingly every Bay Area resident who had caught a glimpse of either Roscoe or Virginia during that Labor Day weekend had a story to tell. The media made stars out of Arbuckle's estranged wife and

Rappe's grieving fiance. There were charges of evidence tampering and witness coercion, as well as a controversial autopsy.

Trumping all newsmakers was the aforementioned Maude Delmont. With the eyes of the world upon her, this drama queen was in her element, soaking up the attention. The press could always count on her to supply them with freshly remembered "facts" every time her spotlight showed signs of dimming. Before the trial was over, she would serve prison time on the bigamy charge. Later she tried to extend her 15 minutes of fame by touring the lecture circuit as "The Woman Who Accused Fatty Arbuckle."

The proceedings finally opened on November 18, 1921. Brady's team called more than 40 witnesses and turned the courtroom into a display of moral high ground grandstanding. Yet there was little of substance to prove that Arbuckle was a killer. The "million-dollar defense" made fine work of the DA's paper-thin case. Roscoe took the stand and explained to the jury how he entered his bedroom to change clothes and was surprised to find a drunk and ill Virginia Rappe in the adjoining bathroom. The time spent alone with her was to administer care. At no time did he violate the woman.

To observers in the courtroom, the case seemed one-sided for acquittal. But it was not so clear-cut in the jury room. The majority reached a quick conclusion of Arbuckle's innocence, but one juror was steadfast in her resolve that she would "vote guilty until hell freezes over." In the course of the proceedings, the defense learned that this juror was married to a man who had connections in Brady's office. A mistrial was declared and a second jury was assembled.

So confident was the Arbuckle defense during round two that they presented no rebuttal or witnesses; they merely submitted the transcript from the first trial. This legal hubris resulted in a second hung jury, and the case went back for a third trial. It had been four months since the first trial began. An exhausted and dispirited prosecution increasingly unraveled, while the defense pulled out all the stops. It took the jury a mere five minutes to return its not-guilty verdict, much of the time spent drafting a statement to be read into the court record, to leave no doubt about the veracity of the jurors' feelings: "Acquittal is not enough for Roscoe Arbuckle. We feel that a great injustice has been done him. We feel also that it was only our plain duty to give him this exoneration, under the evidence, for there was not the slightest proof adduced to connect him in any way with the commission of a crime. . . ."

Perhaps Arbuckle's career could have recovered had his been the only movieland scandal at the time. Yet the Jazz Age brought with it tales of drug addiction, alcoholism and ruined lives among a galaxy of lesser-known stars. Most significant, shortly after Arbuckle's second deadlocked trial, a scandal erupted that remains one of Hollywood's most notorious unsolved mysteries. On February 1, 1922, William Desmond Taylor, the erudite and charming president of the Motion Picture Director's Guild and a frequent spokesman for the industry on censorship, was discovered murdered in his Hollywood bungalow. A crime scene investigation unveiled hundreds of illicit photographs the director had taken of many of filmdom's most well-known starlets. Further investigation revealed that Taylor was not who he claimed to be. He was, in fact, a "missing person," an Irishman named William Deane-Tanner, who had abandoned his family, reinvented himself as an English sophisticate and successfully integrated himself into the thick of the film industry. Suspicion was high that his dual identity and eventual murder were related to a criminal past.

Because the Taylor killing took place in the heart of the film capital, a cloak of protective secrecy stonewalled the investigation's attempts to tie the murder to the movie business. Charges were never filed. Arbuckle's acquittal on the heels of this only

made matters worse. There was sentiment that despite the presence of the MPPDA, Hollywood was using its power and influence to thumb its nose at justice. The moralistic public was clamoring for accountability. Without it, the moguls feared widespread box office boycotts.

Again, Hollywood took its cue from professional baseball. The previous summer eight players for the Chicago White Sox had been acquitted of charges that they had fixed the 1919 World Series. Nevertheless, the organization handed out lifetime bans to the players as an act of public contrition. Therefore, Lasky and Zukor decided that their star comedian would be the film industry's scapegoat, not just for the Taylor scandal, but for all of Hollywood's real or imagined sins. After all, the trial and bad press rendered Roscoe damaged goods. Despite the fact that several Fatty Arbuckle films had been re-released to record-setting business upon news of the verdict, it was determined advantageous to sacrifice his career for the industry's long-term health.

Zukor presented the idea to Hays, but Hays demurred. Should it be the business of the MPPDA, Hays questioned, to deny an innocent man the right to earn a living? Zukor pressed the case, stating that a ban could only strengthen public perception that the organization was a legitimate power, and simultaneously send a message throughout the film colony that the MPPDA meant business. Hays took the bait. On April 18, 1922, his office announced that Roscoe Arbuckle was banned from working in motion pictures, effective immediately.

It hardly mattered that less than a year later Hays, in a crisis of conscience, partially lifted the ban and permitted Arbuckle to work behind the scenes using the pseudonym William Goodrich (or sometimes presented as the ultimate in-joke: "Will B. Goode"). The plan had succeeded: With Fatty Arbuckle's presence removed from American movie screens, the hottest flashpoint in the moralist vs. Hollywood war had been defused. With the MPPDA now seen as an effective watchdog, the motion picture industry had in its own hip pocket the ability to control public perception. The social reformers who had been hounding Hollywood from the start kept one eye on the film business but gradually toned down their attacks.

Roscoe Arbuckle understood the need for him to take the fall for the industry he helped build. In the remaining 11 years of his life, his spirits fluctuated between stoic acceptance and bitterness. His good name never recovered, mostly due to the damage done by the Hearst news organization. A decade after the scandal, Hays felt Arbuckle had been punished enough and allowed the star, as the character "Fatty," to appear again on screen. A fatal heart attack in June of 1933 ended the comeback. Because many of Arbuckle's most ambitious films were destroyed in the wake of his banishment, his legacy has not benefited from a modern day evaluation of his screen work. Instead, he is best remembered for the scandal that bears his name.

Yet the ripple effect of the Arbuckle affair had a wide reach. Shortly after the trial, the moguls had Hays investigate the rest of filmland's denizens for behavior that could embarrass the studios. It uncovered a culture of drug use, sexual depravity and more. The result was the industry's first blacklist, and more than 120 careers were ended without public hearings or announcements. Morals clauses became a common part of every performer's contract. The MPPDA drew up guidelines for language, law and order, patriotism, religion and on-screen depictions of sex, all of which adhered to a minimum standard that would be acceptable among the most prudish of audiences. Those guidelines were formalized in 1930 as the Motion Picture Production Code, which stayed in effect until the 1960s, when changing times and tastes necessitated its replacement with the current G-through-X rating system.

Study Questions

1. How did the Arbuckle trial change Hollywood?

2. What role did Will Hays serve in Hollywood?

3. Why did Hollywood studio leaders embrace self-censorship?

4. How did the personal ambitions of San Francisco political and cultural leaders influence the Arbuckle case?

5. What part did William Randolph Hearst and his newspaper philosophy play in the Arbuckle case?

6. How did the trial underscore the deep cultural conflict in America?

7. What happened to Arbuckle after the trial?

Bibliography

The Arbuckle case is covered in Andy Edmonds, *Frame Up!: The Untold Story of Roscoe "Fatty" Arbuckle* (1991) and David Yellop, *The Day the Laughter Stopped: The True Story of Fatty Arbuckle* (1976). Lary May, *Screening Out the*

Past: The Birth of Mass Culture and the Motion Picture Industry (1980), presents a vivid cultural portrait of the origins of the motion picture industry in the context of the revolt against Victorian culture. Richard deCordova, *Picture Personalities: The Emergence of the Star System in America* (1990), shows how the star system developed. Neal Gabler, *Life the Movie: How Entertainment Conquered Reality* (1998), is particularly insightful about the role that stars and Hollywood play in American culture.

READING 13

★ ★ ★

Organized Crime in Urban Society: Chicago in the Twentieth Century

Mark Haller

In 1919 Congress adopted the Eighteenth Amendment, which prohibited "the manufacture, sale, or transportation of intoxicating liquors." Prohibition, however, did not stop Americans from manufacturing, selling, or transporting alcohol; it simply made the actions illegal. During the 1920s and early 1930s, criminals rather than businessmen supplied the public's thirst, and often the distinction between the two occupations grew fuzzy. As "Scarface" Al Capone once noted, "I make my money by supplying a public demand. If I break the law, my customers, who number hundreds of the best people in Chicago, are as guilty as I am. . . . Everybody calls me a racketeer. I call myself a businessman. When I sell liquor it's bootlegging. When my patrons serve it on a silver tray on Lake Shore Drive, it's hospitality."

For many Americans, Capone's point was well taken. As a result, criminals achieved a certain social respect and were able to spread their influence into legitimate business. A 1926 congressional investigation demonstrated that organized crime had made significant inroads into the worlds of labor unions, industry, and city governments. By 1933 when Congress repealed the Eighteenth Amendment, organized crime had become a permanent part of the American scene.

In the following essay, historian Mark Haller examines the role of crime in ethnic communities and urban society. Like sports and entertainment, crime served as an avenue out of the ethnic ghettoes and played an important role in the complex urban environment.

Many journalists have written exciting accounts of organized crime in American cities and a handful of scholars have contributed analytical and perceptive studies. Yet neither the excitement in the journalistic accounts nor the analysis in the scholarly studies fully captures the complex and intriguing role of organized criminal activities in American cities during the first third of the twentieth century. The paper that follows, although focusing on Chicago, advances hypotheses that are probably true for other cities as well. The paper examines three major, yet interrelated, aspects of the role of organized crime in the city: first, the social worlds within which the criminals operated and the importance of those worlds in providing social mobility from immigrant ghettos; second, the diverse patterns by which different ethnic groups became involved in organized criminal activities and were influenced by those activities; and third, the broad and pervasive economic impact of organized crime in urban neighborhoods, and the resulting influence that organized crime did exert.

Crime and Mobility

During the period of heavy immigrant movement into the cities of the Northeast and Midwest, organized crime provided paths of upward mobility for many young men raised in ethnic slums. The gambling kings, vice lords, bootleggers, and racketeers often began their careers in the ghetto neighborhoods; and frequently these neighborhoods continued to be the centers for their entrepreneurial activities. A careful study of the leaders of organized crime in Chicago in the late 1920s found that 31 percent were of Italian background, 29 percent of Irish background, 20 percent Jewish, and 12 percent black; none were native white of native white parents. A recognition of the

"Organized Crime in Urban Society: Chicago in the Twentieth Century" by Mark Haller, from *Journal of Social History 5* (Winter, 1971–1972), pp. 210–234. Copyright © 1971 by The Regents of the University of California. Reprinted by permission.

ethnic roots of organized crime, however, is only a starting point for understanding its place in American cities.

At a risk of oversimplification, it can be said that for young persons in the ethnic ghettos three paths lay open to them. The vast majority became, to use the Chicago argot, "poor working stiffs." They toiled in the factories, filled menial service and clerical jobs, or opened mom-and-pop stores. Their mobility to better jobs and to home ownership was, at best, incremental. A second, considerably smaller group followed respectable paths to relative success. Some of this group went to college and entered the professions; others rose to management positions in the business or governmental hierarchies of the city.

There existed, however, a third group of interrelated occupations which, although not generally regarded as respectable, were open to uneducated and ambitious ethnic youths. Organized crime was one such occupational world, but there were others.

One was urban machine politics. Many scholars have, of course, recognized the function of politics in providing mobility for some members of ethnic groups. In urban politics, a person's ethnic background was often an advantage rather than a liability. Neighborhood roots could be the basis for a career that might lead from poverty to great local power, considerable wealth, or both.

A second area consisted of those businesses that prospered through political friendships and contacts. Obviously, construction companies that built the city streets and buildings relied upon government contracts. But so also did banks in which government funds were deposited, insurance companies that insured government facilities, as well as garbage contractors, fraction companies and utilities that sought city franchises. Because political contacts were important, local ethnic politicians and their friends were often the major backers of such enterprises.

A third avenue of success was through leadership in the city's labor unions. The

Irish in Chicago dominated the building trade unions and most of the other craft unions during the first 25 years of this century. But persons of other ethnic origins could also rise to leadership positions, especially in those unions in which their own ethnic group predominated.

Another path of mobility was sports. Boxing, a peculiarly urban sport, rooted in the neighborhood gymnasiums, was the most obvious example of a sport in which Irish champions were succeeded by Jewish, Polish and black champions. Many a fighter, even if he did not reach national prominence, could achieve considerable local fame within his neighborhood or ethnic group. He might then translate this local fame into success by becoming a fight manager, saloon keeper, politician or racketeer.

A fifth area often dominated by immigrants was the entertainment and night life of the city. In Chicago, immigrants—primarily Irish and Germans—ran the city's saloons by the turn of the century. During the 1920s, Greek businessmen operated most of the taxi-dance halls. Restaurants, cabarets and other night spots were similarly operated by persons from various ethnic groups. Night life also provided careers for entertainers, including B-girls, singers, comedians, vaudeville and jazz bands. Jewish comedians of the 1930s and black comedians of our own day are only examples of a larger phenomenon in which entertainment could lead to local and even national recognition.

The organized underworld of the city, then, was not the only area of urban life that provided opportunities for ambitious young men from the ghettos. Rather, it was one of several such areas. Part of the pervasive impact of organized crime resulted from the fact that the various paths were interrelated, binding together the worlds of crime, politics, labor leadership, politically related businessmen, sports figures and the night life of the city. What was the nature of the interrelationships?

To begin with, organized crime often exerted important influences upon the other social worlds. For aspiring politicians, especially during the early years after an ethnic group's arrival in a city, organized crime was often the most important source of money and manpower. (By the turn of the century, an operator of a single policy wheel in Chicago could contribute not only thousands of dollars but also more than a hundred numbers writers to work the neighborhoods on election day.) On occasion, too, criminals supplied strongarm men to act as poll watchers, they organized repeat voters, and they provided other illegal but necessary campaign services. Like others engaged in ethnic politics, members of the organized underworld often acted from motives of friendship and common ethnic loyalties. But because of the very nature of their activities, criminal entrepreneurs required and therefore sought political protection. It would be difficult to exaggerate the importance of organized crime in the management of politics in many of the wards of the city.

Furthermore, it should not be thought that the politics of large cities like Chicago was peculiarly influenced by organized crime. In a large and heterogeneous city, there were always wards within which the underworld exercised little influence and which could therefore elect politicians who would work for honest government and law enforcement. But in the ethnic and blue-collar industrial cities west or southwest of Chicago, the influence of organized crime sometimes operated without serious opposition. In Cicero, west of Chicago along major commuting lines, gambling ran wide open before the 1920s; and after 1923 Capone's bootlegging organization safely had its headquarters there. In other towns, like Stickney and Burnham, prostitution and other forms of entertainment often operated with greater openness than in Chicago. This symbiotic relationship, in which surrounding blue-collar communities provided protected vice and entertainment for the larger city, was not limited to Chicago. Covington, Kentucky, had a similar relationship to Cincinnati, while East St. Louis serviced St. Louis.

The organized underworld was also deeply involved in other areas of immigrant mobility. Organized criminals worked closely with racketeering labor leaders and thus became involved in shakedowns, strike settlements and decisions concerning union leadership. They were participants in the night life, owned many of the night spots in the entertainment districts, and hired and promoted many of the entertainers. (The comedian Joe E. Lewis started his career in Chicago's South Side vice district as an associate and employee of the underworld; his case was not atypical.) Members of the underworld were also sports fans and gamblers and therefore became managers of prize fighters, patrons at the race tracks and loyal fans at ball games. An observer who knew many of Chicago's pimps in the 1920s reported:

The pimp is first, last and always a fight fan. He would be disgraced if he didn't go to every fight in town. . . .

They hang around gymnasiums and talk fight. Many of them are baseball fans, and they usually get up just about in time to go to the game. They know all the players and their information about the game is colossal. Football is a little too highbrow for them, and they would be disgraced if they played tennis, but of late the high-grade pimps have taken to golf, and some of them belong to swell golf clubs.

However, criminals were not merely sports fans; some ran gambling syndicates and had professional interests in encouraging sports or predicting the outcome of sports events. Horse racing was a sport conducted primarily for the betting involved. By the turn of the century, leading gamblers and bookmakers invested in and controlled most of the race tracks near Chicago and in the rest of the nation. A number of successful gamblers had

stables of horses and thus mixed business with pleasure while becoming leading figures in horse race circles. At a less important level, Capone's organization in the late 1920s owned highly profitable dog tracks in Chicago's suburbs.

The fact that the world of crime exerted powerful influences upon urban politics, business, labor unions, sports and entertainment does not adequately describe the interrelations of these worlds. For many ambitious men, the worlds were tied together because in their own lifetimes they moved easily from one area to another or else held positions in two or more simultaneously. In some ways, for instance, organized crime and entertainment were barely distinguishable worlds. Those areas of the city set aside for prostitution and gambling were the major entertainment districts of the city. Many cabarets and other night spots provided gambling in backrooms or in rooms on upper floors. Many were places where prostitutes solicited customers or where customers could find information concerning local houses of prostitution. During the 1920s, places of entertainment often served liquor and thus were retail outlets for bootleggers. In the world of entertainment, the distinction between legitimate and illegitimate was often blurred beyond recognition.

Take, as another example, the career of William Skidmore. At age fourteen, Billie sold racing programs at a race track near Chicago. By the time he was twenty-one, in the 1890s, he owned a saloon and cigar store, and soon had joined with others to operate the major policy wheels in Chicago and the leading handbook syndicate on the West Side. With his growing wealth and influence, he had by 1903 also become ward committeeman in the thirteenth ward and was soon a leading political broker in the city. In 1912 he was Sergeant-at-Arms for the Democratic National Convention and, afterwards, aided Josephus Daniels in running the Democratic National Committee. Despite his success as gambler and politician, his saloon, until well into the 1920s, was a hangout for pickpockets and con men; and "Skid" provided bail and political protection for his criminal friends. In the twenties Skidmore branched into the junk business and made a fortune selling junk obtained through contracts with the county government. Not until the early 1940s did he finally go to prison, the victim of a federal charge of income tax evasion. In his life, it would be impossible to unravel the diverse careers to determine whether he was saloon keeper, gambler, politician or businessman.

The various social worlds were united not simply by the influence of organized crime and by interlocking careers; the worlds also shared a common social life. At local saloons, those of merely local importance met and drank together. At other restaurants or bars, figures of wider importance had meeting places. Until his death in 1920, Big Jim Colossimo's restaurant in the South Side vice district brought together the successful from many worlds; the saloon of Michael (Hinky Dink) Kenna, first ward Alderman, provided a meeting place in the central business district. Political banquets, too, provided opportunities for criminals, police, sports figures and others to gather in honor of a common political friend. Weddings and funerals were occasions when friends met to mark the important passages through life. At the funeral of Colossimo—politician, vice lord and restauranteur—his pallbearers included a gambler, two keepers of vice resorts, and a bailbondsman. Honorary pallbearers were five judges (including the chief judge of the criminal courts), two congressmen, nine resort keepers or gamblers, several aldermen and three singers from the Chicago Opera. (His good friend, Enrico Caruso, was unable to be present.) Such ceremonial events symbolized the overlapping of the many worlds of which a man like Colossimo was a part.

Thus far we have stressed the social structure that linked the criminal to the wider parts of the city within which he operated. That social world was held together by a system of values and beliefs widely shared by those who participated in crime, politics, sports and the night life of the city. Of central importance was the cynical—but not necessarily unrealistic—view that society operated through a process of deals, friendships and mutual favors. Hence the man to be admired was the smart operator and dealer who handled himself well in such a world. Because there was seen to be little difference between a legal and an illegal business, there was a generally tolerant attitude that no one should interfere with the other guy's racket so long as it did not interfere with one's own. This general outlook was, of course, widely shared, in whole or in part, by other groups within American society so that there was no clear boundary between the social world of the smart operators and the wider society.

In a social system held together by friendships and favors, the attitude toward law and legal institutions was complex. A basic attitude was a belief that criminal justice institutions were just another racket—a not unrealistic assessment considering the degree to which police, courts and prosecutor were in fact used by political factions and favored criminal groups. A second basic attitude was a belief that, if anyone cooperated with the law against someone with whom he was associated or to whom he owed favors, he was a stoolpigeon whose behavior was beneath contempt. This does not mean that criminal justice institutions were not used by members of organized crime. On a day-to-day basis, members of the underworld were tied to police, prosecutors and politicians through payments and mutual favors. Criminal groups often used the police and courts to harass rival gangs or to prevent the development of competition. But conflicts between rival groups were also resolved by threats or violence. Rival gambling syndicates bombed each others' places of business, rival union leaders engaged in bombing and slugging, and rival bootlegging gangs after 1923 turned to assassinations that left hundreds dead in the streets of Chicago. The world of the rackets was a tough one in which a man was expected to take his knocks and stand up for himself. Friendship and loyalty were valued; but so also were toughness and ingenuity.

Gangsters, politicians, sports figures and entertainers prided themselves for being smart guys who recognized how the world operated. They felt disdain mixed with pity for the "poor working stiffs" who, ignorant of how the smart guys operated, toiled away at their menial jobs. But if they disdained the life of the working stiffs, they also disdained the pretensions of those "respectable" groups who looked askance at the world within which they operated. Skeptical that anyone acted in accordance with abstract beliefs or universalistic principles, the operators believed that respectable persons were hypocrites. For instance, when Frank J. Loesch, the distinguished and elderly lawyer who headed the Chicago Crime Commission, attacked three criminal court judges for alleged political favoritism, one politician declared to his friends:

Why pick on these three judges when every judge in the criminal court is doing the very same thing, and always have. Who is Frank Loesch that he should holler? He has done the same thing in his day. . . . He has asked for plenty of favors and has always gotten them. Now that he is getting older and is all set and doesn't have to ask any more favors, he is out to holler about every one else. . . . There are a lot of these reformers who are regular racketeers, but it won't last a few years and it will die out.

In short, the worldview of the operators allowed them to see their world as being little different from the world of the respectable persons who looked down upon them. The whole world was a racket.

Ethnic Specialization

Some have suggested that each ethnic group, in its turn, took to crime as part of the early adjustment to urban life. While there is some truth to such a generalization, the generalization obscures more than it illuminates the ethnic experiences and structure of crime. In important respects, each ethnic group was characterized by different patterns of adjustment; and the patterns of involvement in organized crime often reflected the particular broader patterns of each ethnic group. Some ethnic groups—Germans and Scandinavians, for instance—appear not to have made significant contributions to the development of organized crime. Among the ethnic groups that did contribute, there was specialization within crime that reflected broader aspects of ethnic life.

In Chicago by the turn of the century, for example, the Irish predominated in two areas of organized crime. One area was labor racketeering, which derived from the importance of the Irish as leaders of organized labor in general.

The second area of Irish predominance was the operation of major gambling syndicates. Irish importance in gambling was related to a more general career pattern. The first step was often ownership of a saloon, from which the owner might move into both politics and gambling. Many Irish saloon keepers ran handbooks or encouraged other forms of gambling in rooms located behind or over the saloon. Those Irishmen who used their saloon as a basis for electoral politics continued the gambling activities in their saloons and had ties to larger gambling syndicates. Other saloon keepers, while sometimes taking important but backstage political positions such as ward committeeman, developed the gambling syndicates. Handbooks required up-to-the-minute information from race tracks across the country. By establishing poolrooms from which information was distributed to individ-

Ben Shahn's "Prohibition Alley" portrays whiskey barrels, delivered by ship, being stacked under a portrait of Chicago gangster Al Capone, a victim of gang warfare at lower left, and patrons outside a speakeasy at lower right.

ual handbooks, a single individual could control and share in the profits of dozens or even hundreds of handbooks.

The Irish also predominated in other areas of gambling. At the turn of the century they were the major group in the syndicates that operated the policy games, each with hundreds of policy writers scattered in the slum neighborhoods to collect the nickels and dimes of the poor who dreamed of a lucky hit. They also outfitted many of the gambling houses in the Loop which offered roulette, faro, poker, blackjack, craps and other games of chance. Furthermore, many top police officers were Irish and rose through the ranks by attaching themselves to the various political factions of the city. Hence a complex system of Irish politicians, gamblers and police shared in the profits of gambling, protected gambling interests and built careers in the police department or city politics. Historians have long recognized the importance of the Irish in urban politics. In Chicago, at any rate, politics was only part of a larger Irish politics-gambling complex.

The Irish politics-gambling complex remained intact until about World War I. By the 1920s, however, the developing black ghetto allowed black politicians and policy operators to build independent gambling and political organizations linked to the Republicans in the 1920s and the Democratic city machine in the

1930s. By the 1920s, in addition, Jewish gamblers became increasingly important, both in the control of gambling in Jewish neighborhoods and in operations elsewhere. Finally, by the mid-1920s, Italian bootleggers under Capone took over gambling in suburban Cicero and invested in Chicago gambling operations. Gambling had become a complex mixture of Irish, Negro, Jewish and Italian entrepreneurship.

Although the Irish by the twentieth century played little direct role in managing prostitution, Italians by World War I had moved into important positions in the vice districts, especially in the notorious Levee district on the South Side. (Political protection, of course, often had to be arranged through Irish political leaders.) Just as the Irish blocked Italians in politics, so also they blocked Italians in gambling, which was both more respectable and more profitable than prostitution. Hence the importance of Prohibition in the 1920s lay not in initiating organized crime (gambling continued both before and after Prohibition to be the major enterprise of organized crime); rather, Prohibition provided Italians with an opportunity to break into a major field of organized crime that was not already monopolized by the Irish.

This generalization, to some extent, oversimplifies what was in fact a complex process. At first, Prohibition opened up business opportunities for large numbers of individuals and groups, and the situation was chaotic. By 1924, however, shifting coalitions had emerged. Some bootlegging gangs were Irish, including one set of O'Donnell brothers on the far West Side and another set on the South Side. Southwest of the stockyards, there was an important organization, both Polish and Irish, coordinated by "Pollack" Joe Saltis. And on the Near North Side a major group— founded by burglars and hold-up men—was led by Irishmen . . . and Jews. . . . There were, finally, the various Italian gangs, including the Gennas, the Aiellos, and, of course, the Capone organization.

The major Italian bootlegging gang, that associated with the name of Al Capone, built upon roots already established in the South Side vice district. There John Torrio managed houses of prostitution for Big Jim Colossimo. With Colossimo's assassination in 1920, Torrio and his assistant, Capone, moved rapidly to establish a bootlegging syndicate in the Loop and in the suburbs south and west of the city. Many of their associates were persons whom they had known during humbler days in the South Side vice district and who now rose to wealth with them. Nor was their organization entirely Italian. Very early, they worked closely with Irishmen like Frankie Lake and Terry Druggan in the brewing of beer, while Jake Guzik, a Jew and former South Side pimp, became the chief business manager for the syndicate. In the bloody bootlegging wars of the 1920s, the members of the Capone organization gradually emerged as the most effective organizers and most deadly fighters. The success of the organization brought wealth and power to many ambitious Italians and provided them with the means in the late 1920s and early 1930s to move into gambling, racketeering and entertainment, as well as into a broad range of legitimate enterprises. Bootlegging allowed Italians, through entrepreneurial skills and by assassination of rivals, to gain a central position in the organized underworld of the city.

Although Jewish immigrants in such cities as Cleveland and Philadelphia were major figures in bootlegging and thus showed patterns similar to Italians in Chicago, Jews in Chicago were somewhat peripheral figures. By World War I, Chicago Jews, like Italians, made important inroads into vice, especially in vice districts on the West Side. In the 1920s, with the dispersal of prostitution, several Jewish vice syndicates operated on the South and West Sides. Jews were also rapidly invading the world of gambling. Although Jews took part in vice, gambling and bootlegging, they made a special contribution to the organized underworld by providing professional or expert services. Even before World War I, Jews were becoming a majority of the bailbondsmen in the city. By the 1920s, if not before, Jews constituted over half the fences who disposed of stolen goods. (This was, of course, closely related to Jewish predominance as junk dealers and their importance in retail selling.) Jews were also heavily overrepresented among defense attorneys in the criminal courts. It is unnecessary to emphasize that the entrepreneurial and professional services of Jews reflected broader patterns of adaptation to American urban life.

Even within relatively minor underworld positions, specialization by ethnicity was important. A study of three hundred Chicago pimps in the early 1920s, for instance, found that 109 (more than one-third) were black, 60 were Italian, 47 Jewish and 26 Greek. The large proportion of blacks suggests that the high prestige of the pimp among some elements of the lower-class black community is not a recent development but has a relatively long tradition in the urban slum. There has, in fact, long been a close relationship of vice activities and Negro life in the cities. In all probability, the vice districts constituted the most integrated aspect of Chicago society. Black pimps and madams occasionally had white girls working for them, just as white pimps and madams sometimes had black girls working for them. In addition, blacks held many of the jobs in the vice districts, ranging from maids to entertainers. The location of major areas of vice and entertainment around the periphery and along the main business streets of the South Side black neighborhood gave such activities a pervasive influence within the neighborhood.

Black achievements in ragtime and jazz had their roots, at least in part, in the vice and entertainment districts of the cities. Much of the early history of jazz lies among the talented musicians—black and white—who performed in the famous resorts in the Storyville district of New Orleans in the 1890s and early 1900s. With the dissolution of Storyville as a segregated vice district, many talented black musicians carried their styles to Chicago's South Side, to Harlem, and to the cabarets and dance halls of other major cities. In the 1920s, with black performers like King Oliver and Louis Armstrong and white performers like Bix Beiderbecke, Chicago was an important environment for development of jazz styles. Just as Harlem became a center for entertainment and jazz for New Yorkers during prohibition, so the black and tan cabarets and speakeasies of Chicago's South Side became a place where blacks and whites drank, danced and listened to jazz music—to the shock of many respectable citizens. Thus, in ways that were both destructive and productive, the black experience in the city was linked to the opportunities that lay in the vice resorts, cabarets and dance halls of the teeming slums. In the operation of entertainment facilities and policy rackets, black entrepreneurs found their major outlet and black politicians found their chief support.

Until there has been more study of comparative ethnic patterns, only tentative hypotheses are possible to explain why various ethnic groups followed differing patterns. Because many persons involved in organized crime initiated their careers with customers from their own neighborhood or ethnic group, the degree to which a particular ethnic group sought a particular illegal service would influence opportunities for criminal activities. If members of an ethnic group did not gamble, for instance, then ambitious members of that ethnic group could not build gambling syndicates based upon local roots. The general attitude toward law and law enforcement, too, would affect opportunities for careers in illegal ventures. Those groups that became most heavily involved in organized crime migrated from regions in which they had developed deep suspicions of government authority—whether the Irish fleeing British rule in Ireland, Jews escaping from Eastern Europe, Italians migrating from southern Italy or Sicily, or blacks leaving the American

South. Within a community suspicious of courts and government officials, a person in trouble with the law could retain roots and even respect in the community. Within a community more oriented toward upholding legal authority, on the other hand, those engaged in illegal activities risked ostracism and loss of community roots.

In other ways, too, ethnic lifestyles evolved differently. Among both Germans and Irish, for instance, friendly drinking was part of the pattern of relaxation. Although the Irish and Germans by 1900 were the major managers of Chicago's saloons, the meaning of the saloon was quite different for the two groups. German saloons and beer gardens were sometimes for family entertainment and generally excluded gambling or prostitution; Irish saloons, part of an exclusively male social life, often featured prostitution or gambling and fit more easily into the world of entertainment associated with organized crime. Finally, it appears that south Italians had the highest homicide rate in Europe. There was, in all probability, a relationship between the cultural factors that sanctioned violence and private revenge in Europe and the factors that sanctioned the violence with which Italian bootleggers worked their way into a central position in Chicago's organized crime.

There were, at any rate, many ways that the immigrant background and the urban environment interacted to influence the ethnic experience with organized crime. For some ethnic groups, involvement in organized crime was not an important part of the adjustment to American urban life. For other groups, involvement in the organized underworld both reflected and influenced their relatively unique patterns of acculturation.

Economic Impact

The economic role of organized crime was an additional factor underlying the impact of organized crime upon ethnic communities and urban society. Organized crime was important because of the relatively great wealth of the most successful criminals, because of the large numbers of persons directly employed by organized crime, and because of the still larger numbers who supplemented their income through various part-time activities. And all of this does not count the multitude of customers who bought the goods and services offered by the bootleggers, gambling operators and vice lords of the city.

During the first thirty or forty years after an immigrant group's arrival, successful leaders in organized crime might constitute a disproportionate percentage of the most wealthy members of the community. In the 1930s at least one-half of the blacks in Chicago worth more than $100,000 were policy kings; Italian bootleggers in the 1920s may have represented an even larger proportion of the very wealthy among immigrants from southern Italy. The wealth of the successful criminals was accompanied by extensive political and other contacts that gave them considerable leverage both within and outside the ethnic community. They had financial resources to engage in extensive charitable activities, and often did so lavishly. Projects for improvement of ethnic communities often needed their support and contacts in order to succeed. Criminals often invested in or managed legitimate business enterprises in their communities. Hence, despite ambiguous or even antagonistic relations that they had with "respectable" members of their ethnic communities, successful leaders in organized crime were men who had to be reckoned with in the ethnic community and who often represented the community to the outside world.

In organized crime, as in other economic activities, the very successful were but a minority. To understand the economic impact of crime, it is necessary to study the many persons at the middle and lower levels of organization. In cities like Chicago the number of persons directly employed in the activities of organized crime was considerable. A modest estimate of the number of full-time prostitutes in Chicago about 1910 would be 15,000—not counting madams, pimps, procurers and others in managerial positions. Or take the policy racket. In the early 1930s an average policy wheel in the black ghetto employed 300 writers; some employed as many as 600; and there were perhaps 6,000 policy writers in the ghetto. The policy wheels, in this period of heavy unemployment, may have been the major single source of employment in the black ghetto, a source of employment that did not need to lay off workers or reduce wages merely because the rest of the economy faced a major depression. Finally, during the 1920s, bootlegging in its various aspects was a major economic activity employing thousands in manufacture, transportation and retailing activities.

Yet persons directly employed constituted only a small proportion of those whose income derived from organized crime. Many persons supplemented their income through occasional or part-time services. While some prostitutes walked the streets to advertise their wares, others relied upon intermediaries who would direct customers in return for a finder's fee. During certain periods, payments to taxi drivers were sufficiently lucrative so that some taxi drivers would pick up only those passengers seeking a house of prostitution. Bellboys, especially in the second-class hotels, found the function of negotiating between guests and prostitutes a profitable part of their service. (Many of the worst hotels, of course, functioned partly or wholly as places of assignation.) Bartenders, newsboys and waiters were among the many helpful persons who provided information concerning places and prices.

Various phases of bootlegging during the 1920s were even more important as income supplements. In the production end, many slum families prepared wine or became "alky cookers" for the bootlegging gangs—so much

so that after the mid-1920s, explosions of stills and the resulting fires were a major hazard in Chicago's slum neighborhoods. As one observer reported:

During Prohibition times many respectable Sicilian men were employed as "alky cookers" for the Capones, the Aiellos or for personal use. Many of these people sold wine during Prohibition and their children delivered it on foot or by streetcar without the least fear that they might be arrested. . . .

During the years of 1927 to 1930 more wine was made than during any other years and even the "poorest people" were able to make ten or fifteen barrels each year—others making sixty, seventy, or more barrels.

Other persons, including policemen, moonlighted as truck drivers who delivered booze to the many retail outlets of the city. Finally, numerous persons supplemented their income by retailing booze, including bellboys, janitors in apartment buildings and shoe shine boys.

The many persons who mediated between the underworld and the law were another group that supplemented its income through underworld contacts. Large numbers of policemen, as well as bailiffs, judges and political fixers, received bribes or political contributions in return for illegal cooperation with the underworld. Defense attorneys, tax accountants and bailbondsmen, in return for salaries or fees, provided expert services that were generally legal.

For many of the small businessmen of the city, retailing the goods or services of the underworld could supplement business income significantly. Saloons, as already mentioned, often provided gambling and prostitution as an additional service to customers. Large numbers of small businesses were outlets for handbooks, policy, baseball pools, slot machines and other forms of gambling. A substantial proportion of the cigar stores, for example, were primarily fronts for gambling;

barber shops, pool halls, newsstands, and small hotels frequently sold policy or would take bets on the horses. Drug stores often served as outlets for cocaine and, during the 1920s, sometimes sold liquor.

The organized underworld also influenced business activity through racketeering. A substantial minority of the city's labor unions were racketeer-controlled; those that were not often used the assistance of racketeer unions or of strongarm gangs during strikes. The leaders of organized crime, as a result, exercised control or influence in the world of organized labor. Not so well known was the extensive racketeering that characterized small business organizations. The small businesses of the city were generally marginal and intensely competitive. To avoid cutthroat competition, businessmen often formed associations to make and enforce regulations illegally limiting competition. The Master Barbers Association, for example, set minimum prices, forbad a shop to be open after 7:30 P.M. and ruled that no shop could be established within two blocks of another shop. Many other types of small businesses formed similar associations: dairies, auto parts dealers, garage owners, candy jobbers, butcher stores, fish wholesalers and retailers, cleaners and dyers, and junk dealers. Many of the associations were controlled, or even organized, by racketeers who levied dues upon association members and controlled the treasuries; they then used a system of fines and violence to insure that all businessmen in the trade joined the association and abided by the regulations. In return for control of the association's treasury, in short, racketeers performed illegal services for the association and thereby regulated much of the small business activity of the city.

Discussion of the economic influence of organized crime would be incomplete without mentioning the largest group that was tied economically to the underworld, namely, the many customers for the illegal goods and ser-

vices. Like other retailers in the city, some leaders of organized crime located their outlets near the center of the city or along major transportation lines and serviced customers from the entire region; others were essentially neighborhood businessmen with a local clientele. In either case, those providing illegal goods and services usually attempted to cultivate customer loyalty so that the same customers would return on an ongoing basis and advertise among their friends. Organized crime existed because of wide customer demand, and a large proportion of the adult population of the city was linked to organized crime on a regular basis for purchase of goods and services.

Heroism and Ambiguity

Because of the diverse ways that successful criminal entrepreneurs influenced the city and ethnic communities, many of them became heroes—especially within their own communities. There were a variety of reasons for the admiration that they received. Their numerous philanthropies, both large and small, won them reputations as regular guys who would help a person in need. Moreover, they were often seen as persons who fought for their ethnic communities. They aided politicians from their communities to win elections in the rough and often violent politics of the slums and thereby advanced their ethnic group toward political recognition. Sometimes they were seen as fighters for labor unions and thus as friends of labor. And, on occasion, they fought directly for their ethnic group. There was, for instance, the case of the three Miller brothers from Chicago's West Side Jewish ghetto. In typical ghetto pattern, one became a boxer, one a gangster and one a policeman. The boxer and gangster were heroes among Jews on the West Side, where for many years Jewish peddlers and junk dealers had been subjected to racial slurs and violent attacks by young hoodlums from other ethnic groups. "What I have done from the time I was a boy," Davy Miller told a reporter,

was to fight for my people here in the Ghetto against Irish, Poles or any other nationality. It was sidewalk fighting at first. I could lick any five boys or men in a sidewalk free-for-all.

When the Miller brothers and their gang protected the Jews of the West Side, the attacks against them abated.

Particularly for youngsters growing up in the ghettos, the gangsters were often heroes whose exploits were admired and copied. Davy Miller modestly recognized this when he said:

Maybe I am a hero to the young folks among my people, but it's not because I'm a gangster. It's because I've always been ready to help all or any of them in a pinch.

An Italian student at the University of Chicago in the early 1930s remembered his earlier life in the Italian ghetto:

For 26 years I lived in West Side "Little Italy," the community that has produced more underworld limelights than any other area in Chicago. . . .

I remember these men in large cars, with boys and girls of the neighborhood standing on the running board. I saw them come into the neighborhood in splendor as heroes. Many times they showered handfuls of silver to youngsters who waited to get a glance at them—the new heroes—because they had just made headlines in the newspapers. Since then I have seen many of my playmates shoot their way to the top of gangdom and seen others taken for a ride.

Nevertheless, despite the importance of gangsters and the world within which they moved, their relations to ethnic groups and the city were always ambiguous. Because many of their activities were illegal, they often faced the threat of arrest and, contrary to common belief, frequently found themselves behind bars. Furthermore, for those members of the ethnic community who pursued respectable paths to success, gangsters gave the ethnic group a bad name and remained a continuing source of embarrassment. St. Clair Drake and Horace R. Cayton, in their book on the Chicago black ghetto, describe the highly ambiguous and often antagonistic relations of the respectable black middle class and the policy kings. In his book on Italians in Chicago, Humbert S. Nelli explains that in the 1920s the Italian language press refused to print the name of Al Capone and covered the St. Valentine's Day massacre without suggesting its connection with bootlegging wars.

The respectable middle classes, however, were not the only ones unhappy about the activities or notoriety of gangsters. Organized crime sometimes contributed to the violence and fear of violence that pervaded many of the ghetto neighborhoods. Often local residents feared to turn to the police and lived with a stoical acceptance that gangs of toughs controlled elections, extorted money from local businesses and generally lived outside the reach of the law. Some immigrant parents, too, resented the numerous saloons, the open prostitution and the many gambling dens—all of which created a morally dangerous environment in which to raise children. Especially immigrant women, who watched their husbands squander the meager family income on liquor or gambling, resented the activities of organized crime. Within a number of neighborhoods, local churches and local leaders undertook sporadic campaigns for better law enforcement.

Organized crime, then, was an important part of the complex social structure of ethnic communities and urban society in the early twentieth century. For certain ethnic groups, organized crime both influenced and reflected the special patterns by which the groups adjusted to life in urban America. Through organized crime, many members of those ethnic groups could achieve mobility out of the ethnic ghettos and into the social world of crime, politics, ethnic business, sports, and entertainment. Those who were successful in organized crime possessed the wealth and contacts to exercise broad influence within the ethnic communities and the city. The economic activities of the underworld provided jobs or supplemental income for tens of thousands. Despite the importance of organized crime, however, individual gangsters often found success to be ambiguous. They were not always able to achieve secure positions or to translate their positions into respectability.

Study Questions

1. What were the primary occupational paths out of the ghetto for uneducated but ambitious ethnic youths? How were the paths interrelated?

2. How did organized crime exert influence upon other social worlds? What, in particular, was the relationship between organized crime and urban politics?

3. What social values did criminals share with the leaders in politics, sports, labor unions, entertainment, and business? What was the attitude of the men in these professions toward law and legal institutions?

4. What does Haller mean by "ethnic specialization" in crime? What factors account for the criminal specialization of the different ethnic groups?

5. What was the economic impact of organized crime on the ethnic and urban environment?

6. Why did a number of criminals become ethnic heroes? What role did the "criminal heroes" play in their ethnic neighborhoods?

Bibliography

Because of the secretive nature of organized crime, it has proven an elusive subject for scholars. Nevertheless historians and sociologists have produced several valuable studies. Andrew Sinclair, *Prohibition: The Era of Excess* (1962), examines the impact of the Eighteenth Amendment on the rise of organized crime. Works by Humbert S. Nelli, *The Italians in Chicago, 1880–1930: A Study in Ethnic Mobility* (1970) and *The Business of Crime* (1976), deal admirably with the subject of ethnic crime. John A. Gardiner, *The Politics of Corruption: Organized Crime in the American City* (1970), is also valuable. William F. Whyte, *Street Corner Society: The Social Structure of an Italian Slum* (1955), is a classic sociological study of an ethnic urban environment. Finally, Daniel Bell, *The End of Ideology* (1961), considers crime as a means of social and economic mobility. Thomas Reppetto, *American Mafia: A History of Its Rise to Power* (2004), seeks to dispel common myths of mafia action and connect organize crime to political power struggles.

PART

5

★ ★ ★

Depression and War

Despite all the talk about prosperity and progress in the 1920s, there were disturbing signs that the economy was not as healthy as people assumed. Throughout the decade, agricultural prices steadily declined as production rose, in what many called a "poverty of abundance." In face of high protective tariffs, foreign trade gradually declined, and the production of durable, domestic goods peaked in 1927. When the bubble burst with the crash of the stock market in October 1929, most Americans were shocked. The shock soon turned to despair as banks failed in record numbers, small businesses closed their doors, and unemployment reached unheard-of levels. How could it have been? For three centuries the world viewed America as the land of opportunity. Suddenly, people were losing their jobs, homes, and life savings. The American dream had become a nightmare.

Bewildered with their plight, most Americans were desperate for answers. Socialists and Communists blamed capitalism, arguing that, just as Karl Marx had predicted, the system was collapsing under the weight of its own corruption and exploitation. The technocrats claimed that industrialization had run its course and that a new social order, based on science and technology, would soon emerge out of the rubble of the Depression. Businessmen blamed politicians for the trouble. Farmers saw bogeymen in bankers and commodities speculators. Some Americans even blamed Jews for the collapse. Abandoning laissez-faire economics, Hoover modestly tried to reorganize the federal government to fight the Depression, but his efforts failed. In the next presidential election, Americans put Franklin D. Roosevelt into the White House.

Roosevelt was an unlikely hero for an impoverished nation. Born to old wealth and raised in splendor, he had little understanding of economics and no empathy for poverty. But he did have keen political instincts and few philosophical inhibitions. In a whirlwind of activity, the New Deal greatly increased relief spending, attacked specific problems in the money markets, and tried, usually in a haphazard way, to stimulate an industrial recovery. Although it took World War II to finally lift the country out of the Depression, Franklin D.

Roosevelt nevertheless became one of the most beloved presidents in American history, popular enough to win reelection in 1936, 1940, and 1944. People remembered him for the spark in his eye, his smiling face and cocked head, and his uncompromising exuberance. To men working on government projects, it was Roosevelt who took them away from the soup lines. To farm wives living in poverty, it was Roosevelt who brought the electric transmission lines, the subsidy check, and the refinanced mortgage. To mass production workers, it was Roosevelt who sanctioned their labor unions and brought minimum wages. And to old people, it was Roosevelt who provided for their futures with Social Security.

But just as Roosevelt was easing fears about the economic future, political developments in Europe were bringing new tensions to a weary nation. Adolf Hitler's designs on Austria, Czechoslovakia, and Poland in 1938 and 1939 convinced many that another war was imminent and that the problems of the Depression, as bad as they were, would only be child's play compared to a new global conflagration. Hitler's conquest of France and the Low Countries in 1940, the assault on Great Britain, and the invasion of the Soviet Union in 1941 only confirmed those fears. For a brief time, the United States was caught between its historic need for isolation and its responsibilities as a global leader. On December 7, 1941, Japan resolved America's uncertain position.

READING 14

★ ★ ★

F.D.R.'s Extra Burden

Bernard Asbell

When President Franklin D. Roosevelt collapsed and died of a stroke on April 12, 1945, the nation went into a state of depression unknown since the death of Abraham Lincoln. Like Lincoln, Roosevelt had become inseparably linked with a series of national crises—in his case the Great Depression and World War II. And like Lincoln, Roosevelt was viewed as a savior, a man who had redeemed his people, first from starvation and then from the specter of fascist oppression. Put simply, FDR enjoyed the elusive charisma so prized by politicians. Blessed with enormous self-confidence and an ingratiating personality, he inspired tremendous loyalty among most Americans. They loved him and put him in the White House on four separate occasions—1932, 1936, 1940, and 1944. But like all charismatic leaders, Roosevelt also generated tremendous hostility in some circles, particularly in corporate boardrooms and the parlors of the well-to-do. They viewed him as a "traitor to his class," a politician so seduced by power that he posed a threat to property and the social order.

Franklin D. Roosevelt was a complicated man, a beloved acquaintance of thousands but an intimate of very few. Born rich and raised in pampered splendor, he nevertheless led a virtual revolution in public policy, giving ethnic minorities, labor unions, and poor people their first taste of influence at the federal level. Although Roosevelt inspired a legion of intellectuals to invest their energies in public service, he was not an innovative thinker himself. He preferred the give and take of politics, and the inherent excitement of its risks, to the intricate must and bolts of social and economic policy. His public persona was overwhelming, but there was also a private side to his life that the American people understood only superficially. During the summer of 1921, little more than a decade before he became president, Roosevelt contracted polio, or infantile paralysis, a disease that crippled him for the rest of his life. In "F.D.R.'s Extra Burden," Bernard Asbell describes that paralysis and how Roosevelt, the press, and the nation handled it.

Every campaigner, especially for leadership of a large and complex state or for national office, is a cripple.

His legs are bound against running faster than his constituents are able to keep in step. His hands are tied by the limited powers of the office he seeks; he had better not promise what he knows he cannot deliver. His tongue is gagged against pronouncements that may make new friends if those pronouncements will also make new enemies. His balance is threatened by the pulls and tugs of conflicting demands for justice—shall money go for this urgent need or that one?—shall this group's freedom be expanded at the expense of that one's?

Immobilized by these paralyzing constraints, the candidate has to make himself appear able-bodied, attractive, confident, and powerful. At least more so than his opponent.

Being crippled—not in metaphor, but in reality—is perhaps good schooling for politics.

To this day, more than a quarter century after his death, people keep wondering aloud and speculating, "If Roosevelt had not been a cripple, would he have been the same kind of President?" Of course not. "If a different kind, how?" Impossible to say. "If he had not been a cripple, would he have become president at all?" Again, imponderable.

Did F.D.R.'s private battle teach him to identify with those who suffer? Unquestionably. Moreover it taught him the uses of patience (never a strong suit with crusaders who relied upon him, upon whom he relied, yet who continually harassed him). It heightened his sense of time and timing. "It made him realize"—an observation of Egbert Curtis, a Warm Springs companion—"that he was not infallible, that everything wasn't always going to go his way." More than anything, it forced him to study the uses of handicap, paradoxi-

cally giving him a leg up in a profession of able-bodied crippled men.

Let's not carry theory and speculation too far. Instead, let's try to observe firsthand, insofar as the written word permits, the connections between suffering and Roosevelt's acquired capacity for patience, for tolerance and respect of the wills and ambitions of others, for turning handicap into power.

We begin with his own words. A sufferer identifies with sufferers; and "Doctor" Roosevelt of Warm Springs also identified with other doctors. In F.D.R.'s early days at Warm Springs a South Carolina physician wrote to Roosevelt for a personal case report that might help him treat any polio patients who came his way. Roosevelt's reply is the only detailed personal account of what he had recently endured. The letter, dictated to Missy Le-Hand, his private secretary, during their first stay at Warm Springs, says in part:

. . . I am very glad to tell you what I can in regard to my case and as I have talked it over with a great many doctors can, I think, give you a history of the case which would be equal to theirs.

First symptoms of the illness appeared in August, 1921. . . . By the end of the third day practically all muscles from the chest down were involved. Above the chest the only symptom was a weakening of the two large thumb muscles making it impossible to write. There was no special pain along the spine and no rigidity of the neck.

For the following two weeks I had to be catheterized and there was slight, though not severe, difficulty in controlling the bowels. The fever lasted for only 6 or 7 days, but all the muscles from the hips down were extremely sensitive to the touch and I had to have the knees supported by pillows. This condition of extreme discomfort lasted about 3 weeks . . . [but] disappeared gradually over a period of six months, the last remaining point being the calf muscles.

"F.D.R.'s Extra Burden" by Bernard Asbell, from *American Heritage* (June, 1973). Reprinted by permission of Curtis Brown, Ltd. Copyright © 1973 by Bernard Asbell.

As to treatment—the mistake was made for the first 10 days of giving my feet and lower legs rather heavy massage. This was stopped by Dr. Lovett, of Boston, who was, without doubt, the greatest specialist on infantile paralysis. In January, 1922, 5 months after the attack, he found that the muscles behind the knees had contracted and that there was a tendency to footdrop in the right foot. These were corrected by the use of plaster casts during two weeks. In February, 1922, braces were fitted on each leg from the hips to the shoes, and I was able to stand up and learned gradually to walk with crutches. At the same time gentle exercises were begun, first every other day, then daily, exercising each muscle 10 times and seeking to avoid any undue strain by giving each muscle the correct movement with gravity. These exercises I did on a board placed on the bed.

The recovery of muscle paralysis began at this time, though for many months it seemed to make little progress. In the summer of 1922 I began swimming and found that this exercise seemed better adapted than any other because all weight was removed from the legs and I was able to move the legs in the water far better than I had expected. . . .

I still wear braces, of course, because the quadriceps are not yet strong enough to bear my weight. One year ago I was able to stand in fresh water without braces when the water was up to my chin. Six months ago I could stand in water up to the top of my shoulders and today can stand in water just level with my arm pits. This is a very simple method for me of determining how fast the quadriceps are coming back. Aside from these muscles the waist muscles on the right side are still weak and the outside muscles on the right leg have strengthened so much more than the inside muscles that they pull my right foot forward. I continue corrective exercises for all the muscles.

To sum up I would give you the following "Don'ts".

Don't use heavy massage but use light massage rubbing always towards the heart.

Don't let the patient over-exercise any muscle or get tired.

Don't let the patient feel cold, especially the legs, feet or any other part affected. Progress stops entirely when the legs or feet are cold.

Don't let the patient get too fat.

The following treatment is so far the best, judging from my own experience and that of hundreds of other cases which I have studied:

1. Gentle exercise especially for the muscles which seem to be worst affected.

2. Gentle skin rubbing—not muscle kneading—bearing in mind that good circulation is a prime requisite.

3. Swimming in warm water—lots of it.

4. Sunlight—all the patient can get, especially direct sunlight on the affected parts. It would be ideal to lie in the sun all day with nothing on. This is difficult to accomplish but the nearest approach to it is a bathing suit.

5. Belief on the patient's part that the muscles are coming back and will eventually regain recovery of the affected parts. There are cases known in Norway where adults have taken the disease and not been able to walk until after a lapse of 10 or even 12 years.

I hope that your patient has not got a very severe case. They all differ, of course, in the degree in which the parts are affected. If braces are necessary there is a man in New York . . . who makes remarkable light braces of duraluminum. My first braces of steel weighed 7 lbs. apiece—my new ones weigh only 4 lbs. apiece. Remember that braces are only for the convenience of the patient in getting around—a leg in a brace does not have a chance for muscle development. This muscle development must come through exercise when the brace is not on—such as swimming, etc.

At Hyde Park, before discovering Warm Springs, this powerful man, to the shock of his children and friends, practiced dragging himself crablike across the floor, explaining that the one fear he ever knew was that of being caught in a fire. Then, showing off his inordinately strong shoulders and arms, he filled the house with laughter, wrestling his boys on the floor two at a time. His mother ordered an electric tricycle from Europe, but F.D.R. used it only once. He didn't want his muscles worked; he wanted to work them himself.

John Gunther describes Roosevelt's determination to get from floor to floor unaided: "Day after day he would haul his dead body weight up the stairs by the power of his hands and arms, step by step, slowly, doggedly; the sweat would pour off his face, and he would tremble with exhaustion. Moreover he insisted on doing this with members of the family or friends watching him, and he would talk all the time as he inched himself up little by little, talk, and make people talk back. It was a kind of enormous spiritual catharsis—as if he had to do it, to prove his independence, and had to have the feat witnessed, to prove that it was nothing."

At Warm Springs in 1924 he concentrated on the day he would be able to walk unaided with braces. Braces, which he once said he "hated and mistrusted," which he could not put on or take off by himself, made him like a man on stilts. Unable to flex his toes, he had no balance. In 1928, after seven years of immobility and more than four years of daring and persevering, one day, finally, triumphantly, he hobbled most of the way across the living-room floor of his cottage—with braces, but without human help. The achievement was exhausting—and was never to be accomplished again. Years later, according to Grace Tully, "Missy's eyes filled up when on occasions she reminisced about those days." Roosevelt liked to maintain the belief that if he had had another year before the demand that he run for governor, he'd have mastered walking with a single brace.

In the summer of 1928 at Warm Springs, shortly after Roosevelt agreed to address the Democratic National Convention at Houston, his son Elliott, eighteen, was visiting. One

Throughout his presidency, the press seldom printed pictures showing FDR in a wheelchair or with leg braces. This photograph humanizes him and would have been seen by few Americans.

evening Roosevelt was lost in concentrated thought when suddenly he burst out:

"With my hand on a man's arm, *and one cane*—I'm sure. Let's try it!"

A fellow polio victim, Turnley Walker, Roosevelt's dinner guest, described what then happened and was repeated over and over:

First Roosevelt would get over to the wall and balance there with his cane. It was an ordinary cane but he held it in a special way, with his index finger extended down along the rod from the handle. This finger acted as a rigid cleat . . . so that the strenght of the massive arm and shoulder rammed straight along the cane to its tip against the floor.

"Now, Elliott, you get on the left, my weak side." Elliott watchfully took his place and [Helena] Mahoney [a physiotherapist] came forward to show him how to hold his right arm against his middle at the proper angle and lock it there with a clenching of his biceps.

"Remember that a polio needs more than a fingertip of guidance—he needs an iron bar," said Mahoney, *"Make a habit of holding that arm there. Never forget the job it's got to do."*

"Let's go," said Roosevelt, and he reached out to find the proper grip. Elliott had never felt his father's hand touching him that way. He had been grabbed and hugged, and even tossed and caught with wild energy when he was younger. But now the fingers sought their grip with a kind of ruthless desperation. . . . The pressure became stronger than he had expected as his father pressed down to hitch one braced leg forward for the first step. "You must go right with him," said Mahoney sternly. "Watch his feet. Match your strides with his." Elliott stared down as the rigid feet swung out slowly, and through the pressing hand he could feel the slow, clenching effort of his father's powerful body.

"Don't look at me, Son. Keep your head up, smiling, watching the eyes of people. Keep them from noticing what we're doing."

The cane went out, the good leg swung, the pressure came, the weak leg hitched up into its arc and then fell stiffly into the proper place against the floor. Elliott carefully coordinated his own legs, and they moved across the room.

Roosevelt set his hips against the far wall and told Elliott to rest his arm. "We'll do beautifully," he said.

They went across the room and back again. It was becoming somewhat easier.

"As soon as you feel confident, Son, look up and around at people, the way you would do if I weren't crippled."

"But don't forget," Mahoney warned, "if he loses his balance, he'll crash down like a tree."

"Don't scare us," said Roosevelt.

. . . The cane, the swing, the pressure, the swing. Elliott found that he could look up now and then as they advanced. He caught his father's eyes, the broad smile which was held with a very slight rigidity. . . . Only then did he notice that his father was perspiring heavily.

Yet except when a public show required such extraordinary exertion, Roosevelt was as helpless as a baby. When no strangers were around to see, he let himself be carried by practiced attendants. When F.D.R. became governor, his cousin Nicholas Roosevelt spent a weekend at Hyde Park and later recalled: "His mother and I stood on the veranda watching his son Elliott and Gus Gennerich, the state trooper who acted as his personal bodyguard, carry him down the steps and place him in the car. As they turned and left him, he lost his balance (his powerful torso was much heavier than his crippled legs), and he fell over on the car seat. I doubt if one man in a thousand as disabled and dependent on others would have refrained from some sort of reproach, however mild, to those whose carelessness had thus left him in the lurch. But Franklin merely lay on his back, waved his strong arms in the air and laughed. At once they came back and helped him to his seat behind the wheel, and he called me to join him."

Louis Howe, F.D.R.'s indispensable factotum, set an iron rule—one that F.D.R. was not inclined to resist—that he never be carried in public.

Frances Perkins remembered the gubernatorial campaign.

I saw him speak in a small hall in New York City's Yorkville district. The auditorium was crowded. . . . The only possible way for any candidate to enter the stage without being crushed by the throng was by the fire escape. I realized with sudden horror that the only way he could get over that fire escape was in the arms of strong men. That was how he arrived.

Those of us who saw this incident, with our hands on our throats to hold down our emotion, realized that this man had accepted the ultimate humility which comes from being helped physically. . . . He got up on his braces, adjusted them, straightened himself, smoothed his hair, linked his arm in his son Jim's, and

walked out on the platform as if this were
nothing unusual. . . . I began to see what the
great teachers of religion meant when they
said that humility is the greatest of virtues, and
that if you can't learn it, God will teach it to
you by humiliation.

Was humility—or humiliation—Roosevelt's
great teacher? Many have speculated. Harold
Ickes, after a day in a campaign car with press
secretary Steve Early:

"[Early] recalled the campaign trips that he
had made with Roosevelt when the latter was
a candidate for vice president in 1920. He said
that if it hadn't been for the President's affliction, he never would have been President of
the United States. In those earlier years, as
Steve put it, the President was just a playboy. . . . He couldn't be made to prepare his
speeches in advance, preferring to play cards
instead. During his long illness, according to
Steve, the President began to read deeply and
study public questions."

Perkins: ". . . He had become conscious of
other people, of weak people, of human frailty.
I remember thinking that he would never be so
hard and harsh in judgment on stupid people—even on wrongdoers. . . . I remember
watching him [as governor] in Utica. . . . Certainly some of the Democratic rank-and-file
were pretty tiresome, with a lot of things to
say that were of no consequence. However, he
sat and nodded and smiled and said, 'That's
fine,' when they reported some slight progress. I remembered, in contrast, how he had
walked away from bores a few years earlier
when he was in the State Senate.

"Now he could not walk away when he was
bored. He listened, and out of it learned. . .
that 'everybody wants to have the sense of belonging, of being on the inside,' that 'no one
wants to be left out' as he put it years later in
a Columbus, Ohio, speech. . . . "

A considerably more speculative observation by Noel F. Busch, childhood neighbor of
the Oyster Bay Roosevelts who grew up to be

a *Time* correspondent and avid F.D.R.-
watcher: "Loss of the use of one's legs has several effects on the human psyche. One is that,
when deprived of the power to move around,
the mind demands a substitute or compensa-
tion for this power, such as the ability to command other people to move around. That is
why almost all invalids tend to be peevish and
demanding. However . . . Roosevelt sublimated
and refined the pardonable peevishness of the
normal invalid into an administrative urge
which would have had profound consequences for him even if he had never become
President."

Biographer Emil Ludwig: "The privilege of
remaining seated, which everyone concedes
him because of his affliction, starts him off with
an advantage in his intercourse with others, in
the same way as the smallness of Napoleon's
stature compelled everyone standing before
him to bend his back a little. Certainly giants
like Bismarck or Lincoln had an advantage
when they appeared before men, but the same
effect can be produced by the opposite, by a
weakness, and as Roosevelt looks up at everyone standing in front of him, he has accustomed himself to an upward and therefore very
energetic gesture of the chin which counteracts
the danger of his conciliatory smile."

While never mentioning his paralysis in
public (until his last speech to Congress in
1945) and seldom privately, F.D.R. could
come down fiercely on those he felt mentioned
it unfairly. Huey Long's tapping a straw hat on
the useless Presidential knee he could take as
bad manners—the other fellow's problem, not
his. But when Fulton Oursler brought him a
manuscript of a profile of F.D.R. by Jay
Franklin to be published in *Liberty*—the editor
courteously seeking F.D.R.'s reaction—
Oursler saw "a red flush rise on his neck like
the temperature in a thermometer." Assuming
that Roosevelt was angered over some political needing, he learned otherwise:

"Mr. Oursler, there is only one statement in
this article that I want corrected. The author

says in this line here that I have 'never entirely recovered from infantile paralysis.' *Never recovered what?* I have *never recovered* the complete use of my knees. Will you *fix* that?"

His reticence to mention it—and the released heat that accompanied exceptions—was shared by Mrs. Roosevelt. At an Akron, Ohio, lecture she was asked: "Do you think your husband's illness has affected his mentality?" Betraying no emotion as she read the written question aloud, she paused for an extra cooling moment and replied:

"I am glad that question was asked. The answer is yes. Anyone who has gone through great suffering is bound to have a greater sympathy and understanding of the problems of mankind." The audience rose in an ovation.

He was frequently torn between keeping his silence and protesting his case. On April 6, 1938, he wrote to an "old friend"—Elliott's description—mentioning his affliction. The important thing is not what he wrote but his decision not to mail it. Instead, he marked it "Written for the Record" and filed it away. It said in part:

. . . I do not mind telling you, in complete 100% confidence, that in 1923, when I first went to Florida . . . my old running mate, Jim Cox, came to see me on my house-boat in Miami. At that time I was, of course, walking with great difficulty—braces and crutches. Jim's eyes filled with tears when he saw me, and I gathered from his conversation that he was dead certain that I had had a stroke and that another one would soon completely remove me. At that time, of course, my general health was extremely good. . . .

Jim Cox from that day on always shook his head when my name was mentioned and said in sorrow that in effect I was a hopeless invalid and could never resume any active participation in business or political affairs.

As late as 1931—I think it was—when I was coming back from the Governor's Conference in Indiana, I stopped off at Dayton to see Jim Cox. He had had a very serious operation, followed by a thrombosis in his leg, and was very definitely invalided. His whole attitude during the two hours I spent with him alone was the same—that it was marvelous that I could stand the strain of the Governorship, but that in all probability I would be dead in a few months. He spent the greater part of the time asking me solicitously how I was, though he was a much sicker man than I was.

He made a fine come-back and is furious today if anybody ever refers to the thrombosis he had in his leg—but I still think he expects me to pop off at any moment.

While deciding not to mail that letter, at other times he could be as open as a billboard. Son Jimmy recalls that on one of Madame Chiang Kaishek's visits to the White House the grande dame thoughtlessly told the President not to stand up as she rose to leave the room. He gently replied, "My dear child, I couldn't stand up if I had to."

In a wheelchair or an automobile, getting F.D.R. into or out of an overcoat was an awkward exercise. With a stage sense of costume, F.D.R. took to a velvet-collared, braid-looped regulation Navy cape that, along with his cigarette holder, became a personal mark. Again, disadvantage was the fabric from which, with flair and style, he fashioned advantage.

Out of deference to his office as well as personal affection, newsmen virtually never mentioned the President's disability. So effective was their conspiracy even upon themselves, that, as John Gunther recalled, "hard-boiled newspaper men who knew that he could not walk as well as they knew their own names could never quite get over being startled when F.D.R. was suddenly brought into a room. The shock was greater when he wheeled himself and, of course, was greatest when he was carried; he seemed, for one thing, very small. . . . During the 1930s when I lived in Europe I repeatedly met men in important positions of state who had no idea that the President was disabled."

The people of the United States—his constituents, those from whom he drew strength and, more importantly, those who drew strength from him—knew, yet didn't know. They, too, waiting at tiny railroad depots, straining to see through the autumn sunshine the commanding figure of their President, froze at the sight of the painfully slow-motion, brace-supported step-pause-step across what seemed a torturous mile of observation platform from the train's rear door to the microphone.

It was an unexpected, unforgettable drama of frailty and strength.

Study Questions

1. Did Roosevelt's illness give him the capacity to identify with the suffering of others? How much? Why?

2. Describe the physical course of Roosevelt's disease. How physically restricted was he in his activities?

3. What would you say about his mental attitude? What does it reveal about his personality?

4. How did the press handle the illness? Why were they so respectful of Roosevelt's privacy? Would today's press be equally respectful? Why or why not?

5. Why was Roosevelt so secretive of his illness? What were the possible political ramifications of the public understanding the extent of his handicap?

Bibliography

The best survey of the era of Franklin D. Roosevelt is William E. Leuchtenburg, *Franklin D. Roosevelt and the New Deal, 1932–1940* (1963). For a critical approach to the Roosevelt administration, see Paul Conkin, *The New Deal* (1967). Arthur M. Schlesinger Jr.'s pro-Roosevelt trilogy still makes for outstanding reading. See *The Crisis of the Old Order* (1957), *The Coming of the New Deal* (1959), and *The Politics of Upheaval* (1960). An excellent political biography of Roosevelt is James Macgregor Burns, *Roosevelt: The Lion and the Fox* (1956). Also see Burns's *Roosevelt: The Soldier of Freedom* (1970) for a discussion of World War II. Joseph Lasch, *Eleanor and Franklin* (1971), describes the relationship between President Roosevelt and his wife. For descriptions of opposition to Roosevelt and the New Deal, see George Wolfskill, *Revolt of the Conservatives* (1962); Donald McCoy, *Angry Voices* (1958); and Alan Brinkley, *Voices of Protest: Huey Long, Father Coughlin, and the Great Depression* (1982). Also see Robert McElvaine, *The Great Depression: America 1929–1941* (1984).

READING 15

★ ★ ★

The Black Blizzards Roll In

Donald Worster

Early in 1935, clouds black as night began to rumble across the southern plains. These waves of dirt rose from the ground, sometimes to a height of 7,000 or 8,000 feet, and they obscured the sun. They filled streets and houses with dirt, sandblasted paint from automobiles, and covered the exposed faces of men and women with a layer of grime. All the while they kept moving, some making their way to the Atlantic seaboard and the ocean beyond. The year before they had dumped millions of pounds of dirt on Boston, New York, Washington, and Atlanta; ship captains 300 miles out in the Atlantic reported decks coated with dust. They were part of the worst ecological disaster in the 1930s— the "dirty thirties"—part of what came to be known simply as the Dust Bowl.

Nature helped form the Dust Bowl, but humans made it. The ecology of the high plains had always been fragile, but farmers had moved into the area and exploited the land, transforming millions of acres of grasslands into wheat fields. They overplanted, used the wrong sort of plows, and prayed for plenty of rain. But in an area known more for drought than rain, they badly miscalculated. Soon strong winds lifted the dry topsoil and sent it east, leaving dust pneumonia, ruined crops, and shattered lives in its wake.

While Franklin D. Roosevelt's New Deal confronted the economic and physical costs of the Dust Bowl, artists focused on the human suffering. Pare Lorentz's documentary *The Plow That Broke the Plains*, Woody Guthrie's song "The Great Dust Bowl," Alexandre Hogue's painting "Drought Survivors," and John Steinbeck's novel *The Grapes of Wrath* were all inspired by the Dust Bowl. In the following essay, historian Donald Worster eloquently describes what the dust storms looked, tasted, smelled, and felt like. People who lived through such a storm, where as one writer observed, "Lady Godiva could ride thru the streets without even the horse seeing her," did not soon forget the experience.

160

The thirties began in economic depression and in drought. The first of those disasters usually gets all the attention, although for the many Americans living on farms drought was the more serious problem. In the spring of 1930 over 3 million men and women were out of work. They had lost their jobs or had been laid off without pay in the aftermath of the stock market crash of the preceding fall. Another 12 million would suffer the same fate in the following two years. Many of the unemployed had no place to live, nor even the means to buy food. They slept in public toilets, under bridges, in shantytowns along the railroad tracks, or on doorsteps, and in the most wretched cases they scavenged from garbage cans—a Calcutta existence in the richest nation ever. The farmer, in contrast, was slower to feel the impact of the crash. He usually had his own independent food supply and stood a bit aloof from the ups and downs of the urban-industrial system. In the twenties that aloofness had meant that most farm families had not fully shared in the giddy burst of affluence—in new washing machines, silk stockings, and shiny roadsters. They had, in fact, spent much of the decade in economic doldrums. Now, as banks began to fail and soup lines formed, rural Americans went on as before, glad to be spared the latest reversal and just a little pleased to see their proud city cousins humbled. Then the droughts began, and they brought the farmers to their knees, too.

During the spring and summer of 1930, little rain fell over a large part of the eastern United States. A horizontal band on the map, from Maryland and Virginia to Missouri and Arkansas, marked the hardest hit area of wilting crops, shrinking groundwater supplies, and uncertain income. Over the summer months in this drought band the rainfall shortage was 60,000 tons for each 100-acre farm, or 700 tons a day. Seventeen million people were affected. In twelve states the drought set record lows in precipitation, and among all the Eastern states only Florida was above normal. Three years earlier the Mississippi River had overflowed its banks and levees in one of the most destructive floods in American history. Now captains there wondered how long their barges would remain afloat as the river shrank to a fraction of its average height.

During the thirties serious drought threatened a great part of the nation. The persistent center, however, shifted from the East to the Great Plains, beginning in 1931, when much of Montana and the Dakotas became almost as arid as the Sonoran Desert. Farmers there and almost everywhere else watched the scorched earth crack open, heard the gray grass crunch underfoot, and worried about how long they would be able to pay their bills. Around their dried-up ponds the willows and wild cherries were nearly leafless, and even the poison ivy dropped. Drought, of course, is a relative term: it depends upon one's concept of "normal." But following the lead of the climatologists of the time, we can use a precipitation deficiency of at least 15 percent of the historical mean to qualify as drought. By that standard, of all the American states only Maine and Vermont escaped a drought year from 1930 to 1936. Twenty states set or equaled record lows for their entire span of official weather data. Over the nation as a whole, the 1930s drought was, in the words of a Weather Bureau scientist, "the worst in the climatological history of the country."

Intense heat accompanied the drought, along with economic losses the nation could ill afford. In the summer of 1934, Nebraska reached 118 degrees, Iowa, 115. In Illinois thermometers stuck at over 100 degrees for so long that 370 people died—and one man, who had been living in a refrigerator to keep cool,

From *Dust Bowl: The Southern Plains in the 1930s* by Donald Worster, © 1979 Oxford University Press, Inc. Used by permission of the publisher.

was treated for frostbite. Two years later, when the country was described by *Newsweek* as "a vast simmering caldron," more than 4,500 died from excessive heat, water was shipped into the West by diverted tank-cars and oil pipelines, and clouds of grasshoppers ate what little remained of many farmers' wheat and corn—along with their fence posts and the washing on their clotheslines. The financial cost of the 1934 drought alone amounted to one-half the money the United States had put into World War I. By 1936, farm losses had reached $25 million a day, and more than 2 million farmers were drawing relief checks. Rexford Tugwell, head of the Resettlement Administration, who toured the burning plains that year, saw "a picture of complete destruction"—"one of the most serious peacetime problems in the nation's history."

As the decade reached its midpoint, it was the southern plains that experienced the most severe conditions. During some growing seasons there was no soil moisture down to three feet over large parts of the region. By 1939, near Hays, Kansas, the accumulated rainfall deficiency was more than 34 inches—almost a two-year supply in arrears. Continued long enough in such a marginal, semiarid land, a drought of that magnitude would produce a desert. Weathermen pointed out that there had been worse single years, as in 1910 and 1917, or back in the 1890s, and they repeatedly assured the people of the region that their records did not show any modern drought lasting more than five years, nor did they suggest any long-range adverse climatic shift. But farmers and ranchers did not find much comfort in statistical charts; their cattle were bawling for feed, and their bank credit was drying up along with the soil. Not until after 1941 did the rains return in abundance and the burden of anxiety lift.

Droughts are an inevitable fact of life on the plains, an extreme one occurring roughly every twenty years, and milder ones every three or four. They have always brought with them blowing dust where the ground was bare of crops or native grass. Dust was so familiar an event that no one was surprised to see it appear when the dry weather began in 1931. But no one was prepared for what came later: dust storms of such violence that they made the drought only a secondary problem—storms of such destructive force that they left the region reeling in confusion and fear.

"Earth" is the word we use when it is there in place, growing the food we eat, giving us a place to stand and build on. "Dust" is what we say when it is loose and blowing on the wind. Nature encompasses both—the good and the bad from our perspective, and from that of all living things. We need the earth to stay alive, but dust is a nuisance, or, worse, a killer. On a planet such as ours, where there is much wind, where there are frequent dry spells, and where we encounter vast expanses of bare soil, dust is a constant presence. It rises from the hooves of animals, from a wagon's wheels, from a dry riverbed, from the deserts. If all the continents were an English greensward, there would be no dust. But nature has not made things so. Nor has man, in many times and places.

Dust in the air is one phenomenon. However, dust storms are quite another. The story of the southern plains in the 1930s is essentially about dust storms, when the earth ran amok. And not once or twice, but over and over for the better part of a decade: day after day, year after year, of sand rattling against the window, of fine powder caking one's lips, of springtime turned to despair, of poverty eating into self-confidence.

Explaining why those storms occurred requires an excursion into the history of the plains and an understanding of the agriculture that evolved there. For the "dirty thirties," as they were called, were primarily the work of man, not nature. Admittedly, nature had something to do with this disaster too. Without winds the soil would have stayed put, no matter how bare it was. Without drought, farmers would have had strong, healthy crops capable of checking the wind. But natural factors did not make the storms—they merely made them possible. The storms were mainly the result of stripping the landscape of its natural vegetation to such an extent that there was no defense against the dry winds, no sod to hold the sandy or powdery dirt. The sod had been destroyed to make farms to grow wheat to get cash. But more of that later on. It is the storms themselves we must first comprehend: their magnitude, their effect, even their taste and smell. What was it like to be caught in one of them? How much did the people suffer, and how did they cope?

Weather bureau stations on the plains reported a few small dust storms throughout 1932, as many as 179 in April 1933, and in November of that year a large one that carried all the way to Georgia and New York. But it was the May 1934 blow that swept in a new dark age. On 9 May, brown earth from Montana and Wyoming swirled up from the ground, was captured by extremely high-level winds, and was blown eastward toward the Dakotas. More dirt was sucked into the airstream, until 350 million tons were riding toward urban America. By late afternoon the storm had reached Dubuque and Madison, and by evening 12 million tons of dust were falling like snow over Chicago—4 pounds for each person in the city. Midday at Buffalo on 10 May was darkened by dust, and the advancing gloom stretched south from there over several states, moving as fast as 100 miles an hour. The dawn of 11 May found the dust settling over Boston, New York, Washington, and Atlanta, and then the storm moved out to sea. Savannah's skies were hazy all day 12 May; it was the last city to report dust conditions. But there were still ships in the Atlantic, some of them 300 miles off the coast, that found dust on their decks during the next day or two.

"Kansas dirt," the New York press called it, though it actually came from farther north. More would come that year and after, and some of it was indeed from Kansas—or Nebraska or New Mexico. In a later spring, New Hampshire farmers, out to tap their maples, discovered a fresh brown snow on the ground, discoloration from transported Western soil. Along the Gulf Coast, at Houston and Corpus Christi, dirt from the Llano Estacado collected now and then on windowsills and sidewalks. But after May 1934 most of the worst dust storms were confined to the southern plains region; less frequently were they carried by those high-altitude currents moving east or southeast. Two types of dusters became common then: the dramatic "black blizzards" and the more frequent "sand blows." The first came with a rolling turbulence, rising like a long wall of muddy water as high as 7,000 or 8,000 feet. Like the winter blizzards to which they were compared, these dusters were caused by the arrival of a polar continental air mass, and the atmospheric electricity it generated helped lift the dirt higher and higher in a cold boil, sometimes accompanied by thunder and lightning, other times by an eerie silence. Such storms were not only terrifying to observers, but immensely destructive to the region's fine, dark soils, rich in nutrients. The second kind of duster was a more constant event, created by the low sirocco-like winds that blew out of the southwest and left the sandier soils drifted into dunes along fence rows and ditches. Long after New York and Philadelphia had forgotten their taste of the plains, the people out there ate their own dirt again and again.

In the 1930s the Soil Conservation Service compiled a frequency chart of all dust storms of regional extent, when visibility was cut to less than a mile. In 1932 there were 14; in 1933, 38; 1934, 22; 1935, 40; 1936, 68; 1937, 72; 1938, 61—dropping as the drought relented a bit—1939, 30; 1940, 17; 1941, 17. Another measure of severity was made by calculating the total number of hours the dust storms lasted during a year. By that criterion 1937 was again the worst: at Guymon, in the panhandle of Oklahoma, the total number of hours that year climbed to 550, mostly concentrated in the first six months of the year. In Amarillo the worst year was 1935, with a total of 908 hours. Seven times, from January to March, the visibility there reached zero—all complete blackouts, one of them lasting eleven hours. A single storm might rage for one hour or three and a half days. Most of the winds came from the southwest, but they also came from the west, north, and northeast, and they could slam against windows and walls with 60 miles-per-hour force. The dirt left behind on the front lawn might be brown, black, yellow, ashy gray, or, more rarely, red, depending upon its source. And each color had its own peculiar aroma, from a sharp peppery smell that burned the nostrils to a heavy greasiness that nauseated.

In the memory of older plains residents, the blackest year was 1935, particularly the early spring weeks from 1 March to mid-April, when the Dust Bowl made its full-blown debut. Springtime in western Kansas can be a Willa Cather world of meadowlarks on the wing, clean white curtains dancing in the breeze, anemones and wild verbena in bloom, lilacs by the porch, a windmill spinning briskly, and cold fresh water in the bucket—but not in 1935. After a February heat wave (it reached 75 degrees in Topeka that month), the dust began moving across Kansas, Oklahoma, and Texas, and for the next six weeks it was unusual to see a clear sky from dawn until sundown. On 15 March, Denver reported that a serious dust storm was speeding eastward. Kansans ignored the radio warnings, went about their business as usual, and later wondered what had hit them. Small-town printer Nate White was at the picture show when the dust reached Smith Center: as he walked out the exit, it was as if someone had put a blindfold over his eyes; he bumped into telephone poles, skinned his shins on boxes and cans in an alleyway, fell to his hands and knees, and crawled along the curbing to a dim houselight. A seven-year-old boy wandered

away and was lost in the gloom; the search party found him later, suffocated in a drift. A more fortunate child was found alive, tangled in a barbed wire fence. Near Colby, a train was derailed by dirt on the tracks, and the passengers spent twelve dreary hours in the coaches. The Lora-Locke Hotel in Dodge City overflowed with more than two hundred stranded travelers; many of them bedded down on cots in the lobby and ballroom. In the following days, as the dust kept falling, electric lights burned continuously, cars left tracks in the dirt-covered streets, and schools and offices stayed closed. A reporter at Great Bend remarked on the bizarre scene: "Uncorked jug placed on sidewalk two hours, found to be half filled with dust. Picture wires giving way due to excessive weight of dust on frames. Irreparable loss in portraits anticipated. Lady Godiva could ride thru streets without even the horse seeing her."

The novelty of this duster, so like a coffee-colored winter snow, made it hard for most people to take it seriously. But William Allen White, the Emporia editor, called it "the greatest show" since Pompeii was buried in ashes. And a Garden City woman described her experience for the *Kansas City Times:*

All we could do about it was just sit in our dusty chairs, gaze at each other through the fog that filled the room and watch that fog settle slowly and silently, covering everything— including ourselves—in a thick, brownish gray blanket. When we opened the door swirling whirlwinds of soil beat against us unmercifully. . . . The door and windows were all shut tightly, yet those tiny particles seemed to seep through the very walls. It got into cupboards and clothes closets; our faces were as dirty as if we had rolled in the dirt; our hair was gray and stiff and we ground dirt between our teeth.

By the end of the month conditions had become so unrelenting that many Kansans had begun to chew their nails. "Watch for the

Second Coming of Christ," warned one of Topeka's unhinged, "God is wrathful." Street-corner sects in Hill City and other towns warned pedestrians to heed the signs of the times. A slightly less frenetic Concordian jotted in her log: "This is ultimate darkness. So must come the end of the world." The mood of the people had begun to change, if not to apocalyptic dread in every case, at least to a fear that this was a nightmare that might never end.

By 24 March southeastern Colorado and western Kansas had seen twelve consecutive days of dust storms, but there was worse to come. Near the end of March a new duster swept across the southern plains, destroying one-half the wheat crop in Kansas, one-quarter of it in Oklahoma, and all of it in Nebraska— 5 million acres blown out. The storm carried away from the plains twice as much earth as men and machines had scooped out to make the Panama Canal, depositing it once again over the East Coast states and the Atlantic Ocean. Then the wind slackened off a bit, gathering strength, as it were, for the spectacular finale of that unusual spring season— Black Sunday, 14 April.

Dawn came clear and rosy all across the plains that day. By noon the skies were so fresh and blue that people could not remain indoors; they remembered how many jobs they had been postponing, and with a revived spirit they rushed outside to get them done. They went on picnics, planted gardens, repaired henhouses, attended funerals, drove to the neighbors for a visit. In midafternoon the summery air rapidly turned colder, falling as many as 50 degrees in a few hours, and the people noticed then that the yards were full of birds nervously fluttering and chattering— and more were arriving every moment, as though fleeing from some unseen enemy. Suddenly there appeared on the northern horizon a black blizzard, moving toward them; there was no sound, no wind, nothing but an immense "boogery" cloud. The storm

struck Dodge City at 2:40 P.M. Not far from there John Garretson, a farmer in Haskell County, Kansas, who was on the road with his wife, Louise, saw it coming, but he was sure that he could beat it home. They had almost made it when they were engulfed; abandoning the car, they groped for the fencewire and, hand over hand, followed it to their door. Down in the panhandle Ed and Ada Phillips of Boise City, with their six-year-old daughter, were on their way home too, after an outing to Texline in their Model A Ford. It was about five o'clock when the black wall appeared, and they still had fifteen miles to go. Seeing an old adobe house ahead, Ed realized that they had to take shelter, and quickly. By the time they were out of the car the dust was upon them, making it so dark that they nearly missed the door. Inside they found ten other people, stranded, like themselves, in a two-room hut, all fearing that they might be smothered, all unable to see their companions' faces. For four hours they sat there, until the storm let up enough for them to follow the roadside ditch back to town. By then the ugly pall was moving south across the high plains of Texas and New Mexico.

Older residents still remember Black Sunday in all its details—where they were when the storm hit, what they did then. Helen Wells was the wife of the Reverend Rolley Wells, the Methodist minister in Guymon. Early that morning she had helped clean the accumulated dust from the church pews, working until she was choking and exhausted. Back in the parsonage she switched on the radio for some inspiring music, and what she heard was the hymn "We'll Work Till Jesus Comes." "I just had to sit down and laugh," she recalls; she had worn out her sweeper but still had a broom if that was needed. Later that day her husband, partly to please two visiting *Saturday Evening Post* reporters, held a special "rain service," which concluded in time for the congregation to get home before the dust arrived.

A Kansas cattle dealer, Raymond Ell-saesser, almost lost his wife that day. She had gone into Sublette with her young daughter for a Rebekah lodge meeting. On the way home she stopped along the highway, unable to see even the winged hood ornament on her car. The static electricity in the storm then shorted out her ignition, and, foolishly, she determined to walk the three-quarters of a mile home. Her daughter plunged ahead to get Raymond's help, and he quickly piled into a truck and drove back down the road, hallooing out the window. Back and forth he passed, but his wife had disappeared into the fog-like dust, wandering straight away from the car into the field, where she stumbled about with absolutely no sense of direction. Each time she saw the truck's headlights she moved that way, not realizing her husband was in motion too. It was only by sheer luck that she found herself at last standing in the truck's beams, gasping for air and near collapse.

The last of the major dust storms that year was on 14 April, and it was months before the damages could be fully calculated. Those who had been caught outside in one of the spring dusters were, understandably, most worried about their lungs. An epidemic of respiratory infections and something called "dust pneumonia" broke out across the plains. The four small hospitals in Meade County, Kansas, found that 52 percent of their April admissions were acute respiratory cases—thirty-three patients died. Many dust victims would arrive at a hospital almost dead, after driving long distances in a storm. They spat up clods of dirt, washed the mud out of their mouths, swabbed their nostrils with Vaseline, and rinsed their bloodshot eyes with boric acid water. Old people and babies were the most vulnerable to the dusters, as were those who had chronic asthma, bronchitis, or tuberculosis, some of whom had moved to the plains so they might breathe the high, dry air.

Doctors could not agree on whether the dust caused a new kind of pneumonia, and some even denied that there were any unusual health problems in their communities. But the Red Cross thought the situation was so serious that it set up six emergency hospitals in Kansas, Colorado, and Texas, and it staffed them with its own nurses. In Topeka and Wichita volunteers worked in high school sewing rooms to make dust masks of cheesecloth; over 17,000 of those masks were sent to the plains, especially to towns where goggles had been sold out. Chewing tobacco was a better remedy, snorted some farmers, who thought it was too much of a bother to wear such gadgets when driving their tractors. But enough wore the Red Cross masks or some other protection to make the plains look like a World War I battlefield, with dust instead of mustard gas coming out of the trenches.

On 29 April the Red Cross sponsored a conference of health officers from several states. Afterward the representatives of the Kansas Board of Health went to work on the medical problem in more detail, and eventually they produced a definitive study on the physiological impact of the dust storms. From 21 February to 30 April they counted 28 days of "dense" dust at Dodge City and only 13 days that were "dust free." Dirt deposited in bakepans during the five biggest storms gave an estimated 4.7 tons of total fallout per acre. Agar plate cultures showed "no pathogenic organisms" in the accumulation, only harmless soil bacteria, plant hair, and microfungus spores. But the inorganic content of the dust was mainly fine silicon particles, along with bits of feldspar, volcanic ash, and calcite; and "silica," they warned, "is as much a body poison as is lead"—"probably the most widespread and insidious of all hazards in the environment of mankind," producing, after sufficient contact, silicosis of the lungs. These scientists also found that a measles outbreak had come with the black blizzards, though why that happened was not clear; in only five months there were twice as many cases as in any previous twelve-month period. The death rate from acute respiratory infections in the 45 western counties of Kansas, where the dust was most intense, was 99 per 100,000, compared with the statewide average of 70; and the infant mortality was 80.5, compared with the state's 62.3.

The medical remedies for the dust were at best primitive and makeshift. In addition to wearing light gauze masks, health officials recommended attaching translucent glass-cloth to the inside frames of windows, although people also used cardboard, canvas, or blankets. Hospitals covered some of their patients with wet sheets, and housewives flapped the air with wet dish towels to collect dust. One of the most common tactics was to stick masking tape, felt strips, or paraffin-soaked rags around the windows and door cracks. The typical plains house was loosely constructed and without insulation, but sometimes those methods proved so effective that there was not enough air circulation inside to replenish the oxygen supply. Warren Moore of southwestern Kansas remembers watching, during a storm, the gas flame on the range steadily turn orange and the coal-oil lamp dim until the people simply had to open the window, dust or no dust. But most often there was no way to seal out the fine, blowing dirt: it blackened the pillow around one's head, the dinner plates on the table, the bread dough on the back of the stove. It became a steady part of one's diet and breathing. "We thrived on it," claim some residents today; it was their "vitamin K." But all the same they prayed that they would not ingest so much it would maim them for life, or finish them off, as it had a neighbor or two.

Livestock and wildlife did not have even those crude defenses. "In a rising sand storm," wrote Margaret Bourke-White, "cattle quickly become blinded. They run around in circles until they fall and breathe so much dust that they die. Autopsies show their lungs caked with dust and mud." Newborn calves could suffocate in a matter of hours, and the older cattle ground their teeth down to the gums trying to eat the dirt-covered grass. As the dust buried the fences, horses and cattle climbed over and wandered away. Where there was still water in rivers, the dust coated the surface and the fish died too. The carcasses of jackrabbits, small birds, and field mice lay along roadsides by the hundreds after a severe duster; and those that survived were in such shock that they could be picked up and their nostrils and eyes wiped clean. In a lighter vein, it was said that prairie dogs were now able to tunnel upward several feet from the ground.

Cleaning up houses, farm lots, and city stores after the 1935 blow season was an expensive matter. People literally shoveled the dirt from their front yards and swept up bushel-basketfuls inside. One man's ceiling collapsed from the silt that had collected in the attic. Carpets, draperies, and tapestries were so dust-laden that their patterns were indiscernible. Painted surfaces had been sand-blasted bare. Automobile and tractor engines operated in dust storms without oil-bath air cleaners were ruined by grit, and the repair shops had plenty of business. During March alone, Tucumcari, New Mexico, reported over $288,000 in property damage, although most towns' estimates were more conservative than that: Liberal, Kansas, $150,000; Randall County, Texas, $10,000; Lamar, Colorado, $3,800. The merchants of Amarillo calculated from 3 to 15 percent damage to their merchandise, not to mention the loss of shoppers during the storms. In Dodge City a men's clothing store advertised a "dust sale," knocking shirts down to 75 cents. But the heaviest burdens lay on city work crews, who had to sweep dirt from the gutters and municipal swimming pools, and on housewives, who struggled after each blow to get their houses clean.

The emotional expense was the hardest to accept, however. All day you could sit with your hands folded on the oilcloth-covered table, the wind moaning around the eaves, the fine, soft, talc sifting in the keyholes, the sky a coppery gloom; and when you went to bed the acrid dust crept into your dreams. Avis Carlson told what it was like at night:

A trip for water to rinse the grit from our lips. And then back to bed with washcloths over our noses. We try to lie still, because every turn stirs the dust on the blankets. After a while, if we are good sleepers, we forget.

After 1935 the storms lost much of their drama; for most people they were simply a burden to be endured, and sometimes that burden was too heavy. Druggists sold their supplies of sedatives quickly. An Oklahoman took down his shotgun, ready to kill his entire family and himself—"we're all better off dead," he despaired. That, to be sure, was an extreme instance, but there were indeed men and women who turned distraught, wept, and then, listless, gave up caring.

The plains people, however, then as now, were a tough-minded, leather-skinned folk, not easily discouraged. Even in 1935 they managed to laugh a bit at their misfortunes. They told about the farmer who fainted when a drop of water struck him in the face and had to be revived by having three buckets of sand thrown over him. They also passed around the one about the motorist who came upon a ten-gallon hat resting on a dust drift. Under it he found a head looking at him. "Can I help you some way?" the motorist asked, "Give you a ride into town maybe?" "Thanks, but I'll make it on my own," was the reply, "I'm on a horse." They laughed with Will Rogers when he pointed out that only highly advanced civilizations—like ancient Mesopotamia—were ever covered over by dirt, and that California would never qualify. Newspaper editors could still find something to joke about, too: "When better dust storms are made," the *Dodge City Globe* boasted, "the Southwest will make

them." Children were especially hard to keep down; for them the storms always meant adventure, happy chaos, a breakdown of their teachers' authority, and perhaps a holiday. When darkness descends, as it did that April, humor, bravado, or a childlike irresponsibility may have as much value as a storm cellar.

Whether they brought laughter or tears, the dust storms that swept across the southern plains in the 1930s created the most severe environmental catastrophe in the entire history of the white man on this continent. In no other instance was there greater or more sustained damage to the American land, and there have been few times when so much tragedy was visited on its inhabitants. Not even the Depression was more devastating, economically. And in ecological terms we have nothing in the nation's past, nothing even in the polluted present, that compares. Suffice it to conclude here that in the decade of the 1930s the dust storms of the plains were an unqualified disaster.

At such dark times the mettle of a people is thoroughly and severely tested, revealing whether they have the will to go on. By this test the men and women of the plains were impressive, enduring, as most of them did, discouragements the like of which more recent generations have never had to face. But equally important, disasters of this kind challenge a society's capacity to think—require it to analyze and explain and learn from misfortune. Societies that fail this test are sitting ducks for more of the same. Those that pass, on the other hand, have attained through suffering and hardship a more mature, self-appraising character, so that they are more aware than before of their vulnerabilities and weaknesses. They are stronger because they have been made sensitive to their deficiencies. Whether the dust storms had this enlarging, critical effect on the minds of southern plainsmen remains to be seen.

Study Questions

1. When did the dust storms begin and when did they end? What areas of the country did they affect the most?

2. Describe the size, color, and smell of the dust storms. How long did they last? Were they uniform?

3. Describe the impact that the dust storms had on humans and animals. How did people cope with them?

4. What kinds of destruction did the dust storms cause?

Bibliography

This selection is from Donald Worster, *Dust Bowl: The Southern Plains in the 1930s* (1979), an award-winning study that combines passion and outrage with scholarly distance and fine writing. Also valuable are Paul Bonnifield, *The Dust Bowl: Men, Dirt, and Depression* (1979); R. Douglas Hurt, *The Dust Bowl: An Agricultural and Social History* (1981); and James N. Gregory, *American Exodus: The Dust Bowl Migration and Oke Culture in California* (1991). An outstanding overview of the Great Depression is Robert S. McElvaine, *The Great Depression* (1984). For a new perspective on the Depression, see Gene Smiley, *Rethinking the Great Depression* (2003). In their own ways, the works of John Steinbeck, Pare Lorentz, Woody Guthrie, and Alexandre Hogue also document the era of the Dust Bowl and the Depression.

READING 16

★ ★ ★

Night of the Martians

Edward Oxford

It's a truism today that the mass media influences the lives of Americans. Society is constantly barraged with questions and criticism about such issues as the quality of children's television programming, the political bias of newscasters, the ethics of television advertising, the domination of political campaigns by the media, and the decline of literacy and the written word. More than any other technological innovation, the development first of radio and then of television has transformed American life, changing the way people live and relate to one another. The first radio station in the United States began broadcasting out of Pittsburgh in 1920. Three years later there were more than 500 stations doing the same thing, and by 1929 more than 12 million families listened to the radio at home every night. The communications revolution that radio stimulated contributed to the creation of a mass, national culture.

The influence of the radio, however, did not immediately dawn on people. In 1927 the National Broadcasting Company became the first national network, and by 1933 President Franklin D. Roosevelt was effectively using the radio for his famous "fireside chats." But it was not until 1938, when Orson Welles broadcast his famous "War of the Worlds" program, that Americans realized the potential of radio to shape public attitudes. With Adolf Hitler making his designs on Czechoslovakia well known, Americans were worried that another global conflict was in the making. Battered by the frustration of the Great Depression and nervous about the safety of the world, millions of people panicked when Orson Welles described over national radio an invasion of the East Coast by Martians. In the following essay, historian Edward Oxford describes the broadcast and the controversy it inspired.

A little after eight P.M. on Halloween eve 1938, thirteen-year-old Dick Stives, his sister, and two brothers huddled around their family's radio. They were in the dining room of their grandfather's farmhouse near the hamlet of Grovers Mill, four miles east of Princeton, New Jersey. Their mother and father had dropped them off there and gone to the movies.

Dick worked the radio dial, hunting for the station that carried the *Chase and Sanborn Hour,* his—and the nation's—favorite Sunday evening program. As he scanned the airwaves, Dick tuned in the local affiliate of the Columbia Broadcasting System (CBS). A commanding voice—that of Orson Welles—riveted his attention.

". . . across an immense ethereal gulf, minds that are to our minds as ours are to the beasts of the jungle, intellects vast, cool, and unsympathetic, regarded this earth with envious eyes and slowly and surely drew their plans against us. . . . "

Dick Stives turned the dial no further. Instead, during the next hour he and millions of other listeners sat glued by their radios, convinced by an alarming series of "news bulletins" that monster aliens from Mars were invading America. Dick's village of Grovers Mill—the supposed landing site for these invaders—became the focal point of a panic wave that rapidly swept across the nation.

The program—the *Mercury Theatre on the Air* adaptation of H. G. Wells's *The War of the Worlds*—would later be remembered as the most extraordinary radio show ever broadcast. And Orson Welles, its brilliant young producer, director, and star, would be catapulted to nationwide fame overnight.

As the wonder boy of the performing arts, Orson Welles had by age twenty-three already appeared on the cover of *Time* magazine; built a considerable reputation as a radio actor; set the stage world on its ear with a *Julius Caesar* set in Fascist Italy, an all-black *Macbeth,* and a production of Marc Blitzstein's opera *The Cradle Will Rock;* and founded—with his partner-in-drama John Houseman—the revolutionary and often controversial Mercury Theatre.[1]

In midsummer 1938, the Columbia Broadcasting System, impressed by Welles's meteoric success, offered him and his repertory company a grand stage, radio—"the Broadway of the entire United States"—on which to deliver a sixty-minute dramatization each week.

Broadcast from the twenty-second floor of the CBS building in midtown Manhattan, the *Mercury Theatre on the Air* had no commercial sponsor. The show was subsidized by the CBS network, and its bare-bones budget provided no money for expensive, original plays. "We offered the audience classic works from the public domain—*Julius Caesar, Oliver Twist, The Heart of Darkness, Jane Eyre,* and such," recalls John Houseman. "Orson and I would select the book. Sometimes it was my task to fashion the original into a workable radio script."

For the last program of October, the seventeenth in their series, Welles and Houseman wanted to "throw in something of a scientific nature." They settled on an adaptation of *The War of the Worlds,* a science-fiction novel written in 1898 by British author H. G. Wells. Houseman assigned the script to a recent addition to the company, writer Howard Koch.

"Night of the Martians" by Edward Oxford. This article is reprinted from the October 1988 issue of *American History Illustrated* 23, pp. 14–23, 47–48 with the permission of Cowles History Group, Inc. Copyright *American History Ilustrated* magazine.

---

[1] Up to this time Welles was probably best known to radio audiences as "Lamont Cranston," alias "The Shadow," on the popular Sunday afternoon mystery program of the same name. But he also appeared frequently on many other shows including "The March of Time," and was said to be earning $1,000 a week from his radio commitments alone.

For the fall season CBS had moved the *Mercury Theatre on the Air* from Monday evening to the Sunday night eight-to-nine-o'-clock slot, an "unsold" time period. During this hour much of America tuned in to the competing NBC Red network for the *Chase and Sanborn Hour,* which featured ventriloquist Edgar Bergen and his wooden-headed "dummy" Charlie McCarthy. The Crossley ratings of listenership gave Charlie McCarthy a "thirty-five" (roughly 35 percent of radio listeners at that hour tuned in), while the *Mercury* usually scored about "three."

During the week before the October 30 broadcast, Welles nonchalantly put in his own typically frantic week while Houseman, Koch, and the cast struggled to ready the show. Welles spent much of his time not in the CBS studios at 485 Madison Avenue, but on the stage of the Mercury Theatre on West 41st Street, rehearsing his repertory company for the opening of a new play. He hurried back to CBS at odd hours to try out some of his lines, listen to run-throughs by the radio show's cast, and render his inimitable revisions.

Welles and his company spent much of Sunday amid a litter of sandwiches and coffee cups in Studio One, adding final touches to their version of *The War of the Worlds* and conducting a dress rehearsal with full music and sound effects.

Just before eight P.M., Eastern Standard Time, Welles, conductor-like, stood poised on his platform in the middle of the studio. He had at his command not only his loyal band of actors, but also a small symphony orchestra. Wearing a headset, the multifaceted genius was prepared to read his own lines, cue the other actors, signal for sound effects, summon the orchestra, and also keep in touch with the control room.

At the stroke of eight o'clock, he gave the cue for the start of the *Mercury* theme—the Tchaikovsky Piano Concerto No. 1 in B-Flat Minor.

For the next unforgettable hour, Dick Stives at Grovers Mill, along with several million other Americans, sat transfixed as the airwaves brought word of weird and almost incomprehensible events that seemed to unfold with terrifying reality even as they listened.

It was not as though listeners hadn't been warned. Most simply didn't pay close attention to the program's opening signature (or tuned in a few seconds late and missed it altogether): "The Columbia Broadcasting System and its affiliated stations present Orson Welles and the Mercury Theatre on the Air in *The War of the Worlds* by H. G. Welles. . . . "

Many in the radio audience failed to associate what they heard with prior newspaper listings of the drama. And, by the time a single station break came late in the hour with reminders that listeners were hearing a fictional story, many others were too agitated to comprehend that they had been deceived.

Skillfully choreographed by Welles and Houseman, the program—a play simulating a montage of real-life dance band "remotes" and news bulletins—began with deliberate calm. Millions of listeners, conditioned by recent news reports of worldwide political turmoil—and by their inherent trust in the medium of radio—believed what they heard.

Just two minutes into the show, audience perception between fantasy and reality began to blur when, following Welles's dramatic opening monologue, the microphone shifted to a "network announcer" reading an apparently routine report from the "Government Weather Bureau."

Programming then shifted to "Ramon Raquello and his orchestra" in the "Meridian Room" at the "Hotel Park Plaza" in downtown New York City.

During rehearsals for the show, Welles had insisted—over the objections of his associates—on increasing the broadcast time devoted to the fictional orchestra's soothing renditions of "La Cumparsita" and "the ever-popular 'Stardust.'" As he had anticipated, the resulting "band remote" had a disarming air of reality—and provided emotional contrast to the intensity of later news bulletins.[2]

Just when Welles had calculated that listeners might start tuning out the music in search of something more lively, an announcer broke in with a bulletin from the "Intercontinental Radio News": "Professor Farrell of the Mount Jennings Observatory" near Chicago had reported observing "several explosions of incandescent gas occurring at regular intervals on the planet Mars. . . . The spectroscope indicates the gas to be hydrogen and moving towards the earth with tremendous velocity."

The dance music resumed, only to be interrupted repeatedly during the next several minutes by other bulletins. The tempo of events—and listeners' interest—began to intensify.

From a "remote pickup" at the "Princeton Observatory," reporter "Carl Phillips" interviewed famous astronomer "Richard Pierson" (played by Welles). As the clockwork of mechanism of his telescope ticked in the background, Professor Pierson described Mars as a red disk swimming in a blue sea. He said he could not explain the gas eruptions on that planet. But skeptical of anything that could not be explained by logic, the astronomer counted the chances against living intelligence on Mars as being "a thousand to one."

Then Phillips read a wire that had just been handed to Pierson: a seismograph at the "Natural History Museum" in New York had registered a "shock of almost earthquake intensity occurring within a radius of twenty miles of Princeton." Pierson played down any possible connection with the disturbances on Mars: "This is probably a meteorite of unusual size

and its arrival at this particular time is merely a coincidence."

Again the program returned to music, followed by yet another bulletin: an astronomer in Canada had observed three explosions on Mars, confirming "earlier reports from American observatories."

"Now, nearer home," continued the announcer, "comes a special announcement from Trenton, New Jersey. It is reported that at 8:50 P.M. a huge, flaming object, believed to be a meteorite, fell on a farm in the neighborhood of Grovers Mill, New Jersey, twenty-two miles from Trenton. The flash in the sky was visible within a radius of several hundred miles and the noise of impact was heard as far north as Elizabeth."

Listeners leaned closer to their sets. In Grovers Mill, Dick Stives stared at the radio and gulped.

Again the broadcast returned to dance music—this time to "Bobby Millette and his orchestra" at the "Hotel Martinet" in Brooklyn. And again the music was interrupted by a news flash. Having just arrived at the scene of "impact" on the "Wilmuth farm" near Grovers Mill, reporter Carl Phillips, accompanied by Professor Pierson, beheld police, state troopers, and onlookers crowding around what appeared to be a huge metallic cylinder, partially buried in the earth.

About this time, some twelve minutes into the broadcast, many listeners to the *Chase and Sanborn Hour*, momentarily bored by a guest musical spot, turned their dials. A lot of them stopped in sudden shock as they came upon the CBS wavelength. The events being described seemed real to listeners—quite as real to them as reports, not many months before, that Adolf Hitler's troops had marched into Austria.

"I wish I could convey the atmosphere . . . the background of this . . . fantastic scene," reported Phillips. "Hundreds of cars are parked in a field back of us. . . . Their headlights throw an enormous spot on the pit where the object is half-buried. Some of the

---

[2]The format was a familiar one to radio listeners. "Big band remotes"—network broadcasts featuring America's best-known dance bands as they played at one-night stands in ballrooms from coast to coast—were a staple of broadcasting during the 1930s.

more daring souls are venturing near the edge. Their silhouettes stand out against the metal sheen. . . . "

Professor Pierson described the object as "definitely extraterrestrial . . . not found on this earth. . . . This thing is smooth and, as you can see, of cylindrical shape." Then Phillips suddenly interrupted him:

"Just a minute! Something's happening! Ladies and gentlemen, this is terrific! The end of the thing is beginning to flake off! The top is beginning to rotate like a screw! The thing must be hollow! [shouts of alarm] Ladies and gentlemen, this is the most terrifying thing I have ever witnessed. . . . Wait a minute! Someone's crawling out of the hollow top. Someone or . . . something. I can see peering out of that black hole two luminous disks—are they eyes? Good heavens, something's wriggling out of the shadow like a gray snake. . . . I can see the thing's body. It's large as a bear and it glistens like wet leather. But that face. It . . . it's indescribable. I can hardly force myself to keep looking at it. The eyes are black and gleam like a serpent. The mouth is V-shaped with saliva dripping from its rimless lips that seem to quiver and pulsate. . . . "

Thirty state troopers, according to the reporter, now formed a cordon around the pit where the object rested. Three policemen carrying a white handkerchief of truce walked toward the cylinder. Phillips continued:

"Wait a minute . . . something's happening. [high-pitched, intermittent whine of machinery] A humped shape is rising out of the pit. I can make out a small beam of light against a mirror. . . . What's that? There's a jet of flame springing from the mirror, and it leaps right at the advancing men! It strikes them head on! Good Lord, they're turning into flame! [screams and shrieks] Now the whole field by the woods has caught fire! [sound effects intensify] The gas tanks, tanks of automobiles . . . it's spreading everywhere! It's coming this way now! About twenty yards to my right [abrupt silence]."[3]

Now terror was afoot. A series of voices—fictional "announcers," "militia commanders," "network vice presidents," and "radio operators"—took up the narrative. At least forty people, according to the radio bulletins, lay dead at Grovers Mill, "their bodies burned and distorted beyond all possible recognition." And in a Trenton hospital, "the charred body of Carl Phillips" had been identified.

A current of fear flowed outward across the nation. Real-life police switchboards, first in New Jersey, then, steadily, throughout the whole Northeast, began to light up: "What's happening?" "Who's attacking America?" "When will they be here?" "What can we do?" "Who are they—these Martians?"

By now, according to the broadcast, "eight battalions of infantry" had surrounded the cylinder, determined to destroy it. A "Captain Lansing" of the "Signal Corps"—calm and confident at first, but with obviously increasing alarm—described what happened next:

"Well, we ought to see some action soon. One of the companies is deploying on the left flank. A quick thrust and it'll all be over. Wait a minute, I see something on top of the cylinder. No, it's nothing but a shadow. . . . Seven thousand armed men closing in on an old metal tube. Tub, rather. Wait, that wasn't a shadow. It's something moving . . . solid metal. Kind of a shield-like affair rising up out of the cylinder! It's going higher and higher! Why, it's . . . standing on legs! Actually rearing up on a sort of metal framework! Now it's reaching above the trees and searchlights are on it! Hold on [abrupt silence]."

In a matter of moments, a studio "announcer" gave America the incredible news:

". . . Those strange beings who landed in the Jersey farmlands tonight are the vanguard of

---

[3]Phillip's narrative bore a perhaps-not-coincidental resemblance to a famous eyewitness report by Chicago radio newsman Herb Morrison, who on May 6, 1937, had described the explosion and destruction of the German dirigible Hindenburg as it was about to moor at Lakehurst, New Jersey.

an invading army from the planet Mars. The battle which took place tonight at Grovers Mill has ended in one of the most startling defeats ever suffered by an army in modern times; seven thousand men armed with rifles and machine guns pitted against a single fighting machine of the invaders from Mars. One hundred and twenty known survivors. The rest strewn over the battle areas from Grovers Mill to Plainsboro crushed and trampled to death under the metal feet of the monster, or burned to cinders by its heat ray. . . . "

Grovers Mill's couple of hundred real-life residents hardly knew what to make of it all. Young Dick Stives was stunned. He and his sister and brothers pulled down the shades in the farmhouse. Their grandfather shoved chairs against the doors.

Teen-aged Lolly Dey, who heard about the "invasion" while attending a church meeting, consoled herself by saying: "I am in the Lord's House." Another resident, seeing what he thought to be a Martian war machine among the trees (actually a water tower on a neighbor's property), peppered it with shotgun blasts. One man packed his family into the car, bound for parts unknown. He backed right through his garage door. "We're never gonna be needing that again anyway," he muttered to his wife.

"The monster is now in control of the middle section of New Jersey," proclaimed the voice on the radio. "Communication lines are down from Pennsylvania to the Atlantic Ocean. Railroad tracks are torn and service from New York to Philadelphia discontinued. . . . Highways to the north, south, and west are clogged with frantic human traffic. Police and army reserves are unable to control the mad flight. . . . "

Life was soon to imitate art. A wave of terror, unprecedented in its scope and rapidity, swept across New Jersey. A New Brunswick man, bound for open country, had driven ten miles when he remembered that his dog was tied up in the backyard of his home.

Daring the Martians, he drove back to retrieve the dog.

A West Orange bar owner pushed customers out into the street, locked his tavern door, and rushed home to rescue his wife and children.

Twenty families began to move their belongings out of a Newark apartment house, their faces covered by wet towels to repel Martian rays. Doctors and nurses volunteered to come to hospitals to help handle the "war casualties."

At Princeton University, the chairman of the geology department packed his field equipment and headed into the night to look for whatever it was that was out there. The governor of Pennsylvania offered to send troops to help New Jersey. A Jersey City man called a bus dispatcher to warn him of the fast-spreading "disaster." He cut their conversation short with: "The world is coming to an end and I have a lot to do!"

Meanwhile, on the radio, the "Secretary of the Interior," speaking in a voice much like that of President Franklin D. Roosevelt, announced that he had faith in the ability of the American military to vanquish the Martians.[4] He solemnly intoned:

". . . placing our trust in God we must continue the performance of our duties each and every one of us, so that we may confront this destructive adversary with a nation united, courageous, and consecrated to the preservation of human supremacy on this earth."

A Trenton store owner ran out screaming, "The world is ending! The world is ending!" Another man dashed into a motion-picture theater in Orange, crying out that "the state is being invaded! This place is going to be

---

[4]Network censors, concerned that the drama might sound too factual, had earlier requested more than thirty changes in the script. Thus, although he still sounded like Franklin Roosevelt, the "President" became the "Secretary of the Interior." The "U.S. Weather Bureau" was changed to the "Government Weather Bureau," the "National Guard" became the "State Militia," etc.

blown up!" The audience hurriedly ran out to the street.

A woman in a Newark tenement just sat and cried. "I thought it was all up with us," she said. A man driving westward called out to a patrolman: "All creation's busted loose! I'm getting out!"

More grim reports issued from the radio. Scouting planes, according to the broadcast, had sighted three Martian machines marching through New Jersey. They were uprooting power lines, bridges, and railroad tracks, with the apparent objectives of crushing resistance and paralyzing communications. In swamps twenty miles south of Morristown, coon hunters had stumbled upon a second Martian cylinder.

In the Watchung mountains, the "22nd Field Artillery" set down a barrage against six tripod monsters—to no avail. The machines soon let loose a heavy black poisonous gas, annihilating the artillerymen. Then eight army bombers from "Langham Field, Virginia," attacked the tripod machines, only to be downed by heat rays.

Thousands of telephone calls cascaded into radio stations, newspaper offices, power companies, fire houses, and military posts throughout the country. People wanted to know what to do . . . where to go . . . whether they were safer in the cellar or the attic.

Word spread in Atlanta that a "planet" had struck New Jersey. In Philadelphia, all the guests in one hotel checked out. Students at a college in North Carolina lined up at telephones to call their parents for the last time. When a caller reached the CBS switchboard, the puzzled operator, asked about the end of the world, said: "I'm sorry, we don't have that information."

Radio listeners soon heard an "announcer," said to be atop the "Broadcasting Building" in Manhattan, describe a doomed New York City:

"The bells you hear are ringing to warn the people to evacuate the city as the Martians approach. Estimated in the last two hours three million people have moved out along the roads to the north. . . . No more defenses. Our army wiped out . . . artillery, air force, everything wiped out. . . . We'll stay here to the end."

Something like madness took hold among radio listeners in New York City. People stood on Manhattan street corners hoping for a glimpse of the "battle." Thirty men and women showed up at a Harlem police station wanting to be evacuated. A woman had her husband paged at a Broadway theater and told him of the Martian landings; word spread quickly and a throng of playgoers rushed for the exits.

The radio voice continued: "Enemy now in sight above the Palisades! Five great machines. First one is crossing the river . . . wading the Hudson like a man wading through a brook. . . . Martian cylinders are falling all over the country. One outside Buffalo, one in Chicago, St. Louis. . . . Now the first machine reaches the shore! He stands watching, looking over the city. His steel, cowlish head is even with the skyscrapers. He waits for the others. They rise like a line of new towers on the city's west side. . . . "

A Bronx man dashed into the street and saw people running in all directions. One New Yorker claimed he heard the "swish" of Martian flying vehicles. Another told of machine-gun fire. Atop a midtown Manhattan building, a man with binoculars "saw" the firing of weapons. In Brooklyn, a man called the police station: "We can hear the firing all the way here, and I want a gas mask. I'm a taxpayer."

An NBC executive was upset because *his* network wasn't carrying the ultimate news event. One man sped at eighty miles an hour to reach a priest before the "death rays" overtook him; his car flipped over twice, but he lived.

The program played out the drama of doom right to its end.

From atop his fictional building, the "broadcaster" continued his "eyewitness" report: "Now they're lifting their metal hands. This is the end now. Smoke comes out. . . .

People in the streets see it now. They're running towards the East River . . . thousands of them, dropping in like rats. . . . It's reached Times Square. . . . People trying to run away from it, but it's no use. They . . . they're falling like flies. . . ."

Meanwhile, in real life, Boston families gathered on rooftops and thought they could see a glow in the sky as New York burned. A horrified Pittsburgh husband found his wife with a bottle of poison, screaming: "I'd rather die this way than that!"

People called the electric company in Providence, Rhode Island, to turn off all the city lights to make it a less visible target. A motorist rode through the streets of Baltimore, Paul Revere-fashion, blowing his horn and warning of the Martian invasion.

The staff of a Memphis newspaper readied an extra edition on rumored landings in Chicago and St. Louis. In Minneapolis, a woman ran into a church yelling: "This is the end of the world! I heard it on the radio!"

Back on the broadcast, the forlorn announcer carried on: "Now the smoke's crossing Sixth Avenue . . . Fifth Avenue . . . [coughing] a hundred yards away . . . it's fifty feet . . . [thud of falling body, then only sound of ships' whistles]."

In Salt Lake City, people started to pack before heading into the Rocky Mountains. One man, in Reno for a divorce, started to drive east, hoping to aid his estranged wife. A man and woman who'd run out of gas in northern California just sat and held hands, expecting any minute to see the Martian war machines appear over the tops of trees. Electric power failed in a village in Washington; families started to flee.

In Hollywood, John Barrymore downed a drink, went to his kennels and released his Great Danes. "Fend for yourselves!" he cried.

Then, from the radio, came the mournful call of a "radio operator": "2X2L calling CQ . . . New York. Isn't there anyone on the air? Isn't there anyone?"

Forty minutes into the broadcast, Welles gave his distraught audience a breather—a pause for station and program identification.

In the control room, CBS staffer Richard Goggin was startled as telephones there began to ring. That would only happen in an emergency. "Tension was becoming enormous in Studio One," he later recalled. "They had a tiger by the tail and couldn't let go."

For those brave enough to stay tuned, Welles was able to match the program's stunning first portion with an equally remarkable concluding sequence. In what amounted to a twenty-minute soliloquy, he, in the role of Professor Pierson, chronicled the events that followed the Martians' destruction of New York City. Welles's spellbinding voice—magnetic, doom-filled, stirring—held listeners mesmerized.[5]

In the script, a stoic Pierson, still alive in the rubble, made his solitary way toward the ruins of New York, hiding from the invaders as he went.

Along the way he met a "stranger," a former artilleryman. This survivor feared that the Martians would cage and enslave any humans still alive. The stranger was determined to outwit and outlast the Martians and, in time, to turn the heat-rays back on the invaders and even—if need be—upon other humans. And so, one day, new leaders would rule a new world.

Pierson, unwilling to join the stranger's cause, continued his lonely journey. Entering Manhattan through the now-empty Holland Tunnel, he found a lifeless city:

"I wandered up through the Thirties and Forties . . . stood alone on Times Square. I caught sight of a lean dog running down Seventh Avenue with a piece of dark brown meat

---

[5]Welles's closing narrative, fictionally dramatic in style and compressing months of events into twenty minutes, contrasted sharply with the realism of the first portion of the program. Nevertheless, many listeners apparently remained convinced that Martians had landed.

in his jaws, and a pack of starving mongrels at his heels. . . . I walked up Broadway . . . past silent shop windows, displaying their mute wares to empty sidewalks. . . . "

There seemed to be little hope left for the human race. Then Pierson "caught sight of the hood of a Martian machine, standing somewhere in Central Park, gleaming in the late afternoon sun":

"I rushed recklessly across Columbus Circle and into the park. I climbed a small hill above the pond at Sixtieth Street, and from there I could see standing in a silent row along the mall, nineteen of those great metal Titans, their cowls empty, their steel arms hanging listlessly by their sides. I looked in vain for the monsters that inhabit those machines. Suddenly my eyes were attracted to the immense flock of black birds that hovered directly below me . . . and there before my eyes, stark and silent, lay the Martians, with the hungry birds pecking and tearing brown shreds of flesh from their dead bodies."

The mighty Martians had fallen: ". . . it was found that they were killed by the putrefactive and disease bacteria against which their systems were unprepared . . . slain, after all man's defenses had failed, by the humblest thing that God in His wisdom put upon this earth."

In a sprightly epilogue, Welles then explained away the whole unsettling broadcast as the Mercury Theatre's "way of 'dressing up in a sheet and saying Boo!' . . . We annihilated the world before your very ears, and utterly destroyed the CBS. You will be relieved, I hope, to learn that we didn't mean it, and that both institutions are still open for business."

He tried cheerily to dispel the darkness: "So goodbye everybody, and remember . . . the terrible lesson you learned tonight. . . . And if your doorbell rings and nobody's there, that was no Martian . . . it's Hallowe'en."

The joke was on the listeners. More than one hundred and fifty stations affiliated with CBS had carried the broadcast. About twelve million people had heard the program. Newspapers estimated that at least a million listen-

ers, perhaps many more, had thought the invasion real.

Back in Grovers Mill, disenchantment began to take hold. Twenty-year-old Sam Goldman and three pals had been playing cards when they heard that the Martians were on the move down by the mill. They had thrown down their cards and jumped into a car, ready to face the invaders. "We got there and looked around," Sam said, "and nothing was going on."

A squad of New Jersey state troopers equipped with riot guns had deployed near the crossroads. They found little more than the dilapidated old mill itself.

Nearby, in their grandfather's farmhouse, Dick Stives, his sister, and brothers talked excitedly about the "men from Mars." Then their mother and father came home from the movies and told the children about the "make believe" on radio that everyone was talking about. Dick, more confused than ever, went upstairs to go to sleep, still half-sure that what he heard was "really real."

For the players who had inadvertently just made radio history, the next hours turned into a nightmare. As soon as Welles left the twenty-second-floor studio, he was called to a telephone. He picked it up, to hear the irate mayor of Flint, Michigan, roar that his city was in chaos because of the program and that he, the mayor, would soon be on his way to New York to punch one Orson Welles in the nose.

"By nine o'clock several high-ranking CBS executives had arrived or were in full flight toward 485 Madison. We were in trouble," recalled Larry Harding, a CBS production supervisor for the *Mercury Theatre* show.

Policemen hurried into the CBS building. Welles, Houseman, and the cast were held under informal house arrest. Staffers hastily stashed scripts, memoranda, and the sixteen-inch acetate disks upon which the show had been recorded.

Welles was taken to a room on the seventeenth floor, where reporters battered him with questions about whether he knew of the deaths and suicides his broadcast had caused (none have ever been documented), whether he knew ahead of time how devastating an effect his show would have (he said he didn't), and whether he had planned it all as a publicity stunt (he said he hadn't).

Finally, at about one o'clock Monday morning, Welles and the cast were "released," free to go out into the streets of New York where not a Martian was stirring. Welles walked a half-dozen blocks to the Mercury Theatre, where, even at that hour, members of the stage company were still rehearsing their new play.

Welles went up on stage, where news photographers were lurking. They caught him with his eyes raised, his arms outstretched. The next day his photograph appeared in newspapers throughout the country, over a caption that blurted: "I Didn't Know What I Was Doing!," or words to that effect.

The next morning headlines in major city newspapers reported the hoax: "Radio Listeners in Panic, Taking War Drama as Fact" (*New York Times*); "U.S. Terrorized by Radio's 'Men From Mars'" (*San Francisco Chronicle*); "Radio Drama Causes Panic" (*Philadelphia Inquirer*); "Listeners Weep and Pray, Prepare for End of World" (*New Orleans Times-Picayune*).

Many of the listeners who had been deluded laughed good-naturedly at one another—and at themselves. Some professed not to have been taken in by what one woman called "that Buck Rogers stuff." But others turned their wrath on Welles, on the network, and on the medium that had turned their Sunday evening into a time of unsolicited terror.

CBS apologized to the public, but also pointed out that during the program no fewer than four announcements had been made stating that it was a dramatic presentation, not a news broadcast.

A subdued Welles, believing his career was ruined, dutifully followed suit. "I don't think we will try anything like this again," he stated.

For two or three days, the press would not let Welles, nor radio, off the front page. Media rivalry played its part; newspaper publishers seemed anxious to portray radio—and Welles—as villains. The clipping bureau that served CBS delivered condemnatory editorials by the pound.

While newsmen "tsk-tsked," government officials fumed. Senator Clyde Herring of Iowa, reflecting the anger of many citizens, stated his support for legislation to curb such "Halloween bogymen." The Federal Communications Commission (FCC), flooded with complaint letters, tried to find a philosophical stance somewhere between imposing severe censorship and permitting unbridled expression.

Novelist H. G. Wells cabled his disregards from London. Although he had given CBS permission to air his novel, he complained that "it was not explained to me that this dramatization would be made with a liberty that amounts to a complete reworking of *The War of the Worlds*."

But some columnists and editorialists began to perceive significant merit in the program. Essayist Heywood Broun interpreted the broadcast as a cautionary tale: "Jitters have come home to roost. The peace of Munich hangs heavy over our heads like a thundercloud." *Variety*, under a headline stating "Radio Does U.S. a Favor," described the program as a warning to Americans of the danger of unpreparedness.

In a column that turned the tide of public opinion in favor of Welles and company, Dorothy Thompson called the broadcast "the news story of the century—an event which made greater contribution to an understanding of Hitlerism, Mussolinism, Stalinism, anti-Semitism, and all the other terrorism of our time than all the words about them that have been written by reasonable men."

Welles, to his relief, soon learned that he would not be consigned to durance vile. "Bill Paley, the head of CBS, brought Orson and me up on the carpet and gave us a reprimand," Houseman later recalled. "But there was ambivalence to it. The working stiffs thought we were heroes. The executives thought of us as

Orson Welles, besieged by reporters after the 1938 brodcast of War of the Worlds. *Welles expressed amazement and regret that his dramatization had created panic among millions of radio listeners.*

some sort of anarchists. But reason—and revenues—prevailed. A few days after the broadcast, when it was announced that Campbell's Soup had become a sponsor, the boys at the top began to think of us as heroes, or at least as employable persons, as well."

Some critics continued to decry the credulity of the American people. They spoke of the compelling power of the human voice emanating from the upper air. Radio, ominously, seemed able to reduce an entire country to the size of one room; it exerted unexpected power over susceptible millions.

For a book-length study titled *The Invasion from Mars,* Princeton University psychology professor Hadley Cantril interviewed scores of persons who had listened to the program. Speaking with them shortly after "that night," he received responses ranging from insecure to phobic to fatalistic.

"The coming of the Martians did not present a situation where the individual could pre-

serve one value if he sacrifices another," Professor Cantril concluded from his research. "In this situation the individual stood to lose all his values at once. Nothing could be done to save any of them. Panic was inevitable."

Did Welles intend the panic? Had he hoped, by means of his magnificent dramatic powers, to gain all those headlines?

Houseman dismisses such conjecture as "rubbish." He declares: "Orson and I had no clear presense of the mood of the audience. *The War of the Worlds* wasn't selected as a parable of invasion and war in the 1930s, but just as an interesting story unto itself. Only after the fact did we perceive how ready and resonant the world was for the tale. Our intent was theatre, not terror."

Welles and his players could not know that they had portrayed the shape of things to come. The program was, in a way, quite prophetic. Barely two weeks later, German foreign minister Joachim von Ribbentrop chillingly commented: "I would not be surprised if in the United States eyewitness reports are under consideration in which the 'Giants from Mars' marched up in brown shirts waving swastika flags."

Sooner than the peoples of the world could guess, a true nightmare—that of World War II—would be upon them.

Welles, of course, went on to memorable successes in motion pictures and theater. And his *War of the Worlds* broadcast became the most famous radio program of all time.

These days, the crossroads village of Grovers Mill is much the way it was that spectral night half a century ago. There are, however, signs of strangers nearby—new homes sprouting up among what had been potato fields. And futuristic shapes—sleek, glass-walled, high-technology industrial buildings—stand amid the trees.

But the old mill itself is still at the intersection of Millstone and Cranbury roads—a dot east of Princeton on the highway map. The weather-worn wooden structure, with a few of its millstones scattered about, stands lonely vigil.

Here fate tossed its random lightning-bolt. Here the "Martians" made their landing on what is now a municipal park. Nearby, ducks glide on a big, placid pond.

The former Wilson farm (the script spoke of the "Wilmuth" farm, but sightseers made do with the Wilson place) has long since been cut up into smaller properties. Here Martian-hunters once tramped across the cornfields looking for traces of the invaders.

Wayfarers from all parts of the world still occasionally wander the roads and fields of Grovers Mill. They know they will see no Martians, find no burn marks on the earth left by war machines from outer space, nor come upon charred ruins wrought by the aliens' devastation. Still, drawn by curiosity, they come and look and wonder.

Not all Grovers Mill residents find such doings fascinating. The proprietor of a nearby gas station, for example, remembers the night of the "invasion," but didn't think much of it then and thinks as little of it now. "It doesn't make sense," he says with disdain. "Never has. Never will."

But for Dick Stives, now sixty-three, the "panic broadcast" till holds disquieting memories. Not long ago he walked around the "Martian landing ground."

"When I was a kid," he recalled, "I would crawl down near the wheel of the old mill, just by the pond there, and shuck my clothes and go in swimming. It was just a pond on a farm. But now, looking at it, I have to wonder why people still come so far to find a place where something that was supposed to happen didn't happen."

"I still remember," he said, "how I felt that night, up there in the bedroom in my granddad's place, in the dark, trying to sleep, thinking about what we had heard on the radio. The nighttime would make me think about how almost anything, just about anytime, could happen anywhere—even in Grovers Mill. Things in the shadows. Things I didn't understand."

Study Questions

1. Describe the early career of Orson Welles. Did he realize that his *War of the Worlds* broadcast would create such a controversy?

2. Describe how the show was structured to create tension and heighten suspense.

3. How did Americans react to the broadcast? What do their reactions suggest about the power of radio?

4. In your opinion, was the broadcast unethical or dangerous?

5. How did the struggles going on in Europe affect how Americans received the broadcast?

Bibliography

For discussions of the role of advertising in the 1920s, see Stuart Ewen, *Captains of Consciousness* (1976) and Roland Marchand, *Advertising the American Dream: Making Way for Modernity, 1920–1940* (1986). The influence of films on American culture is ably portrayed in Robert Sklar, *Movie-Made America: A Cultural History of American Movies* (1975) and Larry May, *Screening Out the Past* (1980). Paul Carter's *Another Part of the Twenties* (1977) is an excellent description of popular social attitudes during the infancy of the radio industry. Although there is not much literature on the history of radio, see Erik Barnouw, *A Tower of Babel: A History of Broadcasting in the United States* (1966). Francis Chase, *Sound and Fury: An Informal History of Broadcasting* (1942); and Michele Hilmes and Jason Loviglio, eds., *Radio Reader: Essays in the Cultural History of Radio* (2001). The broadcast itself is discussed in Howard Koch, *The Panic Broadcast* (1970) and Barbara Leaming, *Orson Welles* (1985).

READING 17

★ ★ ★

Superman in Depression and War

David Welky

In the comic book, Superman may have been born on the doomed planet of Krypton, but in reality, he was a product of the Great Depression. He was the creation of Jerry Siegel and Joe Shuster, two sons of Jewish immigrants. In the midst of the Depression Siegel and Shuster maintained their faith in the American Dream, and Superman expressed that faith. The most appealing quality of Superman is that he was both average and extraordinary. As Clark Kent, the mild-mannered reporter, he was the American common man, a person who blended anonymously into a crowd. As Superman, however, he was endowed with the power to avenge wrongs, eradicate evils, and triumph over inequities. Superman debuted in DC's *Action Comics* in June 1938. He was the "champion of the oppressed," an action hero for a country that desperately needed action, and as a commercial venture a super success. As historian David Welky shows, however, Superman also expressed the anxieties and fears, as well as the hopes and dreams, of Americans during the crisis years of the Depression and World War II. At a time when Adolf Hitler spoke of a Nazi superman, America's Superman became a democratic hero.

Yes, Superman, strange visitor from another planet, a handsome man in red boots and cape with one lock of dark hair curling across his forehead and a bold "S" emblazoned upon his chest. Even the most cultured and all but the most ignorant Americans know who is faster than a speeding bullet and more powerful than a locomotive, and few can honestly say that they have never tied a towel around their neck, thrust out their arms, and run around a room in an approximation of flight. From his obscure origins on the doomed planet Krypton, Kal-El, or Superman, has achieved a level of popularity here on Earth greater than any other figure in mass culture save perhaps Mickey Mouse. He has fought for truth, justice, and the American way in films, cartoons, comic strips, a Broadway musical, television shows, novels, and a radio program, and his image has been emblazoned on products ranging from T-shirts to moccasins to peanut butter. He has even had his own exhibit at the Smithsonian Institute.

Superman emerged during the depths of the Great Depression of the 1930s. The decade's economic dislocation was not only unprecedented, it also occurred against a backdrop of wrenching social and political transformations. Many worried that Franklin Roosevelt's ambitious New Deal marked the first step toward an American dictatorship. The rise of Hitler and Mussolini, the specter of Joseph Stalin, and the growth of militarism in Japan seemed to confirm that totalitarianism was on the march and democracy was on the run. This climate of fear, uncertainty, and suffering raised loud calls for sweeping changes in American life. Proletarian authors like James T. Ferrell, Michael Gold, and John Dos Passos produced novels that vividly portrayed the psychological, economic, and social damage done by the Depression. Much more common and much more popular, however, was literature that upheld long-standing American values and insisted that there was no need for dramatic reforms. Middle-class magazines, newspapers, and books demonstrated the continuing relevance of the rags-to-riches ethos of hard work, upheld traditional gender roles, and expressed suspicion of foreigners and outsiders. They also envisioned a homogenous society without class divisions and assured Americans that their country was still uniquely blessed and had a distinct Way of Life. This middlebrow ideology had deep roots in the past and offered comforting and familiar landmarks to a nation reeling from domestic and overseas disasters.

Although Superman did not appear until 1938, his instant popularity and strong identification with many common Depression-era themes make him a valuable figure to study. He is also noteworthy because, perhaps more than any other figure in popular culture, he transmitted many of the themes of middlebrow ideology to the next generation of Americans. And yet he ignited a firestorm of controversy when he first appeared. Although his early adventures were far from radical, they often challenged the status quo and called for social revision. His rebellious side attracted the notice of parental and educational groups, who launched a very public campaign to quiet him and the new medium he represented, the comic book, which violated accepted ideals of childrearing and awakened fears for the future of democracy in an age of dictatorship. Superman rapidly evolved in response to these attacks, shifting from a culturally marginal figure known only to children as a mainstream character and a lucrative cash cow for his corporate handlers. He dropped his dangerous elements and completely embraced the safety of tradition. Just as Clark Kent transformed himself into the Man of Steel, Superman shed his reformer role to become a booster of middle-class Americanism, providing a notable example of how cultural products alter their messages when they move from the periphery to the center of the popular consciousness.

Original Essay. Copyright David Welky.

The adventures of Superman are also instructive for those who argue for the primacy of radicalism in 1930s-era culture. The forces of respectability and the lure of profits made it impossible for culture to be both popular and subversive. The pressures to conform were too powerful even for Superman to resist. They were the kryptonite that weakened his original message and rendered him socially harmless.

Superman arrived at a time when his young readers desperately needed someone to admire. The comic magazine's primary audience, boys aged eight to twelve, had never known good times. Their lives had been marked by want and militarism, and disorder seemed the normal state of affairs. Economic dislocation exacted a psychological toll on many children. They often lost respect for fathers who were unemployed or had trouble providing for the family. The accompanying damage to family status made many more self-conscious and often led to withdrawal, underachievement, and feelings of shame. The belief that their parents had failed led many children and young adults to look beyond them for positive examples. Younger children typically use older peers and siblings as role models, but comic-book readers often had little reason to admire big brother, for teenagers keenly felt their own economic shortcomings. Even well-educated teenagers struggled to find work and felt that they were a drag on their families. Many unsuccessful jobseekers left home for the life of a transient or grew apathetic toward their own lives and events in the outside world. With their parents and older siblings proving inadequate role models and with only hardship looming in the future, it is no wonder that children wanted a hero who spoke directly to them and offered hope for a better tomorrow.

That hero came not from Washington, D.C. and not even from the United States, but rather from the faraway planet of Krypton. Superman was the brainchild of Jerry Siegel and Joe Shuster, two youths who were

Superman was a product of the late 1930's comic book industry. He spoke directly to the fears and dreams of American's during the Great Depression and World War II.

as obscure and hopeless as millions of others in their generation. Had their formative years not been so bleak, it is unlikely that the Man of Steel would have arrived on Earth, for Superman was not just the creation of two inventive minds. He was the product of and the answer to the problems of a troubled generation, a hero sent from above who helped to alleviate the anxieties spawned by a world in turmoil.

Jerry Siegel was an awkward introvert who spent much of his life in a world of his own imagination. Born into a lower-middle-class family in Cleveland in 1914, the "slightly built, slope-shouldered" boy seemed bound for nowhere. He was a poor student who usually showed up late for school, often still wearing his pajamas beneath his clothes, and made few close friends. But the mediocre student had what comic book historian Dennis Dooley called "the soul of a D'Artagnon imprisoned in the body of an undernourished delivery boy." Siegel secretly loved dime detective novels and adventure stories and devoured Edgar Rice Burroughs, Jules Verne, and H. G. Wells novels. He also adored action films and fantasy comic strips like *Tarzan, Buck Rogers,* and *Flash Gordon.* Philip Wylie's 1930 novel, *Gladiator,* featuring a hero who could leap forty feet, lift cars, and deflect bullets with his body, heavily influenced the young man. He considered becoming a writer or a newspaper reporter, but his future was still very much in question when he met Joe Shuster in 1930.

Also born in 1914, Shuster was as unremarkable as his future collaborator. He moved with his family from Toronto to Cleveland when he was ten, settling in a run-down area just twelve blocks from Siegel's modest home. He was as awkward as Siegel and resembled an "undernourished, bewildered schoolboy of sixteen" despite his earnest efforts to bulk up. Burdened with the additional handicap of thick-lensed glasses, he was painfully shy around girls. Schuster shared Siegel's interest in science fiction, but he was more attracted to pictures than words. He drew comic strips for his school newspaper, including one prophetically titled *Jerry the Journalist*. The strip's author introduced Shuster to his cousin, Jerry Siegel, when he learned of their common love.

Siegel and Schuster were on the fringe of American life. They were poor, socially inept, and far from the culture centers of New York and Hollywood. They both sensed that they were misfits and outsiders, and the two hit it off instantly. Their relationship was, Siegel later remarked, "like the right chemicals coming together." Thrilled to have found kindred spirits, they dreamed of launching a comic strip and submitted innumerable proposals with no success. They started a fantasy pulp of sorts in 1933, a mimeographed publication entitled *Science Fiction*. One of their best stories, "The Reign of the Superman," in which a bald, villainous megalomaniac gains super powers and threatens to conquer the earth, appeared in the third issue. But their work accomplished little, and *Science Fiction* died after five issues. They graduated from high school with no career prospects and worked odd jobs to pay for postage for comic-strip submissions. Shuster was so poverty-stricken that he had to draw their proposals on brown wrapping paper or on the back of wallpaper.

Their lives could have gone the way of a proletarian novel. They could have grown dis-

affected and radical. They could have ended up drunk and penniless in a dank urban pool hall like James Farrell's antihero Studs Lonigan. But as Jerry Siegel lay in bed one summer night in 1933, he was struck by a simple yet profound epiphany. "I conceive[d]," he later wrote, of "a character like Samson, Hercules, and all the strong men I ever heard of rolled into one. *Only more so.*" He got Shuster to give his inspiration a visual form the next morning. Schuster drew a powerful man, clad in a T-shirt and jeans, holding a thug over his head as another futilely fired a machine gun at him. A one-word logo arched across the top of the page, each letter getting smaller as it gently descended to the right: "SUPERMAN." Unlike the "Superman" from their *Science Fiction* story, he was a hero, not a villain (an "infinitely more commercial" proposition, remarked Siegel). The two fleshed out their creation in the Shusters' unheated apartment through 1933 and 1934. Superman shed his civilian garb in favor of a garish, skintight outfit, complete with a flowing cape and the trademark "S" on his chest. After properly outfitting him, Siegel and Shuster developed Superman's mild-mannered alter ego, named for two of their favorite actors, Clark Gable and Kent Taylor, and loosely modeled in looks and personality on the film comedian Harold Lloyd. They also gave Superman a home, named in honor of Fritz Lang's 1926 science-fiction film *Metropolis*.

Siegel and Shuster had not designed a character for the middle-class America of the *Saturday Evening Post* and the *Ladies' Home Journal*. They consciously created a character who spoke to the disaffected and the disenfranchised and bore direct relevance to the current economic crisis. "Both of us were children of the Depression," Siegel once remarked, "so we knew how the people felt who were having a rough time of it." Siegel deeply sympathized with those in need and felt a powerful sense of "compassion . . . for the downtrodden." Seeing nothing but dislocation at home and growing discord abroad, he pondered how he could make the world a better place for them. "What would I do," he asked, "if I weren't so meek and mild, and if I were stronger than anyone else on Earth?" Superman was Siegel and Shuster's gift to America, a fictional figure who did more to restore hope than his creators ever could on their own. They wanted him to be the protector of the little man, the defender of common folk struggling in a world gone mad. He also marked the ultimate expression of "wish fulfillment." As Clark Kent, he was no more remarkable than his creators—shy, bespectacled, and awkward around women. But suddenly and without warning, this mild-mannered reporter became the most powerful being on Earth, saving lives and catching crooks while maintaining a nonchalant air towards the women who worshiped him—most notably, the ever-adoring Lois Lane. Superman addressed the inadequacies of a hopeless generation by instilling a belief that ordinary people could be special, that they could succeed in an unforgiving world that offered little hope for the future. In a way it was a very traditional message that incorporated the dreams of hundreds of years of Americans, the dream of finding a special gift that will make you an extraordinary person. By pitching his appeal to the underclass, however, Superman would end up making many conservative thinkers very uncomfortable.

The budding cartoonists labored for five years to get Superman into the public eye. They sent samples to numerous comic-strip syndicates to no avail. Superman seemed too marginal and immature for these engines of middlebrow culture. Finally accepting that *Superman* would not appear in newspapers any time soon, Siegel and Shuster pursued employment in a new and little-known medium—the comic magazine.

The comic-book industry was not much of an industry. Comic books had existed since the turn of the century, but publications like *Yellow Kid Magazine* (1897), *Comic Monthly* (1922), and *Famous Funnies* (1934) contained reprints of newspaper comics rather than original material. Some appeared on newsstands and others served as giveaway premiums—purchasers of Phillips' Dental Magnesia, for example, received a free copy of *Skippy Comics*. *New Comics* broke new ground in 1935 by including original material. That same year, *New Fun Comics* (later renamed *More Fun Comics*) followed its lead and became the first regularly issued comic to feature all-new work.

The shift from reprints to first-run comics created a pressing need for artists and storywriters. Drawing from a large pool of unemployed, often-inexperienced, and sometimes-incompetent artists and writers, companies established assembly lines that focused on quantity rather than quality of output. Artist Will Eisner recalled that employees "worked buttock-to-buttock and communicated like cell-block inmates" as they performed their assigned tasks—inking, lettering, drawing backgrounds or main characters—for about one dollar per page. It was not always pleasant work, but it was work. When asked why he worked in such conditions, Eisner responded: "malnutrition."

The two youngsters from Cleveland traveled to New York in 1935 to get a toehold in this still-primitive business. *Superman* came with them, but no publisher wanted to use such an absurd feature in their book. Siegel and Shuster convinced National Allied Publishing (later DC Comics) head Major Malcolm Wheeler-Nicholson to run their "Henri Duval," the story of a swashbuckling adventurer (submitted on brown wrapping paper), in *New Fun Comics*. The pair later contributed "Federal Men," which followed the lives of G-Men, and "Dr. Occult the Ghost Detective" to Wheeler-Nicholson's comics. Dr. Occult's superhuman powers, long cape, and triangular chest insignia indicate that Superman had not left their minds. The duo's wisecracking vigilante sleuth, "Slam Bradley," became a fan favorite in National's new *Detective Comics* and gave them enough clout to get the Man of Steel in print. In 1938, National featured Superman in the first issue of *Action Comics.* Conceived during the first days of the New Deal, Superman was finally born at the bottom of the Roosevelt Recession. He appeared at exactly the time when Americans began a quest to discover strength in the ordinary citizen. Like Steinbeck's Tom Joad and Capra's Jefferson Smith, he was an average-looking man who could do great things for the country, a vivid expression of the capabilities of the everyday American riled in support of a just cause.

Action Comics had an instant impact upon the business. Kids snatched up the first edition of 200,000 and dealers begged for more. The fourth installment of *Action Comics* sold almost 500,000 issues, far more than any other comic on the market. Surveys revealed that kids bought the magazine mostly because of the Man of Steel. It was not *Action Comics* they wanted, it was *Superman Comics.* National gave the buyers what they wanted; the first issue of *Superman,* featuring four stories about the man from Krypton, hit newsstands in early 1939, making him the first comic character to have his own magazine. The quarterly *Superman* moved about 1.25 million copies per issue by the next year, while sales of the monthly *Action Comics* skyrocketed to about 900,000 copies per issue, far outreaching their closest competitors. Both magazines reached far larger audiences than sales indicate. Far from being a private commodity, kids treated comic books as "a sort of currency," exchanging them with peers for ones that they had not yet read. Statisticians estimated that about three children read each comic book.

Superman and the other "costumed characters" who soon cropped up around him— Batman, Captain America, Green Arrow, Hawkman, Wonder Woman—put the business upon solid financial footing. But Super-

man was clearly the star of the medium. Superman deserves most of the credit for this. Comic-book insider Carmine Infantino argued that he "literally *created* this industry. . . . He's the key, the granddaddy of them all."

Comic books are built on fantasy, and there were of course differences between the comic world and the real world. Obviously, there were no caped superheroes patrolling the skies over Depression-era America, and much of the technology in Superman comics went far beyond contemporary capabilities. But more interesting are the ways that they twisted the reality of American demographics to better conform to conservative traditions. Although it was more willing to show the lower class than many other publications, the comic offered a world populated almost entirely by WASPy whites, who accounted for the bulk of comic book sales. Not one African American appeared in the pre-war issues of *Superman* and *Action Comics.* Although a few stories included native peoples, they rarely had personalities and acted primarily as colorful backdrops for Superman's exploits. Siegel and Shuster appealed to their largely male, youthful audience by including very few women in their stories, most notably Lois Lane. Lois was a career woman—a rarity in 1930s literature—but her job serves mostly as a gateway to trouble. Her journalistic efforts generally get her kidnapped or into some other scrape that Superman has to extract her from. One wonders if she would have been better off at home, and her constant fawning over the Man of Steel makes one wonder if she would have chosen a man over a career.

Superman upheld other conservative priorities. Though he is a unique figure, he embodies many of the attributes Americans traditionally ascribed to themselves. Superman continued a tradition of superheroes that stretched back to the ancient Babylonians, whose Gilgamesh epic told the story of a half-human, half-god creature, but the cowboy, who embodied independence and rugged individualism as he created order out of lawlessness in the Old West, was a much more important influence for Superman's creators. Pulp characters like Doc Savage propelled the ideals of the cowboy into a modern, urban environment, and Superman carried them into the realm of science fiction. Like all white Americans, he was an immigrant, and he quickly shed any vestige of his alien nature to blend seamlessly into the mainstream. He applied his talents to lift himself from an obscure midwestern town to become nationally renowned, and he works to preserve the social order, preventing chaos and disaster from wracking the lives of the innocent.

Even though the comic was in many ways aligned with the conservative tradition, its social rebelliousness placed it beyond respectability. Unlike most middlebrow sources, it realistically depicted the country's economic woes and pinned blame for them squarely upon the business class, which was in turn tied to notorious criminals and devious foreigners—even America's most famous immigrant shared the nation's traditional suspicion of outsiders. Restoring tranquility meant shattering the capitalist class' stronghold on power. In one story, Superman investigates the murder of Paul Dorgan, a prominent sociologist who believed that "sinister persons or forces" wanted to "stave off the return of national prosperity." Superman learns that Dorgan's killers work for J. F. Curtis, a powerful industrialist whose henchmen are hard at work sabotaging factories and sowing labor discord. Superman digs further and discovers that a "foreign nation" has promised to give Curtis "important concessions if he'll wreck America's economic structure" by crashing the stock market. Superman visits the capitalist, who inhospitably tries to electrocute him. But the current has no effect on the Man of Tomorrow. He grabs Curtis as it surges through him, "instantly electrocuting" him and allowing the United States to resume its "march toward prosperity."

Another story posits an even more sinister plot to devastate America. With the country in the midst of "the worst depression" in history, the *Daily Planet* dispatches Clark Kent to interview some leading financiers. Not unlike Herbert Hoover, they all assure Clark that the downturn is just "a temporary panic." Clark overhears one of them laughing with his cronies about the profits he is making "while the rest of the country goes bankrupt." Changing into Superman, he follows the "ruthless financial giant" to a strange meeting headed by his mortal enemy, Lex Luthor, who uses a "narcotic incense" to control the capitalists' minds and pocketbooks. They have been manipulating the stock market while under his influence, creating huge profits for Luthor and driving the rest of the country to ruin. Superman breaks up Luthor's ring and knocks his airplane from the sky when he flees, presumably ending his career in crime. With Luthor gone, Clark assures his publisher that "the menace is removed" and "the nation" will soon return "to its former prosperity."

Metropolis's moguls engaged in an array of dubious ventures that were not directly tied to the Depression but nevertheless wreaked havoc on ordinary people. Businessmen masterminded numerous stock swindles and had a nasty habit of using low-grade materials in construction projects. Thornton Blakely was the most repulsive of the lot. Workers at the Blakely Coal Mine had long complained about unsafe conditions. The boss, however, paid little heed to their concerns and the miners had to either stay on or starve. Their fears are confirmed when a shaft collapses and traps a miner. Superman saves his life, but the accident leaves the miner crippled. Blakely blames the accident on the worker's "own carelessness" in an interview with Clark Kent and offers a mere fifty dollars in severance pay. Angrily denying charges that he is running an unsafe business, he retorts that even if there are "safety hazards" in the mine, they are not his problem. "I'm a businessman, not a humanitarian," he remarks. That night, Clark disguises himself as a miner and crashes a party at the boss's mansion.

Watchmen capture him and bring him before Blakely. Inspired by this unexpected arrival, the host decides to move the gathering into the mine. After the assembly dutifully troops beneath the earth to continue the fete, their new miner friend interrupts their revelry by yanking down the supports holding up their shaft and imprisoning them. Blakely remains calm until he discovers that the alarms that signal the world above have broken due to years of neglect. His party assails the "blasted skinflint" for his greed. "If you'd have had the mine equipped with proper safety-precautions," screams one tuxedo-clad prisoner, "we might have gotten out alive!" They futilely claw at the rubble, exhausting themselves without making any progress. Superman finally frees the panicked group, and when Clark visits Blakely for a follow-up interview, he discovers a changed man. "Henceforth," he insists, "my mine will be the safest in the country, and my workers the best treated."

The various crimes of corrupt businessmen were one part of a bleak picture painted by the first Superman comics. Siegel and Shuster placed their hero in a gritty urban landscape full of vice, crime, and official ineptitude, a blasted-out mockery of America's City on a Hill. It was an image that stretched all the way back to Thomas Jefferson, but anti-city rhetoric found many expressions in Depression-era mass culture. Hollywood issued a spate of films portraying the city as a seedbed of corruption and moral decay, populated by devious slicksters, shyster lawyers, and politicians on the take. Urbanites like radio's Amos and Andy lived in a world full of tricksters and con-artists. Countless B-Westerns identified the city with greedy businessmen and bankers eager to cheat common folk out of their money. Even though middle-class sources generally avoided this world, the marginalized comic-book industry identified much more with John Wayne than the *Saturday Evening Post*. Batman and other comic-book heroes existed in climates similar to Super-

man's, but none were as good at uncovering and crushing wickedness as the Man of Steel.

Malicious capitalists were not the only threat to social tranquility in this malevolent environment. Murders and kidnappings occur with frightening regularity. Racketeers impose protection schemes on innocent storekeepers and cab drivers. Many of the institutions designed to expose and halt crime are ineffective or, even worse, assist the bad guys. Although Clark Kent's *Daily Planet* remains squeaky-clean, the tabloid *Morning Herald* cooperates with crooks to get lurid scoops, and its equally yellow competitor, the *Morning Pictorial*, uses its influence to denounce critics of its politician-owner, Alex Evell (who could very easily be viewed as a caricature of William Randolph Hearst), who plans to dominate the city for his own benefit. The police are always at least one step behind the Man of Tomorrow and repeatedly prove incapable of solving a crime without his help. Further, even with all the confessions he extracts and all of the felons he deposits at Police Headquarters, the cops still consider him an enemy. Figuring that anyone who is around so many crimes must be involved somehow, they spend more time trying to capture Superman than tracking down criminals.

In Superman's world, inept police officers were indicative of larger failings. He resolved to do something about the problems in local government in late 1940. An opening caption shrieks the setup:

Crooked politics sabotages the very foundations of democratic government! When **SUPERMAN** *finds the city of Metropolis infested by evil, conniving public officeholders, he begins a cleanup campaign which for sheer thoroughness and unorthodox procedure has never before been witnessed in the annals of representative government!*

Clark and Lois suspect that city prosecutor Ralph Dale is "working hand-in-hand with the underworld" and convince the *Daily Planet* to endorse opposition candidate Bert Runyan in the upcoming election. The evildoings of Nat Burly, a "corrupt political boss" whose shady regime depends upon Dale's lax prosecution of criminals, hampers Runyan's campaign. Superman thwarts Burly's efforts to bump him off and to use corrupt police officers to frame and discredit him. Runyan keeps up his attacks on Burly, who retaliates by using "strongarm men" to bust up his rallies. Prosecutor Dale wins the election with the help of some vigorous ballot-box stuffing, but Superman, infuriated by this perversion of democracy, forces a pivotal pro-Burly ward leader to confess his chicanery on the radio, thereby nullifying the fraudulent results and returning "good government" to Metropolis. Good government was apparently tough to preserve. Superman was again battling "crooked politicians" with links to organized crime by mid-1941.

The little guy needed help in this brutal world, so Superman dedicated much of his energy to assisting ordinary citizens who were down on their luck. Just because the Man of Steel was super-powerful did not mean that he always concentrated on super-important issues; no problem is too small for the man in the sky. In one early story, he helps a washed-up boxer regain his form and win the title. In another, he takes the place of a bench-warming college football player, partly to bring down a crooked coach and partly to help the second-stringer keep his girlfriend from running off with another athlete. In a third tale, he poses as a strongman to drum up business for the struggling Jordan Circus. Mr. Jordan is a kindly old man who maintains "an optimistic front" despite facing "bitter disappointment and certain defeat." "A guy like that," Superman concludes, "deserves a break." And what a break. Superman's remarkable feats of strength pack the big top and save Mr. Jordan from bankruptcy.

His desire to help those in need and his drive for social reform reach an interesting peak in *Action Comics* #8, cover-dated January 1939 but written on the heels of the Roosevelt Recession. The story, which shows the influence of social-problem films like *Dead End* (1937) and *Angels With Dirty Faces* (1938), again revolves around children. Always on the lookout for a story, Clark watches as Frankie Marello, a hardened street urchin of perhaps twelve, is found guilty of assault and battery. He listens intently as Frankie's mother begs the court for leniency. "He's my only son," she tells the judge. "He might have been a good boy, except for his environment." The reporter agrees with Frankie's distraught mother but notes that "if I know the court of law . . . her plea hasn't a chance!" Sure enough, the judge sentences Frankie to two years in the reformatory. Clark discovers that Frankie was part of a child-crime syndicate straight from the pages of *Oliver Twist*, with "Gimpy," a "loathsome corrupter of youth," standing in for Dickens's Fagin. Appalled by the scheme, Superman roughs up Gimpy and exiles him from Metropolis, then scares the slum kids straight. He is satisfied that they will live "clean an' honest" lives yet hopes to do more. "It's not entirely your fault that you're delinquent," he explains, "these slums—your poor living conditions" are the real culprit. He sends the children through the slums to tell residents to gather their possessions and leave the area, then rips down dilapidated buildings and single-handedly clears the slum while ignoring the gunfire of troops brought in to stop him. After the dust settles, emergency crews replace the tenements with decent apartments, allowing the children to live in "splendid housing conditions" and putting a major dent in juvenile crime.

As this story implies, Superman did not merely fight crime. He instead took a proactive approach by reforming the environment and misguided morals that led to felonious behavior. Nor was he reluctant to use force to get what he wanted. The May 1939 edition of *Action Comics* presented the most violent and dictatorial vision of Superman during the pre-war era. Clark Kent arrives at a crash scene to find that a negligent driver has killed a friend of his. The ineffective mayor refuses to improve the city's traffic situation, so he takes the matter into his own hands. Bursting through the door of a radio station, the Man of Tomorrow snatches the microphone from a startled announcer and proclaims that "the auto-accident death rate of this community . . . should shame us all! It's constantly rising and due entirely to reckless driving and inefficiency! . . . From this moment on, I declare war on reckless drivers—Henceforth, homicidal drivers answer to *ME!*" He "systematically" destroys every vehicle in the city's impound lot as he chuckles about his "private little war." Next, he accuses the owner of the Bates Motor Company, whose cars are involved in more accidents than any other make, of using inferior parts to save money at the cost of human lives, then dismantles the entire factory without a thought for the jobs to be lost. Finally, he catches the mayor himself driving recklessly. Hurling himself into the car, Superman grabs the wheel and mashes the accelerator. The mayor panics as the car lurches forward. "Do you want to kill us?" he screams. "Why not?" Superman replies. "You didn't worry much about killing the others! . . . By not seeing to it that the speed laws were strictly enforced." He yanks the mayor out of the vehicle a split second before it collides with a boulder and drags him to the morgue to show him the bodies of recent auto-accident victims. Shaken by Superman's actions, the mayor agrees to "rigidly" enforce the traffic laws. Clark finds a parking ticket on his car soon after, proving the effectiveness of his tactics and demonstrating that sometimes people need a strongman, not a bureaucracy, to set them right.

Superman's social ethos set him apart from other comic-book heroes. He outmuscled all of his comic competitors, but this was merely a matter of shading. Batman, Captain Marvel, Wonder Woman, and the other superheroes could approach Superman physically. None, however, were nearly as committed to helping the unfortunate as the self-proclaimed "champion of the weak and helpless," and none were so concerned with improving morals and standards of conduct. Cosmo, the Phantom of Disguise, mostly helped rich people and never explained why he was so eager to help. Batman, Superman's closest rival in sales, was less interested in the welfare of others than in satisfying his own dark and mysterious urges. He wanted vengeance, not a better world.

As the leading voice in a marginal industry, Superman challenged authority, demonized the rich, exposed class differences, demanded social reform, and worked on behalf of common people. But by making the comic book a phenomenon among American youth, he also brought it to the attention of adult critics who viewed it as a threat to children and even to the nation.

Parents, educators, and librarians agreed that "virtually no child escape[d] the influence of the comics," and set about to combat the menace. *Chicago Daily News* literary editor Sterling North contributed one of the most vociferous attacks against the genre with a 1940 editorial entitled "A National Disgrace," in which he denounced the comic book as "a poisonous mushroom growth" growing upon the American social body. These "sex-horror serials" pushed "mayhem, murder, torture and abduction" into impressionable minds, making children more likely to live reckless lives. They imbalanced "young nervous systems" by portraying an unnaturally tinted landscape and crudely drawn characters that ruined "the child's natural sense of color." Comics also prevented children from discovering the "better" class of literature that all educated people should be acquainted with. Ultimate blame for the comic menace lay not with kids, but rather with adults and, by implication, society:

The shame lies largely with the parents who don't know and don't care what their children

*are reading. It lies with unimaginative teach-
ers who force stupid, dull twaddle down eager
young throats, and, of course, it lies with the
completely immoral publishers of the
'comics'—guilty of a cultural slaughter of the
innocents.*

Over forty newspapers and magazines reprinted North's jeremiad. Preachers read it
from pulpits, teachers posted it on school-
house walls, and concerned adults nationwide
wrote in its support.

Most who commented on comic books seconded North's argument. Literary critic Lovell
Thompson found the comics to be brutal, sadistic, and fantastic, and wondered how kids
would ever "learn concentration on such a
reading diet." The *Wilson Library Bulletin* declared that any child "conditioned by the jerky,
jiggling, inflamed world of the comics is a damaged child." Writing in the *Horn Book,* Louise
Bechtel urged parents to blunt the comics' appeal by reading their children more mind-
expanding books and taking a more active
interest in their schooling. Parents should feel
"ashamed that in an America which above all
cares for education, such a phenomenon as Superman should be so successful." Perhaps the
most trenchant analysis came from James
Frank Vlamos, one of the few commentators
who actually studied his subject before assault-
ing it. Writing in the *American Mercury* in 1941,
he expressed his concerns in terms that reflected a profound concern for the traditional
social and political fabric of America and an
awareness of how events in Europe could unravel that fabric. "You can't go through an issue
of a 'comic' magazine," he declared,

*without realizing that the lawful processes of
police and courts have disappeared and that
only the heroism of superheroes keep us from
being annihilated by divers[e] disasters and
crimes. The 'hero' has no hesitancy, in these
tracts for the kiddies, in subjecting the 'villain'
to third-degree tortures and mental terror. . . .
His methods may be those of a bully, but his al-*

*leged motives make him a hero. He is a law
unto himself, this super-hero. . . . 'Politician' in
these child stories means 'crook' and 'policeman' means 'idiot.' Expressions like 'racketeering union' and 'war-mongering industrialist'
and 'Fifth Columnist' are used indiscrimi-
nately. If any hope for normal democratic society exists at all, it is in the goodness and might
of some superman.*

Vlamos worried that figures such as Superman subverted respect for traditional institutions of authority without offering any
appropriately American substitute. Superheroes, who settled problems without strictly
adhering to the law, seemed anti-democratic
at a time when democracy desperately needed
defending.

The anxieties raised by comic books reflected broader social attitudes toward the
youth and youth leisure. Critics who connected comic books to totalitarianism tapped
into widespread worries for the future of
America's youth. Herbert Hoover feared that
continued deprivation would cause the youth
to lose faith in democracy and Americanism.
Roosevelt shared Hoover's concern and established several agencies designed to neutralize
impoverished young people's rebelliousness.
The National Youth Administration (NYA)
and the Civilian Conservation Corps (CCC)
furnished jobs and job training for adolescents and young adults, provided an introduction to middle-class values of thrift and hard
work, and acted as a primer course on Americanism. These programs, explained NYA executive Charles Taussig, existed to teach the
young to adopt a "democratic approach" to
the world.

But government programs did not alleviate
Americans' fears of and for their children. The
spread of fascism only enhanced adults' suspicions that dictators would seduce their children. Thatcher Winslow noted the prominent
role that young people played in elevating
Hitler and Mussolini to power and concluded
that there was "no reason to suppose" that

American youth would prove "any more immune to the appeal of the dictator than the youth of other countries." George Lawton, a psychologist writing for *Scholastic Magazine*, proposed a similar argument. Because of the difficulty in finding jobs, adolescents could not become independent adults and instead remained in a sort of perpetual childhood. Their frustration made them more susceptible to the false charms of demagogues who promised them the chance to "play an active part in our economic and social system," even if that meant the "sacrifice of democracy." In this climate of fear, Superman appeared as an enabling figure, a benevolent *Übermensch* who could facilitate a generational switch in allegiance from democracy to dictatorship.

Comic books also offended current attitudes toward recreation. Many in the 1930s echoed a sentiment that first gained strength in the Progressive-era Playground Movement by arguing that play should be organized and meaningful, not unstructured and anarchistic. The federal government contributed to this effort by spending hundreds of millions of dollars constructing playgrounds, swimming pools, and athletic fields where play could take place under adult direction. Supervised contests in which nobody kept score or declared a winner offered excellent opportunities to instill "socially desirable conduct" in children by teaching them teamwork and cooperation. Proper recreation developed social skills, physical prowess, and creativity, and produced "useful citizens" by teaching kids "justice and fair play." Games that relied on teamwork and cooperation trained children to serve as the next generation of leaders. Children who did not spend their free time properly would likely suffer from a stunted mind and body and never reach "the full stature of manhood." No wonder the perceived rise of more passive and solitary forms of recreation dismayed experts. Instead of absorbing valuable social lessons, kids sat alone and listened to the radio, watched movies, and read comic books—one survey revealed that nine- to fourteen-year-olds spent three-quarters of their leisure time reading comic books—that did not teach kids how to get along in society or assist in acquiring the skills necessary to ensure the smooth development of an American community. Many feared that the next generation would be "soft" and socially inept, resulting in a nation of weak individuals who had no sense of togetherness or ability to lead.

Superman and the fledgling comic-book industry were therefore open to assault on several fronts, and a business just able to stand on its own had no stomach for a vigorous counterattack that would at best leave it marginalized and unstable and at worst demonized and bankrupt. Sales of *Superman* and *Action Comics* were bringing in big money, and DC was finding ways to milk their hero for even more. It could use Superman's endorsement to sell other comics in its line or new toys like the "Krypto Ray Gun." As the medium's standard bearer, Superman had to harmonize his focus with middle-class morality to deflect criticisms that could cut into sales and sink the trade. In response to these pressures, DC Comics hired an advisory board of child psychiatrists, social workers, and educators, and watered down the content of comic books. "With millions of parents ready to ban Superman from the house should his high moral sense falter," noted the *Saturday Evening Post*, "the company takes its civic responsibilities seriously." DC also changed the personnel behind Superman. The strain of churning out artwork day after day overwhelmed Joe Shuster, who was so near-sighted that he almost had to press his face onto the paper to see the pages on his desk. His staff did most of the drawing by mid-1940. Once free to develop plots from his office in Cleveland, Jerry Siegel found himself attending more policy meetings in New York and facing tougher editing of story proposals. The B-movie-style class conflict was no longer acceptable. No more destruction of private property, unless absolutely necessary. No more deaths, unless absolutely necessary. No more evil capitalists, unless absolutely necessary. After the start of 1941, it was rarely necessary. A new Superman emerged, one palatable to a middle-class audience. He abandoned his concerns for social reform and the common man and became a super-patriot, proudly selling Americanism for ten cents a shot. It was now the Man of Steel's job to bring young people into tune with the trend of middle-class culture as it prepared to face the global challenge to the American Way of Life.

This shift began almost as soon as Superman landed in children's hands. He started to embrace his role as the bringer of traditional values when DC Comics formed the Supermen of America Club in 1939. The Club allowed the Man of Steel to directly share his views with readers while making his handlers a few extra dollars. For a dime, enrollees received a certificate of membership, a Supermen of America pin, and a decoder ring. DC also set aside a special "Supermen of America" page in *Action Comics* and *Superman* in which the Man of Steel personally addressed his fans. Anyone could read the page, but only members, about 250,000 of them by 1941, had the decoder rings necessary to read the encrypted message included in each edition. He created an air of intimacy with readers by signing his note, "Sincerely, Clark Kent"—although everyone knew that it was Superman speaking. "I regard each and every one of you as a real part of my family," he told them. He sometimes used this page to promote a new contest or giveaway ("I will soon announce a gigantic contest for Superman club members only," read one secret directive), but typically used it to imbue readers with the values that he considered important. In 1940, Superman cautioned kids to "remember to play fair and live honestly," a theme he returned to many times in his notes. He often built his messages

around the three central principles of the club—strength, courage, and justice—arguing that one needed equal shares of each to be a true Superman. He also offered kids advice on physical conditioning—critical, since "mental health" was "inextricably linked with physical health." Perhaps, with good diet, moderate exercise, lots of sleep, and clean living, they too could be Supermen.

The new Superman stopped talking about the economy and social change and focused more and more of his attention on the looming threat to democracy and Americanism. To do this, he had to renounce some of his earlier views. The first two Superman adventures, which appeared about the time that Germany annexed Austria, contain an unmistakably anti-war message. Clark is sent to cover a war in the tiny South American country of San Monte but, for reasons left unclear, instead hastens to Washington, D.C., where he finds the powerful Senator Barrows cohorting with Alex Greer, "the slickest lobbyist in Washington." His suspicions aroused, the "champion of the oppressed" overhears the Senator agreeing to Greer's plan to embroil the United States in a war and net themselves a tidy profit. The enraged Superman kidnaps the lobbyist and demands to know who is behind the plot. The terrified Greer confesses that he is the pawn of "munitions magnate" Emil Norvell. The Man of Steel releases Greer and hunts down Norvell, then drags the arms dealer to San Monte and forces him to enlist in the army. Norvell cowers as bombs explode around him. His nerves in tatters, he begs Superman to let him go home. "Let me return to the U.S.," he pleads, "I've grown to hate war. . . . From now on, the most dangerous thing I'll manufacture will be a firecracker!" Superman next kidnaps the leaders of the rival armies and demands that they settle their differences with a one-on-one fistfight ("Or I'll clean up on both of you myself!"). But the two generals quickly discover that they have no real differences and no good reason for fighting. Sensing their bewilderment, he explains that it is "obvious you've been fighting only to promote the sale of munitions!" They agree to end the war, bringing peace to the beleaguered nation and ending the rule of the arms dealers.

Superman's anti-war philosophy supported the findings of the 1934 Nye Committee investigation of the causes of World War I, but middle-class culture had evolved since then, and the new Man of Steel followed the flow. As Roosevelt guided the United States closer to intervention, Superman paralleled other middle-class reading by loudly voicing the merits of Americanism. Once a critic of the status quo, he reinvented himself as "patriot number one." He used his "Supermen of America" column to inspire readers to become true believers in America's cause. More and more, his messages focused on patriots like Washington and Lincoln and on the greatness of democracy, "the best and truest form of government." He informed kids of the wonders of a free society and contrasted it with life in fascist nations. With freedom, however, comes obligations. The Man of Steel reminded readers to do their part to make their families and communities stronger, for "in these crucial days each of us, young or old, has responsibilities to be shouldered." He warned them not to take their own loyalty for granted, but rather work to keep "the fierce fires of love of country and liberty alive" within them by upholding democratic principles and living up to the ideals of the Supermen of America Club: strength, courage, and justice. Taking loyalty and duty to country lightly, he cautioned, would bring dire consequences upon America—in Superman's mind, France fell because its citizens had taken democracy "so much for granted that they allowed the forces of fascism within France herself to betray their nation." Small wonder then, that his Secret Message for August 1941 read: "True Americanism becomes more important to us all every day."

Making it clear that "sinister forces" wanted to "impede America's effort to arm itself," he spent much of 1941 battling saboteurs, fifth columnists, and other "secret foes of our nation." Nothing was safe from terrorists, who targeted factories, individuals, and even the *Daily Planet*. Superman prevented these strikes from succeeding, but they were frightening nonetheless. What was most unsettling is that anyone, no matter their public reputation, could be a spy—prominent patriots and "ultra-respectable" citizens headed many of the espionage rings that Superman busted up. The "traitorous activities of fifth columnists," however, were usually directed by highly-visible members of the anti-war movement, who were in turn guided by fascists. In early 1941, Superman attended a meeting of the "Volunteers for Peace," an anti-war group led by Stuart Pemberton. He looks on in disgust as the crowd, in a scene reminiscent of Hitler's rallies, "goes berserk in fanatical applause" when Pemberton urges the crowd to oppose rearmament. Superman later spies on a meeting of the group's leaders and is horrified to learn that they are in league with "Nation X," which is plotting an immediate strike against the United States. The Volunteers plan to "prepare the way by sabotaging important strategic centers." Superman foils Nation X's attempts to destroy a train, poison the water supply, and bomb Metropolis, then goes after the traitorous Pemberton, who has taken over a radio station and proclaimed that "democracy's death is at hand!" Unwilling to submit to a foreign dictatorship, the Man of Steel captures the rogue and puts both his organization and Nation X's invasion out of commission.

Superman's writers made Germany their primary enemy. Spies resembled northern Europeans, and insignia on enemy weaponry often imitated the markings on Nazi arms. A story from *Superman* #10 (May/June, 1941) cleared up any lingering doubts as to who was America's most dangerous foe. The *Daily Planet* sends Clark and Lois to cover a sports festival pitting American athletes against a team from Dukalia, a country whose relations with the United States have been strained in recent years. The tall and blond Dukalian athletes epitomize the Aryan ideal. The crowd notes the symbol they wear on their chests (which resembles a cross with an extra set of arms) and their extended right-arm salute as they enter the stadium. Convinced that these sportsmen actually represent "an organization fomenting unamerican activities," Clark listens as Karl Wolff, the Dukalian Consul, regales the crowd with a speech taken straight from *Mein Kampf*. "Present here," he intones, "is the flower of Dukalian youth! You have seen them perform physical feats which no other human beings can. Proof, I tell you, that we Dukalians are superior to any other race or nation! Proof that we are entitled to be the masters of America!" Sensing "a menace to American democracy," Clark changes into Superman and leaps onto the field to find out "just how superior you **really** are!" Superman proves that Americans are not so inferior after all, hurling the Dukalian shotput champion farther than his record throw, lifting the pole-vault champion over his record height, dragging the sprint champion on a two-second hundred-yard dash, and carrying the hurdler champion over the whole course with one great leap. Finally, with total disregard for the niceties of diplomacy, he seizes Wolff and deposits him on top of a flagpole. But the Man of Steel is not finished. After some top-notch spy work, he foils a Dukalian plot to use their newest weapon, an invisible submarine that is also capable of flight, to blow up the Panama Canal.

Superman's subversive spirit was gone, not to return until the more permissive 1960s. He had always illustrated some elements of the conservative American tradition, but social, political, and economic pressures forced him to jettison any controversial or divisive story lines. Gone were the socially incendiary plots of his first few years, replaced by patriotic stories that never opposed the status quo. He exchanged his class-based social vision for one that stressed the unified agenda of all Americans, neatly folding himself into the middle-class tradition of imagining a classless and essentially homogenous society. He also accepted the mainstream's insistence that America was a special and unique nation with a divinely granted mission to spread its ideals around the globe. Superman faced a career crisis in the early 1940s. He could preserve his original principles and remain condemned to the fringes of American culture, or abandon his convictions and join the cultural center by becoming middle class. His continuing presence provides ample evidence of his ultimate decision and demonstrates the coercive power of the middlebrow tradition in American life.

Study Questions

1. What social and economic conditions best describe America when the Superman character was introduced to the American public?

2. What does the age of Superman's creators and audience reveal about the impact of the Great Depression on young America?

3. What attributes of American society did Superman embody?

4. What ailments of American society did Superman strive to correct?

5. The author tells us that Superman changed over the years. Why did he change, and what do these changes reflect about American politics, economy, and society from the Great Depression through World War II?

Bibliography

The scholarship on the role of comic books in American society has proliferated over the past few decades. Bradford W. Wright, *Comic Book Nation: The Transformation of Youth Culture in America* (2001), impressively outlines the connections between the genre and one element of American society. For general histories of the comic book in American society, see Joseph Witek, *Comic Book as History* (1989) and Michael Benton, *The Comic Book in America* (1989). Historians are also beginning to examine the role of children in American society. For a good recent overview of the changing place of children in the twentieth century, see Judith Sealander, *The Failed Century of the Child: Governing America's Young in the Twentieth Century* (2003). See also Eric Rauchway, *The Refuge of Affections: Family and American Reform Politics, 1900–1920* (2001).

READING 18

★ ★ ★

Edward R. Murrow and World War II

Inventing Broadcast Journalism
Mark Bernstein

For Most of It I Have No Words
Edward R. Murrow

Edward R. Murrow looked the part. Fedora worn at slanting angle, trench coat with a turned-up collar, cigarette moving from hand to mouth in a thoughtless, compulsive manner—Murrow looked the part of foreign correspondent. In fact, he was once described as "the only foreign correspondent who could play a foreign correspondent in the movies and give all the glamour Hollywood wants." Though only in his late 20s when he began broadcasting from London for CBS, he looked as if he had seen it all. His face and most of all his voice seemed beyond surprise. His good looks had a flinty quality, an ageless, honorable honesty. Americans learned to trust what Murrow said. They sensed that he would not embellish the facts or dramatize himself. Instead, he would look about and report exactly what he saw.

Murrow first came to America's attention in 1938 during the Austrian and Czechoslovakia crises, and he and his team of reporters—dubbed "Murrow's Boys"—kept Americans informed about Hitler's drive for European supremacy. Once the war in Europe started, Murrow reported from London, describing the feel and the effect of the Blitz, Germany's air war against Great Britain. Poet Archibald MacLeish said that Murrow "burned the city of London in our houses and we felt the flames . . . [he] laid the dead of London at our door. . ." The following two selections explore the impact of Edward R. Murrow. In the first, Mark Bernstein describes Murrow's work during the Blitz. The second selection is a 1945 report Murrow gave after visiting the concentration camp of Buchenwald.

In 1937 Edward R. Murrow sailed with his wife, Janet, to London where he was to take up the post of chief CBS radio correspondent in Europe. At the time, Murrow had never written a news story in his life, and he had never made a scheduled radio broadcast. He was 29 years old.

During the next three years, Murrow would oversee the birth of foreign news broadcasting, and he would make his own clipped baritone voice one of the most recognized by his countrymen. More important, Murrow, utilizing the new medium, would report from beleaguered London during the Blitz of 1940, dramatizing Britain's stand-alone defense against Adolf Hitler to an America that slowly rallied to England's cause. In so doing, he virtually invented modern broadcast journalism.

Murrow was a somewhat unlikely champion for the British. He had traveled to England before, but had been thoroughly unimpressed and later told one English audience: "I thought your streets narrow and mean, your tailors over-advertised, your climate unbearable, your class-consciousness offensive. You couldn't cook. Your young men seemed without vigor or purpose. I admired your history, doubted your future."

Edward R. Murrow was that peculiarly American thing, a self-made man. In Britain during the war, London hostesses came to regard him as a prized dinner guest—handsome and intelligent, an elegant dresser who displayed an understated wit that appealed to local tastes. But there was little in his background to suggest such style and panache. Murrow was born Egbert Roscoe Murrow on April 24, 1908, in Polecat Creek, N.C., a place no more sophisticated than its name might suggest. When he was young, his family moved to Blanchard, Wash., a small logging town near the Pacific. In high school the self-making began with a self-naming. He dropped the Egbert and eventually rechris-tened himself Edward R. He worked at timbering during summers while in high school and for a year after graduation to secure the funds to attend a Washington state college.

When Murrow entered college, the field of foreign radio correspondence did not exist. Still, his undergraduate interests did much to prepare him for his future work. His best subjects were speech, debate and ROTC. He was a natural leader; on graduation he became president of the National Student Federation, through which he met his future wife, Janet Brewster. He took an interest in European politics, uncommon in young Americans at the time. At age 25, he worked for a tiny organization that attempted to relocate persecuted scholars from Germany to the United States. In 1933 fear of Hitler in the United States was not great, so funds were limited and visas difficult to obtain. Still, the 335 refugees brought to the States included novelist Thomas Mann, theologian Martin Buber and philosopher Herbert Marcuse. All this was in Murrow's background when he went to Europe in 1937.

If war was to be Murrow's coming-of-age, it was also the coming-of-age of radio. Murrow's lack of reporting credentials meant little when he went to London in 1937. He was sent to the British capital to be "director of talks," and his task was to schedule interviews with notables from government, business and the arts. At the time, CBS did not report the news from London; CBS, and radio generally, barely reported the news from New York. News coverage was largely limited to radio commentators, like H.V. Kaltenborn, and to announcers who read the headlines on the hour. It was the Depression, and the public turned to radio not for news, which was mostly bad, but for escape—the humor of Jack Benny and Burns and Allen and the singing of Bing Crosby and Kate Smith.

Murrow was among the first to see serious journalistic possibilities in the airwaves. In August 1937, Murrow decided to hire an itinerant American journalist as CBS' "man on

"Inventing Broadcast Journalism," by Mark Bernstein, *American History* Vol. 40, No. 2 (June 2005), pp. 40–46.

No American ever looked better in a trench coat than Edward R. Murrow. During World War II, Murrow's radio broadcasts from England and Europe brought the war to America with jolting intimacy.

the Continent." The reporter, William L. Shirer, having fled Prohibition-era Iowa for a place "where a man could drink a glass of wine or a stein of beer without breaking the law," had been knocking about Europe for a decade. By chance, on the same day that Shirer was laid off from his post as a correspondent for Universal Service in Berlin, Murrow offered him a job. Shirer accepted, but a hurdle remained. With CBS brass listening in from New York, Shirer made a voice audition. His speaking voice was midwestern, nasal and flat, and CBS executives thought he was terrible. Murrow put his foot down: He was not hiring announcers, he said, but people who could think and write. That was Murrow's personal standard, and Shirer was the first to meet it.

(The issue would resurface in 1939, when Murrow wanted to hire a young American newspaperman who had gone to Paris in 1937 to be near the war that he, though few others, expected. Not wanting to be a famous war cor-

respondent named Arnold, the young journalist dropped his first name and presented himself to the world as "Eric" Sevareid. His voice audition was worse than Shirer's. Shirer had been monotone; Sevareid was a mumbler. So he was, and—hired at Murrow's insistence—so he remained through an illustrious four-decade-long broadcast career.)

Events pressed the new medium into a new role. On March 12, 1938, Shirer traveled to Vienna—coincidentally, the same day the Germans were marching in, adding Hitler's native country to his Nazi state. The day's top story had landed in Shirer's lap, but he could not report it. German officials refused to let him broadcast and escorted him out of the radio station. At Murrow's suggestion, Shirer flew to London to report his story on air from there. Murrow then headed for Vienna to cover subsequent events. From New York, CBS news director Paul White called Shirer to say he wanted reports from London, Vienna, Paris, Berlin and Rome, using American newspaper correspondents: "A half-hour show, and I'll telephone you the exact time for each capital in about an hour. Can you and Murrow do it?" "I said yes," Shirer recorded in his diary, "and we hung up. The truth is I didn't have the faintest idea."

In eight hours, and on a Sunday, Murrow and Shirer lined up newsmen to make reports, found the needed shortwave facilities and went on the air—live. The broadcast, a great success, soon became a standard feature. Shortly thereafter, Shirer recorded in his diary: "The [Austrian] crisis has done one thing for us. Birth of the 'radio foreign correspondent' so to speak."

The basic forms were set early. Correspondents would write their stories, clear them through censorship, then go to a government-operated shortwave facility to transmit them live back to CBS in New York. The programs sounded more organized than they were. In New York, announcer Robert Trout might say, "We take you now to William Shirer in Berlin." In Berlin, Shirer could not hear Trout's voice;

rather, he simply started speaking live into a microphone at an assigned time.

The seizure of Austria was bad news; worse news followed. The Western democracies deserted Czechoslovakia at Munich. Murrow had a world scoop on the settlement, but took little consolation in it. He was not so much a newsman as a citizen of the world. The rise of Hitler was, to him, less a story to be covered than an unraveling catastrophe he could do little to stem. Post-Munich, Murrow met up with Shirer in Paris, where the pair tried without success to drink themselves into a better frame of mind.

America seemed largely indifferent. To Murrow, it was as though the greatest drama in history was playing to an empty and deserted theater. In July 1939, Shirer was briefly back in New York. His wife, Tess, told him he was "making [him]self most unpopular by taking such a pessimistic view [of Europe]. They *know* there will be no war." And Americans clearly wanted none. At year's end, more than 95 percent of Americans polled were against war with Germany. By then Poland had fallen. In April 1940, Denmark and Norway followed. In May, German tanks rolled into the Netherlands, Belgium and France, with resistance quickly subdued. On June 22, the French surrendered at Compiègne, an event for which Shirer again gained a world scoop. With the French surrender, England stood alone.

England's future was never more in doubt than in the summer and fall of 1940 when Hitler, master of the Continent, unleashed his *Luftwaffe* on Great Britain, his sole opponent still standing. For Murrow, nothing less than the future of civilization was at stake in that battle. For millions in America, news of that conflict came each evening in a report that began with Murrow's signature phrase, "This. . . is London."

England's south coast awaited invasion. In Berlin two Nazi officials placed bets with Shirer: The first wagered that the German swastika would be flying over Trafalgar Square by August 15; the second said by

September 7. Along the French and Belgian coasts, the Germans concentrated the small craft—1,700 by mid-August—with which they planned to transport the initial invasion wave of 90,000 soldiers and 650 tanks. In London a newspaper vendor posted a placard that typified English resolve: "We're in the final. And it's on the home pitch."

The German attack had two phases. In the first—lasting from mid-August to early September 1940—the *Luftwaffe* sought to destroy the Royal Air Force. If the RAF was defeated, it could not provide air cover for the British navy, which would then be forced to withdraw from the English Channel. A German crossing would follow. In Germany, invasion planning proceeded. On September 2, Shirer noted that German press officers had removed a gigantic illuminated map of France that had been used to help reporters track the invasion of that country. "That map has been taken down," Shirer reported, "and an equally large one substituted. It was a map of England."

From opposite sides of the Channel, Murrow in London—assisted by his colleague, Larry LeSueur, another of Murrow's young hires—and Shirer in Berlin tracked the first battle in history to be fought solely in the air. Or at least they tried. All acknowledged that with aircraft so small flying so high, it was all but impossible to tell what was happening. Though many current military historians believe the *Luftwaffe* was gaining an edge, Hitler was impatient; he wanted the invasion to be accomplished by late September, before the October fogs cut visibility in the Channel. He decided that bombing civilian London would quickly cow the British.

On September 7, wave after wave of German bombers struck London in a 12-hour attack. Murrow was southeast of the city, trying to get a bead on the action. He interviewed Englishmen in a variety of places, including spending part of the day near an RAF air base. After writing his script, the following day he broadcast live from the studio: "On the airdrome ground crews swarmed over those

British fighters, fitting ammunition belts and pouring in gasoline. As soon as one fighter was ready, it took to the air, and there was no waiting for flight leaders or formation. The Germans were already coming back, down the river, heading for France." He spoke of "the hollow grunt of the bombs, [the] huge pear-shaped bursts of flame." He talked to a pub owner who "told us these raids were bad for the chickens, the dogs and the horses." And for a time, he simply took cover, hunkering down with Vincent Sheean, an American writer whom Murrow pressed into service from time to time, and Ben Robertson of the short-lived New York newspaper *PM*. As Murrow described it: "Vincent Sheean lay on one side of me and cursed in five languages. . . . Ben Robertson . . . lay on the other side and kept saying in that slow South Carolina drawl, 'London is burning, London is burning.'" London, indeed, was burning. Four hundred were dead, triple that many injured, and fires blazed throughout the city.

London's stand against the bombing became the focus of world attention; eventually, 120 reporters—a huge number at the time— came to the British capital to report it. Murrow stood out as unmatched. This was so, first, because of the manner in which he portrayed the English—not as heroes but as human: unflappable, dogged, quirky. He reported how life among the many citizens continued after the bombing of residential London began: "Walking down the street a few minutes ago, shrapnel stuttered and stammered on the rooftops and from underground came the sound of singing, and the song was 'My Blue Heaven.'"

He reported on Londoners' solidarity in the shelters, but noted that even there, the rich fared better than the working classes. He spoke of a cluster of "old dowagers and retired colonels" who took refuge at the Mayfair Hotel. There, he remarked, the protection was not great, but "you would at least be bombed with the right sort of people." He reported on casual courage. He described an official

adding a name to a list of firefighters killed battling fires the bombing had caused. The list, Murrow noted, contained 100 names.

Added to Murrow's empathy for the British people was his mastery of language. He was, his colleague Sevareid said, "the first great literary artist of a new medium." Murrow, through reflection and intuition, had a keen appreciation of broadcasting's power and nature. Radio, he said, was essentially intimate. It was not an announcer speaking to an audience, but Murrow as an individual speaking to fellow individuals who had gathered by their Philcos in living rooms in Kansas or New Hampshire. He believed that radio was visual, and he had a gift for the evocative phrase. When Winston Churchill was made prime minister, Murrow introduced him as "Britain's tired old man of the sea." Knowing that moonlight made London more visible to attacking aircraft, he referred to one night sky as being brightened by "a bomber's moon."

And Murrow believed that radio's task was not to bring the story to the listener, but to bring the listener to the story. On August 24, two weeks before the "On the airdrome" program, he had made a remarkable nighttime broadcast from London's Trafalgar Square, standing just outside the entrance to a bomb shelter. Live and unscripted, his words painted the scene: the searchlights splashing white on the bottom of clouds; a red double-decker bus—most of its lights extinguished in the blackout—passing like a ship at night; a driver calmly stopping for a red light on a totally deserted street. Murrow said he could see almost nothing in the blackout. But he could hear something. Bringing his listeners to the scene, he lowered the microphone to street level so that people in America could hear the footsteps of Londoners taking shelter from bombs.

Through it all, Murrow was battling on a second front. That August 24 coverage of the bombing had raised questions about the propriety of such live, on-the-scene reporting of the attacks. As bombing continued, Murrow pressed British officials hard for permission to do regular, unscripted, live, on-the-street broadcasts of the events. Initially, British officialdom was dismissive—Murrow was not even a citizen, and live broadcasts could give valuable information to an enemy that would presumably be listening in. Murrow pressed the matter, explaining that his broadcasts would be transmitted from his microphone through the BBC headquarters, where they would still be subject to censorship. More important, he gained an ally, Prime Minister Churchill. Forty years earlier Churchill had been a correspondent in the Boer War, and he had a newsman's residual compassion for getting the story out. More to the point, he believed that anything done to dramatize London's struggle would build American sympathy for England's cause.

By mid-September, Murrow gained permission. With the live broadcasts, he became the star of his own drama, standing exposed on rooftops. The sounds of bombs exploding near him were clearly audible. In narrow terms, the work was quite remarkably dangerous. In broader terms, his accounts of a city under siege made compelling listening. Murrow's reports from London helped make radio America's dominant news media. In one 1940 survey, 65 percent of respondents said radio was their best source of news. His own audience grew to 22 million, reportedly including President Franklin Roosevelt and members of his cabinet. Many were swayed by what they heard. During September 1940, the bombing's first month, the share of Americans telling Gallup pollsters that their nation should aid Britain increased from 16 to 52 percent. That month, President Roosevelt went to Congress to repeal the Neutrality Act that barred military support to the British.

Hitler had good reason to believe that the bombing of civilian London would soon break Britain's will to resist. Prewar, most military experts held that aerial bombardment would quickly devastate any city. In 1932 British Prime Minister Stanley Baldwin had famously stated, "The bomber will always get through"—a remark that did little to bolster British self-assurance. As events in London and elsewhere were to prove, such bombing more generally strengthened than broke resolve. The London Blitz was, however, the first sustained bombing of a major city. And when, contrary to expectations, that city did not fall, respect for its stand grew. Murrow shared the sentiment, and he broadcast that admiration. From one bombed location, he reported: "The girls in light, cheap dresses were strolling along the streets. There was no bravado, no loud voices, only a quiet acceptance of the situation. To me those people were incredibly brave and calm."

London sent its children to the countryside, ate powdered eggs rather than fresh ones and endured the nightly attacks, sleeping in bomb shelters. At year's end, Londoners were underfed, under-rested and under bombardment. Murrow's December 29 broadcast caught the grimness of the hour: "No one expects the New Year to be happy. We shall live hard before it is ended. The immediate problems are many and varied: Something must be done about the night bombers and the submarines; improved facilities for life underground must be provided." He added: "Probably the best summary—written by Wordsworth [when England was at war with Napoleon] in 1806: 'Another year, another blow, another mighty empire, overthrown, and we are left, and shall be left, alone, the last that dared to struggle with the foe.'"

The bombing affected people strangely, noted Sevaried, who joined Murrow in London after the fall of France. Those who were walking when the first bombs dropped would halt. Those who were standing would begin to walk. Murrow once awakened CBS correspondent LeSueur, who was bunking at the Murrow's, with the news that the building was on fire. LeSueur picked up his clothes and walked into a closet to get dressed.

Murrow refused to go into shelters, saying that once you did you lost your nerve. With considerable nonchalance, Murrow, LeSueur and a young *New York Times* reporter, James Reston, played golf on a nine-hole course on London's Hampstead Heath. If a ball rolled near an unexploded bomb, it was declared an unplayable lie.

The hazards were all too real. Out walking one evening, Murrow suddenly stepped into a doorway. Two colleagues instantly followed suit. Seconds later, a shell casing landed where they had been standing. CBS was repeatedly bombed out of its tiny London office—always without serious casualty. Another evening, Ed and Janet Murrow were walking home and he suggested stopping in the Devonshire Arms, a pub frequented by journalists. Janet said she was tired, so they continued home. Ten minutes later the pub received a direct hit—and everyone inside was killed.

Sevareid did not share that bravado. He lived a few blocks from the BBC, and wrote: "To get to the underground broadcasting facility meant a walk of a couple blocks for me. I would shuffle cautiously through the inky blackness to each curbing where the guns would make the crossing street a tunnel of sudden, blinding light. [Then,] I would plaster myself against the nearest wall, and, however sternly I lectured myself, I not infrequently found myself doing the last 50 yards at a dead run."

If Murrow was not frightened, he was nonetheless exhausted. Sleeping little, eating less and smoking four packs of cigarettes a day, he was driven by his sense of the importance of the event. Among other problems, Murrow had to reconcile his own views with CBS' strict policy of nonpartisanship. In part he did this simply by presenting the British as the underdog, relying on his countrymen's natural sympathies to take England's side. Further, however, he was inclined to attribute his own point of view to others, then report it as news. He spoke of the attitudes of unnamed Englishmen who, he said, had given up on the notion that victory could be achieved without American aid. Now, Murrow reported, such Englishmen had come to admit: "British victory, if not British survival, will be made possible only by American action. There are too many Germans, and they have too many factories. It seems strange to hear English, who were saying, 'we'll win this one without America,' admitting now that this world—or what's left of it—will be largely run either from Berlin or from Washington."

Of Murrow's influence, Sevareid later wrote: "The generality of British people will probably never know what Murrow did for them in those days. . . . Murrow was not trying to 'sell' the British cause to America; he was trying to explain the universal human cause of men who were showing a noble face to the world. In so doing he made the British and their behavior human and thus compelling to his countrymen at home."

The German air assaults varied in intensity. The strength of the attacks depended in part on the demands made by German operations elsewhere and, apparently, by Germany's periodic shortage of lubricating fluids for its aircraft. After a lull, the *Luftwaffe* returned in April 1941. Murrow reported: "They came over shortly after blackout time, and a veritable show of flares and incendiaries. One of those nights where you wear your best clothes, because you're never sure that when you come home you'll have anything other than the clothes you were wearing." Given the size of the city, Murrow added, it was difficult to judge the severity of an attack from one's own vantage. If the bombs fall close to you, he added: "You are inclined to think the bombing is very severe. Tonight, having been thrown against the wall by blasts—which feels like nothing so much as being hit with a feather-covered board—and having lost our third office, which looks like some crazy giant had been operating an eggbeater in its interior, I naturally conclude that the bombing has been heavy." Actually, it was the heaviest single attack of the war. The following month, CBS lost its fourth office.

Toward the end of 1941, Murrow returned to New York to receive what one observer called the greatest welcome given a journalist since Henry Morton Stanley returned, having found David Livingstone. One thousand gathered for a testimonial dinner at New York's Waldorf Astoria. There, poet and Librarian of Congress Archibald MacLeish praised Murrow's work: "But it was not in London really that you spoke. It was in the back kitchens and the front living rooms and the moving automobiles and the hot-dog stands. . . that your voice was truly speaking." What Murrow had done, MacLeish added, was to destroy the belief that what happened 3,000 miles away was not really happening. "You burned the city of London in our houses and we felt the flames that burned it. You laid the dead of London at our doors and we knew the dead were our dead—were all men's dead. . . . Without rhetoric, without dramatics, without more emotion than needed be, you destroyed the superstition of distance and of time."

Murrow's own remarks were those of a man making a case. He told the audience: "If you were in London now, you would be surprised at the number of people who would say to you, 'Tell your fellow countrymen not to make the same mistakes we made. We didn't want anything of this world except to be let alone—until it was almost too late.'" And, again making reference to "thoughtful Englishmen," Murrow used the podium to issue a challenge: "The question most often asked by thoughtful Englishmen is this: 'If America comes in, will she stay in? Does she have any appetite for the greatness that is being thrust upon her?'"

On the night that dinner was held—December 2, 1941—America's role in the conflict was still unsettled. Five days later, in an act that astonished Murrow, Pearl Harbor was bombed, and America was at war.

With the United States at war, Americans leaned more strongly into the day's events. CBS expanded its European news team. In time, those reporting with Murrow included many who would make great careers in broadcasting: along with Shirer, LeSueur and Sevareid were Charles Collingwood, Howard K. Smith, Richard C. Hottelet, Cecil Brown, William Downs and Winston Burdett. When Murrow hired them, they were little more than kids—bright boys in their mid-20s—as inexperienced at radio news reporting as Murrow had been. They did, however, meet Murrow's personal standard: They could think and they could write. And most modeled their approach to gathering the news on Murrow's approach. Customarily, their reports would be part fact, part essay, part color and part editorial, all wrapped up in a crisply written two- or three-minute account that became the standard format for CBS journalism. Many others in the field regarded their work as the best ever done in broadcasting.

Murrow, who defined their task and directed their efforts, never made any great claims for himself—not for his efforts during the Blitz, or for what followed. Writing to Charles Collingwood in the immediate post-war period, Edward R. Murrow said, "For a few brief years a few men attempted to do an honest job of reporting under difficult and sometimes hazardous conditions and they did not altogether fail."

APRIL 15, 1945.

During the last week, I have driven more than a few hundred miles through Germany, most of it in the Third Army sector—Wiesbaden, Frankfurt, Weimar, Jena and beyond. It is impossible to keep up with this war. The traffic flows down the superhighways, trucks with German helmets tied to the radiators and belts of machine-gun ammunition draped from fender to fender. The tanks on the concrete roads sound like a huge sausage machine, grinding up sheets of corrugated iron. And when there is a gap between convoys, when the noise dies away, there is another small noise, that of wooden-soled shoes and of small iron tires grating on the concrete. The power moves forward, while the people, the slaves, walk back, pulling their small belongings on anything that has wheels.

There are cities in Germany that make Coventry and Plymouth appear to be merely damage done by a petulant child, but bombed houses have a way of looking alike, wherever you see them.

But this is no time to talk of the surface of Germany. Permit me to tell you what you would have seen, and heard, had you been with me on Thursday. It will not be pleasant listening. If you are at lunch, or if you have no appetite to hear what Germans have done, now is a good time to switch off the radio, for I propose to tell you of Buchenwald. It is on a small hill about four miles outside Weimar, and it was one of the largest concentration camps in Germany, and it was built to last. As we approached it, we saw about a hundred men in civilian clothes with rifles advancing in open order across the fields. There were a few shops; we stopped to inquire. We were told that some of the prisoners had a couple of SS men cornered in there. We drove on, reached the main gate. The prisoners crowded up behind the wire. We entered.

And now, let me tell this in the first person, for I was the least important person there, as you shall hear. There surged around me an evil-smelling horde. Men and boys reached out to touch me; they were in rags and the remnants of uniform. Death had already marked many of them, but they were smiling with their eyes. I looked out over that mass of men to the green fields beyond where well-fed Germans were ploughing.

A German, Fritz Kersheimer, came up and said, "May I show you round the camp? I've been here ten years." An Englishman stood to attention, saying, "May I introduce myself, delighted to see you, and can you tell me when some of our blokes will be along?" I told him soon and asked to see one of the barracks. It happened to be occupied by Czechoslovakians. When I entered, men crowded around, tried to lift me to their shoulders. They were too weak. Many of them could not get out of bed. I was told that this building had once stabled eighty horses. There were twelve hundred men in it, five to a bunk. The stink was beyond all description.

When I reached the center of the barracks, a man came up and said, "You remember me. I'm Peter Zenkl, one-time mayor of Prague." I remembered him, but did not recognize him. He asked about Benes and Jan Masaryk. I asked how many men had died in that building during the last month. They called the doctor; we inspected his records. There were only names in the little black book, nothing more—nothing of who these men were, what they had done, or hoped. Behind the names of who those who had died there was a cross. I counted them. They totalled 242. Two hundred and forty-two out of twelve hundred in one month.

As I walked down to the end of the barracks, there was applause from the men too weak to get out of bed. It sounded like the hand clapping of babies; they were so weak. The doctor's name was Paul Heller. He had been there since 1938.

"For Most of It I Have No Words," Edward R. Murrow, *Reporting World War II: Part Two American Journalism, 1944–1946.* New York Library of America, 1995.

As we walked out into the courtyard, a man fell dead. Two others—they must have been over sixty—were crawling toward the latrine. I saw it but will not describe it.

In another part of the camp they showed me the children, hundreds of them. Some were only six. One rolled up his sleeve, showed me his number. It was tattooed on his arm. D-6030, it was. The others showed me their numbers; they will carry them till they die.

An elderly man standing beside me said, "The children, enemies of the state." I could see their ribs through their thin shirts. The old man said, "I am Professor Charles Richer of the Sorbonne." The children clung to my hands and stared. We crossed to the courtyard. Men kept coming up to speak to me and to touch me, professors from Poland, doctors from Vienna, men from all Europe. Men from the countries that made America.

We went to the hospital; it was full. The doctor told me that two hundred had died the day before. I asked the cause of death; he shrugged and said, "Tuberculosis, starvation, fatigue, and there are many who have no desire to live. It is very difficult." Dr. Heller pulled back the blankets from a man's feet to show me how swollen they were. The man was dead. Most of the patients could not move.

As we left the hospital I drew out a leather billfold, hoping that I had some money which would help those who lived to get home. Professor Richer from the Sorbonne said, "I should be careful of my wallet if I were you. You know there are criminals in this camp, too." A small man tottered up, saying, "May I feel the leather, please? You see, I used to make good things of leather in Vienna." Another man said, "My name is Walter Roeder. For many years I lived in Joliet. Came back to Germany for a visit and Hitler grabbed me."

I asked to see the kitchen; it was clean. The German in charge had been a Communist, had been at Buchenwald for nine years, had a picture of his daughter in Hamburg. He hadn't seen her for almost twelve years, and if I got to Hamburg, would I look her up? He showed me the daily ration—one piece of brown bread about as thick as your thumb, on top of it a piece of margarine as big as three sticks of chewing gum. That, and a little stew, was what they received every twenty-four hours. He had a chart on the wall; very complicated it was. There were little red tabs scattered through it. He said that was to indicate each ten men who died. He had to account for the rations, and he added, "We're very efficient here."

We went again into the courtyard, and as we walked we talked. The two doctors, the Frenchman and the Czech, agreed that about six thousand had died during March. Kersheimer, the German, added that back in the winter of 1939, when the Poles began to arrive without winter clothing, they died at the rate of approximately nine hundred a day. Five different men asserted that Buchenwald was the best concentration camp in Germany; they had had some experience of the others.

Dr. Heller, the Czech, asked if I would care to see the crematorium. He said it wouldn't be very interesting because the Germans had run out of coke some days ago and had taken to dumping the bodies into a great hole nearby. Professor Richer said perhaps I would care to see the small courtyard. I said yes. He turned and told the children to stay behind. As we walked across the square I noticed that the professor had a hole in his left shoe and a toe sticking out of the right one. He followed my eyes and said, "I regret that I am so little presentable, but what can one do?" At that point another Frenchman came up to announce that three of his fellow countrymen outside had killed three S.S. men and taken one prisoner. We proceeded to the small courtyard. The wall was about eight feet high; it adjoined what had been a stable or garage. We entered. It was floored with concrete. There were two rows of bodies stacked up like cordwood. They were thin and very white. Some of the bodies were terribly bruised, though there seemed to be little flesh to bruise. Some had been shot through the head, but they bled but little. All except two were naked. I tried to count them as best I could and arrived at the conclusion that all that was mortal of more than five hundred men and boys lay there in two neat piles.

There was a German trailer which must have contained another fifty, but it wasn't possible to count them. The clothing was piled in a heap against the wall. It appeared that most of the men and boys had died of starvation; they had not been executed. But the manner of death seemed unimportant. Murder had been done at Buchenwald. God alone knows how many men and boys have died there during the last twelve years. Thursday I was told that there were more than twenty thousand in the camp. There had been as many as sixty thousand. Where are they now?

As I left that camp, a Frenchman who used to work for Havas in Paris came up to me and said, "You will write something about this, perhaps?" And he added, "To write about this you must have been here at least two years, and after that—you don't want to write any more."

I pray you to believe what I have said about Buchenwald. I have reported what I saw and heard, but only part of it. For most of it I have no words. Dead men are plentiful in war, but the living dead, more than twenty thousand of them in one camp. And the country round about was pleasing to the eye, and the Ger-

mans were well fed and well dressed. American trucks were rolling toward the rear filled with prisoners. Soon they would be eating American rations, as much for a meal as the men at Buchenwald received in four days.

If I've offended you by this rather mild account of Buchenwald, I'm not in the least sorry. I was there on Thursday, and many men in many tongues blessed the name of Roosevelt. For long years his name had meant the full measure of their hope. These men who had kept close company with death for many years did not know that Mr. Roosevelt would, within hours, join their comrades who had laid their lives on the scales of freedom.

Back in 1941, Mr. Churchill said to me with tears in his eyes, "One day the world and history will recognize and acknowledge what it owes to your president." I saw and heard the first installment of that at Buchenwald on Thursday. It came from men from all over Europe. Their faces, with more flesh on them, might have been found anywhere at home. To them the name "Roosevelt" was a symbol, the code word for a lot of guys named "Joe" who are somewhere out in the blue with the armor heading east. At Buchenwald they spoke of the president just before he died. If there be a better epitaph, history does not record it.

EDWARD R. MURROW, CBS RADIO BROADCAST,
APRIL 15, 1945

Study Questions

1. How was Edward R. Murrow a self-made man? What was his background for journalism?

2. How did Murrow and radio news "come of age" together? What did Murrow look for in his radio correspondents?

3. What impact did Murrow's reports from London have on Americans' attitudes toward Great Britain and the war? What impact did the Blitz have on Murrow?

4. How important were Murrow's reports in inching the United States toward involvement in the war?

5. What were Murrow's motives in his report from Buchenwald? What response did he try to arouse?

Bibliography

Erik Barnouw, *Tube of Plenty: The Evolution of American Television* (1990) is a standard source for the development of radio and television. Edward J. Bliss, *Now the News: The History of Broadcast Journalism* (1975) and Bob Edwards, *Edward R. Murrow and the Birth of Broadcast Journalism* (2004) put Murrow's career into context. For full treatments of Murrow's career see Norman Finkelstein, *With Heroic Truth: The Life of Edward R. Murrow* (2005); Alexander Kendrick, *Prime Time: The Life of Edward R. Murrow* (1969); Joseph E. Persico, *Edward R. Murrow: An American Original* (1988); and A. M. Sperber, *Murrow: His Life and Times* (1986). Murrow's work during the Blitz is covered in Philip Seib, *Broadcasts from the Blitz: How Edward R. Murrow Helped Lead America into War* (2006). David Halberstam, *The Powers That Be* (1979) looks at the news business.

READING 19

★ ★ ★

Okinawa: Of Mud and Maggots

E. B. Sledge

Okinawa was one of the final steps on the route to Japan. Lying about 330 miles southwest of Japan, the long, narrow island was perfectly situated for what the U.S. Pacific forces needed: an air and supply base to launch an invasion of the Japanese home islands. It had airfields, harbors, and Japanese defenders determined to give their lives, if necessary, to keep Americans from capturing the island. The Japanese were not the only obstacles for Americans. Like so many other Pacific islands where Americans and Japanese soldiers fought, Okinawa was a hothouse of spiders, mosquitoes, black flies, leeches, lizards, centipedes, crabs, and other small, biting, sucking, and stinging pests. It was a terrain overgrown with ferns, vines, and mushrooming growth, drenched by rain and all but empty of comfort. Battle on such islands was simply terrible, a hellish place of nightmares.

American forces stormed the beaches of Okinawa on Easter Sunday, April 1, 1945. At first the U.S. Marine and Army troops encountered limited opposition, but when they reached the defensive Shuri line on the southern end of the island, they faced the full force of the Japanese resistance. The Japanese were dug in, surrounded by valleys and gorges that they used to their advantage. American soldiers literally fought for every yard of territory. Before the battle ended in an American victory, 107,000 Japanese and 15,500 Americans were dead. Those numbers do not even approximate the reality of Okinawa. E. B. Sledge fought there and recounts what the battle was like for the soldiers of the war.

The boundary between the III Amphibious Corps (Marines) and the XXIV Corps (Army) ran through the middle of the main Japanese defensive position on the heights of Shuri. As the Marines moved southward, the 1st Marine Division remained on the left in the III Amphibious Corps' zone of action with the 6th Marine Division on the right. Within the 1st Marine Division's zone of action, the 7th Marines occupied the left flank and the 5th Marines the right. The 1st Marines was in reserve.

Beyond Awacha-Dakeshi, the Marines next faced Wana Ridge. On the other side of Wana Ridge lay Wana Draw, through which meandered the Asato Gawa. Forming the southern high ground above Wana Draw was yet another ridge, this one extending eastward from the city of Naha and rising to the Shuri Heights. This second ridge formed a part of the main Japanese defensive positions, the Shuri Line.

Wana Draw aimed like an arrow from the northwest directly into the heart of the Japanese defenses at Shuri. Within this natural avenue of approach, the Japanese took advantage of every difficult feature of terrain; it couldn't have provided a better opportunity for their defense if they had designed it. The longest and bloodiest ordeal of the battle for Okinawa now faced the men of the 1st Marine Division.

For the attack against Wana on 15 May 1945, the 5th Marines sent 2/5 forward with 3/5 in close support. The 1st Battalion came behind in reserve.

Before 2/5's attack began, we moved into a position behind that battalion. We watched tanks firing 75s and M7s firing 105s thoroughly shell the draw. The tanks received such heavy Japanese fire in return that the riflemen of 2/5 assigned to attack with the tanks had to seek any protection they could in ditches and holes while they covered the tanks from a distance; no man on his feet could have survived the hail of shells the enemy fired at the tanks. And the tanks couldn't move safely beyond the cover the riflemen provided because of Japanese suicide tank-destroyer teams. Finally, we saw the tanks pull back after suffering some hits. Our artillery and naval gunfire threw a terrific barrage at the Japanese positions around the draw. Shortly after that the tanks withdrew. Then an air strike was made against the draw. The bombardment of the draw seemed very heavy to us, but it wasn't anything compared to what was to become necessary before the draw was taken.

We moved from one position to another behind 2/5 until I was so confused I had no idea where we were. Late in the afternoon, we halted temporarily along a muddy trail running along the treeless slope of a muddy ridge. Marines of 2/5 moved past us going the other direction. Japanese shells whistled across the ridge and burst to the rear. Our artillery roared and swished overhead, the explosions booming and thundering out in the draw across the ridge.

Nearby our regimental Protestant chaplain had set up a little altar made out of a box from which he was administering Holy Communion to a small group of dirty Marines. I glanced at the face of a Marine opposite me as the file halted. He was filthy like all of us, but even through a thickly mudcaked dark beard I could see he had fine features. His eyes were bloodshot and weary. He slowly lowered his light machine gun from his shoulder, set the handle on his toe to keep it off the mud, and steadied the barrel with his hand. He watched the chaplain with an expression of skepticism that seemed to ask, "What's the use of all that? Is it gonna keep them guys from gettin' hit?" That face was so weary but so expressive that I knew he, like all of us, couldn't help but have doubts about his God in the presence of constant shock and suffering. Why did it go on and on? The machine gunner's buddy held the

E. B. Sledge, *With the Old Breed: At Peleliu and Okinawa* (New York: Oxford University Press, 1990).

gun's tripod on his shoulder, glanced briefly at the muddy little communion service, and then stared blankly off toward a clump of pines to our rear—as though he hoped to see home back there somewhere.

"Move out," came along their file.

The machine gunner hoisted the heavy weapon onto his shoulder as they went slipping and sliding around a bend in the trail into the gathering dusk.

We were told to spread out, take cover, and await further orders. Some of us found holes. Others scooped out what they could. Soon several Japanese shells exploded not far from me. I heard a shout for a corpsman and then, "Hey, you guys, Doc Caswell got hit!"

I forgot about the shells and felt sick. I ran in the direction of the shout to look for Kent Caswell, praying with every step that he wasn't hurt badly. Several other Marines were already with Doc, and a fellow corpsman was bandaging his neck. Doc Caswell lay back in the foxhole and looked up at me as I bent over him and asked him how he was doing (no doubt a stupid question, but my throat was constricted with grief). He opened his lips to speak, and blood trickled out from between them. I was heartbroken, because I didn't see how he could possibly survive. I feared that vital blood vessels in his neck had been severed by the shell fragments.

"Don't talk Doc, they'll get you outa here, and you'll be OK," I managed to stammer.

"OK you guys, let's get him outa here," the corpsman said as he finished his aid.

As I said so long to Doc and got up to leave, I noticed a cloverleaf of 60mm mortar shells lying on the side of the foxhole. A shell fragment had sliced a gash through the thick black metal endplate. I shuddered as I wondered whether it had passed first through Doc's neck.[1]

---

[1]Some time later we learned that Doc had survived the trip to the aid station with the stretcher team and that he would live. He returned to his native Texas where he remains one of my most faithful friends from our days in K/3/5.

Our massive artillery, mortar, naval gunfire, and aerial bombardment continued against Wana Draw on our front and Wana Ridge on our left. The Japanese continued to shell everything and everybody in the area, meeting each tank-infantry attack with a storm of fire. A total of thirty tanks, including four flamethrowers, blasted and burned Wana Draw. Our artillery, heavy mortars, ships' guns, and planes then plastered the enemy positions all over again until the noise and shock made me wonder what it was like to be in a quiet place. We had been under and around plenty of "heavy stuff" at Peleliu, but not on nearly so massive a scale or for such unending periods of time as at Wana. The thunderous American barrages went on and on for hours and then days. In return, the Japanese threw plenty of shells our way. I had a continuous headache I'll never forget. Those thunderous, prolonged barrages imposed on me a sense of stupefaction and dullness far beyond anything I ever had experienced before.

It didn't seem possible for any human being to be under such thunderous chaos for days and nights on end and be unaffected by it—even when most of it was our own supporting weapons, and we were in a good foxhole. How did the Japanese stand up under it? They simply remained deep in their caves until it stopped and then swarmed up to repulse each attack, just as they had done at Peleliu. So our heavy guns and air strikes had to knock down, cave in, or otherwise destroy the enemy's well-constructed defensive positions.

At some time during the fight for Wana Draw, we crossed what I supposed was the draw itself, somewhere near its mouth. To get to that point, we fought for days. I had lost count of how many. Marines of 2/5 had just gone across under fire, while we waited in an open field to move across. We eased up to the edge of the draw to cross in dispersed order. An NCO ordered three men and me to cross at a particular point and to stay close behind the 2/5 troops directly across the draw from us. The other side looked mighty far away.

A U.S. Marine of the 1st Division takes aim and fires with his machine gun at a Japanese sniper as his comrade ducks for cover, during the division's advance to take Wana Ridge near the town of Shuri, on Okinawa, in 1945. (AP Photo)

Japanese machine guns were firing down the draw from our left, and our artillery was swishing overhead.

"Haul ass, and don't stop for anything til you get across," said our NCO. (We could see other Marines of our battalion starting across on our right.) He told me to leave my mortar ammo bag and that someone else would bring it. I had the Thompson (submachine gun) slung over my shoulder.

We left the field and slid down a ten-foot embankment to the sloping floor of the draw. My feet hit the deck running. The man ahead of me was a Company K veteran whom I knew well, but the other two were replacements. One I knew by name, but the other not at all. I ran as fast as I could, and was glad I was carrying only my Tommy, pistol, and combat pack.

The valley sloped downward toward a little stream and then upward to the ridge beyond. The Japanese machine guns rattled away. Bullets zipped and snapped around my head, the tracers like long white streaks. I looked neither right nor left, but with my heart in my throat raced out, splashed across the little stream, and dashed up the slope to the shelter of a spur of ridge projecting out into the draw to our left. We must have run about three hundred yards or more to get across.

Once behind the spur I was out of the line of machine-gun fire, so I slowed to a trot. The veteran ahead of me and a little to my right slowed up, too. We glanced back to see where the two new men were. Neither one of them had made more than a few strides out into the draw from the other side. One was sprawled in a heap, obviously killed instantly. The other was wounded and crawling back. Some Marines ran out, crouching low, to drag him to safety.

"Jesus, that was close, Sledgehammer," said the man with me.

"Yeah," I gasped. That was all I could say.

We went up the slope and contacted a couple of riflemen from 2/5.

"We got a kid right over there just got hit. Can you guys get him out?" one of them said. "There's some corpsmen set up in a ravine along the ridge there." He pointed out the location of the casualty and then the dressing station.

We hailed two Company K men coming along the ridge, and they said they would help. One ran back along the ridge to get a stretcher. We other three moved up the ridge and into some brush where we found the wounded Marine. He lay on his back still clutching his rifle. As we came up he said, "Boy, am I glad to see you guys."

"You hit bad?" I asked as I knelt beside him.

"Look out you guys! Nips right over there in the bushes."

I unslung my Tommy and, watching where he indicated the Japanese were, I talked to him. My two buddies knelt beside us with their weapons ready, watching for enemy soldiers through the brush while we waited for the stretcher.

"Where you hit?" I asked the wounded Marine.

"Right here," he said, pointing to the lower right portion of his abdomen.

He was talkative and seemed in no pain—obviously still shocked and dazed from his wound. I knew he would hurt badly soon, because he was hit in a painful area. I saw a smear of blood around a tear in his dungaree trousers, so I unhooked his cartridge belt and then his belt and his trousers to see how serious the wound was. It wasn't the round, neat hole of a bullet, but the gash characteristic of a shell fragment. About two inches long, it oozed a small amount of blood.

"What hit you?" I asked.

"Our company sixty mortars," answered the wounded Marine.

I felt a sharp twinge of conscience and thought some 60mm mortarman in the poor guy's own company fouled up and dropped some short rounds.

Almost as though he had read my thoughts, he continued, "It was my own damn fault I got hit, though. We were ordered to halt back there a way and wait while the mortars shelled this area. But I saw a damn Nip and figured if I got a little closer I could get a clear shot at the sonofabitch. When I got here the mortars came in, and I got hit. Guess I'm lucky it wasn't worse. I guess the Nip slipped away."

"You better take it easy now," I said as the stretcher came up.

We got the young Marine on the stretcher, put his rifle and helmet alongside him, and moved back down the ridge a little way to a corpsman. Several corpsmen were at work in a deep ravine cut into the ridge by erosion. It had sheer walls and a level floor and was perfectly protected. About a dozen wounded, stretcher cases, and walking wounded were there already.

As we set our casualty onto the floor of the ravine, he said, "Thanks a lot you guys; good luck." We wished him luck and a quick trip to the States.

Before we left, I paused and watched the corpsmen a moment. It was admirable how efficiently they handled the wounded, with more coming in continuously as stretcher teams left for evacuation centers with those already given field first-aid.

We split up, moved apart a little, and sought shelter along the slope to await orders. I found a commodius two-man standing foxhole commanding a perfect wide view of the draw for a long distance right and left. It obviously had been used as a defensive position against any movement in the draw and probably had sheltered a couple of Japanese riflemen or perhaps a light machine gunner. The hole was well dug in dry clay soil; the ridge sloped up steeply behind it. But the hole and its surroundings were devoid of any enemy equipment or trash of any kind. There wasn't so much as an empty cartridge case or ammo carton to be seen. But there were enemy tracks in the soft soil thrown out of the hole, tracks of tabi sneakers and hobnail-sole field shoes.

The Japanese had become so security conscious they not only removed their dead when possible but sometimes even picked up their expended "brass" just as we did on a rifle range. Sometimes all we found were bloodstains on the ground where one had been killed or wounded. They removed everything they could when possible to conceal their casualties. But when they removed even empty cartridge cases, and we found only tracks, we got an eerie feeling—as though we were fighting a phantom enemy.

During their battle on the Motobu Peninsula in April, Marines of the 6th Division had seen evidence of increased security consciousness on the part of the Japanese. But we had seen nothing like it on Peleliu, and Guadalcanal veterans had told me nearly every Japanese they "field stripped" had a diary on him. The same was said about Gloucester.

After sitting out another thunderous barrage of friendly artillery fire, the three of us shouldered our weapons and moved along the ridge to rejoin Company K. Once together, our company formed into extended file and headed westward toward the regimental right flank. (I lost track of the date, as we moved about for several days.) The shell-blasted terrain was treeless and increasingly low and flat. We dug in, were shelled off and on, and were thoroughly bewildered as to where we were, other than we were said to be still somewhere in Wana Draw. Shuri loomed to our left front.

About that time Burgin was wounded. He was hit in the back of the neck by a shell fragment. Fortunately, he wasn't killed. Burgin was a Texan and as fine a sergeant as I ever saw. He

was a Gloucester veteran whose luck had run out. We would miss him from the mortar section, and were delighted when he returned later after eighteen days of convalescence.

The weather turned cloudy on 21 May, and the rains began. By midnight the drizzle became a deluge. It was the beginning of a ten-day period of torrential rains. The weather was chilly and mud, mud, mud was everywhere. We slipped and slid along the trails with every step we took.

While the 1st Marine Division was fighting the costly, heartbreaking battle against the Wana positions, the 6th Marine Division (on the right and slightly forward) had been fighting a terrible battle for Sugar Loaf Hill. Sugar Loaf and the surrounding pieces of prominent terrain—the Horse Shoe and Half Moon—were located on the main ridge running from Naha to Shuri. Like Wana, they were key Japanese defensive positions in the complex that guarded the Shuri Heights.

During the morning of 23 May, the boundary between the 1st Marine Division and the 6th Marine Division shifted to the right (west) so the latter could rearrange its lines. The 3d Battalion, 5th Marines went into line on the right to take over the extended front.

I remember the move vividly, because we entered the worst area I ever saw on a battlefield. And we stayed there more than a week. I shudder at the memory of it.

We shouldered our weapons and gear and the column telescoped its way circuitously through muddy draws, slipping and sliding along the slopes of barren hills to avoid observation and consequent shelling by the enemy. It rained off and on. The mud got worse the farther we went. As we approached our destination, the Japanese dead, scattered about in most areas since 1 May, became more numerous.

When we had dug in near enemy dead and conditions permitted, we always shoveled soil over them in a vain effort to cut down the stench and to control the swarming flies. But the desperate fighting for ten days against and around Sugar Loaf Hill and the continued, prolonged Japanese artillery and mortar fire had made it impossible for the Marine units there to bury the enemy dead.

We soon saw that it also had been impossible to remove many Marine dead. They lay where they had fallen—an uncommon sight even to the veterans in our ranks. It was a strong Marine tradition to move our dead, sometimes even at considerable risk, to an area where they could be covered with a poncho and later collected by the graves registration people. But efforts to remove many Marines killed in the area we entered had been in vain, even after Sugar Loaf Hill had been captured following days of terrible fighting.

The rains had begun 21 May, almost as soon as Sugar Loaf Hill had been secured by men of the 6th Marine Division. Because of the deep mud, the able-bodied could scarcely rescue and evacuate their wounded and bring up vital ammo and rations. Regrettably, the dead had to wait. It couldn't have been otherwise.

We slogged along through a muddy draw around the base of a knoll. On our left we saw six Marine corpses. They were lying face down against a gentle muddy slope where they apparently had hugged the deck to escape Japanese shells. They were "bunched up"—in a row, side by side, scarcely a foot apart. They were so close together that they probably had all been killed by the same shell. Their browning faces lay against the mud in an even row. One could imagine the words of fear or reassurance that had been passed among them as they lay under the terror of the shelling. Each clutched a rusting rifle, and every sign indicated that those tragic figures were new replacements, fresh to the shock of combat.

The first man's left hand was extended forward, palm down. His fingers clutched the mud in a death grip. A beautiful, shiny gold watch was held in place around the decaying wrist by an elaborate gold metal stretch band. (Most of the men I knew—and myself—wore plain, simple luminous-dial, waterproof, shockproof wristwatches with a plain green cloth wristband.) How strange, I thought, for a Marine to wear a flashy, conspicuous watch while on the front lines, stranger still that some Japanese hadn't slipped out during a dark night and taken it.

As we filed past the dead Marines, each of my buddies turned his head and gazed at the horrible spectacle with an expression that revealed how much the scene inwardly sickened us all.

I had heard and read that combat troops in many wars became hardened and insensitive to the sight of their own dead. I didn't find that to be the case at all with my comrades. The sight of dead Japanese didn't bother us in the least, but the sight of Marine dead brought forth regret, never indifference.

Half Moon Hill

While the artillery swished and whined overhead in both directions, we moved to our new positions in the westernmost extension of Wana Draw. By twos and threes, the Company K men forming the front line eased onto a barren, muddy, shell-torn ridge named Half Moon Hill and into the foxholes of the company we were relieving. Our mortar section went into place behind a low rise of ground below the ridge and about a hundred yards back of the front lines. The terrain between us and Half Moon was nearly flat. The little elevation behind which we emplaced our guns was so low that when we stood up beside the gun pit, we could see clearly up to the company's forward lines on the ridge.

Readily visible beyond that, to the left front, were the still higher, smoke-shrouded Shuri Heights, the heart of the Japanese defensive system. That ominous and formidable terrain feature was constantly under bombardment of varying intensity from our artillery, heavy mortars, and gunfire support ships. No matter, though. It didn't seem to deter the enemy observers from directing their artillery and heavy mortars in shelling our whole area frequently, every day and every night.

We faced south on Half Moon. A narrow-gauge railroad track lay a short distance to our right and ran south through a flat area between Half Moon and a ridge to our right known as the Horse Shoe. Beyond that it swung westward toward Naha. An officer told us that the ridge to our right (west) and slightly to our rear across the railroad was Sugar Loaf Hill.

Company K was on the right flank of 3/5 and moved up onto the western part of the base of Half Moon. The Japanese still occupied caves in both of the southward-pointing tips of the crescent. The right-flank foxhole of our company was dug on the crest at the western edge of the end of the base of Half Moon. Below it to the right the ridge dropped away to low flat ground.

Our company CP was situated in the sunken railroad bed to the right of our mortar section's position. A nice tarpaulin was stretched over the CP from one side of the railroad embankment to the other. This kept the post snug and dry while torrents of chilly rain kept shivering riflemen, machine gunners, and mortarmen soaked, cold, and miserable day and night in open foxholes. The rain greeted us as we moved into our assigned area.

The almost continuous downpour that started on 21 May turned Wana Draw into a sea of mud and water that resembled a lake. Tanks bogged down and even amtracs could not negotiate the morass. Living conditions on the front lines were pitiful. Supply and evacuation problems were severe. Food, water, and ammunition were scarce. Foxholes had to be bailed out constantly. The men's clothing, shoes, feet, and bodies remained constantly wet. Sleep was nearly impossible. The mental and physical strain took a mounting toll on the Marines.

Making an almost impossible situation worse were the deteriorating bodies of Marines and Japanese that lay just outside the foxholes where they had fallen during the five days of ferocious fighting that preceded Company K's arrival on Half Moon. Each day's fighting saw the number of corpses increase. Flies multiplied, and amoebic dysentery broke out. The men of Company K, together with the rest of the 1st Marine Division, would live and fight in that hell for ten days.

We dispersed our guns and dug gun pits as best we could in the mud. Snafu and I took compass readings and set aiming stakes based on the readings from our observer. As soon as we fired a couple of rounds of HE to register in my gun, it was obvious we had a bad problem with the base plate of our mortar being driven farther into the soft soil with the recoil of each shell. We reasoned the rain would soon stop, however, or if it didn't, a couple of pieces of ammo box under the base plate would hold it firm. What a mistake!

After digging in the gun, registering in on the aiming stakes, and preparing ammo for future use, I had my first opportunity to look around our position. It was the most ghastly corner of hell I had ever witnessed. As far as I could see, an area that previously had been a low grassy valley with a picturesque stream meandering through it was a muddy, repulsive, open sore on the land. The place was choked with the putrefaction of death, decay, and destruction. In a shallow defilade to our right, between my gun pit and the railroad, lay about twenty dead Marines, each on a stretcher and covered to his ankles with a poncho—a commonplace, albeit tragic, scene to every veteran. Those bodies had been placed there to await transport to the rear for burial. At least those dead were covered from the torrents of rain that had made them miserable in life and from the swarms of flies that sought to hasten their decay. But as I looked about, I saw that other Marine dead couldn't be tended properly. The whole area was pocked with shell craters and churned up by explosions. Every crater was half full of water, and many of them held a Marine corpse.

The bodies lay pathetically just as they had been killed, half submerged in muck and water, rusting weapons still in hand. Swarms of big flies hovered about them.

"Why ain't them poor guys been covered with ponchos?" mumbled my foxhole buddy as he glanced grimly about with a distraught expression on his grizzled face. His answer came the moment he spoke. Japanese 75mm shells came whining and whistling into the area. We cowered in our hole as they crashed and thundered around us. The enemy gunners on the commanding Shuri Heights were registering their artillery and mortars on our positions. We realized quickly that anytime any of us moved out of our holes, the shelling began immediately. We had a terrible time getting our wounded evacuated through the shell fire and mud without the casualties and stretcher-bearers getting hit. Thus it was perfectly clear why the Marine dead were left where they had fallen.

Everywhere lay Japanese corpses killed in the heavy fighting. Infantry equipment of every type, U.S. and Japanese, was scattered about. Helmets, rifles, BARs, packs, cartridge belts, canteens, shoes, ammo boxes, shell cases, machine-gun ammo belts, all were strewn around us up to and all over Half Moon.

The mud was knee deep in some places, probably deeper in others if one dared venture there. For several feet around every corpse, maggots crawled about in the muck and then were washed away by the runoff of the rain. There wasn't a tree or bush left. All was open country. Shells had torn up the turf so completely that ground cover was nonexistent. The rain poured down on us as evening approached. The scene was nothing but mud; shell fire; flooded craters with their silent, pathetic, rotting occupants; knocked-out tanks and amtracs; and discarded equipment—utter desolation.

The stench of death was overpowering. The only way I could bear the monstrous horror of it all was to look upward away from the earthly reality surrounding us, watch the leaden gray clouds go skudding over, and repeat over and over to myself that the situation was unreal—just a nightmare—that I would soon awake and find myself somewhere else. But the ever-present smell of death saturated my nostrils. It was there with every breath I took.

I existed from moment to moment, sometimes thinking death would have been preferable. We were in the depths of the abyss, the ultimate horror of war. During the fighting around the Umurbrogol Pocket on Peleliu, I had been depressed by the wastage of human lives. But in the mud and driving rain before Shuri, we were surrounded by maggots and decay. Men struggled and fought and bled in an environment so degrading I believed we had been flung into hell's own cesspool.

Not long after 3/5 took over Half Moon, several of us were on a work party, struggling through knee-deep mud to bring ammo from the rear up to the mortar positions. We passed near the company CP in the railroad bed.

"Hey, you guys, looka there; Stumpy's in bad shape!" said a Marine in an excited low voice. We all stopped and looked toward the CP. There was our CO, Stumpy Stanley, just outside the edge of the tarpaulin, trying to stand by himself. But he had to be supported by a man on each side. He looked haggard and weary and was shaking violently with malarial chills. He could barely hold up his head. The men supporting him seemed to be arguing with him. He was objecting as best he could. But it was a feeble effort, because he was so sick.

"Po' Stumpy got that goddamn bug so bad he can't hardly stand up. But looka there; he's all man, by God. He don't wanna be 'vacuated," said Snafu gravely.

"He's a damn good Joe," someone else said.

We thought highly of Stumpy and respected him greatly. He was a good skipper, and we had confidence in him. But malaria made him too ill to stay on his feet. The chilly rain, the emotional stress, and the physical exertion and strain of those days were enough to make a well man collapse. Obviously those who had malarial infections couldn't possibly keep going. So, for the second time in May, we lost our commanding officer. Stumpy was the last of our Peleliu officers, and his evacuation ended an era for me. He was the last tie to Capt. Andy Haldane. For me, Company K was never the same after that day.

As we feared, Shadow became the CO. It's best that I don't record what we said about that.

At daybreak the morning after we took over the line on Half Moon, George Sarrett and I went up onto the ridge to our observation post. Half Moon was shaped like a crescent, with the arms pointing southward. Our battalion line stretched along the crest of the ridge as it formed the base of the crescent. The arms extended outward beyond our front lines, and Japanese occupied caves in the reverse slopes of those arms, particularly the one on the left (east). They made our line a hot spot.

To our front, the ridge sloped down sharply from the crest then more gently all the way to a big road embankment approximately three hundred yards out and running parallel to our lines. A large culvert opened toward us through the embankment. The area to our front was well drained and as bare as the back of one's hand. It wasn't heavily cratered. Two shallow ditches about fifty yards apart ran across the area between the southern tips of the Half Moon. These ditches were closer to the road embankment than to our lines. The sloping area leading to the culvert resembled an amphitheater bordered by the base of the crescent (where we were) to the north, the arms of the crescent extending southward, and the high road embankment running east and west at the southern end. Our visibility within the amphitheater was perfect (except for the reverse slopes of the arms of the crescent).

Marines of 2/4 had warned us as they departed that the Japanese came out of the caves in the reverse slopes of the crescent's arms at night and generally raised hell. To combat that, our ships kept star shells aloft, and our 60mm mortars kept flares burning in the wet sky above the ridge all night every night we were there.

As the dawn light grew brighter, we could see the lay of the land through the drizzle and thin fog. So we registered the mortar section's three guns with an aiming stake on one of each of three important terrain features. We had one gun register in on the reverse slope of the left-hand extension of the Half Moon. A second mortar we registered on the reverse slope of the road embankment. We registered the third gun to cover the area around the mouth of the culvert.

No sooner had we registered the guns than we got a reaction. Big 90mm Japanese mortar shells began crashing along the crest of the ridge. They came so thick and so fast we knew an entire enemy mortar section was firing on us, not an isolated gun. They were zeroed in on the ridge and traversed along the crest from my left to the far right end of the company's line. It was an awful pounding. Each big shell fluttered and swished down and went off with a flash and an earsplitting crash. Shrapnel growled through the air, and several men were wounded badly. Each shell threw stinking mud around when it exploded. The wounded were moved down behind the ridge with great difficulty because of the slippery, muddy slopes. A corpsman gave them aid, and they were carried to the rear—shocked, torn, and bleeding.

An uneasy quiet then settled along the line. Suddenly, someone yelled, "There goes one." A single Japanese soldier dashed out of the blackness of the culvert. He carried his bayoneted rifle and wore a full pack. He ran into the open, turned, and headed for shelter behind the tip of the southern end of the crescent arm on our left front. It looked as though he had about a thirty-yard dash to make. Several of our riflemen and BARmen opened up, and the soldier was bowled over by their bullets before he reached the shelter of the ridge. Our men cheered and yelled when he went down.

As the day wore on, more Japanese ran out of the culvert in ones and twos and dashed for the shelter of the same ridge extension. It was obvious they wanted to concentrate on the reverse slope there from where they could launch counterattacks, raids, and infiltration attempts on our front line. Obviously, it was to our best interest to stop them as quickly as possible. Any enemy soldier who made it in behind that slope might become one's unwelcome foxhole companion some night.

When the Japanese ran out of the culvert, our men fired on them and nearly always knocked them down. The riflemen, BARmen, and machine gunners looked on it as fine target practice, because we received no return small-arms fire, and the Japanese mortars were quiet.

I kept busy with the field glasses, observing, adjusting range, and calling fire orders onto the slope and the road embankment. I had the Tommy with me, but it wasn't as steady and accurate at the two- to three-hundred-yard range as an M1 Garand rifle. We had an M1 and an ammo belt in our OP, though, and I wanted to throw down that phone and the field glasses and grab up that M1 every time an enemy popped into view. As long as our mortar section was firing a mission, I had no choice but to continue observing.

The Japanese kept up their efforts to move behind the slope. Some made it, because our men missed them. Our 60mm mortar shells crashed away steadily on the target areas. We could see Japanese emerge from the culvert and be killed by our shells.

The longer this action continued without our receiving any return fire, the more relaxed my buddies became. The situation began to take on certain aspects of a rifle range, or more likely, an old-fashioned turkey shoot. My buddies started making bets about who had hit

which Japanese. Lively arguments developed, but with rifles, BARs and several machine guns firing simultaneously, no one could tell for sure who hit which enemy soldier.

The men yelled and joked more and more in one of their few releases from weeks of tension under the pounding of heavy weapons. So they began to get careless and to miss some of the Japanese scurrying for the slope. Shadow saw this. He ran up and down our firing line cursing and yelling at everybody. Then the men settled down and took more careful aim. Finally the enemy stopped coming, and I received orders to call "cease firing" to our mortars. We sat and waited.

During the lull, I moved over into the machine-gun emplacement next to our mortar OP to visit with the gunner. It contained a Browning .30 caliber water-cooled heavy machine gun manned by a gunner who had joined Company K as a replacement after Peleliu. On Pavuvu, he and I had become good friends. We called him "Kathy" after a chorus girl he knew in California. He was married and very much in love with his wife, so he bore a heavy burden of guilt because he had had an affair with Kathy on his way overseas and couldn't get her out of his mind.

As we sat alone in the machine-gun pit, he asked me whether I wanted to see a picture of Kathy. I said yes. He carefully and secretively picked up his rain-soaked combat pack and took out a waterproof plastic map holder. Folding back the canvas cover, he said, "Here she is."

My eyes nearly popped out of my head. The eight- by ten-inch photo was a full-length portrait of one of the most beautiful girls I ever saw. She was dressed, or undressed, in a scanty costume which exposed a good portion of her impressive physical endowments.

I gasped audibly, and "Kathy" said, "Isn't she a beauty?"

"She really is!" I told him, and added, "You've got a problem on your hands with a girl like that chorus girl and a wife you love." I kidded him about the possible danger of getting the letters to his wife and his girl crossed up and in the wrong envelopes. He just laughed and shook his head as he looked at the photo of the beautiful girl.

The scene was so unreal I could barely believe it: two tired, frightened young men sitting in a hole beside a machine gun in the rain on a ridge, surrounded with mud—nothing but stinking mud, with so much decaying human flesh buried or half buried in it that there were big patches of wriggling fat maggots marking the spots where Japanese corpses lay—looking at the picture of a beautiful seminude girl. She was a pearl in a mudhole.

Viewing that picture made me realize with a shock that I had gradually come to doubt that there really was a place in the world where there were no explosions and people weren't bleeding, suffering, dying, or rotting in the mud. I felt a sense of desperation that my mind was being affected by what we were experiencing. Men cracked up frequently in such places as that. I had seen it happen many times by then. In World War I they had called it shell shock or, more technically, *neuresthenia*. In World War II the term used was combat fatigue.

Strange that such a picture provoked such thoughts, but I vividly recall grimly making a pledge to myself. The Japanese might kill or wound me, but they wouldn't make me crack up. A peaceful civilian back home who sat around worrying about losing his mind probably didn't have much to occupy him, but in our situation there was plenty of reason for the strongest-willed individuals to crack up.

My secret resolve helped me through the long days and nights we remained in the worst of the abyss. But there were times at night during that period when I felt I was slipping. More than once my imagination ran wild during the brief periods of darkness when the flares and star shells burned out.

"There comes another one," somebody yelled. "Kathy" quickly stowed his picture in his pack, spun around, gripped the machine-gun handle in his left hand, poised his trigger finger, and grabbed the aiming knob with his right hand. His assistant gunner appeared from out of nowhere and jumped to his post to feed the ammo belt into the gun. I started back to the OP hole but saw that George had phone in hand, and the mortars were still "secured." So I grabbed up an M1 rifle "Kathy" had in the machine-gun emplacement.

I saw enemy soldiers rushing out of the culvert. Our line started firing as I counted the tenth Japanese to emerge. Those incredibly brave soldiers formed a skirmish line abreast, with a few yards between each other, and started trotting silently toward us across open ground about three hundred yards away. Their effort was admirable but so hopeless. They had no supporting fire of any kind to pin us down or even to make us cautious. They looked as though they were on maneuvers. They had no chance of getting close to us.

I stood up beside the machine gun, took aim, and started squeezing off shots. The Japanese held their rifles at port arms and didn't even fire at us. Everybody along our line was yelling and firing. The enemy soldiers wore full battle gear with packs, which meant they had rations and extra ammo, so this might be the beginning of a counterattack of some size.

Within seconds, eight of the ten enemy soldiers pitched forward, spun around, or slumped to the deck, dead where they fell. The remaining two must have realized the futility of it all, because they turned around and started back toward the culvert. Most of us slackened our fire and just watched. Several men kept firing at the two retreating enemy soldiers but missed, and it looked as though they might get away. Finally one Japanese fell forward near one of the shallow ditches. The surviving soldier kept going.

Just as "Kathy" got his machine-gun sights zeroed in on him, the order "cease firing" came along the line. But the machine gun was making so much noise we didn't hear the order. "Kathy" had his ammo belts loaded so that about every fifth cartridge was a tracer. He squeezed off a long burst of about eight shots. The bullets struck the fleeing Japanese soldier in the middle of his pack and tore into him between his shoulders.

I was standing directly behind "Kathy," looking along his machine-gun barrel. The tracers must have struck the man's vertebrae or other bones and been deflected, because I clearly saw one tracer flash up into the air out of the soldier's right shoulder and another tracer come out of the top of his left shoulder. The Japanese dropped his rifle as the slugs knocked him face down into the mud. He didn't move.

"I got him; I got the bastard." Kathy yelled, jumping around slapping me on the back, and shaking hands with his assistant gunner. He had reason to be proud. He had made a good shot.

The enemy soldier who fell near the ditch began crawling and flopped into it. Some of the men started firing at him again. The bullets kicked up mud all around the soldier as he slithered desperately along in the shallow ditch which didn't quite hide him. Machine-gun tracers ricocheted off the ground like vicious red arrows as the Japanese struggled along the shallow ditch.

Then, on one of the rare occasions I ever saw compassion expressed for the Japanese by a Marine who had to fight them, one of our men yelled, "Knock it off, you guys. The poor bastard's already hit and ain't got a snowball's chance in hell."

Someone else yelled angrily, "You stupid jerk; he's a goddamn Nip ain't he? You gone Asiatic or something?"

The firing continued, and bullets hit the mark. The wounded Japanese subsided into the muddy little ditch. He and his comrades had done their best. "They died gloriously on the field of honor for the emperor," is what their families would be told. In reality, their lives were wasted on a muddy, stinking slope for no good reason.

Our men were in high spirits over the affair, especially after being pounded for so long. But Shadow was yelling, "Cease firing, you dumb bastards." He came slipping and sliding along the line, cursing and stopping at intervals to pour out storms of invective on some smiling, muddy Marine. He carried his helmet in his left hand and periodically took off his cap and flung it down into the mud until it was caked. Each man looked glum and sat or stood motionless until Shadow had finished insulting him and moved on.

As Shadow passed the machine-gun pit, he stopped and screamed at "Kathy," who was still jumping around in jubilation over his kill. "Knock it off, you goddamn fool!" Then he glared at me and said, "You're supposed to be observing for the mortars; put that goddamn rifle down, you bastard."

I wasn't impetuous, but, had I thought I could get away with it, I would certainly have clubbed him over the head with that M1 rifle.

I didn't, but Shadow's asinine conduct and comment did make me rash enough to say, "The guns are secured, sir. We were all sent out here to kill Nips, weren't we? So what difference does it make what weapon we use when we get the chance?"

His menacing expression turned into surprise and then doubt. With a quizzical look on his face, he cocked his head to one side as he pondered my remark, while I stood silently with the realization that I should have kept my mouth shut. The fine sergeant accompanying Shadow half glared and half smiled at me. Suddenly, without another glance, Shadow strode off along the ridge crest, cursing and yelling at the Marines in each foxhole as he passed them. I resolved to keep my mouth shut in the future.

As daylight waned, I looked out to our front through the drizzling rain falling through the still, foul air. A wisp of smoke rose straight up from the pack of the Japanese soldier "Kathy" had shot. The tracers had set something on fire. The thin finger of smoke rose high and then spread out abruptly to form a disc that appeared to rest on the column. So delicate and unreal, the smoke stood in the stagnant, fetid air like a marker over the corpse. Everything out there was motionless, only death and desolation among the enemy bodies.

George and I got orders to return to our mortar gun pits. Someone else would man the OP for the night. Getting back to the mortar emplacements from the company's front line was a major effort and an extremely dangerous one. From the moment we stepped to the rear of the crest of the ridge to descend the muddy slope, it was like trying to walk down a greased slide.

A large and unknown number of Japanese all over the ridge had been killed during the early counterattacks. They had been covered with soil as soon as possible. And Japanese were still being killed out front. Infiltrators also were being killed all along the ridge at night. Our men could only spade mud over them.

The situation was bad enough, but when enemy artillery shells exploded in the area, the eruptions of soil and mud uncovered previously buried Japanese dead and scattered chunks of corpses. Like the area around our gun pits, the ridge was a stinking compost pile.

If a Marine slipped and slid down the back slope of the muddy ridge, he was apt to reach the bottom vomiting. I saw more than one man lose his footing and slip and slide all the way to the bottom only to stand up horror-stricken as he watched in disbelief while fat maggots tumbled out of his muddy dungaree pockets, cartridge belt, legging lacings, and the like. Then he and a buddy would shake or scrape them away with a piece of ammo box or a knife blade.

We didn't talk about such things. They were too horrible and obscene even for hardened veterans. The conditions taxed the toughest I knew almost to the point of screaming. Nor do authors normally write about such vileness; unless they have seen it with their own eyes, it is too preposterous to think that men could actually live and fight for days and nights on end under such terrible conditions and not be driven insane. But I saw much of it there on Okinawa and to me the war was insanity.

Study Questions

1. What tactics did the Japanese use to hide casualties, and what was its psychological impact on U.S. soldiers?

2. How did the author and other American soldiers cope with the dead and wounded—both Japanese and American?

3. What impact did the island's geography and weather conditions have on the mentality of soldiers?

4. How had the fighting near Sugar Loaf Hill and Half Moon Hill changed the landscape?

5. How do you explain the difference in soldier attitudes between times of combat and periods of lull in battle?

6. What different ways did soldiers resolve to remember life back home in the States?

7. What attitudes did soldiers hold toward the enemy?

Bibliography

This piece first appeared in E. B. Sledge, *With the Old Breed: At Peleliu and Okinawa* (1981). John W. Dower, *War Without Mercy: Race and Power in the Pacific War* (1986), details the feelings of soldiers who fought in the Pacific. Hiromichi Yahara, *The Battle for Okinawa* (1997), is the personal account from a Japanese soldier and provides an interesting counterpoint to Sledge. John Frayn Turner, ed., *Fight for the Sea: Naval Adventures from World War II* (2001), is a collection of American reminiscences of the war in the Pacific. Other good personal narratives and firsthand accounts of World War II are Studs Terkel, ed., *The Good War: An Oral History of World War Two* (1984); and Jack Stenbuck, ed., *Typewriter Battalion: Dramatic Front-Line Dispatches from World War II* (1995). For a general overview of the battles for Iwo Jima and Okinawa, see Roy Appleman, *Okinawa: The Last Battle* (1948); and Robert Leckie, *Okinawa: The Last Battle of World War II* (1995). John Keegan, *The Second World War* (1989), is an excellent place to begin study of World War II.

6

★ ★ ★

America in the Age of Anxiety: 1945–1960

The fallout of Hiroshima lasted many years. The most immediate result of the atomic bombs that America dropped on Japan on August 6 and August 9, 1945, was the end of World War II. V-J Day was celebrated with an emotional outpouring of relief. Most Americans believed that the United States had saved the world from the totalitarian threat of the Axis powers. They also assumed that America would now return to its traditional foreign policy posture of isolationism. Such was not the case. World War II had made the United States the most powerful country in the world. Retreat into isolationism was impossible. During the next few years, America accepted the responsibilities that went with being a world power and replaced Great Britain as the globe's police force.

Almost as soon as the war was over, the Soviet Union emerged as America's leading rival. Joseph Stalin, Russia's leader, was by nature suspicious, and the complexities and uncertainties of Soviet politics made him even more so. He resented America and Great Britain for delaying the second front against Germany during World War II. He was also upset that the United States refused to share its nuclear secrets with the Soviet Union. Fears, anxieties, and ambitions degenerated into a new type of power conflict. Called the cold war, the object was to control, either through economic or military means, as much of the world as possible.

America originated the policy of containment as a strategy for the cold war. The policy was essentially defensive in nature, and it forced America to react to Soviet movements. Although the policy scored several notable successes—particularly in Turkey, Greece, and Western Europe—it had a number of real weaknesses. Most important, it committed American troops to prevent the expansion of Communism. In Korea and later in Vietnam, Americans came to understand the limitations and constraints of the containment doctrine.

The cold war and the fear of a nuclear confrontation shaped domestic politics as well as foreign affairs. If Americans distrusted Stalin's motives, they also questioned the actions of their own leaders. They asked pointed and complex questions, yet sought simple answers. Why had Stalin gained so much territory at Yalta? How was Russia able to develop its own atomic weapons so rapidly? Who lost China? Politicians such as Senator Joseph McCarthy of Wisconsin and Congressman Richard Nixon of California provided easy answers. They said that Communist sympathizers in the American government had worked to ensure the success of the Soviet Union. The publicity lavished on the trials of Alger Hiss and Julius and Ethel Rosenberg and the activities of McCarthy and the House Un-American Activities Committee increased the public's distrust of its own officials.

In the following section, the essays deal with the fallout of Hiroshima and the cold war. Although they examine very different subjects—Korean War POW's, race questions, highways, and television scandals—they contain a unifying theme. They all discuss Americans' attitudes toward themselves. The underlying assumption was that something deep and troubling was happening, that the American character had changed for the worse. The search for exactly what was wrong took many different turns and helped illuminate the psychological, cultural, and social landscape of the 1950s.

READING 20

★ ★ ★

American Prisoners of War in Korea: A Second Look at the "Something New in History" Theme

H. H. Wubben

Contrary to what most people had anticipated, the end of World War II did not bring a feeling of security to the United States. The war was barely over when the Soviet Union replaced the Germans and Japanese as mortal enemies of the Americans. The Soviet threat seemed particularly ominous because of the Marxist prediction of revolutionary upheavals in capitalist countries. In the late 1940s, U.S. foreign policy revolved around the idea of containment, an economic and military commitment to keep Russian influence behind the Iron Curtain. The Truman Doctrine of 1946, the Marshall Plan of 1947–1948, the North Atlantic Treaty Organization, and the Berlin Airlift of 1948–1949 were all directed at stopping Soviet expansion in Western Europe. To secure congressional funding of that foreign policy, the Truman administration talked unceasingly of the international Communist conspiracy, and in the process created a tense, suspicious political atmosphere inside the United States. Many Americans became convinced there was a subversive, internal Communist plot to overthrow the U.S. government.

The American fear of the Soviet Union and Communism intensified in 1950 with the outbreak of the Korean War. North Korean troops poured across the 38th parallel into South Korea, and the United States implemented the containment policy by sending hundreds of thousands of troops into the peninsula. When the armistice was reached three years later, the United States had had its first taste of undeclared war—a "police action." And when the prisoners of war began filtering home with their horror stories of deprivation, torture, and "brainwashing," Communism became even more sinister to the American people. The experiences of the POWs also aroused serious doubts about the "American character." In the following selection, historian H. H. Wubben discusses the significance of the POW problem in the context of the cold war.

Americans have long been intrigued by speculations about their national character. In particular they have been receptive to assessments which credit them with immunity against certain human frailties, an immunity not possessed by most other peoples. Out of the Korean War came a controversy which impinged annoyingly upon such assessments and which provided grist for the mill of those who now preferred to believe that in recent decades the character had deteriorated.

Throughout the conflict reports coming out of North Korea indicated that the communists were subjecting American prisoners of war to a re-education process popularly described as "brainwashing." Prisoner returnees during Operation Little Switch in May and Operation Big Switch in August and September 1953 corroborated some of these reports. But it also became clear that such re-education was largely ineffective. Nevertheless, 21 prisoners chose not to return home. A few who did return admitted that they were "progressives," that is, men partially converted by the Chinese re-education program. Some who did not confess to such leanings faced accusations from other prisoners that they had taken the "progressive" line.

In addition it became apparent that a number of men had engaged in collaborative or criminal behavior detrimental to the welfare of their fellows. Consequently, the armed services made special efforts to find out what had happened. Psychiatrists and psychologists interviewed the newly freed prisoners during the repatriation process and on the journey home. Intelligence officers also interviewed them, compiling dossiers on each man. Information acquired by these specialists eventually provided the data upon which subsequent formal studies of the prisoners and their behavior in captivity were based.

In 1955 came the official government view of the POW behavior issue, the report of the Secretary of Defense's Advisory Committee on Prisoners of War. But the committee's judgment was hardly definitive. On the one hand, the group declared, "the record [of the prisoners] seems fine indeed . . . they cannot be found wanting." On the other it concluded, "The Korean story must never be permitted to happen again." Then in 1956 the Army issued a training pamphlet on the subject of POW behavior. It was even more ambiguous. Readers learned that the Chinese "lenient policy" designed to lessen resistance "resulted in little or no active resistance to the enemy's indoctrination." Later, however, they read that the "large majority . . . resisted the enemy in the highest tradition of the service and of our country."

Findings of the major formal studies, financed by or undertaken by the armed services in most cases, are much more satisfying to the scholar who desires more consistency in both raw material and analysis. These include research projects done for the Department of the Army, the Surgeon General's Office, the Air Force, and the Walter Reed Army Institute of Research. Also engaged in examination of POW experiences was the Society for the Investigation of Human Ecology. The studies never achieved wide circulation although the research scientists who engaged in them reported their substance in professional journals. Eventually one scholarly book-length treatment appeared, Albert Biderman's *March to Calumny*. Biderman, a sociologist who was active in several of these projects, demolished in a convincing manner those interpretations which accused the prisoners of being singularly deficient in the attributes expected of American servicemen unfortunate enough to become prisoners of war.

The work of such specialists, however, has had little impact compared with that of those whose reports convey a largely, if not exclusively, negative version of the prisoners'

H. H. Wubben, "American Prisoners of War in Korea: A Second Look at the 'Something New in History' Theme" in *American Quarterly*, Vol. 22 (Spring, 1970). © The Johns Hopkins University Press, Reprinted by permission.

actions during captivity. That version, in general, declares that American prisoners of war in Chinese and North Korean hands were morally weak and uncommitted to traditional American ideals. Consequently, some, though not a majority, were infected to a degree with the virus of communism. Furthermore, they were undisciplined. They were unwilling to aid each other in their travail. And they succumbed too easily under limited duress or no duress at all to the pressures of their captors to engage in collaborative behavior, including informing on each other. Their death rate, 38 percent, was the highest in history, and most deaths resulted from "give-up-itis" and lack of concern for one another among the prisoners themselves, not from communist mistreatment. Also, no prisoners successfully escaped from communist prison camps, a "first" in U.S. military experience. Other nationality groups, particularly the Turks, successfully resisted communist blandishments, and only the Marines among the Americans consistently adhered to patterns of honorable conduct. Finally, the POWs in Korea were the first Americans in captivity to so act, a "fact" which calls for a reassessment of mid-century American values and the culture which spawned them.

Among those who accepted this as history, in part or in whole, were President Dwight Eisenhower, FBI Director J. Edgar Hoover, and Senator Strom Thurmond of South Carolina. Political scientist Anthony Bouscaren saw the "record" as evidence that American education had flunked a significant test. Another critic of education, Augustin Rudd, viewed the prisoner performance as evidence that the chickens of progressive education had come home to roost. The editors of *Scouting* magazine in 1965 cited it in urging continued efforts to implant the ideals of the Boy Scout Code among youth in that organization. And as late as 1968, California educator and political figure Max Rafferty employed it in some of his campaign literature during his senatorial race.

These individuals, however, have not been so influential as two others in promoting this "history." They are the late Eugene Kinkead, a freelance writer, and Lt. Col. William E. Mayer, one of the psychiatrists who participated in the interviewing of the repatriates. Kinkead's major contribution was a book entitled *In Every War But One* which sold around fifteen thousand copies. Col. Mayer's contributions, mainly public addresses, have won even wider circulation than Kinkead's, thanks to the tape recorder and the mimeograph. Both men have modified from time to time their indictment of the prisoners, if not of recent trends in American society. Mayer, for instance, toward the end of one of his speeches said, "Finally, the great majority of men didn't become communists, didn't suffer any kind of moral breakdown, no matter what the communists did to them." But by then the negative point had been so strongly stressed that few listeners were aware of his significant caveat.

That they were not aware resulted from a number of circumstances. Many conservative Americans were disgruntled at the absence of a decisive American victory in the war. They blamed communist subversion at home for the result. This subversion in turn they blamed on "socialistic" influences originating in the 1930s which, they charged, had weakened the capacity and will of home, church, and school to develop good character among the nation's youth. Thus, the prisoners served as evidence to verify their beliefs. Many liberals accepted the prisoners as examples of societal sickness also, although they rejected the communist subversion theme. They claimed that American materialism lay at the root of the problem. Both groups professed to view the prisoners with pity rather than scorn, as men who through no fault of their own were simply unfortunate products of a society on the verge of decay. Both were impressed by Mayer's credentials and the literate, entertaining manner in which he employed tendentious illustrations to document a general picture of moral and morale breakdown resulting from defective precaptivity nurture. Given these general dispositions on the part of many Mayer listeners, it is no wonder that they let his muted but significant qualifier slip by. They weren't interested in it. Finally many Americans, including academicians who would ordinarily have demanded more intellectual rigor in their own disciplines, simply took Mayer's and Kinkead's revelations at face value because they seemed to meet the test of reasonableness.

Historians have long known a great deal about the behavior of Americans in prisoner camps prior to the Korean War, particularly about prison behavior in World War II camps. As Peter Karsten wrote in the spring of 1965 issue of *Military Affairs*, the motivation and conduct of American servicemen, in or out of prison camps, have been a source of concern from the American Revolution to the present. George Washington had numerous unkind words for defectors, mutineers, and those of his forces who lacked "public spirit." The activities of the reluctant warriors of the War of 1812, the defectors and the short-term volunteers who departed the service when their time was up—if not sooner—wherever they were during the Mexican and Civil Wars, are a matter of record. "Give-up-itis," called "around the bends," was not unknown at Andersonville and Belle Isle. Draft dodgers and deserters numbered over 170,000, in World War I. By the early 1940s, "around the bends" had several new names, the most common being "Bamboo disease" and "fence complex."

Even in a "popular" war, World War II, the Army worried about the lack of dedication among its troops. Indoctrination programs were overhauled and beefed up with negligible success. A Social Science Research Council team which analyzed data collected by the Army during the war concluded that the average soldier "gave little concern to the conflicting values underlying the military struggle. . . . [and] Although he showed a strong but tacit patriotism, this usually did not lead him in his thinking to subordinate his personal interests to the furtherance of ideal aims and values."

As to moral and morale breakdown under severe conditions, two military physicians reported that in Japanese POW camps "moral integrity could be pretty well judged by inverse ratio to one's state of nutrition." And, they added, "Although some of these prisoners sublimated their cravings by giving aid to their fellows, there was, in general, a lowering of moral standards. Food was often obtained by devious means at the expense of other prisoners." Though a buddy system did function to some extent, particularly among small cliques who shared both companionship and food, there were few group activities, and most men tended to be taciturn and seclusive. Being unable to defy their captors and survive, they expressed considerable verbal resentment toward each other. In particular they disparaged their own officers and their behavior. Another physician, who was a prisoner himself in the Philippines and Japan, wrote that most POWs, whether sick or well, suffered periods of apathy or depression which, if not countered forcefully, would lead to death. "Giving up" occurred earliest and easiest among younger men in Korea. In a sentence strikingly reminiscent of the Kinkead-Mayer critique, except that he omitted the "something new in history" theme, the physician wrote, "Failures in adjustment were most apparent in the 18-to-23-year-old group who had little or no previous experience and much overprotection. These men demonstrated marked inability to fight physical diseases and the initial shock of depression of captivity."

Dr. Harold Wolff, a consultant to the Advisory Committee, reported that in World War II German prison camps where the pressures were much less severe than in Japanese and Korean camps, about 10 percent of the Americans "offered remarkably little resistance, if not outright collaboration." Wolff also noted that the escape record of Americans in World War II was not exceptional. Less than a dozen prisoners of the Japanese out of twenty-five to thirty thousand escaped from permanent camps, all in the Philippines. Less than one hundred out of ninety-four thousand Americans captured by the Nazis successfully escaped from camps, of which less than half returned to Allied control.

Autobiographical accounts of former World War II prisoners also tell much which shows that the Korean POW behavior was not unique. Edward Dobran, an airman held by the Germans, reported that a GI mess hall crew at his camp took care of itself well but skimped on the rest of the men's rations. Nor could those who apportioned food in the squads be trusted to do their job honestly more than a few days at a time. Dobran concluded, "In a place such as this, every man is strictly for himself. This sort of living and hardships showed what a human being is really made of. If you didn't look out for yourself here, nobody else did."

Physician Alfred Weinstein's book-length recital of prison-camp life in the Philippines and Japan tells about a Marine officer's extensive collaboration with the Japanese and about the stealing of medicine by the same officer and some enlisted men medics at Cabanatuan. Some POW mechanics and truck drivers, put to work by the Japanese, lived high, using their positions to smuggle from Manila desperately needed food and medicine which they then sold for outrageous prices to the rest of the prisoners who were in dire need of both. Nor was Weinstein complimentary about behavior in an officers' ward at a prisoner hospital at Cabanatuan. These officer-patients demanded so many special privileges, food, and medicine because of their rank that the senior American officer had to break up the group by distributing the men throughout the other wards. Also not complimentary about the self-keeping of a few officers incarcerated in Japan is Hugh Myers in a recently published memoir. Myers has described how four veteran Navy chiefs from the garrison at Guan assumed control over prison life at one stage in his POW experience when

it became apparent that the officers were too concerned about their privileges, too inexperienced, or both, to do the job fairly or well.

Nevertheless, in all the accounts discussed above which were written by men who had been POWs there is no tendency to denigrate American civilization because of the failings of a greater or lesser number of men in prison camps. Nor is it assumed by them that men under conditions of stress will uniformly conduct themselves in exemplary fashion. Weinstein, for instance, wrote, "Hard living, disease, and starvation made heroes out of few men. More frequently does it make animals out of men who, in the normal course of living would go through life with a clean slate."

Two aspects of the Korean POW story, then, should be of particular interest to the historian. First, there is the fact that a poorly understood historical experience is interpreted in such a way that it makes a thoroughly inaccurate comparison between Americans past and Americans present. Second, there is the acceptance by the general public of this "nonhistory" as history, largely without the aid of historians. Critical to the development of these two aspects is the misuse of the data derived from the prisoners' experiences. This data, largely collected at the time of their repatriation, was not originally intended to provide raw material for behavioral or historical studies per se. It was, rather gathered with the intention of providing information for possible court martial action against men accused of collaboration or criminal activity while in captivity, to identify men who merited commendation and decoration, and to identify repatriates who needed psychiatric care.

Consequently, the generally accepted percentage classification of POWs by behavior, 5 percent resistor, 15 percent participator (or collaborator), and 80 percent middlemen, needs to be viewed more as suggestive than as absolutely definitive. Biderman, for instance, reports that placement of a POW in the collaborator category required only that he be "accused of committing isolated but serious acts in collaboration" which could be corroborated. Placement in this category remained firm, moreover, even if the prisoner were otherwise regarded as having been a hard-case resistor throughout his captivity, as some of them were.

With regard to the evidence that the POWs were peculiarly weak in moral fibre, uncommitted to American ideals and ignorant of the institutions and history of their country, a change in perspective is revealing. If one accepts the idea that it takes moral fibre to resist, actively and passively, ideological conversion attempts by a captor who is very concerned about "correct thoughts" and who has overwhelming power which he uses as it suits his purpose, then one must grant that most prisoners had it to some meaningful degree. The Chinese regarded passive resistance to indoctrination, including "going through the motions," as "insincere" and "stupid," if not actually reactionary behavior, as many of the scholars of POW behavior have noted. They made strenuous efforts to overcome such "insincerity" and "stupidity." But in May of 1952 they abandoned compulsory indoctrination, keeping classes only for the relatively small number of progressives. Their extensive efforts had resulted in disappointing returns among their stubborn captives.

Many prisoners did supply evidence that there was often a lack of discipline in their ranks. Autobiographies, both American and British, speak of a dog-eat-dog system prevailing during several of the "death marches" and in the temporary holding camps during the harsh winter of 1950–1951. They also tell of prisoners in need being refused assistance by other prisoners. In these respects, however, they differ little from World War II POW memoirs which described the same kind of reaction to stress during those periods in which captivity conditions were the worst. Conversely, those who give testimony to such animalistic behavior also testify to behavior of a different order. Morris Wills, one of the original 21 who refused repatriation, only to return over a decade later, has written: "You really can't worry about the other fellow; you are at the line of existence yourself. If you go under that, you die. You would help each other if you could. Most would try; I wouldn't say all."

"Reactionary" Lloyd Pate wrote in a similar, if more positive, vein. "After the first shock of our capture wore off, the G.I.'s with me on those Korean mountain roads began to act like soldiers this country could be proud of." He told of prisoners helping each other to keep up the pace when dropping out meant death; and he credited two such good Samaritans with saving his life. Captive British journalist Philip Deane in one poignant passage revealed the context within which many prisoners faced life or death under brutal march conditions. In it he inadvertently answers many who charge that the prisoners "shamefully" abandoned their weaker fellows en route. A young American lieutenant, faced with a bitter choice, allowed five men to drop out, in effect "abandoning" them, contrary to the orders of the North Korean march commander. He could not, he told the North Korean, order them carried because "That meant condemming the carriers to death from exhaustion." For this decision, the lieutenant's captors executed him on the spot.

The same kinds of sources, supplemented again by the studies of research scientists and journalists, reveal that the physical duress to which prisoners allegedly succumbed so easily, presumably leading to widespread collaboration, ranged all the way from calculated manipulation of necessities of life to murder. One former prisoner labeled a reactionary by his captors told the author of many instances of physical brutality practiced by the Chinese. Among those brutalized were Chinese-appointed squad leaders who couldn't or wouldn't promote group compliance with the indoctrination program. Some, he maintained, were murdered. Others were subjected to severe beatings and then denied medical treatment for the injuries inflicted; death sometimes resulted. Some bad treatment, he declared, resulted from caprice, citing a case of one man in his squad, a "middleman" who underwent several nighttime beatings over a period of one month for no apparent reason. Nevertheless, those who disparage prisoner behavior tend to take at face value the Chinese contention that they did not commit atrocities or torture their captives. An official U.S. Army report issued in June 1953, however, declared that after Chinese entrance into the war they were "fully as active as the North Koreans" in commission of war crimes.

So far as the POW death rate, 38 percent, is concerned, this figure is speculative. It does not include atrocity deaths, which numbered over a thousand. Nor does it include well over two thousand missing in action. The Chinese kept no dependable records, and throughout much of the first year of the war the prisoners were in no position to do so themselves. Whatever the true death rate, critics of the prisoners and of the alleged "softness" of American society see it as "too high." By implication they blame most of the deaths on prisoner negligence, or worse, on loss of will to live. Five prisoner physicians, however, reported otherwise shortly after the war. They wrote:

The erroneous impression has been created that prisoners of war who were in good physical health gave up and died; this is not true. Every prisoner of war in Korea who died had suffered from malnutrition, exposure to cold, and continued harassment by the Communists. Contributing causes to the majority of deaths were prolonged cases of respiratory infection and diarrhea. Under such conditions, it is amazing not that there was a high death rate, but that there was a reasonably good rate of survival.

Another example of misuse of data to demonstrate weakness on the part of the POWs and their nurture is the "no escape" theme. While it is true that no American successfully escaped from permanent prison camps in the Yalu River region, several hundred did escape before permanent camps were established, some after several months of captivity. From these camps, furthermore, at least 46 verifiable escape attempts involving nearly 4 percent of the POWs have been authenticated. Nevertheless, both Mayer and Kinkead have insisted that failure to escape from permanent camps is significant. Mayer, in one speech, praised American prisoners in the Philippines for attempting and completing escapes despite the Japanese practice of putting prisoners in blood-brother groups of ten. If one escaped the rest were to be shot. But, according to Weinstein, the POWs took the Japanese at their word and established MP patrols to halt just such escape attempts.

The assumption of Turkish superiority in POW camps also rests on a misreading of evidence. Turkish prisoners were, in the first place, a select group of volunteers. Furthermore, half of them were captured after the worst period of captivity was over, the winter of 1950–1951. Well over 80 percent of the American POWs were not so fortunate. Turkish prisoners, unlike the Americans, were not split up. Officers and enlisted men remained together most of the time, an aid to maintenance of discipline. Nor were the Turks the objects of intense re-education efforts as the Americans were. Yet, one Turk served on a peace committee. One refused to accept repatriation until he had a late change of heart. And some communist propaganda materials show Turkish involvement in communist-sponsored POW programs. In 1962, Brigadier General S. L. A. Marshall (ret.), military historian and author of *The River and the Gauntlet* and *Pork Chop Hill* bluntly told a Senate subcommittee that the Turks were overrated. Said Marshall, "The story about the Turks being perfect prisoners is a continuation of the fable that they were perfect soldiers in the line which was not true at all."

The assumption of Marine superiority to soldiers in prisoner-camp behavior also rests upon misreading of evidence. Marines may have retained more esprit de corps as prisoners, but they, like the Turks, were more of an elite unit. However, at Kangyye in 1951, some Marines made speeches, signed peace petitions (often with illegible signatures and wrong or misspelled names); and wrote articles for a "peace camp" paper called *The New Life*. Told by the Chinese that rewards for being a "good student" could include early release, some made up stories of hungry childhood and living on relief. Others said they joined the Corps in order to get decent food and clothing. Two described the criteria for a satisfactory article: "All you had to do was string stuff together in fairly coherent sentences, such words as 'war-mongers' . . . 'Wall Street big shots' . . . 'capitalistic bloodsuckers' and you had it made." Eighteen Marines and one soldier who convinced the Chinese of their "sincerity" eventually were selected for early repatriation. Taken close to the front, they crossed up their captors by escaping ahead of schedule.

The experience of the eighteen Marines is discussed in a University of Maryland history master's thesis on Marine POWs in Korea by Lt. Col. Angus MacDonald. MacDonald notes with disapproval that the Marines gave far more information to their captors than name, rank, and serial number. But he correctly views these as gambits designed to secure release from captivity. The Army, however, seems to have taken a less pragmatic, and, consequently, more humorless view of similar efforts by its enlisted men. MacDonald, on the other hand, does not deal adequately with the joint investigations of all services which, when concluded, revealed that only 11 percent of the Army repatriates compared with 26 percent of the Marine repatriates warranted further investigation on possible misconduct charges. Instead he quotes with approval an address by Col. Mayer which praised Marine performance, and by implication, criticized that of Army POWs. Eventually both services made the further investigations suggested, the Army possibly applying a broader set of standards to define misconduct, since it initially cleared only 58 percent of the 11 percent thought to warrant further investigation. The Marines cleared 94 percent. Finally, only fourteen cases came up for trial, all Army cases, out of which eleven convictions resulted.

In view of the commonly accepted belief that the Marines performed better than soldiers as POWs, it is interesting to note the comment by retired Air Corps Major General Delmar T. Spivey in a John A. Lejeune Forum on prisoner behavior. In this Marine-sponsored forum, Spivey, who while imprisoned in Germany during World War II was senior officer in the Center Compound of Stalag III, made the unrebutted statement that:

Even with all these things ["survival courses, physical conditioning programs, instruction in our American heritage, information about the enemy, courses and exercises designed to instill pride and self-respect and belief in one's service and country, and the assurance that our country will stand by an individual, both in combat and as a prisoner"] . . . we cannot assume that every fighting man will be completely prepared for his responsibilities as a prisoner. History is not on our side, and neither is human nature when we consider the past conduct of prisoners of war.

The conclusions of professional and semi-professional scholars and writers about American POW behavior are mixed. Stanley Elkins in his search for suggestive experience to support his description of the effects of a closed system on slave psychological development turned to the POWs. Unfortunately he exaggerated some of the findings of his source, Edgar Schein, one scholar involved in the POW studies. Elkins wrote of "profound changes in behavior and values" being "effected without physical torture or extreme deprivation" and of "large numbers" of American informers and men who cooperated in the indoctrination program. But Schein said only that mandatory discussion and mutual criticism sessions which followed communist indoctrination lectures probably created "considerable doubt concerning ideological position in some of the men." They were, as a whole, he declared, "not very effective." Nor did he give any estimates of the numbers of informers or cooperators relative to the total POW population.

Betty Friedan has seen the average Korean prisoner as an "apathetic, dependent, infantile, purposeless being . . . a new American man . . . reminiscent of the familiar 'feminine' personality." Edgar Friedenberg described the POW as a new model of being, but an international one, not just American. He wrote, "this sort of young man is a character in existentialist novels and post-World War II Italian films." Miss Friedan, however, discovered parallels closer to home. She found them in the youth of the 1950s, in their "new passivity," bored and passionless, demonstrated variously in: the annual springtime collegiate riots at Fort Lauderdale; a teenage call girl service in a Long Island suburb; adolescent grave defiling in Bergen Country, New Jersey; drug-taking parties in Westchester County, New York, and Connecticut; and the "helpless, apathetic state" of the female student body at Sarah Lawrence College.

It is doubtful whether the typical Korean POW would recognize himself in all this. His schooling averaged somewhat less than nine years. His social class was hardly comfortable middle. And his withdrawal from activity was certainly in part a shrewd way of fending off the ubiquitous Chinese indoctrinators.

Among historians, Walter Hermes, author of the second volume of a projected five-volume official history of the war, took note of the Kinkead book. But he accepted Biderman's view, calling it a "convincing rebuttal" of Kinkead's thesis. Robert Leckie, however, relied heavily on Kinkead and called the POW record "sorry. . . the worst in American history." Apathy, he declared, was responsible for

the failure of any men to escape. But in the same paragraph he asserted that the Caucasian appearance of the Americans was the "more likely reason for this failure." T. R. Fehrenbach, too, has generally taken a dim view of the prisoners' behavior. "Chemistry and culture," the Doolittle Board's democratization reforms and American education, among other culprits, were at fault, he wrote. His analysis of sources, like Leckie's, was less than rigorous.

Harry Middleton, while acknowledging that the percentage of collaborators was small, also looked askance at the prisoners' record. His book, though published later (1965) than Fehrenbach's narrative, displayed less acquaintance with or close reading of the available literature on the subject. An English scholar, David Rees, in *Korea: The Limited War*, after devoting a lengthy chapter to the subject, leaned to the point of view that POW behavior was not unusual considering the fallible nature of man and considering the unique nature of the prisoner's experiences. S. L. A. Marshall, a consultant to the Advisory Committee, is a defender of the prisoners. And Russell Weighley in his *History of the United States Army* also concluded that the Korean POWs were not a discredit to the nation.

In 1962, 21 scholars familiar with the POW behavior materials signed a paper entitled "Statement: to Set Straight the Korean POW Episode." This paper, drawn up by two of the signers, Edgar Schein and Raymond Bauer, who had worked extensively on the subject, directly refuted the popular version of the POW story expounded by Kinkead and Mayer. The "Statement" included these challenging assertions:

The behavior of the Korean prisoners did not compare unfavoraby with that of their countrymen or with the behavior of people of other nations who have faced similar trials in the past.

Instances of moral weakness, collaboration with the enemy, and failure to take care of fellow soldiers in Korea did not occur more

During the Korean War stories of American prisoners of war raised questions about brutal enemy behaviors, brain washing, and the character of American soldiers. In truth, however, American soldiers in Korea fought just as bravely as U.S. soldiers did during World War II.

frequently than in other wars where comparable conditions of physical and psychological hardship were present. Indeed, such instances appear to have been less prevalent than historical experience would lead us to expect. . . .

It is our opinion that any serious analysis of American society, its strengths and weaknesses, should rest on historically correct data. It is unfortunate that the Korean POW episode has been distorted to make the case for one view of American society. We hope that this Statement will be the first step toward setting the historical facts of this episode straight.

Historically correct data, however, were insufficient for many Americans in the 1950s and 1960s. They seemed to feel that any communist success at eliciting collaborative behavior or inducing ideological doubt among any American soldiers, no matter how small

the number, signified a general American failure. Such failure to them was not to be taken lightly. It might reflect, after all, the existence of a more dangerous cancer in the American character than even they had suspected.

What is really "new in history," then, about the whole Korean POW episode?

First, never before Korea were American POWs confronted by a captor who worked hard to change their ideological persuasion. This point is worth a brief examination. Had American POWs of the Germans, for instance, been subjected to ideological thought reform efforts designed to inculcate virulent racist attitudes or to inculcate the idea that Germany was fighting the West's battle against communism, had these efforts taken place over the length of time and under circumstances comparable to those endured by the Korean POWs, there might be a rough basis for comparison. But those American

POWs weren't so subjected. Dobran did report some anti-Semitism among his POW group upon which the Germans might have capitalized. But one can speculate a little in the other direction that the American reaction to this divisive ploy might have been similar to that in one group of Negro POWs in Korea among whom the Chinese tried to foment ideological change by hammering upon the existence of racial discrimination in the United States. Wrote Lloyd Pate, "A few colored guys got up and said it was our business what we did in the United States and for the Chinks to mind their own damn business."

Second, never before had the American public been so gullible as to believe that such a chimera as the enemy's self-proclaimed "lenient policy" was, in fact, lenient. During the first year of the war in particular the Chinese and North Koreans, often in systematic fashion, fostered brutalizing captivity conditions which were in significant part responsible for prisoner behavior which did not measure up to "ideal" standards.

And, finally, for the first time the public seemed to assume that such selfish, undisciplined behavior as existed among the POWs was something new in American military experience and that it was a direct consequence of a characterological deterioration in the nation itself.

Whether or not such a deterioration has been taking place in American society, from the advent of the New Deal and the impact of progressive education as the critics strongly imply, is not under contention here. What is being contended, rather, is that if one really believes this and wants evidence to prove it, one will have to find examples other than among those Americans who died and those who survived in the prison camps of North Korea, 1950–1953.

Study Questions

1. What is the meaning of "brainwashing" and "re-education"?

2. By the mid-1950s, what was the prevailing opinion about the behavior of American POWs in Korea? Why did this issue seem to be so important to the American public? How did Americans explain the behavior and "failure" of the POWs?

3. Compare the behavior of American POWs in German prison camps during World War II with the Americans in Japanese or Korean prisoner of war camps. Was there much difference? Why or why not?

4. Does POW behavior reveal anything about American civilization? Why or why not?

5. Did large numbers of POWs die because of a "loss of the will to live"? Why or why not? Was the behavior of U.S. Marines any different from other groups of POWs? Why or why not?

6. Summarize Wubben's feelings about the behavior of American POWs during the Korean War.

Bibliography

For a general discussion of the Korean War, see Joseph C. Goulden, *Korea: The Untold Story of the War* (1982). Also see Bruce Cummings, *The Origins of the Korean War* (1980). Ronald Caridi's *The Korean War and American Politics* (1969) analyzes the domestic impact of the conflict. The internal tension inspired by the cold war is discussed in Edward Shils, *The Torment of Secrecy* (1956); David Caute, *The Great Fear* (1978); and Alan Harper, *The Politics of Loyalty* (1969). The most critical account of American POW behavior during the Korean War is Eugene Kinkead, *In Every War But One* (1959). For a devastating critique of Kinkead's book, see Albert D. Biderman, *March to Calumny: The Story of American POWs in the Korean War* (1963). Also see Louis J. West, "Psychiatry, 'Brainwashing,' and the American Character," *American Journal of Psychiatry* CXX (1964). Also see Robert J. Donovan, *Tumultuous Years* (1982).

READING 21

★ ★ ★

The Man Who Changed His Skin

Ernest Sharpe Jr.

For millions of African Americans the early 1960s were years of pain mixed with glimpses of promise. Compared to white Americans, they faced a grim set of statistics. The 1960 census reported that African Americans died seven years younger than did white Americans, had half the chance of completing high school, one-third the chance of finishing college, and one-third the chance of entering a profession. On the average, African Americans earned half as much as whites and were twice as likely to be unemployed. Yet events like the *Brown v. The Board of Education* decision, the Montgomery bus boycott, and the various Freedom Rides, "sit-ins," "wade-ins," "pray-ins," and "apply-ins" sent the message that the time to change was at hand. For demanding no more than what was guaranteed them by the Constitution of the United States and a general sense of decency, African Americans were hosed, set on by dogs, arrested, beaten, and even murdered, yet they continued their march toward justice.

How ironic, then, with so many examples of injustice and inhumanity toward African Americans, that many white Americans had to be told by another white American what it was like to be black. In 1959 John Howard Griffin chemically darkened his skin, shaved his head, and traveled through the heart of Dixie as a black man. He experienced humiliations large and small, occasionally feared for his life, and came to know racism on very personal terms. After a few months he returned to his white world and wrote a book about his experiences. Published in 1961, *Black Like Me* became a national sensation, selling over five million copies, angering millions of white Americans, and opening the eyes of millions more. On television shows and radio programs, Griffin heard variations of the same line by whites: "I never knew what it was like to be black."

Probably Griffin never did either. In "The Man Who Changed His Skin," Ernest Sharpe Jr. explores the life of the unusual man who passed for a brief time as black.

O n a sunny November day in 1959, a tall, brown-haired Texan entered the home of a New Orleans friend. Five days later an unemployed, bald black man walked out. The name of both was John Howard Griffin, and the journey he began that Louisiana evening was to take him to a country farther than any he had ever been in, one bordered only by the shade of its citizens' skin.

For four weeks Griffin, his skin chemically darkened, posed as an itinerant black. He wandered the South, hitchhiking, seeking work, and talking and listening to people black and white. His journal of those weeks became a series of magazine articles and then a book, *Black Like Me*. In passionate first-person prose it brought home to millions of American whites the misery and injustice daily endured by American blacks. It opened eyes and seized hearts and changed minds.

It also changed lives, including Griffin's own. Abandoning a promising literary career, he devoted the next eight years to the civil rights movement. He saw authorship of a single book eclipse all his other achievements. He became for the rest of his life the man who had turned himself black. But *Black Like Me* was only the most prominent event in a life filled with drama and transformation. By the time of his death, in 1980, Griffin had left behind the sloughed skins of a dozen careers and identities. Born to a middle-class Dallas family, he was schooled in France, where he joined in the soirées of European aesthetes and aristocrats. He served in the French Resistance and soldiered in the South Pacific, where he lived for a year as an aborigine islander. He converted to Catholicism, and he thirsted for a life of prayer and chastity even while he wrote a novel banned in Detroit for its sexual explicitness. He lost his sight, lived

for ten years as a blind man, and then miraculously recovered his vision. He was a musical scholar, a religious intellectual, a working journalist, a livestock breeder, a professional photographer, a social activist, and a controversial novelist.

And, of course, for a few weeks in 1959 he was a black man.

Griffin was a product of two disparate cultures, Texan and French, and was never totally at home in either. He was born on June 16, 1920, the second of four children. His father was a religious, hardworking wholesale-grocery salesman utterly devoted to his refined, delicate wife. Years later Griffin recalled waking each morning to the sound of his mother practicing the piano sonatas of Mozart and Schubert and Bach preludes and fugues.

When Griffin was fifteen, he came upon a magazine ad for the Lycée Descartes, a boarding school in France, and wrote to the headmaster begging for admission. He had no money, he confessed, but he would do anything to pay his way, even scrub floors. Several weeks later a reply came back: If the young man wanted to learn so badly, he was by all means welcome. Griffin presented the letter to his flabbergasted parents; they responded predictably, but he was already a person of considerable will, and he was soon aboard an ocean liner.

Griffin was a gifted student. He graduated from the Lycée, then stayed in France to study medicine and the humanities. He spent his seventeenth summer at the country home of a wealthy French family. Evenings he played Ravel, Debussy, and Schubert on the phonograph or lay in bed reading Balzac, Gide, and Rabelais.

By the spring of 1939 his future seemed bright. Having decided on a career in psychiatry, he began work after his first year of medical school as an "extern" at the Tours insane asylum. A student of religious music, he conducted experiments using Gregorian chants as therapy for patients considered beyond cure. Then, in September, Germany invaded

"The Man Who Changed His Skin" by Ernest Sharpe Jr. in *American Heritage*, Vol. 40/No. 1, February 1989, pp. 44–55. Reprinted by permission of *American Heritage* Magazine, a division of Forbes, Inc. © Forbes, Inc., 1989.

Poland. France declared war, and virtually all the medical staff at the asylum was immediately conscripted. Griffin was placed in charge of the hospital's female wing, responsible, along with eight nuns, for 120 patients. He was nineteen years old.

It was a harrowing time. He was often dragged from his bed to treat wounded soldiers trucked from the front. German and Austrian Jews began trickling into the city; officially enemy aliens, many did not speak French and most lacked safe-conduct papers. As the French fell back, the young American volunteered to help the refugees. He strapped them into strait-jackets and smuggled them in an asylum ambulance to the port of St. Nazaire for passage to England. Their faces haunted him: he never forgot the encounter with racism.

After the French surrender in 1940, Griffin himself fled. He returned to the United States and joined the Army Air Corps. Leaving for what would become a three-year stint in the Pacific, he stuffed his duffel bag full of books by Molière and Racine and scores by Mozart and Beethoven. His initial assignments were light. For a while he served as a disc jockey, broadcasting classical concerts to front-line troops. Bored, he volunteered for a post on a remote island, to set up liaison in the event of an American occupation.

He lived on Nuni, as the natives called it, for a year. His charge was not only to learn the local tongue but to gain the islanders' trust. To do so, he became one of them: fishing with the men, chewing betel nut, observing tribal customs and ceremonies, and even taking a wife. "They were one of the few truly primitive tribes left in the world," he later wrote, "in a land where there was no sense of time or goal." But life there was far from innocent. Behind the apparent languor Griffin discovered a harsh existence where children sometimes perished in brutal rites of initiation. When his year was up, he was ready to leave.

He was reassigned to Morotai, a tiny spot of land in the Moluccas close to several is-

lands held by the Japanese. Manning the radar tent there alone one night, he was caught in an air raid and artillery barrage. He described the scene in his unpublished autobiography: "A shell shrieked downward and I threw myself to the ground. . . . The shell exploded nearby and shrapnel whizzed unseen around me. Relief and exhaustion overwhelmed my senses. . . . I wanted to lie still and rest, to ignore some gigantic urgency in the atmosphere. A new wave of mortars, ack-ack explosions and shell screeches swept toward me. I hurried to my feet to run ahead of it." He didn't make it; knocked unconscious, he was at first taken for dead by medics and later rescued by an alert burial crew.

Griffin regained consciousness, apparently suffering from nothing worse than a concussion, and except for sensitivity to light and difficulty reading his mail, he quickly recovered. Sick of the service and fearful of a prolonged hospital stay, he kept his vision problems to himself. Back in the United States he was given a last physical, including a cursory eye exam. Unable to make out the results on his discharge papers, he asked another soldier to read them to him. He was staggered to learn that his vision was 20/200. He was legally blind.

He soon realized that his blindness would be more than legal. He was losing his sight completely. Specialists were unable to help; he had apparently suffered some kind of brain damage. They outfitted him with thick, dark spectacles, but they weren't strong enough. Wanting to hide his affliction, he took to reading with the help of a small, easily hidden magnifying glass.

Medicine was obviously no longer a viable profession, so in 1946 Griffin returned to France to pursue a career as a musicologist. He spent the summer at the conservatory at Fontainebleau. Each day his eyes were a little worse, but still he told no one: "I felt that losing my sight was a thing I had to do alone."

In the fall he left for Paris to visit an old school friend who had become a monk in a

Dominican convent. At first he found the monastery dismal, reeking of "the odors of cabbages and onions and mop water," but distaste gradually turned to respect, and respect to reverence. "The poverty of my unlighted cell warmed with delight," he wrote. "I had imagined that men seeking union with God more or less languished in a state of mystical trauma, soaring above the baser aspects of their own daily living. But here men lived in intimacy with the things of the earth—cold, fasting, labor. . . . I saw they were men like me. I lived with them, saw them bleary-eyed at dawn, smelled them sweating after labors, and yet sanctity lay there within them."

It was to be five years before Griffin left the Episcopal Church for the Catholic, but by the time he departed the Couvent St. Jacques he was already very much converted. Moreover, he had discovered a part of himself that yearned for the devotional solitude of a monastic life. In the years to come he would often retreat to the sanctuary of monastery walls.

From Paris Griffin went to the Abbey of Solesmes, to research medieval church music. When he returned to the United States in the spring of 1947, he was twenty-six and totally blind. He was also engaged. During his year in France he had fallen in love with a woman several years his senior named Françoise Longuet.

The two faced obvious obstacles; the first was Griffin's physical helplessness. Françoise decided to remain in France for the time being. Back in Texas Griffin and his parents escaped the city's noise and hazardous traffic by moving to a farm outside Mansfield, a small town near Fort Worth. To earn an income, Griffin turned from musicology to animal husbandry. After some tutoring by teachers at Texas A&M, he purchased four Ohio Improved Chester sows and began breeding them. He also began tutoring local children in advanced piano. One of his first students was the thirteen-year-old daughter of a local insurance agent, Clyde Holland. Elizabeth Holland— "Piedy" to friends and family—was already a talented pianist.

She proved an apt pupil and was soon a regular visitor to the Griffin farm.

By 1949 Griffin was earning a respectable income as a breeder of prize livestock, but his yeoman days were already numbered. That spring he met the New York drama critic John Mason Brown, who was in Texas on a lecture tour. Brown suggested that Griffin try his hand at writing; he certainly talked like a writer. Griffin, intrigued, asked how he should start. You get some paper and write, Brown curtly replied. Griffin did just that, converting a room in the barn behind his parents' house into an office. It was a cramped space, "about three long steps each way," but it suited Griffin's anchoritic temperament. It also suited his subject, a novel about a young American man studying Gregorian chant in a French monastery. Neglecting his hogs, Griffin sometimes worked all night, dictating in French on a wire recorder and later transcribing his dictation in English on his mother's ancient Underwood. In seven weeks he had completed a first draft and launched a new career for himself.

He had also precipitated a series of events that eventually changed the law of the land. He called the book *The Devil Rides Outside*, borrowing from a French proverb: "The devil rides outside the monastery walls." The six-hundred-page novel is a study of the struggle between faith and temptation, a raw, sprawling work that seems to have sprouted like a mushroom in the garden of Texas letters. In 1981 the novelist Larry McMurtry wrote of it as "a strange, strong book whose verbal energy . . . still seems remarkable after almost 30 years. In the mostly all-too-healthy and sunlit world of Texas fiction, the book remains an anomaly, dark, feverish, introverted, claustrophobic, tortured."

Issued by a fledgling Fort Worth publisher, *The Devil Rides Outside* received surprising attention for a first novel by an unknown. Reviews were mixed. "Most of the novel's sound and fury is bound up with the medieval notion that sex is the domain of Satan," complained the *Atlantic Monthly*, but the noted literary critic Maxwell Geismar was impressed. He called the book one of the best novels of the decade and dubbed its author "a Texas Balzac."

The Legion for Decent Literature, a Catholic organization, succeeded in getting *The Devil Rides Outside* banned in Detroit on the grounds that it was unfit for children and adolescents. While little in the book would shock a contemporary reader, the novel was daring for the fifties. It contains a pair of passages that describe in exactly the same language sexual climax and spiritual rapture.

Postwar censorship laws were a welter of local and state statutes, many of which, despite the historic 1934 circuit court ruling on *Ulysses*, still banned whole works based on isolated passages. In the spring of 1954 the book's paperback publisher, Pocket Books, arranged to challenge the Detroit ban. A bookstore manager was arrested for selling a copy to a police inspector; the court convicted, the bookseller appealed, and *Butler v. Michigan* began a two-and-a-half-year march to the Supreme Court.

Despite the praise and attention, the fall of 1952 found the thirty-two-year-old Griffin utterly miserable. After six years of delay Françoise had bitterly broken their engagement. In his grief he received solace from an unexpected source, Piedy Holland, now a seventeen-year-old high school senior. Despite Griffin's disability and the gap in their ages, the two found themselves increasingly drawn to each other. After a genteel courtship of several months, he proposed to Piedy at midnight mass on Christmas Eve. She happily accepted, and the two were married the following June after Griffin received dispensation from the Vatican for his Pacific marriage. They moved into a cottage behind the Hollands' house, and Griffin went to work on a second novel.

That fall Griffin noticed a growing numbness in his fingers. The doctor diagnosed malaria, a souvenir of his days in the tropics.

The numbness progressed until by December he was not only blind but confined to a wheelchair, effectively paralyzed except in his left arm. He began taking minute doses of strychnine as a stimulant, but the prognosis was uncertain. To compound his troubles, he had been diagnosed as diabetic.

Despite these afflictions, he continued to labor on *Nuni*, a Robinson Crusoe tale of a middle-aged English professor struggling for survival on an island of savages. In his journal he wrote: "I am aware perhaps that I am putting the problems of my life into the lap of Professor Harper and I am desperate for him to solve them. I am stripping him of everything that men generally consider necessary to a man's ability to function at the human level."

Professor Harper overcame his predicament, and so, after a long ordeal, did Griffin. By May 1956, when *Nuni* was published, he was not only fully recovered from the malaria but perhaps more content than he had ever been. *Nuni* was receiving favorable reviews, translations of his first novel were selling well in Europe, and he was close to finishing a third. He was the happy husband of a loving wife and the doting father of two small children. He seemed finally to have achieved a measure of peace.

All that changed one morning the following January. As with everything in his life, he described it in his daily journal:

"Wednesday, four days ago, I was walking to the house for lunch. Redness swirled in front of my eyes. Then I thought I saw the back door, cut in portions, dancing at crazy angles. I stood dumbfounded. Angles continued to dance and there was pain in the eyes and head.

"I stumbled inside, found the telephone. Somehow I got the number dialed. I heard my wife's voice.

"'I think . . .' I began, and then collapsed into weeping.

"'What is it? What's happening?' she asked.

"'I think I can see.'" He could. By the time Piedy and the family physician reached the

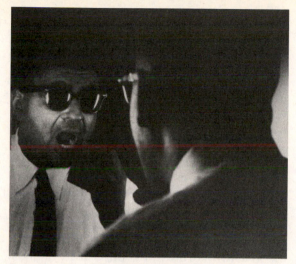

Portrait of John Howard Griffin.

farmhouse, he was able to make out forms and colors. He was euphoric. The sight of his two-year-old daughter was "like looking at the sun—blinding me to everything else."

The strychnine, he was told, had apparently unstopped blocked blood vessels. The flow of blood in turn had unknotted twisted vessels. A month later he wrote to a friend: "We have, on this near-lethal dosage . . . brought my vision to a plu-perfect 20/15 in each eye. I am overwhelmed by details seen with the utmost clarity—every glass flaw, every pebble."

The singularity of his recovery brought Griffin national attention and some local gibes. Many in Mansfield had never taken to Griffin's cosmopolitan background and cultured air, and some suggested that maybe he had never been blind at all. *Time*, echoing the skeptics, reported in its medicine section that Griffin's recovery was unprecedented, but his blindness might have been "mainly, if not entirely, hysterical."

On February 25, 1957, a little more than a month after he regained his sight, the sun broke on Griffin again. The Supreme Court of the United States unanimously struck down the Michigan law banning *The Devil Rides*

Outside. Speaking for the Court, Justice Felix Frankfurter wrote, "The state insists that, by thus quarantining the general reading public against books not too rugged for grown men and women in order to shield juvenile innocence it is exercising its power to promote the general welfare. Surely this is to burn the house to roast the pig." The decision effectively reversed an 1868 British ruling that for almost a century had remained the principal guide to Anglo-American jurisprudence on censorship and obscenity.

Moral triumphs do not pay bills, however, and the income from his novels was not enough to support Griffin and his growing family. Several months before his sight returned, he had found employment in Fort Worth as a staff writer at *Sepia*, a black monthly modeled loosely after *Life*. Griffin fit in easily at the magazine, whose publisher, George Levitan, practiced a policy of equal opportunity long before it became a national slogan.

In the fall of 1959 he began research on a piece about the high suicide rate among Southern blacks. He sent out questionnaires to black professionals, but the few who responded simply returned them blank. The article stalled. He vented his frustration on Adelle Martin, the magazine's editorial director. Why wouldn't Negroes trust him? He was on their side. Mrs. Martin, black herself, responded bluntly: Negroes knew that no matter how he tried, he would never understand. The only way he could know what it was like to be a Negro was by being one.

The remark triggered the return of an old, odd thought: If a white man became a Negro in the Deep South, what adjustments would he have to make? A few days later he proposed a series of articles to Levitan. He would dye his skin and travel the South. He wouldn't change his name or hide his background or education. He would still be John Howard Griffin—author, teacher, musicologist—but with one difference: he would be black.

The publisher warned Griffin of the dangers involved, but he couldn't hide his enthusiasm. Go ahead, he told Griffin; *Sepia* would foot the bill. Piedy was less enthusiastic. It sounded dangerous, but if he felt he had to do it, then he should. He would be gone for a month.

Two days later Griffin flew to New Orleans. He arranged to stay at the house of a friend, and the next morning he explained his project to a sympathetic dermatologist. The physician prescribed Oxsoralen, a drug usually used to treat vitiligo, a condition that causes milky patches on the skin. The process would take a couple of months. Griffin explained there wasn't time, so the physician suggested a higher dosage coupled with exposure to a sunlamp; the drug worked through reaction to ultraviolet light. There was some chance of liver damage, but as long as Griffin was monitored through frequent blood tests, he was probably safe.

For four days Griffin lay in his room under a sunlamp, his eyes protected by cotton pads. The Oxsoralen produced lassitude and nausea and didn't entirely work; by the evening of the fourth day his skin was dark but mottled. Determined to see the project through, he touched up the light patches with vegetable dye and then shaved his head. The whole process took hours. Finally he was done.

"Turning off all the lights, I went into the bathroom and closed the door. I stood in the darkness before the mirror, my hand on the light switch. I forced myself to flick it on.

"In the flood of light against white tile, the face and shoulders of a stranger—a fierce, bald, very dark Negro—glared at me from the glass. He in no way resembled me.

"The transformation was total and shocking. I had expected to see myself disguised, but this was something else. I was imprisoned in the flesh of an utter stranger, an unsympathetic one with whom I felt no kinship. All traces of the John Griffin I had been were wiped from existence."

Toting a pair of duffel bags, Griffin stepped out of the house and walked to the corner to catch a streetcar to downtown New Orleans. Trembling, he bought a ticket and moved down the aisle to take a seat in the back. No one gave him a glance. After a few moments he sighed with relief; he had passed the first test of his new identity.

He stayed the night in a shabby hotel, and the next morning he made a confidant of a street-corner shoe shine boy. The "boy," a gray-haired World War I veteran named Sterling Williams, cackled with delight at Griffin's charade. He agreed to let the writer work at his stand for a few days. Then he pointed at the giveaway brown hair on Griffin's hands. Griffin grabbed a razor from his duffel and scurried for the nearest lavatory. In his haste he almost entered a whites' washroom, forgetting he was black even as he rushed to eliminate the last sign of his whiteness.

Griffin worked as a shoe-shine boy for several days, learning when to smile, when to laugh, when to shrug, and when to be silent. One of his earliest lessons was that the friendliest customers were those looking for black women. "When they want to sin, they're very democratic," his mentor observed. After gaining some confidence, Griffin began searching for a regular job, applying for clerical work at local businesses. The responses were polite but consistent. After three days he had failed to obtain even an interview. At the end of each day he plodded back to the shine stand, and as Williams dolloped out a supper of raccoon stew, Griffin told the old man what he already knew: nobody would hire a black man for anything but manual labor.

After a week in New Orleans, Griffin decided to travel to Mississippi, where, despite massive evidence collected by the FBI, a grand jury had recently refused to return indictments in a race lynching. New Orleans had proved outwardly affable, but as he bought a ticket at the Greyhound station, Griffin had his first encounter with the "hate stare," a cold, irrational gaze long familiar to blacks that struck Griffin like a blow in the face. It was on the bus ride that he first experienced the petty tyranny regularly visited on Southern blacks. Pulling into a small town for a rest stop, the driver let out the white passengers but ordered the blacks to stay in their seats. They grumbled and objected but complied. Griffin saw that one of the unexpected requirements of blackness was an impressive ability to hold one's urine.

He stayed in Mississippi only a few days. Overwhelmed by the oppressive poverty and climate of violence, he returned to New Orleans and then took a bus along the Gulf to Biloxi. From Biloxi he hitchhiked to Mobile, traveling beside miles of white, sandy beaches forbidden to blacks. In Mobile he again sought work and also spent much of his time seeking out the things he had once taken for granted: "a place to eat, or somewhere to find a drink of water, a restroom, somewhere to wash my hands." He had no better luck with jobs there than in New Orleans. "No use trying down here," one plant foreman told him. "We're gradually getting you people weeded out. . . . We're going to do our damndest to drive every one of you out of the state."

Unable to find a room one evening, Griffin accepted the offer of an elderly black preacher to share a thin mattress in his small, bare room. Night had come to be a time of comfort for Griffin. The strain of the day was over, and he could, like blacks throughout the South, relax in darkness's enveloping anonymity. The two men lay under quilts, gazing at the ceiling and chatting about Bible miracles. The old man was especially fond of the raising of Lazarus. When it came to prospects for Southern blacks, however, his faith was less secure. He had two sons who had gone north. He hoped they would never return.

From Mobile Griffin hitchhiked to Montgomery. The white men who gave him lifts were friendly, but invariably they turned the conversation to the same topic: "All but two picked me up the way they would pick up a pornographic photograph or book. . . . Some were shamelessly open, some shamelessly subtle. All showed morbid curiosity about the sexual life of a Negro, and all had, at base, the same stereotyped image of the Negro as an inexhaustible sex machine with oversized genitals and a vast store of experiences, immensely varied."

The situation might almost have been comic had not Griffin, despite the earthiness of his writing, possessed an almost nineteenth-century sense of modesty. He found the conversations increasingly loathsome and grew increasingly curt, a dangerous tone for a black in rural Alabama. One farmer asked Griffin if he was one of those out-of-state "troublemakers." Griffin replied that he was just passing through. The farmer patted the shotgun by his knee and gestured at the swampy forest on either side of the road. "You can kill a nigger and toss him into that swamp and no one will ever know what happened to him." Griffin nodded, "Yes, sir."

Arriving in Montgomery, Griffin found the atmosphere electric with racial tension. Blacks there seemed less passive and deferential than in other towns. The difference, he decided, was due to the influence of the city's prominent black minister, Martin Luther King, Jr. But if Montgomery's blacks seemed less defeated, its whites seemed more actively hostile. Griffin saw the hate stare everywhere. Looking into a washroom mirror, he discovered a change in his own gaze: "My face had lost animation. In repose, it had taken on the strained, disconsolate expression that is written on the countenance of so many Southern Negroes. My mind had become the same way, dozing empty for long periods."

The strain of Griffin's appropriated identity was taking its toll. He began having nightmares. Then he stopped taking the Oxsoralen pills, and his skin began daily turning lighter. His hair grew to a heavy fuzz. He decided to see if he could cross the border back into whiteness. He scrubbed off the vegetable dye, donned a dark shirt to stand off against his lightening skin, and headed for the city's white section. He strolled into a segregated restaurant and ordered a meal. "I ate the white meal, drank the white water, received the white smiles and wondered how it all could be. What sense could a man make of it?"

He returned to the black section and discovered that blacks had a subtle but definite hate stare of their own. He reapplied the dye and found himself once again accepted by one race, spurned by the other. He began zigzagging back and forth across Montgomery, shifting skins like a chameleon, deliberately testing the limits of his disguise. It was, he sadly concluded, impenetrable. He gave up and boarded the bus for Atlanta, the last station in his tracing of the black cross.

Atlanta was a surprise for Griffin. Leaving Montgomery, he had given up hope for the lot of Southern blacks, but Georgia's capital changed his mind. The city, he found, had made "great strides." He professed to see hope for the South in Atlanta, but his optimism sounds forced. Despite thoughtful interviews with black and white civic leaders and a tour of black colleges, Griffin's picture of Atlanta is overwhelmed by the shadows of New Orleans, Mississippi, and Alabama.

Nearly three decades have gone by since Griffin made his journey through the South, but *Black Like Me*'s power to move and outrage remains undiminished. Still in print, it has sold more than twelve million copies and been translated into fourteen languages. Most recently it was published in South Africa. Part of its enduring appeal comes from what seems the very transparency of the author's imposture.

It is hard to imagine a person worse suited than Griffin to pass for black. A cultural epicure who had spent his adolescence in France and lived a blind, sheltered existence for the previous decade, Griffin had remarkably little in common with most Southern whites, let alone with blacks. In the book his relations with blacks are cordial but never intimate. He practically shudders every time his ears are assaulted by jazz or the blues. Griffin was able to change his color, but not his heritage.

Which makes it all the harder to see how he pulled it off. Naturally he fooled whites; whites didn't look at blacks. But how did he dupe blacks? Surely somebody should have seen through such a thin disguise. No one did. His transformation was skin-deep, but neither whites nor blacks ever looked deeper. As readers we are in on the secret. Griffin's voice—courtly, refined, educated—is so evident throughout the book that we are amazed at the blindness of bus drivers and shopkeepers and all the others. We hear him secretly wail, "I'm just like you," at each new indignity or abuse, and we cannot believe that no one else hears him.

It is on this level of moral protest that *Black Like Me* is best known and most celebrated, as a work of civil rights advocacy and a tract on man's inhumanity to man. But also it was one of the first works of a new kind of journalism—what was called in the sixties the New Journalism—with its personal, participatory, novelistic approach. In fact, the book is arguably the genre's first masterpiece, even though Griffin was really less a journalist than a personal essayist. Judged as reporting, *Black Like Me* is an imperfect work. There is too much of the author, too little of others; too much earnest discussion of issues and too little personal observation and encounter. Assuming they had Griffin's bull-headed courage, one can imagine other writers—Norman Mailer, Tom Wolfe—rendering the experience with more nuanced insight and elegance of style.

What one cannot imagine is these masters of irony abandoning their strategic distance for the raw, racked emotion that powers Griffin's prose. *Black Like Me* is not simply a record of oppression and injustice; it is an account of painful personal discovery. Griffin began his experiment as an adventure. He assumed he would find racism, but he did not expect to find it everywhere, least of all in himself. By the end of his four weeks, he ached with hurt and humiliation. The adventure had turned into an ordeal. In discovering the brutal reality of racism, however, he also discovered compassion for the fierce stranger he had first seen three weeks before, the one with whom he had felt no kinship.

"I switched on the light and looked into a cracked piece of mirror bradded with bent nails to the wall. The bald Negro stared back at me from its mottled sheen. I knew I was in hell. Hell could be no more lonely or helpless. . . .

"I heard my voice, as though it belonged to someone else, hollow in the empty room, detached, say: 'Nigger, what you standing up there crying for?'

"I saw tears slick on his cheeks in the yellow light."

The initial installment of Griffin's series appeared in *Sepia* in April 1960, two months after the first lunch-counter sit-in and seven months before Kennedy's election. It was an instant sensation. Griffin went to New York for television interviews with Dave Garroway, Mike Wallace, and other hosts. Letters poured in—six thousand of them, mostly from Southern states, and only nine hostile.

Closer to home, friends and a few townspeople were warmly congratulatory, but most of Mansfield was silent. One night in April an effigy of Griffin—half black, half white, a yellow stripe down its back—was hung next to the downtown traffic light. A few days later a cross was burned in front of the town's predominantly black elementary school. Anonymous phone calls warned Griffin that "they" were coming to castrate him. Griffin's father came to the house to keep watch with a shotgun.

For a month the Griffins hid out in the homes of friends; in August he decided to move to Mexico. There he worked on a book version of the *Sepia* articles. Published in 1961, *Black Like Me* became an immediate best seller and was soon sold to Hollywood.

(The film, a mediocre melodrama starring James Whitmore, was released in 1964.)

Griffin stayed in Mexico for nine peaceful months and began a scholarly history of the Tarascan Indians. Then, in the spring of 1961, anti-American riots erupted near his home in Morelia, and the Griffins were forced to take refuge in a Benedictine monastery. They returned north to Fort Worth.

Soon Griffin was swallowed up in the civil rights movement. He had an authority among whites and a credibility among blacks that made him a persuasive and much sought-after speaker. He lectured, marched, investigated, worked as a mediator, argued against violence, and grieved with the families of those claimed by violence. To the dismay of his literary friends, he shelved his autobiography and two nearly finished novels. What time he had for writing he devoted to essays and articles on racism, culminating with his book *The Church and the Black Man*, an outspoken criticism of the failure of the Christian churches to act on their creeds.

During this time Griffin met Thomas Merton, the Trappist monk and author of the best-selling *The Seven Storey Mountain*. The two had much in common. Both were French-educated and Catholic converts: Merton a contemplative with a lively interest in the world outside, Griffin an activist with a yearning for the cloister. Not surprisingly, a close friendship blossomed.

After Merton's death, in 1968, the Merton Legacy Trust asked Griffin to write the monk's official biography. He accepted the task gladly. Recurrent foot tumors and bone deterioration from diabetes kept him largely confined to a wheelchair, and he welcomed a return to purely literary labor. He spent the next nine years working on the book. As he had done before, he sought to understand his subject by slipping inside his skin. For nearly three years he spent two weeks out of every month at Merton's Kentucky hermitage, faithfully observing the monastic routine, a

Spartan schedule of prayer and work beginning each morning at three. He discovered a tranquillity there that made these among the happiest days of his life.

By 1973 Griffin was too ravaged by diabetes to work away from home. As his health declined, the work proceeded more and more slowly. He missed his first deadline and then a second. Finally, in 1978, despite Griffin's pleadings, the Merton Legacy Trust named Michael Mott as Merton's official biographer. To compound Griffin's woes, his publisher demanded the return of its substantial advance. The settlement left him virtually bankrupt.

For the last two years of his life, Griffin was tortured by pain and despair. Emotionally he never recovered from the loss of what he thought would be his masterpiece, his contribution to the world's spiritual literature. Physically he suffered from kidney trouble, lung congestion, impaired circulation, and regular heart attacks, sometimes several a week. A bearish man, he dwindled to a hundred and fifty pounds. In 1979 his left leg was amputated and he was confined to bed.

He, Piedy, and their youngest daughter were forced to live on overextended credit cards and Piedy's secretarial job. When he could, Griffin worked on his thirty years of daily journals, with an eye toward eventual publication. Sometimes he rallied to give interviews or entertain friends or even cook a meal. But more often he had neither the wind nor the fire to do more than rest and reflect.

He died on September 9, 1980. When a friend asked the cause, Piedy said simply, "Everything." In the years since his death, a myth has spread that Griffin died from cancer cause by the Oxsoralen he had taken years before. He did not, and the suggestion of martyrdom would have offended him. He was in pain, though, in his last days, and perhaps he often thought of a favorite poem by Langston Hughes. He had used it for his most famous title:

> *Rest at pale evening ...*
> *A tall slim tree ...*
> *Night coming tenderly*
> *Black like me.*

Study Questions

1. What experiences and adventures contributed to the development of John Howard Griffin's racial attitudes? What obstacles in life did he personally face?

2. What does the novel *The Devil Rides Outside* tell us about Griffin's inner world and American society in the early 1950s?

3. Why did Griffin decide to temporarily change his skin color to better understand discrimination? Why did some people consider his experiment dangerous?

4. What conclusions did Griffin reach? What privations, small and large, did he experience? How did skin color alter the way he was received and treated by both races?

5. What impact did *Black Like Me* have on American society and American journalism?

Bibliography

The best place to start a search for John Howard Griffin is in his book *Black Like Me* (1961). A good starting point for literature on the general struggles and everyday life of African Americans during the late 1950s and early 1960s is Taylor Branch, *Parting the Waters: America in the King Years* (1988). Also insightful are John Dittmer, *Local People: The Struggle for Civil Rights in Mississippi* (1994); Eric R. Burner, *And Gently He Shall Lead Them: Robert Parris Moses and Civil Rights in Mississippi* (1994); William H. Chafe, *Civilities and Civil Rights* (1980); David Garrow, *Bearing the Cross: Martin Luther King, Jr. and the Southern Christian Leadership Conference* (1986); Doug McAdam, *Freedom Summer* (1988); and Stephen Oates, *Let the Trumpet Sound: The Life of Martin Luther King, Jr.* (1982). Anne Moody, *Coming of Age in Mississippi* (1968), is also a deeply moving document of the period.

★ ★ ★

Intellect on Television: The Quiz Show Scandals of the 1950s

Richard S. Tedlow

In 1854, Henry David Thoreau wrote, "We are in great haste to construct a magnetic telegraph from Maine to Texas; but Maine and Texas, it may be, have nothing important to communicate." More than one hundred years later, Thoreau's observation, greatly expanded, is still valid. Possessing the technological means of communication is no guarantee of meaningful communication. Nowhere is this situation more evident than in the commercial television industry. In the following essay, Richard S. Tedlow examines the problems inherent in commercial broadcasting, especially as they relate to the television quiz scandals of the late 1950s. The picture he presents is not a flattering one; the object of commercial television is quite simply to sell products, not to educate or uplift its audience. The result is an industry dominated by monetary values and generally oblivious to all ethical or moral consideration. In the specific case of quiz shows, television has produced an additional side effect: it has cheapened the meaning of education and intelligence. As Tedlow cogently observed, "If any crime had been committed in the quiz show episode, it was surely the broad conspiracy to portray as genuine intellectual activity the spouting of trivia." In today's America where books of lists and trivia make the best-sellers list, Tedlow's discussion of the quiz shows has a haunting familiarity.

On the seventh of June, 1955, *The $64,000 Question* made its debut on the CBS television network. No programming idea could have been more thoroughly foreshadowed by previous shows. Since the mid-1930s radio had been exploiting the American passion for facts with contests and games. For years, small amounts of cash or manufacturer-donated merchandise had been given away through various formats. What was new about *Question* was the size of the purse. The giveaway had taken a "quantum jump"; losers received a Cadillac as a consolation prize.

Question's format was simple. The producers selected a contestant who chose a subject about which he or she answered increasingly difficult questions which were assigned monetary values ranging from $64 to $64,000. The contestants could quit without attempting the succeeding plateau, but if he chose to continue and missed, he forfeited his winnings and was left with only his Cadillac.

By a few deft touches, the producers heightened the aura of authenticity and tension. The questions used were deposited in a vault of the Manufacturers Trust Company and brought to the studio by a bank officer flanked by two armed guards. As the stakes increased, the contestant entered a glass-enclosed "isolation booth" on stage to the accompaniment of "ominous music which hinted at imminent disaster" in order to prevent coaching from the audience. Since the contestant returned week after week rather than answering all the questions on one broadcast, the audience was given time to contemplate whether he would keep his winnings or go on to the next plateau and also a chance to worry about how difficult the next question might be.

The program became an immediate hit. In September, an estimated 55 million people, over twice as many as had seen the Checkers speech, viewing 84.8 percent of the television sets in operation at the time, saw Richard S. McCutchen, a 28-year-old Marine captain whose category was gourmet foods, become the first grand prize winner.

Most early contestants were seemingly average folks who harbored a hidden expertise in a subject far removed from their workaday lives. Thus McCutchen was asked about *haute cuisine* rather than amphibious assault. This separation was no accident. Its purpose was not only to increase the novelty of the show by providing something odd to the point of being freakish but also to integrate the viewer more intimately into the video melodrama. Everyone who had ever accumulated a store of disconnected, useless information could fantasize about transforming it into a pot of gold.

In a few months, *Question* had created a large new "consumption community," Daniel Boorstin's label for the nonideological, democratic, vague, and rapidly shifting groupings which have characterized twentieth-century American society. Suddenly, a third of the country had a common bond about which total strangers could converse. Paradoxically, in order to belong to this community, the individual had to isolate himself physically from others. Families stayed at home to watch the show, rather than celebrating it in the company of a large crowd. Movie theaters reported a precipitous decline in business, and stores and streets were empty when it came on the air.

Everyone whose life was touched by the show seemed to prosper. In addition to their prize money, some contestants received alluring offers to do public relations work for large companies or to star in movies. *Question's* creator, an independent program packager named Louis Cowan, became president of CBS-TV, an indication of how pleased the network executives were to present so successful a show. Even the banker who brought the sealed questions from the vault found himself promoted to a vice presidency. But the greatest beneficiary was the sponsor.

Richard S. Tedlow, "Intellect on Television: The Quiz Show Scandals of the 1950s" in *American Quarterly*, Vol. 27/No. 4 (Fall, 1979). © The Johns Hopkins University Press. Reprinted by permission.

In March of 1955, the show was purchased by Revlon, which soon began reaping the rewards of well-constructed advertising on a popular television program. Several products quintupled their sales, and advertising for one had to be discontinued because it sold out nationally. George F. Abrams, the company's vice president in charge of advertising, gloated that *Question* ". . . is doing a most fantastic sales job. It certainly is the most amazing sales success in the history of the cosmetics industry. There isn't a single Revlon item that hasn't benefitted. . . ." Net sales for 1955 increased 54 percent over the previous year, and in 1956 they soared another 66 percent. When Revlon shares were first offered on the New York Stock Exchange at the end of 1955, the issue's success was "so great it was almost embarrassing."

Question's greatest liability was its own success; it spawned imitators around the world. In the United States, a spate of programs featuring endless variations of gift-giving for answering questions further retarded "TV's already enfeebled yearning to leaven commercialism with culture." Most of these have mercifully been consigned to oblivion, but one rivaled *The $64,000 Question* in the impact it made upon the nation.

The *21* program was developed by another firm of independent program packagers, Barry and Enright, Inc. The format was different, especially in having two contestants compete against each other and no limit on their winnings, but the basic idea was the same. Questions were given point values, and the points were worth money. Once again, the "wiles of a riverboat gambler" were combined with the memory of sundry bits of information which was passed off as intellectual acumen, with the result a spectacularly profitable property.

Barry and Enright leased the show to Pharmaceuticals, Inc., now known as the J. B. Williams Company, and it first appeared on NBC on October 12, 1956. Pharmaceuticals, whose most well-known product was Geritol, soon had good reason to be pleased with its quiz show. *21* did not attain quite the ratings of *Question*, but it competed successfully against *I Love Lucy*, one of the most popular programs in television history, and attracted much notice. Although its advertising director was reluctant to give complete credit to the program for the increased sales of Geritol, it could hardly have hurt. Sales in 1957 bettered the previous year's mark by one-third.

Unlike *Question*, *21* did not shun the highly educated, and one of its contestants became a symbol to the nation of the profitability of intellectual achievement. Charles Van Doren provided evidence that an intellectual could be handsome, that he could get rich, and that he could be a superstar. Like a football player, the intellectual athlete could win fame and wealth. Van Doren's family could lay genuine claim to membership in an American aristocracy of letters. Descended from seventeenth-century Dutch immigrants, Van Doren's uncle Carl was a literary critic whose 1939 biography of Benjamin Franklin won a Pulitzer Prize. His father Mark won the Prize for poetry the following year, and he was equally famous for his accomplishments in the classroom as a professor of English at Columbia. The wives of the Van Doren brothers were also literary, rounding out a remarkably cultivated quartet. Van Doren's family divided its time between a country estate in Connecticut and a Greenwich Village townhouse where guests over the years included Sinclair Lewis, Mortimer Adler, Joseph Wood Krutch, and Morris Ernst. The family was the symbol of intellectual vitality.

Van Doren established himself on the program by defeating the swarthy, seemingly impoverished previous champion Herbert Stempel on December 5, 1956, after having played three tie matches with Stempel on November 28. It was smooth sailing for the weeks that followed.

On the TV screen [Eric Goldman has written] he appeared lanky, pleasant, smooth in dress and manner but never slick, confident but with an engaging way of understating himself. The

*long, hard questions would come at him and
his eyes would roll up, squeeze shut, his forehead furrow and perspire, his teeth gnaw at his
lower lip. Breathing heavily, he seemed to coax
information out of some corner of his mind by
talking to himself in a kind of stream-of-
consciousness. Like a good American, he fought
hard, taking advantage of every rule. . . . Like a
good American, he won without crowing. And,
like a good American, he kept on winning,
drowning corporation lawyers or ex-college
presidents with equal ease on questions ranging from naming the four islands of the
Balearic Islands to explaining the process of
photosynthesis to naming the three baseball
players who each amassed more than 3,500
hits. Charles Van Doren was "the new All-
American boy," the magazines declared, and to
millions he was that indeed. . . .*

Van Doren's victories on the quiz show
brought him greater rewards than had ac-
crued to any of his predecessors. He received
thousands of letters from parents and teachers around the world, thanking him for popu-
larizing the life of the mind. Little services
such as dry cleaning, which he had had to pay
for when supporting himself on his $4,400
yearly salary as an English instructor at
Columbia, were now donated *gratis* by starstruck shopkeepers. Several colleges expressed an interest in hiring him away from
Columbia, and he found himself referred to in
print as "Doctor" despite not yet having
earned his Ph.D. And then, of course, there
was the money. Van Doren won $129,000 dur-
ing his 14 weeks on *21*. Soon after he left, he
was awarded a $50,000 contract to appear on
the *Today* show, where for five minutes each
morning he would speak of science, literature,
and history. "I think I may be the only
person," he once remarked, "who ever read
seventeenth-century poetry on a network television program—a far cry from the usual diet
of mayhem, murder, and rape."

Rumors of improper practices surfaced
soon after the quiz shows made their debut.

By the end of 1956, articles were appearing in
the trade and general circulation press discussing the "controls" exercised by the producers to keep popular contestants alive and
eliminate the unpopular. "Are the quiz shows
rigged?" asked *Time* magazine in the spring of
1957, a year in which the networks were in-
vesting a small fortune in them. The answer:
producers could not "afford to risk collusion
with contestants," and yet, because of pretest-
ing, they were able to ask questions which
they knew the contestants would or would not
know. They could thus manipulate the outcome "far more effectively than most viewers
suspect." The report noted, however, that Van
Doren "feels certain that no questions were
being formfitted to his phenomenal mind."

A number of contestants had been disappointed at their treatment on the shows. The
most important of these, and the John Dean of
this piece, was the man Van Doren first defeated, Herbert Stempel.

Stempel's motives were very mixed. One
was money. He had quickly squandered his
winnings and had failed in an attempt to
blackmail more out of producer Dan Enright.
A more important reason was his bruised ego.
Stempel had been forced to portray himself as
a poor boy from Brooklyn, when in fact he
had married into a well-to-do family and was
from Queens. Enright insisted that he wear
ratty suits and a cheap wristwatch to project
this image and that he address the emcee,
Jack Barry, deferentially as Mr. Barry while
other contestants called him Jack. He had an
I.Q. of 170 and was infuriated by having to
"miss" answers he knew "damn well." And he
was beside himself at the unearned praise accorded to Van Doren. Here was ". . . a guy that
had a fancy name, Ivy League education, parents all his life, and I had the opposite. . . . " He
would hear passing strangers remark that he
was the man who had lost to this child of light,
and he could not stand it. But it was more
than greed or envy that prompted Stempel to
turn state's evidence. Even before he was ordered to "take a dive" and before he had ever

heard of Charles Van Doren, he was telling friends that the show was fixed. Stempel knew all the real answers about the quiz shows, and he was bursting to show the nation how smart he was.

In 1957, Stempel tried to interest two New York newspapers in the truth, but both papers refused to print what would have been one of the biggest scoops of the decade because they feared libel action. It is a commentary on the state of investigative journalism at the time that not until August, 1958, after the discovery that a giveaway show called *Dotto* was fixed, was Stempel able to make his charges in public. At this time also, New York County District Attorney Frank Hogan began an investigation, and the inexorable process of revelation had been set in motion. For almost a year, the grand jury interviewed about 150 witnesses. The producers tried to arrange a cover-up by persuading the show's alumni to perjure themselves. Many of the most well known did just that. It was one thing to fix a quiz show, however, and quite another to fix a grand jury probe. Realizing that the day of reckoning was at last approaching, the producers hurried back to change their testimony. This they did without informing the contestants, leaving them, to put it mildly, out on a limb.

For reasons which remain unclear, the judge sealed the grand jury's presentment, but the Subcommittee on Legislative Oversight (over the FCC) of the House Interstate and Foreign Commerce Committee was determined to get to the bottom of the matter. Its public hearings, held in Washington in October and November of 1959, attracted worldwide attention.

On October 6, a bitter Herbert Stempel exposed the whole sordid story of *21*. He had originally applied to take part in what he thought was an honest game but was approached by Enright who talked him into becoming an actor rather than a riverboat gambler. Every detail of his performances was prearranged: his wardrobe, his diffidence, his hesitations, and his answers. He was in-

structed on the proper way to mop his brow for maximum effect, and he was guaranteed to sweat because the air conditioning in the isolation booth was purposely kept off. From his testimony, it became clear that Van Doren was implicated as well. On the following two days, other contestants, producer Enright, and his assistant Albert Freedman testified to the fix. No one contradicted Stempel.

In the months preceding the hearings Van Doren had consistently and ever more vehemently proclaimed that no matter what others had done, his appearances on *21* had been strictly legitimate. When Stempel's charges were first published in the papers, Van Doren was "... horror struck.... I couldn't understand why Stempel should want to proclaim his own involvement." A representative of D. A. Hogan interviewed him toward the end of the year, and he denied everything. He retained a lawyer, to whom he lied about his involvement, and then proceeded to perjure himself before the New York County Grand Jury in January, 1959. He was assured by Enright and Freedman that they too would cover up.

Van Doren's day of reckoning came on November 2, 1959, before the subcommittee. Herb Stempel hurried down from New York City to get a seat from which he could clearly see his former adversary. Pale and jittery, Van Doren walked into the crowded hearing room and delivered himself of one of the most pathetic confessions in the history of American public speech.

He wished that he could erase the past three years but realizing the past may be immutable resolved to learn from it. When he had first contacted Barry and Enright, he had assumed that their programs were honest. Before his appearance on *21*, Albert Freedman summoned him to his apartment and, taking him into the bedroom, explained that Stempel had to be defeated in order to make the show more popular. Van Doren asked to go on the air honestly, but Freedman said he had no chance to defeat the brilliant Stempel. "He also told me that the show was merely entertainment and that giving help to quiz contestants was a common practice and merely a part of show business." Besides, said Freedman, Van Doren had an opportunity to help increase respect for intellectual life and education. "I will not," said Van Doren, "bore this committee by describing the intense moral struggle that went on inside me." The result of that struggle was history. Freedman coached him on how to answer questions to increase suspense and several times gave him a script to memorize. When Van Doren missed the questions which were slated for the evening, Freedman ". . . would allow me to look them up myself. A foolish sort of pride made me want to look up the answers when I could, and to learn as much about the subject as possible."

As time went on the show ballooned beyond my wildest expectations. . . . [F]rom an unknown college instructor I became a celebrity. I received thousands of letters and dozens of requests to make speeches, appear in movies, and so forth—in short, all the trappings of modern publicity. To a certain extent this went to my head.

He realized, however, that he was misrepresenting education and was becoming more nervous about the show. He urged the producers to let him quit, but it was only after they could arrange a sufficiently dramatic situation that he was defeated.

Van Doren's brief testimony was the climax of the subcommittee's investigation as it was of this scandal as a whole. Nevertheless, the hearings continued, including an investigation of *The $64,000 Question*. *Question* was also fixed, and although the details differed from the *21* case, the deception was no less pervasive.

It is no exaggeration to say that the American public was transfixed by the revelation of quiz show fraud. A Gallup poll found the highest level of public awareness of the event in the history of such surveys. Questioned about the shows at successive news conferences, President Eisenhower said he shared "the

American general reaction of almost bewilderment" and compared the manipulations to the Black Sox scandal of 1919. The quiz show episode affords an opportunity to discuss feelings toward Van Doren, the hero unmasked, and also the general arguments which swirled around television at decade's turn.

For Van Doren, humiliation came in the wake of confession. Just as institutions had been happy to associate themselves with quiz show geniuses, they hurried to dissociate themselves when the geniuses turned out to be hustlers. NBC fired Van Doren, while Columbia "accepted his resignation." The actions of these two institutions were scrutinized along with those of Van Doren in the period following his confession.

From the first, both NBC and CBS had maintained the highly implausible stand that they were fooled about the shows along with the public. They unquestionably could have uncovered the rigging had they really wanted to, and in the end they were left holding the bag. They had lost millions of dollars and, what was worse, had suffered what at the time loomed as a potentially mortal blow to a very pleasant way of making a lot of money. The popular uproar threatened to force government to restrict the broadcasting prerogatives of management. In this state of affairs, Van Doren had to go. CBS took the next step, eliminating quiz shows altogether, from which NBC refrained.

Few were surprised by NBC's stand. The network was, after all, a business, and Van Doren had become a liability. Columbia's treatment of him aroused different issues. Some students had no patience with him, but hundreds rallied to his defense with petitions and demonstrations. They pointed out that his teaching was excellent and that having made public relations capital out of his victories, Columbia would be craven to desert him now. The Columbia College dean, however, maintained, "The issue is the moral one of the honesty and integrity of teaching." The dean found Van Doren's deceptions contrary to the principles a teacher should have and should try to instill in his students.

The academic community holds in especial contempt, as *Love Story* author Erich Segal was to discover, those "willing to play the fool" for limitless publicity. In defense of Columbia's action, political scientist Hans J. Morgenthau published two essays purporting to show that Van Doren had actually violated "the moral law" as handed down from Moses, Plato, Buddha, and other worthies. Apparently no such law would have been violated had Van Doren's participation in what thinking people very well knew was a cheap stunt been unrigged. If any crime had been committed in the quiz show episode, it was surely the broad conspiracy to portray as genuine intellectual activity the spouting of trivia. But while the shows were on and winning high ratings, there was neither from Morgenthau nor Columbia a peep of protest.

The most devastating but also perhaps the fairest indictment of Van Doren's role was penned by a Columbia colleague, Lawrence S. Hall, who demonstrated that Van Doren's confession had been as thoroughly fraudulent as his conduct on *21*. He had not confessed because of a letter from a fan of his on the *Today* show as he had claimed but only because of a congressional subpoena. "To the very end he never did perform the ethical free act of making up his mind. . . . Van Doren did not *decide* to tell the truth; what he did was adapt himself to the finally inescapable necessity of telling it." Worst of all, asserted Hall, was his "concealing under [the] piously reflexive formulas" of his silken prose "the most maudlin and promiscuous ethical whoredom the soap opera public has yet witnessed."

Unlike Hall the average American seemed rather sympathetic. A Sindlinger poll asked respondents to rate those most blameworthy for the fixes. Asked to assess the responsibility of network, sponsor, producer, and Van Doren, only 18.6 percent blamed Van Doren the most while 38.9 percent blamed him the least. A substantial number even favored a continuation of the shows, rigged or not. Many man-in-the-street interviewees said they would have done no differently, and most newspaper editorials treated him extraordinarily gently.

Investigators discovered not a single contestant on *21*, and only one on *The $64,000 Question*, who refused to accept money once they learned the shows were fixed. Most were quite "blithe" about it. Pollsters at the end of the 1950s were finding the belief widespread that the individual did not feel it was his place to condemn. Moral relativism, it seemed, rather than adherence to Professor Morgenthau's moral absolutism, was the rule. So many people lived polite lies that though it may have been titillating to discover them, they were hardly worth preaching about.

Other factors, in addition to this general willingness to partake in a fraud such as the quiz shows, help explain why the outrage was muted and transient. First, as Boorstin has pointed out, television unites many people in a community, but their union is tenuous and easily forgotten. Secondly, although many were taken in by the seeming reality of the shows, they had believed and been disabused so many times in the past that the shock soon wore off. For underneath the belief in the shows there probably lingered skepticism. Robert Merton observed in 1946 that cynicism about public statements from any source, political or commercial, was pervasive. Television was a new medium which some may have thought was simply too big to play by the rules of the old-time newspaper patent medicine advertiser. The quiz shows taught them that it was not, and some critics asserted that it was the naked selfishness of commercial radio and television, more than the machinations of particular producers or contestants, that was truly to blame. The quiz shows excited to a new pitch of intensity long-running arguments about commercial broadcasting and the public interest.

The growth of commercial broadcasting cannot be explored here at length, but suffice it to say that it was opposed every step of the way by intellectuals, educators, and journalists who deplored what they saw as the perversion of a medium of great potential for the sake of the desire of private business to push products. As early as the 1920s, when radio was first coming into its own, articulate voices spoke up against its use for advertising. Bruce Bliven thought such "outrageous rubbish" should be banned from the air, and at least one congressman considered introducing legislation to that end. Herbert Hoover, whose Commerce Department supervised the granting of broadcast licenses, felt that radio would die if it allowed itself to be "drowned in advertising chatter," but he favored self-regulation rather than government action. The Radio Act of 1927 demanded that licensees operated their stations not solely for profit but with due regard for the "public interest, convenience, and necessity."

As charted by broadcasting's foremost historian, Erik Barnouw, the ascendancy of commercial programming was established in a fit of absence of mind. "If such a system [as exists today] had been outlined in 1927 or 1934, when our basic broadcasting laws were written," he concluded, "it certainly would have been rejected." Critics believed that the quiz shows and the radio "payola" scandals that followed proved that broadcasting was too important to be left in the hands of those whose primary, if not sole, motive was to turn a profit for the stockholders.

Television executives insisted that the scandals were the exception in a generally well-run industry, but critics thought they were the tip of the iceberg. In themselves, the scandals were relatively unimportant, held the *New Republic*. "A real investigation would center on the simple question: why is television so bad, so monstrous?" It was the thirst

for profit which forced the industry to a state of thralldom to the ratings. It was profit which mandated such dreadful children's programming. Advertising agencies and their clients, with profit always uppermost in mind, forced absurd restrictions on what could be broadcast. When commentators complained about the astounding amount of violence on the tube, defenders warned of the danger of censorship. Critics replied that the most stultifying censorship was already being exercised on behalf of the manufacturers of the pointless nostrums of an overindulgent society. In its quest for ratings, television seemed consistently to avoid satisfying the intelligent minority.

The industry had now been caught redhanded, Walter Lippmann wrote, in ". . . an enormous conspiracy to deceive the public in order to sell profitable advertising to the sponsors." The situation which had made this shameful occurrence possible could not be allowed to survive intact. Television had "to live up to a higher, but less profitable, standard." What America needed was prime-time TV produced "not because it yields private profits but because it moves toward truth and excellence." What was needed, said Lippmann, was public service television.

Industry spokesmen had traditionally defended themselves as true democrats. The president of CBS, Frank Stanton, soon after *The $64,000 Question* was first aired, declared, "A program in which a large part of the audience is interested is by that very fact . . . in the public interest." By such a standard, the quiz shows can be seen not as "cynical malpractices . . . in one corner of television," as Robert Sarnoff tried to represent them, but rather as the perfect expression of the industry.

Sarnoff recognized the charges being hurled at TV in 1959 and 1960 as the "long-familiar [ones] of mediocrity, imbalance, violence, and overcommercialism." These charges had been unjustified in the past and were unjustified in 1960, but because ". . . those who press them are now armed with the cudgels represented by the quiz-show deceptions" they could not be sloughed off. Sarnoff's response was to promise careful scrutiny of such programs in the future and vigorous self-regulation. As a special bonus to the viewing public in a gesture to wipe the slate clean, he offered to donate time for a series of debates between the major presidential candidates of 1960, which eventually resulted in the televised confrontations between Kennedy and Nixon.

Sarnoff's offer was enthusiastically welcomed by such politicians as Stewart Udall, who had been working for a suspension of equal time regulations in order to permit broadcast debates between Democratic and Republican presidential nominees in the upcoming election. Paradoxically, the four "Great Debates" which ensued showed unmistakably the influence of the supposedly discredited quiz programs. The similarity in formats was obvious. As in *21*, two adversaries faced each other and tried to give point-scoring answers to questions fired at them under the glare of klieg lights. The debates bore as little relationship to the real work of the presidency as the quiz shows did to intellectuality. Boorstin has remarked on how successful they were ". . . in reducing great national issues to trivial dimensions. With appropriate vulgarity, they might have been called the $400,000 Question (Prize: a $100,000-a-year job for four years)." No president would act on any question put to him by the reporters without sustained and sober consultation with trusted advisors. But the American people, conditioned by five years of isolation booth virtuosity, expected the "right" answer to be delivered pithily and with little hesitation. They did not want to be told that some questions did not have simple answers—or any answers at all.

The technological advances which led to radio and television grew out of the tinkerings of amateur experimenters. These two new forms of mass communication, with unprecedented drama and immediacy, developed independently of the desire to say

anything. In 1854, Henry David Thoreau wrote, "We are in great haste to construct a magnetic telegraph from Maine to Texas; but Maine and Texas, it may be, have nothing important to communicate." This observation has been yet more relevant during the last half century. Except for the military, which was always seeking more direct means for locating ships at sea and soldiers on the battlefield, no one knew what to broadcast and telecast. The federal government, dominated by the ideology of free enterprise, declined to fill this void. To be sure, regulations did prohibit certain messages over the air, but there has never been a national statement on the positive purposes of the new media which the industry was obliged to take seriously.

Businessmen soon discovered that broadcasting was a powerful instrument for increasing sales. Those advertisers who had financed the print media, including manufacturers of patent medicines, cosmetics, and cigarettes, quickly adopted the same role with radio and television. Left to their own devices, they sought programs which would constitute a congenial frame for their selling message. They soon hit upon the idea, among others, of parlor games, of which the quiz shows were direct descendants.

Such programs had been popular since the thirties, but in the 1950s, clever producers learned how to make them even more so. They combined large sums of money with the American fondness for facts, dressed up as intellectuality, and the result was *The $64,000 Question* and *21*. When these programs were exposed as frauds, a jaded public, inured to mendacity, was quick to forgive.

Critics have often complained, as they did with vigor after the scandals, that television—"a medium of such great potential"—was being so ill-used. But no one seems to have a clear vision of what that potential is. The lack of direction which characterized the early years of American broadcasting has never been overcome. Commentators such as Lippmann have won their public broadcasting sys-

Charles Van Doren, winner of $129,000 in a rigged TV quiz show, pleaded guilty to perjury in his testimony to the New York County Grand Jury and received a suspended sentence in 1962.

tem, but commercial television has not up-graded its fare in order to compete. If any-thing, public TV may act as a lightning rod deflecting complaints about the commercial industry by providing an outlet for those de-manding alternative viewing.

For its part, the industry has usually ignored what enlightened guidance has been available in favor of traditional forms of entertainment guaranteed not to distract the viewer from the advertisements. Thus, recently, quiz and game shows have made a comeback. There has even been talk of resurrecting *The $64,000 Question,* despite the risk of reviving along with it mem-ories of past chicanery. Such programming represents a distressing devotion to Philistin-ism and a failure of imagination, the solution for which is not in sight.

Study Questions

1. What is implied by the concept of a "consumption community"? How is this sort of a community different from any other community?

2. Compare how Charles Van Doren and Herbert Stempel were presented on the television quiz show *21.* Why was Stempel told to appear poor and deferential on the show? Is there a political statement in the images of both men?

3. How did most Americans respond to the disclosure that *21* and other quiz shows were rigged?

4. What does Tedlow mean by the concept of "moral relativism"? Is morality ever absolute?

5. What issues are involved in the debate between advocates of commercial broadcasting and proponents of public service broadcasting?

6. How were the Nixon-Kennedy television debates in 1960 similar to or different from the format of the television quiz show *21?* What does this say about the importance of television in a political campaign?

Bibliography

The television industry has received far less historical attention than the film industry. This is perplexing, considering that television "touches" more people—American as well as non-American—than the movies. The fact that some movie directors have consciously cultivated reputations as "artists" undoubtedly has something to do with academic interest in their product that is not apparent with television. There are, however, several very good books on television. Among the best are Erik Barnauw, *The Golden Web* (1968) and *The Image Empire: A History of Broadcasting in the United States* (1970); Raymond Williams, *Television: Technology and Cultural Form* (1975); and Robert Sklare, *Prime-Time America: Life on and Behind the Television Screen* (1980). Also of interest are two books by Daniel Boorstin, *The Americans: The Democratic Experience* (1974) and *The Image: A Guide to Pseudo-Events in America* (1961). The Van Doren case is dealt with in Kent Anderson, *Television Fraud* (1978) and Eric Goldman, *The Crucial Decade and After: America, 1945–1960* (1960). Douglas Miller and Marian Novak discuss social and cultural developments in the 1950s in *The Fifties: The Way We Really Were* (1977) as does Karal Ann Marling's *As Seen on TV: The Visual Culture of Everyday Life in the 1950s* (1996).

READING 23

★ ★ ★

"Broader Ribbons Across the Land": The Creation of the Interstate Highway System

Logan Thomas Snyder

In the 1920s the automobile began to alter the shape of American culture. From work to play, automobiles changed the ways Americans went about their lives. After the passage of the National System of Interstate and Defense Highways Act in 1956, the pace of the automotive revolution accelerated. The act earmarked $26 billion for the construction of 41,000 (later raised to 42,500) miles of multilane interstate highways. The legislation created hundreds of thousands of jobs and became the largest public works program in American history. It also changed the landscape of America by fostering the growth of suburbs, hastening the decline of inner cities, and giving rise to thousands of motels, service stations, drive-in theaters, and mobile home parks.

In the following essay Logan Thomas Snyder surveys the origins of the Interstate and Defense Highways Act. In particular, he demonstrates that President Dwight Eisenhower had long been concerned with the state of American roads. A military man with a keen eye for the logistics of moving armies, Ike fully understood that good highways were essential to modern life. He considered the Interstate and Defense Highways Act the crowning achievement of his administration. Economically, socially, politically, and culturally, no other piece of legislation had such a long-lasting impact.

Whether it is commuting to work, embarking on the great American road trip or something as simple as receiving a product that has wended its way across hundreds, perhaps thousands of miles of highway, nearly everyone in America benefits from the Eisenhower Interstate System on a day-to-day basis. Most Americans, however, do not know the history behind one of the country's greatest public works projects, and fewer still understand the motivation of the man whose personal experience and vision brought the massive and challenging project to fruition. The story of the creation of the Interstate Highway System spans two world wars and the life of one of America's most famous leaders.

In 1919, following the end of World War I, an Army expedition was organized to traverse the nation from Washington, D.C., to San Francisco. The First Transcontinental Motor Convoy (FTMC) left the nation's capital on July 7, following a brief ceremony and the dedication of the "Zero Milestone" at the Ellipse just south of the White House. Joining the expedition as an observer was a young lieutenant colonel, Dwight D. Eisenhower.

Only eight months earlier the Allied powers and Germany had signed an armistice ending World War I, a conflict that is today synonymous with savage trench fighting, the chilling call to "fix bayonets!" and so many blighted and blood-soaked fields. Yet as Secretary of War Newton D. Baker noted during the FTMC's ceremonial send off: "The world war was a war of motor transport. It was a war of movement, especially in the later stages. . . . There seemed to be a never-ending stream of transports moving along the white roads of France."

Baker's important observation factored directly into the departing convoy's primary objectives. As stated in one official report, those objectives included: "To service-test the special-purpose vehicles developed for use in the first World War, not all of which were available in time for such use, and to determine by actual experience the possibility and the problems involved in moving an army across the continent, assuming that railroad facilities, bridges, tunnels, etc., had been damaged or destroyed by agents of an Asiatic enemy."

At its starting point, the massive convoy consisted of 34 heavy cargo trucks; four light delivery trucks; two machine shops; one blacksmith shop; one wrecking truck; two spare-parts stores; two water tanks; one gasoline tank; one searchlight; one caterpillar tractor; four kitchen trailers; eight touring cars; one reconnaissance car; two staff observation cars; five sidecar motorcycles; and four motorcycles; all of which were operated and maintained by 258 enlisted men, 15 War Department staff observation officers and 24 expeditionary officers. By the time the expedition reached San Francisco on September 6—62 days after setting out, the convoy had traveled 3,251 miles, at an average of 58.1 miles per day and 6.07 miles per hour.

It was truly an unprecedented undertaking in every regard, and although the mission was a success, the numbers were disappointing if not dismal. According to a report by William C. Greany, captain of the Motor Transport Corps, the convoy lost nine vehicles—"so damaged as to require retirement while en route"—and 21 men "thru various casualties" (mercifully there was no mention of fatalities). During the course of its journey, the convoy destroyed or otherwise damaged 88 "mostly wooden highway bridges and culverts" and was involved in 230 "road accidents" or, more precisely, "instances of road failure and vehicles sinking in quicksand or mud, running off the road or over embankments, overturning, or other mishaps due entirely to the unfavorable and at times appalling traffic conditions that were encountered."

Logan Thomas Snyder, "'Broader Ribbons Across the Land': The Creation of the Interstate Highway System," in *American History* Vol. 41/No. 2 (June 2006), pp. 32–39.

The construction of the interstate highway system in the 1950's and 60's changed the face of America. It also changed American economic, social, and cultural life.

The after-action report of Lt. Col. Eisenhower, one of the 15 War Department staff observation officers, noted: "In many places excellent roads were installed some years ago that have since received no attention whatsoever. Absence of any effort at maintenance has resulted in roads of such rough nature as to be very difficult of negotiating." Even more vexing, many of what otherwise would have been considered "good roads" were simply too narrow for military vehicles. Others were too rough, sandy or steep for trucks that in some cases weighed in excess of 11 tons. Eisenhower claimed, "The train operated so slowly in such places, that in certain instances it was noted that portions of the train did not move for two hours."

The July 30 entry in the FTMC's daily log, for example, shows it covered 83 miles in 10 hours through Nebraska, not exactly burning up the track but a good clip nonetheless at about 8 miles per hour. Just three days later, however, the convoy became mired in "gumbo roads," which slowed the rate of progress to 30 miles in 10 grueling hours—at one point even causing 25 of the expedition's trucks to go skidding into a ditch. "Two days were lost in [the] western part of this state," Eisenhower later recorded.

For all involved, the military convoy was a learning experience, a sharp illustration of the disrepair and, more often than not, complete lack of highway infrastructure in many areas of the country, particularly the heartland. The majority of the nation's roads and highways were simply a mess. Even the Lincoln Highway, the most famous transcontinental highway of its day, had been described as nothing more than "an imaginary line, like the equator"!

Eisenhower's experience with the FTMC provided him with great insight into the logistics of moving large quantities of men and material across vast stretches of land and convinced him of the necessity of building and maintaining the infrastructure to do so more efficiently. Yet, as educational as his experience with the convoy had been, it would be dwarfed by the greater and far more serious challenges of World War II.

In November 1942, 21 years after the FTMC and nearly a year after the United States had entered the war, Eisenhower was appointed to command Allied forces in Operation Torch, aimed at evicting the Axis powers from North Africa.

There was much about Operation Torch to dislike from a command standpoint. Given the physical geography and the incredibly poor infrastructure of the lands he and his forces were invading, the operation was a logistical nightmare.

Torch required three amphibious landings spread over 800 miles: at Casablanca, on the western coast of Morocco, and at Oran and Algiers, along the Algerian coast in the Mediterranean Sea. Each group was to hit the ground running and make all due haste east, toward the ultimate goal of Tunis, the capital of Tunisia. Unfortunately for the Allies, North Africa was not well suited to the rapid movement of military convoys. The Atlas Mountains, where elevation at places exceeds 13,000 feet, spanned virtually the entire area of operations, and the infrastructure, where it existed, was generally poor at best.

The fact that Casablanca was more than 1,000 miles west of its objective meant a longer, more vulnerable supply line and much slower going when speed was essential. According to historian Stephen Ambrose, many, including Eisenhower, "could see no good reason to terminate the seaborne phase of the amphibious assault 1,000 miles away from the objective, which itself was on the coast and could be reached quicker on ship than on foot." Chief of Staff General George C. Marshall, however, was concerned that if all three landing sites were within the Mediterranean it might tempt Adolf Hitler to invade Spain, giving him the opportunity to blockade the Straits of Gibraltar and strangle the seaborne Allied supply lines.

The race to reach Tunis before it could be reinforced with Axis troops found the Allies at a decided disadvantage. Axis troops moved with ease through Benito Mussolini's Italy and onto Sicily, approximately 150 miles off the Tunisian coast, little more than a long ferry ride. The Allies, according to Ambrose, were, by comparison, "dependent on unimproved dirt roads and a poorly maintained single-track railroad." When the Allied heads of state began to lament the slow advance, Eisenhower barked back that, in spite of commandeering every vehicle that would move, he was hindered by the complete absence of organized motor transport. Moreover, the *Luftwaffe's* strong presence over the Mediterranean prevented shipping supplies that far into the sea.

According to Ambrose, Eisenhower privately confided to Marshall that his situation was so hodgepodge and patchwork it would "make a ritualist in warfare go just a bit hysterical." Some did; others got creative. Lieutenant General Sir Kenneth Anderson of the British First Army became so fed up with the logistical situation that he resorted to bringing supplies into the Tunis area by pack mule. Every bit as slow and obstinate as the four-wheeled alternative, a good mule was at least much less likely to break down in the mountains.

Although the Allies failed to beat the Axis reinforcements to Tunis, they did eventually win the race to resupply. Germany was so invested in stalemating the Soviet Union along the Eastern Front that the material it was allocating to *Afrika Korps* represented little more than the barest scraps of an almost incalculably vast resource pool. Ultimately, the fact that Allied supplies had to travel much greater distances to the front weighed little against the sheer volume of output coming from American production capacity at its peak. Operation Torch was a success, albeit belatedly. With French North Africa free from the Axis powers, Eisenhower and the Allies were finally able to turn their attention toward the big picture, namely a full-scale Allied invasion of Europe the following year.

As harrowing and dramatic as any single event during the war could be, D-Day was also, by its very nature, only the beginning of the Crusade in Europe (as Eisenhower later titled the memoirs of his experience in-the-ater). As jubilant as the Allied forces were after having successfully penetrated Hitler's so-called Atlantic Wall—the layered network of coastal defenses protecting occupied France—there was an even greater challenge facing them on the other side. Several hundred miles of terrain, which the *Wehrmacht* had occupied for nearly four years, remained between the Allies and their ultimate objective, Berlin. Much of the worst fighting still lay ahead—not far ahead, either.

Normandy's famous hedgerows stymied Allied advances almost from the beginning. The densely packed hedgerows and narrow roads slowed tank movements to a crawl, making them easy pickings for German units wielding the *Panzerfaust* (an early model of rocket-propelled grenade). The great majority of the advancing, therefore, had to be done piecemeal by slow-moving infantry. Nearly two months later, all that the Allies had to show for their efforts to push farther into the continent was a skimpy front 80 miles wide, extending 30 miles inland at its deepest points. In an ominous throwback to World War I, commanders again began to measure their advances in yards instead of miles.

Once the Allies emerged from hedgerow country, however, the terrain significantly opened up. Lieutenant General George S. Patton was the first to break out, on August 1; by the 6th he was halfway to Paris. "The nightmare of a static front was over," Ambrose wrote. "Distances that had taken months and cost tens of thousands of lives to cross in World War I" were being crossed in mere hours with minimal casualties. Even so, isolated sections of terrain proved nearly impassable. According to Ambrose, the Hürtgen Forest, "where roads were nothing more than forest trails," and the Ardennes Mountains, with their "limited road network," were hell on both tanks and infantry. There would be further setbacks not attributable to infrastructure, primarily the German counteroffensive at the Battle of the Bulge, but the Allies were headed full-bore for the Rhine,

while on the Eastern Front the Red Army was bearing down on Berlin.

It was not until the Allies broke through the Western Wall and tapped into Germany's sprawling autobahn network that Eisenhower saw for himself what a modern army could do with an infrastructure capable of accommodating it. The enhanced mobility that the autobahn provided the Allies was something to behold, and years later was still cause for reminiscing. "The old convoy," Eisenhower wrote, referring to his experience with the FTMC, "had started me thinking about good, two-lane highways, but Germany had made me see the wisdom of broader ribbons across the land."

Eisenhower's experience commanding and directing the movements of massive quantities of troops and equipment, added to his early experience with the FTMC, strengthened his recognition that America was sorely lacking in a national highway defense system. In a situation requiring the mass exodus of an entire city or region or the urgent mobilization of troops for purposes of national defense, the federal government, to say nothing of state and local entities, would have been hard-pressed to adequately respond. Moreover, the need for such critical infrastructure became that much more urgent as the Soviet Union eagerly stepped into the power vacuum created by the fall of Nazi Germany. The idyllic Allied notion that all would be right with the world following the death of Hitler and the smashing of the German armies quickly gave way to the painful realization that there is always reason to remain prepared, always someone else to fight.

Not surprisingly, therefore, when Eisenhower became the 34th U.S. president in 1953, he pushed for the building of an interstate highway system. Although Congress had first authorized a national highway system in 1944, it had always been woefully underfunded. Throwing the full weight of his presidency behind the project, Eisenhower declared to Congress on February 22, 1955: "Our unity as a nation is sustained by free communication of thought and by easy transportation of people and goods. The ceaseless flow of information throughout the Republic is matched by individual and commercial movement over a vast system of interconnected highways crisscrossing the country and joining at our national borders with friendly neighbors to the north and south.

"Together, the uniting forces of our communication and transportation systems are dynamic elements in the very name we bear— United States. Without them, we would be a mere alliance of many separate parts."

More than a year later, on June 29, Eisenhower signed the Federal-Aid Highway Act of 1956, guaranteeing full, dedicated funding for the project. The National Highway Defense System (NHDS), as it was initially known, has been referred to as one of the "Seven Wonders of the United States," among other such notable structures as the Golden Gate Bridge, the Hoover Dam and the Panama Canal. What sets the NHDS apart from those wonders, and what Eisenhower addressed as one of its greatest selling points, is the fact that it truly has strengthened and enhanced the Union (including noncontiguous states Alaska and Hawaii, as well as the territory of Puerto Rico). Only the Panama Canal, which similarly made the United States more accessible to itself by greatly reducing the time required to ship goods from coast to coast, can claim anything approaching a similar distinction.

The scope of the NHDS is underscored by its individual components. The longest east-west route, I-90, stretches more than 3,000 miles, linking Seattle to Boston. I-95 serves a similar end for north-south travel: Extending from Miami to Maine, its nearly 2,000 miles of highway cross through 15 states—including all 13 of the original colonies—and the District of Columbia. (It is also estimated to have been the most expensive route to construct, at a cost of nearly $8 billion.) Texas boasts the most interstate mileage within a single state, with more than 3,200; New York claims the

most interstate routes, with 29. California is second in both categories, with just under 2,500 miles of interstate on its 25 routes.

The structural achievements involved are no less staggering than the numbers. Although the "highway" is often declaimed as an eyesore at worst and bland at best, the NHDS is actually composed of many unique wonders of modern engineering and ingenuity. Some of the most spectacular cross large bodies of water or ride alongside the Pacific Coast. The Sunshine Skyway Bridge across Tampa Bay, Fla., a so-called cable-stayed bridge, has been lauded by *The New York Times* for its "lyrical and tensile strength"— indeed rows of small cables attached to two single-column pylons support the weight of the bridge below "like the strings of a harp."

Several interstate routes in California and Hawaii hug the coasts, offering panoramic views of stunning Pacific seaside vistas to passing motorists.

Other achievements in interstate construction are closely associated with the "Not In My Backyard" movement. Many urban areas have "gone green" in recent decades, improving their routes to meet increased environmental concerns and the aesthetic needs of citizens; some projects were even forced to halt construction entirely until such concerns were addressed in advance. Worries about the safety of the endangered and much beloved Florida panther led to the construction of special underpasses along Alligator Alley, the portion of I-75 that connects Naples and Miami in Florida, allowing panthers and other wildlife to cross safely beneath the flow of traffic. One section of I-10 in Arizona that opened in 1990, the Papago Freeway, runs beneath "19 side-by-side bridges that form the foundation for a 12-hectare [29.6 acre] urban park," according to Richard F. Weingroff, a former official at the Federal Highway Administration. Known as the Margaret T. Hance Park, the space was conceived as a unique solution to the vexing problem of how to maintain connections between neighborhoods divided by the interstate. In other areas, simpler concerns required simpler solutions, such as tree-lined medians, noise-reducing berms and walls, lowered speed limits and prohibitions against large trucks.

A frequent complaint leveled against the NHDS is that it has stripped the adventure and romanticism from long-distance traveling. Upon the completion of I-40 (Barstow, Calif., to Wilmington, N.C.), the late CBS News commentator Charles Kuralt observed: "It is now possible to travel from coast to coast without seeing anything. From the Interstate, America is all steel guardrails and plastic signs, and every place looks and feels and sounds and smells like every other place." While the criticism is to an extent justified, it is also true that the NHDS directly serves nearly every major metropolitan area (as well as countless smaller areas of population) and is home to, or otherwise conveniently located near, thousands of tourist destinations across the country.

Some of the most intriguing and impressive tourist stops are those that are not content to simply nestle alongside the highway, but those that, like the Great Platte River Road Archway Monument, literally straddle it. The Archway Monument, a 1,500-ton structure spanning 308 feet across I-80 in Kearney, Neb., is a celebration of frontier culture designed to resemble a covered bridge. Built to honor the thousands of pioneers who had followed the arduous route from Missouri to the West Coast during the 19th century, the Archway Monument is a living bridge to history over a modern river of asphalt, a testament to the wisdom of and need for well-planned, well-constructed infrastructure. Eisenhower would have approved of the symbolism.

Whatever else these features may be in and of themselves, they are ultimately incidental to the system's much more vital main purpose. The NHDS, according to a 1996 report written by Wendell Cox and Jean Love 40 years after Eisenhower signed the Federal-Aid Highway Act of 1956, was con-

ceived and marketed as the best possible way to facilitate "the quick and efficient movement of military equipment and personnel" in the event of a Soviet invasion or nuclear strike. Inspired by the autobahn, Eisenhower envisioned multilane highways—"broader ribbons across the land," as he called them— yet even at its narrowest points, the system can still accommodate all but the most cumbersome wheeled or tracked military vehicles. Also, most military bases are situated within close proximity to the NHDS, adding to the already unequaled in-country response capability of the U.S. armed forces— a fact that is every bit as comforting as the fact that there has never been occasion to use this capability to its utmost.

One widely held dual-use-related belief is that one out of every five miles of the NHDS is mandated to be straight and level, capable of functioning as an emergency airstrip. Aside from the fact that, according to Weingroff, "no law, regulation, policy, or sliver of red tape requires that one out of every five miles of the interstate highway system be straight," it is virtually impossible from an engineering standpoint. The NHDS is composed of nearly 50,000 miles of road, meaning that almost 10,000 miles would need to be straight and level to conform to the supposed one-in-five-mile rule, a figure that is wildly unrealistic. In addition, from an aerial standpoint, an airstrip every five miles is superfluous, given the speed at which modern aircraft travel. Although there are long and level stretches of highway that could function as an emergency landing strip in a pinch, they are nowhere near as evenly parceled out as the one-in-five-mile rule would suggest. (The use of highway infrastructure for an airstrip is not unheard of, however: Nazi Germany did use limited stretches of the autobahn for such purposes during World War II.)

One cannot discuss the NHDS without also mentioning its impact on the U.S. economy. It is, quite literally, the economic engine that drives this country's prosperity. No other industrialized nation has such a sprawling and comprehensive system of roadways, though many are now seeking to emulate the U.S. model as a means toward becoming more competitive in the international marketplace. One look at the figures in the Cox and Love report and it is not hard to understand why. By 1996 the interstates, comprising just over 1 percent of the miles of public road in this country, carried "nearly one-quarter of the nation's surface passenger transport and 45 percent of motor freight transport." During the course of its first 40 years, the system was responsible for an increase of "approximately one-quarter of the nation's productivity." Highway transportation and directly related industries accounted for more than 7 million jobs.

Indirectly related industries have felt the uptick, as well. In the restaurant business alone, employment "has increased more than seven times the rate of population growth," according to the Cox and Love report. By making " 'just in time' delivery more feasible" while simultaneously reducing tractor-trailer operating costs by as much as 17 percent compared with other roadways, the NHDS has played a major role in making the electronic marketplace a workable phenomenon for all parties involved: retailers, delivery companies and consumers alike. Perhaps the most telling figure is the return rate of $6 for every $1 spent on highway construction. Consider also that in the 10 years since those figures were generated, several factors—population expansion, the advent of e-commerce, our national reluctance to fly following the terrorist attacks of September 11, 2001—have conspired to place an even greater share of traffic onto our nation's highways. The many differences separating 2006 from 1996 notwithstanding, the conclusion of the Cox and Love report concerning the economic impact of the NHDS remains as true today as the day it was written: "By improving inter-regional access, the interstate highway system has helped to create a genuinely national domestic market with companies able to supply their products to much larger geographical areas, and less expensively."

For most of us, though, the dual-use military features and the economic benefits of the NHDS are barely an afterthought. The interstate is a way to get to work, to go downtown, to shave 30 minutes off the drive to grandma's house. Often it is the backbone of that uniquely American pastime, the road trip. Sometimes it's just a headache. Occasionally it becomes a lifeline out of harm's way.

In 1990 the National Highway Defense System was renamed the Dwight David Eisenhower National System of Interstate and Defense Highways under an act of Congress signed into law by President George H. W. Bush. As tributes go, it was perfectly appropriate. "Of all his domestic programs," Ambrose wrote, "Eisenhower's favorite by far was the Interstate System."

For all its detractors' criticism, the interstate system, more than any other project in the past 50 years, has encouraged an unprecedented democratization of mobility. It has opened up access to an array of goods and services previously unavailable to many and created massive opportunities for five decades and three generations of Americans. It has made the country more accessible to itself while also making it safer and more secure, outcomes that in almost any other undertaking would prove mutually exclusive.

"More than any single action by the government since the end of the war, this one would change the face of America," Eisenhower wrote in 1963. "Its impact on the American economy—the jobs it would produce in manufacturing and construction, the rural areas it would open up—was beyond calculation." The clarity of his vision and the resiliency of his words are inarguable. The Eisenhower Interstate System has grown to be valuable beyond its original intent and is a lasting tribute to American ingenuity, ability and strength of purpose.

Study Questions

1. What role did World War I and World War II play in the origins of the Interstate Highway System?

2. What did the 1919 First Transcontinental Motor Convoy reveal about American roads? What impact did it have on Dwight Eisenhower?

3. What did Eisenhower learn about roads during World War II?

4. What importance did military planning have in the creation of the Interstate Highway System?

5. What were some of the complaints voiced against the Interstate Highway System? What were some of its successes?

6. What was—and is—the economic impact of the Interstate Highway System?

7. How did the Interstate Highway System help to create modern America?

Bibliography

Robert A. Caro, *The Power Broker: Robert Moses and the Fall of New York* (1974) and Kenneth Jackson, *The Crabgrass Frontier: The Suburbanization of United States* (1985) contain valuable information about the importance of highways in the creation of modern America. For the role automobiles have played in American life see Clay McShane, *Down the Asphalt Path: The Automobile and the American City* (1994); James Flink, *The Car Culture* (1975); and John B. Rae, *The Road and the Car in American Life* (1971). Mark H. Rose, *Interstate: Express Highway Politics, 1939–1989*, rev. ed. (1990) presents an overview of the subject. Stephen E. Ambrose, *Eisenhower: President* (1984) details Eisenhower's concerns about American highways.

7

★ ★ ★

Coming Apart: 1960–2000

The era began innocently enough. In an extremely close election, John F. Kennedy defeated Richard M. Nixon for the presidency and quickly became one of the most admired men in the country. Blessed with brains, charisma, money, and a lovely young family, Kennedy epitomized America, particularly the rise and triumph of the immigrant. In public rhetoric, he cultivated a tough idealism, one that offered a courageous challenge to the Russians and hope for democracy and prosperity in the rest of the world. When Kennedy assumed the presidency in 1961, Americans believed their moral hegemony would last forever. They believed that their values deserved to govern the world by virtue of their success—an equality of opportunity and a standard of living unparalleled in human history. In closing his inaugural address, Kennedy even invoked the divine by claiming that "God's work must truly be our own."

What few people realized was that Kennedy was sitting on a powder keg, both at home and abroad. His liberal idealism, so self-righteous and yet so naive, barely survived his own life. From the mid-1960s through the mid-1970s, the country passed through a period of intense turmoil and doubt. Smug convictions about the virtues of equality and opportunity in the United States succumbed to the shrill criticisms of racial, ethnic, and gender groups. Beliefs in the virtues, safeguards, and stability of the American government were shattered by the lies exposed in the controversies over Watergate and the Pentagon Papers. By the late 1960s and early 1970s, the explosion in oil prices, the appearance of stagflation, and the worries about the future of the environment all undermined the prevailing confidence about the American economy. Finally, the moral complacency so endemic to Kennedy liberalism died in the jungles of Southeast Asia. Like few other events in American history, the Vietnam War tore the country apart. At home, America was characterized by bit-

terness, demonstrations, and widespread disaffection from the country's leaders. A counterculture of young people scornful of conventional values appeared, and the symbols of their rebellion were drugs and rock and roll. As far as world opinion was concerned, the country seemed to be a superpower out of control, employing the latest military technology in a futile effort to impose democracy on a nation barely out of the stone age.

Between 1964 and 1977, four American presidents struggled with these overwhelming problems. Lyndon Johnson's Great Society was eventually destroyed by what he called "that bitch of a war." Richard Nixon left the White House in disgrace after the Watergate tapes proved his complicity in perjury and obstructing justice. Gerald Ford failed in his WIN campaign—whip inflation now—and then watched helplessly as the last Americans, fleeing the invading North Vietnamese troops, took off in helicopters from the roof of the U.S. embassy in Saigon. Jimmy Carter left the White House in 1977 after trying unsuccessfully to get Americans to accept the idea of austerity, shortages, and reduced expectations. The hostage crisis in Iran seemed the final symbol of American impotency. Not until the late 1980s, with Vietnam receding into history, oil prices dropping, inflation subsiding, and Ronald Reagan in the White House, did the United States recapture its legendary optimism about the future.

READING 24

★ ★ ★

Why the Shirelles Mattered

Susan J. Douglas

Rock and roll in the 1950s and 1960s was charged with testosterone. Sung by Elvis Presley, Chuck Berry, Jerry Lee Lewis, and the Beatles, it emphasized rebellion and sexuality. Rockers dressed in leather, rejected bourgeois culture, and viewed monogamy as a capital crime. Women, though occasionally idealized, were generally treated as objects designed for the satisfaction of males. Consider a few of Presley's Gold records—"I Want You, I Need You, I Love You," "Don't Be Cruel," "Love Me Tender," "Any Way You Want Me," "Treat Me Nice," "It's Now or Never," "Surrender," "Are You Lonesome Tonight?" The titles suggest sex but not marriage, satisfaction but not commitment. They act as windows to a world of male fantasies—selfish, aching, insistent.

In the 1960s, Top 40 radio stations also gave females' fantasies air time. Such groups as the Bobbettes, the Chantels, the Crystals, the Marvelettes, the Chiffons, the Shangri-Las, the Supremes, the Ronettes, and the Shirelles— collectively known as "girl groups"—recorded songs that spoke to the dreams and fears of teenage girls. In such songs as "Will You Love Me Tomorrow?" "He's So Fine," "Sweet Talkin' Guy," "I Will Follow Him," "I Wanna Be Bobby's Girl," and "Wishin' and Hopin'," female singers address female audiences, asking questions about sex, independence, and longings. In the following selection from her book *Where the Girls Are: Growing Up Female with the Mass Media*, Susan J. Douglas presents an insightful reading of the girl groups, suggesting that they were a bridge toward an important liberation movement.

O K—here's a test. Get a bunch of women in their thirties and forties and put them in a room with a stereo. Turn up the volume to the "incurs temporary deafness" level and play "Will You Love Me Tomorrow" and see how many know the words—all the words—by heart. If the answer is 100 percent, these are bona fide American baby boomers. Any less, and the group has been infiltrated by impostors, pod people, Venusians. But even more interesting is the fact that non–baby boomers, women both older and younger than my generation, adore this music too, and cling to the lyrics like a life raft.

Why is it that, over thirty years after this song was number one in the country, it still evokes in us such passion, such longing, such euphoria, and such an irresistible desire to sing very loudly off key and not care who hears us? And it's not just this song, it's girl group music in general, from "He's So Fine" to "Nowhere to Run" to "Sweet Talkin' Guy." Today, the "oldies" station is one of the most successful FM formats going, in no small part because when these songs come on the radio, baby boomers get that faraway, knowing, contented look on their faces that prompts them to scream along with the lyrics while running red lights on the way home from work. None of this is silly—there's a good reason why, even on our deathbeds, we'll still know the words to "Leader of the Pack."

First of all, girl group music was really about us—girls. When rock 'n' roll swiveled onto the national scene in the mid-1950s and united a generation in opposition to their parents, it was music performed by rebellious and sexually provocative young men. Elvis Presley was, of course, rock 'n' roll's most famous and insistently masculine star—in 1956, five of the nine top singles of the year were by Elvis. At the same time, there would be weeks, even months, when no woman or female group had a hit among the top fifteen records.

When women in the fifties did have hits, they were about the moon, weddings, some harmless dreamboat, like Annette's "Tall Paul," or maybe about kissing. But they were never, ever about doing the wild thing.

Then, in December 1960, the Shirelles hit number one with "Will You Love Me Tomorrow"; it was the first time a girl group, and one composed of four black teenagers, had cracked the number one slot. And these girls were not singing about doggies in windows or old Cape Cod. No, the subject matter here was a little different. They were singing about whether or not to go all the way and wondering whether the boyfriend, so seemingly full of heartfelt, earnest love in the night, would prove to be an opportunistic, manipulative, lying cad after he got his way, or whether he would, indeed, still be filled with love in the morning. Should the girl believe everything she'd heard about going all the way and boys losing respect for girls who did? Or should she believe the boy in her arms who was hugging and kissing her (and doing who knows what else) and generally making her feel real good?

Even though this song was about sex, it didn't rely on the musical instrument so frequently used to connote sex in male rockers' songs, the saxophone. Saxes were banished, as were electric guitars; instead, an entire string section of an orchestra provided the counterpoint to Shirley Owens's haunting, earthy, and provocative lead vocals. The producer, Luther Dixon, who had previously worked with Perry Como and Pat Boone, even overlaid the drumbeats with violins, so it sounded as if the strings gave the song its insistent, pulsing rhythm. While Owens's alto voice vibrated with teen girl angst and desire, grounding the song in fleshly reality, violin arpeggios fluttered through like birds, and it was on their wings that our erotic desires took flight and gained a more acceptable spiritual dimension. It was this brilliant juxtaposition of the sentimentality of the violins and the sensuality of the voice that made the song so perfect, because it was simultaneously lush and

Susan J. Douglas, *Where the Girls Are: Growing Up Female With the Mass Media* (New York: Random House, 1994).

In the 1960s, the Shirelles used the cross-over look and lyrics that spoke to young female listeners to climb the pop charts.

spare, conformist and daring, euphemistic yet dead-on honest. The tens of millions of girls singing along could be starry-eyed and innocent, but they could also be sophisticated and knowing. They could be safe and sing about love, or dangerous and sing about sex. "Will You Love Me Tomorrow" was about a traditional female topic, love, but it was also about female longing and desire, including sexual desire. And, most important, it was about having a choice. For these girls, the decision to have sex was now a choice, and *this* was new. This was, in fact, revolutionary. Girl group music gave expression to our struggles with the possibilities and dangers of the Sexual Revolution.

What were you to do if you were a teenage girl in the early and mid-1960s, your hormones catapulting you between desire and paranoia, elation and despair, horniness and terror? You didn't know which instincts to act on and which ones to suppress. You also weren't sure whom to listen to since, by the age of fourteen, you'd decided that neither your mother nor your father knew anything except how to say no and perhaps the lyrics to a few Andy Williams songs. For answers—real answers—many of us turned to the record players, radios, and jukeboxes of America. And what we heard were the voices of teenage girls singing about—and dignifying—our most basic concern: how to act around boys when so much seemed up for grabs. What were you to do to survive all those raging hormones? Why, dance, of course.

There's been a lot of talk, academic analysis, and the like about how Elvis Presley and rock 'n' roll made rebelliousness acceptable for boys. But what about the girls? Did girl group music help *us* become rebels? Before you say "no way" and cite "I Will Follow Him," "Chapel of Love," and "I Wanna Be Bobby's Girl" to substantiate your point, hear me out. Girl group music has been denied its rightful place in history by a host of male music critics who've either ignored it or trashed it. Typical is this pronouncement, by one of the contributors to *The Rolling Stone History of Rock & Roll:* "The female group of the early 1960s served to drive the concept of art completely away from rock 'n' roll. . . . I feel this genre represents the low point in the history of rock 'n' roll." Nothing could be more wrong-headed, or more ignorant of the role this music played in girls' lives. It would be ideal if this section of the book were accompanied by a customized CD replaying all these fabulous songs for you. Since that's not possible, I do urge you to listen to this music again, and to hear all the warring impulses, desires, and voices it contained.

By the late 1950s, Tin Pan Alley realized that Perry Como, Doris Day, and Mantovani and his orchestra weren't cutting it with the fastest-growing market segment in America, teenagers. Even Pat Boone was hopelessly square, having foisted on us the insufferable "April Love" and his goody-two-shoes advice book to teens, *'Twixt Twelve and Twenty,* which said kissing "for fun" was dangerous. Music publishers and producers grasped two key trends: rock 'n' roll was here to stay, and

there was this flourishing market out there, not just boys, but girls, millions of them, ready and eager to buy. And they were not buying the Lennon Sisters or Patti Page. At the same time, the proliferation of transistor radios meant that this music could be taken and heard almost everywhere, becoming the background music for our desires, hopes, and fears, the background music to our individual and collective autobiographies.

Teenage songwriters like Carole King and Ellie Greenwich got jobs in the Brill Building in New York, the center of pop music production in America, and in the aftermath of the Shirelles hit, all kinds of girl groups and girl singers appeared, from the pouf-skirted Angels ("My Boyfriend's Back") to the cute and innocent Dixie Cups to the eat-my-dirt, in-your-face, badass Shangri-Las. There was an explosion in what has come to be called "girl talk" music, the lyrics and beat of which still occupy an inordinately large portion of the right—or is it the left?—side of my brain.

The most important thing about this music, the reason it spoke to us so powerfully, was that it gave voice to all the warring selves inside us struggling, blindly and with a crushing sense of insecurity, to forge something resembling a coherent identity. Even though the girl groups were produced and managed by men, it was in their music that the contradictory messages about female sexuality and rebelliousness were most poignantly and authentically expressed. In the early 1960s, pop music became the one area of popular culture in which adolescent female voices could be clearly heard. They sang about the pull between the need to conform and the often overwhelming desire to rebel, about the tension between restraint and freedom, and about the rewards—and costs—of prevailing gender roles. They sang, in other words, about getting mixed messages and about being ambivalent in the face of the upheaval in sex roles. That loss of self, the fusing of yourself with another, larger-than-life persona that girls felt as they sang along was at least as powerful as what they felt in a darkened movie theater. And singing along with one another, we shared common emotions and physical reactions to the music.

This music was, simultaneously, deeply personal and highly public, fusing our neurotic, quivering inner selves with the neurotic, quivering inner selves of others in an effort to find strength and confidence in numbers. We listened to this music in the darkness of our bedrooms, driving around in our parents' cars, on the beach, making out with some boy, and we danced to it—usually with other girls—in the soda shops, basements, and gymnasiums of America. This music burrowed into the everyday psychodramas of our adolescence, forever intertwined with our most private, exhilarating, and embarrassing memories. This music exerted such a powerful influence on us, one that we may barely have recognized, because of this process of identification. By superimposing our own dramas, from our own lives, onto each song, each of us could assume an active role in shaping the song's meaning. Songs that were hits around the country had very particular associations and meanings for each listener, and although they were mass-produced they were individually interpreted. The songs were ours—but they were also everyone else's. We were all alone, but we weren't really alone at all. In this music, we found solidarity as girls.

Some girl group songs, like "I Will Follow Him," allowed us to assume the familiar persona *Cinderella* had trained us for, the selfless masochist whose identity came only from being some appendage to a man. As we sang along with Dionne Warwick's "Walk On By," we were indeed abject martyrs to love, luxuriating in our own self-pity. But other songs addressed our more feisty and impatient side, the side unwilling to sit around and wait for the boy to make the first move. In "tell him" songs like "Easier Said Than Done," "Wishin'

and Hopin'," and, of course, "Tell Him," girls were advised to abandon the time-wasting and possibly boy-losing stance of passively waiting for *him* to make the first move. We were warned that passivity might cost us our man, and we were urged to act immediately and unequivocally, before some more daring girl got there first. Girls were urged to take up a previously male prerogative—to be active agents of their own love lives and to go out and court the boy. Regardless of how girls actually behaved—and I know from personal experience that what was derisively called "boy chasing" was on the rise—now there were lyrics in girls' heads that said, "Don't be passive, it will cost you."

Was being cautious too safe? Was being daring too risky? Girl group music acknowledged—even celebrated—our confusion and ambivalence. Some of us wanted to be good girls, and some of us wanted to be bad. But most of us wanted to get away with being both, and girl group music let us try on and act out a host of identities, from traditional, obedient girlfriend to brassy, independent rebel, and lots in between. We could even do this in the same song, for often the lead singer represented one point of view and the backup singers another, so the very wars raging in our own heads about how to behave, what pose to strike, were enacted in one two-minute hit single.

Few songs capture this more perfectly than one of the true girl group greats, "Sweet Talkin' Guy" by the Chiffons. Here we have a tune about a deceitful and heartless charmer who acts like he loves you one day and moves on to another girl the next. Nonetheless, since he's "sweeter than sugar" (ooh-ooh) with "kisses like wine (oh he's so fine)," this heel is irresistible. The lead singer warns other girls to stay away from such a boy, since he'll only break their hearts, but she also confesses he is "my kinda guy." The female chorus backs her up, acknowledging that it is indeed understandable to be swept up by such a cad.

On the face of it, we have lyrics about the unrequited love of a young woman with, no doubt, a few masochistic tendencies. But the song achieves much more. With the layering of voices over and against one another, some of them alto and some of them soprano, we have a war between resisting such boys and succumbing to them. The music, with its driving beat and a tambourine serving as metronome, is dance music. At the end of the song the layered vocal harmonies run ecstatically up the octaves, like girls running jubilantly across a field, ending with a euphoric chord that suggests, simultaneously, that young female love will win in the end and that it will transcend male brutishness. Singing along to a song like this, girls could change voice, becoming singing ventriloquists for different stances toward the same boy, the same situation. As altos, sopranos, or both, back and forth, we could love and denounce such boys, we could warn against our own victimization, yet fall prey to its sick comforts. We could feel how desire—irresistible, irrational, timeless—was shaping our destinies. The euphoric musical arrangement made us feel even more strongly that the power to love and to dream would enable us somehow to burst through the traps of history. In "Sweet Talkin' Guy," being divided against yourself is normal, natural, true: the song celebrates the fact not just that girls *do* have conflicting subjective stances but that, to get by, they *must*. Yes, we can't help loving them, even when they're bastards, but we have to be able to name how they hurt us, and we must share those warnings with other girls. And if we're dancing while we do it, moving our bodies autonomously, or in unison with other girls, well, maybe we'll escape after all.

Girl group songs were, by turns, boastful, rebellious, and self-abnegating, and through them girls could assume different personas, some of them strong and empowering and others masochistic and defeating. As girls listened to their radios and record players,

they could be martyrs to love ("Please Mr. Postman"), sexual aggressors ("Beechwood 4–5789"), fearsome Amazons protecting their men ("Don't Mess with Bill" and "Don't Say Nothin' Bad About My Baby"), devoted, selfless girlfriends ("My Guy," "I Will Follow Him"), taunting, competitive brats ("Judy's Turn to Cry," "My Boyfriend's Back"), sexual sophisticates ("It's in His Kiss"), and, occasionally, prefeminists ("Don't Make Me Over" and "You Don't Own Me"). The Shirelles themselves, in hit after hit, assumed different stances, from the faithful romantic ("Soldier Boy," "Dedicated to the One I Love") to knowing adviser ("Mama Said," "Foolish Little Girl") to sexual slave ("Baby, It's You"). The songs were about escaping from yet acquiescing to the demands of a male-dominated society, in which men called the shots but girls could still try to give them a run for their money. Girls in these songs enjoyed being looked at with desire, but they also enjoyed looking with desire themselves. The singers were totally confident; they were abjectly insecure. Some songs said do and others said don't. Sometimes the voice was of an assertive, no-nonsense girl out to get the guy or showing off her boyfriend to her friends. At other times, the voice was that of the passive object, yearning patiently to be discovered and loved. Often the girl tried to get into the boy's head and imagined the boy regarding her as the object of his desire. Our pathetic struggles and anxieties about popularity were glamorized and dignified in these songs.

In girl group music, girls talked to each other confidentially, primarily about boys and sex. The songs took our angst-filled conversations, put them to music, and gave them a good beat. Some songs, like "He's So Fine" (doo lang, doo lang, doo lang), picked out a cute boy from the crowd and plotted how he would be hooked. In this song the choice was clearly hers, not his. Songs also recreated images of a clot of girls standing around in their mohair sweaters assessing the male talent and, well, looking over boys the way boys had always looked over girls. Other songs, like "Playboy" or "Too Many Fish in the Sea," warned girls about two-timing Romeo types who didn't deserve the time of day, and the sassy, defiant singers advised girls to tell boys who didn't treat them right to take a hike. Opening with a direct address to their sisters— "Look here, girls, take this advice"—the Marvelettes passed on what sounded like age-old female wisdom: "My mother once told me something/And every word is true/Don't waste your time on a fella/Who doesn't love you." Urging the listener to "stand tall," the lead singer asserted, "I don't want nobody that don't want me/Ain't gonna love nobody that don't love me."

The absolute necessity of female collusion in the face of thoughtless or mystifying behavior by boys bound these songs together, and bound the listeners to the singers in a knowing sorority. They knew things about boys and love that they shared with each other, and this shared knowledge—smarter, more deeply intuitive, more worldly wise than any male locker room talk—provided a powerful bonding between girls, a kind of bonding boys didn't have. And while boys were often identified as the love object, they were also identified as the enemy. So while some of the identities we assumed as we sang along were those of the traditional, passive, obedient, lovesick girl, each of us could also be a sassy, assertive, defiant girl who intended to have more control over her life—or at least her love life. In numerous advice songs, from "Mama Said" to "You Can't Hurry Love," the message that girls knew a thing or two, and that they would share that knowledge with one another to beat the odds in a man's world, circulated confidently.

Other songs fantasized about beating a different set of odds—the seeming inevitability, for white, middle-class girls, of being married off to some boring, respectable guy with no sense of danger or adventure, someone like David Nelson or one of Fred MacMurray's

three sons. Here we come to the rebel category—"Leader of the Pack," "Uptown," "He's a Rebel," "Give Him a Great Big Kiss," and "He's Sure the Boy I Love." Academic zeros, on unemployment, clad in leather jackets, sporting dirty fingernails, and blasting around on motorcycles, the boy heroes in these songs were every suburban parent's nightmare, the boys they loved to hate. By allying herself romantically and morally with the rebel hero, the girl singer and listener proclaimed her independence from society's predictable expectations about her inevitable domestication. There is a role reversal here, too—the girls are gathered in a group, sharing information about their boyfriends, virtually eyeing them up and down, while the rebel heroes simply remain the passive objects of their gaze and their talk. And the girls who sang these songs, like the Shangri-Las, dressed the part of the defiant bad girl who stuck her tongue out at parental and middle-class authority. The Ronettes, whose beehives scraped the ceiling and whose eyeliner was thicker than King Tut's, wore spiked heels and skintight dresses with slits up the side as they begged some boy to "Be My Baby." They combined fashion rebellion with in-your-face sexual insurrection.

In "Will You Love Me Tomorrow," Shirley Owens asked herself, Should she or shouldn't she? Of course, the question quickly became Should I or shouldn't I? The answer wasn't clear, and we heard plenty of songs in which girls found themselves smack in the grip of sexual desire. Sexuality emerged as an eternal ache, a kind of irresistible, unquenchable tension. But in the early 1960s, sex and sexual desire were still scary for many girls. The way many of these songs were produced—orchestrated with violins instead of with electric guitars or saxophones—muted the sexual explicitness and made it more romantic, more spiritual, more safe. "And Then He Kissed Me" alluded to some kind of new kiss tried on the singer by her boyfriend, one she really liked and wanted to have a lot more of. In "Heat Wave," Martha Reeves sang at the top of her lungs about being swept up in a sexual fever that just wouldn't break, and the whispering, bedroom-voiced lead in "I'm Ready" confessed that she didn't really know quite what she was supposed to do but that she was sure ready to learn—right now. Claudine Clark desperately begged her mother to let her go off to the source of the "Party Lights," where one helluva party was happening, and she sounded like someone who had been in Alcatraz for twenty years and would simply explode if she didn't get out.

The contradictions of being a teenage girl in the early and mid-1960s also percolated from the conflict between the lyrics of the song and the beat of the music. Girl group music had emerged at the same time as all these new dance crazes that redefined how boys and girls did—or, more accurately, did not—dance with each other. Chubby Checker's 1960 hit "The Twist" revolutionized teenage dancing, because it meant that boys and girls didn't have to hold hands anymore, boys didn't have to lead and girls didn't have to follow, so girls had a lot more autonomy and control as they danced. Plus, dancing was one of the things girls usually did much better than boys. As the twist gave way to the locomotion, the Bristol stomp, the mashed potatoes, the pony, the monkey, the slop, the jerk, and the frug, the dances urged us to loosen up our chests and our butts, and learn how to shimmy, grind, and thrust. This was something my friends and I did with gleeful abandon.

Many of us felt most free and exhilarated while we were dancing, so bouncing around to a song like "Chains" or "Nowhere to Run" put us smack-dab between feelings of liberation and enslavement, between a faith in free will and a surrender to destiny. Both songs describe prisoners of love, and if you simply saw the lyrics without hearing the music, you'd think they were a psychotherapist's notes from a session with a deeply paranoid young

woman trapped in a sadomasochistic relationship. Yet with "Chains," sung by the Cookies, girls were primed for dancing from the very beginning by the hand clapping, snare drums, and saxophones, so that the music worked in stark contrast to the lyrics, which claimed that the girl couldn't break free from her chains of love. Then, in a break from the chorus, the lead singer acknowledged, "I wanna tell you pretty baby/Your lips look sweet/I'd like to kiss them/But I can't break away from all of these chains." At least two personas emerge here, coexisting in the same teenager. One is the girl who loves the bittersweet condition of being hopelessly consumed by love. The other is the girl who, despite her chains, has a roving and appreciative eye for other boys. The conflict between the sense of entrapment in the lyrics and the utter liberation of the beat is inescapable. The tension is too delicious for words.

It was the same for one of the greatest songs ever recorded, "Nowhere to Run." The opening layers of drums, horns, and tambourines propelled us out onto the dance floor—I mean, you couldn't not dance to this song. While we were gyrating and bouncing around to a single about a no-good boy who promised nothing but heartache yet had us in his sadistic grip, we were as happy as we could be. The best part was the double entendre lyrics in the middle, which we belted out with almost primal intensity. "How can I fight a love that shouldn't be?/When it's so deep—so deep—it's deep inside of me/My love reaches so high I can't get over it/So wide, I can't get around it, no." In the face of our entrapment, Martha Reeves made us sweat, and celebrated the capacity of girls to love like women. She also articulated a sophisticated knowingness about how sexual desire overtakes common sense every time, even in girls. In a very different kind of song, the effervescent "I Can't Stay Mad at You," Skeeter Davis told her boyfriend that he could treat her like dirt, make her cry, virtually grind her heart under the heel of his boot, and she'd still love him anyway, and all this between a string of foot-tapping, butt-bouncing shoobie doobie do bops. So even in songs seemingly about female victimization and helplessness, the beat and euphoria of the music put the lie to the lyrics by getting the girl out on the dance floor, moving on her own, doing what she liked, displaying herself sexually, and generally getting ready for bigger and better things. Dancing to this music together created a powerful sense of unity, of commonality of spirit, since we were all feeling, with our minds and our bodies, the same enhanced emotions at the same moment.

While a few girl groups and individual singers were white—the Angels, the Shangri-Las, Dusty Springfield—most successful girl groups were black. Unlike the voices of Patti Page or Doris Day, which seemed as innocent of sexual or emotional angst as a Chatty Cathy doll, the vibrating voices of black teenagers, often trained in the gospel traditions of their churches, suggested a perfect fusion of naivete and knowingness. And with the rise of the civil rights movement, which by 1962 and 1963 dominated the national news, black voices conveyed both a moral authority and a spirited hope for the future. These were the voices of exclusion, of hope for something better, of longing. They were not, like Annette or the Lennon Sisters, the voices of sexual repression, of social complacency, or of homogenized commercialism.

From the Jazz Age to rap music, African American culture has always kicked white culture upside the head for being so pathologically repressed; one consequence, for black women, is that too often they have been stereotyped as more sexually active and responsive than their white-bread sisters. Because of these stereotypes, it was easier, more acceptable, to the music industry and no doubt to white culture at large that black girls, instead of white ones, be the first teens to give voice to girls' changing attitudes toward sex.

But since the sexuality of black people has always been deeply threatening to white folks, black characters in popular culture also have been desexualized, the earth-mother mammy being a classic example. The black teens in girl groups, then, while they sounded orgiastic at times, had to look feminine, innocent, and as white as possible. Berry Gordy, the head of Motown, knew this instinctively, and made his girl groups take charm school lessons and learn how to get into and out of cars, carry their handbags, and match their shoes to their dresses. They were trapped, and in the glare of the spotlight, no less, between the old and new definitions of femininity. But under their crinolined skirts and satin cocktail dresses, they were also smuggling into middle-class America a taste of sexual liberation. So white girls like me owe a cultural debt to these black girls for straddling these contradictions, and for helping create a teen girl culture that said, "Let loose, break free, don't take no shit."

The Shirelles paved the way for the decade's most successful girl group, the Supremes, who had sixteen records in the national top ten between 1964 and 1969. But of utmost importance was the role Diana Ross played in making African American beauty enviable to white girls. As slim as a rail with those cavernous armpits, gorgeous smile, and enormous, perfectly made-up eyes, Diana Ross is the first black woman I remember desperately wanting to look like, even if some of her gowns were a bit too Vegas. I couldn't identify with her completely, not because she was black, but because when I was fourteen, she seemed so glamorous and sophisticated. Ross has taken a lot of heat in recent years as the selfish bitch who wanted all the fame and glory for herself, so it's easy to forget her importance as a cultural icon in the 1960s. But the Supremes—who seemed to be both girls and women, sexy yet respectable, and a blend of black and white culture—made it perfectly normal for white girls to idolize and want to emulate their black sisters.

Another striking trend that grew out of the girl group revolution was the proliferation of the male falsetto. From Maurice Williams in "Stay" to Lou Christie in "Two Faces Have I" to Roy Orbison in "Crying" and Randy and the Rainbows in "Denise" (ooo-be-ooo), and most notably with The Four Seasons and The Beach Boys, boys sang in high-pitched soprano ranges more suited for female than for male sing-along. What this meant was that girls belting out lyrics in the kitchen, in the car, or while watching *American Bandstand* had the opportunity to assume *male* roles, male subjective stances as they sang, even though they were singing in a female register.

This was nothing less than musical cross-dressing. While the male falsettos sang of their earnest love for their girls, about how those girls got them through the trials and tribulations of parental disputes, loneliness, drag-car racing ("Don't Worry Baby"), or being from the wrong side of the tracks, girls could fantasize about boys being humanized, made more nurturing, compassionate, and sensitive through their relationships with girls. This is an enduring fantasy, and one responsible for the staggeringly high sales of romance novels in America. It was a narcissistic fantasy that the girl was at the center of someone's universe, that she did make a difference in that universe, and that that difference was positive. This practice of assuming male voices later enabled girls to slip in and out of male points of view, sometimes giving girls a temporary taste of power. Several years later, in a song much maligned by feminists, "Under My Thumb," girls could and did sing not as the one under the thumb but as the one holding the thumb down.

While girl group music celebrated love, marriage, female masochism, and passivity, it also urged girls to make the first move, to rebel against their parents and middle-class conventions, and to dump boys who didn't treat them right. Most of all, girl group music—precisely because these were groups, not just individual singers—insisted that it was critically important for girls to band together, talking about men, singing about men, trying to figure them out.

What we have here is a pop culture harbinger in which girl groups, however innocent and commercial, anticipate women's groups, and girl talk anticipates a future kind of women's talk. The consciousness-raising groups of the late sixties and early seventies came naturally to many young women because we'd had a lot of practice. We'd been talking about boys, about loving them and hating them, about how good they often made us feel and how bad they often treated us, for ten years. The Shirelles mattered because they captured so well our confusion in the face of changing sexual mores. And as the confusion of real life intersected with the contradictions in popular culture, girls were prepared to start wondering, sooner or later, why sexual freedoms didn't lead to other freedoms as well.

Girl group music gave us an unprecedented opportunity to try on different, often conflicting, personas. For it wasn't just that we could be, as we sang along first with the Dixie Cups and then the Shangri-Las, traditional passive girls one minute and more active, rebellious, even somewhat prefeminist girls the next. Contradiction was embedded in almost all the stances a girl tried on, and some version, no matter how thwarted, of prefeminism, constituted many of them. We couldn't sustain this tension forever, especially when one voice said, "Hey, hon, you're equal" and the other voice said, "Oh no, you're not."

The Shirelles and the other girl groups mattered because they helped cultivate inside us a desire to rebel. The main purpose of pop music is to make us feel a kind of euphoria that convinces us that we can transcend the shackles of conventional life and rise above the hordes of others who do get trapped. It is the euphoria of commercialism, designed to get us to buy. But this music did more than that; it generated another kind of euphoria as well. For when tens of millions of young girls started feeling, at the same time, that they, as a generation, would not be trapped, there was planted the tiniest seed of a social movement.

Few symbols more dramatically capture the way young women in the early 1960s were pinioned between entrapment and freedom than one of the most bizarre icons of the period, the go-go girl dancing in a cage. While African American performers like the Dixie Cups or Mary Wells sang on *Shindig* or *Hullabaloo*, white girls in white go-go boots pranced and shimmied in their cages in the background. Autonomous yet objectified, free to dance by herself on her own terms yet highly choreo-graphed in her little prison, seemingly indifferent to others yet trapped in a voyeuristic gaze, the go-go girl seems, in retrospect, one of the sicker, yet more apt, metaphors for the teen female condition during this era. It's not surprising that when four irreverent, androgynous, and irresistible young men came over from England and incited a collective jailbreak, millions of these teens took them up on it. For we had begun to see some new kinds of girls in the mass media—some perky, some bohemian, some androgynous—who convinced us that a little anarchy was exactly what we, and American gender roles, needed.

Study Questions

1. What were Americans' popular views on sexuality in the late 1950s and early 1960s?

2. How did the lyrics and beat of music in the early and mid-1960s reflect the contradictions of being a teenage girl?

3. Why did African-American females become the popular choice for the voice and look of the new sexualized music?

4. What was it about girl groups, like the Shirelles or Supremes, that attracted young white female audiences?

5. How did girl groups of the 1960s pave the way for other music in that decade?

Bibliography

This piece comes from Susan J. Douglas, *Where the Girls Are: Growing Up Female with the Mass Media* (1994). For more on the Shirelles and other girl groups of this period, see Charolette Greig, *Will You Still Love Me Tomorrow* (1989). Susan McClary, *Feminine Endings: Music, Gender, and Sexuality* (1991) provides an impressive examination of the interconnections between female artists and sexuality in this period. Nelson George, *Where Did Love Go?: The Rise and Fall of the Motown Sound* (1985) and Suzanne Smith, *Dancing in the Street: Motown and the Cultural Politics of Detroit* (1999) present wonderful studies on the conditions of African-American artists in the 1950s and 1960s. Several excellent general overviews of the history of rock and roll have been published in recent years, including Paul Friedlander, *Rock and Roll: A Social History* (1996) and David P. Szatmary, *Rockin' in History: A Social History of Rock and Roll* (2000). For a general overview of the 1960s, see Alexander Broom, ed., *"Takin' It to the Streets": A Sixties Reader* (2004).

READING 25

★ ★ ★

Boomer Century

Joshua Zeitz

In the last half-century we have become accustomed to speaking of generations—"the Greatest Generation," "the Baby Boomers," "Generation X"—as if every member of the particular group enjoyed a common cultural gene pool. One generation willingly sacrificed, another sought self-fulfillment and self-satisfaction, and yet another searched for a defining characteristic. Are such generational generalizations merely glib labels, or do they contain more than a germ of truth? Certainly the Baby Boomers—the Americans born between 1946 and 1964—have been poked and prodded like laboratory mice. Historians, political scientists, sociologists, psychologists, and cultural critics have studied them. Self-appointed experts have credited them with ennobling flights of idealism and pitiful spirals of greed.

In "Baby Boomers," Joshua Zeitz reexamines this already much-examined generation. It was America's largest generation, a generation raised in a time of prosperity and rising expectations. It was the generation that bought Hula-Hoops, Davy Crockett raccoon-skin hats, and Barbie and Ken dolls; that listened to the Beatles, Beach Boys, and Rolling Stones; that watched *The Graduate, Easy Rider,* and *American Graffiti*; that fought in and protested against the war in Vietnam; and that marched for civil rights for African Americans, women, gays, and other groups who were not sharing in the American Dream. It displayed the best and worst of American culture. But was it unique in that regard?

On December 31, as millions of Americans don party hats and pop champagne corks to usher in the New Year, Kathleen Casey, the Philadelphia-born daughter of a Navy machinist and his wife, will likely find her phone once again ringing off the hook. It happens every decade or so. Journalists and academics and earnest civic leaders, family and friends, all find their way to Casey's doorstep, hoping for just a few minutes of her time, eager to glean a little bit of wisdom about *what it all means* and *where it's all going*.

Kathleen Casey, you see, bears the unique distinction of having launched the baby boom.

Born at 12:01 A.M. on January 1, 1946, she was the first of 76 million Americans brought into the world between 1946 and 1964, when, in a sharp reversal of a steady century-long decline, the national birthrate skyrocketed, creating a massive demographic upheaval.

So this year the very first baby boomer, the vanguard of that endlessly youthful generation, turns 60. But hers is not like other generations. If its last, unrecorded member was born at 11:59 P.M. on December 31, 1964, he or she will just be turning 41. Certainly this person, the Unknown Boomer, will have encountered very different cultural signposts than did Kathleen Casey (say, Pat Boone vs. the Sex Pistols), but together the two of them bracket a group that, despite its immensity, is strangely unified, and whose influence today defines both the limits and the promise of American life—and will for years to come.

Last summer, 40 years after "(I Can't Get No) Satisfaction" climbed to the top of *Billboard's* singles chart and earned the Rolling Stones their first gold release in the United States, the Stones launched their 2005 World Tour at Boston's Fenway Park. For tens of thousands of boomers who came to see Mick Jagger and Keith Richards perform the greatest hits of yesteryear, age really *is* just a number.

Their kids might have been mortified to see these graying veterans of the 1960s filling a ballpark for one last great rock 'n' roll show. But in many ways, it all makes sense. There is still no more fitting anthem for the baby-boom generation than the Stones' signature hit.

Raised in an era of unprecedented affluence and national omnipotence, but coming of age in a time that perceived more limited resources and diminished American power, the boomers have long been defined by a vain search for satisfaction. No matter how much they have, they can't ever seem to get enough. This quest for satisfaction has at times led to nadirs of narcissism and greed. As a generation the boomers have always seemed to want it all: cheap energy, consumer plenty, low taxes, loads of government entitlements, ageless beauty, and an ever-rising standard of living. They inherited a nation flush with resources and will bequeath their children a country mired in debt.

But their quest for personal satisfaction has also pushed the boundaries of civic life in radical and unusual directions. In their youth, black and white boomers took to the streets to tear down the walls of racial segregation. They strove toward greater equality of opportunity between men and women, made it harder for policymakers to choose war over peace without first convincing a skeptical electorate of its merits, and created a nation that was more accepting of diversity.

For all their faults and all their virtues, they remain exemplars of what Henry Luce called the American Century. The social commentators Neil Howe and William Strauss got it exactly right when they wrote that "from V-J Day forward, whatever age bracket Boomers have occupied has been the cultural and spiritual focal point for American society as a whole. Through their childhood, America was child-obsessed; in their youth, youth-obsessed; in their 'yuppie'

Joshua Zeitz, "Boomer Century," in *American Heritage* (October 2005), pp. 32–48.

Dr. Benjamin Spock, shown here with a group of children, influenced the way children were raised in post-1945 America. His book, The Common Sense Book of Baby and Child Care *was a runaway bestseller and the primary handbook for new mothers.*

phase, yuppie-obsessed." Maybe Luce had it wrong. It wasn't the American Century. It was the Boomer Century.

Scholars continue to marvel at the phenomenon known as the baby boom. It seemed then, and seems now, to fly in the face of modern demographic and social history. Between 1800 and 1920 the number of children borne by the average American woman fell by more than half, from roughly seven to three. As America transformed itself from a nation of small farmers into an urban, industrial behemoth, increasing numbers of parents no longer needed small armies of children to work the family farm. In this new world of machine and factory, surplus children were a liability. They required much in the way of food, clothing, and shelter but contributed very little in turn to the economic well-being of their families.

The national birthrate, long on the decline, bottomed out in the 1930s. With unemployment running as high as 25 percent, many young Americans, facing an uncertain economic future, decided to put off marriage and parenthood until better days.

When those better days finally arrived in 1940, courtesy of America's swift and total mobilization for war, most commentators expected only a temporary upsurge in births. The editors of *Life* magazine worried that by 1970 the Soviet Union's population would outstrip that of the United States, Britain, France, and Italy combined. They were taken completely by surprise at the magnitude and duration of what actually followed.

Beginning in 1942 with so-called furlough babies, taking off in May 1946—nine months after V-J Day—and peaking around 1947 or 1948, when an American child was born every eight seconds, the GI generation broke sharply with a century-long demographic trend toward smaller families. The population boom also hit Australia, Canada, and New Zealand, whose economies enjoyed a postwar expansion similar to (though not on scale with) America's, but not Europe, large portions of which lay in ruins. Little wonder, then, that a British visitor traveling in the United States in 1958 observed with something like amazement that "every other young housewife I see is pregnant."

Though its causes continue to puzzle scholars, the baby boom probably grew from three distinct trends.

First, in the prosperous 1940s and 1950s, thirtyish Americans who had postponed marriage and children during the Great Depression were eager to make up for lost time and start building families. They crowded the field 10 years after they would normally have contributed their share of progeny to the national population.

Second, they were joined by a younger cohort, including many recently demobilized GIs who had come home to find economic prosperity, generous government assistance in the form of housing and educational benefits for veterans, and a general sense of optimism born of conquering global fascism. For these young victors, many still in their early twenties, it made little sense to put off marriage and family. Like their older brothers and sisters, they understood that the years of Depression scarcity and wartime sacrifice were over.

Finally, and in a more subtle way, the general euphoria that drove up marriage and birthrates was soon complemented by Cold War–era anxieties over nuclear competition. In an uncertain world, the comforts of home and hearth could provide a salve against atomic angst, just as the stabilizing influence of marriage and parenthood offered a strategic advantage in the nation's struggle against communism.

Noting the dangers posed by the Cold War, two Harvard sociologists informed the Ford Foundation that the "world is like a volcano that breaks out repeatedly. . . . The world approaches this critical period with a grave disruption of the family system. . . . The new age demands a stronger, more resolute and better equipped individual. . . . To produce such persons will demand a reorganization of the present family system and the building of one that is stronger emotionally and morally." Ultimately, if Americans wanted to do their part in this new global war, they'd settle down, have lots of kids, and raise them to do well in school and well in life.

Even household architecture seemed to reinforce the relationship between Cold War worries and the cult of domesticity in which the baby boom prospered. The standard suburban ranch house favored by many young families in the 1950s was set back from the street and protected by a fence, and it had a low-slung roof and an attached carport, lending it a bit of the appearance of a well-fortified bunker.

Not just homes, but the children who were starting to crawl through them, formed a "defense—an impregnable bulwark" against the horrors of the atomic age, the social commentator Louisa Randall Church argued in 1946. Many Americans seemed to agree, and out of this vague combination of economic optimism and atomic unease, they were fruitful, and they multiplied.

Their children—the boomers—were necessarily a heterogeneous lot. America still suffered from deep racial and economic divisions. A country as large as the United States contained a host of distinctive regional folkways. Still, as the cultural critic Annie Gottlieb has observed, for all their differences, the baby boomers formed a distinctive "tribe with its roots in time, rather than place or race." By any measure, the America in which they grew up was more abundant, more powerful, and more enraptured with its own glory than ever before. When John F. Kennedy called on his countrymen to "explore the stars, conquer the deserts, eradicate disease, tap the ocean depths, and encourage the arts and commerce," he echoed the optimism that helped forge the new generation's outlook.

Part of this confidence grew out of America's total victory in World War II and the country's scientific and medical achievements, including Jonas Salk's discovery of a polio vaccine in the early 1950s. But most of it was due to the nation's dynamic economy. Between 1940 and 1960 our gross national product doubled; real wages—and real purchasing power—increased by 30 percent; the portion of owner-occupied homes climbed to 61 percent; four-fifths of American families kept at least one car in the driveway; average life expectancy rose by almost 11 percent; most employees of large firms enjoyed such new benefits as private health insurance, paid vacations, and retirement pensions; and the typical American house held seven times more gadgets and goods than in the 1920s. By 1957 the energy of the American economy led *U.S. News & World Report* to declare that "never had so many people, anywhere, been so well off." When Richard Nixon famously sparred with Nikita Khrushchev at the 1959 American National Exhibition in Moscow and proclaimed the superiority of the American suburban kitchen, with its sleek electric appliances in their myriad styles and models, he articulated a vague but popular sense that America's consumer abundance was a sure sign of its Cold War advantage.

For boomer children, this cornucopia translated into billions of dollars' worth of Hula-Hoops, Davy Crockett raccoon-skin hats, Hopalong Cassidy six-shooters, bicycles and tricycles, Slinkys, Silly Putty, and skateboards (and, in California, the shining lure of

Disneyland). The writer Joyce Maynard remembered that when the Barbie doll made its debut in 1959, her world changed "like a cloudburst, without preparation. Barbie wasn't just a toy, but a way of living that moved us suddenly from tea parties to dates with Ken at the soda shoppe." Relatively speaking, to grow up a middle-class American kid in the 1950s meant wanting for nothing.

It also meant television in just four years, between 1948 and 1952, the number of American households with TV sets jumped from 172,000 to 15.3 million. T. S. Eliot observed that television was "a medium of entertainment which permits millions of people to listen to the same joke at the same time, and yet remain lonesome," but for the millions of children raised on it, the new device offered up endless hours of entertainment in the form of family sitcoms like "The Adventures of Ozzie and Harriet," "Father Knows Best," and "Leave It to Beaver," all of which idealized the carefree, child-centered world of suburban America.

More popular still were the Westerns: "Gunsmoke," "Wyatt Earp," "Bonanza," "The Texan," "Wagon Train," "Cheyenne," "The Rifleman," "The Outcasts," "Wanted: Dead or Alive," "Have Gun, Will Travel." Together, these serial epics captured close to half of America's weekly television audience and, by the end of the decade, constituted 7 of the 11 most popular shows on the small screen. The programs mythologized the rugged individualism and physical strength of the American frontiersman, who tamed both his enemy (the Indian or outlaw standing in for the Soviet menace) and the natural environment. It was a genre well suited for a country confident of its ability to reach the stars, vanquish disease, and collapse the limits of time and space.

Complementing this message of abundance and conquest were new vogues in child rearing and pedagogy rooted in John Dewey's ideas about the merits of progressive education. They entered the mainstream in 1946, when Benjamin Spock published *The Common Sense Book of Baby and Child Care*. His book instructed the parents of the baby-boom generation to go light on punishment and heavy on reason and persuasion, and to bear in mind that their daughters' and sons' happiness was the paramount objective of child rearing. If Johnny steals someone's toy, don't hit him. Explain that stealing is wrong, and buy him the toy that he coveted. If Suzie misbehaves at the dinner table, don't worry. Table manners are overrated.

Spock was enormously influential. A study conducted in 1961 revealed that two-thirds of new mothers surveyed had read his book. He made permissive or child-centered parenting mandatory for millions of new postwar middle-class families. By the mid-1950s his message was routinely echoed in the pages of *Parents* magazine and found confirmation in countless sociological studies.

In later years critics would decry the effects of progressive child rearing, some of them crediting it with an entire generation's egotism. The iconoclastic historian Richard Hofstadter worried that America would be overrun by the "overvalued child." Writing of the typical GI generation mother, the novelist Lisa Alther lamented: "If anything had been drummed into her in years of motherhood, it was that you mustn't squelch the young. It might squelch their precious development. Never mind about your own development."

Hyperbole aside, millions of boomers *did* grow up in prosperous, nurturing homes in which children formed the core of the family. Raised amid plenty, taught to value their needs and satisfy their wants, and imbued with a sense of national greatness and purpose, it would have been odd had they not entered young adulthood with at least some sense of entitlement.

In 1956, noting the connection between postwar vogues in Freudian analysis and progressive child rearing, the literary critic Alfred Kazin was bemused by the national "insistence on individual fulfillment, satisfaction and happiness." Years later the pollster Daniel Yankelovich observed that grown boomers, instead of asking themselves, "Will I be able to make a living?," as their parents, raised in the Depression years, often did, were more prone to wonder, "How can I find self-fulfillment?"

No American generation has been so intensely studied, so widely celebrated, and so roundly condemned as this one. Out of the cacophony of analysis, two standard criticisms—one from the left, the other from the right—stand out.

For contemporary liberals, popular films like *The Big Chill* and television series like "thirty-something" follow a familiar narrative line in which idealistic, socially committed children of the sixties grow into self-centered, blandly acquisitive adults. In the words of the former sixties activist Todd Gitlin, by the 1980s a generation that once raged against "banality, irrelevance, and all the ugliness which conspire to dwarf or extinguish the human personality" had graduated from "*J'accuse* to Jacuzzi."

Even when television boomers retained their fundamental goodness—think, for instance, of Michael J. Fox's parents, Elise and Steven Keaton, in the popular 1980s sitcom "Family Ties"—they remained painfully conscious of their generation's potential drift toward self-absorption.

To conservatives, on the other hand, the generation embodies the evils of secular liberalism. In *Slouching Towards Gomorrah*, Robert Bork credits the pampered baby-boom generation with virtually every insidious social trend in recent American history. "The dual forces of radical egalitarianism . . . and radical individualism (the drastic reduction of limits to personal gratification)," explains the book's back cover, have "undermined our culture, our intellect, and our morality."

Of course, traditionalists don't have to look far to make their case. Boomers are certainly more tolerant than their parents of looser personal mores. In 1983, 44 percent of them approved of cohabitation outside marriage, 29 percent supported legalizing marijuana, and 37 percent endorsed casual sex. Whereas only a quarter of Americans approved of premarital sex in the 1950s, by the 1970s that figure had climbed to three-quarters.

More recently, boomers from left and right have begun weaving a third critique. In an effort of historical revision that comes close to self-flagellation, they have begun to worship their parents' generation. That the "GI Generation" has become "the Greatest Generation" is evident everywhere—in popular television series like "Band of Brothers," in films like *Saving Private Ryan*, and in official tributes, such as the World War II memorial in Washington, D.C. Offered by the children of G.I. Joe and Rosie the Riveter, these accolades carry an implicit message: Try as we may, we will simply never measure up to our parents' self-sacrificing greatness.

The problem with all these critiques is that they ignore both the creative use to which the generation has sometimes put its terrific sense of entitlement and the continuities between sixties idealism and eighties excess.

In February 1960, when four black college students staged a sit-in at a Woolworth's lunch counter in Greensboro, North Carolina, sparking a national campaign and inaugurating a decade of youth-driven political activism, they were doing nothing so much as demanding access to the same entitlements that other children of the postwar era claimed as their American birthright. A sympathetic advertisement appearing in three Atlanta newspapers in March 1960 hit the nail on the head when it explained "the meaning of the sit-down protests that are sweeping this nation": "Today's youth will not sit by submissively, while being denied all of the rights, privileges, and joys of life." Raised on the same television advertisements and political rhetoric as their white peers, young black Americans were determined to get their piece of satisfaction.

In a country where happiness and dignity were so inextricably bound up with the individual's right to enjoy the blessings of the national wealth, this argument resonated. In his "Letter from Birmingham Jail," Martin Luther King Jr., the father of young baby boomers of his own, drove home this point. He spoke of finding your "tongue twisted and your speech stammering as you seek to explain to your six-year-old daughter why she can't go to the public amusement park that has just been advertised on television, and see tears welling up in her eyes when she is told that Funtown is closed to colored children."

The legions of junior high and high school students who heeded his call in Birmingham—who filled the jails, attended the prayer meetings, and drove King himself to embrace more radical tactics and demands—ultimately compelled the nation to confront long-standing inequities that "the Greatest Generation" had been content to ignore.

They were the shock troops of the 1960s rights revolution. Like their white peers, these boomer kids had seen an average of 500 hours of television advertisements by the age of 6 and over 300,000 commercials by the age of 21. (King's daughter had clearly seen an ad for Funtown.)

In the aftermath of the Newark riots of 1967, the black poet Amiri Baraka told a state investigatory commission that the "poorest black man in Newark, in America, knows how white people live. We have television sets; we see movies. We see the fantasy and the reality of white America every day." The schism between fantasy and reality could inspire a truly creative tension.

And so it went for other boomers as well. Young black activists influenced women, gays and lesbians, students, welfare recipients, Latinos, and American Indians to appreciate the gap between America's lofty democratic promise and its imperfect reality, and to work to narrow that gap.

By the 1970s boomer rights activists forced changes in credit laws, so that married women could have their own credit cards, and pushed for the enactment of Title IX, which broke down gender barriers in education and athletics. In forcing a new liberalization of sex and romance, they insisted on everyone's right to satisfaction and self-realization—not just married couples but also unmarried partners, no matter what their sexual orientation. They played an instrumental role in bringing down a U.S. President, Lyndon Johnson, and in making the Vietnam War increasingly untenable for his successor, Richard Nixon.

In other words, the generation raised on Spock, television, and abundance put its sense of privilege and entitlement to work for the better good. Today most scholars agree that the boomers will leave their children and grandchildren a country that's a little more just, a little more humane, and a little more inclusive than the one they inherited from their parents.

These accomplishments notwithstanding, it's a small wonder that the generation has accumulated mixed reviews. The radical left is no happier with the boomers than is the reactionary right. In their youth they effected so massive an upheaval in politics and culture that they were bound eventually to fall in the public's esteem. Apostles of what Gitlin has called "the voyage to the interior," and what the late historian and social critic Christopher Lasch derided as a "culture of narcissism," they seemed after the 1960s to place an unusually high premium on self-discovery and personal satisfaction.

The generation that had raged against authority, vowing with Bob Dylan, "I ain't gonna work on Maggie's farm no more," was now swinging to Andrea True's refrain "More, more, more. How do you like it, how do you like it?" They bought minivans, microwaves, and self-help books, embraced transcendental meditation, embarked on various diets, visited tanning salons and fat

farms, and filled their homes with more durable goods than their prosperous parents could ever have imagined.

Even their politics seemed to change. In 1980 it was an eleventh-hour swing among boomer voters that turned Ronald Reagan's razor-thin margin into a landslide victory. In fact, there was always more continuity than the critics liked to admit. Even in 1972, the first year that 18-year-olds were allowed to take part in national elections, fewer than half the eligible new voters bothered to show up at the polls, and just half of those who did cast their lot with the liberal antiwar Democrat George McGovern.

Popular memory notwithstanding, the sixties generation has never been a political monolith. Nor was it uniformly engaged by public issues. Only 20 percent of students who attended college in the late 1960s participated in marches or protests, and far fewer—2 or 3 percent—regarded themselves as activists.

The antiwar movement, which many liberal boomers fondly remember as embodying the altruistic, public spirit of the era, was always more self-interested than its veterans might wish to admit. Whereas virtually every able-bodied, draft-eligible man of the GI generation served in the military during World War II, only 10 percent of the 27 million draft-eligible boomers were in uniform while America fought the Vietnam War. The rest, most of them white and middle class, found creative ways to stay safe. They claimed medical dispensations and student deferments, became schoolteachers or entered defense industries, or married and had children before their local draft boards could sweep them up.

In opposing the war, which many activists did sincerely view as both immoral and unwinnable, protesters betrayed as much selfish entitlement as noble intent. They wanted the United States out of Southeast Asia, but they also wanted to keep *themselves* out of Southeast Asia. Richard Nixon understood this when he shifted the draft burden away from men in their twenties and back onto 18- and

19-year-olds. Suddenly college campuses quieted down. Why bother to protest once you're safely out of the woods?

In effect, for all their racial, economic, and cultural diversity, if the boomers shared anything, it was that perpetual search for satisfaction. In their best moments, and in their worst, they demanded that the country make good on the promises it had handed them in the 1950s. The problem was that when they began to come of age in the 1970s, the bottom fell out on the American economy. Even as they clamored for "more, more, more," what they found was less, less, less. Between the 1960s and 1980s the income of young men just entering the job market declined by 50 percent. This mostly was due to forces beyond anyone's control: Government expenditures for the Vietnam War caused runaway inflation; economic restructuring took a toll on manufacturing; oil shortages in the 1970s drove up energy costs and interest rates. The long slump also came from the gradual erosion of progressive tax policies and growth in entitlements like health insurance.

Ironically, the baby boom was itself a major cause of the nation's economic slide. So many young people seeking jobs drove down wages and accounted for as much as half of the unemployment rate during the 1970s and 1980s. So boomers made the necessary adjustments. To maintain a standard of living that reflected their upbringing, they, like their Depression-bred parents, postponed marriage and children. Though women's wages, once adjusted for changing education and skill levels, remained stagnant in the 1970s and 1980s, the proportion of young married women in the workforce more than doubled, from roughly 30 percent to 70 percent. Two-earner households helped keep pace with the generation's material expectations, but at the expense of outsourcing Generation X to after-school daycare and sports programs.

Even these adjustments fell short. The generation that couldn't get no satisfaction could hardly be expected to live within its means. In 2002 baby boomers spent between 20 percent and 30 percent more money each year than did the average American consumer. In part, this was out of necessity. They had children to feed, houses to furnish, and college tuitions to pay. But the boomers have long stretched the limits of sound household economy. According to the economist Robert Samuelson, between 1946 and 2002 consumer debt climbed from 22 percent of household income to 110 percent. In other words, we've become a debtor nation, and the boomers have presided over this transition.

Now at the height of their political influence (the 2000 presidential election saw the first-ever race between two baby boomers, and the commentators Neil Howe and William Strauss estimate that boomers will hold a plurality in Congress until 2015) they are also presiding over the creation of a national debt that their children and grandchildren will be left to pay off in coming years.

In the end the boomers may be less culpable, less praiseworthy, and less remarkable than they, and everyone else, think. Their cohort was so big, arrived so suddenly, and has grown up so closely alongside the modern broadcast media that they have always struck us as standing apart from larger historical forces that drive the normal workings of states and societies. Yet much about this seeming exceptionalism just isn't new.

When the husband-and-wife sociologist team Robert and Helen Lynd visited Muncie, Indiana, in the early 1920s, they found many of the same traits popularly associated with the boomers already evident among Jazz Age youth. Their famous, pathbreaking book, *Middletown: A Study in Modern American Culture*, reported a younger generation in the thrall of movies and music, willing to stretch the limits of romantic and sexual propriety, obsessed with clothes and cosmetics, and eager to stake out shocking new degrees of personal autonomy.

And if the children of the 1950s were technically the first generation raised on Spock, they weren't the first generation raised on the *ideas* of Spock. By the mid-1930s upward of 75 percent of middle-class men and women were reading advice books that, more often than not, counseled unprecedented attention to the child. Most experts in the 1920s and 1930s had figured out Spock before Spock figured out Spock.

Nor were the boomers the first generation to make therapeutic self-discovery a competitive sport. In their parents' youth, in the twenties and thirties, Freud was already all the rage. Popular books of the day included *The Psychology Golf*, *Psychology of the Poet Shelley*, and *The Psychology of Selling Life Insurance*. Bookstores and mail-order houses peddled new titles like *Psychoanalysis by Mail*, *Psychoanalysis Self-Applied*, *Ten Thousand Dreams Interpreted*, and *Sex Problems Solved*.

Long before the boomers arrived on the scene, Americans were drawn to a new cult of self-improvement that celebrated the mastery of one's deepest impulses and thoughts. In the 1920s millions followed the advice of the French wonder guru, Emile Coué, faithfully repeating the simple catechism "Day by day, in every way, I am getting better and better." The explosion of self-help literature peaked in 1936 with the publication of Dale Carnegie's *How to Win Friends and Influence People*.

If the boomers weren't entirely original in their loosened sexual standards, emphasis on physical appearance and youth, or search for a therapeutic mind cure, neither were they all that unusual in their resistance to collective sacrifice. It hardly diminishes the decisive effort of the World War II generation to note that civilians traded on the black market, deeply resented rationing and wage and labor controls, and often worked in defense production as much for profit as for patriotism.

Even the era's soldiers had mixed reasons for going to war. When *The Saturday Evening Post* ran a series of articles by American GIs entitled "What I Am Fighting For," readers learned that their sons and brothers were in Europe "for that big house with the bright green roof and the big front lawn," their "nice little roadster," pianos, tennis courts, and "the girl with the large brown eyes and the reddish tinge in her hair, that girl who is away at college right now, preparing herself for her part in the future of America and Christianity."

The same conflation of private and public interests drove home-front advertisers to pitch their wares as a just reward for wartime sacrifice—as in an ad promising that "when our boys come home . . . among the finer things of life they will find ready to enjoy will be Johnston and Murphy shoes. Quality unchanged."

None of this suggests that the boomers aren't a distinct category of Americans. If many of the character traits popularly assigned them were in evidence long before they were born—if the boomers were, in fact, walking along the arc of history rather than outside it—still, they have, for good and for ill, made a lasting imprint on the nation.

Social commentators have long been inclined to make sense of the world in generational terms. Writing about his travels in the United States in the 1830s, Alexis de Tocqueville argued that "among democratic nations each new generation is a new people." Roughly 100 years later the social scientist Karl Mannheim similarly observed: "Early impressions tend to coalesce into a natural view of the world."

The boomers—a generation born into national wealth and power, raised on the promise of their limitless potential and self-worth, reared on television and advertising, enthralled by the wonders of modern science and medicine—are, for all their differences, a most potent emblem of the long American Century.

Even today they remain characteristically unfulfilled. Looking for "more, more, more"—for that "satisfaction" that seems forever to elude them—they will, as they have since 1946, stretch the limits of America's possibilities and its resources.

In 2046 we'll still be appraising their work.

Study Questions

1. Why is "(I Can't Get No) Satisfaction" the ideal anthem for the Baby Boom generation?

2. How was the Baby Boom generation a demographic oddity?

3. How did economic prosperity influence the expectations of the Baby Boomers?

4. How did the ideas of Dr. Benjamin Spock influence the Baby Boomers?

5. How is the Baby Boom generation different from the GI generation? What were the greatest accomplishments of each generation?

6. How unique are the Baby Boomers? Were their defining characteristics new?

Bibliography

James T. Patterson, *Grand Expectations: The United States, 1945–1974* (2005), provides a basic narrative of America during the coming of age of the Baby Boomers. Steve M. Gillon, *Boomer Nation: The Largest and Richest Generation Ever and How It Changed America* (2004), examines representatives of the Baby Boom generation and suggests new ways of looking at the whole. Susan Faludi, *Backash: The Undeclared War Against American Women* (1991), explores the trials of female Baby Boomers. Rick Atkinson, *The Long Gray Line: The American Journey of West Point's Class of 1966* (1999), follows the lives of a group of West Point cadets, Baby Boomers who had far more in common with their father's generation than their own.

READING 26

★ ★ ★

Ms. America: Jane Fonda

Peter Braunstein

Jane Fonda was the daughter of a major Hollywood star and the sister of a minor one. As a child John Wayne bounced her on his knee, Jimmy Stewart was a household fixture, and she was familiar with many of the leading actors and actresses of the day. It was natural that after a stint at Vassar, a brief career in modeling, and an education at the Actors' Studio, she too became an actress, making her debut in 1960 in an innocent piece of fluff entitled *Tall Story*. She played the cheerleader girlfriend of her college's basketball star, and she demonstrated a wonderful screen presence. During the next 40 years, she played a series of roles. She was a sex goddess in *Barbarella* (1968), a fragile, destructive call girl in *Klute* (1971), a disillusioned Vietnam veteran's wife in *Coming Home* (1978), and an alcoholic in *The Morning After* (1986). Off the screen, she has also played a series of very public roles, from the political activist wife of radical Tom Hayden to video workout guru to the oddly "traditional" wife of conservative media mogul Ted Turner. Historian Peter Braunstein asks the right question about Jane Fonda: "Who *is* she?" In fact, in her ability to continually reinvent herself, she is a classic example of modern culture.

On the cusp of turning 60 in 1997, Jane Fonda decided to compile a video of highlights in her notably eventful life to present to guests at her forthcoming birthday party. In search of a guiding concept, she turned to her daughter Vanessa and asked for her input. She wasn't prepared, however, for her daughter's reply. "She said to me, 'Why don't you just get a chameleon and let it crawl across the screen?'," Fonda recounts. "Ouch. And so I thought to myself, Is that true. Am I simply a chameleon that changes color according to the times and the men in my life?" Of course, compared with some of the things Jane Fonda has been called, cultural chameleon is positively mild—even flattering. After all, most celebrities enjoy a relatively brief vogue before disappearing from the cultural landscape. By contrast, Jane Fonda's unusual staying power as an active public figure stems from her uncanny ability to adopt the foliage of successive eras of American culture. She was libertine in the mid-sixties, radical by decade's end, progressive in the seventies, entrepreneurial in the eighties, and corporate *grande dame* in the nineties.

It is in fact possible to trace the vicissitudes of American history over the past four decades simply by watching Fonda's public persona multiply and subdivide like so many stock splits. Her nineties incarnation as "Mrs. Ted Turner" might seem an apotheosis, but it was just another identity pit stop for a public figure who is part Zeitgeist receptacle, part historical timeline, and part cultural encyclopedia.

Fonda's tendency to intersect with the larger forces of history may be hereditary. The ancestors of her actor father Henry Fonda were among the first Dutch settlers of what is now upstate New York, where the town of Fonda still stands today. The family of Frances Fonda, Jane's mother, claimed direct descent from Edward Seymour, Duke of Som-

erset, whose sister, Lady Jane Seymour, was the third of King Henry VIII's unfortunate wives. So infatuated was Frances with her regal ancestry that when the Fondas' baby girl was born, in December 1937, Frances christened her Jane Seymour Fonda. It wasn't long before the tomboyish girl rejected her "Lady Jane" epithet because, as she recalls, "It made me feel different."

When Henry Fonda announced in late 1949 that he was leaving his wife for a much younger woman, Frances had a nervous breakdown and was institutionalized in a sanitarium, where she committed suicide. Because Jane was 12 at the time, and her brother, Peter, 10, Henry thought it best to tell them that their mother had died of a heart attack. Jane learned the truth a year later, when a classmate leafing through a movie magazine stumbled on the real story. "I was very powerful for the first 10 years of my life," she recalls today. "I was feisty, I was brave, I had ambition. Then, at the beginning of puberty, it disappeared, and you could have put what was left of me in a thimble."

While Peter learned to act out his childhood trauma, Jane followed her father's lead and dissembled. During her adolescence, she nursed tightly packed emotions that might be let out at a moment's notice—a psychological foundation fit for the soon-to-be actress. She entered Vassar College in the fall of 1955 and quickly earned a reputation as what one observer called a "sophisticated delinquent." Her college antics, such as sneaking off to spend time with boys at Yale, seem mild enough today, but that hasn't kept a rumor from circulating among subsequent generations of Vassar students. It holds that Fonda was once barred from the daily afternoon tea service at Rose Hall because she wasn't wearing the requisite white gloves and pearls, so she promptly left the scene and returned wearing gloves, pearls—and nothing else. "Totally untrue," Fonda insists. Still, it wouldn't be the last time that Fonda's subsequent notoriety would be retroactively projected onto the rest of her life.

Peter Braunstein "Ms. America," *American Heritage* (July/August 2001).

Fonda's ongoing habitation of the American moment began in 1958. Having dropped out of college after her second year, she toyed with the idea of becoming an actress and soon found a teacher in Lee Strasberg, the famous dean of the Actors Studio. Strasberg's "Method" acting regime was at the zenith of its cultural visibility, having influenced such film stars as Montgomery Clift, Paul Newman, and Anne Bancroft. Aspiring actors clamored for entry into the Studio, which accepted only five new members a year for every thousand applicants. Many settled for Strasberg's more accessible private classes, which were seen as a way to get one's foot in the Studio door. Fonda met Strasberg while he was working with Marilyn Monroe, his favorite protégé, on *Some Like It Hot*. After a short interview, she was accepted into the Strasberg fold. "The only reason I took her," Strasberg said, "was her eyes. There was such panic in her eyes."

Strasberg's approach to acting has often been criticized for producing a generation of mumbling, self-enclosed islands of subjectivity, Marlon Brando being a chief example. Yet despite its excesses, Strasberg's philosophy centered on the belief that actors shouldn't play a role so much as inhabit it. As he put it in a 1956 *New York Times Magazine* article, "I stress the difference between the actor who thinks acting is an imitation of life and the actor who feels acting is living. Unless the actor on stage really comes alive, really lives a character, he gives a superficial interpretation." The Method emphasized the importance of empathy, not imitation: One student who was to play a prostitute in a movie was told to go out and sleep with sailors. It was very possibly under Strasberg's tutelage—part dramatic training and part group psychoanalysis—that Fonda mastered the two elements that would make her such an effective harbinger and exemplar of her times: empathy and exhibitionism. The technique that allowed her intuitively to appropriate someone else's subjectivity for the purposes of a screen role would later enable her to conform to, and inhabit, the changing configurations of American culture—to "become" the culture, as it were.

From the high-minded rigor of the Actors Studio, Fonda descended in 1960 into a morass of shallow, forgettable roles, playing a cheerleader in her debut, *Tall Story*, and a "bad girl" in *Walk on the Wild Side*. Fearful of becoming just another Hollywood studio player, she made a bold career move in 1963: She accepted the director René Clément's offer to star in a French film, *Joy House*, opposite Alain Delon. Although eager to work with Clément, Fonda worried about the repercussions of a cinematic identity crafted abroad. "Nobody's ever heard of an American actress making a name for herself by taking off to Europe," her future husband Roger Vadim recalled her saying at the time. But as it turned out, she had unwittingly located the pulse of 1960s cinema.

Fonda chose Paris, which at the time was the capital of New Wave filmmaking, the home of the avant-garde directors Jean-Luc Godard and François Truffaut. "Hollywood had already embarked on a desperate effort to become Europeanized," notes her biographer Thomas Kiernan. "In their attempt to recover their audiences, American films rapidly became infiltrated by the mannerisms of the French style."

One of the masters of the "French style" was the director Roger Vadim, who had launched the career of his wife Brigitte Bardot in the 1956 film *And God Created Woman*. Vadim's entire cultural mission seemed to center on provoking audiences with movies about sexual frankness. He had mastered the art of embedding risqué adult content in scenarios drawn from classic French novels, thereby coating it with a varnish of respectability. As a result, his movies gained distribution in France and the United States under the guise of "art films." Interwoven with his film work was Vadim's reputation as the self-described "pope of hedonism," a reputation reinforced by his fathering children with two of France's most famous female stars, Bardot and Catherine Deneuve. Vadim mused on his ability to attract high-profile women in his notorious autobiography *Bardot Deneuve Fonda*: "For some, the secret was my performance in bed; for others, I was only a vehicle for success; and for still others, I was a Svengali capable of bewitching innocent young girls and molding them as I wished." Repulsed by and then attracted to Vadim for precisely these reasons, Jane Fonda married him in 1965—which also meant starring in his films and serving as iconographic ammunition in Vadim's ongoing crusade against bourgeois sexual morality. "I needed someone to teach me how to be a woman," Fonda remarks today with a laugh, "and I was stupid enough—no, I take that back—superficial enough to think that Vadim would do it. And he taught me a lot, but it's a certain version of womanhood."

It was during the Vadim years that Fonda became, in both France and America, a kind of shorthand signifier for hedonism, decadence, and public nudity. Although she bore no resemblance to Brigitte Bardot either physically or stylistically, the French press quickly dubbed Fonda "la BB americaine" and, fond of animal metaphors, described her as "a young wild thing, galloping too fast" and "the black panther I used to watch in the zoo."

The films she made in France, while successfully endowing her with sought-after European cachet, also tended to reinforce her association with free-loving nudism. American critics like Judith Crist ignored the plot of Vadim's 1966 film *The Game Is Over* and dwelled instead on the near-nudity, dubbing Fonda a "Miss Screen Nude of '67." (Fonda later remarked that, in the United States, "if you do a Dostoyevsky film and take your bra off, you're a sex symbol.") The American distributors of another Vadim/Fonda movie,

Circle of Love, placed an eight-story-high billboard of a nude Fonda atop a Broadway theater, an image not even drawn from the film itself. "What shocked me personally was that the poster was extremely ugly," remarked the relentlessly casual Vadim.

Another example of the almost subliminal association made between Jane Fonda and the new morality was *Newsweek*'s decision to feature a barebacked photo of the actress for a cover story titled "The Permissive Society," evoking her as the child of Eros even though the article barely mentioned her. Questioned by the press about whether she had exhibitionist tendencies, Fonda spontaneously realized that she had been Method living—applying Method acting to the entirety of her life. "I do in life exactly what I do when I act," she admitted, "talking like the character, and so on—as an experiment." The fact that the American public and media conflated her with her vixenish film roles, that she tended to "become" her on-screen self in real life, and that her films reflected the sexual libertinism of the sixties, produced a unique synergy in which Jane Fonda the actress, the person, and the cultural phenomenon all melded into one entity. This fusion of self, image, and culture took hold at the very moment *Barbarella* was released, in 1968.

Barbarella, the kitschy sci-fi hit about a sexually uninhibited space woman, emblazoned her sex-symbol image forever after in the public mind. While *Barbarella* wasn't a "movement movie" like *Bonnie and Clyde*, its free-love ethic implicated it in the cultural revolt sweeping the United States in the form of the hippie counterculture. Looking back on his *Barbarella*-era theories of sexual revolution from the vantage point of the 1980s, Vadim recalled the "aura of intoxication" of the late sixties, where "ancestral rules were on shaky ground," and concluded, "Jane and I were guinea pigs of an unstable era, and we did not know it." As it turned out, it was this very instability that would separate Fonda from Vadim and launch her into the most controversial phase of her life/career.

She had spent several years justifying American foreign policy to Vadim and his French friends, all of whom relentlessly criticized America's intervention in Vietnam. Indeed, she had once been bestowed the title of "Miss Army Recruiting of 1962," whereupon she gave an animated acceptance speech on America's need for a strong military. "I was very defensive," she recalls. "My father had fought in World War II, and I really believed that if our flag was flying somewhere, what we were doing in the name of the flag must be noble." But gradually she came to oppose the Vietnam War. In 1968, pregnant with her first child, Vanessa, during the near-collapse of the de Gaulle government in France, she underwent an epiphany: "In the streets there was revolution, and then there was my own revolution—which childbirth is. I was seeing people in the United States putting their lives on the line to try to end the war, and I realized I wanted to be there." Taking her newborn child with her, she abruptly terminated the French phase of her life, returning to a Hollywood brimming with radical activism.

Nineteen sixty-nine was the year of the radical celebrity in Hollywood. Fonda's brother, Peter, starred in *Easy Rider,* the youth-culture hit that expressed hippie fears of a silent-but-deadly majority, while actors like Marlon Brando and Paul Newman lent support to groups ranging from the Black Panthers to antiwar activists and Native Americans. Fonda landed on U.S. soil and dove headfirst into radical politics, holding press conferences for Huey Newton, visiting Native Americans who had seized Alcatraz, and devoting particular attention to the G.I. Coffeehouse movement, which was attempting to instill antiwar sentiment in U.S. soldiers. This abrupt shift in personas was replicated on-screen. At her most campy and frivolous in *Barbarella,* her next part was that of misanthropic, suicidal Gloria in *They Shoot Horses, Don't They,* perhaps the

most brutally realistic role of her film career. In a prescient commentary, the film critic Pauline Kael wrote, "Jane Fonda stands a good chance of personifying American tensions and dominating our movies in the seventies as Bette Davis did in the thirties." Nominated Best Actress for her harrowing performance, Fonda flashed a Black Panther fist-salute as she strode into the Oscars.

Despite her attempts to distance herself from the frivolity of the Vadim years, the public perceived her newfound radicalism through the prism of her immediately preceding incarnation. "Jane Fonda represented unrestrained sexuality to American audiences," observed the historian David Farber, author of *The Age of Great Dreams: America in the 1960s,* "and now supporters of the war found that sexuality turned against them." Tom Hayden, the antiwar activist whom Fonda married in 1973, theorized that her sex-kitten image, combined with her radical antiwar activism, had left her open to charges of "sleeping with the enemy"—both literally and metaphorically: "All these people expected her to be a certain kind of person who occupied, probably, a large part of their fantasies, and when your fantasy life is threatened, and Barbarella becomes revolutionary, it's very upsetting."

Apart from her being perceived as a Barbarella-gone-bad, much anti-Fonda animus stemmed from the fact that her immersion in radical politics transcended and defied the public roles traditionally assigned to celebrities, film stars, pin-up girls, daughters of famous people, and women in general. Of course, for Fonda herself, this broadening of her public persona was quite intentional— "being a movie star," she was fond of saying at the time, "is not a purpose"—but others believed she had ventured into forbidden territory. Henry Fonda took to referring to her as "my alleged daughter," while Vadim made it clear that she had violated his version of womanhood: "I prefer to be married to a soft and vulnerable woman rather than to an American Joan of Arc." A sardonic 1971 *Life* magazine profile depicted her as a bubble-headed dilettante whose superficial espousal of left-wing politics was everything one would expect from a sex kitten–turned–radical. The misogynist article, entitled "Nag, Nag, Nag! Jane Fonda has become a nonstop activist," ended with the derisory summation, "If Jane Fonda only had a sense of humor, a sense of history and a power base, she could cause a real commotion."

As it turned out, Fonda caused quite a commotion during her infamous visit to Hanoi in the summer of 1972. The trip, conceived as a mission to uncover whether the Nixon administration was in fact bombing the dikes of North Vietnam, ended up as the crucible of her public life. Subjected to routine bombing by American planes, and awed by the determination of the North Vietnamese people, she went completely Method; she "became" North Vietnam. All the earmarks of her actress training came into play: a radical immersion in the subject experience resulting in profound empathy, followed by an exhibitionist portrayal of this newly adopted perspective. But this time, Jane completely forgot about the audience. In one fateful moment, she was photographed laughing with her North Vietnamese hosts while seated on an antiaircraft gun. On the index of self-inflicted character assassination by photograph, the Hanoi image ranked somewhere between the *Life* magazine cover photo of Oswald holding the rifle and the 1988 footage of a helmeted Dukakis inside the Army tank. "The worst thing I ever did in my life" is how Fonda assesses that moment today. "It's the most stupid, naive thing I could have done. I was so swept up in what was happening that I didn't even think that there were photographers there and how it could be interpreted. I will go to my grave regretting that—not going to North Vietnam," she qualifies, "but that photograph."

Ironically, in Barbarella *Jame Fonda struck blows for both the sexual revolution and the feminist movement.*

She returned to an enraged nation. Several states immediately began introducing legislation that would have made "Hanoi Jane" *persona non grata* within their borders. The conservative Manchester (N.H.) *Union-Leader* urged that she be tried for treason and, if found guilty, shot. Some congressmen took this proposal to heart and attempted to prosecute her for treason, sponsoring a House bill—unofficially called the Fonda Amendment to the 1950 Internal Security Act—that would have made it a felony for any citizen to visit a country at war with the United States. Such initiatives foundered on the question of whether the United States was constitutionally at war with Vietnam; nonetheless, Fonda's Hanoi trip transformed her from a wayward celebrity to a permanently controversial national figure.

Whereas the explicit phase of Jane Fonda's activism can be regarded as the death rattle of sixties-era New Left radicalism, her political career during the liberal sunset of the Carter years testified to a burgeoning political maturity. By the mid-1970s, a more pragmatic, less impulsive Fonda now characterized herself as a "progressive Democrat"; this repositioning was consistent with the new ambitions of former sixties radicals who now sought a place in the "system," be it electoral or corporate. Her husband Tom Hayden even bought a suit and ran (unsuccessfully) for the Senate in 1976 with the slogan "The radicalism of the 1960s is becoming the common sense of the 1970s." To fund the political arm of the Fonda-Hayden alliance, called the Campaign for Economic Democracy (CED), Fonda launched her own film production company, IPC (for Indochina Peace Campaign).

"If you want to send a message," the film mogul Samuel Goldwyn once said about political movies, "use Western Union." Fonda's cinematic successes of the late seventies proved, quite to the contrary, that message films could ride high at the box office. The key was subtlety and audience appeal. "You can't propagandize," she insisted, cognizant of her mistakes earlier in the decade. "It has to be a good, well-told story. If you don't have that, people won't go." Having learned the hard way that audiences took her on-screen persona as her real one, she mastered the art of casting herself against type, playing apolitical characters on-screen and thereby confounding her reputation as a left-wing rabble-rouser. Her film roles belied her public image, enabling her to finesse her political agenda for easy, almost subliminal consumption by a mass audience. In IPC's first feature film, *Coming Home* (1978), she played the politically neutral wife of a career Army officer who falls in love with a handicapped veteran who comes to oppose the war. The film's implicit message—that an antiwar conscience actually translates into a superior masculinity—was conveyed through the two men, not through

Fonda, but her performance earned her a second Oscar for Best Actress.

This calibration of her political and cinematic identities netted her critical acclaim and box-office success even while rehabilitating her public image. At the same time, her political concerns had a knack for shadowing, and at times even anticipating, the cultural and political permutations of the late seventies. In 1979 she coproduced *The China Syndrome*, cannily playing a politically apathetic, career-minded TV reporter who accidentally witnesses a meltdown while visiting a nuclear power plant. No sooner had the film opened than a real-life nuclear accident occurred in Pennsylvania, producing a bizarre convergence in which audiences went to see *The China Syndrome* in order to understand Three Mile Island. Fonda's antinuke message was so effective that the "father of the H-bomb," Edward Teller, actually blamed her for the heart attack he suffered at the time. The 1980 hit *Nine to Five* took on the issues of sexual harassment and women's workplace grievances through the easily palatable formula of slapstick comedy, and Fonda cast the film's players with the strategic care of a presidential candidate choosing a running mate. Knowing that "there are still a lot of people out there who would like to see me dead," especially in more conservative regions of the country, she picked Dolly Parton because "Dolly gets us the South."

By 1980, the year her political nemesis Ronald Reagan was elected President, Jane Fonda had staged a remarkable comeback: a Gallup poll ranked her among the world's 10 most admired women. But despite the success of her films, she foresaw the diminished earning potential she could expect as an actress in her mid-forties and worried about securing new funding sources for the CED. As it turned out, the answer to her financial concerns would launch her next, and most lucrative, cultural incarnation. "This was at the height of Lyndon Larouche, and I discovered that he funded his organization through a computer business," Fonda recalls. "So I said to Tom,

'Let's borrow a page from the right wing and figure out a business that we can start.' Now, I'm about as far from a businesswoman as anybody could possibly be. But one day it just hit me: There's one thing I understand, and that's exercise. I know what works, and I know what it can do for a woman. Why don't I turn it into a business?" Drawing from an exercise routine she had developed over the past twenty years that built on her early ballet training, she launched the "Workout," an interdisciplinary regimen that incorporated calisthenics, dance, and aerobics.

Once again, Jane Fonda had tapped the spirit of the age. She opened her first Workout center in Beverly Hills, in 1979, and the concept took off. Workout centers spread to other cities, and *Jane Fonda's Workout Book* sold nearly two million copies in its first year. Not only did her newest endeavor mesh with, as well as fortify, the fitness craze of the 1980s, it also helped jump-start the infant home-video industry. When the entrepreneur Stuart Karl persuaded her to release a video version of the Workout, her videocassettes quickly became bestsellers. By 1982 her fitness empire had taken in an astonishing $20 million. Like a vertically integrated corporation, the diversification of her professional identities now had a mutually reinforcing, synergistic effect. Showing off her fit, middle-aged body onscreen promoted her Workout routine; the Workout and film roles subsidized Hayden's successful campaign for California State Assembly in 1982. At the same time, Jane Fonda the "political actress" now mutated into an emblem of the fitness-crazed, body-conscious, "say no to drugs" eighties.

It might seem paradoxical that she found her greatest mainstream appeal during the Reagan era, but Jane Fonda's Workout rhetoric also proclaimed a return to a strenuous life and a code of self-discipline that aptly, if perversely, meshed with the president's neoconservative philosophy. Indeed, Fonda once defended her Workout regimen—deemed too rigorous by some critics—by articulating a "zero tolerance" approach to fitness wimpiness worthy of a White House press conference: "I shed no tears for the Beverly Hills matron who cries and drinks and takes drugs. You have the ability to get off your butt and find out what life is about. If you don't, that's your problem, not someone else's."

Part Murphy Brown, part Teddy Roosevelt, the eighties Fonda was a solid role model for entrepreneurial feminists and career moms. But the nineties Fonda was perplexing. Fresh on the heels of her breakup with Hayden after 16 years of marriage, she met the media baron Ted Turner and married him in 1991. Despite their disparate cultural orbits, Fonda and Turner shared a high-profile public presence and similar family tragedies; Turner's father, like Fonda's mother, had taken his own life, when Ted was 24. Fonda chose this turning point to retire gracefully from cinema, her financial independence having spared her from the lesser roles normally allotted to older actresses. She still devoted her time to an array of causes, particularly the Georgia Campaign for Adolescent Pregnancy Prevention. The nineties Fonda also embraced Christianity, after a lifetime of agnosticism. Yet even these ostensibly conservative turns were enacted with characteristic Fonda bravura. In true Civil Rights–era fashion, she frequently attends a black Baptist church. Her inner permutations, though less publicly visible than before, also contributed to the recent disintegration of her marriage. She attributes the rupture with Turner to a continuing pursuit of personal growth and self-definition. "You can lose a marriage when you find your voice," Fonda says, "if you didn't have a voice when you got into the marriage."

Any summation of Jane Fonda's life must begin with the question: Who *is* she? Indeed, in the kaleidoscope of identities that constitute her past, many observers and detractors still attempt to reduce her to one of her many incarnations. Hanoi Jane, for some, is the quintessential Fonda, while others attempt to explain her life through her successive marriages. But she eludes all such interpretations. Vadim titled his autobiography *Bardot Deneuve Fonda,* thereby boiling his life down to the women in it; a Fonda autobiography called *Vadim Hayden Turner* would surely sell, but it wouldn't explain the complexity of her public image. If one factor does stand out, it is that Fonda had her formative training as a Method actress and approached her subsequent personae—from libertine to disciplinarian—like sought-after roles that accorded her a vivid and all-encompassing, if temporary, identity. Yet this only brings us back to her daughter's chameleon remark, and begs the question: Was Fonda's life merely a series of performances, each played with Oscarworthy conviction?

She herself has trouble answering such questions. "It's like my whole life has been a quest for growing up," she muses. "I had no mother, my father was remote, I had to invent myself, and I used men to do it." What is unique, however, is that Fonda also used the shifting configurations of our culture to assemble her identities. One consequence of this symbiosis with great national currents is that Fonda the historical figure now affords us a guided tour of nearly 40 years of American history. This unique historical utility, in turn, points to what is perhaps the greatest meaning of her life.

During the making of *Klute,* in 1970, Fonda's antiwar militancy placed her at odds with much of the film's crew, and one day she arrived to find the set decorated with American flags. Still, by the end of the shoot she had won over the crew because, as the director, Alan Pakula, put it, "above all else, she is quintessentially an American." When one adds up all of her incarnations—sixties sex kitten, seventies feminist, eighties fitness drill sergeant, nineties church lady—and factors in her ability to thrive in conservative and radical times alike, what emerges is a highly visible existence that has managed to encompass the country's moral, cultural, and political contradictions without being overwhelmed by them. Whether evinced in her moralistic politics, her entrepreneurial zeal, her thirst for novelty, or her capacity for self-reinvention, the larger message of Jane Fonda's life may just be: Jane Fonda is America.

Study Questions

1. How did Jane Fonda's youth influence her adulthood?

2. How did Americans react to Fonda's early film career in Paris?

3. What was America like in 1968 when Fonda returned to the United States? What were other actors in the States doing?

4. How did Fonda's career in the 1970s reflect her real life? How had she changed since the 1960s?

5. How did Jane Fonda's rise as a workout icon reflect national attitudes in the 1980s and the growth of neoconservatism?

6. Why has the author argued that Jane Fonda reflects American life throughout the past four decades?

Bibliography

This piece came from *American Heritage* (July/August, 2001). Much has been written on the Fonda family and their role in Hollywood. For an overview of the Fonda family's legacy, see Jack Stewart, *The Fabulous Fondas: Henry, Jane, and Peter* (1976) and Peter Collier, *The Fondas: A Hollywood Dynasty* (1991). For Fonda's journey to Vietnam, see Henry Mark Holzer and Erica Holzer, *"Aid and Comfort": Jane Fonda in North Vietnam* (2002) and Russell Sorto, *Jane Fonda: Political Activism* (1991). For a general biography of Jane Fonda, see Bill Davidson, *Jane Fonda: An Intimate Biography* (1990). For a good overview of the sixties, see Alexander Broom, ed., *"Takin' It to the Streets": A Sixties Reader* (2004); for the seventies, Brice Schulman, *The Seventies: The Great Shift in American Culture, Society, and Politics* (2001); and the eighties, Gilbert Sewall, ed., *The Eighties: A Reader* (1997).

READING 27

★ ★ ★

Arabs, Israelis, and American Orientalism

Douglas Little

In his 1869 best-selling travel account of a trip to the Holy Land entitled *The Innocents Abroad*, Mark Twain characterized the Muslims as "a people by nature and training filthy, brutish, ignorant, unprogressive, [and] superstitious." For him, the entire region was trapped between the romance of the *Arabian Nights* and the bloodthirsty tyranny of the Ottoman Empire. American readers of *The Innocents Abroad* readily accepted Twain's crude, vicious stereotypes because they accurately reflected common Western beliefs. From at least the late-seventeenth century, Americans had conceived of the Middle East as a land of ancient prophets and modern-day pirates, a backward region of sand, brutality, and political inefficiency.

Groundbreaking scholar Edward Said has employed the term *Orientalism* to describe this attitude toward the Middle East. Orientalism, Said argues, is a distorted lens through which the West has viewed the East. On one hand, Westerners have viewed the Middle East as the land of Scheherazade and Aladdin, a wonderful, romantic landscape of magic carpets, genies, and harems. On the other hand, they have described the region as a place of decadence and backwardness, a land of greed, violence, repression, and irrationality. The binary Said describes contrasts the Western "Us" against the Eastern "Them." It allows the West to define itself in opposition to the East. In the following essay, Douglas Little explores how images of the Middle East in American popular culture have helped to shape U.S. policy in the region.

David, Goliath, and the Arab-Israeli Conflict, 1948–1967

During the nineteen years between the founding of Israel in May 1948 and the stunning Israeli victory in the June 1967 Six Day War, the U.S. public and policymakers gradually came to see the tiny Jewish state's confrontation with its much larger Arab rivals as a reenactment of the biblical story of David and Goliath. Cast by much of the American media as a geopolitical underdog whose occidental values were anathema to its oriental neighbors, Israel relied on courage, ingenuity, and increasingly, Western weapons to defeat people whose Muslim faith and tribal culture seemed to magazines such as *National Geographic* more and more out of step with twentieth-century realities. The November 1948 issue of *National Geographic*, for example, included "Sailing with Sindbad's Sons," an account of the voyage of the *Bayan*, a square-rigged "Winged Galleon of Araby" that retraced the route of the old slave and spice trade from Aden at the mouth of the Red Sea to Zanzibar off the East African coast. The description of the *Bayan*'s crew reaffirmed the classic orientalist myth of the primitive but happy native. "Like Monkeys in Treetops, Arabs Climb a 130-Foot Yard," reads one caption. "Their pay is a pittance and their food poor, yet they are cheerful."

The sharp contrast that *National Geographic* drew for its readers between westernized Israelis and backward Arabs came through most clearly, however, in a pair of articles that appeared in the autumn of 1947. In "An Archaeologist Looks at Palestine," photographs of Bronze Age skeletons and biblical ruins alternate with snapshots of Zionist irrigation projects that "Make the Desert Bloom" and sun-drenched Tel Aviv beachgoers clad in Bermuda shorts. The color photos at the end of the article, on the other hand, highlight the exotic and dangerous Arab lands to the east. "Sheiks of the Wealthy Majali Bedouins Relax on Rugs and Soft Cushions before Their Tent," reads one caption. A few pages later a Jordanian desert warrior, sporting a rifle, a pistol, two bandoliers, and a silver dagger, stares menacingly at the camera from beneath his red-checkered kaffiyeh.

National Geographic's subscribers got their longest look at the primitivism of the Arab world in October 1947 with the publication of "Yemen: Southern Arabia's Mountain Wonderland," a forty-one-page photoessay written by Harlan B. Clark, a U.S. Foreign Service officer based next door in Britain's Aden protectorate. One aerial shot showed Imam Yahya watching his "Parading Troops Perform the Dagger Dance" amidst racing camels and black stallions, a moment Clark likened to "a scene out of *Arabian Nights*." The article closed with a photo of Harry Truman, clad in a double-breasted suit, chatting in the Oval Office with Yahya's youngest son, Prince Saif, who had arrived at the White House carrying worry beads and wearing a fez and a prayer shawl.

Saif's July 1947 visit doubtless helped persuade Truman that Arabs were exotic figures straight out of *Innocents Abroad*. After meeting with Abdullah Suleiman, King Ibn Saud's minister of finance, in August 1946, Truman had likened the second most powerful man in Saudi Arabia to "a real old Biblical Arab with chin whiskers, a white gown, gold braid, and everything." When Suleiman asked for U.S. help on a Saudi irrigation project, Truman replied that "he should send for a Moses to strike rocks in various places with his staff and he'd have plenty of water."

Other top U.S. officials held the Arabs in even lower esteem. When Saudi Arabia and its Arab allies nearly sidetracked U.S. plans for the early recognition of Israel in the spring of 1948, for example, White House counsel Clark Clifford urged decisive action. "The United States appears in the ridiculous role of trembling before threats of a few nomadic desert

Douglas Little *The United States and the Middle East Since 1945* (2002).

tribes," he wrote Truman in early March. "Why should Russia or Yugoslavia, or any other nation treat us with anything but contempt in light of our shilly-shallying appeasement of the Arabs." Even across town at Foggy Bottom, where State Department Middle East experts had a reputation for being much more sympathetic to Arabs than to Jews, key officials regarded Israel's neighbors as irrational and unrealistic. "As for the emotion of the Arabs, I do not care a dried camel's hump," acid-tongued Palestine desk officer Robert McClintock growled on 1 July. "It is, however, important to the interests of this country that these fanatical and overwrought people do not injure our strategic interests through reprisals against our oil investments." Like McClintock, George Kennan, the State Department's reigning Soviet specialist and newly appointed chief of its Policy Planning Staff, questioned the wisdom of U.S. support for Israel. But he was no friend of the Arabs, who had left a lasting impression on him during a wartime visit to Iraq as a people prone to "selfishness and stupidity" and "inclined to all manner of religious bigotry and fanaticism."

Few U.S. policymakers saw any reason to challenge Clifford's or Kennan's orientalist interpretation of Muslim behavior during Truman's second term. After all, according to a 1949 Central Intelligence Agency (CIA) psychological profile of the Middle East, the Arabs were not only "non-inventive and slow to put theories into practice" and "skillful mainly at avoiding hard work" but also capable of "astonishing acts of treachery and dishonesty." Carleton Coon, a State Department whiz kid whose first assignment abroad had come in Damascus during the early 1950s, recalled long afterward that "the Syrians had a well deserved inferiority complex" that predated the creation of Israel. Adolf Berle, a Democratic Party insider who served in Truman's kitchen cabinet, remarked privately during the summer of 1952 that this well-documented psychological profile of instability

extended to non-Arab Muslims such as the Iranians as well. "Fanatic Mohammedan nationalism" seemed about to sweep away the shah of Iran, opening the door to a "Communist takeover" in Tehran, Berle confided in his diary on 13 August. There was a very real danger, he concluded gloomily, "that the Russians would be on the Persian Gulf by Christmas."

In short, as the Truman administration drew to a close, officials from the bottom to the top of the policymaking pyramid were convinced that the peoples of the Muslim world were an unpredictable lot whose penchant for political and religious extremism constituted a grave threat to U.S. interests in the region. Indeed, most U.S. policymakers would likely have seconded the orientalist assessment that Britain's ambassador to Iraq forwarded to London in late 1952. The Iraqi, like most Arabs, "is embittered, frustrated and fanatical," Sir John Troutbeck cabled Whitehall on 31 October. "Seeing little but squalor and stagnation around him, he will not admit even to himself the obvious answer, that he belongs to a peculiarly irresponsible and feckless race."

The man who replaced Harry Truman in the Oval Office in January 1953 was equally comfortable with such orientalist stereotypes of the Middle East. Dwight Eisenhower's view of the Muslim world was colored by his wartime experiences in North Africa, where a decade earlier he had tried unsuccessfully to bridge the gap between French colonialists and Algerian nationalists. "Arabs are a very uncertain quantity, explosive and full of prejudices," he remarked privately in November 1942. "Many things done here that look queer are just to keep the Arabs from blazing up into revolt." Eisenhower's close encounter with the Arabs during the 1950s did nothing to soften his earlier assessment. Despite Britain's "modern program of independence for countries once part of the Empire," Ike complained in his memoirs, Egyptian president Gamal Abdel Nasser had unleashed a crusade of "virulent nationalism and unreasoning

For years, when Americans thought about the Middle East, they imagined a land of deserts and oasis's. Eventually, simplistic thinking would have profound impact American foreign policy.

prejudice" in which there was "evidence of Communist meddling."

Nasser's seizure of the Suez Canal during the summer of 1956 reinforced Eisenhower's belief that the Arabs were irrational, resentful, and dangerous to Western interests. "Nasser," Ike observed on 31 July, "embodies the emotional demands of the people of the area for independence and for 'slapping the White Man down.'" When Eisenhower sent U.S. marines to Lebanon two years later to shore up a pro-American regime besieged by pro-Nasser dissidents, he reminded the National Security Council (NSC) that "the underlying Arab thinking" remained deeply rooted in "violence, emotion and ignorance." As his term drew to a close, Ike complained that Nasser and like-minded nationalists were little more than oriental despots. "If you go and live with these Arabs, you will find that they simply cannot understand our ideas of freedom or human dignity," he told the NSC in June 1959. "They have lived so long under dictatorships of one form or another, how can we expect them to run successfully a free government?"

Eisenhower's top advisers echoed the president's growing frustration with the Arabs. Shortly after taking over at Foggy Bottom, for example, John Foster Dulles took a two-week fact-finding trip to the Middle East that confirmed all of his Presbyterian fears of the Muslim infidel. Following visits to Cairo and other Arab capitals in May 1953, Eisenhower's secretary of state pronounced Nasser and like-minded Arab nationalists "pathological" in their suspicion of the Western powers and "naive" in their trust of the Kremlin. It is no surprise that in private conversations with U.K. officials in early July, Dulles described Iran's anti-Western prime minister, Mohammed Mossadegh, as "a wily oriental." When anti-Western violence rocked Baghdad, Beirut, and Amman five summers later, White House troubleshooter Robert Murphy undertook a "twenty-nine-day Magic Carpet tour of the fabled East" at the behest of Eisenhower, with whom he had worked to curb "the restiveness of the indigenes" in Muslim North Africa during the Second World War. After visiting "Godforsaken stretches of Iraq," where "mobs whose violence surpassed all expectations" held sway, he informed his boss in August 1958 that little had changed since the early 1940s.

U.S. diplomats stationed in the Middle East helped reinforce the orientalist views of Eisenhower, Dulles, and Murphy. When Ambassador Henry Villard found himself mired down in endless negotiations over a U.S. air base in June 1954, he cabled Washington that the tactics of Libyan officials were "tantamount to blackmail and show[ed] little change from [the] barbary pirate tradition." Two years later Henry Byroade, the U.S. ambassador to Egypt, confirmed that Nasser and his followers were volatile, unpredictable, and quixotic. "Arabs are quite capable of getting completely beside themselves" on matters related to Israel, Byroade warned Dulles on 14 March 1956, "because by nature they [are] inclined to fight windmills." A White House study completed four years later reiterated the importance of "psychological" factors in U.S. relations with the Middle East. American officials, the drafters of NSC-6011 pointed out in July 1960, must underestand that "the Arabs' experience with and fear of Western domination" had generated hostility and suspicion that were in turn exacerbated by "their belief that the United States is the special friend and protector of Israel."

Indeed, by the time that Eisenhower retired to his farm just outside Getysburg, Pennsylvania, in January 1961, the Arabs could see that Israel had won not only a special spot in the hearts of everyday Americans, who identified with the underdog status of the new nation, but also the grudging respect of U.S. policymakers, who were impressed by its military prowess. As they had during the mid-1940s, so too during the Eisenhower era many Americans seemed to regard sympathy for a Jewish homeland in the Middle East as a form of symbolic atonement for having done too little too late to prevent the Holocaust in Europe. For the United States during the 1950s

perhaps the most powerful reminder of Hitler's genocide was a grainy, black-and-white snapshot of a teenage Jewish schoolgirl that graced the cover of her heartbreaking, posthumous account of life and death in Nazi-occupied Holland. When first published in 1952, *Anne Frank: Diary of a Young Girl* became an instant best-seller. By the end of the decade the haunting visage of Anne Frank had been imprinted even more deeply onto U.S. popular culture, first by a Pulitzer Prize–winning play that drew standing-room-only crowds on Broadway in 1956 and then by a Hollywood box-office smash that received two Academy Awards three years later.

The literary and cinematic connections between the nightmare of the Holocaust and the dream of Israel were drawn most clearly for readers and moviegoers in Eisenhower's America, however, in the work of novelist and screenwriter Leon Uris. Few novels have sold 4 million copies faster while winning wide critical acclaim than *Exodus*, a thinly fictionalized account of the tireless Zionist crusade to run food, guns, and Jewish refugees into Palestine after the Second World War. Published in 1958, the book contained a plot that pitted survivors of the Nazi death camps against callous British colonial bureaucrats and ruthless Arab demagogues as well as a message that trumpeted the eventual triumph of good over evil. Hollywood wasted little time producing its version of the heroic founding of Israel. In December 1960 United Artists released *Exodus*, a four-hour epic starring rising young screen idol Paul Newman as an indomitable Jewish freedom fighter and featuring a stirring soundtrack that would win an Oscar for best musical score. Appearing seven months after a well-publicized, stranger-than-fiction operation whereby Israeli intelligence had snatched Adolf Eichmann, one of the chief architects of the final solution, off the streets of Buenos Aires and spirited him to Jerusalem to stand trial as a Nazi war criminal, *Exodus* reminded American audiences that with the creation of a Jewish state in the Holy Land, Anne Frank had not died in vain.

Eighteen months after Paul Newman enthralled friends of Israel with his gallantry and good looks in *Exodus*, a white-robed Peter O'Toole stormed out of the heart of Arabia and into movie theaters from coast to coast as the reincarnation of T. E. Lawrence. Directed by British filmmaker David Lean and shot on location in the desert just outside Seville, where the Spaniards had finally driven the Muslims out of Europe in 1492, *Lawrence of Arabia* recaptured the romance, the adventure, and the orientalism of Britain's errand among the Arabs during the First World War. Despite the bravery and skill of the Bedouin warriors, millions of film-goers went home convinced that without Lawrence's help, the Arabs could never have thrown off the Ottoman yoke. Unlike the Zionists in *Exodus*, whose singleness of purpose ensured the establishment of a strong and independent Jewish state, the Arabs in *Lawrence of Arabia* saw their dreams of self-determination dashed by their self-destructive penchant for tribal infighting and political scheming. *Lawrence of Arabia's* orientalist message, its breathtaking camera work, and its talented cast combined to win six Oscars, including those for best actor, best director, and best picture.

The images of noble Israelis surrounded by unruly Arabs projected by Hollywood were reinforced by mass market monthlies such as *National Geographic*, whose circulation soared during the early 1960s. The magazine's December 1963 issue, for example, included "Holy Land Today," a brief photoessay that described Israeli pioneers, "a trowel in one hand and a Bible in the other," methodically "reversing the ordinary course of history" through "the transformation of ancient ruins into living communities." By way of contrast, a March 1964 *National Geographic* piece on Yemen began with this lead-in: "Wracked by

civil war, an ancient Arabian land struggles to find its place in the world of the twentieth century." Even a brief look at the wild-eyed mountain tribesmen brandishing daggers and submachine guns or the bearded worshipers "pour[ing] out of Yemen's Arabian Nights capital" must have persuaded many American readers that the Yemenis were unlikely to win that struggle without the second coming of T. E. Lawrence. Subscribers thumbing through a March 1965 pictorial on Israel, on the other hand, discovered a "Land of Promise" where "smooth new highways hum with traffic" and where "fields of soft green gleam amid the old desert wastes."

Like the editors of *National Geographic*, the insiders who advised John F. Kennedy and Lyndon B. Johnson on the Middle East seem subconsciously to have embraced a hierarchy of race and culture in which the Arabs ranked far below the Israelis. A June 1961 CIA national intelligence estimate on U.S. relations with Nasser, for example, predicted that his brand of nationalism was likely to grow stronger "because it provides an excuse—the wickedness of the great powers—for a host of deficiencies and inadequacies in Arab society." Nasser was not above employing "an oriental bargaining tactic," White House Middle East expert Robert Komer complained to Kennedy in November 1962, whenever he needed to extract himself from a military or diplomatic tight spot. It was always important, Komer mused a year later, to "tak[e] adequate account of the inferiority of the Arab soldier as compared to the Israeli." Perhaps the most pronounced orientalist views, however, were expressed by U.S. diplomats serving overseas, like Harold Glidden, who was stationed in Iraq. "If Arabs ever took over [the] world, they would start instantly to tear it down," Glidden told a reporter shortly after a bloody military coup rocked Baghdad in early 1963. "Arab values of vengeance, prestige and obsession with feuding are not acclimated to urban society."

The hulking Texan who succeeded Kennedy in the Oval Office later that year did not disagree with this harsh assessment. An ardent friend of the Jewish state and an outspoken foe of radical Arab nationalism since his days as Senate majority leader during the late 1950s, President Lyndon Johnson regarded the Middle East as a backward and exotic corner of the world straight out of *Arabian Nights* and badly in need of westernization. At a White House dinner in April 1964, for example, Johnson toasted King Hussein of Jordan for having "brought that ancient land of the camel, the date, and the palm to the threshold of a bright and a hopeful future." On the other hand, LBJ neither liked nor trusted militant Arab leaders such as Nasser, who seemed to be a cross between Ho Chi Minh and Geronimo. Johnson's sentiments became very clear after Egyptian students staged violent anti-American demonstrations and burned down the U.S. Information Agency (USIA) library in Cairo in December 1964. "One way to react," LBJ told a group of congressmen shortly afterward, was to tell Nasser "to go to hell."

According to Mohamed Heikal, a leading Egyptian journalist and one of Nasser's closest advisers, the feeling was mutual. After Johnson threatened to suspend U.S. economic aid to Egypt in retaliation for the destruction of the USIA facility, Nasser delivered a blistering reply. "Those who do not accept our behavior can go and drink from the sea," he thundered on 23 December. "We will cut the tongues of anybody who talks badly about us." Lest LBJ miss the point, Nasser added, "We are not going to accept gangsterism by cowboys." This outburst helped place America's confrontation with the Arabs into a context any self-respecting Texan could appreciate: cowboys and Indians. While neither Johnson's memoirs nor his private papers make it clear whether he ever cast the problem explicitly in terms of Western civilization versus oriental barbarism, the newly

created Palestine Liberation Organization (PLO) did remind him of the Viet Cong. When PLO raids against Israeli villages along the Syrian frontier lit the fuse for the Six Day War during the spring of 1967, the Johnson administration knew who wore white hats and who wore black. White House aide John Roche probably put it best in late May when he told LBJ in the vernacular of the Lone Star State, "I confess that I look on the Israelis as Texans and Nasser as Santa Ana."

Israel's stunning victory over the combined forces of Egypt, Jordan, and Syrian in June 1967 seemed to confirm a verdict British orientalists had handed down about the Arab East a century earlier. Nasser might invoke the memory of Saladin and appeal to "the 'Holy War' psychology of the Arab world," Secretary of State Dean Rusk prophesied as the clock ticked down toward H-hour in early June, but in the face of superior Western firepower, the Egyptians would cut and run. Israel's swift seizure of the Sinai, the West Bank, and the Golan Heights with the blessing of Lyndon Johnson touched off "a riotous wave of anti-Americanism" from Cairo to Kuwait City that John Badeau, Kennedy's ambassador to Egypt, likened to "the Boxer Rebellion in China" seven decades earlier. The implications of the Six Day War for U.S. policymakers were spelled out several years later in a CIA study of the Arab-Israeli conflict. "The June [1967] war was frequently invoked by analysts as proof," the agency's experts concluded in late 1973, that "many Arabs, as Arabs, simply weren't up to the demands of modern warfare and that they lacked understanding, motivation, and probably in some cases courage as well."

For the U.S. public, however, the lessons of the Six Day War grew out of popular culture rather than foreign policy and probably ran more in the direction of David and Goliath tempered by knowledge of the Holocaust. Opinion polls taken shortly after the shooting stopped showed that Americans sympathizing with Israel outnumbered those sympathizing with the Arabs by a whopping 19-to-1 ratio. Predisposed to siding with the underdog, most Americans seemed to regard Israel's smashing victory as the fulfillment of a biblical prophecy. Indeed, one of the hottest-selling paperbacks in June 1967 was James Michener's *The Source*, a 1,000-page epic recounting 2,000 years of Jewish exile, torment, and eventual redemption symbolized by the creation of Israel. Dismissing the notion that his country should remain "a little enclave that thrills the world because its fighters defend themselves against the Arab circle," Michener's Israeli protagonist insisted that the Jewish state could "become a beacon of pure, burning light, illuminating this entire area, forming an alliance with a prospering Arab world." Readers thumbing through the *National Geographic's* fifteen-page photoessay on the Six Day War six months later were reminded of just how close that light had come to burning out. "I am the only member of my family who survived Buchenwald," reads the caption alongside a snapshot of an Israeli commando who had helped defeat three Arab armies. "This time I have a gun to fight with, a country and a cause to serve."

In short, for Americans Israel's military triumph in June 1967 completed the transformation of Jews from victims to victors while branding the Arabs as feckless, reckless, and weak. For a generation that remembered appeasement as a dirty word and regarded Nasser as a Hitler on the Nile, the Six Day War closed the book on Anne Frank and fulfilled the dream of *Exodus*. The burned-out tanks that littered Egypt's Sinai Desert and Syria's Golan Heights and the angry mobs who burned Uncle Sam in effigy from the Gulf of Sidra to the banks of the Euphrates confirmed for many Americans that the Arabs did not have an inferiority complex; they were simply inferior. As Lyndon Johnson settled into a Vietnam-induced early retirement at the LBJ Ranch in January 1969, his disap-

pointment that the Indians held the upper hand in Southeast Asia was tempered by his realization that, in the Middle East, the cowboys were winning.

True Lies?: From Black September to Desert Storm

For many Americans the darkest and most chilling image to emerge from the Middle East before 11 September 2001 may well date from September 1972. As Richard Nixon mowed inexorably toward a landslide victory in his bid for a second term inside the Beltway, a small band of Palestinian commandos shot their way into the Israeli compound at the Olympic Village just outside Munich, the city that thirty-four years earlier had become synonymous with totalitarianism and appeasement. While the whole world watched in horror, seven Black September terrorists mowed down eleven defenseless Israeli athletes during an airport shootout with German police. For the next twenty years both U.S. popular attitudes and foreign policy toward the Middle East would be preoccupied with combating Palestinian terrorists and their patrons such as Iraqi dictator Saddam Hussein.

Like most Americans, Richard Nixon was appalled by the awful news from Munich. After watching the Olympic tragedy unfold live via satellite, he denounced Black September as "international outlaws of the worst sort who will stoop to anything in order to accomplish their goals" and pledged to help the Israelis rid themselves of the Palestinian terrorists whose cruelty knew no bounds. Indeed, although he occasionally lambasted Jews critical of his administration in language that shocked insiders like national security adviser Henry Kissinger, Nixon was a staunch friend of the Jewish state. "In every crisis Nixon stood by Israel more firmly than almost any other president save Harry Truman," Kissinger recalled in his memoirs. "He admired Israeli guts. He respected Israeli leaders' tenacious defense of their national interest. [And] he considered their military prowess an asset for the democracies." Speaking for himself, Kissinger confessed that Israel was also an intensely personal issue. "I could never forget that thirteen members of my family had died in Nazi concentration camps," he noted grimly. "I had no stomach for encouraging another Holocaust by well-intentioned policies that might get out of control."

For both Kissinger and Nixon this meant working quietly behind the scenes to broker an Arab-Israeli truce with moderates such as Egypt's Anwar Sadat while isolating extremists like the Black September guerrillas. Despite his role in masterminding the Syro-Egyptian attack on Israel in October 1973, by the end of the decade Sadat was regarded by most Americans and by many Israelis as the quintessential "good Arab." In Egyptian-Israeli disengagement parleys extending through three U.S. administrations, Sadat struck American policymakers as shrewd, pragmatic, and willing to take enormous risks for peace. Nixon praised Sadat's "great subtlety and sophistication" and called him "a constructive and essential influence for any future Middle East negotiations." Gerald Ford, who had once inadvertently toasted Sadat as the leader of "the great people of the Government of Israel," appreciated the Egyptian president's sense of humor, his straight forward manner, and his diplomatic flexibility. Jimmy Carter, who without Sadat's help could never have launched the Camp David peace process in September 1978, came to admire his Egyptian friend "more than any other leader" and called him "a man who would change history."

Carter, Ford, Nixon, and most other Americans were shocked and saddened on 6 October 1981 when Anwar Sadat was gunned down in Cairo by "bad Arabs," Muslim militants linked to the shadowy Islamic Group. The funeral three days later produced a media frenzy reminiscent of Valentino's death fifty-four years earlier, with a sad-eyed Barbara Walters beaming an informal eulogy of her friend Anwar into millions of American living rooms. The *National Geographic* crew that witnessed Sadat's assassination never forgot the "exceptional beauty about his dark, complex face, noble as a pharaoh's," as he rose to confront his killers, and they never forgave the Bedouin tribesmen who shortly thereafter celebrated the Islamic Group's awful deed. "Sadat was a great and good man," Jimmy Carter remarked upon hearing the sad news, a victim of "his most bitter and dangerous enemies," anti-Western extremists "obsessed with hatred for his peaceful goals." A latter-day pharaoh, Carter added four years later, Anwar Sadat had died "at the hands of misguided religious fanatics."

Although few Americans realized that "assassin" was an Arabic word, many probably believed that the brutal act of terrorism in the streets of Cairo, like Black September's bloody raid outside Munich nine years earlier, was very much in keeping with the Arab character. Seven months before the Olympic massacre, a retired State Department Middle East expert had published a psychological profile warning that the repeated humiliations inflicted by Israel would unleash a "collective need for vengeance" deeply rooted in Arab culture. "It is difficult to describe the depth of the Arabs' emotional need for revenge, but suffice it to say that Islam itself found it necessary to sanction revenge," Harold Glidden observed in February 1972. "The felt need for revenge is as strong today as it was in pre-Islamic times."

Other orientalist broadsides followed in quick succession. Raphael Patai, an Israeli-educated anthropologist who had taught Middle Eastern studies at Princeton, Columbia, and other American universities, offered his readers a bleak view of the "backwardness, cultural decline, indeed, fossilization" of the Arab world in 1973. The troubled relationship with the West, Patai explained, was the result of everything from prolonged breast-feeding to faulty toilet training, all of which "produced a disturbing inferiority complex in the

Arab mind which in itself made it more difficult to shake off the shackles of stagnation." Two years later British orientalist John Laffin informed the American public that "violence exists at every level of Arab life," thanks mainly to "poverty and frustration—sexual, economic, [and] political." Long ago, Laffin added, "history 'turned wrong' for the Arabs," leaving them subordinate to the Western powers. The "consequent trauma," he concluded, was "a principal reason for the great psychological sickness which fell like a plague upon the Arab race." William Brown, a U.S. diplomat posted to Cairo and Beirut during the 1960s, confirmed Patai's and Laffin's orientalist diagnoses in a 1980 retrospective aptly titled *The Last Crusade*. Arab nationalism was "beyond the control apparatus of any state" and had "a reactive quality arising from the Arabs' experience with the West," Brown observed. "A relative and tolerant perspective is not possible within the Arab's world of absolute and God-given truth."

Critics such as Edward Said were quick to challenge these orientalist assumptions. As early as 1978 Said insisted that such pathological stereotypes of the Arabs constituted little more than self-serving rationalizations for Western cultural and economic imperialism. "Lurking behind all of these images is the menace of *jihad*," he observed bluntly. "Consequence: a fear that the Muslims (or Arabs) will take over the world." The net effect of this fear was ignorance, Said concluded in the final chapter of *Orientalism*, ignorance that seemed destined "to keep the region and its people conceptually emasculated, reduced to 'attitudes,' 'trends,' statistics: in short, dehumanized." Throughout the 1980s and into the early 1990s Said broadened his critique, stressing that America's habit of viewing "Arabs as basically, irrecusably, and congenitally 'Other'" clearly reflected "racist overtones in its elaboration of an 'Arab' anti-democratic, violent, and regressive attitude to the world." This, Said pointed out in *Culture and Imperialism* in 1993, "contributed to the polarity that was set up between democratic Israel and a homogeneously non-democratic Arab world, in which the Palestinians, dispossessed and exiled by Israel, came to represent 'terrorism' and little beyond it."

Said's trenchant criticism notwithstanding, the reading public was treated to a steady diet of orientalism American style during the Reagan and George Bush years. In a revised edition of *The Arab Mind* that appeared in 1983, Raphael Patai saw little hope for peace or progress in the Middle East unless the children of Ishmael could "devote their best talents not to fighting windmills, but to constructing the new Arab man." Six years later David Pryce-Jones, a crusty veteran of Britain's Suez War and a self-styled orientalist, published *The Closed Circle*, a scathing anti-Arab diatribe that recycled many of the stereotypes popularized by Glidden, Patai, and Laffin. Because the Arabs remained trapped in a brutal, patriarchal, and tribal society whose members "really believe in their inalienable right to be exploited by people of their own nationality," Pryce-Jones concluded that autocracy, not democracy, would always carry the day: "Instead of construction, destruction; instead of creativity, wastefulness; instead of body politic, atrocities."

The most widely disseminated orientalist screed of the decade, however, was probably Bernard Lewis's "The Roots of Muslim Rage," *Atlantic Monthly's* cover story for September 1990. A British-born, Princeton-based founding father of the modern academic discipline of Middle Eastern studies, Lewis attributed the wave of anti-Americanism sweeping the Muslim world to an irrational hatred of Judeo-Christian civilization exacerbated by "the revival of ancient prejudices" among Islamic extremists. Reminding the *Atlantic's* readers that "America had become the archenemy, the incarnation of evil," for theocratic zealots from Lebanon to Iran, Lewis prophesied that Islam's "war against modernity" would eventually escalate into "a clash of civilizations."

Anyone studying the magazine's cover, which showed a bearded and turbaned Muslim whose scowling eyes were riveted on the stars and stripes, might reasonably have concluded that the clash was already under way. Anyone reading the blurb in the *Atlantic's* table of contents, which insisted that the "intense—and violent—resentment of the West" was merely the latest in "a long series of attacks and counterattacks, jihads and crusades, conquests and reconquests," might well have wondered whether Lewis had uttered a self-fulfilling prophecy. Indeed, critics such as Georgetown University's John Esposito have suggested that academic orientalists, U.S. policymakers, and the American media had, like twentieth-century Scheherazades, conjured up the genie of rampaging "Islamic fundamentalism" to fill a "threat vacuum" created by the collapse of the Soviet Union and the end of the Cold War.

A quick look at how Arabs have been depicted in everything from pulp fiction to television during the past twenty years confirms that orientalism American style remained alive and well in both popular culture and the mass media. A "Saturday Night Live" spoof during the 1979 oil shortage, for example, featured "The Bel Airabs," poor Bedouins transplanted to California like latter-day Beverly Hillbillies thanks to the dumb luck of Abdul, the leader of the clan: "And then one day he was shootin' at some Jews, and up through the sand came a bubblin' crude." Nor was such imagery uncommon in prime time, where during the late 1970s Arabs were the frequent butt of jokes delivered by everyone from Sonny and Cher to Archie Bunker on "All in the Family." Angered by the shoddy treatment he received from an Arab dry cleaner, Archie orders Edith, "Don't go near that Ay-rab again unless you got a dirty camel to wash." When son-in-law Michael objects to the nasty stereotype, Archie retorts, "They're born pirates, all of 'em."

Arabs have fared little better in American cartoons. When Tarzan inadvertently insulted a thin-skinned sheik during the 1980s, a sword-wielding comic-book Arab shrieked, "Only this blade will satisfy me ... letting flow your coward's blood!" Later that decade Marvel Comics' *GI Joe* and a band of U.S. commandos rescued two Americans held hostage by a stereotypical Arab potentate who "has been known to behead jaywalkers." In 1985 one political cartoonist provided a nasty portrait of "the Arab mind" that included "vengeance," "fanaticism," and "blackmail" among its many lobes. "What is the difference between a rat and [Yasser] Arafat?" another asked after sketching two vermin, only one of whom was a rodent, crawling out of the garbage. "Answer: The rat has more friends." Still another humorist drew a captionless panel showing a white-robed Arab executioner holding a bleeding globe in one hand and a bloody scimitar in the other.

This orientalist imagery was no less pronounced among newspaper reporters and television journalists. "It became very clear to me," Jim Hoaglund of the *Washington Post* recalled in early 1982, "that in Western writing in general—not just newspapers but in books and certainly in cartoons—there was quite a distorted image" of a Middle East peopled by "Arabs sneaking about with knives in their teeth." A year later John Cooley of the *Christian Science Monitor* agreed that "certainly Arabs have been unfairly portrayed" in both print and electronic media. Indeed, Cooley added, "Arabs are probably still the only group in the U.S. that anyone dares to portray in pejorative terms." As early as 1975 ABC television anchorman Peter Jennings acknowledged that "there is definitely an anti-Arab bias in America," a bias that had led "unfortunately, [to] stereotyping in the media." In the early 1980s Jim Lehrer, cohost of the PBS evening news hour, agreed that network television's fascination with terrorism and sectarian strife in the Middle East "feeds the stereotype that many Americans have of Arabs as bloody people who just go out killing each other all the time."

When pressed by an interviewer to suggest what Arabs and, more generally, Muslims might do to counteract this stereotype, Lehrer did not mince words. "This is not a public relations image problem," he observed archly, his mind's eye doubtless riveted on the fifty-two Americans recently released from 444 days of captivity in Iran and on the never-ending civil war in Lebanon; "it's a reality problem." Anthony Lewis of the *New York Times* agreed. "When Mr. Arafat goes on an American television program," Lewis told Arab American media consultant Edmund Ghareeb, "he comes through as a mixture of that romantic desert Arab you spoke of, but without the romance." When Ghareeb retorted that many Americans mistakenly seemed to regard Arafat as "a bloodthirsty terrorist," Lewis shot back, "But you know, he does look a bit bloodthirsty."

What Lehrer termed "a reality problem" was clearly exacerbated, however, by how Arabs were portrayed in pulp fiction. Beginning in 1975 with the publication of Thomas Harris's *Black Sunday*, which revolved around a Palestinian plot to commandeer the Goodyear blimp and terrorize the Super Bowl, a slew of paperback potboilers with titles such as *Jihad*, *Phoenix*, and *On the Brink* rountinely depicted Arabs as either ruthless and brutal thugs or greedy sheiks eager to bankroll their bloodthirsty brethren. But the most widely read mass market novel extolling orientalist stereotypes of the Arabs was probably *The Haj*, a prequel written by Leon Uris in 1984, a quarter-century after the publication of *Exodus*. Set in the Holy Land during the 1930s, *The Haj* describes Palestinians in language that would have made even right-wing Israeli leaders like Menachem Begin blush. "Every last Arab is a total prisoner of his society," a British officer tells Uris's proto-Israeli protagonist. "The Arabs will never love you for what good you've brought them. They don't know how to really love. But hate! Oh God, can they hate!"

Lest readers miss the point, Uris hammered home this orientalist verdict in terms that pre-figured those employed by Bernard Lewis six years later. The Arabs "have a deep, deep, deep resentment because you have jolted them from their delusions of grandeur and shown them for what they are—a decadent, savage people controlled by a religion that has stripped them of all human ambition . . . except for the few cruel enough and arrogant enough to command them as one commands a mob of sheep." This anti-Arab soliloquy ends with a message intended not only for Zionists during the 1930s but also for Americans during the 1980s: "You are dealing with a mad society and you'd better learn how to control it." With nearly 2 million copies of *The Haj* in print by 1985, that message seems to have been well received by the reading public.

As it had for more than a generation, the film industry projected orientalist images from the printed page onto the silver screen throughout the 1980s and into the 1990s. As early as 1977, when the big-budget *Black Sunday* became the summer's hottest hit, Hollywood's Arabs were consistently depicted as homicidal fanatics who were, more often than not, too clever by half. Occasionally Arabs came across as comical, as in *Back to the Future*, a 1985 blockbuster in which bungling Libyan hitmen out to steal enough plutonium to build an atomic bomb shoot Christopher Lloyd and inadvertently send Michael J. Fox and his nuclear-powered De-Lorean back to 1955.

U.S. audiences, however, were more likely to cringe than chuckle when an Arab appeared on the screen. In *Delta Force*, a 1986 action film loosely based on the brutal murder of a U.S. sailor aboard a hijacked TWA jetliner a year earlier in Beirut, Chuck Norris and a team of commandos rescued a planeload of Americans held hostage by psychopathic Palestinian terrorists. Eight summers later in *True Lies*, a CIA superman played by Arnold Schwartzenegger single-handedly thwarted "Crimson Jihad," a gun-toting band of Arab wildmen planning to launch a nuclear attack on Miami from their base in the

Florida Keys. Despite protests from Arab Americans, at the end of the twentieth century the film industry continued to offer orientalist fare like *Executive Decision* (1996) or *The Mummy* (1999), with Arabs depicted as airborne fanatics or feckless and foul-smelling opportunists. "To Hollywood, the Arab is the wife-abuser who wants to buy Steve Martin's house in *Father of the Bride II*," Ray Hanania complained in *Newsweek* in late 1998. "We Arabs murder innocent airline passengers in *Executive Decision* simply because it makes us feel good."

The Israelis, by contrast, tended to fare somewhat better than the Arabs at the hands of Hollywood and the mass media. To be sure, the *New York Times* and the major television networks were highly critical of both Israel's invasion of Lebanon in June 1982 and its repression of the Palestinian "Intifada" uprising that erupted on the West Bank in December 1987. Ze'ev Chafets and Stephen Karetzky responded by publishing stinging exposés in which they charged that the media were employing a double standard. Why was there so much coverge of the massacre of nearly 1,000 Palestinian refugees just outside Beirut in September 1982 by Lebanese Christians allied with Israel, Chafets and Karetzky wondered, and so little outcry over the far greater slaughter seven months earlier at Hama, a city 100 miles north of Damascus, where Syria's President Hafez al-Assad ordered his troops to kill more than 10,000 Syrians whose only crime was to oppose his dictatorship? Israeli foreign minister Moshe Arens reacted in a similar fashion to U.S. criticism of Israel's crackdown on the West Bank. "The media coverage of the Intifada," Arens told U.S. Jewish leaders in early 1989, "had successfully switched the focus from the Arab-Israeli conflict—in which Israel appeared as little David—to the Israeli-Palestinian conflict, in which Israel was being made to appear as Goliath."

Yet despite a tendency among militantly pro-Israeli pundits such as *Commentary's*

Norman Podhoretz to imply that media figures critical of the Jewish state were closet anti-Semites, journalists at NBC, *Newsweek*, and the *Los Angeles Times* found fault with Israel because of what its government was doing in Lebanon and on the West Bank, not because most of its citizens were Jews. In any case, Moshe Arens's complaint notwithstanding, most Americans still seemed to identify Israel as more like David than Goliath. Much of the reason probably lies in Hollywood. The 1981 made-for-television movie *Masada*, for example, retold the legendary story of a besieged Jewish fortress on the shores of the Dead Sea whose heroic defenders, like Davy Crockett at the Alamo, had chosen death rather than submission to Roman imperialism almost 2,000 years earlier.

It was the Holocaust, however, painfully and painstakingly relived with the help of Hollywood, that probably did the most to reaffirm subconsciously Israel's status as an underdog in the hearts and minds of most Americans. The eight-hour miniseries *The Holocaust*, which starred Meryl Streep as a beautiful but doomed twenty-something version of Anne Frank, won the network ratings war during sweeps week in 1978 and later captured eight Emmys. Four years later Streep won an Oscar for her moving performance in *Sophie's Choice*, where she played a concentration camp survivor haunted by having had to choose which of her two children would die at Auschwitz. Once television and film viewers turned their attention from these emotionally charged histories of the Holocaust to the here and now of the modern Middle East, more than a few must have taken comfort from the knowledge that, whatever Israel's faults, it remained the best insurance available against a replay of Hitler's final solution.

An even more riveting cinematic treatment of the Holocaust appeared a decade later with the premiere of *Schindler's List* in December 1993. Shot on location just outside Auschwitz in grainy black and white and directed by Hollywood wunderkind Steven Spielberg, the film told the story of Oskar Schindler, a German businessman whose growing doubts about Nazism and whose simple humanity led him to risk everything to save several hundred Jewish slave-laborers imprisoned at the death camp. Although *Schindler's List* won seven Oscars, including those for best director and best picture, the film was banned in April 1994 by many Islamic countries, less because its brief nude scenes and graphic violence offended Muslim sensibilities than because its subliminal message ran counter to the abiding anti-Israel and anti-Semitic sentiments of some Arab audiences.

A year earlier a very different movie, Disney's *Aladdin*, had won two Oscars while offending the sensibilities of many Arab Americans. Ostensibly an animated love story about two rather westernized Arabs, Aladdin and Princess Jasmine, whose English was flawless, Disney's animators and lyricists depicted most of the other inhabitants of their imaginary oriental sheikdom as frightful thugs sporting turbans, daggers, and thick accents. The Academy Award–winning soundtrack written by Alan Menken and Howard Ashman summed up *Aladdin*'s subconscious orientalism most succinctly. The first song, "Arabian Nights," contains an opening lyric straight out of *Innocents Abroad*. "Oh I come from a land, from a faraway place, where the caravan camels roam," a swarthy merchant croons, "where they cut off your ear if they don't like your face, it's barbaric, but hey, it's home." The second tune, "A Whole New World," won a Grammy in March 1993 as "song of the year." Evoking images of a patriarchal oriental past and an egalitarian Western future, Aladdin serenades Jasmine with the promise of "a new fantastic point of view," if only she will let her heart decide. Although repeated protests from the Arab-American Anti-Discrimination Committee persuaded Disney Studios to remove the most offensive lyrics from the home video distributed later

that year, *Aladdin* revised still reflected the orientalism deeply embedded in U.S. popular culture during the preceding two centuries.

As it did for many people living next door to hostile neighbors, xenophobia came naturally to most citizens of the fledgling United States, surrounded as they were by Spanish imperialists, British provocateurs, and Indian infidels who seemed determined to destroy God's American Israel. Because Jews and Muslims were neither Christian nor Anglo-Saxon, both groups were suspect in the eyes of most Americans, who throughout the nineteenth century and into the twentieth relied on a well-defined hierarchy of race and culture in dealing with foreigners who looked and prayed differently. The missionaries, merchants, and archaeologists who shaped America's understanding of the Middle East from the Barbary Wars through the discovery of King Tut's tomb reaffirmed orientalist stereotypes as old as the Crusades depicting Arabs as exotic, fanatical, and congenitally predisposed toward autocracy. Likewise, America's blue-blooded elite and its blue-collar workforce usually greeted the millions of Jewish immigrants who arrived in the United States between the Civil War and the Balfour Declaration with anti-Semitic epithets and ethnic slurs.

Beginning in the 1920s, however, the images of Muslims and Jews as represented in U.S. popular culture began to diverge sharply. Well into the last quarter of the twentieth century, films, books, and magazines continued to depict Arabs as primitive, untrustworthy, and malevolent figures who bore close watching. By contrast, the eagerness of Jewish newcomers to assimilate themselves into Main Street's mainstream and the awfulness of the Holocaust combined to reduce American anti-Semitism and to stimulate U.S. support for the creation and preservation of Israel, despite Arab objections.

Down through the 1990s, media giants as diverse as *National Geographic* and Disney Studios presented a Middle East in which

Israel was cast as an occidental David while Arabs, and Muslims in general, were depicted as oriental Goliaths. Predictably, the Oscar for best documentary in March 2000 went to *One Day in September*, the heartbreaking story of the Israeli Olympians massacred at Munich twenty-eight years earlier. Meanwhile the season's first box-office smash, *Rules of Engagement*, saw Samuel L. Jackson mow down a wild-eyed mob of Islamic zealots in Yemen, and Nelson DeMille's *The Lion's Game*, a potboiler recounting the fictional exploits of a ruthless Libyan terrorist, topped the *New York Times* best-seller list.

Nevertheless, in the wake of the airborne terrorist attacks on Washington and New York City on 11 September 2001 there were some reassuring signs that life need not always imitate art. Three summers earlier Twentieth Century Fox had released *The Siege*, an eerily prescient film about an ever escalating Muslim reign of terror in the streets of Manhattan that culminates with a group resembling al-Qaeda attacking a skyscraper with a truck bomb and killing 600 New Yorkers. "You have to learn the consequences of telling the world how to live," the terrorist ringleader informs the FBI's Denzel Washington in words that must have made Osama bin Laden smile. Shortly thereafter the Pentagon's Bruce Willis rounds up Arab Americans and briefly places them in detention centers.

Despite causing many more deaths, however, bin Laden's real-life assault on the World Trade Center generated a relatively mild orientalist backlash against America's Muslims.

Sadly, there was some racial profiling at airports, a few hate crimes, and even one or two murders. But there was no wholesale violation of the civil liberties of Arab Americans. Indeed, during a visit to Washington's Islamic Center on 17 September, George W. Bush took pains to emphasize that "Islam is peace" and reminded all Americans that they "must treat each other with respect," regardless of race or religion. "The terrorists are traitors to their own faith," Bush told a joint session of Congress three days later, "trying to hijack Islam itself."

Yet lurking just beneath Bush's rhetoric of toleration was a subliminal impulse to demonize Islamic terrorists that echoed earlier orientalist diatribes. "By sacrificing human life to serve their radical visions—by abandoning every value except the will to power—they follow in the path of fascism, and Nazism, and totalitarianism," America's forty-third president concluded. "And they will follow that path all the way, to where it ends: in history's unmarked grave of discarded lies." As the grim task of recovering the remains of thousands of Americans entombed beneath the ruins of the World Trade Center entered its sixth month, a truck bomb here or an oil embargo there seemed very likely to resurrect ugly anti-Arab prejudices from the not so distant past. With popular culture saturated by an American-style orientalism dating from the nineteenth century, it should come as no surprise that since 1945 the U.S. public and policymakers have ostracized Arab radicals who threaten Israeli security or challenge Western control over Middle East oil.

Study Questions

1. How did Americans view the Israeli-Arab conflict? How did the popular American image of Arabs influence U.S. policy in the Middle East?

2. What were the attitudes of the Truman, Eisenhower, Kennedy, and Johnson administrations toward the Middle East?

3. What impact did the novel and film *Exodus* have on American attitudes toward Israelis?

4. How did the film *Lawrence of Arabia* portray Arabs? What role did it suggest the West should play in the Middle East?

5. What impact did the Munich Massacre have on American attitudes toward the Middle East?

6. How have Arabs and Israelis been characterized in American popular culture during the last 20 years? What has been the effect on U.S. foreign policy?

Bibliography

"Arabs, Israelis, and American Orientalism" comes from Douglas Little's insightful *American Orientalism: The United States and the Middle East since 1945* (2004). Melani McAlister, *Epic Encounters: Culture, Media, and U.S. Interests in the Middle East since 1945* (2005), also blends popular culture with political culture and foreign policy. Three books by Edward Said are particularly influential: *Orientalism* (1979), *Covering Islam: How the Media and Its Experts Determine How We See the Rest of the World* (1981), and *Culture and Imperialism* (1993). Ali Behdad, *Belated Travelers: Orientalism in the Age of Colonial Dissolution* (1994), expands on Said's themes. Daniel Yergin, *The Prize: The Epic Quest for Oil, Money, and Power* (1991), treats vital economic relations between the United States and the Middle East.

READING 28

★ ★ ★

Perfect Bodies, Eternal Youth: The Obsession of Modern America

Randy Roberts and James S. Olson

The message comes at Americans from every direction, every hour of the day. The American obsession with body image has never been stronger. Diet books perennially occupy the top tier of best-seller book lists; plastic surgery "make-over" shows garner top Nielsen ratings on television; infomercials hawk a bewildering array of mechanical devices to shape the customers. Incidence rates of bulimia and anorexia nervosa among young women have never been higher. Yet, obesity is a national epidemic.

Sports programming dominates television, as if Americans have an insatiable need to watch football, baseball, basketball, bowling, bodybuilding, and a host of other competitions. Future linguists and anthropologists will study what have become the highlights of contemporary American popular culture—diet sodas, low-calorie beers, Lean Cuisine, sugarless gum, half-the-calories bread, Nautilus, jogging, Iron Man marathons, "fun runs," tennis, bicycling, 10 K races, Superbowls, play-offs, World Series, Grand Slams of golf and tennis, Little League, Pop Warner football, and championship after championship.

Modern America is not the first society to indulge in the emptiness of narcissism, but no other society has ever had such resources to spend on a fruitless crusade to prevent aging and deny death. In "Perfect Bodies, Eternal Youth: The Obsession of Modern America," Randy Roberts and James S. Olson examine the preoccupation with health, fitness, and youth in the United States, explaining how and why the members of an entire culture have become infatuated with their own bodies.

Fewer and fewer people these days argue that running shortens lives, while a lot of people say that it may strengthen them. If that's all we've got for the time being, it seems a good enough argument for running. Not airtight, but good enough.

—*Jim Fixx*

It was a perfect July day in Vermont—clear and cool. Jim Fixx, on the eve of a long-awaited vacation, put on his running togs and headed down a rural road for his daily run, expecting to do the usual twelve to fifteen miles. At fifty-two years of age, Fixx was a millionaire, the best-selling author of *The Complete Book of Running*, and the reigning guru of the American exercise cult. In 1968 he had weighed 214 pounds, smoked two packs of cigarettes a day, and worried about his family health history. Fixx's father had died of a heart attack at the age of forty-three. So Fixx started running and stopped smoking. He lost 60 pounds and introduced America to the virtues of strenuous exercise: longevity, freedom from depression, energy, and the "runner's high." He regularly ran 80 miles a week. When he hit the road on July 21, 1984, Fixx weighed 154 pounds and seemed the perfect image of fitness. Twenty minutes into the run he had a massive heart attack and died on the side of the road. A motorcyclist found his body later that afternoon.

Fixx's death shocked middle- and upper-class America. Of all people, how could Jim Fixx have died of a heart attack? Millions of joggers, runners, swimmers, cyclists, triathletes, walkers, weightlifters, and aerobic dancers had convinced themselves that exercise preserved youth and postponed death. It was the yuppie panacea; "working out" made them immune to the ravages of time.

From Randy Roberts and James S. Olson, "Perfect Bodies, Eternal Youth: The Obsession of Modern America" in *Winning Is the Only Thing*. The Johns Hopkins University Press, Baltimore/London, 1989, pp. 213–34. Reprinted by permission.

The autopsy on Fixx was even more disturbing. In spite of all the running, his circulatory system was a shambles. Fixx's cholesterol levels had been dangerously high. One coronary artery was 98 percent blocked, a second one 85 percent blocked, and a third one 50 percent blocked. In the previous two to eight weeks, the wall of his left ventricle had badly deteriorated. On that clear Vermont day, Jim Fixx shouldn't have been running; he should have been undergoing triple-bypass surgery.

Even more puzzling, Fixx had been complaining for months of chest pains while running—clear signs of a deadly angina, the heart muscle protesting lack of oxygen. Friends had expressed concern and urged him to get a check-up. He resisted, attempting to will good health. In January 1984 he had agreed to a treadmill test, but he skipped the appointment that afternoon, running 16 miles instead. Why had someone so committed to health ignored such obvious warnings? How had sports, exercise, and fitness become such obsessions in the United States?

Modern society was the culprit. In an increasingly secular society, church membership no longer provided the discipline to bind people together into cohesive social groups. Well-integrated neighborhoods with long histories and strong identities had given way after World War II to faceless suburbs. Corporate and professional elites tended to be highly mobile, relocating whenever a pay raise was offered. The new American community had become fifty suburban homes and a 7–11 convenience store. New organizations, especially business and government bureaucracies, had assumed power in the United States, but those were hardly places where most Americans could feel comfortable and in control. Blessed with money but deprived of community in the 1970s and 1980s, Americans began to use sports to rebuild their sense of community and fitness and to define individual happiness and individual pleasure, creating a culture of competitive narcissism supported by a host of therapeutic panaceas, such as EST, psychotherapy, Scientology, and strenuous exercise.

For individuals, families, groups, and communities, sports had become a new cultural currency, a common ground upon which a diverse people could express their values and needs. Unlike European society, where such traditional institutions as the church, the aristocracy, and the monarchy had maintained order through established authority, America had been settled by lower-class working people and small farmers. The traditional institutions anchoring European society were absent. Without those same moorings, America had always confronted the centrifugal forces of individualism, capitalism, Protestantism, and ethnicity, using the culture of opportunity to stave off social disintegration. Social mobility, the westward movement, the abundance of land, and ruralism helped stabilize a highly complex society.

But in the twentieth century, when industrialization, urbanization, and the disappearance of the frontier changed the definitions of opportunity and progress, the values of individualism, community, and competition had to find new modes of expression, and sports became a prominent one. At the local, regional, and national levels, sports evolved into one of the most powerful expressions of identity. Outside observers marveled, for example, at the "religion" of high school football in the more than eleven hundred independent school districts of Texas. When viewed simply as sport, of course, the obsession with football seems absurd, but when viewed in terms of community identity, it becomes more understandable. In hundreds of rural areas, where scattered farms surround tiny county seats, the local high school, with its arbitrarily drawn district lines, was the central focus of community life. Rural Texans passionately opposed school district consolidations, even when it made good economic sense, because it threatened the high school, high school football, and community identity. For hundreds of small Texas towns—and rural areas

throughout much of the rest of the country—high school athletics was literally the cement of community life.

It wasn't just high school sports which provided new identities in the United States. After World War II, social and economic pressures worked against the nuclear family. More and more women were working outside the home; more and more men were working at jobs that were long commutes from the suburbs; and divorce rates were way up. Childhood play became less spontaneous and more organized as schools, government, and communities assumed roles once played by the family. The most obvious consequence was the appearance of organized youth sports. Little League grew by leaps and bounds beginning in the 1950s; child's play, once the domain of the home and immediate neighborhood, became a spectator sport complete with uniforms, umpires, scoreboards, leagues, play-offs, drafts, and championships. By the 1980s, Little League was competing for time with Pop Warner football, Little Dribblers basketball, soccer, and swimming, with organized competition beginning in some sports at the age of three. In 1987 sports sociologists estimated that thirty million children under sixteen years of age were competing in organized sports.

Sports functioned as identity on the regional level as well. In an age when television, movies, and mass culture threatened regional distinctiveness, sports emerged as the single most powerful symbol of localism and community loyalty. That was obviously true of high school and college sports, but even in professional sports, when ownership shifted away from local businesses and entrepreneurs to conglomerates and national corporations, the regional identity of teams remained critically important to gate receipts and television revenues. The rivalries between the Chicago Bears and the Green Bay Packers, or the Boston Red Sox and the New York Yankees, or the Boston Celtics and the Los Angeles Lakers, filled stadiums, arenas, and living rooms with fans desperate for the home team to win. Five hundred years ago, European cities dedicated all their surplus capital over the course of 100 to 200 years to build elaborate cathedrals to God. In the United States during the 1970s and 1980s, the modern equivalent of the medieval cathedral was the domed stadium. For sports, not for God, American communities would sell bonds and mortgage themselves for the next generation.

Even on the national level, sports competition reflected and promoted American nationalism. Sports was a mirror of federalism, at once local in its community loyalties but national in its collective forms. The 1984 Olympic Games in Los Angeles did not just expose a rising tide of patriotism and national pride; they became a major force in stimulating a new American nationalism. Unlike the recent Olympic Games in Montreal, Moscow, and Seoul, the Los Angeles Games did not accumulate billion-dollar deficits and require the resources of national governments to prop them up. In 1984, "free enterprise capitalism" organized and conducted the Games, used existing facilities, and turned a profit. The Los Angeles Coliseum was filled with flag-waving Americans cheering every native athlete winning a medal. On television back home, Europeans watched the proceedings with astonishment and not a little fear, worrying about the burst of American patriotism, nationalism, and even chauvinism. Nearly a decade after the debacle in Vietnam, American pride and optimism were on the rebound, and the 1984 Olympic Games was center stage for the resurrection of the American sense of mission.

Modern sports in the United States also provided a sense of identity cutting across class, racial, and ethnic lines. In penitentiaries throughout the country, intense struggles were waged every evening over television and radio programming, black convicts wanting to watch soul stations and black sitcoms and whites demanding MTV or white sitcoms. But there was no trouble or debate on

Sunday afternoon or Monday nights during the fall. It was football, only football, and blacks and whites watched the programs with equal enthusiasm. On Monday evenings in the fall, whether in the poorest ghetto tenement of the South Side of Chicago or the most tastefully appointed living room in the Lake Forest suburbs, televisions were tuned in to football, and discussions at work the next morning revolved around the game, who won and who lost, and why.

For ethnic minorities and immigrants, sports similarly became a way of identifying with the new society, a powerful form of acculturation. During the 1980s, for example, Los Angeles became the second largest Mexican city in the world, behind only Mexico City in Spanish-speaking population and larger now than Guadalajara in terms of Mexican residents. At Dodger Stadium in Los Angeles, Mexicans and Mexican Americans became an increasingly large part of the evening box office, helping to sustain Dodger attendance at its three million-plus levels each year. In September 1986, when Dodger pitcher Fernando Valenzuela won his twentieth game of the season, the Spanish cable network SIN broke into its regular programming nationwide for live interviews. The fact that sports was making its way to the headlines and front pages of major newspapers was no accident in the United States. It had become, indeed, a new cultural currency in modern America, a way to interpret change and express traditional values.

Women, too, used sports as a vehicle in their drive for equality and identity. The development of women's and men's sports in America has varied considerably. From the first, men's sports have emphasized fierce competition and the ruthless pursuit of expertise. Early male and female physical educators, however, believed women were uncompetitive and decided that women's sports should promote a woman's physical and mental qualities and thus make her more attractive to men. They also believed that sports and exercise should sublimate female sexual drives. As renowned nineteenth-century physical educator Dudley A. Sargent noted, "No one seems to realize that there is a time in the life of a girl when it is better for her and for the community to be something of a boy rather than too much of a girl."

But tomboyish behavior had to stop short of abrasive competition. Lucille Eaton Hill, director of physical training at Wellesley College, urged women to "avoid the evils which are so apparent . . . in the conduct of athletics for men." She and her fellow female physical educators encouraged widespread participation rather than narrow specialization. In short, women left spectator and professional sports to men. Indeed, not until 1924 were women allowed to compete in Olympic track and field events, and even then on a limited basis.

During the 1920s the tennis careers of Suzanne Langlen and Helen Wills were used to demonstrate the proper and improper pursuit of victory by athletic women. Tennis, for the great French champion Langlen, was not only a way of life: it was life. Her only object on a tennis court was to win, and between 1919 and 1926, when she turned professional, Langlen lost only two sets of singles and won 269 of 270 matches. But at what cost? Bulimic in her eating habits and subject to dramatic swings in emotions, she suffered several nervous breakdowns and lived in fear of losing. In addition, male critics noted that, far from keeping her looking young, tennis cruelly aged Langlen. Journalist Al Laney remarked that by the mid-1920s Langlen looked thirty years older than she actually was and that her complexion had turned dull and colorless. Her friend Ted Tinling agreed that before she turned twenty-five, "her face and expression had already the traces of deep emotional experiences far beyond the normal for her age."

In contrast, Helen Wills was a champion of great physical beauty. Before Wills, Americans tended to agree with journalist Paul Gallico that "pretty girls" did not excel in sports and that outstanding female athletes were simply compensating for their lack of beauty. Summarizing this school of thought, Larry Engelmann observed: "Athletics was their way of getting attention. If Suzanne Langlen were really beautiful, for instance, she wouldn't be running around like crazy on the tennis courts of Europe. She would have been quietly at home, happily married. Athletics proved a refuge and a last chance for the desperate female ugly duckling."

Yet Wills was beautiful, and she was great, winning every set of singles competition she played between 1927 and 1933. Journalists explained Wills's success and beauty by stressing the fact that tennis was only a game for her, not a way of life and certainly not life itself. Losses did not worry her. She always appeared composed. "My father, a doctor," she explained, "always told me not to wince or screw up my face while I was playing. He said it would put lines on my face." And no victory was worth a line.

Women were not fully emancipated from the older ideal until the 1970s, when they asserted their right to be as ruthless and competitive in athletics as men. Tennis champion Billy Jean King symbolized on the court as well as off this new attitude. Like Langlen, she single-mindedly pursued victory. And she was no more concerned with sweating and grimacing than Pete Rose. Unlike Wills, King was not interested in art or starting a family. When asked why she was not at home, she replied, "Why don't you ask Rod Laver why he isn't at home?" It was as eloquent a statement of athletic liberation as could be asked for.

To develop fully as an athlete, King had to earn money. Along with Gladys Heldman and Philip Morris Tobacco Company, King helped to organize the Virginia Slims women's tennis circuit in 1971. That year she became the first female athlete to earn $100,000 in a single year. More importantly, she labored to get women players a bigger share of the prize money at the major championships. In the early 1970s women's purses at Wimbledon and the U.S. Open were about 10 percent of the men's. By the mid-1980s the prize money split was equal. As if to punctuate the point that women's tennis had arrived, King defeated the former Wimbledon triple-crown champion (1939) Bobby Riggs 6–4, 6–3, 6–3, in a highly publicized match in the Houston Astrodome in 1973.

Even more important than King for the future of women's athletics was Title IX of the 1972 Educational Amendments Act. It outlawed sexual discrimination by school districts or colleges and universities which received federal aid. Certainly, athletic budgets in high schools and universities are not equally divided between male and female athletics. But women have made significant gains. Before Title IX less than 1 percent of athletic budgets went to women's sports. By the 1980s that figure had increased to over 10 percent. No longer is there a serious argument over the road women's sports should travel. Instead, the battle is over what portion of that pie they should receive.

But it wasn't just countries, cities, colleges, small towns, high schools, and ethnic groups which turned to sports in the 1980s as the most powerful way of defining their values. The most extraordinary development in contemporary popular culture was the extent to which individuals turned to athletics, exercise, and body image as a way of finding meaning in an increasingly dislocated society. In the mid-1980s, a Louis Harris poll indicated that 96 percent of all Americans found something about their bodies that they didn't like and would change if they could. Harris said that the "rampant obsessions of both men and women about their looks have produced an obvious boon for the cosmetics industry, plastic surgery, diet doctors, fitness and shape advisers, fat farms, and exercise clubs." The cult of fitness and the cult of individual happiness went hand in hand. Politicians used international sports at the Olympic level to confirm the superiority of various political systems or prove the equality of their Third World cultures; they mustered professional sports to project the quality of life in major American cities; collegiate sports touted the virtues of different universities; and in the 1970s and 1980s, millions of Americans embraced the cult of fitness to discover the meaning of life, retreating into the fantasy that they are how they look.

The cult of fitness and preoccupation with physical appearance first emerged in the United States during the John Kennedy administration. In the election of 1960, Kennedy used television as it had never been used before when he challenged Richard Nixon to a series of debates. Kennedy faced formidable odds. Young, handsome, and wealthy, he was considered perhaps too young, too handsome, and too wealthy to make an effective president. His Roman Catholicism seemed another albatross. Behind the polls, Kennedy needed a boost. The televised debates were perfect.

Nixon arrived in Chicago for the first debate looking tired and ill. He had injured his knee six weeks before, and a hospital stay had weakened him. On the eve of the debate a chest cold left him hoarse. He looked like a nervous corpse—pale, twenty pounds underweight, and haggard. Makeup experts suggested covering his heavy beard with a thick powder, but Nixon accepted only a thin coat of Max Factor's "Lazy Shave," a pancake cosmetic.

Kennedy looked better, much better. He arrived at Chicago from California with a suntan. He didn't need makeup to look healthy, nor did he need special lighting to hide a weak profile. He did, however, change suits. He believed that a dark blue rather than a gray suit would look better under the bright lights. Kennedy was right, of course, as anyone who watches a nightly news program must realize. Once the debate started, Kennedy intentionally slowed down his delivery and watered down his ideas. His face was controlled and cool. He smiled with his eyes and perhaps the corners of his mouth, and his laugh was a mere suggestion of a laugh. Although Nixon marshalled a mountain of facts and closely reasoned arguments, he looked bad. Instead of hearing a knowledgeable candidate, viewers saw a nervous, uncertain man, one whose clothes didn't fit and whose face looked pasty and white. In contrast, Kennedy *looked* good, scored a victory in the polls, and went on to win the election by a razor-thin margin.

The first president born in the twentieth century, Kennedy had claimed in his inaugural address that "the torch had been passed to a new generation of Americans . . . tempered by war, disciplined by a hard and bitter peace, proud of our ancient heritage." Life around the White House soon reflected the instincts of a new generation. It wasn't just little Caroline and later John-John frolicking on the White House lawn. The Kennedys were fiercely competitive and obsessed with sports. At the family compound at Hyannisport or Robert Kennedy's "Hickory Hill" home in Virginia, the days were filled with tennis, golf, sailing, isometric exercise, swimming, horseback riding, badminton, and a brutal form of touch football, which overweight and overaged visitors dreaded, since the Kennedys expected everyone to give it a try. An atmosphere of youthful virility surrounded the Kennedy administration. To impress the Kennedys, one associate remembered, you had to "show raw guts, fall on your face now and then. Smash into the house once in a while going after a pass. Laugh off twisted ankles or a big hole torn in your best suit."

The whole country became infatuated with the sense of vitality, and the fifty-mile hike became the symbol of fitness. Marine Corps commandant General David M. Shoup, whom Kennedy especially admired, accepted Kennedy's challenge to see if his Marines could duplicate a feat of Theodore Roosevelt's 1908 Marines—march fifty miles in less than twenty hours. Shoup met the challenge, as did Attorney General Robert Kennedy, who

walked his fifty miles along the path of the C & O canal. Kennedy's secretaries took up the challenge, and once the newspapers had picked up the story, tens of thousands of Americans tried it too. The spring of 1963 became the season of the fifty-mile hike.

These were also years of giddy infatuation with the Mercury astronauts, whose crew-cut fitness first came to public attention at their introductory press conference in 1959. All of them were military pilots, and John Glenn of Ohio emerged as their leader. Square-jawed with ramrod perfect posture, Glenn had a personality and value system to match. He was the ultimate "goody-goody," and America loved him. The country was also astounded at his daily fitness regimen—vigorous calisthenics followed by a two-mile jog along the beach. Two miles—every day! Even when it rained.

If John Glenn was the leading jogger of the 1960s, the scientific father of running was Kenneth Cooper, an Air Force physician. A high school track star in Oklahoma City, Cooper finished medical school and joined the Air Force as a physician at the School of Aerospace Medicine in San Antonio. He tested fitness levels in thousands of potential Air Force pilots and in the process developed new standards of conditioning. To really benefit from exercise, Americans had to get their heart rate above 130 beats a minute for a sustained period. Jogging, running, racquetball, squash, cycling, walking, and swimming were the best exercises.

To please an increasingly technical, postindustrial clientele whose faith in science was unrivaled, Cooper even charted fitness, providing a quantified methodology to guarantee fitness. An aerobically fit person had to "earn 30 points a week." He or she could do this by walking three miles in no more than forty-one minutes five times a week; by swimming 700 yards in fifteen minutes five times a week; or by running a mile in eight minutes only twice a week. To measure fitness, Cooper recommended the "twelve minutes test." If a person can run or walk less than a mile in twelve minutes, he or she is in "very poor shape"; 1 to 1.25 miles is "poor"; 1.25 to 1.5 miles is "fair"; 1.5 to 1.75 miles is "good"; and more than 1.75 miles is "excellent." Cooper also warned people to watch out if their pulse rate exceeded 80 beats a minute. Fewer than 60 beats was "excellent." Vigorous exercise would reduce the heart rate. In Cooper's own words, "You might just save your heart some of those 20,000 to 30,000 extra beats you've forced on it every day."

The country was more than ready for Cooper's message. Early in the 1960s the first of the baby-boom generation hit college. The "don't trust anyone over thirty" culture had appeared, protesting war and inequality and proclaiming the virtues of brotherly love and sexual liberation. In 1961 half the American population was under thirty. By 1964 the median age had dropped to twenty-seven and in 1966 to twenty-five. America fell in love with youth, health, sex, and pleasure. Hippies, protests, "love-ins," "teach-ins," Woodstock, drugs, rebellion, and loud, self-righteous rejections of materialism emanated from college campuses.

But in 1967 the first baby-boom class graduated from college. The transformation of hippies into "yuppies" was underway. By 1971 those 1946 babies were twenty-five years old. The cruel tricks of gravity and heredity commenced. Bellies started to thicken, hairlines to recede. Women with babies looked despairingly at abdominal stretch marks and the faint beginnings of "crow's feet." The youth culture still survived, but individual youth was proving to be a temporary state. Middle age loomed as large as death.

Dr. Kenneth Cooper had the answer. Late in 1968, he coined a new word and wrote a book by the same name—*Aerobics.* By 1972 the book had sold nearly three million copies to anxious yuppies bent on postponing the inevitable. By the early 1970s, Cooper had an estimated eight million Americans, including astronaut John Glenn, adding up their weekly

points, counting their pulse, testing their speed, taking their blood pressure, and weighing their bodies.

Throughout the 1970s and 1980s the cult of fitness reached extraordinary dimensions in the United States. More than twenty million Americans regularly exercised, and along with the running boom came a boom in racquetball, tennis, swimming, cycling, weightlifting, and "aerobic" dancing. In 1970 only 125 people entered the first New York City marathon, which took runners over a 26-mile course through all four boroughs; but in the 1986 marathon, 20,000 officially entered the race, and 19,412 finished it. The race was so popular that organizers had to reject thousands of applicants. Marathons became common events on every weekend all across the country.

The triathlon endurance was an even better gauge of the fitness cult. Known as the ultimate of the "ultrasports," the triathlon combined a 2-mile swim with a 112-mile cycle ride and a 26-mile run. In 1986 more than one million Americans competed in triathlon events around the country. And in what can only be considered the absurd limit of the fitness craze, Stu Mittleman won the "Sri Chinmoy 1,000 Mile Marathon" in New York City in 1986. His time of just under fifteen days "was my best ever."

The cult of fitness was rivaled only by the obsession with youth and body image which swept through American culture in the 1970s and 1980s. To be sure, this was nothing new. Americans had long been preoccupied with their bodies, and attempts to stay young had centered on staying thin, as if slenderness were in itself a foundation of youth. In the 1860s Harriet Beecher Stowe had written: "We in America have got so far out of the way of a womanhood that has any vigor of outline or opulence of physical proportion, that, when we see a woman made as a woman ought to be, she strikes us as a monster. Our willowy girls are afraid of nothing so much as growing stout."

To stay thin, nineteenth-century American women dieted and corseted their bodies. "It ain't stylish for young courting gals to let on like they have any appetite," admitted one female. And through tightlacing their corsets, women could maintain the proper girlish waistline of eighteen inches, with only such acceptable side effects as headaches, fainting spells, and uterine and spinal disorders.

If tightlacing and dieting led to serious health problems, illness was in itself admired. Consumptive women were romanticized and imbued with spiritual qualities. Little Eva in *Uncle Tom's Cabin*, Beth in *Little Women*, Mimi in *La Bohème*—all were thin, romantic consumptives who radiated spirituality and sensuality. Perhaps the ideal was the romantic ballerina—thin, ethereal, pale, pure, as certain to die young as poor broken-hearted Giselle.

Throughout the twentieth century, thinness has largely remained the feminine ideal, although sickliness generally declined as an attractive characteristic. The Gibson Girl of the turn of the century touted athletics, and during the 1920s the flapper exuded energy, vitality, and youth. And if the breast-bound flapper did not survive the 1929 stock market crash, an emphasis on thinness did. Indeed, only during the 1950s, when Marilyn Monroe was at her height, was there a serious challenge to the slender ideal.

Post–World War II culture has enshrined both thinness and youth for men as well as women. Advertisers have aided the process. Since photographers maintain that clothes look best on lean bodies, leading fashion models have always been thin and generally young. But since the 1960s, advertisers have used youth and thinness to sell other products as well. The evolution of Pepsi-Cola slogans illustrates this point:

> 1935: "Twice as Much."
> 1948: "Be Sociable—Have a Pepsi."
> 1960: "Now it's Pepsi for those who think young."
> 1965: "The Pepsi Generation."
> 1984: "Pepsi: The Choice of a New Generation."

Appeals to abundance ("twice as much") and social interaction ("be sociable") were replaced by the promise of eternal youth. As if to reinforce this appeal, Pepsi paid magnificent amounts to two thin, youthful Michaels as spokesmen: Michael Jackson and Michael J. Fox. Far from being sociable, Jackson is a virtual recluse, obsessed with personality change through plastic surgery. And Fox, as sure as Peter Pan, is the perpetual adolescent.

To fit the culture's procrustean mold, advertisers encourage Americans to binge and purge, consume and diet. Consume because "you are someone special" and "you can have it all." Diet because "you can never be too thin or too rich." In his perceptive book *Never Satisfied*, Hillel Schwartz argues that "dieting is an essentially nostalgic act, an attempt to return to a time when one *could* be satisfied, when one *was* thinner, when the range of choices in the world neither bewildered nor intimidated. To restrict one's range of choices, as all dieters must do, is not so much deficient as it is regressive. . . . Imagining a miraculous future, the dieter is always looking back."

In a secular, materialistic age, dieting has become an ascetic religion. Seventeenth-century poet and preacher John Donne wrote, "The flesh that God hath given us is affliction enough, but the flesh that the devil gives us, is affliction upon affliction and to that, there belongs a woe." To be fat in America has become a religious as well as a secular sin. Christian diet books emphasize John 3:30—"He must increase, but I must decrease."

In 1957 Charlie Shedd in his *Pray Your Weight Away* confessed, "We fatties are the only people on earth who can weigh our sin." His book inspired some Christians to lose weight and others to write diet books. Such works as Deborah Price's *I Prayed Myself Thin*,

John Cavanaugh's *More of Jesus and Less of Me*, Reverend H. Victor Kane's *Devotion for Dieters,* and Francis Hunter's *God's Answer to Fat—Lose It!* emphasized that godliness is in league with thinness. Capturing the temper of her times, columnist Ellen Goodman wrote in 1975 that "eating has become the last bona fide sin left in America." And on this point, religion and secular humanism are in complete accord.

The fitness boom and body-image obsession financed a huge growth industry. To support their new interest in fitness, Americans needed equipment and clothes—shoes, shorts, shirts, racquets, bicycles, balls, paddles, bats, cleats, gloves, goggles, weights, scales, blood-pressure cuffs, timing watches, clubs, socks, headbands, wristbands, and leotards. Between 1975 and 1987 sporting goods sales in the United States increased from $8.9 billion to $27.5 billion. Americans spent $4 billion on athletic shoes alone in 1987. Health clubs, once the domain of the wealthy and a small clique of bodybuilders, multiplied in number from 350 in 1968 to more than 7,000 in 1986. Gross revenues in 1987 exceeded $650 million.

Exercise and fitness revenues were matched by those of the weight loss industry. Jean Nidetch founded Weight Watchers in 1962 and eventually franchised it, making sure that group leaders had been through the diet program and reached "maintenance" levels. Attendance doubled between 1983 and 1987, the gross revenues went past $200 million that year. Sybil Ferguson's Diet Center, Inc., founded in 1969, had two thousand franchises in 1987 and nearly $50 million in gross revenues. Americans spent $6 billion for diet soda in 1986, $5 billion for vitamins and health foods, and $350 million for diet capsules and liquid protein. The president's council on physical fitness estimated that 65 million Americans were dieting in 1987. Diet Coke, Diet Pepsi, Diet Dr Pepper, Lean Cuisine, Bud Light, Miller Lite, "lite" bread, sugarless gum, NutraSweet, Cambridge, and a host of other diet products entered American popular culture.

What dieting and exercise couldn't fix, plastic surgery could. Americans went on a plastic surgery binge in the 1980s—not to repair real damage to their bodies or birth defects, but to improve their appearance cosmetically and recapture the illusion of youth. In 1987 more than 500,000 Americans underwent cosmetic plastic surgery. The most popular procedures were abdominoplasty (tummy tucks), breast augmentation, liposuction (fat removal), blepharoplasty (eyes), and rhinoplasty (nose). Plastic surgeons were also beginning to perform "total body contour" procedures. To postpone middle age, yuppies made plastic surgery a $3 billion industry.

Americans also changed a number of their habits in the 1970s and 1980s. Cigarette consumption began to decline in 1982. In 1965, 52 percent of men and 34 percent of women smoked. By 1985 only 33 percent of men and 28 percent of women smoked, and at the end of 1987 the American Cancer Society estimated that only 27 percent of Americans were still smoking. Per capita whiskey consumption dropped nearly 20 percent between 1976 and 1986 as Americans turned to lower-alcohol-content beer and wine coolers. Beef and pork consumption dropped in favor of chicken and fish when cholesterol-conscious Americans turned away from "red meat." Caffeine was also suspect. Americans under twenty-five drank only a third of the coffee their parents did; sales of decaffeinated coffee and drinks like Pepsi Free and Pepper Free symbolized the new health consciousness.

The results were impressive, even though some of the gains had to be attributed to better drug therapy, the rise of heart bypass surgery, and improvement of cardiac care units in American hospitals. But the bottom line was that between 1950 and 1985, the death rate per 100,000 people from cardiovascular and cerebrovascular disease declined from

511 to 418, a dramatic improvement. The cult of fitness seemed to be paying dividends.

But there was an underside to the cult of fitness, an obsessive perfectionism which was the antithesis of good health. Jim Fixx and his daily runs in spite of chest pains were one example. Kathy Love Ormsby was another. The North Carolina State University junior, who held the U.S. collegiate women's record for 10,000 meters, had difficulty dealing with failure. In the 1986 NCAA championships, after 6,400 meters, she was struggling along in fourth place, running a bad race. Then, as she approached a turn, she decided to keep going straight. She ducked under a railing and ran straight past Wisconsin team coach Peter Tegen. "It was eerie," he said. "Her eyes were focused straight ahead." She kept going—out of Indiana University's track stadium in Indianapolis, across a softball diamond, over a seven-foot fence, down New York Street, toward the bridge that spans the White River. Seventy-five feet onto the bridge she stopped, climbed over the railing, and jumped. After falling thirty-five feet, she landed on the soggy ground close to the river. She broke a rib, collapsed a lung, and fractured vertebrae. The doctor who attended her said that she would be permanently paralyzed from the waist down: "Given the distance that she fell, she's very lucky she's not a quadriplegic," Dr. Peter Hall noted. "She could have easily died."

Why? Ormsby was a high school valedictorian, a straight-A student, the record holder for the 800, 1,600, and 3,200 meters. At North Carolina State she was a track star and promising premed student. She was raised in a strong Christian family and was deeply religious herself. After her record-breaking 10,000-meter run, she told a reporter: "I just have to learn to do my best for myself and for God and to turn everything over to Him." Her leap had turned everything over to Him.

Some observers blamed Ormsby's consuming pursuit of perfection. Others blamed the pressure of world-class sport competition. Her father commented, "I believe . . . that it had something to do with the pressure that is put on young people to succeed." Certainly society's emphasis on the importance of sports places tremendous strains on young athletes. Often isolated from the world outside gyms and tracks and stadiums, they begin to think that their world has real, lasting meaning. Failure, then, becomes equated with death itself.

Such obsessive perfectionism also affected millions of other people, only a tiny fraction of whom were competitive athletes. For many people, exercise and weight loss became forms of psychological discipline, proof that the individual was in charge of his or her life. A 1986 Gallup poll estimated that three million Americans, most of them women, suffered from eating disorders—anorexia nervosa and bulimia. In anorexia nervosa, victims virtually starve themselves to death, using laxatives, exercise, and absurdly low calorie intake to lose body weight. Most psychologists attribute the eating disorder to a sense of powerlessness in the victim. They strive for a sense of weightlessness, and in that weightlessness they find a sense of control missing from other areas of their lives. In 1984 the soft-rock vocalist Karen Carpenter brought the disease to national attention when she died of a heart attack induced by extreme weight loss. Even when their weight drops below 85 pounds and they resemble concentration camp victims, anorectics still look in the mirror and see themselves as fat, with round faces and flabby skin. Breasts disappear, menstruation stops, and their bodies return momentarily, just before death, to preadolescence.

Bulimia is a related disorder. The Gallup poll concluded that nearly 10 percent of all American women between the ages of sixteen and twenty-five practice bulimia, an eating disorder characterized by huge calorie intake followed by self-induced vomiting. The Food and Drug Administration said that bulimic episodes may last up to eight hours, with an intake of 20,000 calories (an equivalent of 210 brownies, or 6 layer cakes, or 35 Big Macs), involve 25 to 30 vomiting episodes, and cost up to $75 a day for food purchases. If untreated, the disease causes irregular heartbeats, cramps, fatigue, and seizures by destroying the body's electrolyte balance. The gastric acid from vomiting will also erode teeth away.

In a country which historically has been keenly competitive and has periodically affirmed a belief in perfectionism, the idea of a better life through sports has been carried to obsessive lengths. Often the object of physical fitness has not been to produce health and well-being but to test or even to escape the limits of one's body. Ultradistance runner Stu Mittleman, one of the leaders in his field during the 1980s, was the epitome of this tendency. For him a 26-mile marathon was unsatisfactory, a flat, almost meaningless endeavor. The 100-mile event was better, and in the early 1980s he established the American record with a 12:56:34 run. Better still was the six-day event, in which his 488 miles was also an American record.

In ultra-distance running Mittleman saw man rediscovering his lost past. "Our culture forces us to eliminate sensory input so that we can cope," he observed. "Sports re-sensitizes. I want to live life intensely. . . . Long slow running has a heritage in hunting and gathering. Sprinting is based on retreat, on flight." Life, then, is best experienced at the limits of endurance, well past what is good for one's health. Yet, sometimes even that does not seem enough. As Mittleman told an interviewer, "I plan to do a 12-hour run tomorrow. You know, it seems like so little now."

Among world-class athletes, performance is more important than health. During the nineteenth century athletes occasionally took drugs to enhance their performances. Cyclists, in particular, used drugs to extend their pain and endurance barriers. As early as 1869 some cyclists used "speed balls" of heroin and cocaine to increase endurance. Others used caffeine, alcohol, nitroglycerine, ethyl ether, strychnine, and opium to achieve the same effect.

Of course, not all athletes survived such experimentation. And in the twentieth century, as drug use became more frequent, the casualty rate climbed. In 1960 Danish cyclist Knut Jensen collapsed and died during the Rome Olympics. He had taken amphetamines and nicotinyl tartrate to improve his chances of victory. In 1967 Thomas Simpson died during the ascent of Mount Ventoux in the Tour de France. Amphetamines were discovered in his jersey pockets and luggage.

Since World War II, however, stimulants have done less damage than muscle-building drugs. During the 1920s American scientists isolated the male hormone testosterone. By the 1940s testosterone was being hailed as a potential fountain of youth. Science writer Paul de Kruif in *The Male Hormone* (1945) noted that the newly developed synthetic testosterone "did more than give [the subjects] more energy and a gain in weight. . . . It changed them, and fundamentally . . . after many months on testosterone, their chest and shoulder muscles grew much heavier and stronger. . . . In some mysterious manner, testosterone caused the human body to synthesize protein, it caused the human body to be able to build the very stuff of its own life." There is evidence that during World War II testosterone was administered to German storm troopers to increase their strength and aggressiveness.

In 1945 de Kruif speculated, "It would be interesting to watch the productive power of [a] . . . professional group [of athletes] that would try a systematic supercharge with testosterone." By the 1952 Helsinki Olympics the Soviet Union had embarked on just such a campaign. That year Soviet weightlifters won seven Olympic medals, and U.S. Olympic weightlifting coach Bob Hoffman told reporters, "I know they're taking the hormone stuff to increase their strength."

At the 1954 World Weightlifting Championships in Vienna, a Soviet team physician confirmed Hoffman's belief. Upon returning home, Dr. John Ziegler, the U.S. team physician, acquired some testosterone and tested it on himself, Hoffman, and several American lifters. Concerned about the hormone's side effects—heightened aggression, increased libido, prostatic problems, and hirsutism—Ziegler approached the CIBA pharmaceutical company about producing a drug that would have testosterone's anabolic (muscle-building) effects without its androgenic (masculine characteristics) problems. The unsatisfactory result was the anabolic steroid Dianabol, a drug intended to aid burn victims and certain postoperative and geriatric patients.

Dianabol soon became the candy of the athletic world. By the 1960s nearly every world-class weightlifter was taking some form of anabolic steroid. In fact, steroids became the *sine qua non* of lifting. American superheavyweight weightlifting champion Ken Patera announced in 1971 that he was anxious to meet his Russian counterpart Vasily Alexiev in the 1972 Olympics: "Last year, the only difference between me and him was that I couldn't afford his pharmacy bill. Now I can. When we hit Munich next year, I'll weigh in at about 340, maybe 350. Then we'll see which are better—his steroids or mine."

Track and field athletes, football players, and bodybuilders similarly improved their performances with the aid of drugs. Jay Sylvester, a member of the 1972 U.S. Olympic track and field team, polled his teammates and found that 68 percent had used steroids to prepare for the Games. They believed that without them they would be at a competitive disadvantage. The same was true in football. One San Diego Charger player told team psychiatrist Arnold J. Mandell, "Doc, I'm not about to go out one-on-one against a guy who's grunting and drooling and coming at me with big dilated pupils unless I'm in the same condition."

Testosterone and anabolic steroids have led to athletes' experimenting with other performance-enhancing drugs. One of the more popular recent additions to this drug array is human growth hormone (hGH), a hormone manufactured from the pituitary. As the authors of *The Underground Steroid Handbook* claimed, hGH could "overcome bad genetics. . . . We LOVE the stuff." Of course, it may also cause elongation of the chin, feet, and hands; thickening of the rib cage and wrists; and heart problems.

Risk is part of taking drugs. Anabolic steroids can cause a rare, fatal type of kidney tumor, high blood pressure, sterility, intestinal bleeding, hypoglycemia, heart problems, acne, a deepened voice, and a change in the distribution of body hair. Steroids and testosterone also make users more aggressive and irritable. One NFL player confessed that testosterone "definitely makes a person mean and aggressive. . . . On the field I've tried to hurt people in ways I never did before. . . . A lot of guys can't handle it. I'm not sure I can. I remember a while back five of the guys on our team went on the juice at the same time. A year later four of them were divorced and one was separated. I've lost a lot of hair from using it, but I have to admit it's great for football. . . . I lost my family, but I think I'm a better player now. Isn't that a hell of a trade-off?"

By the 1970s steroids had become part of America's drug culture, and athletes asserted the right to decide what could or could not go into their own bodies. Frederick C. Hatfield in *Anabolic Steroids: What Kind and How Many* (1982) wrote: "As pioneers, these athletes carefully weigh the risk-to-benefit ratio and proceed with caution and with open minds. Can there be much wrong with getting bigger and/or stronger?" Users, then, have been transformed into pioneers, "adventurers who think for themselves and who want to accomplish something noble before they are buried and become worm food."

Ironically, however, most of the users are not world-class athletes. In the 1980s use of steroids expanded out of the realm of world-class athletes to college and high school playing fields. An estimated one million young American men and women were consuming large amounts of anabolic steroids in 1987. The praise they received for "bulking up" was irresistible. When they reduced steroid use and lost muscle tissue, friends immediately commented on how "much smaller you are," and they would return to the pills. Like bulimia and anorexia nervosa, anabolic steroids were addictions linked inseparably with body image.

Steroid use was most pronounced in the subculture of body building. Most of these men and women are not competitive athletes trying to break a world record or win an Olympic gold metal—"to accomplish something noble"—but people who want to look "pumped." Like dieting and cosmetic surgery, steroid use has become a means to a better-looking body, and looks—not health—is the real objective.

The quest for the "ideal" body has been taken to its furthest pharmaceutical extremes by bodybuilders. Not only do they take steroids to build up muscle mass, but they also diet and take diuretics to achieve maximum muscular striation, or the "cut up" look. For weeks or even months before an important competition, bodybuilders eat as little as 1,000 calories a day and still work out eight or more hours a day. The result may be "the picture of health," but there is no reality behind the image. As one professional commented, "When we walk on stage we are closer to death than we are to life." And after a contest, in a bulimic binge, bodybuilders "pig out," often putting on fifteen pounds in one evening of eating.

Furthermore, to support their quest, many bodybuilders resort to homosexual "hustling." In theory, male bodybuilders have enshrined heterosexuality. Charles Atlas advertisements emphasized that the prize for the biggest biceps was the woman in the bathing suit. *Muscle and Fitness,* the leading bodybuilder magazine, reinforces this mythology by always picturing beautiful women hanging onto the biceps and thighs of "pumped," oiled men. "Ya know," said *Muscle and Fitness* editor Joe Weider, "in every age the women, they always go for the guy with the muscles, the bodybuilder. [The women] never go for the studious guy."

In fact, gay men have been a continual source of financial support for bodybuilders. Since serious bodybuilding is a full-time pursuit, the men involved need some source of income. Anthropologist Alan M. Kline estimated that 50 to 75 percent of Southern California bodybuilders "hustle" the gay community for living expenses. Hustling ranges from posing for "beefcake" photographers and dancing nude at all-male events to pornography and sexual acts. Most bodybuilders, however, insist that they are not homosexual, that they have to hustle only to finance their bodybuilding habit. And besides, they insist, almost everyone does it. "People don't realize," noted one bodybuilder, "that in any given line-up of twenty competitors ten are hustling."

Many serious bodybuilders sacrifice heterosexual relationships as well as good health for their obsession. As one admitted, "On any given day I can go out with a woman, but it is not very satisfying. . . . Women demand time. I don't have that right now." Time, commitment, women, and even other men—all are obstacles to be mastered or avoided in the pursuit of a narcissistic ideal. To echo Michael Jackson's popular 1988 song, life for these bodybuilders starts and ends with the man in the mirror.

By the end of the 1980s, sports had become the secular religion of America. The stadiums, tanning salons, health spas, and gymnasiums had become the new cathedrals; jogging, running, aerobic dancing, cycling, weightlifting, and dieting the new rituals; and televised events, newspapers, radio talk shows, and sports and health magazines the new liturgies. The most obsessive athletes have a disciplined devotion that even the most ascetic medieval saints would have envied. Alberto Salazar, the world-class marathoner, bragged about his willingness to run 105 miles a week on stress-fractured legs. In the heat of one marathon, he kept running even when his body temperature had reached 108 degrees, collapsed in heat prostration, and while being packed in ice, received the last rites of the Roman Catholic Church.

Sports in the 1980s holds out secular salvation for nations, communities, and individuals. In competition and fitness, they locate the holy grail, the meaning of life in a world where God, church, and state no longer reign supreme. In *The Complete Book of Running*, Jim Fixx wrote: "It is here with my heart banging against my ribs that I discover how far beyond reason I can push myself. Furthermore, once a race has ended, I know what I am truly made of. Who can say how many of us have learned life's profoundest lessons while aching and gasping for breath?" On that Vermont road in 1986, with his body aching, his lungs gasping for breath, and his heart pounding against his ribs, Jim Fixx may have discovered the meaning of life.

Study Questions

1. Why did sports assume such an important dimension in American culture after World War II?

2. To what extent does sports in America reflect the aggressive, competitive spirit of the American culture?

3. What are the advantages and disadvantages to the new American obsession with sports?

4. In rural areas, why are high school sports so important to the community?

5. Why has plastic surgery become so popular in modern America?

6. How can anorexia nervosa and bulimia be seen as cultural, not merely physical, extremes?

7. What does the concept *cultural currency* mean? How do sports assist American society in transcending ethnic and religious divisions?

8. What is the connection between the cult of fitness and the post–World War II baby boom generation of yuppies?

Bibliography

For an extraordinary look at American values in the contemporary period, see Christopher Lasch, *The Culture of Narcissism: American Life in the Age of Diminishing Expectations* (1975); Bruce J. Schulman, *The Seventies: The Great Shift in American Culture, Society, and Politics* (2002); and David Frum, *How*

We Got Here: The 70's: The Decade That Brought You Modern Life—for Better or Worse (2000). Also see Peter Clecak, *America's Quest for the Ideal Self* (1983). Randy Roberts and James S. Olson analyze the American obsession with sports in *Winning Is the Only Thing* (1989). Studs Terkel's *American Dreams: Lost and Found* (1980) is an oral history of how Americans coped with the social and economic changes of the 1970s and 1980s. Hillel Schwartz's *Never Satisfied: A Cultural History of Diets, Fantasies and Fat* (1986) is an outstanding examination of the American preoccupation with youth and body image. Also see Kim Chernin, *The Obsession: Reflections on the Tyranny of Slenderness* (1981). For the dangerous, pathologic dimension of weight consciousness in history, see Rudolph M. Bell, *Holy Anorexia* (1985).

READING 29

★ ★ ★

O.J. Simpson: The Trial of the Century

Haynes Johnson

O.J. Simpson had spent his career in the national spotlight. In 1967 as a running back for the University of Southern California, he led the Trojans to a Rose Bowl. The following year, he became everybody's All-American, flashing across the nation's televisions with a combination of speed and moves unmatched in the history of football. He won the Heisman Trophy, the Maxwell Award, and the AP and UPI Player of the Year honors. As a professional he was equally spectacular. Not only did he become the first runner to rush for more than 2,000 yards in one season, he also set National Football League records for the most 100-yard games and the most yards in one game. But O.J. was always more than his statistics indicated. His charm, smile, and charisma made him an icon. He was the first African-American athlete to become a major corporate spokesman, and after he retired, he became a film and television celebrity. Unlike previous black athletes, it seemed that every door in America was open to O.J.

All this changed on Friday, June 17, 1994. First, the Los Angeles County Police Department charged Simpson with the murder of his ex-wife, Nicole Brown Simpson, and her friend Ronald Goldman. Next, reporters tracked Simpson to a white Ford Bronco, driven by O.J.'s friend Al Cowlings. Followed by a flotilla of police cars and television helicopters, Cowlings drove Simpson along various Los Angeles freeways. Cheering spectators lined several stretches of highway, and all the major networks covered the entire drama. The trial that followed, which historian Haynes Johnson termed the "trial of the century," became a media event that shed light on more than Simpson's innocence or guilt. It illuminated American culture in the late twentieth century.

Everyone thinks they know him: O.J., the good guy, always smiling, always charming, always nonthreatening, always ready to sign one more autograph for adoring fans; O.J., the all-American sports hero, the amiable athlete turned affable TV commentator; O.J., the entertaining pitchman who is constantly seen in American living rooms, courtesy of TV commercials, leaping over barricades and racing through airports as he promotes his sponsor's products; O.J., the loving father and family man; O.J., the black man, who plays so long and successful a role as an appealing, self-effacing American icon, that he's no longer seen as black. In fact, he doesn't see himself as black—he's often quoted as saying, "I'm not black, I'm O.J." In manner, language, lifestyle, and personal association he passes, seemingly effortlessly, into the upper echelons of the white world. Exposed to the good life, courted by the powerful, he belongs to the best country clubs, moves in the best social circles, golfs with the corporate elite, travels on private jets to fabulous resorts, rubs shoulders with influential deal makers.

So nonblack, so nonthreatening racially is O.J. that he becomes the first black athlete to be employed by corporate sponsors to endorse products not marketed solely to blacks. His marriage to a beautiful young blonde, a familiar golden girl of the nineties type, draws none of the sneers and hatred and jealousies that mark other interracial celebrity marriages. In the American heart and mind, O.J. is colorless. His celebrity status is such that even some who resent him do not express their feelings publicly. That is particularly true, and particularly complicated, when it comes to blacks.

After O.J.'s arrest for the murders, some of these hidden emotions surface. "He forgot that he was black," one black woman says when she phones a Dallas talk-radio show de-

Haynes Johnson, *The Best of Times: The Boom and Bust Years of America Before and After Everything Changed,* Harvest Books, Harcourt Inc., 2002.

Never had an athelete risen and fallen as far as O. J. Simpson. From his days at USC to his trial for murder, he captured the attention of the nation.

voted solely to the O.J. case. "He didn't show love to us that he should have showed. But deep in our hearts, all of us loved him. He left us years ago." Another black woman calls the same show to say: "Even though he was with a white woman, he was something for our race to be proud of. I feel hurt. I feel hurt."

O.J., the reality, is infinitely more complicated. His life story illuminates the continuing struggles of African Americans to escape the obstacles that keep them separated from the predominant white mainstream. O.J. Simpson, the gentle sports hero fans think they know, is, in fact, the product of a tough, violent upbringing in the slums of San Francisco.

His is a raw and painful childhood, but typical of blacks like him who live in the dismal public projects of the inner city. In the tough Potrero Hill district where he grew up,

70 percent of the blacks are on welfare, and, as in O.J.'s case, a majority of the children are raised without a father in the home. It's common for them to join a gang, as O.J. does at the age of thirteen when he becomes a member of the Gladiators. A year later, at fourteen, he experiences his first arrest—for robbing a liquor store. In junior high he joins what he once described as his "first *fighting* gang," the Persian Warriors. With them, he participates in pitched battles, usually on weekends, with rival gangs. In their world, violence is commonplace; brawling and stoning cars are part of a normal weekend. Witnessing sudden death is also a common experience. Years later, O.J. remembers being in gang fights "where a couple of guys got croaked."

By the age of fifteen, he has earned a reputation as being especially good with his fists. "I only beat up dudes who deserved it," he once explained, "at least once a week, usually on Friday or Saturday night. If there wasn't no fight, it wasn't no weekend." It was then, barely into his teens, that he wins renown within the gang culture for the manner in which he beats an older, much feared, leader of a rival gang, the Roman Gents, the toughest gang in the city.

After he ends his pro-football career, O.J. recalls that fistfight in a 1976 *Playboy* interview that reveals much about him the public would later be forced to confront, but does not want to. His fight is with Winky, then a battle-hardened twenty-year-old. "One night I was at a dance in the Booker T. Washington Community Center," O.J. remembers, "when, all of a sudden, this *loud* little sucker—an older O.J.—comes up to me and says, 'What did you say about my sister?' I'd heard of Winky—just about everyone had—but I didn't know that was who this cat was, so I just said, 'Hey, man, I don't know your sister. I don't even know *you*.' It wasn't cool to fight in the community center, so the guy started walking away, but he was still talkin' crap to me and I yelled back, 'Fuck you, too, man!'

"Well, a few minutes later, I see a whole bunch of Roman Gents trying to get this cat to be cool, but nope, he's comin' over to me and he shouts, 'Motherfucker, I'm gonna kick your ass!!' And then—bingo!—the music stops and I hear everybody whisperin', 'Winky's gettin' ready to fight.' *Winky!* Damn, I didn't want to fight *him*. So as he walks up to me, I say, 'Hey, man, I really didn't say *anything* about your sister.' But before I can say anything else, Winky's on me, and swingin'. Well, I beat his ass—I just cleaned up on the cat—and as I'm givin' it to him, I see this girl Paula, who I just loved, so *I* start getting loud. And as I'm punchin', I'm also shoutin': '*Muthafuckah! You gonna fuck with me??*'"

That's the O.J. his peers know. The public never does. Over the years, as he becomes enshrined among American sports heroes, O.J. adopts the style—and the speech—of the successful white world.

O.J. works hard at transforming his public persona from brawling street tough to smooth, confident member of the successful elite. Long before the brutal murders with which he's charged, Lee Strasberg, the acting coach who helped Marlon Brando, Marilyn Monroe, and other stars, and was then assisting O.J. in his Hollywood roles, says of O.J.: "He already is an actor, an excellent one." Strasberg adds, "A natural one." And once, while shooting a TV commercial with underprivileged black youths in Oakland, in the territory where he grew up, O.J.'s mask slips. Inadvertently, he begins employing the street language of his gang childhood. Furious, he announces he wants to redo the commercial. The second take goes perfectly. "That's what happens when I spend too much time with my boys," O.J. says afterward, in explaining his slip. "I forget how to talk white."

For O.J. and others like him, sports offers the surest path toward that road to success. It's not unusual for a black child from the slums with natural athletic ability to achieve an American Dream lifestyle and public fame.

It is highly unusual, however, to become a superstar athlete in spite of suffering from a severe childhood physical handicap.

As a two-year-old, O.J. Simpson was afflicted with rickets. The disease, resulting from a lack of calcium in the bones, a commentary on his impoverished inner-city diet, withered his legs and left him bow-legged and pigeon-toed. To correct his disability, leg braces were required; his mother, however, couldn't afford them. So for the next three years, O.J. shuffled around his house with an improvised contraption that enabled him to walk, while strengthening his legs. For several hours every day he put on shoes connected to each other by an iron band and struggled to walk. Ultimately, his handicap was corrected. The tenacity and drive displayed by this bow-legged kid with rickets who couldn't walk unaided is as impressive as any of the subsequent stories in the nineties that celebrate the determination to succeed of the new golden entrepreneurs of Technotimes.

From high school on, O.J.'s athletic prowess propels him up, and eventually out, of the world of his birth. His career ambitions are minimal. By his own account, he was "a lousy student" and "didn't exactly kill myself studying." He's so eager to leave the classroom that he thinks of enlisting in the Marines and fighting in Vietnam. By the time he graduates from junior college, he has smashed all existing football rushing records for that level of play and finds himself aggressively courted by recruiters of big-time collegiate athletics. They shower him with offers of full scholarships—and, typically, much more, most of it hidden.

Though ostensibly an amateur endeavor, guided by principles of good sportsmanship, American collegiate athletics, especially football, long since has passed into the realm of high-stakes, high-revenue professional sports. It's the biggest of businesses, awash in cash, commercialism, and corruption. It's all about money. A young potential superstar like O.J. finds himself at the center of a virtual bidding war. "A whole bunch of 'em were offering all kinds of under-the-table shit," he recalls of the college recruiters who besieged him. "In addition to a regular scholarship, most of the schools were talking about $400 or $500 a month and stuff like a car. One school was gonna arrange for my mother to clean up an office for $1,000 a month; another was gonna get my mother a house."

Whatever the offer, O.J. more than proves his worth; he richly rewards those who invest in him. Both in college at USC and then in the National Football League with the Buffalo Bills, his athletic ability attracts legions of paying fans. They fill the stadiums. With them come the networks and the sponsors. They vie for the right to telecast his games, not only locally, but nationally. These generate still more revenue.

Through it all O.J. soars. As his earnings multiply, he acquires more of the taste for and the trappings of the affluent life. To an adoring public, he becomes a self-effacing, beloved superstar. It's an intoxicating role. O.J., like so many sports heroes who achieve celebrity at an early age, takes the fawning worship of starstruck fans and effusive praise of sports announcers as his due. So, too, he takes as his natural right the physical gratification that comes with quick fame and wealth—the easy and endless sexual conquests, the eager girls on their knees, the constant adulation of faithful camp followers. No wonder primal urges are unchecked. Stars believe they can always get away with outrageous behavior, and often do. In the nineties, sports stars become involved in even more notorious cases, often resulting only in slaps on the wrist for the offenders, if that. Rules are made for lesser mortals.

But the idea that such a supposedly familiar public figure could be capable of the monstrous murders with which he's accused is simply inconceivable. Indeed, the public can be excused for being so misinformed about O.J. and the life he's led. The O.J. the public has grown to love is wholesome, charismatic, uncomplicated.

As with so many other celebrities, especially sports celebrities, O.J. has led a charmed life, protected by a cordon of publicists, agents, producers, sponsors, sportswriters, and commentators, and protected no less by the police who treat him as an untouchable. Even in prison, O.J. demonstrates the power of special privilege accorded the celebrated star. In the Los Angeles County Men's Central Jail, where he is incarcerated along with sixty-four hundred other inmates, O.J. lives alone in a row of seven cells. Most of the other inmates are housed two to six in a single cell. They wait in line to use pay phones. O.J. doesn't. They must bathe in communal showers. O.J. showers by himself. Other prisoners are limited to visits of only twenty minutes a day. O.J. sees his lawyers and forty specially designated visitors for up to ten hours a day.

When asked about this special treatment, a sheriff's deputy justifies it by saying: "O.J. Simpson was living in a Brentwood estate worth $5 million, now he's incarcerated in a 9-by-7-foot cell. . . . It's all relative."

Not until the aftermath of the murders do other aspects of his life become widely known.

Within days, former friends and associates tell reporters of his jealousies, his rages, his record of hitting on women, casually, repeatedly, his blatant sexism and possessiveness. Once, in a fine Santa Ana restaurant where O.J. was hosting a group of his friends and his wife for dinner, he grabbed Nicole's crotch and loudly proclaimed, "This belongs to me." On another occasion, as testimony later reveals, he boasted to an acquaintance how easy it would be to kill someone by slashing his neck with a knife—and demonstrated, with gestures, how he would do it. And once, according to information a former Hollywood associate of his tells prosecutors, when the subject of Nicole's boyfriends was raised O.J.

angrily vowed to "cut their fucking heads off" if he ever finds them driving his cars.

The public knows nothing about this side of O.J. It certainly has no knowledge of the devastating record of desperate telephone calls Nicole Brown Simpson made to police emergency numbers over the years, both during her marriage and after her divorce, as she sought protection from a violent, battering O.J. Nicole's police emergency calls document not only O.J.'s explosive violent nature, but also the failure of both police and judicial authorities to take effective action to stop his abusive behavior. Not that such failure is unique in Nicole's case; police routinely fail the battered wife, as numerous court records show. That dreary kind of record was compounded by the circumstances of the O.J. case. O.J.'s a superstar; superstars receive different treatment.

All this changes after The Chase and the arrest. Police and prosecutors, or both, immediately slip tape recordings of many of Nicole's 911 police emergency calls to local TV stations and the networks. Along with the recordings are equally damaging leaked written reports of police investigations of those incidents.

One police report, on New Year's Day 1989, describes how Nicole, wearing only bra and sweatpants, runs from bushes where she's hiding after having called police from inside their Brentwood mansion. Badly beaten, her lip cut, one eye blackened, Nicole keeps telling officers, "He's going to kill me; he's going to kill me." Does he have any guns? police ask. "He's got lots of guns," she replies. Then she bitterly complains to the police: "You never do anything about him. You talk to him and then leave. I want him arrested."

At that point, according to the police account, O.J. appears in a bathrobe. "I don't want that woman in my bed anymore," he screams at police. "I got two other women, and I don't want that woman in my bed anymore." When warned he is going to be arrested, O.J. yells: "The police have been out here eight times before and you're going to arrest me for this? This is a family matter. Why do you want to make a big deal out of it? We can handle it."

Ultimately, Nicole doesn't press charges, but a city attorney files misdemeanor charges of spousal abuse against O.J. He pleads no contest, is fined $970, ordered to perform 120 hours of community service, and attend counseling sessions twice a week for three months. He's also given two years' probation.

The incident attracts little news attention. It has no demonstrable effect on O.J.'s public popularity. "It was perplexing," a female former employee of NBC Sports remarks to *Sports Illustrated* immediately after the murders. "People at NBC Sports used to always remark about the beating, shaking their heads and saying, 'Here's a man who used to beat his wife, and none of America cares or remembers.' People refused to believe because they thought he was such a nice guy."

It isn't just the American people who don't believe or care about such behavior. Neither do O.J.'s corporate bosses. Three months after the 1989 incident, NBC signed O.J. to an annual $400,000 broadcast contract, and he got another contract for more than half a million dollars a year from Hertz rental car, the sponsor of his TV commercials.

Even more damaging are tapes leaked to CNN and then broadcast over that network in prime time days after O.J.'s arrest. These include a 911 call Nicole made to police from inside her home, after her 1992 divorce, on October 25, 1993. The transcript of that phone conversation frighteningly foreshadows her fate on the front steps of her townhouse less than a year later:

911 Operator: *911 emergency.*
Nicole: *Could you get someone over here now, to 325 Gretna Green. He's back. Please.*
911 Operator: *Okay. What does he look like?*

Nicole: *He's O.J. Simpson. I think you know his record. Could you just send somebody over here?*
911 Operator: *Okay, what is he doing there?*
Nicole: *He just drove up again. Can you just send somebody over?*
911 Operator: *He just drove up. Okay, wait a minute. What kind of car is he in?*
Nicole: *He's in a white Bronco. But first of all, he broke the back door down to get in.*
911 Operator: *Okay. Wait a minute. What's your name?*
Nicole: *Nicole Simpson.*
911 Operator: *Okay. Is he the sportscaster or whatever?*
Nicole: *Yeah.*
911 Operator: *Okay. What is—*
Nicole: *Thank you.*
911 Operator: *Wait a minute. We're sending the police. What is he doing? Is he threatening you?*
Nicole: *He's fuckin' going nuts.*

Her furious profane response doesn't stop the police operator from asking still more questions and still not responding swiftly.

In view of what happens later, Nicole's words as she tries to explain her fear of O.J. are especially chilling: "The kids are upstairs sleeping and I don't want anything to happen."

She explains to the police operator how O.J. came to her townhouse earlier, broke down her back door, went upstairs and pounded on her door until she fears it, too, will be broken. "Then he screamed and hollered," she says, "and I tried to get him out of the bedroom because the kids are sleeping in there."

The 911 Operator replies laconically, "Okay." Nicole, her tone increasingly urgent, continues trying to describe the danger she feels. The operator interrupts, maddeningly, to say, "Okay. So basically you guys have just been arguing?"

At that point, the tape picks up the background sound of a male voice, roaring and shouting unintelligibly. The conversation continues:

911 Operator: *Is he inside right now?*
Nicole, desperately: *Yes, yes.*
911 Operator: *Okay, just a moment.*
O.J. Simpson: *[Unintelligible.]*

Through the sound of O.J.'s angry shouting, the tape clearly picks up a fragment of Nicole's plaintive voice: "—the kids. O.J.—O.J., the kids are sleeping."

The police operator interjects with yet another question: "He's still yelling at you? Just stay on the line, Okay?"

The conversation ends with a heartbreaking appeal from Nicole. "O.J. O.J. O.J. Could you please leave. Please leave."

After another frightening encounter with O.J., Nicole expressed the terror she felt in a tape recording. It's entered into the public record, along with a diary she kept in the years prior to her death. The diary details her fears of O.J.; it also describes the beatings and humiliations she suffers, including a vivid account of how O.J. once "beat me for hours." On the tape, she says that during O.J.'s rages he "gets a very animal look in him, his veins pop out and his eyes get black." Looking at him, she fears that "if it happened once more, it would be the last time." Eight months later, she's hacked to death.

In the aftermath of O.J.'s arrest, the revelations about Nicole's terror-stricken emergency calls and O.J.'s prior record for wife abuse initially focus great attention on the issue of domestic violence, particularly violence against women. For years, advocates and activists have been trying to place that issue squarely on the public agenda. Now O.J. gives them the perfect opportunity to get across their message about the prevalence of wife battering and spousal abuse. They appear on television to air the problem. They write op-ed pieces. Congress even holds hearings.

Black women are prominent among these advocates. Many speak out against O.J.'s vio-

lent behavior toward Nicole, as they have been doing repeatedly about violence committed against women by men, whether black men or white men. At this point in the O.J. story, they don't view the case along purely racial lines. As in the highly charged Supreme Court confirmation hearings for Clarence Thomas, women see abuse or harassment, while men see an "electronic lynching." Indeed, just a day after Nicole's body is discovered, the domestic violence issue appears to be creating further sharp divisions between African-American men and women.

On that Monday a female judge in Indiana refuses to free Mike Tyson, the former black heavyweight boxing champion then serving a six-year jail sentence for rape. Immediately, Indianapolis talk shows are besieged by angry callers. Women, many of whom identify themselves as black, praise her decision but add that Tyson should serve more, not less, prison time. Some believe he should have served the full sixty years to which he could have been sentenced after being convicted on two counts of criminal deviant sexual conduct and rape.

African-American male callers, by contrast, are outraged at the judge for not immediately freeing Tyson. The champ is "the greatest," they say. He never should have been imprisoned in the first place. He's the victim of a "scheming woman." The female judge's ruling proves how "the system" castrates and lynches black men. This becomes a theme that repeats itself ever more forcefully during the O.J. trial as the issue of domestic violence against women is overtaken by an even more combustible one—race.

The race card, as exemplified by the character of Mark Fuhrman, plays powerfully on deeply held African-American fears and resentments. It intensifies the already strong belief that blacks cannot expect fair treatment from the nation's criminal justice system. The O.J. case, in this reasoning, becomes an opportunity for racial payback to counter past wrongs extending back to the very beginnings of the American experiment—the wrongs of slavery, of murder, of rape, of castration, of lynching, of segregation, of discrimination, of injustice. Fanning racial flames even higher is the performance of the black press, where O.J. is portrayed as yet another "victim" of white racism perpetrated by the combined conspiratorial efforts of a white legal and police establishment and a "white media."

While O.J. becomes another example of a black hero being destroyed by the white conspiracy, Johnnie Cochran, O.J.'s lead attorney, is hailed as a new black hero. He's even called a new civil rights leader for his defense of O.J. In sharp contrast, one of the key prosecutors, Chris Darden, also black, is condemned in the same black press as being a contemptible "house Negro" for prosecuting O.J.

In the end, race, not domestic violence, not corruption at the core of professional athletics that inspires above-the-law attitudes among its pampered stars, not even murder, becomes the emotional touchstone of the O.J. case.

No thinking American in the nineties could be surprised to learn that the United States still suffers from pervasive racial prejudice. Despite African-American advances in employment and income opportunities; despite the ending of legal segregation in housing, in schools, in the military; despite integration of previously all-white police departments enabling blacks to become chiefs of police in such former racial trouble spots as Birmingham, Alabama, and Charleston, South Carolina; despite anti-discrimination laws and affirmative action programs aimed at combating discrimination nationwide, racial suspicion and racial hostility still afflict the United States. The shock produced by the O.J. case comes not from the discovery that racial resentment and anger exist. The shock comes from the depth and virulence of them.

In the O.J. trial, everything is seen through the distorting prism of race. Blacks and whites examine the same evidence and draw starkly differing conclusions from it. One side sees a murderer; the other sees a victim. One sees clear and compelling evidence of guilt; the other sees a sinister conspiracy that seeks to convict the innocent.

Barely a month after O.J.'s arrest, 63 percent of whites answering a Time/CNN poll say they believe he will get a fair trial. Only 31 percent of blacks feel the same way. While 66 percent of whites believe he received a fair preliminary hearing, only 31 percent of blacks agree. Seventy-seven percent of whites believe the case against O.J. is either "very strong" or "fairly strong." Only 45 percent of blacks agree.

As the trial begins, the racial lines harden. Out of public view, the sequestered jury becomes riven with increasing racial tensions. Black and white jurors use separate gyms, watch movies in separate rooms. Black jurors complain that whites on their panel are given preferential treatment by sheriff's deputies. They suspect the deputies are secretly searching their housing quarters while they are on jury duty seeking evidence of bias against the prosecution or to discover they have been violating the judge's orders not to read news accounts about the case. One black juror, after being removed from the panel, goes on TV to accuse a white juror of kicking her. She says the same white juror stomped on the foot of another black juror in the jury box. Another black juror files a formal protest to Judge Ito about the racism perceived by black jury members.

Six months into the trial, a national survey by Lou Harris and Associates finds that 61 percent of whites believe Simpson is guilty. Sixty-eight percent of blacks think him innocent. Only 8 percent of all blacks surveyed believe that O.J. murdered Nicole and Ron. (Twenty-four percent of blacks polled say they aren't sure about O.J.'s guilt or innocence.)

By trial's end, a state of near total racial polarization exists across America.

In the O.J. case, the public fascination with violent entertainment and courtroom drama mixes with the conjunction between capitalism and celebrity. The case becomes a prime example of how profit seekers can manufacture and exploit a mass audience and how television provides the perfect vehicle to promote that rush to profit. As Walter Lippmann observed in the wake of the TV quiz scandals that rocked the television world at the end of the fifties, "While television is supposed to be 'free,' it has in fact become the creature, the servant, and indeed the prostitute, of merchandising." To that point, Lippmann thought television's major influence had been twofold: first, "to poison the innocent by the exhibition of violence, degeneracy, and crime, and second, to debase the public taste." He should have seen the nineties.

In the O.J. case, everyone cashes in—the media, the lawyers, the judge, the jury, the publishers, the entertainment industry, the marketers of items bearing on the case. Even friends and foes of O.J. profit, eagerly, aggressively, shamelessly. Not least among them is O.J. himself, as well as supposedly bereaved relatives of the victims. The O.J. trial becomes not just "a rush to judgment," as his lawyer dramatically and repeatedly warns; it becomes a rush to capitalize, and capitalize in a way America has not witnessed before.

Not that the phenomenon of exploiting tragedy and sensation is new. . . .

In the O.J. case, the difference from the past lies not in the human instinct that lures crowds and hucksters to scenes of disaster. In the nineties, the difference lies in the ability of everyone, everywhere, to participate vicariously in those scenes as they are occurring.

For this capacity, thank technology. Mobile TV minicams and earth-orbiting satellites provide the technical ability to go live, virtually instantly, from any scene of disaster or scandal. For the decision to bring more and more of these scenes into everyone's living room, credit a number of factors that converged in the nineties. Intense competitive pressures among proliferating cable channels scrambling to wrest market share from the traditional networks created increasing demand to broadcast the latest, most sensational newsbreaks as they hap-

pen—and the more scandalous and lurid the better. As cable channels focused increasingly on the sensational and the scandalous, the old networks adapted by furnishing more of the same in an attempt to hold their declining audience.

The disgraceful attack talk-radio programs, with their growing audience and increasing influence, also affected the electronic and celebrity culture of the nineties. With their daily airing of ideological conspiracies and preoccupation with scandals—proof never necessary and rarely even a consideration—the talk-radio shows demonstrated the impact, and the money, to be made by appealing to the worst in people. Television, especially cable, followed their lead; tabloid TV joined attack radio in filling more of the nation's airwaves. "Trash TV" was on the rise.

None of this readily explains the appeal of these offerings, however, or the paradox they present about American society in the nineties. Americans, after all, were better educated, more sophisticated, more tolerant, more aware of subtlety and nuance and the imperfectability of public and private lives than ever before. They were, in the main, practical and realistic, generally hard-eyed, and not easily swayed by cheap appeals to emotion. So why were so many so captivated by such tawdry daily fare?

Part of the answer rests in the nature of the times. The best of times they may or may not have been, but they were certainly times blessed by an absence of crises—crises domestic or foreign, economic or social, environmental or medical. Freed from the kinds of concerns that compel public attention, Americans were also free to indulge in the titillation of gossip and scandal. They were free to be entertained by the spectacle of celebrities and public figures brought low. And with relentless, nonstop intensity, the electronic media dished up scandal in helpings that enabled every citizen to share in every gory, sordid detail.

Nor was O.J. the first of the great scandalous spectacles Americans witnessed in the nineties. By the time of O.J., Americans were conditioned to witnessing a succession of long-running scandalous episodes. No sooner did one end than another took its place. Each attracted an immense audience; each received frenzied media coverage; each was treated as if it said something significant about American society and thus deserved intense attention; each fueled an appetite for more of the same; each became a springboard for a successor, happily supplied by producers of Teletimes who sought and supplied the latest scandal for public consumption, all in a breakneck race to boost ratings.

So many were there, and so rapidly did they replace each other, that it seemed as if the single most defining characteristic of America in the nineties was an all-consuming preoccupation with scandal—scandal that over time merged into one continuous serial production.

The names of the players and the particulars about the scandals changed, but the object was the same—scandal, always more scandal: Dr. Kevorkian and the first assisted suicide; Rodney King, beaten viciously by Los Angeles policemen; Jeffrey Dahmer, "the homosexual cannibal," and horrific acts of mass murder; Anita Hill, Clarence Thomas, sexual harassment, and pubic hairs; Mike Tyson and rape; Tailhook and sexual assault in the Air Force; the Packwood diaries and sex on Capitol Hill; Michael Jackson and that young boy; Nancy Kerrigan, Tonya Harding, and their violent skating rivalry; Lorena Bobbitt and her husband's severed penis.

All these occurred before O.J. Other episodes flitted across the TV screens during and after the long period when O.J. dominated the national stage: Susan Smith and her two drowned children; the Menendez brothers; JonBenet Ramsey, the pathetic six-year-old pushed by parents to compete in beauty pageants by tarting up and acting like a bud-

ding Lolita, found murdered in the basement of her home; Louise Woodward, the young British nanny, and the death of the child in her care; the murder of fashion designer Gianni Versace in a Palm Beach oceanfront mansion, perfectly providing a spectacle that combined synthetic glamour and glitz with salacious tales of gay sex; the clearly deeply troubled teacher, Mary Kay Letourneau, and her sad, sick affair—naturally labeled by the tabs "forbidden love"—with her thirteen-year-old student; Dick Morris, a president's Machiavellian pollster, sucking the toes of that prostitute on a Washington hotel balcony; Marv Albert, the loudmouth sportscaster, biting a woman in another hotel room near the capitol, providing perfect fodder for the televised celebrity and scandal culture, and being returned to the air as a sports commentator, apparently no less popular, or perhaps more so, than when his scandalous behavior created yet another mass spectacle.

Drawing the most intense media focus and public attention were the trials that resulted from many of those episodes. They were the easiest to cover and offered a convenient running plot line of scandal and suspense.

The cumulative effect of these events was to divert attention from the really great episodes of the nineties, and especially from two that came into play with tremendous force then. One, as we've seen, was the revolution in science, technology, and medicine rapidly changing life on the planet. The other was the growing concentration of great blocs of power through the greatest wave of mergers ever, creating new entities reshaping the basic economic and social structures of the nation.

As time passed, few Americans could recall specific details of the various episodes to which they were exposed or their outcomes. Nonetheless, stamped in the collective public memory was a hazy montage of sensationalized scandals. While people professed to be repelled by media excesses and obsessive attention to scandal, they also took guilty pleasure in watching, and wallowing in, the spectacle.

Two weeks after O.J.'s arrest, CNN dispatched its cameras, and a correspondent, to a popular Atlanta fast-food restaurant, aptly named The Varsity, for a daylong sounding of public attitudes about the O.J. case. The slice of vox populi aired was highly revealing. Virtually every person interviewed expressed the same kinds of underlying ambivalence. They hated what they were seeing, or so they said, but they were watching all of it.

Television provided much more than "updates." It offered a new form of public entertainment—a live, free theater of spectacle and sensation. O.J. had it all, the serious and the sordid. It was irresistible. In the process, old news barriers and taboos were broken; practices previously deemed unacceptable by mainstream news organizations became acceptable amid rapidly evolving standards of the electronic age. Even some talk-radio hosts expressed concern about the negative impact they were having on the public. Days after the murders, during a Los Angeles convention of national talk-show hosts, one of them acknowledged to a *CBS Evening News* interviewer that with the O.J. case talk radio had "gone totally over the line." Then the talk host quickly added: "With each case we say that—and the line gets pushed further." That didn't stop the lines separating accuracy from rumor, fairness from unfairness, good taste from bad, from being driven farther and farther apart.

Distinguished news executives from both print and television bemoaned the lowering of journalistic values, the cheapening of reportage, the omnipresent "gotcha" aspects, the circus atmosphere that typified the coverage. "I don't like the idea that a murder trial has been turned into an entertainment special," Don Hewitt, the executive producer of *60 Minutes*, wrote in a *New York Times* oped article. "There are certain moments in American life that have a certain dignity." Not an O.J. moment, though, especially an O.J. mo-

ment that increases ratings and one that shows the growing public appetite for more of the same—more of the spectacular, more of the sensational, more of the scandalous. Which, of course, is what the public got.

Long before the trial even began, virtually all hope had vanished that it would provide for a watching world an example of the American criminal justice system at its best, a serious civic proceeding that exemplified the most cherished judicial attributes: dignity, decorum, and fairness. It quickly degenerated into a spectacle that demonstrated some of the worst characteristics of Teletimes. No one escaped unscathed. The lawyers fought among themselves, played as much to the TV cameras as to the jury, argued their cases in impromptu press encounters at every opportunity, leaked damaging information to the press, and also exhibited a taste for cashing in on the instant celebrity television had conferred upon them. One attorney on the defense team was involved in a New York trial that conflicted with O.J.'s. He asked for and won a postponement from that engagement; then he asked for another postponement from his New York obligations, in effect arguing it would be unfair to him financially if he were denied the chance to participate in the O.J. show, never mind his East Coast client. This time, his request was denied.

The jurors squabbled among themselves. At times, they, too, acted petulantly. Once, they even acted mutinously. On that occasion, thirteen of the eighteen remaining members of the panel showed up in court dressed in black. They threatened to refuse to enter the jury box until Judge Ito heard their protests about his decision to dismiss three of their guards in the wake of charges the guards gave some jurors favorable treatment. Though it wasn't known until after the trial ended, many of the jurors already had sold their stories to tabloid TV shows, granting exclusive interviews immediately after the verdict. And the judge, despite early expressions of confidence that he would live up to his reputation for ensuring scrupulous courtroom discipline and decorum—Ito would exercise his usual "cool manner and firm hand," one puff piece had predicted before the trial—showed himself to be petty and temperamental, given to angry outbursts against media excesses and threatening often to ban cameras from his courtroom.

Yet Ito himself astounded lawyers and law professors across the country when he permitted himself to be interviewed extensively by a local Los Angeles TV correspondent in the midst of the O.J. proceedings taking place in his court. Portions of the interview, conducted at Ito's home, were then broadcast each night beginning at eleven o'clock Sunday, November 13, for an entire week over L.A.'s KCBS Channel 2. More astonishing yet, these nightly airings on the local "Action News" broadcast took place during one of four so-called sweeps periods each year. The sweeps are the critical times when TV audiences are measured to help set advertising rates—the bigger the audience, the more money stations can charge their advertisers. Nor was the timing of Ito's interview with the commercially crucial sweeps period accidental. The channel promoted those nightly segments of his interview in full-page newspaper ads and in on-air promos, all intended to entice more viewers.

Reaction in the legal community, and in some press circles, was swift and strongly critical. In San Diego, a defense lawyer expressed typical consternation. "It's out of control," Elisabeth Semel told the *San Francisco Chronicle's* legal affairs writer. "The side show is obscuring the heart of the case." In Los Angeles, another prominent defense attorney, Harland Braun, voiced astonishment at how "a garden variety murder involving a celebrity" now is "going off into all kinds of side shows. Ito has become a side show. It's unbelievable."

And in New York, a respected legal scholar on judicial ethics at the New York University School of Law, Stephen Gillers, reflected sadly that "There's something about the big publicity monster. It co-opts everybody."

It certainly did in the O.J. case, nor was that trial the first that raised serious questions about the "publicity monster" that accompanied sensationally televised court hearings. By the time of the O.J. case, forty-seven states permitted TV cameras in courtrooms, and with the advent of the around-the-clock cable telecasts of CNN and such popular programs as "Court TV," the televised trial had become a staple of the electronic media. "Court TV" alone had been televising them for several years before the O.J. trial.

As for the rhetoric about how televising the trial live from Los Angeles would provide a great national civics lesson, and all the pretrial arguments from freedom of the press advocates who urged that cameras be allowed in the courtroom not only as a constitutional right but as a check on abuses, in the end the O.J. Simpson trial produced more public cynicism and disgust.

When it works as it should, the American criminal justice system is a noble, indispensable defender of freedom and individual rights. That it often does not work as well amid the scandal culture of Teletimes is only one of many lessons emerging from the nineties.

O.J.'s saga was over. After riveting the nation for a year and a half, after a trial lasting for nine months, after a jury was sequestered for 265 days facing a virtual ton of overwhelmingly incriminating evidence to assess, it took those O.J. Simpson jurors only three hours of deliberation before rendering their verdict on October 3, 1995—not guilty on all charges.

The same cameras and technology that brought O.J. live into people's homes and offices for all those months now captured America's reaction to the outcome.

Just as in the beginning, the cameras brought Americans together, and then sharply divided them.

In Los Angeles, a deathly silence settled over the courtroom when the clerk began reading the verdict beginning with the words, "In the matter of the people of the State of California versus Orenthal James Simpson, we the jury find the defendant. . . .

Screams of joy and cries of outrage rang out in the courtroom at the pronouncement "not guilty." Those same conflicting emotions were immediately displayed in televised scenes across the country.

Pandemonium swept black neighborhoods in Los Angeles. Worshipers in a black church there began jubilant celebrations. Others took to the streets amid wild cheering.

In Washington, D.C., in black neighborhoods along North Capitol Street in sight of the Capitol, young black men gleefully leaned out of passing cars and high-fived each other, some shouting, "The Juice is loose."

Outside public buildings where throngs gathered with people carrying portable TVs and radios, in public school classrooms where students listened over public address systems, in packed office conference rooms where workers watched the TV screen, news of the verdict showed blacks joyfully cheering and whites shocked into silence.

Of the many public-reaction scenes broadcast live that day and later repeated on evening network telecasts, two in particular showed the immensity of the racial divide the verdict exposed.

At Howard University, black law students, watching the verdict from the vantage of the school that more than any other has provided historic African-American leadership in the civil rights movement, spontaneously burst into prolonged cheers when they heard the words "not guilty." At the same moment, other cameras panning the faces of mostly white law students at Columbia University recorded stunned expressions and gasps of disbelief.

National reaction broke along the same racial fault lines. To an extraordinary degree, whites thought: O.J. literally got away with murder because of a racially biased jury. Blacks believed the verdict just because they

thought sufficient evidence existed of a white police frame-up that more than raised reasonable doubts about his guilt, or because a not-guilty verdict symbolized payback by blacks against whites for past acts of injustice, or because of a combination of these and other factors. Out of the torrent of commentary the verdict unleashed, one remarkable example emerged, though it does not seem to have attracted much notice, certainly not the Pulitzer Prize for commentary it deserved.

Writing on deadline immediately after the verdict that day, Michael Wilbon, a *Washington Post* sports columnist who is black, memorably expressed the greater dimensions and significance of the case. Under the title "A Celebrity Goes Free," Wilbon described the uniformly jubilant reaction of blacks across America and commented:

All over urban America you could find these scenes yesterday. It was as if acquitting O.J. Simpson made up for Rodney King and Emmit Till. For all the black fathers and uncles and grandfathers who'd been jailed unjustly, for every brother who has been framed or railroaded, beaten into a confession or placed at the scene of a crime when he was a million miles away. You know what? It doesn't make up for it. I'm a lot less concerned with O.J. Simpson's guilt or innocence than I am with this unqualified embrace of a man simply because he is a celebrity.

He addressed the greater implications of America's obsession with and glorification of celebrity, placing special emphasis on the effect on black Americans. "All of America has become mesmerized by celebrity in the past 20 years," he wrote.

But nobody buys into celebrity, nobody's suckered inescapably into it like black people, my people, the people who can least afford it. You know what happens every single day in urban courtrooms in this country? Black juries, or pre-

dominantly black juries, convict people of crimes with no more drama than necessary. Ordinary, everyday people. But not the chosen ones. You know who the chosen ones are in black America? People who dunk, tackle or sing. Can't touch them. A black delivery man on trial facing the same evidence Simpson faced is a black delivery man headed to prison for life. . . . I worry that the people who feel overjoyed at Simpson's acquittal don't get it. Simpson is free because he played football, because he turned that into a movie career and he's rich. Period. This doesn't symbolize anything or portend great changes in the judicial system to somehow ensure a better shake in the future for African-American citizens. . . . I worry that we, black people, are so desperate for heroes we'll take the worst candidates on the face of the earth because they ran sweet or had a nice crossover dribble. In the last year we fawned over a drug user (Marion Barry), a convicted rapist (Mike Tyson), and a wife-beater (Simpson), as if those three somehow reflect the best of what we offer to society at-large or our own communities.

Wilbon wanted his readers to know he wasn't "naive about one of the primary emotions involved here: vengeance," adding:

A lot of black people could care less about Simpson and see him truly for what he is. They simply see this as payback, even if the score is still about 1 million to one. They feel the chickens might have come home to roost yesterday for all of our relatives and ancestors who've been beaten and raped and lynched and murdered by whites without any consequence whatsoever. . . . The bigger issue here, of course, is race. It's always race. What we've seen on television and heard on radio before and after the verdict only confirms that blacks and whites have a completely different reality when it comes to some things. You see evidence, I see a plant. I see a racist cop, you see a defense attorney's diversionary tactics. The lines aren't always that clear, but they were in this instance.

With disturbing eloquence, he posed the larger challenge arising from the Simpson case: "Until we as a nation begin to pay attention, those two separate realities will continue to exist. And in one of those worlds, a blind and undying love for anyone famous will continue to drain us of energy that ought to be channeled in another direction."

Study Questions

1. Why did O.J. Simpson become the first black athlete to be employed by corporate sponsors?

2. How did O.J.'s career as a celebrity differ from his childhood?

3. How did O.J.'s celebrity status shield the O.J. his friends knew from the public? Why did his previous actions with Nicole go unnoticed?

4. Why and how did race become the central issue in trials like the O.J. Simpson case?

5. What do trials like Mike Tyson's and O.J. Simpson's say about race relations in the United States?

6. The O.J. Simpson case illustrates the proliferation of the mass media in the 1990s. How has technology affected the way Americans in the 1990s receive and interpret news?

Bibliography

This piece first appeared in Haynes Johnson, *The Best of Times: The Boom and Bust Years of America Before and After Everything Changed* (2002). The debate over O.J. Simpson's guilt continues within the pages of several recent books. Jeffrey Toobin, *The Run of His Life: The People Versus O.J. Simpson* (1997), argues that "overwhelming evidence" proves O.J. guilty, while Donald Freed, *Killing Time: The First Full Investigation into the Unsolved Murders of Nicole Brown Simpson and Ronald Goldman* (1996), offers several alternative scenarios for the murders. Janice E. Schuetz and Lin S. Lilley, eds., *The O.J. Simpson Trial: Rhetoric, Media, and the Law* (1999), discuss the connections between media representation and the Simpson trial. For a general introduction to the issue of race in the media, see Gail Dines and Jean Humez, *Gender, Race, and Class in Media: A Text-Reader* (2002). For an overview of the Mike Tyson trial, see Randy Roberts and J. Gregory Garrison, *Heavy Justice: The State of Indiana v. Michael G. Tyson* (1994).

Credits

★ ★ ★